Global
Marketing
Management

4th Edition

Global
Marketing
Management

4th Edition

John A. Quelch
London Business School

Christopher A. Bartlett
Harvard Business School

Joel Steckel, Consulting Editor
New York University

 **ADDISON-WESLEY**

An imprint of Addison Wesley Longman, Inc.

Reading, Massachusetts • Menlo Park, California • New York • Harlow, England
Don Mills, Ontario • Sydney • Mexico City • Madrid • Amsterdam

Executive Editor: Mike Roche
Associate Editor: Ruth Berry
Editorial Assistant: Adam Hamel
Senior Marketing Manager: Julie Downs
Senior Marketing Coordinator: Joyce Cosentino
Supplements Editor: Deborah Kiernan
Editorial and Production Services/Composition: Compset, Inc.
Production Supervisor: Louis C. Bruno, Jr.
Design Manager: Gina Hagen
Cover Designer: Leslie Haimes
Print Buyer: Sheila Spinney
Printer and Binder: Maple-Vail Book Group
Cover Printer: Coral Graphics

Library of Congress Cataloging-in-Publication Data

Global marketing management / [edited by] John A. Quelch, Christopher A. Bartlett.
   4th ed.
     p.   cm.
   ISBN 0-201-35062-9
   1. Export marketing—Management.   2. Export marketing—Management—Case studies.
I. Quelch, John A.   II. Bartlett, Christopher A., 1943–   .
   HF1416.G56   1998
   658.8'48—dc21

Printed in the United States
12345678910—MV—0201009998

Preface

The organization of this edition is similar to that of its predecessor. Three changes have been made in response to adopter feedback. First, we no longer include articles in this casebook, in order to provide a broader selection of cases. Second, about 40 percent of the cases in this edition are new. Third, an increased emphasis has been placed on cases in emerging markets, including the Middle East, as well as Asia, Latin America, and Central Europe.

An Instructor's Resource Manual, which includes teaching notes for all of the cases, is also available. Please contact your Addison Wesley Longman sales representative to obtain a copy.

Our sincere thanks to those whose collaborations with us have made this fourth edition possible. They include Assistant Professors David Arnold, Ashish Nanda, and Das Narayandas of Harvard Business School, Dr. Christopher Lovelock, and Professor Roderick White of the University of Western Ontario. Our Research Associates and MBA students—Michele Calpin, Claude Cohen, Barbara Feinberg, Yoshinori Fujikawa, Jamie Harper, Jean-Marie Ingea, Lisa Klein, Carin-Isabel Knoop, Nathalie Laidler, Diane Long, Afroze Mohammed, Takia Mahmood, Robin Root, and Kathleen Scharf—each aided in the field research of one or more cases and in the development of case drafts.

Thanks also to Dean Kim Clark and the Division of Research of Harvard Business School for the financial support that made possible the development of the materials included in this text.

Michael Roche, our editor at Addison-Wesley, and his colleagues researched adopter reactions to the previous edition and, thereby, influenced the organization and content of the fourth edition. Barbara Stratton of Compset, Inc. has been especially helpful in the production process.

While many people have assisted us in preparing this book, we remain solely responsible for any inaccuracies or omissions. We wish our readers—whether they be managers, instructors, or students—success and enjoyment in grappling with the exciting challenges faced by the business protagonists in our cases, and we thank them for sharing their problems and experiences with us.

John A. Quelch
London Business School

Christopher A. Bartlett
Harvard Business School

August 1998

Table of Contents

PART I

Designing Strategies for Global Competition

1   INTRODUCTION
5   CASES
5   Ingvar Kamprad and Ikea
    Christopher A. Bartlett and Ashish Nanda
25 Komatsu Ltd.: Project G's Globalization
    Christopher A. Bartlett
47 Skandia AFS
    Christopher A. Bartlett and Takia Mahmood
69 McKinsey & Company: Managing
    Knowledge and Learning
    Christopher A. Bartlett
89 Bayer AG
    John A. Quelch and Robin Root

PART II

Global Expansion Strategies

105 INTRODUCTION
109 CASES
109 Bajaj Auto Ltd.
     John A. Quelch and Nathalie Laidler
135 Mary Kay Cosmetics: Asian Market Entry
     John A. Quelch and Nathalie Laidler
167 Vietnam: Market Entry Decisions
     John A. Quelch and David A. Arnold
181 Air Miles®
     John A. Quelch and Michele Calpin
211 Orbital Sciences Corporation: ORBCOMM
     John A. Quelch and Das Narayandas

PART III

Global Marketing Programs

233 INTRODUCTION
237 CASES

237 Gallo Rice
     John A. Quelch and Nathalie Laidler
265 Sony Corporation: Car Navigation Systems
     John A. Quelch and Yoshinori Fujikawa
301 AB Sandvik Saws & Tools: The Ergo Strategy
     Roderick White and Julian Birkinshaw
321 Planet Reebok
     John A. Quelch and Jamie Harper
353 DHL Worldwide Express
     John A. Quelch and Greg Conley

PART IV

Marketing in Emerging Markets

373 INTRODUCTION
375 CASES
375 Braas GmbH
     John A. Quelch and Carin-Isabel Knoop
391 Koç Holding: Arçelik White Goods
     John A. Quelch and Robin Root
409 Harlequin Romances—Poland
     John A. Quelch and Nathalie Laidler
433 EMDICO
     John A. Quelch and Yoshinori Fujikawa
451 Gillette Indonesia
     John A. Quelch and Diane E. Long

PART V

Managing International Partners and Alliances

465 INTRODUCTION
469 CASES
469 Loctite Corporation—International
     Distribution
     John A. Quelch and David J. Arnold
491 Pechazur
     John A. Quelch and Nathalie Laidler

513   MasterCard and World Championship Soccer
       John A. Quelch and Carin-Isabel Knoop
545   Jurassic Park
       John A. Quelch, Barbara Feinberg,
       and Jeremy Tachau
563   Disney Consumer Products in Lebanon
       John A. Quelch, Jean-Marc Ingea, and
       Barbara Feinberg

PART VI

Organizing and Controlling Global Marketing Operations

577   INTRODUCTION
581   CASES
581   Global Client Management (A1)
       Christopher H. Lovelock
583   Global Client Management (B1)
       John A. Quelch
585   Bausch & Lomb: Regional Organization
       John A. Quelch and Nathalie Laidler
603   Hewlett Packard: European Remarketing
       Operation
       John A. Quelch and Claude Cohen

627   Becton Dickinson: Worldwide Blood
       Collection Team
       Christopher A. Bartlett and Kathleen Scharf
647   ABB's Relay Business: Building and Managing
       a Global Matrix
       Christopher A. Bartlett

PART VII

Special Issues in Global Marketing

669   INTRODUCTION
671   CASES
671   Weissberg GmbH
       John A. Quelch
675   Lexus and the USTR
       John A. Quelch
681   Astra Sports (A)
       John A. Quelch
685   Astra Sports (B)
       John A. Quelch
689   TRADE'ex: The Stock Exchange of
       the Computer Industry
       John A. Quelch and Lisa R. Klein

Global Marketing Management

4th Edition

PART I

DESIGNING STRATEGIES FOR GLOBAL COMPETITION

In the last quarter of the twentieth century, international business has been shaken by a revolution in global competition unlike any previously experienced. It is a revolution that has rocked established multinationals like Philips, Caterpillar, and ITT while providing the emerging basis for challengers like Matsushita, Komatsu, and NEC to take them on. Yet even the forces of change that helped give birth to the Japanese competitive juggernaut of the 1980s is changing in dramatic ways, and as companies head into the twenty-first century, they need to be aware of a range of powerful, dynamic, yet often conflicting forces shaping the emerging competitive environment.

FORCES FOR MULTIPLE-MARKET SCALE

Perhaps the most powerful force driving the globalization revolution has been the need for companies to capture economies at greater than national scale. One of the main triggers of this change was

a technological revolution that swept across many industries, radically transforming both product designs and manufacturing processes. A classic example was the way in which the invention of the transistor and integrated circuit shook up all electronics-based businesses. In color TV set production, for example, minimum efficient scale jumped from 50,000 sets in the early 1970s to 500,000 sets a decade later. Around the world, scores of nationally focused companies that were unable to access new markets quickly enough were either swallowed up in acquisitions, forced to outsource their sets from global-scale competitors, or simply went out of business.

Having revolutionized plants worldwide, the forces of global scale next spread through the R&D laboratories. The technological revolution was putting equal pressure on companies' product development processes, forcing up the cost of new developments while simultaneously shortening product life cycles. In the telecommunications industry, for example, the arrival of powerful electronic switching technology forced companies to replace their old electromechanical designs with central network switches designed around the faster and cheaper digital technology. However, the cost of developing a digital switch exceeded $1 billion, and to recoup that investment, companies either had to dominate a huge market (like AT&T) or they had to have access to global markets. Among the later, those that failed to leverage the global scale development investments—like ITT—did not survive; those that did so—like Ericsson—were able to develop new sources of competitive advantage.

CHANGING COMPETITIVE GAMES

It is important to note that these environmental forces did not trigger the radical change by themselves. They simply provided the potential for a company to capture a new source of competitive advantage, thereby changing the rules of the game. It was Matsushita's aggressive exploitation of the potential scale economies in color TVs that forced Philips, GE, and others to respond; and it was Ericsson and NEC's ability to roll out their new digital switches around the world that challenged the once-dominant position of ITT.

As competitors began taking the battle to the global marketplace, new competitive games emerged. Where once the overseas subsidiaries of multinational companies competed on a local-for-local basis with national companies and other MNC affiliates, some began playing a new, more sophisticated game. Leveraging the strong positions they developed in key markets (particularly at home), they began to increase their share of other key markets worldwide by pricing at or below cost. The strategy was particularly effective when they could force key competitors with major market positions to follow their price lead, thereby draining the competitors' profit source. It was an approach strategists called "global chess" and economists called "cross-subsidization of markets." Politicians called it "dumping."

As many companies in large target markets learned at their cost, it was an extremely effective strategy. In the semiconductor industry, for example, Japanese exporters virtually eliminated U.S. manufacturers of memory chips in the pricing bloodbath that erupted in the mid-1980s. As became the standard response worldwide, such tactics were eventually checked by government-to-government negotiations, and occasionally retaliations. Yet the new rules of the game had been established, and still shape many global competitive battles today, albeit in less blatant form.

NEED FOR NATIONAL RESPONSIVENESS

The response of national governments to companies' competitive global strategies highlights another set of forces often overlooked in the current fascination with cross-market integration. Despite the emergence of regional economic and political entities such as ASEAN and the European Community, we are a long way from seeing the demise of the nation state. And companies operating around the world still must recognize that it is the host government that frames the rules within which they must operate on a country-by-country basis. Frequently, this requires them to make investments, transfer technology, or modify products in a way that is not consistent with their drive to achieve global scale or cross-border competitive advantage.

Beyond the political imperative, there are other powerful reasons why companies must adopt a flexible and responsive approach to local markets. Despite Professor Theodore Levitt's provocative 1983 statement that "the world's needs and desires have been irrevocably homogenized,"[1] wide national variances in consumer tastes and market structures still persist. Many behavioral differences, particularly those with strong ethnic, religious, or nationalistic roots, are very deeply embedded and highly resistant to change.

---

[1]Theodore Levitt, "The Globalization of Markets," *HBR*, Vol. No. 92-102.

As the information age brought a network of electronic commerce to the most developed countries, market differences linked to a country's economic infrastructure have in many cases been diverging rather than converging. To compete effectively, truly global companies needed to develop the ability to sell products and services via the Internet in some markets, and through street bazaars in others.

THE RACE FOR WORLDWIDE INNOVATION

In the new game, developing cross-market scale, global chess positioning, and local flexibility are only the price of admission. In the knowledge-intensive, service-based information age, perhaps the most vital new skill a company must master is the ability to develop and diffuse innovations rapidly. This has led many companies to recognize that the key motivation for expanding abroad is no longer to access cheap labor or raw materials, to capture incremental scales, or even to build strategic positions on the global chess board. Increasingly, the challenge is to tap into worldwide sources of information, knowledge, and expertise—the latest competitive intelligence, the emerging technological trend, the scarce engineering skill—and use them to develop new products or capabilities that can be leveraged and adapted to market needs worldwide.

A classic example was provided by Procter and Gamble's development of its first truly global innovation, a liquid laundry detergent. Developed first in the United States in response to a competitive threat by Colgate's Wisk, the product was substantially improved by P&G Europe, where environmental legislation was challenging the use of phosphates. Then the Japanese sensed a market need for a liquid with cold-water washing power to respond to their market needs. And finally, another U.S. innovation to prevent redisposition of dirt was added. Coordinating all of these market inputs and technological capabilities, the company developed a new generation of products rolled out worldwide—as Tide Liquid in the United States, Ariel Liquid in Europe, and Liquid Cheer in Japan. So successful was the process that P&G now sees its ability to develop and diffuse innovations globally as its prime source of competitive advantage.

BUILDING LAYERS OF COMPETITIVE ADVANTAGE

As these various environmental forces and competitive pressures interact, many companies are changing to their old notions of developing a single dominant source of competitive advantage—low-cost, differentiated, or niche. The reality in the emerging competitive environment is that such rules no longer apply. Recall how Toyota entered the U.S. market—first offering low-cost automobiles produced on a global scale in Toyota City, Japan; then developing the ability to play a sophisticated game of global chess, forcing U.S. manufacturers like Chrysler into crisis; then complying with government pressures to build local plants and market pressures to develop products more adaptable to the U.S. market; and finally, picking off the top-end niches by developing and diffusing innovations on a global basis.

The global strategic challenge in the new millennium will be to continually develop new layers of competitive advantage. It is a challenge that one manager described as "learning how to walk, chew gum, and whistle at the same time."

INGVAR KAMPRAD AND IKEA

With a 1988 turnover of 14 billion Swedish kronor (US $1 ≅ SKr 6 in 1988) and 75 outlets in 19 countries, IKEA had become the world's largest home furnishings retailer. As the company approached the 1990s, however, its managers faced a number of major challenges. Changes in demographics were causing some to question IKEA's historical product line policy. Others wondered if the company had not bitten off too much by attempting major new market entries simultaneously in two European countries (U.K. and Italy), the United States, and several Eastern Bloc countries. Finally, there was widespread concern about the future of the company without its founder, strategic architect, and cultural guru, Ingvar Kamprad.

IKEA Background and History

In 1989, furniture retailing worldwide was still largely a fragmented national industry in which small manufacturers and distributors catered to the demands of their local markets. Consumer preferences varied by region, and there were few retailers whose operations extended beyond a single country. IKEA, however, had repeatedly bucked market trends and industry norms. Over three and a half decades it had built a highly profitable worldwide network of furniture stores. (See Exhibit 1.)

Company Origins

IKEA is an acronym for the initials of the founder, Ingvar Kamprad, his farm Elmtaryd, and his county, Agunnaryd, in Småland, South Sweden. In 1943, at the age of 17, Kamprad began his entrepreneurial career by selling fish, Christmas magazines, and seeds. Within a few years he had established a mail-order business featuring products as diverse as ballpoint pens and furniture. It was in furniture, however, that he saw the greatest opportunity.

Even as the pent-up wartime demand found expression in the postwar boom, the traditional Swedish practice of handing down custom-made furniture through generations was giving way to young householders looking for new, yet inexpensive, furniture. But while demand was growing, interassociation supply contracts and agreements between Swedish manufacturers and retailers kept prices high while foreclosing entry. As a result, between 1935 and 1946 furniture prices rose 41% faster than prices of other household goods.

This case was prepared by Christopher A. Bartlett and Ashish Nanda. Copyright © 1990 by the President and Fellows of Harvard College. Harvard Business School case 390-132.

Exhibit 1   *IKEA Growth and Performance Indicators* *

Year	Turnover (m SKr)	Outlets	Countries	Co-workers	Catalogs (000s)
1954	3	1	1	15	285
1964	79	2	2	250	1,200
1974	616	10	5	1,500	13,000
1984	6,770	66	17	8,300	40,000
1988	14,500	83	20	13,400	44,000

Year	1979–1980	1980–1981	1981–1982	1982–1983	1983–1984	1984–1985	1985–1986	1986–1987	1987–1988
Turnover (billion SKr)	3.6	4.1	4.8	6.0	6.8	8.2	10.7	12.6	14.5
Estimated PAT (million SKr)	250	280	300	420	500	500	630	930	1100
Total surface area (000 sq. m.)	425	458	483	533	606	825	907	953	973
Number of visitors (millions)	25	30	34	36	38	44	53	60	65

Region	% of Sales (1988)	Region	% of Purchases (1988)
West Germany	29.7%	Scandinavia	50%
Scandinavia	27.5	East Europe	20
Rest of Europe	28.5	Rest of Europe	22
Rest of the world	14.3	Rest of the world	8

Sources: 1. Company documents. 2. *Affärsvärlden*, December 8, 1987.
*IKEA was a closely held private company. Accounting data were not made public. The company's capitalized market value was estimated conservatively at SKr 10 billion in 1987. Profits are best-estimates from available information.

Kamprad felt that this situation represented both a social problem and a business opportunity. He commented:

> A disproportionately large part of all resources is used to satisfy a small part of the population. . . . IKEA's aim is to change this situation. We shall offer a wide range of home furnishing items of good design and function at prices so low that the majority of people can afford to buy them. . . . We have great ambitions.

When Kamprad's upstart company started participating in the annual furniture trade fair in Stockholm, traditional retailers complained that

IKEA was selling imitations. In 1951, when the company was explicitly forbidden from selling directly to customers at the fairs, it responded by only taking orders. In 1952, such order taking was banned at the fair, so Kamprad told employees to take down the names of potential customers and contact them after the fair. Subsequently, IKEA was forbidden from showing prices on its furniture. Finally, the retail cartel members pressured the manufacturers cartel not to sell to IKEA. Kamprad responded by buying from a few independent Swedish furniture makers and by establishing new sources in Poland. To his delight, he found that his costs actually fell and he could charge even lower prices.

"[IKEA] resembles the monsters of old times," fumed one retailer in a letter to the cartel. "If we cut one of its heads, it soon grows another."

In 1953, Kamprad converted a disused factory in Älmhult into a warehouse-showroom. Company sales grew from SKr 3 million in 1953 to SKr 6 million in 1955. By 1961, IKEA's turnover was over SKr 40 million—80 times larger than the turnover of an average furniture store. (See Exhibit 2.) Of a total SKr 16.8 million furniture mail-order business in Sweden, IKEA had SKr 16 million.

In 1965, Kamprad opened a second outlet in Stockholm. Sensitive to the impact of the automobile on shopping habits, he gave priority to creating ample parking space rather than the focus, as was traditional, on downtown location. His new store, built on the outskirts of the city, was the largest in Europe at the time. Several of IKEA's basic practices were developed in this period: the self-service concept facilitated by the wide distribution of informative catalogs and the use of explanatory tickets on display merchandise, the knock-down kits that allowed stocks of all displayed items to be kept in store warehouses in flat pack boxes, and the development of suburban stores with large parking lots that brought the cash-and-carry concept to furniture retailing. Each of these practices resulted in economies that reinforced IKEA's position as the industry's low-price leader.

Between 1965 and 1973, IKEA opened seven new stores in Scandinavia, capturing a 15% share of the Swedish market. Rather than appeal to the older, more affluent consumers who had been the prime target of those offering the traditional, more expensive lines of furniture, Kamprad focused on younger buyers, who were often looking to furnish their first apartments. (See Exhibit 3 for customer data.) However, by

Exhibit 2 *IKEA and the Swedish Furniture Industry: 1961*

Personnel Functions in Swedish Furniture Stores in 1961*			
Personnel Occupied with	**IKEA**	**Furniture Stores**	**Furniture Sections of Department Stores**
Selling	29%	42%	65%
Clerical	44	13	6
Warehouse	17	11	16
Transportation	5	13	5
Workshop	5	21	8

Productivity of Swedish Furniture Retailers in 1961*			
Measure	**IKEA**	**Large Store[a]**	**Average Store**
Annual turnover in 1,000 SKr/employee	202	114	93
Annual turnover in SKr/sq. m.	1,453	1,076	704
Rent as percent of annual turnover	0.6%	3.0%	3.4%
Annual stockturn	3.2	2.9	2.3

*Source: R. Marteson, *Innovations in Multinational Retailing: IKEA in Swedish, Swiss, German, and Austrian Markets*, Doctoral Dissertation, (University of Gothenburg: Gothenburg, Sweden, 1981).
[a]Annual turnover SKr 1 million or more.

Exhibit 3   *IKEA Customer Profile and Buyer Behavior* *

Profile of IKEA Customers (Stockholm, 1975)

Age		Children		Status		Income (SKr– thousands)		Education (yrs)		Home	
0–25	47%	0	55%	Married	65	0–2	6%	0–6	24%	House	25%
25–35	32	1	22	Single	35	2–4	31	7–11	63	Apartment	63
35–45	14	2	16			4–6	25	12+	38	Condominium	12
45+	7	3	7			6+	38				

Buyer Behavior at IKEA (1975)

Primary determinants of purchase	%
Design	14%
Price	44
Quality	3
Large assortment	16
Catalog	11
Recommendations	1
Guarantees	0
Others	11
Total	100%

Importance of criteria for store-choice:	High	Low	No Response
Design	69%	5%	26%
Price	54	11	35
Quality	90	0	10
Distance	19	66	15

Consumer attitude to IKEA	Positive	Negative	Neither
Design	51%	10%	39%
Price	73	4	23
Quality	27	29	44
Distance	56	29	1

Purchase decisions were based on:	
Prior visits to the store	37%
Visits to other stores	72
Information from catalog	78

*Source: R. Marteson, (op. cit.)

the early 1970s, growth in the Swedish furniture market was stagnating. Kamprad felt it was time for IKEA to expand internationally.

Entry into Continental Europe

"It is our duty to expand," Kamprad said, dismissing those who insisted that furniture retailing was a strictly local business. "He ignored the economic downturn caused by the 1973 oil shock," remarked an executive, "and oddly, it worked in our favor. Our overhead costs were low, and the customers really appreciated our value-for-money approach." Because the German-speaking countries constituted the largest market for furniture in Europe, they became his priority, with Switzerland being the first target.

As in other European countries, Swiss furniture retailing was highly fragmented, with 67% of all firms employing three people or less. Most were in expensive, downtown locations. IKEA opened a large store in the suburbs of Zurich, in a canton which had about 20% of the country's consumer purchasing power. Ignoring the fact that furniture in Switzerland was of traditional design, very sturdy construction, and made from dark woods, the new store offered IKEA's line of simple contemporary designs in knockdown kits. Besides, rather than conform to the local service-intensive sales norms, the IKEA stores introduced self-service and cash-and-carry concepts. By distributing half a million catalogs and backing them with humorous, off-beat advertising (see Exhibit 4), the new store attracted 650,000 visitors in its first year.

In 1974, IKEA opened near Munich. Not only was West Germany Europe's largest and best organized furniture market (estimated at DM 12 billion in 1973), but it was also the largest furniture producer and exporter. German retailers were set up as elaborate furniture showrooms and they had adopted the role of order takers for manufacturers, holding little inventory of their own. As a result, consumers typically had to wait weeks for delivery, and manufacturers often faced sharp swings in demand as styles changed or the economy slowed. Again IKEA promoted itself as "those impossible Swedes with strange ideas." Promising inexpensive prices, immediate delivery, and the quality image of the Swedish Furniture Institute's Möbelfakta seal, the company attracted 37,000 people to the store during its first three days.

German retailers responded vigorously. Their trade association complained that the Möbelfakta requirements of the Swedish Furniture Institute were "considerably below the minimum requirements for quality furniture in West Germany and neighboring countries." Following legal proceedings against IKEA for deceiving customers with the Möbelfakta seals, the German court put constraints on how IKEA could use the seals. Other retailers initiated legal action challenging the truthfulness of IKEA's aggressive advertising. Again, the courts supported the German retailers and curtailed IKEA's activities.

Nonetheless, business boomed, with IKEA opening 10 new stores in West Germany over the next five years. By the late 1970s, it had built a 50% share in the cash-and-carry segment of the West German market. Retailers who had earlier fought IKEA's entry began to acknowledge the potential of this new retailing concept, and imitators began to mushroom. IKEA continued opening stores in Europe and franchising others outside Europe into the 1980s. (Exhibit 5 details IKEA's worldwide expansion.)

IKEA's Culture, Strategy, and Organization

As IKEA's spectacular growth and expansion continued, its unique management philosophy and organizational approach developed and changed. At the core was the founder, Ingvar Kamprad.

Ingvar Kamprad

Ingvar Kamprad seemed driven by a vision larger than IKEA. "To create a better everyday life for the majority of people," he said, "once and for

Exhibit 4   *Introductory Promotion Campaigns of IKEA in Continental Europe*

Advertising Themes for IKEA Store Opening: Switzerland, 1973
(Six letters from Herr Bunzli)

No.	Theme	Abstract from the Advertisement
1.	The new sales concept	Jokes about Swiss unwillingness to transport and assemble furniture, even for lower prices.
2.	No delivery by IKEA	"That is a stupid thing."
3.	Assembly of knocked-down furniture	"You can't do that to us Swiss."
4.	The wood used for furniture	"No teak . . . we are not Swedes."
5.	The Swiss needing furniture as status-symbol	"Swedes go home."
6.	Swiss quality	"Quality can come only from Switzerland."

Advertising Themes for IKEA Store Opening: Munich, 1974

No.	Theme
1.	Young people have more taste than money.
2.	We achieve the impossible.
3.	On October 17, we'll open Munich's furniture highway.
4.	At long last, the impossible furniture store will open on October 17.
5.	Trees off the ground we take, and furniture for you we make.

Promotion Campaigns: West Germany 1974–1979

No.	Campaign	Theme
1.	The day of the singles	Single visitors could get their socks washed at IKEA.
2.	The day of the baker	Crispy bread straight from the oven to all store visitors.
3.	The day of the barber	Free manicure and haircut to store visitors.
4.	The day of the breakfast	All visitors were offered free breakfasts.
5.	IKEA birthday	Free gifts to visitors.
6.	Rent a Christmas tree	Customers could rent a Christmas tree for 10 D Marks, refundable after Christmas if the tree was returned.
7.	Day of the sleeper	Offered 300 people the opportunity to test the new IKEA mattresses overnight in its store, and buy them the next morning for 10 D Marks.

all, we have decided to side with the many. We know that in the future we may make a valuable contribution to the democratization process at home and abroad." One of his executives said of him, "He focuses on the human aspect. What motivates Ingvar is not profit alone but improving the quality of life of the people."

Throughout IKEA, Kamprad was revered as a visionary. "He consistently turned problems into opportunities and showed us how it is not dangerous to be different," said one executive. But Kamprad also paid extraordinary attention to the details of his business, and could operate simultaneously on multiple levels. "In a group of

Exhibit 5   IKEA's Worldwide Expansion

AUSTRIA — Area in sq.m.*

Year	Location	Area
1977(81)	Vienna	23,500
1981	Wels	11,700
1989	Graz**	14,900

BELGIUM

Year	Location	Area
1984	Ternat (Brussels)	15,100
	Nossegem	11,100
1985	Wilrijk (Antwerp)	14,200
	Hognoul (Liége)	12,900

CANADA

Year	Location	Area
1976(83)	Vancouver	14,700
1977(87)	Toronto	20,000
1978(85)	Edmonton	10,400
1979	Calgary	5,700
	Ottawa	6,600
1982	Quebec	9,600
1982(86)	Montreal	15,400

DENMARK

Year	Location	Area
1969(75)	Tastrup (Copenhagen)	39,500
1980	Arhus	9,700
1982	Aalborg	6,700
1985	Odense	1,400

FRANCE

Year	Location	Area
1981	First establishment no longer in use	
1982(87)	Lyon	18,900
1983	Evry (south of Paris)	24,000
1985	Vitrolles (Marseilles)	15,700
1986	Paris-Nord	24,800
1988	Lomme** (Lille)	15,100

ITALY

Year	Location	Area
1989	Fulvio Testi** (Milano)	11,900

THE NETHERLANDS

Year	Location	Area
1979	Sliedrecht (Rotterdam)	16,600
1982(85)	Amsterdam	19,600
1983	Duiven	10,800

NORWAY

Year	Location	Area
1963(75)	Slependen (Oslo)	19,600
1984	Bergen	10,500
1988	Forus** (Stavanger)	14,000

SWEDEN

Year	Location	Area
1958	Älmhult	18,400
1965	Stockholm	44,000
1966	Sundsvall	11,800
1967(77)	Malmö	19,900

SWEDEN (continued)

Year	Location	Area
1972	Gothenburg	24,700
1977	Linköping	16,000
1981(87)	Jönköping	3,500
	Gävle	6,700
1982(88)	Helsingborg	11,600
1982	Örebro	2,300
1982(86)	Uppsala	13,000
1984	Västerås	10,900

SWITZERLAND

Year	Location	Area
1973(79)	Spreitenbach (Zürich)	25,500
1979	Aubonne (Lausanne)	17,500
1986	Emmen (Lucerne)	3,000

UNITED KINGDOM

Year	Location	Area
1987	Warrington	17,100
1988	Brent Park** (London)	23,300

USA

Year	Location	Area
1985	Philadelphia	15,000
1986	Woodbridge (Washington)	14,500
1988	Baltimore**	19,700
1989	Pittsburgh**	19,900

WEST GERMANY

Year	Location	Area
1974(86)	Eching	24,800
1975(78)	Godorf (Cologne)	16,100
1975	Dorsten	17,600
1976	Grossburgwedel (Hanover)	14,300
1977	Stuhr (Bremen)	12,900
	Kaltenkirchen (Hamburg)	8,000
1977(85)	Wallau (Frankfurt)	23,800
1978	Kamen (Dortmund)	14,200
	Stuttgart	4,300
1979	Berlin	17,700
	Kaarst (Düsseldorf)	14,200
1980	Kassel	4,200
1981	Poppenreuth (Fürth/Nuremberg)	19,100
	Schwalbach-Bous (Saarbrücken)	6,200
	Freiburg	6,100
	Walldorf	18,300
1983	Löhne-Gohfeld	6,200
1989	Schnelsen** (Hamburg)	22,800

Figures in brackets refer to the date of rebuilding.

*Incl. adjacent warehouses.
**Will be inaugurated after 88.08.31. Not included in total figures.

600 items, he will ask about a particular product, know its price, its cost and its source, and he will expect you to know it, too. He checks everything and wants to do everything he can. He does not seem to believe in delegation. He is constantly bypassing formal structures to talk directly with front-line managers, particularly the designers and the purchasing group."

Kamprad's interest in front-line operations also extended to IKEA's staff. Whenever he visited a store he tried to meet and shake hands with every employee, offering a few words of praise, encouragement, or advice as he did so. The simple—some said spartan—values of his native Småland had stayed with Kamprad, and he still rose early, worked hard, lived simply, and took a common-sense approach to management. One executive's account of Kamprad's recent visit to a newly opened store in Hamburg captured much of the founder's management style:

> *During his rounds of the new store, he made points that covered 19 pages of notes. They ranged from comments about the basic design—he felt the building had far too many angles which added to construction costs—to the size of the price tags and the placement of posters in the store.*
>
> *He invited the employees to stay after work—and almost all did—so he could thank them for their efforts, since most had transferred from a distant store site. The dinner was typical IKEA style—the employees went first to the buffet, the managers went next, and Ingvar Kamprad was among the last when only the remnants were left. After dinner, Ingvar shook hands and talked with all 150 present, finally leaving the store well past midnight. That experience will keep the motivation high for weeks. Each employee will go back home and tell his family and his friends that Ingvar shook hands with him.*
>
> *When the store manager arrived at 6:30 the next morning, he found that Ingvar had been in the store for over an hour. Although he was staying in a modest hotel, he remarked that it*

> *was probably priced 5 DM too high. That story will probably circulate through the company as many others do—like the one about Ingvar driving around town late at night checking hotel prices, till he found one economical enough. It's all part of the aura and the legend that surrounds him.*

IKEA's Management Philosophy and Practices

In many ways, IKEA developed as an extension of Kamprad and his view of life. "The true IKEA spirit," he remarked, "is founded on our enthusiasm, on our constant will to renew, on our cost-consciousness, on our willingness to assume responsibility and to help, on our humbleness before the task, and on the simplicity in our behavior." Over the years a very distinct organization culture and management style had emerged.

The company operated very informally. It was reflected in the neat but casual dress of the employees (jeans and sweaters were the norm), in the relaxed office atmosphere with practically everyone sitting in an open-plan office landscape, and in the familiar and personal way the employees addressed each other—with the personal *"du"* rather than the more formal *"sie"* in Germany, and in France, with *"tu"* rather than *"vous."* Kamprad noted, "A better everyday life means getting away from status and conventions—being freer and more at ease as human beings." But a senior executive had another view: "This environment actually puts pressure on management to perform. There is no security available behind status or closed doors."

The IKEA management process also stressed simplicity and attention to detail. "Complicated rules paralyze!" said Ingvar Kamprad. An oft-repeated IKEA saying was "Retail is detail." Store managers and corporate staff alike were expected to fully understand the operations of IKEA's stores. The company organized "antibureaucrat weeks" that required all managers to work in store showrooms and warehouses for at least a week every year. The work pace was such that executives joked that IKEA believed in "management by running around."

Cost consciousness was another strong part of the management culture. "Waste of resources," said Kamprad, "is a mortal sin at IKEA. Expensive solutions are often signs of mediocrity, and an idea without a price tag is never acceptable." Although cost consciousness extended into all aspects of the operation, travel and entertainment expenses were particularly sensitive. The head-office travel department had circulated a pamphlet titled "Travelling for IKEA," which contained tips on qualifying for the most inexpensive air fares, and listed economical, simple "IKEA hotels." "We do not set any price on time," remarked an executive, recalling that he had once phoned Kamprad to get approval to fly first class. He explained that economy class was full, and that he had an urgent appointment to keep. "There is no first class in IKEA," Kamprad had replied, refusing his request. "Perhaps you should go by car." The executive completed the 350-mile trip by taxi.

The search for creative solutions was highly prized within IKEA. Kamprad had written, "Only while sleeping one makes no mistakes. The fear of making mistakes is the root of bureaucracy and the enemy of all evolution." Though planning for the future was encouraged, overanalysis was not. "Exaggerated planning can be fatal!" Kamprad advised his executives. "Let simplicity and common sense characterize your planning."

Kamprad had created company legends out of stories where creative common sense experiments had changed the way the company did business. On opening day of the original Stockholm store, for example, the warehouse could not cope with the rush of customers. The store manager suggested that they be allowed to go into the warehouse to pick up their purchases. The result was so successful that future warehouses were designed to allow self-selection by customers, resulting in cost savings and faster service.

Because it had such a strong and unique culture, IKEA preferred not to recruit those who had already been immersed in another cultural stream. Nor was higher education necessary or even advantageous in IKEA. "The Stockholm-raised, highly educated, status-oriented individuals often find it difficult to adjust to the culture of the company," remarked one executive. "Younger, more open recruits not only keep costs low, but they also absorb and amplify the enthusiasm of the company. We can develop them quickly by delegating responsibilities early, rotating them frequently, and offering rapid promotions to the high performers. The average age of a store manager is only 34." An executive listed the characteristics of the successful new applicants to IKEA:

They are people who accept our values and are willing to act on our ideas. They tend to be straightforward rather than flashy, and not too status-conscious. They must be hard-working and comfortable dealing with everyone from the customer to the owner to the cashier. But perhaps the most important quality for an Ikean is ödmjukhet—a Swedish word that implies humility, modesty and respect for one's fellow man. It may be hard to translate, but we know it when we see it. It's reflected in things like personal simplicity and self-criticism.

The people and the values resulted in a unique work environment of which Kamprad was genuinely proud. "We take care of each other and inspire each other. One cannot help feeling sorry for those who cannot or will not join us," he said.

In 1976, Kamprad felt the need to commit to paper the values that had developed in IKEA during the previous decade. His thesis, *Testament of a Furniture Dealer,* became an important means for spreading the IKEA philosophy during a period of rapid international expansion. (Extracts are given in Exhibit 6.) With the help of this document, the organization strove to retain much of its unique culture, even as it spread into different countries. The big ideas contained in Kamprad's thesis were spread

Exhibit 6   *Extracts from the 11-Page Document,* Testament of a Furniture Dealer

What is good for our customers is also good for us in the long run. . . . We know we can have an important effect on practically all markets. We know that we may make a valuable contribution to the democratization process at home and abroad. . . . That is why it is our duty to expand.

The following section describes our product range and price philosophy, which is the backbone of our work. Furthermore, we describe rules and methods which will continue to make IKEA a unique company.

1. **The Product Range—Our Identity**
    Range: To cover the total home area, indoors as well as outdoors, with loose as well as fixed home furnishings. This range shall always be limited.
    Profile: Our basic range shall be . . . simple and straightforward . . . durable and easy to live with . . . (and) shall express design, color, and joy. In Scandinavia [it] should be regarded as typically IKEA and outside Scandinavia as typically Swedish.
    Quality: Throw-away products is not IKEA. But quality should never be an end in itself. It should always be adapted to the consumer's interests in the long run.
    Changes: Our basic policy to serve the majority of people can never be changed.

2. **The IKEA Spirit—A Strong and Living Reality**
    The true IKEA spirit is still founded on our enthusiasm, on our constant will to renew, on our cost consciousness, on our willingness to assume responsibility and help, on our humbleness before the task, and on the simplicity in our behavior. . . . The IKEA spirit is still here, but it has to be taken care of and developed with time. **Development, however, is not always equal to progress.** It depends upon you, as a leader and a responsible person, to make development progressive.

3. **Profit Gives Us Resources**
    Profit is a wonderful word! Let us rely on ourselves when it comes to creating resources. The aim for accumulating our resources is **to obtain the best results in the long run**.

4. **To Reach Good Results with Small Means**
    Expensive solutions . . . are often a sign of mediocrity. We have no interest in a solution until we know what it costs.

5. **Simplicity is a Virtue**
    Bureaucracy complicates and paralyzes! Exaggerated planning can be fatal. . . . Simplicity in our behavior gives us strength.

6. **The Different Way**
    By daring to be different, we find new ways. . . . I hope we never have two stores completely alike (because) a healthy appetite for experimenting will lead us forward.

7. **Concentration of Energy—Important to Our Success**
    The general who splits up his forces inevitably fails.. . . . We too have to concentrate. We cannot do everything everywhere, at the same time.

8. **To Assume Responsibility—A Privilege**
    To assume responsibility has nothing to do with education, economy or position. In our IKEA family we want to keep the human being in the center, and to support each other. . . . To make mistakes is the privilege of the active person.

9. **Most Things Still Remain to be Done—A Glorious Future**
    Happiness is not to reach one's goal but to be on the way. Experience is the drag on all evolution. . . . Humbleness, will, and strengths are your secret weapons. . . . Time is your most important asset. What we want, we can and will do. Together. A glorious future!

through training and "mouth-to-ear" transfer. Specially trained "IKEA ambassadors" were assigned to key positions in all units to spread the company's philosophy and values by educating their subordinates and by acting as role models. By 1989, about 300 such cultural agents had been trained in a special week-long seminar which covered not only the company's history and culture (presented personally by Kamprad), but also detailed training on how to spread the message.

The Adapting IKEA Strategy

At the heart of the IKEA strategy was its product range. Ingvar Kamprad called it "our identity" and set up clear and detailed guidelines on profile, quality, and price. While leaving considerable flexibility for fringe products, he decreed that IKEA should stand for essential products for the home—simple, durable, and well designed—priced to be accessible to the majority of the people.

IKEA had over 20,000 product offerings, of which 12,000 formed the core of simple, functional items common across IKEA stores worldwide. Of these, the 2,000 to 3,000 items displayed in the catalog received special attention, since the catalog was the centerpiece of the company's product promotion policy. Indeed, management saw it as the principal means of educating consumers to the IKEA product line and concept. By 1988, the annual distribution of 44 million catalogs in 12 languages and 27 editions accounted for half the company's marketing budget.

In order to maintain its low-price reputation and allow catalog prices to be guaranteed for a year, management promoted an organization-wide obsession with cost control. The importance of production flexibility and responsiveness led to the following activities:

- **Finding low-priced materials:** IKEA designers and buyers were always looking for less expensive, good-quality alternative materials, and, in the early 1960s, led the trend to replace traditional teak with less costly oak materials. In the 1970s, IKEA helped win a broader acceptance of inexpensive pinewood furniture.

- **Matching products to capabilities:** "We don't buy products, we buy production capacities," remarked a purchase executive. In an effort to maximize production from available capacity, IKEA constantly searched for unconventional suppliers. For example, it had offered contracts for table manufacture to a ski supplier, and cushion covers to a shirt manufacturer with excess capacity. "If the suppliers have capacity, we ask them to produce first, and then we worry about selling the output. It is by ensuring our suppliers' delivery schedule security and by filling their available manufacturing capacity that we maintain our unique price levels."

- **Developing long-term relations with suppliers:** IKEA supported its suppliers both technically and financially even to the point of designing their factories, buying their machines and setting up their operations. In order to meet cost objectives and maintain long-term supplier relationships, designers worked two to three years ahead of current products. By ensuring a high, steady volume of orders, IKEA encouraged the suppliers to invest and drive down manufacturing costs. In furniture alone, IKEA purchased from about 1,500 suppliers in more than 40 countries. Purchases were consolidated in 12 central warehouses, which maintained high inventories not only because of commitments to suppliers, but also to meet the company's 90% to 95% service-level objective on catalog items.

The most visible aspect of IKEA's strategy was its highly successful retail operations. The distinctive stores with their constant innovations had changed the face of furniture retailing in Europe. As IKEA expanded, tremendous internal competitiveness developed among the stores. "The newly set-up stores would look at the previously developed stores and try their hardest to improve on them," recalled an executive. "One would set up a green plant department, so the next would create a clock section." It was by this process that some of the unique distinguishing characteristics of the typical IKEA store emerged: supervised play areas for children, which featured a large "pool" filled with red styrofoam balls; in-store cafes that served inexpensive exotic meals, such as Swedish meatballs; and fully equipped nursery and baby-changing facilities.

Although this interstore competition resulted in numerous innovative new ideas, it also led to a certain amount of unnecessary differentiation and wheel reinvention. So much so that by the mid-1980s, some senior managers began proposing greater coordination and standardization of the diverse operations and multiple approaches. They argued that not only would such standardization project a clearer IKEA image, but it could also result in considerable savings. An executive recalled:

> *Hans Ax was the major champion of the "IKEA concept." He felt that we were spending too much on diverse development projects instead of taking the best ideas, standardizing our approach, and applying it to all the stores. As a result of this effort, a uniform concept has emerged. Guidelines have developed ranging from the basic color of the IKEA signs to the size of plants sold in our garden shops.*

An important part of the IKEA concept was the development of standard in-store display areas. In every store there were five or six areas called studios which displayed some of the best-selling products. Under the IKEA concept, the locations of the studios within the retail store and their display settings were standardized, down to the last centimeter of layout design.

The concept also specified store architecture more precisely, defining the classic IKEA traffic flow that took customers through the store in a four-leafed clover pattern to maximize their exposure to the product line. It prescribed standard in-store facilities, including baby-changing rooms, a supervised play area for children, information centers, and cafes. "We have become a little like McDonald's in our insistence that all the stores conform on these points," said one headquarters executive. "We want to create a unique ambience that makes IKEA not just a furniture store, but a family outing destination that can compete with the entertainment park and the zoo for family time."

The Evolving Organization

When IKEA started internationalizing, Kamprad organized its non-Scandinavian business into an Expansion Group and an Operations Group. (See Exhibit 7.) The former was responsible for initial planning for new market entry. First, a construction team was sent in to set up the new facility. Then, two months before the opening, a "build-up" team from the first-year group would take charge, training the staff, establishing operations, and managing the opening. After about a year, they would hand responsibility over to the Operations Group.

This organization allowed rapid growth and also propelled many of IKEA's top managers to positions of responsibility. Recalled an IKEA executive:

> *The pioneering spirit of a core group allowed our international expansion to succeed. With no guidelines except Ingvar's thesis and a general objective, young entrepreneurs would buy land, build and set up a store, and quickly move on to the next store. The pace was breathtaking. You could be hired on Monday and sent out on Thursday on a key mission. The company had unbelievable confidence in its people, and this experience created today's leaders in IKEA—Anders Moberg, Thomas Blomquist, and many others.*

Responsibilities shifted frequently and careers progressed rapidly. Most senior executives were in their thirties. Anders Moberg, now IKEA's CEO at 38, had started his career in store administration, moving to work in build-up groups before being appointed store manager in Austria

Exhibit 7   *Organization During the 1970s and Early 1980s*

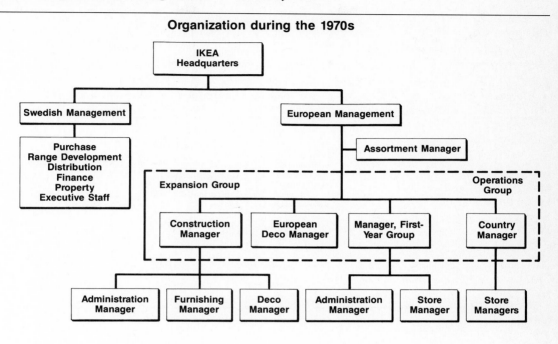

Organization during the 1970s

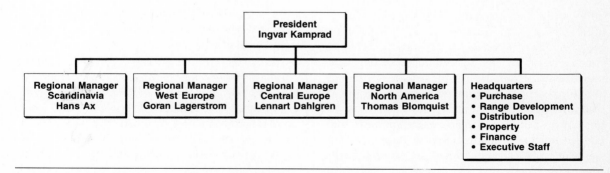

Organization during the early 1980s

and in Switzerland. He then led the IKEA entry into France as country manager.

In the early 1980s, with a well-established international organization, IKEA retail was reorganized into four geographical regions, headed by regional managers. (See Exhibit 7.) However, the purchasing, distribution, and design functions continued to be centrally controlled and were staffed by specialists who rarely migrated to other functions. Most purchasers, for example, came from Småland, Kamprad's home region, whose inhabitants were renowned for their

Exhibit 8   *Ownership Structure of the IKEA Group*

Inter-IKEA Systems. BV Holland	Controlled by the Kamprad Family	**IKEA Stitching Holland**	Charitable Foundation
Inter-IKEA Systems. AS Denmark	Licensor and Franchisor of IKEA Concept and Trademark	**INGKA Holdings Europe**	

Scandinavia   Overseas

Profits   Franchises

IKEA Holdings	**IKEA Holdings**	**IKEA Holdings**	**Non-IKEA Stores**
• Sweden • Norway • Denmark	• West Germany • France • Switzerland • Austria • Belgium • United Kingdom • Netherlands • Italy	• Canada • United States	• Australia • Singapore • Iceland • Kuwait • Saudi Arabia • Canary Islands • Hong Kong

Royalties   Royalties   Royalties   Franchise Fees

thriftiness. They rarely had a college education, and their job rotation and career growth were slower and more specialized than the retailers'.

IKEA's senior management remained predominantly Scandinavian. "There is an efficiency in having a homogeneous group," reasoned a Swedish manager of a foreign operation. "They instinctively follow the Scandinavian management philosophy of simple, people-oriented, nonhierarchic operations." Although there was no overt discrimination, some non-Swedes felt it was important to speak Swedish and understand the Smålandish psyche to be a member of the inner management circle, since the dominant company ethic was viewed internally as systematized Smålandish common sense. Indeed, IKEA's president, Anders Moberg, had been publicly quoted as saying, "I would advise any foreign employee who really wants to advance in this company to learn Swedish. They will then get a completely different feeling for our culture, our mood, our values. All in all, we encourage all our foreign personnel to have as much contact with Sweden as possible, for instance, by going to Sweden for their holidays."

Over the years, the legal ownership structure of the IKEA group had been shaped by several influences. Above all, Kamprad wanted to ensure that the business would live on after him and would not be broken up in some kind of inheritance dispute. He and his family controlled a company whose income derived from franchise fees and royalties paid by IKEA stores. Operating profits were transferred to a charitable foundation Kamprad had set up in the Netherlands to escape stringent Swedish taxes and foreign exchange regulations. (See Exhibit 8.) Kamprad himself had moved to Lausanne, Switzerland, partly to escape the high Swedish taxes.

NEW DIRECTIONS AND FUTURE ISSUES

By the late 1980s, Kamprad and his management team were working on some bold new strategies to take IKEA into the next decade.

Along with the new directions, however, came some questions about how long the company could maintain its remarkable record of growth and expansion.

New Horizons

In 1979, Kamprad had bought a faltering IKEA franchise in Canada, and turned it into a lucrative business within three years. Thereafter, management had been eyeing the United States, the largest furniture market in the world (estimated at $15 billion in 1985). The decision process leading to entry into the United States was in classic IKEA style, as Björn Bayley, head of the Canadian operations at the time, recalled:

The U.S. market had enormous potential. There are 18 million people in New York alone—more than the population of Scandinavia. Once it became known within IKEA that we were planning to open stores in the United States, three or four managers staked out a claim to head the U.S. operations. But Ingvar was not ready to decide and, for several months, confusion reigned. Finally, he called me from a railway station in Stuttgart. He had decided to run the new U.S. stores as part of the Canadian operation. He wanted us to open two stores on the East Coast with as little hoopla as possible, and, once these were successful, follow with further expansion.

As usual, it didn't take long for imitators to appear. Indeed, a California-based retailer calling itself Stör began emulating IKEA's concepts so exactly—from product designs to ball-filled children's play areas—that the company launched legal proceedings against them. To preserve its image and to preempt imitators, management decided to accelerate its national expansion plans. By 1989, stores had been opened in Philadelphia, Washington, Baltimore and Pittsburgh, and six more openings were scheduled by 1992.

In 1987, IKEA entered the U.K., a market estimated at £5 billion, and home of the only other large multinational furniture retailer—the more upscale Habitat. A successful entry in Warrington (in the northwest) was followed by the opening of the country's largest home furnishing store, close to London. Plans for another 10 stores in the U.K. were announced.

In 1989, IKEA opened its first store in Italy—one of Europe's largest furniture markets. Again, its initial reception was excellent. For the first three days of operation, there were hour-long queues outside the store. As soon as it could obtain the necessary permits, the company hoped to expand south from its base in Milan.

IKEA had also taken the first steps in its plans to build a major presence in Russia and Eastern Europe. Not surprisingly, the unconventional idea was hatched by Ingvar Kamprad in the mid-1980s. Recalled an IKEA executive, "Our entire East European strategy was mapped out by Ingvar on a small paper napkin. Just about every aspect of the entry strategy was laid out on this small piece of paper—we call it his Picasso—and for the past few years we have just built on and expanded that original vision."

The bold plans called for new skills and involved different risks. To source from 15 factories in Russia and many others in East Europe would require an investment in excess of SKr 500 million. The limited ability to transfer hard currency from East Europe forced the company to plan for extensive countertrade deals so that dividends and capital repayment could be replaced by furniture exports to the West. Some felt that it was too early to risk heavy resource dependence on the Eastern Bloc countries, given their low reliability of service and poor quality image. Others were concerned that recent economic and political reforms in many of these countries could easily suffer major reversals. However, in face of Kamprad's persistence, IKEA was proceeding with this major thrust.

The site of its first East European outlet was in Budapest, where the company took a 50% share in a joint venture with a Hungarian retail chain. Soon after, it entered an agreement to open a store in Leningrad. In 1988, IKEA Poland decided to build a $25 million warehouse and retail center near Warsaw. As part of that plan,

IKEA would buy furniture and establish a joint-venture woodworking factory in Poland. Outlets were also planned in Yugoslavia. An office in Vienna coordinated the administration of these various East European activities.

New Organization and Leadership

In 1986, Ingvar Kamprad appointed 35-year-old Anders Moberg as president. At the same time, IKEA operations were reorganized on functional lines (see Exhibit 9). At the top of the group was the four-person supervisory board, which reviewed the group's general direction. Under the supervisory board was the executive board, which was responsible for the day-to-day operations of the group. Except for Björn Bayley, all executive board members were based in IKEA's 50-person headquarters in Humlebaek, Denmark. Of the group's key basic functions, product range, purchasing, and distribution service reported directly to Moberg in his operating capacity as head of wholesale. Ingvar Kamprad also continued his deep involvement with the purchase and product range functions and often spent time discussing the intricacies of purchasing or design with managers five or more levels below him.

The leadership shift had an impact on the company's management style. Remarked one executive, "With over 13,000 employees worldwide, some have begun to push for a more formalized approach. Anders is more committed to systematization, and he delegates much more than Ingvar." In 1988, Moberg introduced a formal budgeting and planning process. Business plans from the various country operations and product groups were integrated and modified at the executive board level. A corporate plan with three years' horizon was developed and sent back to the country units and the product groups to ensure their actions were in conformity with the plan.

Blanket cost consciousness at all levels was giving way to cost-benefit studies. Instead of seeking out the least expensive sites, the company was now more willing to locate new stores at A-class sites, where justified. Furthermore, while earlier stores had been built for the mid-week crowds, newer store capacity was being matched with weekend crowds. Although many applauded the changes as overdue, some felt they were not coming fast enough:

There is a time bomb ticking inside IKEA's growing profitability that makes employees less willing to sacrifice and more anxious to share the rewards. There is often a conflict between cost-consciousness and efficiency. It's hard to keep the old spirit of frugality when the business is doing so well.

Future Directions and Concerns

Overall, IKEA hoped to reach a turnover of SKr 19 billion by 1990 and perhaps three times that amount by the year 2000, principally through rapid geographical expansion. But there was some cause for concern. Said one executive, "We are currently making annual risk capital investment of about SKr 500 million, which translates to opening four to six new stores every year. But our expansion plans are much more ambitious. In the United States alone, our rollout plan calls for two to three new stores every year, accelerating to five or six a year by the mid-1990s. I just hope we are not overextending ourselves."

Over the next few years, the median age and income level in most developed countries was expected to rise, while IKEA's target market segment of young, low- to middle-income families would be shrinking. A senior executive reflected:

We have to expand into other segments like office furniture and more traditional designs for the older, richer people. In our advertising also, we have started playing down the image of the "crazy Swedes," replacing it with a superior quality image. In entering the United States, for example, we have tried to project a sober image right from the beginning. But we cannot risk making our profile too diffuse, or distorting the IKEA image.

Exhibit 9 *Organization Structure of IKEA after 1986*

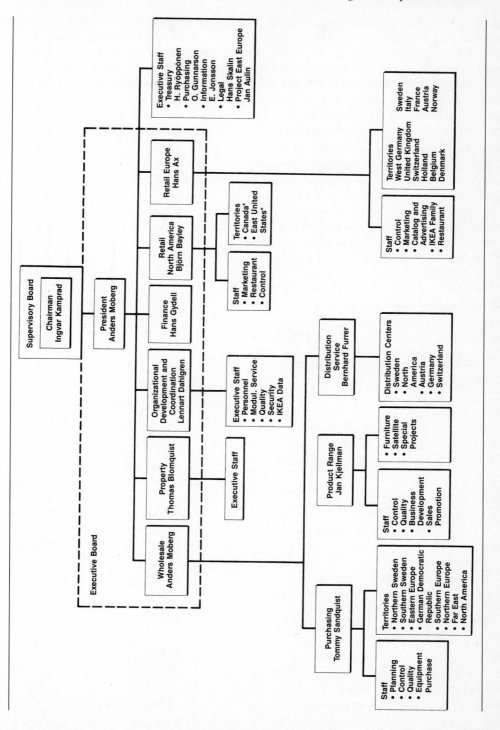

Perhaps the biggest concern was whether the rapid growth and increasing geographic spread of IKEA would make it difficult to retain the company's cultural values. With over 13,000 employees worldwide and 1,000 new recruits being added annually, many newcomers had only a vague sense of the IKEA way. Björn Bayley, head of North American operations, commented:

The only constraint to our growth is people. At the top levels, our commitment to Ingvar's thesis still exists. But these days, the pioneers are having to learn how to fill in forms. IKEA is adding about 10% to its work force every year, in addition to normal personnel turnover, which can be as high as 20% in some departments. Inculcating the IKEA way into such a rapidly growing community is itself a tremendous challenge.

Another barrier we now face is the differences in attitudes between America and Scandinavia. Because of the low job security here, American employees are always looking for guidance—despite their higher education and need to achieve. The IKEA way requires openness and a willingness to take responsibility. We want people to stand up and disagree with authority if they have confidence in their beliefs. Despite intensive training programs, it has been hard making the IKEA way their way of life here in the United States.

Even Kamprad conceded:

Before, it was more concrete, the will to help each other, the art of managing with small means—being cost-conscious almost to the point of stinginess, the humbleness, the irresistible enthusiasm and the wonderful community through thick and thin. Certainly it is more difficult now when the individual is gradually being wiped out in the gray gloominess of collective agreements.

The importance of a homogeneous management group in maintaining this common cultural bond was also being debated within the company. "When we open in a new country, we need the top management to be culture bearers for IKEA," remarked an executive, "so they are Scandinavian." Of the 65 senior executives in IKEA, 60 were Swedish or Danish, and almost all the non-Scandinavians were concentrated in distribution services. Furthermore, most of the senior executives came from the retail side of business. Some in the company felt such similarity of background was no longer in IKEA's best interest, as reflected by the comments of one company executive:

Sometimes, I think there is too much ideology bordering on religion. You sell your soul to IKEA when you start internalizing the culture. Ingvar is obsessed with his own ideas, and there is an element of fanaticism and intolerance towards people who think differently. I, for one, react negatively to the stingy mentality that sometimes shows through our cost-consciousness, or when Ingvar says that we can reach self-fulfillment only through our jobs—we work hard, but there is no reason that our jobs should necessarily dominate our lives.

Concerns were also being raised about how far IKEA could or should push its common concept across all stores even as it rapidly expanded internationally. As one executive put it:

Our common concept should leave sufficient room for creativity and freedom at the individual store level. Very often, market orientation and IKEA concept orientation clash. The U.S. market wants shelves with space for TV sets while European shelves are designed only for books. Should we adapt our line, or continue to sell bookshelves in the United States? The Scandinavian-designed bed and mattress is fundamentally different from the standard approach that is the norm in continental Europe. Should we continue to push the Scandinavian sleeping preferences on the rest of Europe?

But it's more than an issue of product design—it extends to how much we should adapt our organization and culture. Humility may be a virtue in Europe, for example, but should we impose it on our U.S. organization? Or is the attitude of "success breeds success" more appropriate there? Should our business drive our culture, or should our culture drive our business?

Perhaps the deepest concern was one that was often unspoken. How well would IKEA survive Ingvar Kamprad's eventual departure from the company? To this concern, Ingvar Kamprad responded, "The IKEA ideology is not the work of one man but the sum of many impulses from all the IKEA leadership. Its supporting framework is massive." But others were less sanguine. One manager summed up the concerns of many: "Ingvar is a patriarch. His dominating personality has been the life breath of the company, and you have to question how we will survive when he is gone."

KOMATSU LTD.: PROJECT G'S GLOBALIZATION

On a breezy spring day in 1991, passers-by on the bustling street in front of Komatsu's world headquarters stopped, pointed, and stared at the spectacle atop the building. Ten stories above, workers were dismantling one of central Tokyo's most notable landmarks—a giant, yellow Komatsu bulldozer precariously perched on a tall pole. For 25 years, this corporate icon had symbolized Komatsu's overriding strategic aim to surpass Caterpillar (Cat) and become the world's premier construction equipment manufacturer.

President Tetsuya Katada had carefully timed the removal of this corporate symbol to mark recent changes in the company in preparation for Komatsu's spring celebration of its 70th anniversary. Soon, a new electronic beacon would flash a new logo and a new corporate slogan ("The Earth Company, Unlimited"), confirming the changes in strategy and management prac-

tices that Katada and his management had started to implement. The new company president explained:

> Pulling down the bulldozer is just one example showing the strong determination of the president to outsiders and, more importantly, employees that we can't single-mindedly pursue production of the bulldozer. . . . Instead, we have challenged the organization with a new slogan, "Growth, Global, Groupwide"— or the three Gs for short. It's a much more abstract challenge than one focused on catching and beating Cat, but I hope it will stimulate people to think and discuss creatively what Komatsu can be.

Katada's Three Gs slogan challenged managers in all parts of Komatsu to reignite growth through a renewed commitment to global expansion, and an increase in groupwide leverag-

---

This case was prepared by Christopher A. Bartlett. It is adapted from Komatsu Ltd. and Project G (A), Case No. 395-001, and (B), Case No. 395-002, by Professor Christopher A. Bartlett and Research Associate Robert W. Lightfoot. Copyright © 1997 by the President and Fellows of Harvard College. Harvard Business School case 398-016.

ing of resources. For the core construction equipment business, it implied nothing less than a revolution. After three decades of focusing on the goal "to catch up and surpass Cat," this group was now being told to broaden their perspective and define the business on its own terms. In particular, Katada's challenge would require even further expansion of the company's three regionally based operations in the Americas, Europe, and Asia-Pacific. Furthermore, although several parts of this organization were new and untried, management felt it must try to integrate these operations more into a worldwide network of resources. Finally, those in Tokyo recognized that unless they began to elicit the ideas and leverage the expertise of these international operations, Project G would be little more than rhetoric.

KOMATSU COMPANY AND MANAGEMENT HISTORY

Established in 1921 as a specialized producer of mining equipment, Komatsu expanded into agricultural machinery during the 1930s and, during World War II, into the production of military equipment. The heavy-machinery expertise the company developed positioned it well to expand into earth-moving equipment needed for postwar reconstruction. Soon, construction equipment dominated Komatsu's sales.

In the high-demand and capital-constrained Japanese environment, Komatsu held a market share of more than 50%, despite the low quality of its equipment at that time. This comfortable situation changed in 1963 when, after the government decided to open the industry to foreign investors, Cat announced it would enter the market in partnership with Mitsubishi. At this time, Komatsu had sales of $168 million and a product line well below world standards. Local analysts predicted three years of struggle before Cat bankrupted the puny local company.

Emergence and Expansion: The Kawai Era (1964–1982)

It was in this context that Ryoichi Kawai assumed the presidency of Komatsu from his father in 1964.[1] The older man had prepared the company by initiating a Total Quality Control (TQC) program in 1961. Building on this base, Ryoichi Kawai's strategy for the company was straightforward—to acquire and develop advanced technology, to raise quality, and to increase efficiency to the level necessary to "catch up with and surpass Cat." To galvanize the company around his challenge and to focus management on his strategic priorities, Kawai introduced a style of management which he called "management by policy." Kawai explained the philosophy behind his strongly focused and directive approach:

Personally, I believe that a company must always be innovative. To this end, the basic policy and value of the target must be clarified so that all the staff members can fully understand what the company is aiming for in a specific time period. This is the purpose of the management-by-policy system.

Under the umbrella of the TQC philosophy that was now deeply ingrained in Komatsu, management by policy began with Kawai's statement of an overriding, focused priority for the company. Launched the year after Cat announced its entry into the Japanese market, his first policy, "Project A," sought to raise the quality of Komatsu's middle-sized bulldozers to Cat's level. To support this goal, Kawai began an aggressive program to license technology from leading companies such as Cummins, International Harvester, and Bucyrus-Erie. As he implemented his "management by policy" approach, the young CEO instituted a new system of control, the "Plan, Do, Check, Act" (PDCA) cycle. Once

[1]For a detailed description of the Kawai era, see "Komatsu: Ryoichi Kawai's Leadership," HBS case no. 390-037.

Exhibit 1   *Company Description of "Plan, Do, Check, Act" Control Cycle**

	Stage	Actual Activities
What is Control? The term "control" is explained in the concept of a plan-do-check-action circle. Please understand that the concept of control is practice. In short, control means the plan-do-check-action circle.	**Plan (P)**	• In a work shop: arranging daily operation, preparing operation standards, equipment, jigs and tools, and planning for cost reduction. • In a technical department: planning for research and establishing design policy. • In a sales department: preparation of daily or monthly sales and visiting plans according to a given target. • Working out countermeasures for any defects or debts. • Understanding the problem through facts. One must grasp the facts of the matter in order to know the problem. Never adopt false data. To grasp the facts • See the place where the problem exists. • Observe the job and operation. • Investigate the actual problem. • Examine the data. • Listen to people. • Priority principle Treat the gathered facts and problem points on a priority principle, stressing those which are more important in view of expected effects. The Pareto diagram described later will be very helpful. - Maximum effect with minimum labor - 70% of the problem is solved if the planning is properly done.
	Do (D)	Put the plan into practice and operate according to the rules and standards. This includes training on rules and standards.
	Check (C)	• It is your responsibility to check your own work. (Self inspection as well as error checks for drawings, documents, and business forms produce quality products.) Do not hand trouble on to the next person. • Check the result in comparison with the plan.
	Action (A)	• If a result deviates from the standard, correct it. • If any abnormality is found, investigate and remove the cause, and take action to prevent its reoccurrence. (Emergency and preventive measures are necessary.)

*Source: Company records

Exhibit 2   *Selected Data on Komatsu, Caterpillar, and Assorted Other Competitors* *
($ millions, fiscal year ends December 31 unless noted)[a]

	1991	1990	1989	1988	1987	1986	1985
Komatsu							
Company sales	6,915	7,013	5,615	5,961	6,121	4,992	3,581
Construction equipment sales	4,356	4,685	3,824	4,131	4,389	3,592	3,023
Net income	82	222	173	157	79	93	110
Percent of sales outside Japan	30%	30%	31%	31%	39%	47%	49%
Percent of sales from construction equipment	63%	67%	68%	69%	72%	72%	76%
Caterpillar							
Sales (companywide)	9,838	11,103	10,882	10,255	8,180	7,321	6,725
Net income	(404)	21	497	616	350	76	198
Percent of sales from outside the United States	59%	55%	53%	50%	48%	46%	44%
Sales of Other Major Construction and Agricultural Equipment Manufacturers							
Clark Equipment	1,190	1,445	1,392	1,278	1,055	954	964
Deere[b] (FY Oct. 31)	5,060	6,780	6,234	5,365	4,135	3,516	4,061
Hitachi Construction Machinery (FY Mar. 31)	1,812	1,780	1,777	1,725	1,195	824	602
Ingersoll-Rand[c]	1,363	1,445	1,328	1,140	969	865	929
International Harvester[b,d]							
J I Case (Division of Tenneco)	4,449	5,396	5,069	4,309	3,676	3,369	2,697
Shin-Caterpillar Mitsubishi (FY Mar. 31)	1,519	1,810	1,728				

*Sources: Annual reports, Yamaichi Research Institute, company records, forms 10-K, Moody's Industrial Manuals, various years.
"NR" means business segment data not reported.
[a]Komatsu fiscal year ended on Mar. 31 between 1989 and 1991 and on Dec. 31 between 1975 and 1987. Data from 1988 are for the period April to March and correspond with January to December of other companies.

Kawai announced the projects and priorities at the beginning of the year, the continuous PDCA cycle concentrated efforts within the company on attaining the broad policy objective until it was fully implemented (see Exhibit 1).

Kawai's new management approach, as reflected in Project A, was an immediate and outstanding success. Project A enabled Komatsu to double its warranty period within two years while cutting claim rates by two thirds. And, in the face of Cat's entry into Japan, it triggered an increase in sales that raised Komatsu's market share from 50% to 65% by 1970, thereby confounding the experts' forecasts of an early demise.

An avalanche of policies followed, steering Komatsu through the turbulent environment. In response to the economic stagnation that hit Japan in 1965, Kawai targeted a "cost-down" program at slashing costs. In 1966, his five-year "World A" campaign sought to make Komatsu internationally competitive in cost and quality, thus reducing Komatsu's potentially dangerous reliance on domestic sales. And, in rapid succession, Kawai launched Projects B, C, and D to improve reliabil-

Exhibit 2   *(continued)*

1984	1983	1982	1981	1980	1979	1978	1977	1976	1975
2,831	3,235	3,434	3,199	2,944	2,736	1,999	2,118	1,680	1,506
2,177	2,585	2,733	2,488	2,338	2,214	1,597	1,655	1,252	1,137
90	113	138	141	126	116	82	66	63	60
46%	54%	58%	49%	43%	37%	38%	42%	41%	45%
77%	80%	80%	81%	79%	81%	80%	76%	75%	75%
6,576	5,424	6,469	9,154	8,598	7,613	7,219	5,849	5,042	4,964
428	345	180	578	564	491	566	445	383	399
42%	46%	57%	57%	57%	54%	48%	51%	58%	57%
878	702	824	1,077	1,534	1,732	1,503	1,309	1,261	1,425
4,399	3,968	4,608	5,447	5,470	4,933	4,155	3,604	3,134	2,995
876	771	988	1,292	772	686	676	676	615	529
NR	NR	NR	NR	NR	4,069	3,200	3,065	2,930	2,992
1,741	1,752	NR	NR	NR	NR	1,386	1,149	1,054	964

[b]Construction and agricultural machinery segments only.
[c]Standard machinery segment only. Includes some nonconstruction and agricultural equipment.
[d]J I Case acquired agricultural equipment division of International Harvester in 1985. Komatsu data are converted from yen-denominated data at fiscal year-end exchange rates.

ity and durability in large bulldozers and shovels, payloaders, and hydraulic excavators, respectively. Throughout the 1970s, not a year went by without a major project, campaign, or program aimed at catching and surpassing Cat.

By the early 1980s, Komatsu had emerged as the major challenger in the construction equipment industry, putting Cat clearly on the defensive (see Exhibit 2). Nowhere were Cat's concerns clearer than in its 1982 annual report, which opened with a picture of a Komatsu bulldozer and a stern warning that Cat would not be able to compete against its Japanese rival at prevailing exchange and wage rates.

Struggle and Turmoil: The Nogawa Era (1982–1987)

Having guided the organization through an 18-year period of extraordinary growth, Ryoichi Kawai handed over operating leadership to Shoji Nogawa in 1982. Unfortunately for Nogawa, this date also marked the beginning of an era of falling demand, worldwide price wars, a rapidly

Exhibit 3   *Conditions for Komatsu and the Japanese Construction Industry, 1966–1990**

	1990[b]	1989[b]	1987	1986
Average exchange rate (¥/$)	158	133	121	158
Domestic construction investment expenditures				
¥ trillion	72.6	67.4	61.5	53.6
% of GNP	17.7	17.4	17.3	15.8
Komatsu construction equipment (CE)				
• CE segment sales (¥ billion)	603.9	549.5	531.1	567.5
• Overseas CE production (% total CE)	30.2	12.2	8.9	2.4
• Overseas share of CE sales (%)	40.9	38.9	47.9	55.4
• Japanese CE industry, export ratio	27.2	27.8	36.2	44.2
Global unit demand (excl. Japan) for selected types of CE[a]	18,000	22,000	25,000	22,000
• Bulldozers				
• yearly % change	−18%	−4%	+14%	+5%
• Hydraulic excavators	39,000	40,000	33,000	29,000
• yearly % change	−3%	+8%	+14%	0
Global unit demand (excl. Japan) all types of CE	110,500	121,000	112,000	104,000
yearly % change	−9%	+3%	+8%	−3%
Komatsu results:				
Sales (¥ billion)	887	793	741	789
Income (¥ billion)	27	21	10	15
Income (% of sales)	3.0%	2.6%	1.3%	1.9%

*Sources: MITI, company records, *Komatsu Fact Book* (various years), Yamaichi Research Institute of Securities and Economics.
[a]Bulldozers are large pieces of equipment used primarily in road construction, earth moving, agricultural engineering, forestry, mining and waste management. Hydraulic excavators are lighter machinery used in these areas as well as river maintenance, building and demolition, water and sewer main construction, landscaping, and cargo-handling.

appreciating yen, and heightened trade frictions throughout the industry. Nogawa was an engineer who had risen through the manufacturing side of the construction equipment division. A reputedly strong-willed, hands-on manager, he had high expectations of his managers and drove

them hard to meet those expectations. In spite of the growing challenges facing the industry, Nogawa was initially reluctant to change Komatsu's traditional policies, including the company's reliance on its highly efficient, centralized global production facilities. As conditions worsened

Exhibit 3   *(continued)*

1985	1984	1983	1982	1980	1970	1966
200	252	232	236	204	360	360
50.0	48.5	47.6	50.2			
15.4	15.9	16.6	18.3			
604.5	548.7	546.6	646.6	505.3	183.2	64.5
3.2						
58.5	54.3	62.8	67.0	43.3	13.9	10.2
52.3	49.9	55.1	57.0	36.8	10.6	7.6
21,000	21,000	22,000	20,000			
0	−5%	+10%				
29,000	24,000	23,000	20,000			
+21%	+4%	+15%				
107,000	98,000	96,000	86,000			
+9%	+2%	+12%				
796	713	751	810	648	264	28
22	23	26	33	28	13	2
2.8%	3.2%	3.5%	4.1%	4.3%	4.9%	7.1%

[b]Komatsu's results are for year ending December 31 up to 1987, and year ending March 31 from 1989 on.

and external pressures increased (see Exhibit 3), the new president seemed to focus more on cost-cutting and aggressive pricing than on shifting production overseas or reducing Komatsu's dependence on the stagnating construction industry. As the company implemented its aggressive sales strategy worldwide, political pressure mounted. Faced with several antidumping suits, Nogawa introduced new strategic goals in 1984, including faster product introduction and expansion of nonconstruction industrial machinery businesses.

The situation reached a crisis pitch in 1985 and 1986, when the value of the yen surged alarmingly. (See Exhibit 3.) With domestic markets in turmoil, a 25% rise in the value of the yen in nine months exposed Komatsu's foreign exchange vulnerability, putting Nogawa under pressure to internationalize production more rapidly. His short-term strategy included raising prices abroad, expanding overseas parts procurement, and cutting production costs. His medium-term strategy called for developing more marketable construction equipment products through increased R&D spending and capital investments in manufacturing facilities. In the long term, he told shareholders, "Komatsu is gearing itself toward new business areas of high growth potential."

He also responded in 1985 to the growing internal and external pressures for internationalization, approving the establishment of two important overseas plants—one in Chattanooga, Tennessee, and the other in a closed Cat facility in Birtley, United Kingdom. "As a drastic means of efficiently managing the sensitive trade friction and volatile foreign exchange environments," he told shareholders, "we have secured manufacturing bases in the world's major markets." Even after the plants were established, however, Nogawa seemed reluctant to integrate them fully into Komatsu's strategy. For example, when U.S. distributors began lobbying the head office to move additional production overseas, he rejected their proposals outright, finally relenting only when the yen appreciated even further to ¥140 per dollar.

The rising tide of problems, rapidly deteriorating results, Nogawa's apparent resistance to faster and more dramatic change, and the deleterious influence of his unpopular autocratic management style eventually resulted in his replacement. Chairman Kawai explained: "With this serious appreciation of the yen . . . we have no time to lose. We need to have a complete change in people's attitudes so that we can build a new organization, aiming at progress in the 1990s and the twenty-first century."

Steadying the Ship: The Tanaka Transition (1987–1989)

In June 1987, Ryoichi Kawai chose Masao Tanaka to replace Nogawa as president. A former general manager of the domestic sales division and, more recently, three-year general manager of the overseas division, Tanaka responded quickly to the competitive crisis in the domestic market. Chosen, in part, for his diplomatic skills, Tanaka demonstrated his conciliatory approach by emphasizing the need to end price discounting and high-pressure sales practices. In one of his many public statements on the topic, he argued:

> Market share is certainly a source of profit, but there can be no such thing as market share that ignores long-term profitability. We are trying to establish a situation where we can recoup the money spent on development and investment. If Komatsu cannot do this, there is no other company in Japan that can. If business conditions become worse, we should cover this not by carrying out a price war, but by reducing production.

Slowly, the industry responded and Tanaka's efforts culminated in a spate of collective OEM supply agreements within the industry and the creation of the Japan Construction Equipment Manufacturers Association in March 1990. More important from Komatsu's perspective, restoring market order improved the bottom line. While Komatsu's market share fell (from 35% to 31% in the hydraulic excavator market segment, for example), overall profits rose. Tanaka's pricing and sales policies were controversial within the company. When Komatsu developed the first miniexcavator that used advanced microelectronic controls, for example, some managers contended that with its traditional lower prices and aggressive sales methods, the company could capture a 50% market share. But Tanaka's philosophy prevailed, and the product was introduced at a 10% premium to existing prices.

Tanaka also pursued internationalization much more aggressively than his predecessor. More than internationalizing sales or market exposure, Tanaka wished to establish autonomous bases with regional capabilities in manufacturing, sales, and finance in the three core markets—Japan, the United States, and europe. Explained Tanaka: "On the assumption that the yen will further appreciate to, let's say, ¥100 per U.S. dollar, I believe any extension of conventional measures such as management and production rationalization will no longer be effective." Extending its conservative domestic pricing strategy, the company raised U.S. prices 7% in 1988, the seventh mark-up since September 1985. (Collectively, these represented a 40% aggregate price increase.)

Much of the driving force behind this emerging strategy came from Tanaka's director of corporate planning, Tetsuya Katada. Concerned about Komatsu's dwindling growth prospects in construction equipment and its dangerous reliance on domestic production, Katada pushed the company toward regionalizing production in Europe and the United States.

In Europe, Komatsu pursued a number of initiatives to reduce its yen exposure, respond to political pressure, and flesh out its product line. In response to an antidumping suit, the company began producing wheel loaders in its U.K. plant. It began sourcing miniexcavators for the European market—the subject of another antidumping suit—from the Italian company FAI, using engines made by Perkins, a British diesel manufacturer. And it began sourcing articulated dump trucks from Brown (U.K.) and vibratory rollers from ABG Werke (Germany), marketing them around the world under its own name. It even imported backhoe loaders from FAI into Japan.

In the United States, the company's moves were even bolder. In September 1988, Komatsu's U.S. company entered into a 50/50 joint venture with Dresser, the American oil services company that had acquired International Harvester's construction equipment business in 1983. The new $1.4 billion company (Komatsu Dresser Corp., or KDC) combined the U.S.-based finance, engineering, and manufacturing operations of both companies while maintaining separate sales and marketing organizations in KDC. Using all four of the two parent companies' plants in the United States and Brazil, the joint venture produced most major construction products, including hydraulic excavators, bulldozers, wheel loaders, and dump trucks.

The joint venture was controversial within Komatsu, partly because many within the company had heard the industry speculation that Dresser entered the joint venture as a means of exiting this money-losing business segment in which it had a neglected product line, lagging quality, and out-of-date plants. Furthermore, it represented a radical departure from several of Komatsu's closely held strategic maxims and traditional management policies: centralized production, total control over product development, whole ownership of subsidiaries, and Japanese management throughout the Komatsu group. In this way, the KDC deal served notice that the company was committed to a major change in the way it managed its international operations.

ENTERING THE 1990s

New Leadership: Tetsuya Katada

In June 1989, Masao Tanaka stepped down as president and was replaced by his internationally oriented vice president of corporate planning, Tetsuya Katada. With a degree from Kyoto University of Law, Katada had risen through Komatsu's ranks in personnel, labor relations, and corporate planning. After 36 years in the company, Katada was well known. Colleagues saw him as a "quiet and cool-headed commander," who spoke freely and honestly with superiors and subordinates alike. His introduction in the press signaled that he intended to take bold action. In response to questions about yet another change in Komatsu's leadership, the new president differentiated his strategy and style from his predecessor's:

Mr. Tanaka placed defense above anything else in his management policy. [Defense] was necessary because of the persistent high-yen environment. I, however, will be on the offensive in my own management policy.

When pressed on his relationship with Ryoichi Kawai, Mr. Katada added: "I have never hesitated to talk straight with my superiors. . . . [Chairman] Kawai is indispensable at Komatsu. He is, however, nothing more or nothing less than an important advisor."

Questioning the Past

The situation Katada inherited was anything but promising. Despite Komatsu's recent yet belated internationalization, sales were virtually unchanged from their level seven years prior, and profits were only half those of 1982 (see Exhibit 4). This stagnation was made all the more painful by the incredible growth taking place all around Komatsu. In the same 1982 to 1989 period, while Komatsu's profits plunged, Japan's GPN grew 43%. Although the worldwide demand for construction equipment had rebounded since the downturn of 1982 and 1983, a simultaneous shift toward smaller, lighter, and therefore less expensive equipment, such as the hydraulic excavator and the miniexcavator, had dampened the impact of the recovery (see Exhibit 5).

Worse still, worldwide industry demand was expected to dip again, at least over the next few years (see Exhibits 2 and 5). With the global political economy in the midst of major upheaval and large-scale development projects on the wane, Katada was concerned about the suitability of a strategy tightly focused on this declining sector:

There are doubts about the future demand for construction equipment. Central and South America and Africa are having problems with accumulated debt; the Soviet Union and China also have their problems; and the price of oil is [depressing demand for construction equipment]. In the places where

there is latent demand, the market is dormant. As a result, 90% of our demand is in America, Japan, and Europe. . . .

We cannot hope for growth by relying simply on construction equipment. We need to take an objective look at the world economic situation and to discuss concentrating simply on catching up with Caterpillar.

This call to abandon Komatsu's long-established competitive slogan surprised many observers. But Katada went even further. He openly challenged many of the company's deeply ingrained organizational processes and even much of the management philosophy that had made Komatsu the textbook example of management by "strategic intent."[2] The new president expressed his views openly:

The company is now struggling. It has become stereotyped and bureaucratic. The spirit of enterprise and challenge has been lost. . . . When Mr. Kawai was president, the time and our situation allowed him to employ a top-down approach to lead the company. But times have changed. . . . First, the world economy is more and more borderless, and companies must play an important role in developing international harmony. Also, the values of the young people in Japan are changing, and increasingly they question narrow, top-down directions.

A NEW CULTURE; A NEW DIRECTION

Managers at Komatsu confirmed that Katada was less autocratic than prior leaders. Said one colleague, "Mr. Katada believes that one can't manage from the top down, and that any important idea or concept should be fully understood by everyone before a campaign proceeds. . . . His style of free discussion is new in Komatsu."

In keeping with his participatory role, Katada encouraged debate over the company's future

---

[2]See Gary Hamel and C.K. Prahalad, "Strategic Intent," *Harvard Business Review*, Volume 67, Number 3, p. 63.

Exhibit 4 *Komatsu Financial Highlights, 1982–1989* (consolidated, ¥ million)*

	FY Ending December 31 (to 1987) and March 31 (1989 onward):									
	1991	**1990**	**1989**	**1987**	**1986**	**1985**	**1984**	**1983**	**1982**
Net sales	988,897	887,108	792,809	740,599	788,726	796,235	713,472	750,530	810,379
Net income	31,528	27,282	20,833	9,504	14,701	21,915	22,642	26,265	32,639
Net income per share	31.20	27.54	22.71	11.02	17.68	26.49	27.76	32.40	40.78
Total assets	1,319,189	1,230,636	1,128,957	1,027,475	983,682	1,003,560	943,806	894,549	930,685
Shareholders' equity	524,790	490,596	444,975	398,609	381,969	374,320	366,376	337,084	315,701
As a percentage of total assets (%)	39.8%	39.9%	39.4%	38.8%	38.8%	37.3%	37.7%	37.7%	33.9%
Number of consolidated subsidiaries	51	43	37	37	35	36	35	33	30
Number of companies included in account	34	33	28	25	25	24	27	26	26
CE sales (as % of total sales)	63.6%	68.1%	69.3%	71.7%	71.9%	75.9%	76.9%	72.8%	79.8%

*Source: *Komatsu Fact Book*, 1992.

Exhibit 5   *Global Trends in Construction Equipment Demand by Region and Type of Equipment**

Region†	1991 Number of Units	1991 Growth Rate	1990 Number of Units	1990 Growth Rate	1989 Number of Units	1989 Growth Rate
The Americas	28,000	–30%	40,000	–22%	51,000	–6%
Europe	42,000	–7	45,000	–4	47,000	4
Middle East and Africa	9,000	0	9,000	29	7,000	0
Asia and Oceania	13,000	–24	17,000	6	16,000	33
Total	92,000	–17	111,000	–8	121,000	3

Equipment Type†	1991 Number of Units	1991 Growth Rate	1990 Number of Units	1990 Growth Rate	1989 Number of Units	1989 Growth Rate
Bulldozers	14,000	–22%	18,000	–18%	22,000	–4%
Dozer shovels	2,000	–33%	3,000	–40	5,000	–17
Wheel loaders	35,000	–10	39,000	–7	42,000	2
Hydraulic excavators	32,000	–20	40,000	0	40,000	8
Motor graders	7,000	–13	8,000	0	8,000	4
Dump trucks	2,000	–33	3,000	0	3,000	0
Motor scrapers	0	0	0	0	1,000	0
Total	92,000	–17	111,000	–8	121,000	3

*Source: *Komatsu Fact Book*, 1992.
†Note: Figures in both tables exclude those for the Japanese market and show totals for bulldozers, dozer shovels, wheel loaders, hydraulic excavators, motor graders, dump trucks, and motor scrapers only.

direction. In off-site meetings and other forums, he invited a broad spectrum of managers to help shape Komatsu's new mission. During a June 1989 off-site meeting (billed as a "directors' free-discussion camp-out"), Katada proposed a new slogan to help crystallize the nascent consensus of the company's new strategic thrusts: "Growth, Global, Groupwide," or the three Gs. Katada explained:

Top-down management by policy is becoming obsolete. Although it is still useful, we can no longer have TQC at the center of the management process. The future outlook for the industry is not bright. Managers can no longer operate within the confines of a defined objective. They need to go out and see the needs and opportunities, and operate in a creative and innovative way, always encouraging initiative from below. . . .

Although the three Gs slogan is something I came up with when I became president, there's nothing new or unusual about it given the economic conditions we were in—stagnant sales and a bureaucratic and rigidly structured company. These three simple words were intended to promote discussions, directions, and policies at the board level and throughout the organization. The slogan may seem abstract, but it was this abstract nature that stimulated people to ask what they could do, and respond creatively.

Stimulating New Initiatives

Stimulated by the new, open organizational forums, and encouraged by Katada's participative and challenging management style, Komatsu executives struggled to give meaning and definition to the three Gs in a series of meetings that

Exhibit 5 *(continued)*

1988		1987		1986	1985	1984	1983	1982
Number of Units	Growth Rate	Number of Units	Growth Rate	Number of Units	Number of Units	Number of Units	Number of Units	Number of Units
54,000	−2%	55,000	10%	50,000	50,000	45,000	35,000	23,000
45,000	15	39,000	11	35,000	33,000	30,000	30,000	28,000
7,000	−13	8,000	−20	10,000	13,000	13,000	21,000	23,000
12,000	33	10,000	11	9,000	10,000	9,000	9,000	12,000
118,000	5	112,000	8	104,000	106,000	97,000	95,000	86,000

1988		1987		1986	1985	1984	1983	1982
Number of Units	Growth Rate	Number of Units	Growth Rate	Number of Units	Number of Units	Number of Units	Number of Units	Number of Units
23,000	−8%	25,000	14%	22,000	21,000	21,000	22,000	20,000
6,000	−14	7,000	0	7,000	6,000	6,000	6,000	5,000
41,000	14	36,000	6	34,000	37,000	34,000	34,000	31,000
37,000	12	33,000	14	29,000	28,000	24,000	22,000	19,000
7,000	−13	8,000	−11	9,000	10,000	8,000	8,000	7,000
3,000	50	2,000	0	2,000	3,000	3,000	2,000	3,000
1,000	0	1,000	0	1,000	1,000	1,000	1,000	1,000
118,000	5	112,000	8	104,000	106,000	97,000	95,000	86,000

cascaded down the organization from September 1989 to March 1990. By this time, Katada and his top team were ready to formally adopt the new slogan and operationalize it in a long-term strategic plan, known as "Project G."

The most basic element of Project G was that the organization committed itself to return to growth, the first of the three Gs. Following the months of intensive negotiation and debate during 1989 and 1990, Katada announced that the company would aim at achieving a sales level of ¥1,400 billion by the mid-1990s—a level almost double its 1989 revenue level.

The core task in achieving this objective was to begin to grow construction equipment sales that had been stagnating (as reported in yen) since the early 1980s. This was to be the company's major globalization task—the second G—and Katada predicted that by the year 2000, the overseas operations of this business would manufacture over half of Komatsu's total output. To signal his continued commitment to this core business, Katada announced plans to triple the company's capital investment in construction equipment to ¥50 billion per annum and challenged his managers to develop the proposals to justify that commitment.

Beyond revitalizing construction equipment, the third major element in Project G was a belief that Komatsu had to reduce its dependence on its traditional business through the groupwide leveraging of existing assets and resources to apply them to new product and business opportunities. Katada planned to encourage his organization to grow businesses such as electronics, robotics, and plastics, so that by the mid-1990s the nonconstruction part of Komatsu would account for 50% of its sales. (For a representation of Komatsu's diverse business holdings, see Exhibit 6.)

Exhibit 6 *The Komatsu Group*

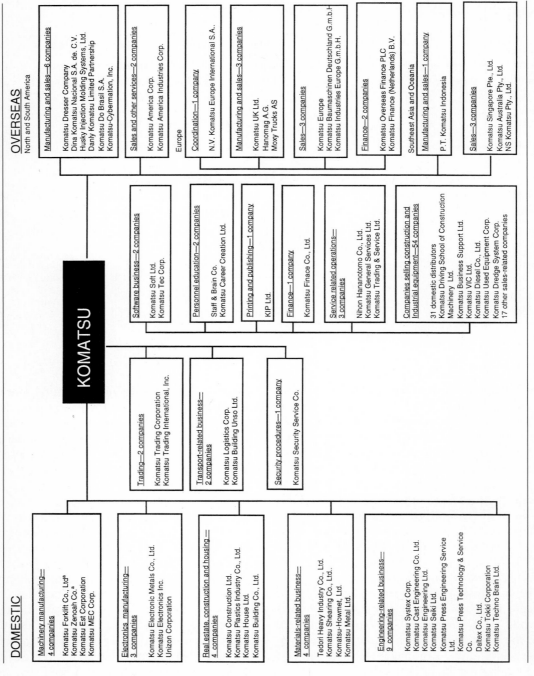

DOMESTIC

KOMATSU

Machinery manufacturing—
4 companies

Komatsu Forklift Co., Ltd[a]
Komatsu Zenoah Co.[a]
Komatsu Est Corporation
Komatsu MEC Corp.

Electronics manufacturing—
3 companies

Komatsu Electronic Metals Co., Ltd.
Komatsu Electronics Inc.
Unizon Corporation

Real estate, construction and housing —
4 companies

Komatsu Construction Ltd.
Komatsu Plastics Industry Co., Ltd.
Komatsu House Ltd.
Komatsu Building Co., Ltd.

Materials-related business—
4 companies

Tedori Heavy Industry Co., Ltd.
Komatsu Shearing Co., Ltd.
Komatsu-Howmet, Ltd.
Komatsu Metal Ltd.

Engineering-related business—
9 companies

Komatsu Systex Corp.
Komatsu Cast Engineering Co. Ltd.
Komatsu Engineering Ltd.
Komatsu Seiki Ltd.
Komatsu Press Engineering Service Ltd.
Komatsu Press Technology & Service Co.
Daltex Co., Ltd.
Komatsu Tokki Corporation
Komatsu Techno Brain Ltd.

Trading—2 companies

Komatsu Trading Corporation
Komatsu Trading International, Inc.

Transport-related business—
2 companies

Komatsu Logistics Corp.
Komatsu Building Unso Ltd.

Security procedures—1 company

Komatsu Security Service Co.

Software business—2 companies

Komatsu Soft Ltd.
Komatsu Tec Corp.

Personnel education—2 companies

Staff & Brain Co.
Komatsu Career Creation Ltd.

Printing and publishing—1 company

KIP Ltd.

Finance—1 company

Komatsu Finace Co., Ltd.

Service related operations—
3 companies

Nihon Hananotomo Co., Ltd.
Komatsu General Services Ltd.
Komatsu Trading & Service Ltd.

Companies selling construction and
industrial equipment—54 companies

31 domestic distributors
Komatsu Driving School of Construction
Machinery Ltd.
Komatsu Business Support Ltd.
Komatsu VIC Ltd.
Komatsu Diesel Co., Ltd.
Komatsu Used Equipment Corp.
Komatsu Dredge System Corp.
17 other sales-related companies

OVERSEAS
North and South America

Manufacturing and sales—6 companies

Komatsu Dresser Company
Dina Komatsu Nacional S.A. de. C.V.
Husky Injection Molding Systems, Ltd.
Danly Komatsu Limited Partnership
Komatsu Do Brasil S.A.
Komatsu-Cybernation, Inc.

Sales and other services—2 companies

Komatsu America Corp.
Komatsu America Industries Corp.

Europe

Coordination—1 company

N.V. Komatsu Europe International S.A..

Manufacturing and sales—3 companies

Komatsu UK Ltd.
Hanomag A.G.
Moxy Trucks AS

Sales—3 companies

Komatsu Europe
Komatsu Baumaschinen Deutschland G.m.b.H.
Komatsu Industries Europe G.m.b.H.

Finance—2 companies

Komatsu Overseas Finance PLC
Komatsu Finance (Netherlands) B.V.

Southeast Asia and Oceania

Manufacturing and sales—1 company

P.T. Komatsu Indonesia

Sales—3 companies

Komatsu Singapore Pte., Ltd.
Komatsu Australia Pty., Ltd.
NS Komatsu Pty., Ltd.

*Source: Company records. The Komatsu Group consists of 185 related companies. This list shows the major affiliates and subsidiaries.
[a]Listed companies

To communicate this new vision, Katada began referring to the company not as a construction equipment manufacturer (and certainly not as one that defined itself in terms of its old rival Caterpillar), but rather as "a total technology enterprise." And the old Japan-centered, engineering-dominated organization was now redefined in futuristic terms as "a globally integrated high-tech organization that integrates hardware and software as systems."

GLOBALIZING CONSTRUCTION EQUIPMENT

The implications of Project G for Komatsu's core construction equipment business were profound. It implied a commitment to globalization that would build on and expend the thrust that had begun in the late 1980s under Katada's urging when he was director for corporate planning. Mr. Aoyama, Katada's new director for corporate planning, commented on the business's new long-term strategic objectives outside Japan:

> We don't want our strategic position to depend just on exchange rate fluctuations or the latest trade frictions. We want a stable, perpetual system of being in the construction equipment business around the world in a more integrated way, starting from development through marketing and sales.

Katada wanted to change the way the construction equipment business was managed, loosening the traditional company policy of whole ownership and control over subsidiaries to allow much more flexibility and local participation. Under his guidance, Komatsu Dresser Corporation (KDC) had not only been structured as a 50/50 joint venture, but was managed jointly. Indeed, despite the fact that it contributed half of the joint venture's equity, Komatsu asked for only two seats on KDC's 12-person board—and it asked Dresser to provide the CEO. (It did, however, still maintain equal management representation on KDC's six-person management committee that oversaw operations and decided the basic policy for the joint venture.) Katada explained the change in thinking behind the new organization:

> We have begun to doubt whether it is possible to become a "localized and international enterprise" using only the capital, management, and engineers of Komatsu. I consider the joint venture to be a combination of Japanese technology with American management and marketing. Of course, Japanese also have pride and confidence in their administrative and marketing skills, but these cannot be fully effective in an American environment. At the same time, Dresser is behind in development and capital investment, so we plan to combine Komatsu's design and development technology with American management and marketing to achieve localization.

With a major presence in North America, the company's attention next focused on Europe. In July 1989, one month after Katada became president, Komatsu acquired an interest in Hanomag, the 154-year-old German niche producer of construction equipment. In addition, the company finalized a supply arrangement with FAI, the Italian producer of miniexcavators. Over the next three years, Komatsu signed no fewer than 18 agreements establishing various partnerships and alliances with local firms. Again, the objective was to obtain a local marketing and management capability.

To oversee the growing number of operations, Katada agreed to the proposal to form Komatsu Europe International SA (KEISA) in November 1989 to develop a more integrated group of European operations, and to coordinate the "mutual supply" of parts and increasingly specialized products. Under KEISA's guidance, for example, Hanomag took over Komatsu U.K.'s (KUK) production of wheel loaders. This arrangement capitalized both on Hanomag's 20% share of the German market for wheel loaders and its 100-outlet-strong distribution network in Europe. It

Exhibit 7 *Specialization of Manufacturing Operations by Region and by Plant, 1992*[*]

Komatsu Plant (year stake taken)	Komatsu Ownership %	Number of Employees (= Japanese Expatriates)	Main Product	Local Content	Regions Supplied
EUROPE:					
Komatsu U.K. (1985)	100% (10)[a]	370	Hydraulic excavators	70–75%	Europe, North Africa
Hanomag, Germany (1988)	64.1 (5)[a]	1,600	Wheel loaders	60–65	Europe, North Africa
FAI, spa, Italy (1991)	10	600	Mini-excavators	85	Europe, North Africa
ASIA (non-Japan):					
Indonesia (1982)	50	530 (24)[a]	Bulldozers, wheel loaders, hydraulic excavators, motor graders, casting and forging products, sheetmetal (for Japan)	15–25	Indonesia, SE Asia, cast metal for Japan
AMERICAS:					
Komatsu Dresser Corp. (1988)[b]	50	2779[b] (15)[a]	Wheel loaders, hydraulic excavators, dump trucks, motor graders	50–65	U.S., Canada
Mexico (1974)	68.4	190 (10)[a]	Small presses, sheet metal to U.S.	NA	Small presses to U.S.; sheet metal
Brazil (1973)	100	1,010 (10)[a]	Hydraulic excavators, bulldozers, wheel loaders, motor graders	8–95	South America, U.S., Indonesia

[*]Source: Company records, *Komatsu Fact Book*, 1992.
[a]Number of Japanese employees as of year-end 1991.
[b]Includes companies in Peoria (1,020 employees), Chattanooga (261), Galion (330), Candac, Canada (110).

Exhibit 8   *Construction Equipment, Overseas Production (¥ million)* *

Overseas Production Subsidiaries	1986	1987	1988	1989	1990	1991	1992
Komatsu Dresser Co.					¥182,000[2]	¥199,000	¥136,000
Komatsu America Mfg. Corp.	NM[1]	¥600	¥17,000	¥25,400	NM	NM	NM
Komatsu Do Brasil SA	¥7,100	7,000	11,700	9,200	NM	NM	1,100[3]
Komatsu UK Ltd.	NM[1]	100	4,400	12,600	19,000	19,200	18,600
Dina Komatsu Nacional SA de CV	6,400	1,600	1,900	1,800	2,200	NM	NM
PT Komatsu Indonesia	3,100	2,400	6,400	5,500	8,600	11,600	9,300
Hanomag AG	NM	NM	NM	NM	NM	26,700	26,300
Overseas production	16,600	11,700	41,500	54,500	211,800	256,500	191,600
Domestic production	500,800	475,500	427,500	447,600	489,400	533,200	437,200
Overseas production as percentage of total production	3.2	2.4	8.9	12.2	30.2	32.5	30.5

*Source: Company records.
"NM" = not meaningful (see Notes)
Notes: [1]Production began in the United States and the United Kingdom at the end of 1986.
    [2]After 1989, Komatsu America Mfg. Corp. and Komatsu Brasil SA were reported as part of the Komatsu Dresser joint venture.
    [3]In October 1991, Komatsu Brasil SA was again separated from Komatsu Dresser.

also freed KUK to specialize in hydraulic excavators. Extending the specialized sourcing network, Italian licensee FAI supplied miniexcavators to all European markets. Exhibit 7 shows the resulting regionalization and specialization that emerged.

As a result of the aggressive expansion of offshore operations, the company's overseas production of construction equipment rose from ¥11.7 billion, or 2.4% of total production in 1987, to ¥256.5 billion, or 32.5% of the total in 1991 (see Exhibit 8). This growth in offshore production, together with an overall slowdown in the market, led to a major decline in the importance of parent company export sales. Accounting for 67% of sales at its peak in 1982 Komatsu Limited's export ratio had fallen to 37.7% by 1992. Nonetheless, exports still re-

mained an important part of Komatsu's sales to all three global regions (see Exhibit 9).

Expanding Overseas Responsibilities

Beyond developing its resource base abroad, the construction equipment management group also began to expand the roles and responsibilities of these offshore operations. With an overall vision of building a three-part, regional geographic structure, these overseas units began to develop not only manufacturing and sales functions, but also purchasing and development capabilities.

In the late 1980s, international production facilities mushroomed from a handful of offshore assembly plants to a worldwide network of sophisticated manufacturing facilities as described briefly above. Much more gradual was

Exhibit 9 *Komatsu, Export Sales Trends by Region (consolidated)* *

| | The Americas | | | Europe, Middle East, and Asia | |
| | Net Sales | | Company | Net Sales | |
	Yen in billions	U.S. $ in millions	Export Share (%)	Yen in billions	U.S. $ in millions
1979	¥ 49	$205	26.8	¥ 88	$ 367
1980	51	248	21.8	128	628
1981	57	261	18.7	203	920
1982	31	131	7.4	274	1,163
1983	41	177	10.9	268	1,157
1984	107	423	34.1	149	591
1985	103	517	31.8	145	723
1986	94	594	29.2	180	1,140
1987	87	718	36.3	98	812
1989	67	505	33.6	80	605
1990	61	385	28.1	81	513
1991	50	354	21.6	94	667
1992	38	282	19.2	97	282

*Source: Company records.
Notes: 1. The exchange rate for each year reflects the Federal Reserve Bank of New York fiscal year-end average.
2. This table excludes the three-month fiscal period ended March 31, 1988, because it represented an extraordinary term caused by the change in the fiscal period.

the shift in responsibilities for product design and development. The company's traditionally centralized development and applications policies were challenged when Hanomag's operations were found to have excellent engineering and development capabilities. The company decided to build on this asset by delegating clear development responsibility to the German company, and eliminating some duplication of effort with Tokyo. For example, management gave Hanomag full responsibility to develop all small wheel loaders for Europe, and a joint-development role with Tokyo on larger models.

In its U.K. company, however, the decision was a more basic one. Up until 1988, KUK had a three-person product engineering office headed by a Japanese manager, whose main task was to make minor modifications to Japanese drawings. Gradually, however, Komatsu began transferring responsibility for the redevelopment of the PW170 wheel excavator to a new development facility in KUK, expanding the department to include 27 design engineers and 12 test engineers by 1992.

Such responsibility transfer had considerable immediate and tangible benefits. Starting with an existing undercarriage from Europe, KUK engineers designed and modified a wheel excavator to satisfy European safety regulations and new work range requirements. Aware of strict local standards on braking and steering performance, these British engineers reduced the engine size and thus maximum speed, avoiding a far more costly redesign of the braking system. German engineers at Hanomag, too, modified basic product dimensions of a different vehicle to meet European road-width standards, creating a model better suited to local conditions

Exhibit 9   *(continued)*

| Asia and Oceania | | | Total | | | |
| Company Export Share (%) | Net Sales | | Company Export Share (%) | Net Sales | | Exchange Rate (Yen/Dollar) |
	Yen in billions	U.S. $ in millions		Yen in billions	U.S. $ in millions	
48.0	¥46	$192	25.2	¥183	$ 764	240
55.3	53	260	22.9	232	1,136	204
66.0	47	214	15.3	307	1,396	220
65.9	111	471	26.7	416	1,753	236
71.3	67	268	17.7	376	1,621	232
47.6	57	227	18.3	313	1,240	252
44.4	78	388	23.8	325	1,627	200
56.1	47	299	14.7	321	2,032	158
41.1	54	445	22.6	239	1,976	121
40.2	53	395	26.2	200	1,505	133
37.4	75	472	34.5	216	1,370	158
40.7	87	617	37.7	231	1,638	141
49.7	61	456	31.1	195	1,466	133

than Tokyo's. Generally, local engineers were also able to simplify the manufacturing process design, and bring the new product to market far faster than if it had been engineered in Tokyo. By operating according to centrally mandated standards covering parts and serviceability concepts, designers ensured that parts for the locally designed product were compatible with others in its product line. Said one former KUK manager:

> Before, if manufacturing had a concern about a drawing, they had no way to complain. Three engineers could not solve the problem. Information had to be transferred to Tokyo asking for a solution from the Osaka test center. Now, locals can decide on design changes as long as they meet commonality requirements.

KUK's recently opened test center and its newly assigned responsibility for two additional projects pointed to a continually expanding role for the group. The impact on local morale was immediate and visible.

Localizing Management

To have enduring value, it was clear to Komatsu's top management—and constantly emphasized by Katada—that this transfer of responsibility had to be accompanied by an equally strong commitment to the recruitment, development and promotion of local managers. This strong belief was formalized in a July 1989 human resources policy that required a substantial increase in the number of foreign nationals in management positions. Komatsu Europe, for example, reduced the number of Japanese managers from 26 out of 180 employees in 1986 to 13 out of 260 by 1992, and planned to reduce that number to six within two years.

Despite the transfer of responsibilities and the replacement of expatriates with locals, Komatsu managers expressed surprise at how long the transition was taking. For example, their strong belief that "bottom-up problem solving" was an essential ingredient of the spirit of Komatsu, led to frustration at the lack of initiative at the local level as responsibility was expanded. When one senior executive routinely began to answer employee reports of problems with the question, "How do you propose we fix it?", he was disappointed to find that typically the employees were surprised—and without answer. Other managers commented on fundamental differences in attitudes toward core values, such as quality and customer service, and how long it took for such values to take deep root in Komatsu subsidiaries.

Those running the business found several causes of these problems and several areas where they needed to take action. Part of the challenge of localizing management entailed changing the way headquarters communicated with the subsidiaries. Mr. Suketomo, a director and former president of KUK, explained his difficulty motivating non-Japanese employees in an environment where all high-level documents were written in Japanese:

When I became KUK's president, there was a real difficulty with the language problem because all important communication with Tokyo was in Japanese. So my first job was to send a letter to Tokyo explaining that all communication from Tokyo would be in English, or I would ignore it! Soon, all official letters to me were in English. It not only allowed me to distribute copies to local managers, but more importantly, it forced expatriate staff to improve their English skills.

The other major problem was that many of the local nationals recruited in the earlier era were not strong managers. The main need prior to the late 1980s was for loyal implementers— "yes men," as one Japanese executive described them. As a result, many were not up to the new challenges being given to them, and overseas units had to undertake major efforts to upgrade their personnel. In 1987, for example, Komatsu Europe had recruited only one university graduate; by 1991, it had recruited 23, including its first two MBAs.

Localization created another unforeseen problem. As the member of Japanese nationals in the overseas operations decreased, the local entities' ability to coordinate their activities with the parent company—and even with each other—began to deteriorate noticeably. Numerous examples of miscommunication began to surface regularly, on issues ranging from market forecasts to product specifications. Said one observer:

Just at the time they need more coordination than ever, they are reducing the number of Japanese managers abroad. For many Japanese companies, the most difficult task for local nationals has been to operate effectively in a linkage or coordinative role due to the high language and cultural barriers within the organization. As they increase their global integration, the intensity of such a role is going to increase dramatically.

Despite these difficulties adjusting, in 1992 some managers believed that Japanese and Western management practices were converging, with each group learning from the other. Said one manager who spent four years in KDC:

Our partner's style is very different from ours. The Komatsu style represents the typical Japanese emphasis on growth potential and market share for long-term survival. Dresser puts the highest priority on ROI [return on investment] and profit measures. Because of these differences, we encountered some friction at first. Recently, Komatsu managers have learned the importance of ROI; and those in Dresser came to under-

stand that they must think beyond the short term. In the future, I think we can expect a hybrid system of management.

Management also began to recognize that their localization program was only one step on a long road to fully internationalizing their management process. As Katada told the Japanese press in November 1990:

Our goal is to transfer management from Tokyo to overseas outlets run by local nationals. As far as nationalities are concerned, this has already been accomplished in such key units as Komatsu Dresser and Hanomag. . . . But this is not enough for doing business. In this regard, what we really need to do is internationalize our headquarters in Tokyo.

Two full years later, Mr. Suketomo felt pride in the achievements, but echoed Katada's concerns:

We have been successful increasing the local management of KUK, but there is a danger here in our thinking. If you ask, "Could the top of KUK or KDC become top of the home office in Japan?", I would have to express my doubt. That reflects a limitation on our part, and I think we should see that as a challenge.

Achievements and Challenges

After three years of growth, Komatsu's construction equipment business experienced a sharp downturn in 1992. Overseas sales fell 10.6% to ¥246 billion, while domestic sales in this segment slipped even further, falling 13.5% to ¥334 billion. Worse, its operating income from construction equipment plummeted 60%.

Management attributed the setback to the downturn in industry demand associated with a recession that seemed to be deepening worldwide in 1992. To some industry observers, however, the continued performance problems also hinted at deeper problems with Komatsu's overall globalization strategy. Said one:

There are clear risks in basing international expansion so heavily on joint ventures with and acquisitions of local and regional players, each of which has different products, capabilities, and approaches. It's going to be hard for them to achieve the same product quality, efficiency, and strategic focus as they had a decade ago. The task is made all the more difficult if we continue to withdraw experienced Japanese expatriates from our overseas operations in the name of localization.

Nonetheless, Katada remained confident. In response to the downturn, he confirmed that Komatsu would continue its long-term globalization investments and its commitment to localization. In the short term, he was preparing major new sales drives for hydraulic excavators, wheel loaders, and dump trucks in all three regional markets. He was clearly prepared to stay the course.

SKANDIA AFS

Jan R. Carendi, deputy chief executive officer (CEO) of Skandia Insurance Company Ltd. (Skandia) and chief operating officer (COO) of Skandia's Assurance and Financial Services (AFS) division, smiled as he reviewed a report on his unit's growth during his 10 years at the helm. Over this time, AFS's sales of private long-term savings and insurance products had grown 45% per year. Once a small unit in the international division of the 140-year-old Stockholm-based insurance and financial services company, AFS currently accounted for almost 50% of Skandia's gross premium revenues. (See Exhibit 1 for Skandia and AFS results 1986–1995.)

Yet to many, Carendi was a maverick who had continually defied conventional wisdom. By redefining the nature of the business, and restructuring it around alliances, some thought he had hollowed out the business and made it less robust than conventional and fully integrated companies. Others in this traditional industry questioned his radical approach of refocusing the business on its intellectual capital, looking at the organization's knowledge rather than finances as its key resources. While the payoffs of his approach were evident, the critics insisted there were also risks.

Carendi recognized that his bold actions were likely to raise eyebrows, but to date AFS's strong performance had been sufficient to silence his critics. However, he was aware that in the turbulent segment of the market his company had carved out, past performance was no guarantee of future success. While financial analysts were focused on the 30% fall in premium income of AFS's flagship U.K. operation in 1995, to Carendi premium growth was a relative measure, and only one indicator of long-term success. His immediate concern was AFS's ability to maintain service quality when resources were constrained. In the medium term, he was focused on AFS's planned expansion into the notoriously difficult Japanese market. And in the long term, he was uncertain how the ability of the Internet to provide increasingly sophisticated consumers with direct access to insurance products would affect

---

This case was prepared by Christopher A. Bartlett and Takia Mahmood. Copyright © 1996 by the President and Fellows of Harvard College. Harvard Business School case 396-412.

Exhibit 1 *Financial Results for Skandia and AFS: 1986–1995**

(MSEK)	1986	1987	1988	1989	1990	1991	1992	1993	1994	1995
Kronor per U.S. $	7.1	6.3	6.1	6.4	5.9	6.0	5.8	7.8	7.7	7.1
Gross Premium Income (MSEK)										
Skandia Group	4,381	4,731	5,282	18,519	24,853	29,031	36,525	43,503	52,248	52,241
AFS:	—	1,919	1,524	1,979	2,868	5,483	7,891	17,240	25,888	23,961
Unit-link assurance	—	1,841	1,464	1,807	2,683	4,306	6,089	16,939	23,898	20,706
Life assurance	—	78	60	172	185	1,083	1,664	119	1,754	3,016
Management Operating Result (MSEK)†										
Skandia Group	4,773	(1,013)	4,410	4,044	(3,205)	(1,098)	(3,721)	4,069	(1,715)	818
AFS:	—	33	28	3	(33)	110	100	389	625	707
Unit-linked assurance	—	25	15	(13)	(47)	88	80	386	530	595
Life assurance	—	8	13	16	14	22	20	3	91	99
Return on Net Asset Value (%)										
Skandia Group	60	(10)	38	24	(19)	(10)	(30)	31	(8)	7
AFS	—	NA	NA	NA	NA	NA	6.5	17.6	19.2	17.6

*Source: Skandia.

†Note: Beginning in 1989, Skandia Group results include Skandia International. Year 1989–92 includes American Skandia Reinsurance (Life Insurance sold 1993). Year 1994–1995 includes Intercaser (Spanish Life Insurance Company.)

He decided to gain control of the U.K. company by buying back 100% of the equity, and to support the U.K. team as it continued to develop its innovative approach. One problem that the young company experienced was that their best in-house funds managers often left for higher pay elsewhere. They had also experienced similar turnover problems with a sales force of dedicated agents. To stem the outflow of talent, the U.K. managers decided to externalize both the fund management and sales functions. They selected local retailers (independent brokers and banks) who were well known to the market and familiar with the environment, and entered into cooperative alliances with them for customer networking and distribution. They did the same with a wide range of highly visible local unit-trust (mutual fund) investment managers who

had superior track records. Carendi began to see in this alliance-based structure the foundation of a new business model for expanding AFS internationally.

Reconceptualizing the Business

The deregulation of the insurance industry in the U.K. turned out to be the first wave of a trend that was spreading worldwide. With barriers to entry falling, new, nontraditional competitors began changing the rules. Carendi became convinced that both the product and the organizational configuration the U.K. subsidiary was developing provided AFS with a means to respond to the changing external environment more easily than traditional insurance companies. He saw that this cooperative model offered several

Exhibit 2   *The "Specialists in Collaboration" Organization Concept**

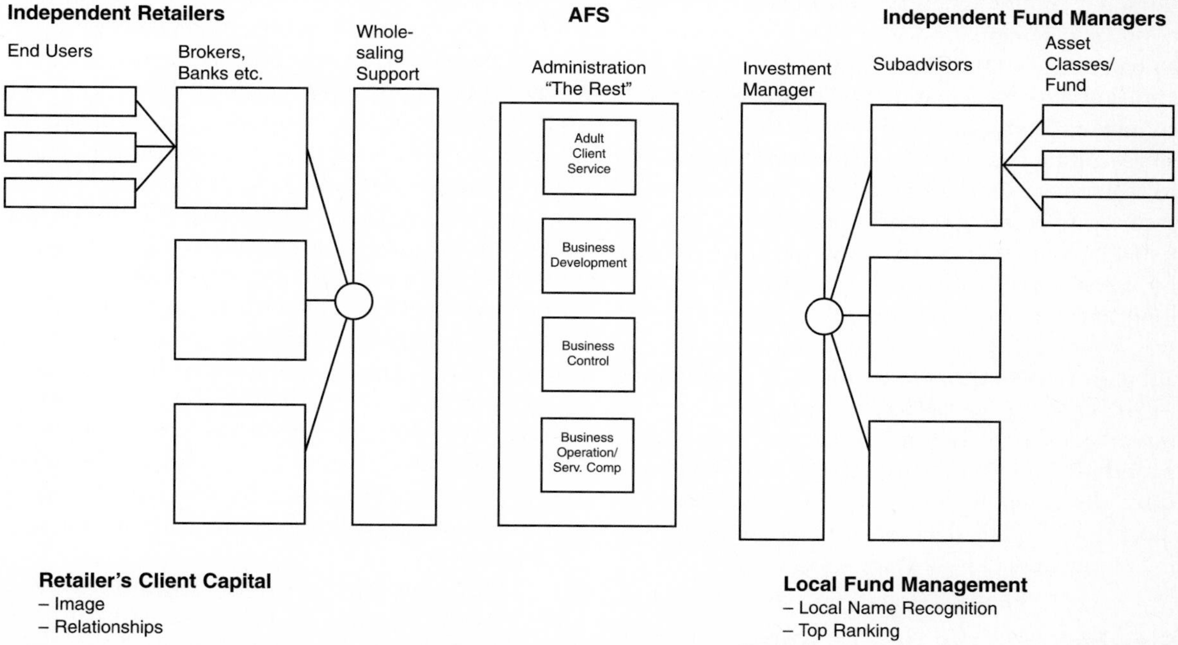

*Source: Skandia.

advantages. First, brokers gave AFS instant access to the market at low cost. Second, independent money managers who were the best in their class not only ensured strong financial management but also gave AFS credibility through a recognized brand where the name Skandia meant little. Finally, the arrangement provided great flexibility, since AFS could form new alliances if the existing ones did not work out.

In this new configuration, Carendi began to redefine AFS's role as the linkage between the distribution and investment functions, packaging long-term savings products for brokers and their clients, and bringing wholesale distribution to brand name money managers. In describing his new business concept, he said, "We must think of ourselves less as insurance specialists, and more as 'specialists in collaboration'." (See Exhibit 2.)

EXPANDING AFS

By the late 1980s, the insurance industry was undergoing major change worldwide. In many countries, deregulation was opening the industry to banks and other financial and nonfinancial institutions. At the same time, cuts in government-sponsored pension and Social Security schemes were leading many people to question their ability to depend on such programs for their retirement security. In some countries, governments were actively encouraging greater long-term self-reliance by creating tax incentives for insurance-backed long-term savings. Behind all of these changes was a worldwide demographic trend towards an aging population that was not only contributing to the crisis in Social Security programs, but simultaneously creating new insurance market opportunities. It was against this background that Carendi wanted to expand his business abroad as quickly and aggressively as he could, initially aiming at one new market entry a year.

Starting up in the United States

Based on a feasibility study that a small group of U.K. executives had put together, Carendi de-

cided in 1988 to leverage the U.K.'s success to enter the very competitive insurance market in the United States. To build the new business, he hired an experienced American insurance industry manager and gave him the support of three relocated executives with specialized expertise—the two who had headed the study of the U.S. market, and Leif Reinius, AFS's international systems controller.

Reinius had been working on a PC-based, modular, software system, designed to support the U.K. investment-linked product and its "partnership model" of management. The software was designed to capture the company's essential administrative processes and coordinative mechanisms, such as policyholder applications, fund selection, daily pricing, commission management, and statements of accounts. Unfortunately, when he tested the system in the U.S. environment, Reinius found that much of the U.K. experience was not transferable. The system was inflexible and difficult to use and maintain in a market with a different set of consumer needs and regulatory requirements.

At the same time, American Skandia was having difficulty establishing the visibility it needed to attract new customers and the credibility it needed to obtain continued support from within. The newly established U.S. company had spent $5 million per year in 1988 and 1989, but had booked no business and had few prospects. Some in the parent company were beginning to question whether AFS should continue to support the struggling operation. Unhappy with the traditional approach being taken by the American subsidiary's president and COO, Carendi decided it was time for a shakeup. In 1989, he removed the U.S. head and some other managers, took on the role of subsidiary president himself, and relocated his new team to Shelton, Connecticut.

Once at Shelton, Carendi's top priority was to reconfigure the distribution structure of American Skandia, which he felt was key to success in a market where Skandia was an unknown. One of his first appointments was Wade

Dokken, a man with extensive industry sales and marketing experience. The two men came to the conclusion that the subsidiary relied too heavily on an external network of wholesalers, who in turn promoted its products to a retail network of brokers. Concerned that these "hired guns" were not giving American Skandia a high enough profile with brokers, they decided to bring the wholesaling function in house. Dokken hired six wholesalers and tied them to an incentive structure that supported their objective of developing market presence for an unknown company. With the new management team and an aggressive new business plan, American Skandia's sales began to take off from $6.3 million in 1989 to $141 million in 1991 and $890.6 million in 1993.

Formalizing the Prototype

Although the initial transfer of the U.K.-based systems had not been successful, Reinius became increasingly certain that a transportable software package would allow AFS to transfer its best administrative processes swiftly and efficiently from one country to another. "Innovation isn't a question of starting out each time with blank yellow pads and pencils in hand," he explained. "Work previously done must be captured and re-used." At the end of 1989, he returned to Stockholm to continue working on the "core prototype system." His objective was to make the system parameter-driven, so that those in the new operation would not be dependent upon IT experts but instead could themselves input variables on risk factors, savings percentage, charges, and other variables and readily see their impact. He also made it more flexible so that it could be adapted to local legal restrictions, reporting requirements and language.

In the process of this continued expansion, Carendi became increasingly convinced of the power of the concept Reinius and his team were developing. In his view, all variable annuity insurance companies were essentially identical at the operational level. They all developed products, issued policies, invested funds, and managed the administrative paperwork. Even at the level of individual products there were similarities—most were assembled from the same elementary processes—the calculation of risk cover, fund value, cash value, charges, and benefits. By capturing cumulative experience, the huge start-up costs of new market entry—to define new products, support distribution efforts, and provide an administrative infrastructure—could be greatly reduced. As he explained: "Applying prototype concepts to business development should enable us to design products for a specific market in half the time, and at a quarter of the cost. That will free time and resources to implement distribution alternatives and solutions tailor-made for the market." And despite the continuing problems in the United States, Carendi intended to keep expanding.

The first chance to use the new prototype came as the company considered entering a new market in Europe. In keeping with his loose, delegating style, Carendi gave the task to an informal group consisting of a team leader, an actuary responsible for product design, someone with local market contacts, and Reinius, who was looking for ways to apply the new prototype systems module. A whole range of individual interests and motivations—from the existence of contacts in Zurich to the image they would develop by operating in the Swiss financial market—brought the group together to focus on Switzerland as a priority for market entry.

In 1990, Reinius completed his work on the prototype and installed it in Switzerland. Breaking away from the model of traditional insurance companies, the AFS prototype was designed to operate on smaller IBM/AS400 computers rather than large mainframes. It now consisted of a core chassis of various financially and administratively oriented modules for applications such as policy administration, product definition, distribution, asset management, accounting, billing, and collection, which together comprised a comprehensive operating environment. (See Exhibit 3.)

Exhibit 3   *Systems Prototype: Components and Integration**

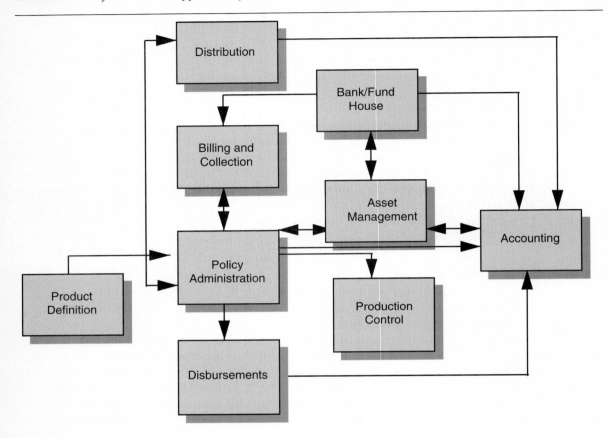

Component	Function
Policy administration	governs all policy activity over the life of a policy, e.g. underwriting, contract issue, financials, changes and terminations.
Accounting	controls all financial events, e.g. maintains ledgers, performs compliance reporting, prepares corporate statements
Product definition	defines products e.g. charges, cost factors, risk cover, calculation methods
Bank/fund house	supports wire transfers, international exchange rates, unit values, corporate financial transactions and balance reporting
Distribution	supports sales by maintaining field organization information, agent license information, sales performance and paying commissions
Production control	provides management information at an operational level, e.g. policies awaiting issue, premiums due and not paid, death claims pending
Asset management	controls balancing policyholder liabilities and fund assets, calculates required purchases or redemptions, provides reporting on funds
Billing and collection	bills for and collects premiums
Disbursements	pays claims, benefits, commissions and expenses

*Source: Skandia.

Despite the excitement that the growth was generating within AFS, Carendi's unconventional approach found its detractors within Skandia. Senior level IT executives were concerned about his investments in non-mainframe-based systems development; others saw his reliance on loose, unfocused teams as a risk in a structured, financially conservative company. But the biggest problem was that AFS was still reporting negative results. Because sales of these products typically generated more expenses than premiums income in early years (due to the heavy front loading of commissions, administrative set-up expenses, etc.), Carendi faced the dilemma that the faster he grew, the more losses he created. Even Hans Dalborg, the head of Skandia International, of which AFS was still a part, was expressing concern about the ongoing negative results in the United States. It was only in 1991, when Dalborg left the company and AFS was made a separate unit reporting directly to Björn Wolrath, the President and CEO of Skandia Group and a strong supporter of AFS strategy, that Carendi was able to continue his radically different approach to international expansion.

Transferring the Model

In 1991, with the fall of the Berlin wall, Carendi and his team decided to open a company in Germany, a large, complex market about which they knew very little. To develop some expertise in analyzing new market entry and starting up new subsidiaries, Carendi tapped Ann-Christin Pehrsson, a young woman he had met at a conference. Impressed by the quality of her thinking, he pursued her until he could convince her to leave her job and join AFS. Looking for a role that would challenge her and use her talents, he named Pehrsson AFS's director of business development, a one-person function based in Stockholm. With the help of local contacts, she developed a three-phase analysis of the new market opportunity: a market study, a legal requirements analysis, and a report on local distribu-

tion and money management networks. Pehrsson described why the three-year preparation for the German startup was so important:

Germans hesitate to speculate and take financial risks. This is a problem which is conditioned by culture, so it's important to interest people in the advantages of a variable annuity—still a relatively unknown form of long-term savings . . . In the beginning, we also had to put a lot of effort into finding the right distribution channels. The German market is traditionally a captive-agent market. They cooperate loyally with domestic companies and sell traditional life insurance products. Broker distribution is a new activity we were trying to help grow.

With the lessons taken from the Swiss entry and with the understanding generated by Pehrsson's business development analysis, Reinius and his team improved the systems prototype, allowing even greater flexibility to adapt to Germany's tax regulations and reporting requirements. Eventually, each local company hired its own IT people to make such adjustments and to maintain its systems, although the staff was kept quite small—three in Germany, three in Switzerland.

CHANGING MANAGEMENT STYLE
Carendi's Evolving Philosophy

As he pursued his international expansion strategy, built on the three-legged stool of unit-linked annuity products, the partnership-based business model, and the prototype-based learning processes, Carendi started to articulate a management philosophy that was radically different from the traditional Skandia approach. The key to success, in his view, lay in developing the knowledge and expertise of people, and in building the systems, processes and culture that would support them and leverage their capabilities. As he described it: "The employee is number one in my book. All my assets are between the ears of my employees, yet they can just walk away. If I want them to give me their best ideas and share their biggest dreams, I have to treat them as volunteers."

In this management model, Carendi described his own role as having two key functions— coach of the team and agent of change. Rather than seeing his job as sitting at the apex of the organization, he took on multiple jobs, allowing him to infiltrate the organization and fulfill his two key roles. In addition to his job as head of AFS, Carendi also served as a member of the parent company's five-person executive committee, as CEO of American Skandia, and as Board Chairman of AFS's holding companies: a continental company that controlled the Swiss, German, and Austrian group; a Mediterranean company that managed the Spanish and Italian groups; a South American company responsible for the group in Colombia; and an American company that controlled the U.S. and Mexican groups. (See Exhibit 4.) Describing himself as "a civil servant in his own organization," Carendi spent 90% of his time internally, and only 10% of his time on outside-focused activities. He traveled constantly, more than 200 days a year by his estimate, spending approximately 40% of the time in the United States, 30% in Sweden, and 30% in the rest of the world.

By taking on so many roles and traveling, Carendi believed he had to manage his various formal positions with a light hand, leaving lots of room for others. In a management style he described as "thrust and trust," he gave people broad directives and empowered them to take action. If someone raised an issue, he was likely to give them responsibility for it, calling an old Swedish adage that if you asked a question you owned the question. When things went wrong, Carendi encouraged open discussion of the problems amongst peers, giving rise to a culture in which people owned up to their errors and the lessons to be drawn from them. "As long as it's based on good faith and careful thinking, it's OK to make a mistake," he explained.

Carendi believed that this strong philosophy of delegation and learning by mistakes put a high premium on recruiting excellent people. "You hire the best people and leave them alone," he said. "If you're not going to leave them alone, you don't need to hire the best people." He often signed people on ahead of his ability to use them effectively, as he did with Pehrsson, and let them poke around the organization for several months until they decided what they wanted to do. "In the end, people are going to do what they like to do," he admitted. Viewing people selection as his greatest strength, Carendi retained the right to veto the hiring decisions of the direct reports of his direct reports; and he acknowledged that the key selection criterion was what he called "chemistry." Having found an individual who was open, honest, willing to question, and able to release the potential in others, he asked himself, "Would I like to have dinner with this person?"

Within AFS there was a well understood norm that "individuals had the responsibility to develop their own capabilities, and the company had the responsibility not to waste them." AFS encouraged personal development through a tuition reimbursement program. People could also volunteer to be on one of the numerous teams that were constantly being assembled in AFS, even if they were in areas outside their own. When forming teams, managers typically sent out e-mail messages to relevant departments, and people nominated themselves. Before defining the final team, managers held an election among the nominees to get their input on who could best serve the team.

To fully utilize the potential of those he recruited, developed, and empowered, Carendi believed he had to maintain AFS's informal and entrepreneurial culture, one that was distinctly different from that of the parent company. "We are a tent in a palace pitched right on top of the Iranian carpet," he said. "When circumstances change, we just take our tent down and put it up

Exhibit 4 *Skandia and AFS: Organizational Structure**

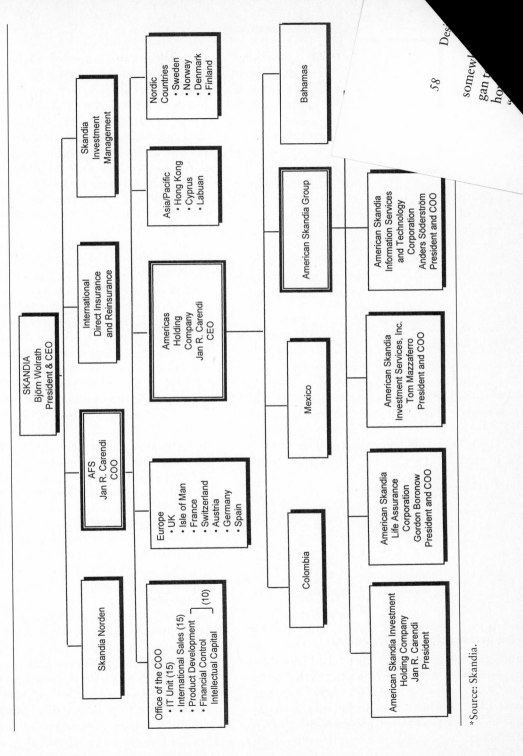

*Source: Skandia.

...here else." Starting in 1992, Carendi be-
...o formalize and communicate his ideas about
...w the organization should work in a series of
..."white papers" published in the internal newspaper. Among the key aspirations of the management model he was aspiring towards were:

- a "high-trust" culture characterized by shared
  values, transparent communications, and the
  encouragement for people to accept responsibility and take risk
- a challenging work environment in which
  learning was driven by people pushing each
  other in open, honest disagreement
- an organization built on identifying and improving processes that were unique to AFS, effective, and created competitive differentiation

ORGANIZING FOR KNOWLEDGE MANAGEMENT

As Carendi's management philosophy evolved,
so too did his strategic and organizational concepts. Increasingly, he became convinced that AFS
would have to compete on its ability to maintain
what he called a "permanent state of advanced
readiness." He told his organization:

> Today, creating bullet-proof products isn't as
> important as building the ability and will-
> power to constantly develop and deploy new
> products that responded to changing cus-
> tomer needs. You have to be able to get in and
> out of products and services with the compet-
> itive energy of a kid playing a video game
> rather than with the analytical consistency of
> a grand master trying to hang on in a three-
> day chess match.

The Federative Organization

For years Lekander and Carendi had been working on transforming AFS into what they described
as a "federative organization." The concept fit
well with Carendi's evolving management philosophy based on delegated responsibility and
individual initiatives. As a result, when a local

company began to develop particular capabilities and expertise in a vital function or activity
from which other units might learn, Carendi
designated it a "strategic competence center" as
a way of recognizing its achievements. For instance, Spain became a competence center for
bank product design, the United States for information technology, and Colombia for administrative support and back-office functions. But
no designation was permanent and lasted only
until another local company bypassed it on the
learning curve.

Since there was no formal structural linkage
to connect the federation of national units in
which AFS's expertise resided, Carendi worked
hard to create informal connections that encouraged information and knowledge sharing across
units. One common way was to use business
projects to draw people together according to
their expertise, regardless of organizational considerations. This was a model used repeatedly
not only in the startup of new subsidiaries but
also in the ongoing management of the business.
The project team assembled to define the specifications of a system to deliver payouts for annuities was typical. Representatives from several
subsidiaries not only captured diverse expertise
from multiple country units, but also ensured
that the system was designed so that the amount
of adaptation required when it was deployed
would be minimal.

Insisting that vital information available in
any part of the organization should be accessible
by all AFS companies, Carendi saw the need to
supplement the organization's informal links with
a sophisticated capability in information technology. After polling subsidiaries to assess their
need and willingness to pay for this capability,
he commissioned the IT units at AFS in Stockholm and Shelton to create an integrative global
area network (GAN) infrastructure. Configured
as a wide area network that connected the local
area networks of individual subsidiaries, the GAN
initially provided the capability for electronic
mail and document and file sharing, even to

those traveling within AFS offices. Later, the GAN was expanded to serve as a conduit for core business applications and operations. For instance, the Austrian subsidiary ran part of its operations on the server in Switzerland, and similarly, Mexico accessed programs housed in the United States. In addition, the GAN provided an electronic venue for the exchange of ideas and experiences about successful and unsuccessful practices and served as a repository of information replicated from external databases, such as those of market research firms.

As he developed this linked federation, Carendi was careful to keep the AFS Stockholm staff at a minimum. Consisting of approximately 40 of the company's 1,700 employees, this group worked on the construction of the IT infrastructure, cross-border sales and marketing projects, business development, and accounting and financial control, largely through resources that had been decentralized to the country units. For example, there were five centers in the IT federation, located in Germany, Colombia, Spain, England, and the United States, each of which not only supported its local operation but also contributed to the broader AFS development priorities. The Stockholm staff also organized knowledge sharing activities and functioned as the center of AFS communications, particularly of its values. "We don't refer to Stockholm as the *head* office," said one senior manager. "The brain power is out in the field. If anything, the center acts as the *heart* office, maintaining the values of the group and helping pump information—our lifeblood—around the organization. It certainly avoids prescribing how businesses should be conducted around the world."

BUILDING KNOWLEDGE

Measuring Intellectual Capital

The more Carendi became convinced of the competitive value of AFS's knowledge assets, the more he became frustrated with the inability of traditional financial reports to focus management attention appropriately. He believed that in companies such as AFS, which did not own machinery and buildings, the entity's value was best represented not in return on investment numbers but in some measurement of the organization's ability to build and leverage intellectual capital to produce revenue. He worried that traditional accounting measures did not even recognize such capital, let alone try to measure it. Because he was committed to making significant investments in precisely these "invisible assets," he gave top priority to finding a way of describing and measuring the effectiveness of such investments.

To help him with this challenge, in 1991 Carendi hired Leif Edvinsson, senior vice president of training and development at a Swedish bank, with an MBA from the University of California at Berkeley, and named him AFS's director of intellectual capital, the world's first. Edvinsson observed that many companies on the Stockholm Stock Exchange were valued at three to eight times their book value, and in the United States at even higher multiples. He argued that these huge hidden values were largely accounted for by a company's intellectual capital. To communicate this core notion to AFS management, Edvinsson often used the metaphor of a tree:

> *Hidden value is the root system for the tree. Healthy, strong roots provide the nutrients and nourishment necessary for its growth and production of fruit. The quality of the fruit, the results you can see, is dependent on the roots, which you cannot see . . . From this perspective, the bottom-line financial results are really the top-line results. The real bottom line is renewal and development, which is the foundation for the future.*

As a first step, Edvinsson felt he needed a taxonomy for "intellectual capital" to help him translate the broad concepts into management specifics. He classified it into human capital (the knowledge, skill and capability of employees in meeting the needs of customers) and structural capital (codified brainpower embedded over time: databases, customer files, software, manuals, trademarks, and organizational structures). Structural capital was in turn composed of customer capital and organizational capital. The former included such assets as existing customer relationships, brand equity, and goodwill, while the latter contained the structured competencies and systems for bringing together the company's innovative abilities and value-creating work processes. See Exhibit 5.

Edvinsson believed that the key management task was developing intellectual capital, which involved leveraging its human capital and transforming it into structural capital through the right combination of management leadership, values and incentives, and supportive infrastructure—thereby creating value for customers, investors, and other stakeholders. Said Edvinsson, "the real aim is to convert IQ into ECU [the European Currency Unit]. Focusing on managing financial resources using only information from

Exhibit 5   *The Building Blocks of Intellectual Capital**

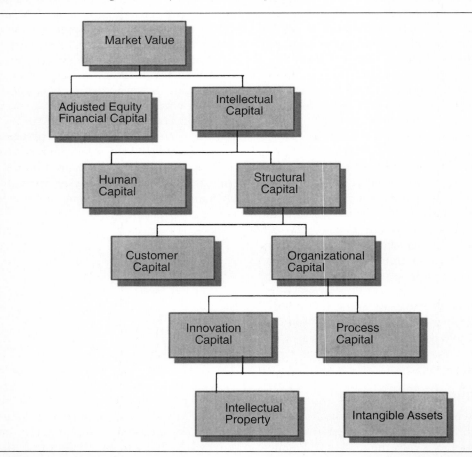

*Source: Skandia.

their accounting systems is a bit like driving into the future while looking in the rear view mirror."

Edvinsson realized, however, that the only way he could have an impact was by having his ideas incorporated into the ongoing decision-making processes. He obtained Carendi's approval to employ what he believed to be the world's first controller for intellectual capital, whose full-time job would be to define measures, gather data, and publish reports that would calibrate AFS's effectiveness in developing and exploiting its human and structural capital. Beginning with modest quarterly reports, Edvinsson and his controller gradually expanded the number of categories of intellectual capital and the means of measuring them, culminating in the publication of AFS's first annual report on intellectual assets for 1993. The report provided baseline measurements of many nontraditional inputs and performance measures, including information technology as a percentage of total expenses, the number of IT-literate employees as a percentage of all employees, gross insurance premiums per employee, and changes in savings per account.

Edvinsson's work touched off a debate within AFS about the utility of using scarce resources, first to identify and define the new indicators, (which were less universal and less readily apparent than traditional financial measures), and then to develop the infrastructure to capture the new data and analyze it. "I'm far too busy already doing what I already have to do," said one manager. Many others suggested that although they understood the effort conceptually, they were unclear about how the additional data would be significant operationally, for instance in setting priorities, allocating resources, or determining compensation and other incentives. Even those who saw the value of highlighting the hidden assets in their operations wondered if that would not be better managed by focusing on the process itself, rather than on creating a standardized "intellectual" balance sheet. "The concept of intellectual capital helps you see what

else to do to stay competitive which a purely financial focus doesn't let you see," said one senior manager. "But accounting for intellectual assets in the same way year after year—that would just be boring."

Nonetheless, Edvinsson continued his mission, eventually developing a new measurement model called the Business Navigator. This was a tool that tracked changes in performance on five key dimensions: the financial focus which represented yesterday's performance; the customer focus; the human focus; the process focus, which represented today's performance; and the renewal and development focus, which represented tomorrow's performance. The Business Navigator used indicators instead of ratios in order not to imply financial values. Edvinsson pointed out, "What's interesting is to measure not just the numbers, but the changes—because direction is more important than precision. It is better to be roughly right than precisely wrong. That is why we call it navigation." In 1993, Carendi announced that each unit would begin to report quarterly performance according to intellectual capital measures along with the standard financial ones, so that the data could be included in the decision making regarding resource allocation and priority setting. (See Exhibit 6 for its application in American Skandia.)

While not everyone on the operational level in AFS was fully sold on the program, Skandia's Direktionen (the top management group), of which Carendi was a member, decided to make this a corporate-wide initiative. In 1994, Skandia became the first company in the world to publish a formal report on intellectual capital as a supplement to its annual report. Although each of Skandia's businesses initially developed its own set of indicators to measure intellectual capital, the company was in the process of developing a consistent reporting format that used the same measurement logic for all business units.

Gradually, the functional units in some AFS companies began to adapt the intellectual capital measures into their front-line operations,

Exhibit 6   *The AFS Business Navigator**

Indicators of American Skandia Life

In this report we have decided to excerpt and illustrate a sampling of indicators for one of AFS's units, the U.S. operating unit American Skandia Life Assurance Corporation.

Since its start in 1989, American Skandia has seen gross premium volume rise to more than MSEK 10,240. The company is thus the 14th largest in the U.S. variable annuity market. The rate of development is high and has resulted in the launching of two to four significant new products or services a year.

FINANCIAL FOCUS

	1994	1993	1992
Return on net asset value	12.2%	24.3%	16.5%
Result of operations (MSEK)	115	96	19
Value added/empl. (SEK 000)	1,666	1,982	976

Comments: *American Skandia's growth remains strong, despite slowing growth in the overall market.*

CUSTOMER FOCUS

	1994	1993	1992
Number of contracts	59,089	31,997	12,123
Savings/contract (SEK 000)	333	371	281
Surrender ratio	4.2%	3.6%	8.0%
Points of sale	11,573	4,805	2,768
Number of fund managers	19	11	8
Number of funds	52	35	24

Comments: *American Skandia has a growing network of brokers, banks and fund managers. All of these have shown growth of about 100 per cent since last year. This growth adds to American Skandia's structural capital.*

HUMAN FOCUS

	1994	1993	1992
Number of employees (full-time)	220	133	94
Number of managers	62	n.a.	n.a.
of whom, women	13	n.a.	n.a.
Training exp./employee (SEK 000)	9.8	10.6	4.0

* n.a. = not available

Comments: *American Skandia's work force has grown rapidly. Many new employees are young. 72 per cent of the employees are under 40 years of age.*

PROCESS FOCUS

	1994	1993	1992
Contracts/employee	269	241	129
Adm. expense/gross premium	2.9%	2.6%	4.8%
PC/employee	1.3	1.4	1.1
IT expense/adm. expense	8.8%	4.7%	13.3%

Comments: *An aggressive IT focus during the year has resulted in low administrative expenses despite a concurrent growth in volume.*

RENEWAL & DEVELOPMENT FOCUS

	1994	1993	1992
Premium from new launches	11.1%	5.2%	49.7%
Increase in net premium	17.8%	204.8%	159.1%
Business development exp. /administrative expense	11.6%	9.8%	3.0%
Share of empl. below age 40	72%	74%	n.a.

Comments: *American Skandia has sustained its rapid pace of growth and presence in a highly competitive total market. The rate of business development is very high, which has become a ballmark of American Skandia. The rate of renewal can be credited, among other things, to IT investments and the build-up of the federative structure.*

AMERICAN SKANDIA'S BUSINESS NAVIGATOR

FINANCIAL FOCUS

| CUSTOMER FOCUS | HUMAN FOCUS | PROCESS FOCUS |

RENEWAL & DEVELOPMENT FOCUS

Return on net asset value	12.2 %
Result of operations (MSEK)	115
Value added/employee (SEK 000)	1,666

Number of contracts	59,089
Surrender ratio	4.2 %
Points of sale	11,573

Contracts/employee	269
Adm. expense/gross premium	2.9 %
IT expense/administrative expense	8.8 %

Premium from new launches	11.1 %
Increase in net premium	17.8 %
Business development exp./adm. exp.	11.6 %
Share of employees below age 40	72 %

albeit at their own pace. For instance, after modifying the Business Navigator for his unit, Anders Söderström, the head of American Skandia's IT unit, discovered that he was not investing enough in training his employees in new rapidly changing technologies. (See Exhibit 7 for his unit's Business Navigator.) "We noticed that our ratio of IT training expenses to IT expense was certainly lower than what we had planned, and lower relative to where we thought our competitors were," said Söderström. "The IC measures pointed me in exactly the opposite direction than the financial measures. While I was minimizing my expenses, I was putting at risk the knowledge and competence of my people at using current and future technologies to their fullest. The Business Navigator let me see that sometimes what looks good is bad, short-term thinking." As a result, Söderström came up with a development plan for each person in his group, and a reward system that weighted training more heavily in awarding bonuses each quarter.

Other American Skandia units were doing likewise. The customer service area began to work on the customer focus dimension of the navigator, developing measures and monitoring trends relating to the promptness and accuracy of responses to telephone requests from the wholesalers and brokers. It was piloting a project where each month, based on the results, representatives could win up to $75 on a debit card based upon the performance of their customer service team. And in marketing and sales, management was trying to measure and monitor the development of customer capital in addition to focusing on current sales. For instance, they started tracking number of brokers who wrote new business or became inactive each quarter, displaying the results on a bulletin board.

Building Broker Relationships

Believing that "strategic ability begins and ends with serving the needs of the customer," in 1992 Carendi redirected the bulk of systems develop-

Exhibit 7   *The American Skandia IT Business Navigator**

AMERICAN SKANDIA'S IT BUSINESS NAVIGATOR

IT expense/administrative expense	19%
Value added*/IT-employees	117
Investments in IT	2,927
Number of internal IT customers	552
Number of external IT customers	14
Number of contracts/IT-employees	1,906
Corporate IT-literacy	+7%
IT capacity (CPU & DASD)	
AS/400 **168,300 trans./hour**	47 GB
PC/LAN **14,055 MIPS**	199 GB
Change in IT inventory	3,639
IT development expense/IT expense	60%
IT expenses on training/IT expense	1%
R&D resources/total resources	5%

All amount in USD 000s.

*Change in IT inventory.

*Source: Skandia.

ment efforts towards meeting the needs of the key brokers and banks, with whom the organization was strategically allied. At first, the focus was simply on building the relationship by providing brokers with excellent service and support. One initiative was the creation of a "concierge desk" to help brokers with whatever they needed: hotel reservations, lost credit cards, theater tickets. "Now the broker thinks of American Skandia when he has a problem to solve," said Carendi. "And the likelihood is that if he continues to think of us, he will also think of us when he has business to write." The customer service function was also reorganized into teams with the objective of providing personal service and building lifetime relationships with their assigned brokers and wholesalers. Carendi invested in the professional development of brokers, establishing a Leader's College in the United States in 1994 whose bimonthly sessions covered an array of financial as well as professional development topics.

Envisioning a day when a broker would provide much greater perceived value to the client by filtering and interpreting the confusing amount of information in the marketplace, American Skandia developed a PC-based software product called ASSESS. Launched in 1994, ASSESS helped brokers become experts on 35 different investment options by providing access to a variety of data sources, including analyst reports, stock listings, and standard indices. It also included an in-depth online questionnaire that helped the broker understand the client's needs, highlighting areas of opportunity or concern. The broker could also use it as an educational tool to help the client understand the relationship of risk and return and the benefits of long-term investing. The software, which was mailed free to 20,000 brokers in the United States, freed them of tedious administrative tasks and allowed them to spend more time advising the client. Equally important, it allowed the broker to address questions, complete paperwork, and close the deal

while the client was still in the office, rather than weeks later when interest might have cooled off.

American Skandia's sales and marketing division also made a sizable investment in creating a database on 250,000 brokers, aimed at reducing the rate of turnover among brokers in its networks. The largest such repository in the industry, the database tracked by broker the types of annuities sold, the commission structure, annual sales, and even the type of software preferred. The area was also developing systems, ranging from one that signaled a slowdown in a broker's underwriting activity, and the need for support, to one that sent brokers automatic thank-yous. "I want to create a process where we're communicating and building an emotional tie with the broker," said Dokken, the subsidiary's marketing chief. "I want to make him think twice about leaving us."

Staying Ahead

Despite AFS's successful growth, Carendi was always cognizant of the uncertainty in the environment and determined to "take charge of change." He was continually trying to identify and test strategic opportunities—what he described as a "dress rehearsal for the future." Recognizing that the world was becoming too complex and dynamic for him to develop clear foresight by himself, Carendi began to see the value of tapping into the ideas of his employees. Not only were they closer to the market, but they also knew AFS and its capabilities. The more he thought about it, the more he wanted to structure a formal process around future scanning. To help him implement it, he enlisted the help of Edvinsson, his director of intellectual capital.

Edvinsson hand-picked a pilot team of nine people from Colombia, the United States, U.K., Germany, and Sweden, deliberately focusing on AFS's "Generation X," the twenty-somethings who were the seed of the future. He gave them a full-time, three-month assignment to develop scenarios of the future for the company and the industry and to be prepared to present their conclusions to the company's Strategic Advisor Board (SAB). After an initial brainstorming session, the team settled on four areas of investigation: the customer, the "igonomy" (economy at the personal and macro level), corporate reality (AFS's resources and constraints), and "valutics," (political systems and national values).

After weeks of intensive reading and discussion to flesh out their ideas, the team made their presentation to the SAB in Stockholm. They asked the senior managers to accept their scenarios at face value, and to come up with the best response for AFS. The Generation Xers foresaw a future in which the customer would be more knowledgeable, have access to information at any time and any place, and demand product flexibility to fit their fast-paced and changing lifestyles. "We will have to offer a totally customized product," said one member of the team. "In other words, there will be no product. There will be as many products as there are clients. The client will be the creator."

The Generation X team and the SAB then compared notes about what AFS's response should be and were surprised at how convergent their ideas were—with one major exception. While the Generation Xers could foresee a fragmented market undermining AFS's carefully designed network, top management believed that there was still value to be added by brokers, because they made clients aware of the need for financial planning. Later, Carendi incorporated the learning into the brokers' Leaders College, devoting one session to the burgeoning field of electronic commerce, alerting brokers to technological advances that could radically alter their present role.

With the success of the pilot attempt in 1995, Carendi supported and enlarged the concept of future scanning through the creation of the Skandia Future Centers (SFC) division, appointing Edvinsson in charge. The centers would act as a meeting place and "greenhouse" for dialog and collaboration. The first iteration created five "future teams," each composed of five full-time members drawn from three populations—the "inpower" generation, the "potential" generation, and Generation X. The groups would meet over several months, convening frequently for a day or two to discuss their assigned topics—the future of information technology, organization and leadership; changing demographics; changes in the insurance market; and the future of the world economy. In addition, the groups would invite "Rolodex groups" of outside experts to present their perspectives on broad conceptual issues in a variety of fields related and unrelated to insurance and financial services. The knowledge gained would be shared throughout the organization via the GAN. The first future center was to be inaugurated near Stockholm in May 1996, and other locations were planned.

CURRENT CHALLENGES

In 1996, AFS was a worldwide organization, with an impressive array of performance statistics. Despite a downturn in 1995, premium income had grown 45% annually during the past five years. Between 1992 and 1995, its customer base had grown from 100,000 to 785,000; its alliance network of brokers, fund managers, and other partners had expanded from 15,000 to 46,000; and its employee base had expanded from 1,130 to 1,700. With only 1 out of 27 people working for it on its payroll, some began to describe AFS as a "virtual corporation." By its own estimate, the company's network-based organization and its use of cutting-edge information technology had reduced its administrative costs to one-third of those of its competitors.

However, despite these accomplishments, Carendi was focused on how to defend and improve AFS's position as a leader in its chosen business. The downturn in the U.K. reflected the growing market turmoil and intensity of competition, and Carendi's main concern was how to maintain the high quality of service and the momentum of innovation when resources were being constrained by growth. Many of AFS's practices were now being imitated widely as other companies built cooperative alliances for money management and distribution. Still others had released their own versions of the ASSESS software, and cloned AFS's products. Furthermore, deregulation had lowered barriers to entry into the market. All of this meant that customer loyalty was eroding. As Carendi explained:

Competition could come from anywhere. Today, we compete with mutual funds. Tomorrow, we are going to compete with software houses ... Consumers couldn't care less about established relationships today if they can get it cheaper elsewhere and at the time of day when they have time rather than when the banker or broker's office is open.

Carendi was particularly intrigued by the ideas generated by the "Generation X" pilot team's future scenario in which potential policyholders would buy insurance very differently than they did in the past. "What implications did this have for AFS?" he wondered.

Another issue on Carendi's mind was AFS's planned entry into Japan—the world's largest life insurance market. In the past, only seven foreign insurance companies had entered Japan. Several of these, including Equitable Life, had eventually sold out their operations to Japanese competitors because of regulatory hurdles and huge problems and costs in adapting their systems to the local market. At the time, there were 30 life insurance companies in Japan, but by 1997 and 1998, when a major reform of Japanese insurance law was due to take effect, the number was expected to rise to 40 or 50. The reform would allow life and nonlife companies to enter each others' domains, simplify the application procedure for new products, abandon the requirement for distribution solely by exclusive agents, and allow a broker channel.

With the help of a local market research firm, AFS had done extensive research on the Japanese assurance market since 1987. Director of business development Ann-Christin Pehrsson found the opportunity very attractive, based on the country's demographics. By the year 2025, the number of people over 65 years of age was expected to increase by 160%. In addition, the Japanese were inclined toward savings and investing, with women often taking a major role in managing the family finances as well as the home.

At present, there were three European insurance companies in Japan, and Skandia was among three others waiting to receive a license, having begun the application process in 1992. According to Pehrsson, the Ministry of Finance in Japan was checking not only the products, but the entire company very closely. The design of AFS's unit-linked product was new to the Japanese market, contrasting with the traditional Japanese variable life policy, which offered a more limited choice in fund management and allocated a larger component of the premium to the insurance rather than the savings segment.

Sales distribution also represented a challenge. Most Japanese companies sold their products through company agents who were linked in turn to a vast network of 400,000 "housewife retailers." Skandia hoped to capitalize on the deregulation process to begin selling its product through a bank. Although it had been negotiating with a bank for some time, as of early 1996 it did not have a final agreement. Another question being addressed within AFS was whether the European or the American IT system should be used as a base, given that the Japanese operation would be managed out of the United States but the product line would be closer to the traditional European one. A complicating factor was that Kanji characters required that all text handling be removed from the core system, while the calculations and product profile and other core elements remained. By the time of the launch, the company was expected to have a staff of 37, with all the attendant expenses. Again, some in Skandia were becoming impatient.

In many ways, this was the ultimate test for the company's notion of transferable knowledge for competitive advantage. Would the lessons in the international expansion over the past decade apply? Would the highly developed AFS organizational model and management philosophy succeed in Japan? These were some of the questions that refocused Carendi's mind from his company's successful past to its uncertain future.

MCKINSEY & COMPANY: MANAGING KNOWLEDGE AND LEARNING

In April 1996, halfway through his first three-year term as managing director of McKinsey & Company, Rajat Gupta was feeling quite proud as he flew out of Bermuda, site of the firm's second annual Practice Olympics. He had just listened to 20 teams outlining innovative new ideas they had developed out of recent project work, and, like his fellow senior partner judges, Gupta had come away impressed by the intelligence and creativity of the firm's next generation of consultants.

But there was another thought that kept coming back to the 47-year-old leader of this highly successful $1.8 billion consulting firm (See Exhibit 1 for a 20-year growth history). If this represented the tip of McKinsey's knowledge and expertise iceberg, how well was the firm doing in developing, capturing, and leveraging this asset in service of its clients worldwide? In his mind, the task of knowledge development had become much more complex over the past decade or so due to three intersecting forces. First,

in an increasingly information- and knowledge-driven age, the sheer volume and rate of change of new knowledge made the task much more complex; second, clients' expectations of and need for leading-edge expertise were constantly increasing, in part because of these developments; and third, the firm's own success had made it much more difficult to link and leverage the knowledge and expertise represented by 3,800 consultants in 69 offices worldwide. Although the Practice Olympics was only one of several initiatives he had championed, Gupta wondered if it was enough, particularly in light of his often-stated belief that "knowledge is the lifeblood of McKinsey."

THE FOUNDERS' LEGACY[1]

Founded in 1926 by University of Chicago professor, James ("Mac") McKinsey, the firm of "accounting and engineering advisors" that bore his name grew rapidly. Soon Mac began recruit-

---

[1]The Founders' Legacy section draws on Amar V. Bhide, "Building the Professional Firm: McKinsey & Co., 1939–1968," HBS Working Paper 95–010.

This case was prepared by Christopher A. Bartlett. Copyright © 1996 by the President and Fellows of Harvard College. Harvard Business School case 396-357.

Exhibit 1   *McKinsey & Company: 20-Year Growth Indicators*

Year	No. of Office Locations	No. of Active Engagements	Number of CSS[a]	Number of MGMs[b]
1975	24	661	529	NA
1980	31	771	744	NA
1985	36	1823	1248	NA
1990	47	2789	2465	348
1991	51	2875	2653	395
1992	55	2917	2875	399
1993	60	3142	3122	422
1994	64	3398	3334	440
1995	69	3559	3817	472

*Source: Internal McKinsey & Company documents.
[a]CSS = Client Service Staff (All professional consulting staff).
[b]MGM = Management Group Members (Partners and directors).

ing experienced executives and training them in the integrated approach he called his General Survey outline. In Saturday morning sessions he would lead consultants through an "undeviating sequence" of analysis—goals, strategy, policies, organization, facilities, procedures, and personnel—while still encouraging them to synthesize data and think for themselves.

In 1932, Mac recruited Marvin Bower, a bright young lawyer with a Harvard MBA, and within two years asked him to become manager of the recently opened New York office. Convinced that he had to upgrade the firm's image in an industry typically regarded as "efficiency experts" or "business doctors," Bower imbued in his associates the sense of professionalism he had experienced in his time in a law partnership. In a 1937 memo, he outlined his vision for the firm as one focused on important management problems; adhering to the highest standards of integrity, professional ethics, and technical excellence; able to attract and develop young men of outstanding qualifications; and committed to continually raising its stature and influence.

Over the next decade, Bower worked tirelessly to influence his partners and associates to share his vision. As new offices opened, he be-

came a strong advocate of the "one firm" policy that required all consultants to be recruited and advanced on a firm-wide basis, clients to be treated as McKinsey & Company responsibilities, and profits to be shared from a firm pool, not an office pool. Through dinner seminars, he began upgrading the size and quality of McKinsey's clients. In the 1945 New Engagement Guide, he articulated a policy that every assignment should bring the firm something more than revenue—experience or prestige, for example. The policies and principles laid down in this era became the basis for McKinsey's values going forward (see Exhibit 2).

Elected managing partner in 1950, Bower led his ten partners and 74 associates to initiate a series of major changes that turned McKinsey into an elite consulting firm unable to meet the demand for its services. Each client's problems were seen as unique, but Bower and his colleagues firmly believed that well-trained, highly intelligent generalists could quickly grasp the issue, and through disciplined analysis find its solution. The firm's extraordinary domestic growth through the 1950s provided a basis for international expansion that accelerated the rate of growth in the 1960s. By the time Bower stepped down as Managing Director in 1967, McKinsey was a well-established and highly respected presence in Europe and North America.

A Decade of Doubt

Although leadership succession was well planned and smoothly executed, within a few years, McKinsey's growth engine seemed to stall. The economic turmoil of the oil crisis, the playing out of the divisionalization process that had fueled the European expansion, the growing sophistication of client management, and the appearance of new, focused competitors like Boston Consulting Group (BCG) all contributed to the problem. Almost overnight, McKinsey's enormous reservoir of internal self-confidence and even self-satisfaction began to turn to self-doubt and self-criticism.

Commission on Firm Aims and Goals

Concerned that the slowing growth in Europe and the United States was more than just a cyclical market downturn, the firm's partners assigned a committee of their most respected peers to study the problem and make recommendations. In April 1971, the Commission on Firm Aims and Goals concluded that the firm had been growing too fast. The authors bluntly reported, "Our preoccupation with the geographic expansion and new practice possibilities has caused us to neglect the development of our technical and professional skills." The report concluded that McKinsey had been too willing to accept routine assignments from marginal clients, that the quality of work done was uneven, and that while its consultants were excellent generalist problem-solvers, they often lacked the deep industry knowledge or the substantive specialized expertise that clients were demanding.

One of the Commission's central proposals was that the firm had to recommit itself to the continuous development of its members. This meant that growth would have to be slowed and

---

Exhibit 2   *McKinsey's Mission and Guiding Principles (1996)*

McKinsey Mission

To help our clients make positive, lasting, and substantial improvements in their performance
and to build a great Firm that is able to attract, develop, excite, and retain exceptional people.

Guiding Principles

SERVING CLIENTS	Adhere to professional standards
	Follow the top management approach
	Assist the client in implementation and capability building
	Perform consulting in a cost effective manner
BUILDING THE FIRM	Operate as one Firm
	Maintain a meritocracy
	Show a genuine concern for our people
	Foster an open and nonhierarchical working atmosphere
	Manage the Firm's resources responsibly
BEING A MEMBER OF THE PROFESSIONAL STAFF	Demonstrate commitment to client service
	Strive continuously for superior quality
	Advance the state of the art management
	Contribute a spirit of partnership through teamwork and collaboration
	Profit from the freedom and assume the responsibility associated with self-governance
	Uphold the obligation to dissent

that the MGM-to-associate ratio be reduced from 7 to 1 back to 5 or 6 to 1. It further proposed that emphasis be placed on the development of what it termed "T-shaped" consultants—those who supplemented their broad, generalist perspective with in-depth competence in an industry or a functional specialty.

Practice Development Initiative

When Ron Daniel was elected managing director in 1976—the fourth to hold the position since Bower had stepped down nine years earlier—McKinsey was still struggling to meet the challenges laid out in the Commission's report. As the head of the New York office since 1970, Daniel had experienced first hand the rising expectations of increasingly sophisticated clients and the aggressive challenges of new competitors like BCG. In contrast to McKinsey's local, office-based model of "client relationship" consulting, BCG began competing on the basis of "thought leadership" from a highly concentrated resource base in Boston. Using some simple but powerful tools, such as the experience curve and the growth-share matrix, BCG began to make strong inroads into the strategy consulting market. As McKinsey began losing both clients and recruits to BCG, Daniel became convinced that his firm could no longer succeed "by trying to out-think our clients in our old generalist model."

Building on an initiative he and his colleagues had already implemented in the New York office, he encouraged the firm-wide development of industry-based "Clientele Sectors" in consumer products, banking, industrial goods, insurance, and so on, cutting across the geographic offices that remained the primary organizational entity. He also encouraged more formal development of the firm's functional expertise in areas like strategy, organization, and operations, where knowledge and experience were widely diffused and minimally codified. There were many, including Marvin Bower, who expressed concern that any move towards a product-driven approach could damage McKinsey's distinctive, client-specific problem-solving approach. They did not want to compromise the advantage of local presence which gave partners strong connections with the business community, allowed teams to work on site with clients, and facilitated implementation. It was an approach that they felt contrasted sharply with the "fly in, fly out" model of consulting.

Nonetheless, Daniel pressed ahead, and the industry sectors quickly found a natural client base. Feeling that functional expertise needed more attention, he assembled working groups to develop knowledge in two areas that were at the heart of McKinsey's practice—strategy and organization. To head up the first group, he named Fred Gluck, a director in the New York office who had been outspoken in urging the firm to modify its traditional generalist approach. In June 1977, Gluck invited a "super group" of younger partners with strategy expertise to a three-day meeting to share ideas and develop an agenda for the strategy practice. One described the meeting:

> We had three days of unmitigated chaos. Someone from New York would stand up and present a four-box matrix. A partner from London would present a nine-box matrix. A German would present a 47-box matrix. It was chaos—but at the end of the third day some strands of thought were coming together. On the final day, an exhausted Gluck put up a slide that read: Christians = 3, Lions = 27, Ohmae = 146.[2]

At the same time, Daniel asked Bob Waterman, who had been working on a Siemens-sponsored study of "excellent companies" and Jim Bennett, a respected senior partner, to assemble a group that could articulate the firm's existing knowledge in the organization arena. One of their first recruits was an innovative young Ph.D. in organizational theory named Tom Peters.

---

[2]Kenichi Ohmae was the energetic and prolific consultant from Tokyo office who had begun generating a stream of ideas that later made him a globally acknowledged strategy guru.

REVIVAL AND RENEWAL

By the early 1980s, with growth resuming and output emerging from the practice development projects, a cautious optimism returned to McKinsey for the first time in almost a decade.

Centers of Competence

Recognizing that the activities of the two practice development projects could not just be a one-time effort, Daniel asked Gluck in 1980 to join the central, small group that comprised the firm office and focus on the knowledge-building agenda that had become his passion. Ever since his arrival at the firm from Bell Labs in 1967, Gluck had wanted to bring an equally stimulating intellectual environment to McKinsey. Against some strong internal resistance, he set out to convert his partners to his strongly held beliefs—that knowledge development had to be a central, not a peripheral firm activity; that it needed to be ongoing and institutionalized, not temporary and project based; and that it had to be the responsibility of everyone, not just a few.

As one key means of bringing this about, he created 15 "Centers of Competence" (virtual centers, not locations) built around existing areas of functional expertise like marketing, change management, and systems. In a 1982 memo to all partners, he described the role of these centers as twofold: to help develop consultants and to ensure the continued renewal of the firm's intellectual resources. For each center, Gluck identified one or two highly motivated, recognized experts in the particular field and named them practice leaders. The expectation was that these leaders would assemble from around the firm a core group of six to ten partners who were active in the practice area and interested in contributing to its development. (See Exhibit 3 for the 15 centers and 11 sectors in 1983.)

However, Gluck acknowledged that the firm's most successful partners were those with the biggest personal networks, and his objective was to leverage, rather than replace, this traditional means of knowledge transfer within McKinsey. He encouraged the core group of each practice to develop a network of agents in each geographic office to facilitate communication of their ideas

---

Exhibit 3   *McKinsey's Emerging Practice Areas: Centers of Competence and Industry Sectors, 1983*

Centers of Competence	Clientele Sectors
Building Institutional Skills	Automotive
Business Management Unit	Banking
Change Management	Chemicals
Corporate Leadership	Communications and Information
Corporate Finance	Consumer Products
Diagnostic Scan	Electronics
International Management	Energy
Integrated Logistics	Health Care
Manufacturing	Industrial Goods
Marketing	Insurance
Microeconomics	Steel
Sourcing	
Strategic Management	
Systems	
Technology	

into the mainstream of practice which was still managed by the offices. To help build a shared body of knowledge, the leadership of each of the 15 centers began to initiate a series of ongoing activities primarily involving the core group and, less frequently, the members of the practice network. A colleague commented on his commitment to establishing the centers:

> Unlike industry sectors, the centers of competence did not have a natural, stable client base, and Fred had to work hard to get them going. . . . He basically told each center, "Spend whatever you can—the cost is almost irrelevant compared to the payoff." There was no attempt to filter or manage the process, and the effect was "to let a thousand flowers bloom."

Gluck also spent a huge amount of time trying to change an internal status hierarchy based largely on the size and importance of one's client base. Arguing that practice development ("snowball making" as it became known internally) was not less "macho" than client development ("snowball throwing"), he tried to convince his colleagues that everyone had to become snowball makers *and* snowball throwers. In endless discussions, he would provoke his colleagues with barbed pronouncements and personal challenges: "Knowing what you're talking about is not necessarily a client service handicap" or "Would you want your brain surgery done by a general practitioner?"

BUILDING A KNOWLEDGE INFRASTRUCTURE

As the Clientele Sectors and Centers of Competence began to formalize existing knowledge and generate new insights, many began to feel the need to leverage the learning. Although big ideas had occasionally been written up as articles for publication in newspapers, magazines, or journals like the *Harvard Business Review*, there was still a deep-seated suspicion of anything that smacked of packaging ideas or creating propri-

etary concepts. (Despite this bias, however, the output of the strategy and organization working groups resulted in the publication in 1982 of two major best-sellers, Peters and Waterman's *In Search of Excellence* and Ohmae's *The Mind of the Strategist*). This reluctance to document concepts had long constrained the internal transfer of ideas, and the vast majority of internally developed knowledge was never captured. The McKinsey Staff Paper series provided another means of documenting important findings, but few made the considerable effort to write one. Believing that the firm had to dramatically lower the barrier to knowledge communication, Gluck introduced the idea of Practice Bulletins: two-page summaries of important new ideas that identified the experts who could provide more detail. A partner elaborated:

> The bulletins were essentially internal advertisements for ideas and the people who had developed them. We tried to convince people that they would help build their personal networks and internal reputations. . . . Fred was not at all concerned that the quality was mixed, and had a strong philosophy of letting the internal market sort out what were the really big ideas.

Although the bulletins facilitated knowledge transfer, Gluck began to question whether the firm's organizational infrastructure needed a major overhaul. He launched a Knowledge Management Project in 1987, and, after five months of study, the team proposed three other recommendadtions. First, the firm had to make a major commitment to build a common database of knowledge, accumulated from client work and developed in the practice areas. Second, to ensure that the databases were maintained and used, they also proposed that each practice area (Clientele Sector and Competence Center) hire a full-time practice coordinator who could act as an "intelligent switch" responsible for both monitoring the quality of the data and helping consultants access the relevant information. Finally, they suggested that the firm expand its hiring practices and promotion policies to create a career path for deep-functional specialists whose narrow expertise would not fit the normal profile of a T-shaped consultant.

The task of implementing these recommendations fell to Bill Matassoni, the firm's director of communications, and Brook Manville, a newly recruited Yale Ph.D. in history with experience in electronic publishing. Focusing first on the Firm Practice Information System (FPIS), a computerized database of client engagements, they installed new systems and procedures to make the data more complete, accurate, and timely so that it could be accessed as a reliable information resource, not just as an archival record. More difficult was the task of capturing the knowledge that had accumulated in the practice areas, since much of it had not been formalized and none of it had been prioritized or integrated. To create a computer-based Practice Development Network (PDNet), Matassoni and Manville put huge energy into begging, cajoling, and challenging each practice to develop and submit documents that represented their core knowledge. After months of work, they had collected the 2,000 documents that they believed provided the critical mass to launch PDNet.

Matassoni and his team also developed another information resource that had not been part of the study team's recommendations. They assembled a listing of all firm experts and key document titles by practice area and published it in a small book, compact enough to fit in any consultant's briefcase. The Knowledge Resource Directory (KRD) became the McKinsey Yellow Pages and found immediate and widespread use firmwide. Although the computerized data bases were slow to be widely adopted, the KRD found almost immediate enthusiastic acceptance.

Making the new practice coordinator's position effective proved more challenging. Initially, these roles were seen as little more than glorified librarians. It took several years before the new roles were filled by individuals (often ex-consultants) who were sufficiently respected that they could not only act as consultants to those seeking information about their area of expertise, but also were able to impose the discipline necessary to maintain and build the practice's databases.

Perhaps the most difficult task was to legitimize the role of a new class of consultants—the specialist. The basic concept was that a professional could make a career in McKinsey by emphasizing specialized knowledge development rather than the broad-based problem-solving skills and client development orientation that were deeply embedded in the firm's value system. While several consultants with deep technical expertise in specialties like market research, finance or steel making were recruited, most found it hard to assimilate into the mainstream. The firm seemed uncomfortable about how to evaluate, compensate or promote these individuals, and many either became isolated or disaffected. Nonetheless, the partnership continued to support the notion of a specialist promotion track and continued to struggle with how to make it work.

Matassoni reflected on the changes:

The objective of the infrastructure changes was not so much to create a new McKinsey as to keep the old "one firm" concept functioning as we grew. Despite all the talk of computerized databases, the knowledge management process still relied heavily on personal networks, old practices like cross-office transfers, and strong "one firm" norms like helping other consultants when they called. And at promotion time, nobody reviewed your PD documents. They looked at how you used your internal networks to have your ideas make an impact on clients.

MANAGING SUCCESS

By the late 1980s the firm was expanding very rapidly again. In 1988, the same year Fred Gluck was elected managing director, new offices were opened in Rome, Helsinki, Brussels, São Paulo, San Jose, and Minneapolis. From the partners' perspective, however, enhancing McKinsey's reputation as a thought leader was at least as important as increasing the demand for its services.

Client Impact

Having led the charge on knowledge management for eight years, Gluck began to focus on a new theme, client impact, when he was elected managing director. In addition to making this a central theme in his early speeches, memos, and his first All Partners Conference, he also created a Client Impact Committee and asked it to explore the ways in which the firm could ensure that its work with each client created measurable, positive results.

One of the most important initiatives of the new committee was to persuade the partners to redefine the firm's key consulting unit from the engagement team (ET) to the client service team (CST). The traditional ET, assembled to deliver a three- or four-month assignment for a client, was a highly efficient and flexible unit, but it tended to focus on the immediate task rather than on the client's long-term need. The CST concept was that the firm could add long-term value and increase the effectiveness of individual engagements if it could unite a core of individuals (particularly at the partner level) who were linked across multiple ETs and commit them to working with the client over an extended period. The impact was to broaden the classic model of a partner "owning" a client to a group of partners with shared commitment to each client.

Although client impact studies indicated the new structure led to a longer-term focus and deeper understanding of issues, it also raised some concerns. In the staff-constrained environment caused by rapid growth, some felt that the new approach biased resource allocation to the largest clients with the biggest CSTs. Others felt that CSTs tended to be more insular, guarding proprietary concepts and reaching out less often for firm-wide knowledge.

In response, Gluck returned to his long-term theme that, "it's all about people." He said:

There are two ways to look at McKinsey. The most common way is that we are a client service firm whose primary purpose is to serve the companies seeking our help. That is legitimate. But I believe there is an even more powerful way for us to see ourselves. We should begin to view our primary purpose as building a great institution that becomes an engine for producing highly motivated, world-class people who in turn will serve our clients extraordinarily well.

Refining Knowledge Management

After 1988, the practice development role Gluck had played since 1980 was taken over by a newly constituted Clientele and Professional Development Committee (CPDC). When Ted Hall took over leadership of this committee in late 1991, he felt there was a need to reflect Gluck's "it's all about people" theme by readjusting the firm from what he saw as growing focus on publication and dissemination to a greater commitment to professional development. He commented:

By the early 1990s, too many people were seeing practice development as the creation of experts and the generation of documents in order to build our reputation. But knowledge is only valuable when it is between the ears of consultants and applied to clients' problems. Because it is less effectively developed through the disciplined work of a few than through the spontaneous interaction of many, we had to change the more structured "discover-codify-disseminate" model to a looser and more inclusive "engage-explore-apply-share" approach. In other words, we shifted our focus from developing knowledge to building individual and team capability.

The CPDC's first step was to change the structure and governance of the industry and functional practices. Over the years, Gluck's philosophy "to let 1,000 flowers bloom" had resulted in the original group of 11 sectors and 15 centers

Exhibit 4   *Group Framework for Sectors and Centers**

Functional Capability Groups	Clientele Industry Sectors
Corporate Governance and Leadership • Corporate organization • Corporate management processes • Corporate strategy development • Corporate relationship design and management • Corporate finance • Post-merger management	**Financial Institutions** • Banking • Insurance • Health care payor/provider
Organization (OPP/MOVE) • Corporate transformation design and leadership • Energizing approaches • Organization design and development • Leadership and teams • Engaging teams	**Consumer** • Retailing • Consumer industries • Media • Pharmaceuticals
Information Technology/Systems • To be determined	**Energy** • Electrical utilities • Petroleum • Natural gas • Other energy
Marketing • Market research • Sales force management • Channel management • Global marketing • Pricing • Process and sector support	**Basic Materials** • Steel • Pulp and paper • Chemicals • Other basic materials
Operations Effectiveness • Integrated logistics • Manufacturing • Purchasing and supply management	**Aerospace, Electronics, and Telecom** • Telecom • Electronics • Aerospace
Strategy • Strategy • Microeconomics • Business dynamics • Business planning processes	**Transportation** **Automotive, Assembly, and Machinery** • Automotive • Assembly
Cross-Functional Management • Innovation • Customer satisfaction • Product/technology development and commercialization • Core process redesign (?)	

*Source: Internal McKinsey & Company document

expanding to become what Hall called "72 islands of activity," (Sectors, Centers, Working Groups, and Special Projects) many of which were perceived as fiefdoms dominated by one or two established experts. In Hall's view, the garden of 1,000 flowers needed weeding, a task requiring a larger group of mostly different gardeners.

The CPDCs proposed that the diverse industry interest groups be integrated into seven closely related sectors, and that the various competence centers be put under the umbrella of seven functional capability groups (See Exhibit 4). These sectors and functional capability groups were to be led by teams of five to seven partners (typically younger directors and principals) with the objective of replacing the leader-driven knowledge creation and dissemination process with a "stewardship model" of self-governing practices focused on competence building.

As it restructured the practice governance model, Hall and the CPDC became aware of a concern within the partnership about a gradual decline in associates' involvement in the firm's efforts to build intellectual capital and their own need for professional development. This was most observable in the skepticism with which some associates viewed participation in functionally oriented practices, which were not seen as having immediate relevance to understanding a particular client's business. Hall firmly believed that the CSTs (by 1993 about 200 firmwide) represented the real learning laboratories and that CST members had to be coopted into the intellectual life of the firm. (See Exhibit 5 for a CPDC conceptualization.)

The CPDC sent memos to the new practice leaders advising them that their practices would be evaluated by their coverage of the firm's

Exhibit 5   *CPDC Proposed Organizational Relationships**

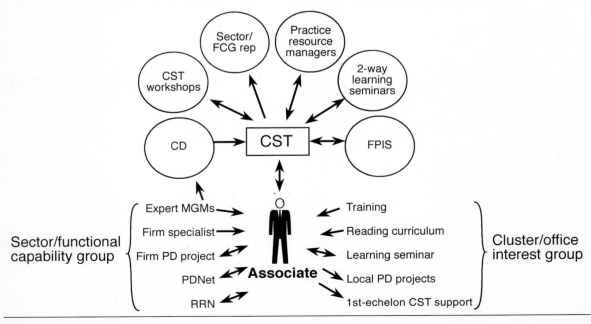

*Source: Internal CPDC presentation.

CSTs. They also wrote to all consultants, emphasizing the importance of the firm's intellectual development and their own professional development, for which they had primary responsibility. Finally, they assembled data on the amount of time consultants were spending on practice and professional development by office, distributing the widely divergent results to partners in offices worldwide. Their hope was that by highlighting the problem that appropriate responses would result.

Developing Multiple Career Paths

Despite (or perhaps because of) all these changes, the specialist consultant model continued to struggle. Over the years, the evaluation criteria for the specialist career path had gradually converged with the mainstream associate promotion criteria. For example, the specialist's old standard of "world-class expertise" in a particular field had given way to a more pragmatic em-

phasis on client impact; the notion of being a consultant to teams had evolved to a need to be "engagement director capable"; and the softer standard of "grow or go" was replaced by the normal associate's "up or out" requirement, albeit within a slightly more flexible time frame.

Although these changes had reduced the earlier role dissonance—specialists become more T-shaped—it also diluted the original objective, and in late 1992 the Professional Personnel Committee decided to create two new career paths for client service support and administrative (CSSA) staff:

- Consultants on the first path were practice-dedicated specialists who built credibility with clients and CSTs through their specialized knowledge and its expert application. Their skills would have them in high demand as consultants to teams (CDs) rather than as engagement directors (EDs).
- The second career path was the practice management track designed to provide a career

---

Exhibit 6   *Alternative Career Path Focus and Criteria**

	CSS Paths		CSSA Paths	
Career Paths/Roles	General Consulting	Specialized Consulting	Practice Expertise	Practice Management Administration
Focus	Perform general problem solving and lead implementation Develop client relationships	Apply in-depth practice knowledge to 1 to 2 studies Develop client relationships Build external reputation	Leverage practice knowledge across studies Create new knowledge	Codify and transfer knowedge Help administer practice

*Source: Internal McKinsey & Company presentation.

progression for practice coordinators who had a key role in transferring knowledge and in helping practice leaders manage increasingly complex networks. Valuable administrators could also be promoted on this track.

Despite the announcement of the criteria and the different nomination and promotion processes, there was still a good deal of skepticism and confusion about the viability of the specialist track to partnership among associates and specialists alike. (See Exhibit 6 for an overview comparison.)

KNOWLEDGE MANAGEMENT ON THE FRONT

To see how McKinsey's evolving knowledge management processes were being felt by those on the firm's front lines, we will follow the activities of three consultants working in three diverse locations and focused on three different agendas.

Jeff Peters and the Sydney Office Assignment

John Stuckey, a director in McKinsey's Sydney office, felt great satisfaction at being invited to bid for a financial services growth strategy study for one of Australia's most successful and respected companies. Yet the opportunity also created some challenges. As in most small- or medium-sized offices, most consultants in Sydney were generalists. Almost all with financial industry expertise had been "conflicted out" of the project due to work they had done for competing financial institutions in Australia.

Stuckey immediately began using his personal network to find how he might tap into McKinsey's worldwide resources for someone who could lead this first engagement for an important new client. After numerous phone calls and some lobbying at a directors' conference, he identified Jeff Peters, a Boston-based senior engagement manager and veteran of more than 20 studies for

financial institutions. The only problem was that Peters had two ongoing commitments that would make him unavailable for at least the first six weeks of the Australian assignment.

Meanwhile, Stuckey and Ken Gibson, his engagement director on the project, were working with the Sydney office staffing coordinator to identify qualified, available, and nonconflicted associates to complete the team. Balancing assignments of over 80 consultants to 25 ongoing teams was a complex process that involved matching the needs of the engagement and the individual consultants' development requirements. A constant flow of consultants across offices helped buffer constraints, and also contributed to the transfer of knowledge. At any one time, 15 to 25 Australian consultants were on short- or long-term assignments abroad, while another 10 to 15 consultants from other offices were working in Australia. (Firmwide, nearly 20% of work was performed by consultants on interoffice loans.)

They identified a three-person team to work with Peters. John Peacocke was a New Zealand army engineer with an MBA in finance from Wharton and two years of experience in McKinsey. Although he had served on a four-month study for a retail bank client in Cleveland, he had worked mostly for oil and gas clients since returning to Australia.Patty Akopianz was a one-year associate who had worked in investment banking before earning an MBA at Harvard. Her primary interest and her developing expertise was in consumer marketing. The business analyst was Jonathan Liew, previously an actuary who was embarking on his first McKinsey assignment.

With Peters's help, Stuckey and Gibson also began assembling a group of internal specialists and experts who could act as consulting directors (CDs) to the team. James Gorman, a personal financial services expert in New York, agreed to visit Sydney for a week and to be available for weekly conference calls; Majid Arab, an insurance industry specialist, committed to a two-week visit and a similar "on-call" availability; Andrew Doman, a London-based financial industry expert, also signed on as a CD. Within the Sydney office, Charles Conn, a leader in the firm's growth strategies practice, agreed to lend his expertise, as did Clem Doherty, a firm leader in the impact of technology.

With Gibson acting more as an engagement manager than an engagement director, the team began scanning the Knowledge Resource Directory, the FPIS and the PDNet for leads on key documents and McKinsey experts. (Firmwide, the use of PDNet documents had boomed in the eight years since its introduction. By early 1996, there were almost 12,000 documents on PDNet, with over 2,000 being requested each month.) In all, they tracked down 179 relevant PD documents and tapped into the advice and experience of over 60 firm members worldwide. A team member explained:

> Ken was acting as EM, but he was not really an expert in financial services, so we were even more reliant than usual on the internal network. Some of the ideas we got off PDNet were helpful, but the trail of contacts was much more valuable . . . Being on a completely different time zone had great advantages. If you hit a wall at the end of the day, you could drop messages in a dozen voicemail boxes in Europe and the United States. Because the firm norm is that you respond to requests by colleagues, by morning you would have seven or eight new suggestions, data sources, or leads.

At the end of the first phase, the team convened an internal workshop designed to keep client management informed, involved, and committed to the emerging conclusions. Out of this meeting, the team was focused on seven core beliefs and four viable options that provided its agenda for the next phase of the project. It was at this point that Peters was able to join the team:

> By the time I arrived, most of the hard analysis had been done and they had been able to narrow the focus from the universe to four core options in just over a month. It was very impressive how they had been able to do that with limited team-based expertise and a demanding client. . . . With things going so well, my main priority was to focus the team on the end product. Once we got a clear logical outline, I assigned tasks and got out of the way. Most of my time I spent working on the client relationship. . . . It was great learning for John and Patty, and both of them were ready to take on a management role in their next engagements.

In November, the team presented its conclusions to the board, and after some tough questioning and challenging, they accepted the recommendations and began an implementation process. The client's managing director reflected on the outcome:

> We're a tough client, but I would rate their work as very good. Their value added was in their access to knowledge, the intellectual rigor they bring, and their ability to build understanding and consensus among a diverse management group . . . If things don't go ahead now, it's our own fault.

John Stuckey had a slightly different postengagement view of the result:

> Overall, I think we did pretty good work, but I was a bit disappointed we didn't come up with a radical breakthrough. . . . We leveraged the firm's knowledge base effectively, but I worry that we rely so much on our internal expertise. We have to beware of the trap that many large successful companies have fallen into by becoming too introverted, too satisfied with their own view of the world.

Warwick Bray and European Telecoms

After earning his MBA at Melbourne University, Warwick Bray joined McKinsey's Melbourne office in 1989. A computer science major, he had worked as a systems engineer at Hewlett Packard and wanted to leverage his technological experience. For two of his first three years, he worked on engagements related to the impact of deregulation on the Asia-Pacific telecommunications industry. In early 1992, Bray advised his group development leader (his assigned mentor and adviser) that he would be interested in spending a year in London. After several phone discussions, the transfer was arranged, and in March the young Australian found himself on his first European team.

From his experience on the Australian telecom projects, Bray had written a PD document, "Negotiating Interconnect" which he presented at the firm's annual worldwide telecom conference. Recognizing this strong, developing "knowledge spike," Michael Patsalos-Fox, telecom practice leader in London, invited Bray to work with him on a cable TV and telecom study. Soon he was being called in as a deregulation expert to make presentations to various client executives. "In McKinsey you have to earn that right," said Bray. "For me it was immensely satisfying to be recognized as an expert."

Under the leadership of Patsalos-Fox, the telecom practice had grown rapidly in the United Kingdom. With deregulation spreading across the continent in the 1990s, however, he was becoming overwhelmed by the demands for his help. Beginning in the late 1980s, Patsalos-Fox decided to stop acting as the sole repository for and exporter of European telecom information and expertise and start developing a more interdependent network. To help in this task, he appointed Sulu Soderstrom, a Stanford MBA with a strong technology background, as full-time practice coordinator. Over the next few years she played a key role in creating the administrative glue that bonded together telecom practice groups in offices throughout Europe. Said Patsalos-Fox:

She wrote proposals, became the expert on information sources, organized European conferences, helped with cross-office staffing, located expertise and supported, and partici-

pated in our practice development work. Gradually she helped us move from an "export"-based hub and spokes model of information sharing to a true federalist-based network.

In this growth environment, supported by the stronger infrastructure, the practice exploded during the 1990s. To move the knowledge creation beyond what he described as "incremental synthesis of past experience," Patsalos-Fox launched a series of practice-sponsored studies. Staffed by some of the practice's best consultants, they focused on big topics like "The Industry Structure in 2005," or "The Telephone Company of the Future." But most of the practice's knowledge base was built by the informal initiatives of individual associates who would step back after several engagements and write a paper on their new insights. For example, Bray wrote several well-received PD documents and was enhancing his internal reputation as an expert in deregulation and multimedia. Increasingly he was invited to consult to or even join teams in other parts of Europe. Said Patsalos-Fox:

He was flying around making presentations and helping teams. Although the internal audience is the toughest, he was getting invited back. When it came time for him to come up for election, the London office nominated him but the strength of his support came from his colleagues in the European telecom network.

In 1996, Patsalos-Fox felt it was time for a new generation of practice leadership. He asked his young Australian protégé and two other partners—one in Brussels, one in Paris—if they would take on a co-leadership role. Bray reflected on two challenges he and his co-leaders faced: "The first was to make telecom a really exciting and interesting practice so it could attract the best associates. That meant taking on the most interesting work, and running our engagements so that people felt they were developing and having fun."

The second key challenge was how to develop the largely informal links among the fast-growing European telecom practices. Despite the excellent job that Soderstrom had done as the practice's repository of knowledge and channel of communication, it was clear that there were limits to her ability to act as the sole "intelligent switch." As a result, the group had initiated a practice-specific intranet link designed to allow members direct access to the practice's knowledge base (PD documents, conference proceedings, CVs, etc.), its members' capabilities (via home pages for each practice member), client base (CST home pages, links to client Web sites), and external knowledge resources (MIT's Multimedia Lab, Theseus Institute, etc.). More open yet more focused than existing firmwide systems like PDNet, the Telecom Intranet was expected to accelerate the "engage-explore-apply-share" knowledge cycle.

There were some, however, who worried that this would be another step away from "one firm" towards compartmentalization, and from focus on building idea-driven personal networks towards creating data-based electronic transactions. In particular, the concern was that functional capability groups would be less able to transfer their knowledge into increasingly strong and self-contained industry-based practices. Warwick Bray recognized the problem, acknowledging that linkages between European telecom and most functional practices "could be better":

> The problem is we rarely feel the need to draw on those groups. For example, I know the firm's pricing practice has world-class expertise in industrial pricing, but we haven't yet learned how to apply it to telecom. We mostly call on the pricing experts within our practice. We probably should reach out more.

Stephen Dull and the Business Marketing Competence Center

After completing his MBA at the University of Michigan in 1983, Stephen Dull spent the next five years in various consumer marketing jobs at Pillsbury. In 1988, he was contacted by an executive search firm that had been retained by McKinsey to recruit potential consultants in consumer marketing. Joining the Atlanta office, Dull soon discovered that there was no structured development program. Like the eight experienced consumer marketing recruits in other offices, he was expected to create his own agenda.

Working on various studies, Dull found his interests shifting from consumer to industrial marketing issues. As he focused on building his own expertise, however, Dull acknowledged that he did not pay enough attention to developing strong client relations. "And around here, serving clients is what really counts," he said. So, in late 1984—a time when he might be discussing his election to principal—he had a long counseling session with his group development leader about his career. The GDL confirmed that he was not well positioned for election, but proposed another option. He suggested that Dull talk to Rob Rosiello, a principal in the New York office who had just launched a business-to-business (B to B) marketing initiative within the marketing practice. Said Dull:

> Like most new initiatives, B to B was struggling to get established without full-time resources, so Rob was pleased to see one. I was enjoying my business marketing work, so the initiative sounded like a great opportunity. . . . Together, we wrote a proposal to make me the firm's first business marketing specialist.

The decision to pursue this strategy was not an easy one for Dull. Like most of his colleagues, he felt that specialists were regarded as second-class citizens—"overhead being supported by real consultants who serve clients," Dull suggested. But his GDL told him that recent directors' meetings had reaffirmed the importance of building functional expertise, and some had even suggested that 15 to 20% of the firm's partners should be functional experts within the next five to seven years. (As of 1995, over 300 associates were specialists, but only 15 of the 500 partners.)

In April, 1995, Dull and Rosiello took their proposal to Andrew Parsons and David Court, two leaders of the Marketing practice. The directors suggested a mutual trial of the concept until the end of the year and offered to provide Dull the support to commit full time to developing the B to B initiative.

Dull's first priority was to collect the various concepts, frameworks, and case studies that existed within the firm, consolidating and synthesizing them in several PD documents. In the process, he and Rosiello began assembling a core team of interested contributors. Together, they developed an agenda of half a dozen cutting-edge issues in business marketing—segmentation, multi-buyer decision making, and marketing partnerships, for example—and launched a number of study initiatives around them. Beyond an expanded series of PD documents, the outcome was an emerging set of core beliefs and a new framework for business marketing.

The activity also attracted the interest of Mark Leiter, a specialist in the Marketing Science Center of Competence. This center, which had developed largely around a group of a dozen or so specialists, was in many ways a model of what Dull hoped the B to B initiative could become, and having a second committed specialist certainly helped.

In November, another major step to that goal occurred when the B to B initiative was declared a Center of Competence. At that time, the core group decided they would test their colleagues' interest and their own credibility by arranging an internal conference at which they would present their ideas. When over 50 people showed up, including partners and directors from four continents, Dull felt that prospects for the center looked good.

Through the cumulative impact of the PD documents, the conference, and word of mouth recommendations, by early 1996 Dull and his colleagues were getting more calls than the small center could handle. They were proud when the March listing of PDNet "Best Sellers" listed B to B documents at numbers 2, 4 and 9 (See Exhibit 7). For Dull, the resulting process was both satisfying and enlightening:

> *We decided that when we got calls we would swarm all over them and show our colleagues we could really add value for their clients. . . . This may sound strange—even corny—but I now really understand why this is a profession and not a business. If I help a partner serve his client better, he will call me back. It's all about relationships, forming personal bonds, helping each other.*

While Dull was pleased with the way the new center was gaining credibility and having impact, he was still very uncertain about his promotion prospects. As he considered his future, he began to give serious thought to writing a book on business-to-business marketing to enhance his internal credibility and external visibility.

A New MD, A New Focus

In 1994, after six years of leadership in which firm revenue had doubled to an estimated $1.4 billion annually, Fred Gluck stepped down as MD. His successor was 45-year-old Rajat Gupta, a 20-year McKinsey veteran committed to continuing the emphasis on knowledge development. After listening to the continuing debates about which knowledge development approach was most effective, Gupta came to the conclusion that the discussions were consuming energy that should have been directed towards the activity itself. "The firm did not have to make a choice," he said. "We had to pursue *all* the options." With that conclusion, Gupta launched a four-pronged attack.

He wanted to capitalize on the firm's long-term investment practice development, driven by Clientele Industry Sectors and Functional Capability Groups and supported by the knowledge infrastructure of PDNet and FPIS. But he

Exhibit 7 *PDNet "Best Sellers": March and Year-to-Date, 1996**

Number Requested	Title, Author(s), Date, PDNet #	Functional Capability Group/Sector

March 1996

21	*Developing a Distinctive Consumer Marketing Organization* Nora Aufreiter, Theresa Austerberry, Steve Carlotti, Mike George, Liz Lempres (1/96, #13240)	Consumer Industries/ Packaged Goods; Marketing
19	*VIP: Value Improvement Program to Enhance Customer Value in Business to Business Marketing* Dirk Berensmann, Marc Fischer, Heiner Frankemölle, Lutz-Peter Pape, Wolf-Dieter Voss (10/95, #13340)	Marketing; Steel
16	*Handbook For Sales Force Effectiveness—1991 Edition* (5/91, #6670)	Marketing
15	*Understanding and Influencing Customer Purchase Decisions in Business to Business Markets* Mark Leiter (3/95, #12525)	Marketing
15	*Channel Management Handbook* Christine Bucklin, Stephen DeFalco, John DeVincentis, John Levis (1/95, #11876)	Marketing
15	*Platforms for Growth in Personal Financial Services (PFS201)* Christopher Leech, Ronald O'Hanley, Eric Lambrecht, Kristin Morse (11/95, #12995)	Personal Financial Services
14	*Developing Successful Acquisition Programs To Support Long-Term Growth Strategies* Steve Coley, Dan Goodwin (11/92, #9150)	Corporate Finance
14	*Understanding Value-Based Segmentation* John Forsyth, Linda Middleton (11/95, #11730)	Consumer Industries/ Packaged Goods; Marketing
14	*The Dual Perspective Customer Map for Business to Business Marketing* (3/95, #12526)	Marketing
13	*Growth Strategy—Platforms, Staircases and Franchises* Charles Conn, Rob McLean, David White (8/94, #11400)	Strategy

Cumulative Index (January – March)

54	*Introduction to CRM (Continuous Relationship Marketing)—Leveraging CRM to Build PFS Franchise Value (PFS221)* Margo Geogiadis, Milt Gillespie, Tim Gokey, Mike Sherman, Marc Singer (11/95, #12999)	Personal Financial Services
45	*Platforms for Growth in Personal Financial Services (PFS201)* Christopher Leech, Ronald O'Hanley, Eric Lambrecht, Kristin Morse (11/95, #12995)	Personal Financial Services
40	*Launching a CRM Effort (PFS222)* Nick Brown, Margo Georgiadis (10/95, #12940)	Marketing
38	*Building Value Through Continuous Relationship Marketing (CRM)* Nich Brown, Mike Wright (10/95, #13126)	Banking and Securities
36	*Combining Art and Science to Optimize Brand Portfolios* Richard Benson-Armer, David Court, John Forsyth (10/95, #12916)	Marketing; Consumer Industries/Packaged Goods
35	*Consumer Payments and the Future of Retail Banks (PA202)* John Stephenson, Peter Sands (11/95, #13008)	Payments and Operating Products
34	*CRM (Continuous Relationship Marketing) Case Examples Overview* Howie Hayes, David Putts (9/95, #12931)	Marketing
32	*Straightforward Approaches to Building Management Talent* Parke Boneysteele, Bill Meehan, Kristin Morse, Pete Sidebottom (9/95, #12843)	Organization
32	*Reconfiguring and Reenergizing Personal Selling Channels (PFS213)* Patrick Wetzel, Amy Zinsser (11/95, #12997)	Personal Financial Services
31	*From Traditional Home Banking to On-Line PFS (PFS211)* Gaurang Desai, Brian Johnson, Kai Lahmann, Gottfried Leibbrandt, Paal Weberg (11/95, #12998)	Personal Financial Services

*Source: *Month By Month* (McKinsey's internal staff magazine)

also wanted to create some new channels, forums, and mechanisms for knowledge development and organizational thinking.

Building on an experiment begun by the German office, Gupta embraced a grass-roots knowledge development approach called Practice Olympics. Two- to six-person teams from offices around the world were encouraged to develop ideas that grew out of recent client engagements and formalize them for presentation at a regional competition with senior partners and clients as judges. The twenty best regional teams then competed at a firmwide event. Gupta was proud that in its second year, the event had attracted over 150 teams and involved 15% of the associate body.

At a different level, the new MD initiated six special initiatives in late 1995—multiyear internal assignments led by senior partners that focused on emerging issues that were of importance to CEOs. The initiatives tapped both internal and external expertise to develop "state-of-the-art" formulations of each key issue. For example, one focused on the shape and function of the corporation of the future, another on creating and managing strategic growth, and a third on capturing global opportunities. Gupta saw these initiatives as reasserting the importance of the firm's functional knowledge yet providing a means to do longer-term, bigger-commitment, cross-functional development.

Finally, he planned to expand on the model of the McKinsey Global Institute, a firm-sponsored research center established in 1991 to study implications of changes in the global economy on business. The proposal was to create other pools of dedicated resources protected from daily pressures and client demands and focused on long-term research agendas. A Change Center was established in 1995 and an Operations Center was being planned. Gupta saw these institutes as a way in which McKinsey could recruit more research-oriented people and link more effectively into the academic arena.

Most of these initiatives were new and their impact had not yet been felt within the firm. Yet Gupta was convinced the direction was right:

We have easily doubled our investment in knowledge over these past couple of years. There are lots more people involved in many more initiatives. If that means we do 5 to 10% less client work today, we are willing to pay that price to invest in the future. Since Marvin Bower, every leadership group has had a commitment to leave the firm stronger than it found it. It's a fundamental value of McKinsey to invest for the future of the firm.

Future Directions

Against this background, the McKinsey partnership was engaged in spirited debate about the firm's future directions and priorities. The following is a sampling of their opinions:

I am concerned that our growth may stretch the fabric of the place. We can't keep on disaggregating our units to create niches for everyone, because we have exhausted the capability of our integrating mechanisms. I believe our future is in developing around CSTs and integrating across them around common knowledge agendas.

Historically, I was a supporter of slower growth, but now I'm convinced we must grow faster. That is the key to creating opportunity and excitement for people, and that generates innovation and drives knowledge development. . . . Technology is vital not only in supporting knowledge transfer, but also in allowing partners to mentor more young associates. We have to be much more aggressive in using it.

There is a dark side to technology—what I call technopoly. It can drive out communication and people start believing that e-mailing someone is the same thing as talking to them. If teams stop meeting as often or if practice conferences evolve into discussion forums on

Lotus Notes, the technology that has supported our growth may begin to erode our culture based on personal networks.

I worry that we are losing our sense of village as we compartmentalize our activities and divide into specialties. And the power of IT has sometimes led to information overload. The risk is that the more we spend searching out the right PD document, the ideal framework, or the best expert, the less time we spend thinking creatively about the problem. I worry that as we increase the science, we might lose the craft of what we do.

These were among the scores of opinions that Rajat Gupta heard since becoming MD. His job was to sort through them and set a direction that would leave the firm stronger than he found it.

BAYER AG

On September 25, 1994, Bayer AG's senior management met at corporate headquarters in Leverkusen, Germany to consider submitting a $1 billion bid that would, if successful, recover, once and for all the Bayer name and Bayer cross trademark in North America. In attendance were Dr. Manfred Schneider, chairman of Bayer AG's Board of Management, Dr. Walter Wenninger, a member of the Board of Management and strategic mentor to Bayer's health care division and the North American region, Werner Spinner, head of Bayer's worldwide consumer health care business, and Hermann J. Strenger, chairman of the Supervisory Board and ex-CEO of the company.

Ten days earlier, SmithKline Beecham Plc (SB) had agreed to pay Eastman Kodak $3 billion for Sterling Winthrop's worldwide over-the-counter (nonprescription) pharmaceutical business. Sterling sold Bayer Aspirin and owned the Bayer cross trademark in North America. Interested only in the North American part of the business, Bayer had offered a conservative bid. Now, Bayer's senior managers learned that SB might be willing to spin off Sterling's North America business for $1 billion. The package included the trademark rights to the Bayer cross logo and aspirin product lines in North America, confiscated by the U.S. government after World War I, and a range of other over-the-counter (OTC) products.

The four Bayer executives knew they were within reach of being able to establish the company under one name worldwide. However, they wanted to be sure that the $1 billion did not overstate the value of the Bayer brand name and Sterling product lines in the United States combined with the synergies Bayer would gain by integrating Sterling's North America OTC business into its own Consumer Healthcare Products business. In doing so, the group also set out to assess the communications challenge the company would face should it decide to go forward with the purchase.

BAYER BRAND HISTORY

Origins and Early Presence in the United States

Established in 1863 by Friedrich Bayer and Johann Friedrich Weskott, a merchant and master dyer, "Friedr. Bayer et comp." began as a

---

This case was prepared by Robin Root (under the direction of John Quelch). Confidential data have been disguised. Copyright © 1997 by the President and Fellows of Harvard College. Harvard Business School case 598-031.

dyestuffs factory in Elberfeld, Germany. From very early on, the company invested in overseas markets. Bayer's investment in a coal tar dye plant in Albany, New York, in 1865, for example, gave the German firm an early stake in the industrialization of the United States. In 1903, Bayer took over the Hudson River Aniline and Color Works factory to manufacture its revolutionary Aspirin product. The decision to expand the company's analgesic business from Europe to the United States was a question of simple arithmetic:

> *Execution of the entire project will cost a total of 198,625 dollars, or about 844,000 marks. Since our liquid assets as of August 31 [1903] amount to 15.1 million marks, payment of the above sum will cause us no difficulties.*

The Bayer cross trademark was registered in Germany in 1904. In 1913, Bayer transferred ownership of its U.S. trademarks, including the Bayer cross logo, and patents to its U.S. subsidiary, The Bayer Co., Inc., to avoid payment of heavy import duties. The tides of Bayer's U.S. fortunes took a dramatic turn on December 12, 1918. On that day, the Alien Property Custodian, who had previously confiscated all of the company's shares and assets, auctioned off The Bayer Co., Inc. as a form of indirect payment for German war reparations. Sterling Products, Inc., one of Bayer's early analgesic competitors, submitted the winning bid of $5.3 million for assets that included not only physical plants but also the rights in the Americas to the trademarks, including Aspirin.

Bayer's Relationship with Sterling

In 1919, Sterling and Bayer entered into negotiations that were to last on and off for many decades. The first round dealt with Latin America, where Sterling had quickly begun registering the Bayer cross trademark and trade names as Sterling property after it purchased The Bayer Co. In 1920, the two firms signed the Latin America Aspirin Treaty, which stipulated that only preparations containing acetylsalicylic as an active ingredient would be sold under the Aspirin name. Also, in exchange for acknowledging Sterling's registration rights to the Bayer name in Latin America, Bayer would split the Latin American earnings of Bayer Aspirin with Sterling, 75–25, for a period of 50 years. As the details of this agreement were being finalized, Sterling acquired Bayer's expropriated trademarks in the United Kingdom, which triggered a second round of complex negotiations.

In 1923, the two firms agreed to the so-called Weiss Treaty. Bayer headquarters recognized Sterling as owner of the Bayer name and Bayer cross trademark in the United States and U.S. territories and agreed to supply Sterling with technology it needed to produce aspirin and other analgesics. In return, Bayer would share in Sterling's profits on sales of products under the Bayer name. A similar solution was arranged for British sales territories, which included Great Britain, Ireland, Australia, New Zealand, and South Africa. Until the Second World War, Sterling and Bayer maintained a cordial relationship, jointly acquiring other firms and sharing profits as well as management responsibilities.

In September 1941, three months before the United States entered World War II, a consent decree from the U.S. Justice Department (in which Bayer was not included) ordered Sterling to pay a $26,000 fine for breach of antitrust laws. The decree also canceled the agreements that had been laboriously worked out between Bayer and Sterling. As a consequence, Sterling became sole owner of the worldwide rights to the patents and trademarks that Bayer had previously transferred to Sterling under joint profit-sharing arrangements.

From 1955 to 1962, Bayer sought through legal proceedings to obtain the return of its rights as set down in the Latin American and Weiss agreements by challenging the 1941 consent decree in U.S. courts. In 1964, Bayer and Sterling agreed that Bayer could conduct business in the United States so long as it did not use the Bayer name or trademark cross, except under extremely tight restrictions.

In 1954 Bayer headquarters in Germany signed a joint-venture agreement with Monsanto Chemical Company of St. Louis, Missouri, which they named Mobay, to produce a wide range of chemicals. In 1967, Bayer acquired Monsanto's 50% interest in the company, making it a wholly owned subsidiary under Bayer's U.S. holding company, which was called Rhinechem Corporation.

The Long Road to Reacquisition

Throughout the 1960s, Bayer (then known as Farbenfabriken Bayer AG) pursued litigation against Sterling in countries where Sterling marketed its aspirin as "Genuine" Bayer Aspirin. "Sterling was pretending," argued Dr. Volker Charbonnier, a member of Bayer AG's legal department since 1969 and, in 1994, its general counsel, "that the product originated from Sterling, which had in fact neither invented nor developed it. We alleged that they were misleading the public." A landmark victory in the Australian courts in 1969 precipitated the 1970 Agreement, because Sterling feared that a series of victories in the Commonwealth courts would eventually threaten the trademark protection it enjoyed in the lucrative U.S. market.

Under the 1970 Agreement, Bayer re-secured its rights to the Bayer name and trademarks, including the Bayer cross, everywhere in the world except Canada, the United States, and U.S. territories, for $2.8 million. Sterling agreed to Farbenfabriken Bayer's wish to change its corporate name to Bayer AG, since dyestuffs, Bayer's original product line (*Farbenfabriken* meant dye factories), accounted by 1970 for only 15% of revenues.

Sterling managers in North America used the Bayer cross in aspirin advertising. They did not wish to share the logo with a German company and, more importantly, with a company that would place the same logo on agrochemicals and many other nonpharmaceutical products. "We found a way to live without the Bayer cross in the United States," continued Dr. Charbonnier. "However, there was still confusion if you looked at the business on a worldwide basis. Sterling was using the cross on Bayer Aspirin in the United States and Canada, and we were using it on all our products marketed everywhere else in the world."

In 1977, to re-enter the pharmaceuticals business in the United States, and to secure U.S. distribution channels for its own pharmaceutical and chemical products, Bayer acquired Miles Laboratories Inc. of Elkhart, Indiana. The Miles brand portfolio included Alka-Seltzer, a combination of bicarbonate-of-soda, citric acid, and aspirin, which, when added to water, provided an effervescent tonic that would settle an upset stomach, and One-A-Day and Flintstones vitamins. Bayer managed the Miles subsidiary at arm's length; Miles retained its corporate identity and reported to Rhinechem, the name of Bayer's U.S. holding company.

The relatively cordial relationship that followed the 1970 Agreement facilitated a second significant agreement in 1986. For $25 million, Bayer AG acquired rights to use the Bayer name in the United States on industrial products that had no relation to pharmaceutical or consumer health products. Bayer also obtained the right to change the name of its U.S. holding company from Rhinechem to Bayer USA, Inc. This change was permitted so long as Bayer agreed to restrict its marketing under that name to industrial customers and to conduct no Bayer corporate advertising to the general public. Proudly displaying "Bayer USA" across its cover, the company's 1987 annual report represented the first use of the Bayer name in U.S. corporate communications in over six decades. A corporate print advertisement announcing the name change is presented in Exhibit 1.

Exhibit 1   *U.S. Corporate Advertisement for Bayer USA*

Meeting a world of needs right here in Pittsburgh.

We're Bayer USA. And we've just established our corporate headquarters here in Pittsburgh.

But in a way, we've been here a long time. One of the companies in the Bayer USA group is the Pittsburgh-based Mobay Corporation, a major force in advanced plastics technology and chemicals.

Other Bayer USA companies include Miles Laboratories, Agfa-Gevaert and Compugraphic. Each is a key factor in its industrial category. Each has touched the lives of Pittsburghers in many important ways. In the areas of chemicals, health and life sciences, and imaging and graphic information systems, the companies of Bayer USA have been bringing unique and progressive answers to a whole spectrum of human needs throughout the U.S. And right here in Pittsburgh.

We may be new here in Pittsburgh, but in a way we've been here all along. And we don't mind saying it's good to be home.

Bayer USA INC.

MEETING A WORLD OF NEEDS.

Optimists within Bayer felt that the 1986 Agreement signaled an important departure from the hodgepodge of holding and subsidiary company names that had previously cluttered the company's annual reports, toward a future corporate identity under a single name worldwide. Others, however, felt the company had shelled out $25 million to adorn an annual report that would circulate only among those who already knew Miles Inc.'s true corporate origins, and for whom the name change would mean little.

Different interpretations of the 1986 agreement and a change in Sterling management after it was acquired by Eastman Kodak in 1988, led to an injunction for breach of contract against Bayer in 1992. In that year, a Sterling trademark lawyer spotted a billboard outside Detroit that advertised an industrial paint protector with the corporate name "Bayer" across the bottom. Although Sterling management had long ignored Bayer's gradually expanding use of its corporate name in non–health care markets, the billboard was perceived as over the line. In its defense, Bayer asserted that the billboard was directed not at the general public, for whom the ad would have little or no relevance, but at its industrial customers in automobile manufacturing, many of whom passed by the billboard on their way to work. Following the injunction, Bayer instructed its U.S. sales force to heed a formal identification policy. "Be fair. Don't confuse the trade. Explain who is who, that Sterling owns Bayer Aspirin but that we are Bayer AG." The policy was viewed as critically important on both sides of the Atlantic.

The question "Was it stickered?" became code among Bayer's corporate communications staff to refer to the censoring with a rectangular sticker of any use of the Bayer name on communications materials that might circulate in the United States.[1] Bayer executives who traveled to the United States carried a second set of business cards without the Bayer AG company name and Bayer cross trademark imprinted on them. Bayer exports into the United States had to be relabeled without the Bayer name while exports of products made by Bayer subsidiaries in the United States had to be relabeled with the Bayer

---

[1] The stickers carried the words "not for release or distribution in the United States," and had to be affixed to every English-language press release issued from headquarters in Germany.

name. "The more international our sales base became," explained Dr. Charbonnier, "the more we realized we could not live with this situation. It was costing us, on average, $2 million a year in legal fees. Our researchers were traveling to scientific conferences in the United States to explain the results of our pharmaceutical research, but were prohibited from mentioning the company they represented. You have to talk about your company at such meetings. You have to say who you are, and where you're coming from." Instead, the company was obliged to refer to itself cryptically as a "German chemical and pharmaceuticals company based in Leverkusen, Germany." The First Amendment of the U.S. Constitution, argued Dr. Charbonnier in U.S. courts, both entitled and obliged Bayer to present itself truthfully to its U.S. customers by its real corporate name.

The 1992 injunction was rescinded on appeal two years later. During this period, however, Bayer streamlined its management structure and, by eliminating the U.S. holding company, merged Bayer USA with its U.S. companies Agfa, Mobay, and Miles, under the name Miles Inc., headquartered in Pittsburgh, Pennsylvania. The Bayer name continued to be used on industrial products, as permitted under the terms of the 1986 agreement, with "Miles Inc." listed as the U.S. operating company. The Mobay name all but disappeared; instead, the name Miles was used on the company's chemical products.

BAYER AND THE OTC MARKET

In 1993, Bayer AG was one of the top three companies in the global chemical and pharmaceutical industry, with total sales of more than $27 billion and a portfolio of 10,000 products. With 400 operating companies in 150 countries, Bayer generated a net pretax income of $2 billion. The Bayer Group comprised 21 worldwide business groups, which were organized into six divisions: polymers (17% of sales), organic products (13%), industrial products (18%), health care (23%), agrochemicals (13%) and the Agfa division (16%). Half of Bayer's revenues were generated in Western Europe, the remainder in North America (24%), Asia/Pacific (12%), Latin America (5%) and the rest of the world. Bayer's U.S. operations contributed $6.5 billion to global sales, of which 40% was accounted for by sales of health care products.

By 1993, the health care division was driving Bayer's growth and accounted for 76% of company profits. Sales of Bayer's OTC products advanced 8% that year. Bayer Aspirin, the company's flagship brand, was second only to Tylenol among OTC brands in worldwide sales, with $355 million in revenues outside North America in 1993. Bayer's aspirin sales were growing strongly in many European and Latin American markets, where the brand[2] was perceived as a strong, premium-priced analgesic for young people "on the go"; for example, in Germany, Aspirin® market share grew from 17% in 1983 to 31% ten years later. Exhibit 2 shows a German advertisement for Aspirin®.

The growth of Bayer's OTC sales was the result of strategic decisions taken in the 1980s. At that time, Bayer managers identified two trends that motivated them to invest heavily in OTC pharmaceuticals: the increased willingness of many consumers to take responsibility for their own health through preventive measures and the simultaneous desire of national governments in developed economies to control state health care expenditures. As a result, some drugs that previously were only available on prescription became available over-the-counter and the proportion of drug sales accounted for by lower-priced generics and private labels increased greatly.

---

[2]Contrary to the United States, Aspirin was still a registered trademark in Canada and in more than 70 other countries.

Exhibit 2   *German Advertisement for Bayer Aspirin*

Translation: Headline, "Don't tell me you've got a cold?" Tagline, "So much more."

By 1993, the global OTC pharmaceutical industry was worth around $30 billion at manufacturer prices, and was growing at 6% per year. North America accounted for sales of $13 billion. The largest OTC categories were cough and cold formulas, analgesics (including aspirin), gastrointestinal, skin care, and vitamin products. A strong presence in analgesics, which accounted for 22% of OTC sales, was considered critical to the success of any OTC company. Many ethical pharmaceutical manufacturers attempted, through acquisitions, to build the criti-

cal mass necessary to perform profitably in the OTC market. Some analysts predicted that two-thirds of global OTC product sales would be accounted for by ten companies in 2000.

Recognizing the growing importance of the OTC market, Bayer AG had, in 1984, established a self-medication business group and consumer products business group, separate from the ethical pharmaceuticals business. The sales growth of these two business groups averaged 8% per year between 1989 and 1993, outpacing the growth of the worldwide OTC market. In

1994, these two business groups merged into the Consumer Care business group. Among Bayer AG's 18 business groups, this new group would rank eighth in sales volume and fourth in profits.

Since the late 1970s, Bayer's OTC presence in the United States depended on its Miles subsidiary. During the 1980s, only a few new products were introduced, notably Alka-Seltzer Plus cold remedy, later introduced in Liqui-Gels[3] form for consumers who preferred the convenience of not having to premix the product with water. The intensity of marketing efforts increased following the appointment of Werner Spinner as head of Miles OTC business in 1991. He directed brand managers to develop robust business plans and restaged several existing brands. For example, the One-A-Day vitamin brand benefited from modernized packaging and new line extensions targeting men, consumers over 55, and those seeking special formulations. Spinner also initiated a supply chain rationalization project and cut the Miles sales force to 53 full-time account managers, supplemented by regional brokers.

In two and one half years, Miles North American OTC sales rose from $240 million to $350 million[4]. Though it ranked as the eighth largest OTC company in the United States, Miles still lacked the critical mass necessary for cost-efficient sales and distribution. Miles' return on sales of 10% in 1993 was only half that of the industry's top players and lower than Sterling's 13%.

STERLING AND BAYER ASPIRIN

Sterling Products, Inc., later renamed Sterling Drug, Inc., was established in the mid-nineteenth century in Wheeling, West Virginia, by a pharmacist, William E. Weiss, and his business

---

[3]Liqui-Gels was a registered trademark of R.P. Scherer International Corp.

[4]In addition, around $100 million worth of Miles OTC products were exported from the United States.

partner, A.H. Diebold. Their company acquired momentum in 1901 with a capital injection of $25,000 to focus on manufacturing and marketing Neuralgine, a pain-relief preparation. With an advertising budget in 1902 of $10,000, Sterling's owners were able to increase the company's sales sixfold within one year, to $60,000. The company subsequently expanded through acquisition. When the Bayer properties were put up for auction in 1918, Sterling submitted its bid in hopes that Bayer Aspirin would serve as the successor product to its near defunct Neuralgine. During the 1920s, with the assistance of Bayer under the Weiss treaty, Sterling marketed Aspirin as a branded OTC product. As patents on Aspirin expired, other competing aspirin brands were launched and aspirin became a generic term for self-administered pain relievers. In other words, Sterling lost the trademark protection for "Aspirin." In order to distinguish itself from other aspirin products, Sterling emphasized "Bayer," still a protected trademark, as part of the product name "Bayer Aspirin."

By 1993, Sterling was the eighth largest OTC company worldwide, and ninth in the United States, with factory sales of around $1 billion. Its analgesics business, which accounted for 51% of its global sales, ranked third worldwide and fourth in the United States. Its Panadol brand led with $214 million in annual sales across 64 markets; Panadol was a very small business in the United States. The company's geographic reach was admired; seventy percent of sales came from nine country markets. In the United States, Sterling sold not only Bayer Aspirin but also Phillips' Milk of Magnesia (an antacid), Stri-Dex (an acne treatment pad), Neo-Synephrine (a nasal decongestant spray), and Midol (an acetaminophen-based analgesic). Sterling's OTC sales in North America were $300 million in 1993.

In 1993, factory sales of OTC analgesics in North America were $2.8 billion. Sales were expected to reach $3 billion by 1994. Analgesics were the largest category of OTC products, accounting for 22% of the total U.S. OTC sales.

Exhibit 3   *Sterling Advertisement for Bayer Aspirin: Pain Relief*

(SFX THROUGHOUT)
AVO: For those who use Ecotrin
for the relief

of the minor aches and pains of
arthritis...
we've got a flash.

You can wait hours for Ecotrin to
start working,

or with Genuine Bayer you can
wait just minutes.

Genuine Bayer Aspirin.

America's number one aspirin.

Forty-five percent of the market comprised non-aspirin analgesic compounds, mainly acetaminophens such as Johnson & Johnson's Tylenol, which held a 33% market share. Twenty-eight percent of the market comprised aspirin and aspirin compounds, of which two-thirds were branded products, notably Bristol Myers Squibbs Excedrin (7%) and Bayer Aspirin (4.5%). Private-label and generic aspirin products accounted for the other third. Twenty-four percent of the analgesic market included ibuprofen compounds such as American Home Products' Advil, which held a 10% share. Bayer Aspirin factory sales in North America were $155 million in 1991, 5% lower than in 1990.

Bayer Aspirin's market share was under attack from nonaspirin analgesics, which often highlighted in their advertising aspirin's gas-

Exhibit 4   *Sterling Advertisement for Bayer Aspirin: Heart Attack Prevention*

MAN (VO): Fortunately, my heart attack wasn't the end of the world . . .

it was kind of a beginning

To help prevent another attack, my Doctor prescribed exercise . . . eating right . . .

and Therapy Bayer. Pure Bayer aspirin that's safety-coated to help prevent stomach upset.

I asked my Doctor

if this regimen with Therapy Bayer

would really make a difference down the road.

"That's why I'm doing it myself," he said.

ANNCR: More and more Doctors are discovering Therapy Bayer. Take it from your doctor.

trointestinal side effects, including irritation of the stomach lining; from other aspirin compounds such as Bufferin, which were safety coated to prevent this from happening; and from private-label and generic aspirin, which forced the branded aspirin marketers to lower or hold their prices. Sterling split its $20 million annual advertising budget for Bayer Aspirin; two-thirds focused on pain relief, comparing Bayer to other brands (see Exhibit 3), and one-third on heart attack prevention (see Exhibit 4).

Market research indicated that Bayer Aspirin was well known, trusted, and seen as a good value, but it was not regarded as especially effective in terms of providing complete long-lasting relief every time. A 1992 survey found unaided advertising awareness of Bayer among analgesic users to be 13%, compared to 43% for Tylenol and 35% for Advil. Table A reports the percentages of respondents indicating that they had used each of these three brands for specific indications during the prior 12 months.

Table A   Use of Analgesic Brands for
Specific Indications: 1992*

Indications	Bayer Aspirin	Tylenol	Advil
Headaches	26%	71%	38%
Arthritis/Joint pain	18	47	36
Back pain	15	57	41
Muscle aches	14	61	36

*Source: Company records.

Detailed attribute ratings of these and other brands are presented in Exhibit 5.

To revitalize the brand, Sterling managers launched the Bayer Select series of line extensions in late 1992. The line comprised five non-aspirin analgesics: a headache formula, a cold and flu formula, a menstrual pain formula, a sinus pain formula, a nighttime formula, and an ibuprofen formula for body pain. The objective

was to recapture sales that Bayer Aspirin had lost to competing analgesics through five higher-priced, higher margin products that addressed specific symptoms in contrast to the cure-all positioning of Bayer Aspirin. Sterling management expected additional annual factory sales of $70 million from the Bayer Select line, with only 7% resulting from cannibalization of regular Bayer. A sample magazine advertisement for Bayer Select, with the tag line "Put the help where it hurts," is presented as Exhibit 6.

By the end of 1993, Bayer Select had achieved 1.4% share of the analgesic market, rather than the hoped-for 3.4%. Total Bayer brand factory sales in North America in 1993 were $145 million, of which 20% were Bayer Select. The share of retail sales accounted for by the Select line was significantly lower. The Sterling sales force, backed by generous promotions, had sold significant inventories of Select to the trade, but consumers saw the products, at best, as niche supplements to their regular analgesics, and only the smaller package sizes sold moderately well. Research indicated that many consumers

Exhibit 5   *Consumer Ratings of Analgesic Brands*

Qualities	Bayer	Store/Generic Aspirin	Excedrin	Tylenol	Advil
Provides fast relief	53%	24%	77%	56%	55%
Relieves muscle aches and pains	49	22	30	31	43
Reduces inflammation	42	28	28	17	32
Provides long-lasting relief	41	26	70	38	44
Is good for severe pain	33	5	50	30	40
Relieves arthritis pain	30	17	19	13	27
Relieves menstrual discomfort	9	18	23	21	35
Causes stomach upset	11	14	7	3	3
Is easy to swallow	62	48	75	66	78
Is good value for money	59	68	55	43	40
Is a modern, up-to-date brand	51	31	64	65	60
Prevents heart attacks or strokes	41	19	12	2	3
Is recommended by doctors	37	16	27	63	45

*Source: Company records. Note: Based on a survey of 460 U.S. analgesics users, July 1992.

Exhibit 6   *Sterling Advertisement for Bayer Select*

(MUSIC) ANNCR: Because all pain is not the same.

MAN SINGS: Put the help where it hurts.

ANNCR: There's aspirin-free Bayer Select.

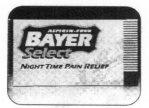

Yes, aspirin-free. They're five completely different products,

for sinus, headache, nighttime, menstrual

and arthritis pain relief.

They're Bayer products, but they're not aspirin.

They're Bayer Select.

Exactly what's right for exactly what's wrong.

MAN SINGS: Put the help where it hurts,

where it hurts--

CHORUS: With Bayer Select! (MUSIC OUT)

equated Bayer with aspirin and were confused or unconvinced by non-aspirin analgesics carrying the Bayer name. Stepped-up advertising by Bayer's competitors and increased competition from private-label and generic aspirin added to the brand's woes.

Trade dissatisfaction that double the normal inventories of Bayer and Bayer Select were stuck in trade pipelines resulted in a 32% drop in Bayer factory sales to $50 million for the first half of 1994 compared to 1993. Sales of other Sterling products in the United States also suffered. Largely as a result, Sterling's worldwide U.S. OTC sales for the 12 months ending in June 1994 were 15% lower, at $250 million, than for the equivalent 1992–1993 period. U.S. operating income fell 50% to $15 million, 29% below the industry average. Cushioned by growth in emerging markets, Sterling's worldwide OTC sales were $980 million, down only 2% and worldwide operating income was $145 million, down 12%.

THE STERLING ACQUISITION

In May 1994, Eastman Kodak announced that it would sell the Sterling Drug business in five separate transactions, one of which was the worldwide OTC business. The announcement prompted a series of senior executive departures, and marketing initiatives almost came to a halt. Bayer AG senior management, having tracked the fortunes of the Sterling OTC business for years, submitted what they thought would be an appropriate bid. However, SB, having just lost out to American Home Products in the race to acquire American Cyanamid, a much larger company than the Sterling OTC business, submitted a higher bid of $3 billion and won the contest. Had Bayer won, it would have supplanted SB as the largest OTC manufacturer worldwide.

It looked like executives at Bayer headquarters in Germany had missed a once-in-a-lifetime opportunity. Those in the United States stoically resolved to search for another acquisition to give Bayer's OTC business in North America critical mass. However, within a week of SB's purchase, discussions were initiated to sell Bayer the North American portion of the acquisition, including the rights to the Bayer name and cross. According to a senior Bayer executive:

SmithKline really wanted the profitable international business including Panadol. They knew the U.S. business was falling apart and figured we would pay anything to get it. Hardly any of Sterling's North American

OTC brands were sold overseas, making any deal with SB easier to execute.

Valuing the Business

In preparing the original bid for Eastman Kodak, Bayer corporate planners had already examined the North American Sterling OTC business and considered how it might be merged with the Miles OTC business. However, they had also cautioned that some of Sterling's worldwide business, especially in Latin America, was not of primary interest. Now they were once again excited about the possible acquisition, which would combine the eighth and ninth largest OTC businesses in North America into a new company that would rank fifth. The combined company would have critical mass and increased clout with the trade. The following annual hard-dollar cost savings were thought realizable from operational efficiencies:

Table B   Projected Cost Savings of U.S. Merger

Sources	Savings
Field sales reorganization (100 fewer staff)	$10,000,000
Marketing reorganization (35 fewer staff)	5,000,000
Research and development reorganization	1,600,000
Collateral and administration reorganization	3,000,000
Distribution warehouse consolidation	4,000,000
Media buying efficiencies	7,000,000
Promotion efficiencies (reduced trade deals and cross-promotions)	13,000,000

Bayer management forecast 180 staff reductions. They believed that $25 million in operating synergies could be realized in 1995, increasing to $44 million per year by 1997. On the other hand, they predicted a maximum of $100 million in restructuring costs, including severance payments and the cost of a new headquarters for the combined company, estimated at $25 million.

Many Bayer and Miles executives felt that the Sterling OTC product line would complement the Miles line as well. By acquiring Sterling, the company would finally gain a position in the U.S. analgesic market. Sterling's Phillips' Milk of Magnesia would add a further gastrointestinal remedy to Miles' Alka-Seltzer line.

Bayer corporate planners estimated Sterling's North American OTC sales at $295 million, of which 90% were in the United States. Combined sales with Miles were estimated at $615 million for 1995, rising to $835 million by 1999. This increase assumed a 3.1% compound annual growth rate for Bayer Aspirin and a 7.9% growth rate for the rest of the brand portfolio. Taking into account the operating synergies already discussed, Bayer corporate planners projected operating income of $75 million in 1995, rising to $182 million by 1999. In calculating net present value Bayer would apply a 10% cost of capital, given the low risk of investing in North America.

Three additional pieces of information were available to the corporate planners. First, they had access to information on comparable acquisitions of OTC businesses from 1991 to 1993. As shown in Exhibit 7, acquisition prices ranged from 1.5 to 3.9 times annual sales and from 18.0 to 25.5 times annual earnings before interest and taxes.

Second, an August 1994 brand valuation survey conducted annually by *Financial World* magazine valued the Bayer brand in the United States at $123 million on sales of $145 million and operating income of $20 million. By contrast, Tylenol was valued at $1.976 million on sales of $1.023 million and operating income of $230 million. The rationale underlying these value estimates is summarized in Appendix A at the end of this case.

Finally, the corporate planners had access to the results of a recent telephone survey which investigated awareness and impressions of OTC manufacturers among U.S. consumers. Aided awareness of Bayer was 73% compared to 96% for Johnson & Johnson and 47% for Miles. Ninety-five% of those aware of the Bayer name associated it with aspirin. Fifty-two% had a high impression of the quality of Bayer products, compared to 74% for Johnson & Johnson and 29% for Miles. Additional questions probed how consumers might respond to the

Exhibit 7   *Valuations of OTC Acquisitions**

Date	Acquiring/Acquired Companies	Valuation millions	Sales (millions)	EBIT[†]	Sales (multiple)	EBIT (multiple)
June 1991	Roche/Nicholas	798	207	41	3.9	19.5
Oct. 1991	Pfizer-Colgate	105	70	NA	1.5	NA
Nov. 1992	Ciba/Fisons (NA)	140	64	5	2.2	25.5
Dec. 1992	Roche/Fisons (UK)	141	41	8	3.4	18.0
July 1993	Warner-Lambert/Fisons (UK)	23	9	NA	2.5	NA

*Source: Company records.
[†]EBIT: Earnings before interest and taxes.

Exhibit 8   *Bayer Brand Consumer Research*

Question 1: "If you knew that the company that makes Bayer aspirin also makes health care products, that is non-prescription products, what effect would this have on your decision of whether or not to purchase . . . ?"	General public aware of Bayer aspirin	Question 2: "Now, for prescription drugs. If you knew that the makers of Bayer aspirin also made a particular drug you had been prescribed, how would you feel about taking it?" "I would . . ."	General public aware of Bayer aspirin
Positive effect	34%	Take it without reservation	72%
Negative effect	3	Take it with some reservation	18
No effect	61	Not take it at all	6
No opinion	2	No opinion	4

*Source: Company records.

knowledge that the makers of Bayer Aspirin also made other products (see Exhibits 8 and 9).

The Discussion

At the senior management meeting, a freewheeling discussion covered the merits of the acquisition, the possible $1 billion price tag, and the implementation implications. Some of the comments were as follows:

It will be wonderful to finally recover ownership of our Bayer cross trademark in North America. We have been working towards this goal for almost 80 years. I've said many times I would gladly swim the Atlantic to regain global control of our company name and logo.

I'm not convinced. True, the Bayer brand name in the United States is well known, but the brand and the Sterling OTC business in North America have been driven into the ground. The latest debacle involving Bayer Select has added to the problem. I question whether the brand franchise is worth anything anymore. But some of our marketing

managers believe the Bayer Aspirin brand can be revitalized in the United States if we just drop the Bayer Select line and apply some of the best practices that are boosting Bayer aspirin sales all over the world. Consumer research in the United States has surfaced a very promising positioning for Bayer as "powerful pain relief and so much more."

Regardless of the potential demand upside for Bayer aspirin, our Miles OTC business in the United States still lacks critical mass, despite all of Spinner's good work to grow sales. We've got to add additional OTC sales volume, especially in a big category like analgesics, to increase our sales force efficiency and our clout with the trade. If we get the Bayer brand back at the same time, so much the better, but the sales synergies are what count.

What synergies? How are Bayer aspirin sales in Germany and the rest of the world going to increase, just because we would now own the brand in North America? Sure, it would make us all proud to own a global brand, but our first priority must be to show a return to our stockholders.

Exhibit 9   *Bayer Brand Consumer Research: "Keeping the company that makes Bayer aspirin in mind, how would it affect your opinion of that company to know that it made ..."* *

Products	Positive	Negative	No effect	No opinion
Prescription medications	41%	3	54	2
Blood glucose testing products	40	4	52	4
Alka-Seltzer	34	3	62	1
One-A-Day Vitamins	34	3	61	2
Flintstones and Bugs Bunny Vitamins	32	3	64	1
Phillips' Milk of Magnesia	30	3	64	3
Neo-Synephrine	30	3	63	4
Herbal extracts for cosmetics	25	8	64	3
Equipment for graphic arts	23	8	65	4
Flavors, fragrances and food ingredients	22	9	66	3
Film, paper, and photography equipment	22	9	65	4
Plastics	20	12	64	4
Synthetic rubber products	19	13	65	3
Polyurethane resins used in producing paint	17	17	62	4
Dyes and organic pigments	13	16	66	5

*Source: Company records.

I agree. The $1 billion purchase price tag is just for starters. Just think of all the implementation problems and restructuring costs involved in merging the Sterling and Miles organizations. Do we know how our trade channels in the United States will react to the acquisition? What about our competitors? Surely they'll try to take advantage of the name confusion. Then, we'll have the expense of a corporate communications campaign to educate everyone in North America that Bayer cures more than just headaches. I've seen estimates of $10 million for three consecutive years.

You're presuming that we'll change the name of the company in the United States from Miles to Bayer. We'll have to take account of the views of the other business units in the United States for example, the chemicals division, Agfa, and the pharmaceuticals business. But I say we pay the $1 billion to SB now, get the name back and worry about the details later.

Appendix A: *Computation of* Financial World *Valuations** *

To value brands, *Financial World* (FW) uses a simplified version of the formula developed by Interbrand Group, the world's premier brand valuation firm. The financial data on brands used by FW was collected with the help of analysts, trade associations and the brands' owners themselves. FW begins by breaking down a company's earnings by brand. Once a brand's earnings have been determined, they are adjusted by an amount equal to what would be earned on a basic unbranded version of the product.

To calculate this, FW estimates the amount of capital it takes to generate a brand's sales. Then FW assumes that a generic version of the product would generate a 5% net return on capital employed. After subtracting that portion of the capital employed, a provision is made for taxes, and the remainder is deemed net brand-related profits.

Then to those profits FW applies a multiple based on a brand's strength. Interbrand defines brand strength as having seven components:

- Leadership: The brand's ability to influence the market.
- Stability: The ability of the brand to survive.
- Market: The brand's trading environment.
- Internationality: The ability of the brand to cross geographic and cultural borders.
- Trend: The ongoing direction of the brand's importance to its industry.
- Support: The effectiveness of the brand's communications.
- Protection: The brand owner's legal title.

Obviously, the stronger the brand, the higher the multiple applied to earnings. Multiples range from 6 to 20, with the highest multiple this year being 18.9. For the third straight year, Coke got the highest multiple.

*Source: Adapted from *Financial World*, August 2, 1994.

PART II

GLOBAL EXPANSION STRATEGIES

The globalization of markets, the increasing homogeneity of customer needs worldwide, and falling tariffs together mean that few companies can continue to afford to remain focused on their domestic markets. The company that has profited for decades serving a single market—thanks perhaps to protectionist tariffs and government regulations—must now face up to the challenge of international expansion as competitors from other countries increasingly invade its home base. In the words of Professor Howard Stevenson of Harvard Business School, today's companies must "eat lunch or be lunch."

There are six main reasons why companies expand beyond the borders of their domestic markets:

- To capitalize on economies of scale and scope and to use additional capacity.
- To leverage a specialist manufacturing or marketing capability, often to a customer niche that can be found in multiple markets worldwide.
- To learn how to compete in foreign markets and thereby develop knowledge and skills that can improve competitiveness in the domestic market.
- To challenge foreign competitors, who may be invading the domestic market, on their own home turf.
- To diversify risk and stabilize sales when the economy in the domestic market is volatile.
- To satisfy the vision or ambition of the chief executive officer and to make employees proud.

Initially, most companies enter international markets opportunistically, responding to rather than developing overseas orders and filling them with products no different than those sold domestically. Over time, international sales may become more integral to success and further penetration of international markets often warrants local adaptation.

This pattern of international sales gradually increasing as a percentage of total revenues is being challenged as a result of globalization. Many small companies marketing specialist-niche products or services are "born global." Using a fax machine, a site on the World Wide Web, and an express delivery service, they are able to reach international customers on a modest sales base without building sales organizations and distribution systems in multiple country markets. Other small companies on the cutting edge of technology find that no matter where they are based, they have to enter the United States early on, since acceptance in this highly competitive market is key to acceptance by customers worldwide.

In selecting which markets to enter, a variety of other criteria are relevant. These range from macroeconomic indicators, political stability and government regulations through industry structure, market size and growth, and competitive intensity to product-market fit and likely customer response. If companies screen markets first on the basis of macroeconomic indicators, fast-growing emerging markets will often be eliminated from further consideration. It is preferable that the market potential and value added to local customers take precedence in the sequence with which market entry criteria are admitted to the market selection decision process.

Sometimes there is a window of opportunity to enter a market ahead of competition that should be exploited. In other cases, it may be appropriate to enter a market to achieve a quick success that will, as a result of learning or increased credibility, facilitate entry into other markets.

Only the largest, wealthiest companies can enter all markets at once. Most must follow a sequential approach that often involves an evolving portfolio of both small and large countries in both emerging and developed markets in all geographic regions of the world.

Once the markets to be entered are decided, the mode and timing of entry must be consid-

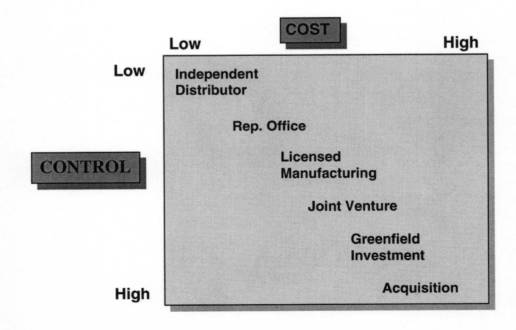

Figure 2.1   Entry Mode.

ered. Many companies work initially through licensed agents, gradually increasing their commitment to establish a representative sales office, perhaps as a joint venture. Later, a wholly owned subsidiary is often set up that may engage in local manufacturing as well as marketing. Throughout this process of progressive commitment, there is a simultaneous increase in the dollars invested and the degree of corporate control, as shown in Figure 1.

Regarding timing, there are clear prime-mover advantages to entering emerging markets early in their development. Brand reputation—like other barriers to entry—can be built cheaply because advertising is inexpensive. Contracts can be signed with the best local suppliers, distributors, and joint venture partners. Early entry often attracts host government goodwill along with favorable regulatory and tax treatment. Finally, early entrants such as Nestlé and Coca-Cola gain experience and confidence and develop a pioneering image that enables them to enter other markets ahead of their competitors.

BAJAJ AUTO LTD.

Rahul Bajaj, chairman and CEO of Bajaj Auto Ltd. (BAL), reflected on the changes that had taken place in the Indian market during the late 1980s and early 1990s and the challenges that his company faced early in 1993. BAL, an Indian manufacturer of two- and three-wheeler vehicles, faced a stagnant domestic market that had declined by 5% in 1991 and 1992 and increasing competition from the major Japanese two-wheeler manufacturers. Bajaj wondered what strategy would both protect BAL's dominant share of the Indian market and permit exports to rise to 15% of total sales by 1998.

COMPANY BACKGROUND

The Bajaj family came from a trading community in Central India. The founder of the current Bajaj Group, Jamnalal Bajaj, set up a sugar factory and steel mill in the 1930s, and his son, Kamalnayan Bajaj, established Bajaj Electricals in 1938 and Bajaj Auto in 1945. Between 1950 and 1956, Bajaj Auto imported scooters and three-wheelers from Piaggio (the Italian manufacturer of the Vespa brand). In 1959, the company was granted a license from the Indian government to produce 6,000 scooters and three-wheelers per annum. In 1960, BAL entered into a technical collaboration with Piaggio to manufacture its products in India, set up a manufacturing unit at Akurdi (near Pune), 170 km south of Bombay, and went public. In 1961, BAL began manufacturing.

During the 1960s, the company concentrated on indigenizing components and establishing a dealer network in India. Initially, local component content was only 26% but, due to the Indian government's emphasis on import substitution, this was gradually increased. By 1966, BAL had become the largest Indian producer of two-wheelers, and product demand exceeded supply. The Piaggio collaboration lasted until 1971, when new government regulations prohibited a continuation of the alliance.

The company's growth had been restricted by the Indian economic and political environment since its inception. In 1969, new regulations made it even more difficult for large private companies to obtain licenses to increase production capacity. Restrictive government import policies also created a protected market for BAL and other domestic two-wheeler manufacturers,

---

This case was prepared by Nathalie Laidler (under the direction of Professor John A. Quelch), with the assistance of Afroze Mohammed. Copyright © 1993 by the President and Fellows of Harvard College. Harvard Business School case 593-097.

permitting BAL to enjoy a high share of a sellers' market for 22 continuous years. During this period, waiting lists for BAL vehicles averaged 10 years.

During the 1970s, both government licensing and price controls remained in place. In 1975, BAL established a manufacturing joint venture with the state government of Maharashtra. BAL held a 24% stake and operating control. In 1982, the government permitted infusion of further foreign technology and expansion of capacity. In 1985, BAL established a second plant at Waluj (near Aurangabad), 225 km north of the Akurdi plant. The 1980s were a period of explosive growth for BAL: production volumes increased from 172,000 in 1981 to 800,000 units a year by 1990. In addition, BAL entered both the motorcycle and moped segments of the two-wheeler market and established a technical collaboration with Kawasaki in 1984. This agreement centered on the development and production of 2-stroke and 4-stroke motorcycles and gave BAL access to Kawasaki motorcycle design and production expertise. The collaboration provided BAL with a full range of two-wheeler products and helped the company respond quickly to competition from other Japanese manufacturers.

Prior to 1993, BAL's business strategy had focused on four objectives: keeping costs and prices low; improving product quality; concentrating on two- and three-wheeler vehicles; and striving for economies of scale. BAL's goals in the 1980s had been to increase product demand and build both volume and market share. As Bajaj described it: "The 1980s were a period of growth for the sake of growth."

BAL IN 1993

In 1993, BAL was the world's largest manufacturer of scooters and the world's third-largest manufacturer of two- and three-wheeler vehicles. Annual revenues placed it among the top 10 manufacturing companies in the Indian private sector and fourteenth in profits before tax. (Exhibit 1 reports past and projected income statements.) Bajaj himself was acclaimed as one of India's most successful entrepreneurs.

Products

In 1993, BAL manufactured 12 different models: five scooter models (Cub, Super, Super FE, Chetak, and Stride); three motorcycle models (M-80, Kawasaki RTZ, and Kawasaki 4S); one moped model (the Bajaj Sunny); and three three-wheeler models (rear-engine Autoriksha, front-engine Autoriksha, and a goods carrier). The two-wheeler market included scooters, motorcycles, and mopeds. (Table A gives a brief description of these products, and Exhibit 2 depicts examples from each product category.) Two-wheeler products were relatively simple in technology, economically priced, and had average lifetimes between 10 to 15 years (scooters averaged 12 to 15 years, motorcycles 10 to 12 years,

Table A   Average Product Profiles Within the Two-Wheeler Market

Product	Retail Price 1992 Rupees[a]	Mileage	Power/Engine Capacity
(50cc) Motorcycles	34,000	65 km/liter	7 HP
(100cc) Scooters	20,000	45 km/liter	6 HP (150cc)
Mopeds	12,000	55 km/liter	2.5 HP

[a]In April 1993, U.S. $1 = 31.6 rupees.

Exhibit 1   *BAL Income Statements: 1986–1996**

	1986	1988	1990	1992	1994E	1996E
Sales (Rs. million)†	4,202	4,997	10,095	12,108	17,391	23,362
Two-wheelers	3,308	3,780	7,849	9,396	14,022	18,990
Three-wheelers	742	1,023	1,929	2,181	2,800	3,734
Spare parts	152	194	317	531	569	638
Sales (units in thousands)	467	510	805	809	1,054	1,182
Two-wheelers	429	460	731	739	975	1,094
Scooters	387	405	641	587	678	748
Motorcycles	42	55	90	117	181	207
Mopeds	0	0	0	34	116	139
Three-wheelers	38	50	74	70	79	88
Average Sales Price (Rs.)†						
Two-wheelers	7,709	8,212	10,745	12,721	14,388	17,367
Three-wheelers	19,405	20,645	26,036	31,200	35,232	42,630
Operating expenditures	3,415	4,562	8,766	10,788	15,878	21,176
Operating profit	787	435	1,329	1,320	1,513	2,186
Net profit after depreciation, interest and taxes	297	293	650	447	831	1,520

*Source: Company records.
†Rs.: Rupees.

and mopeds 8 to 10 years). Ninety percent of three-wheeler vehicles were used as low-cost passenger taxis, known as Autorikshas; the remaining 10% were used as light commercial vehicles. (Examples of both are shown in Exhibit 3.) The average life of three-wheeler products was 10 years.

Manufacturing

By February 1993, BAL was the world's lowest-cost manufacturer of two-wheelers, capable of producing at a rate of over 3,000 vehicles a day in two (rather than three) shifts, six days a week. The Akurdi plant employed 5,800 direct workers and manufactured four scooter models, the M-80 motorcycle, and the front-engine Autoriksha goods carriers. The Waluj plant, with 4,800 workers, made three of the scooter models, the KB 100 and 4S motorcycles, the rear-engine Autoriksha, and Sunny moped. Since 1990, both plants had been modernized and production efficiencies increased. Some stages of the manufacturing process, such as stamping, welding, painting, and assembly, were flexible and could accommodate line changes fairly easily. Machining however, required special-purpose equipment which was less flexible to line changes. Approximately 50% of components were sourced from outside vendors with whom BAL engineers worked hard to achieve consistently high quality. As Kamath, BAL's general manager of manufacturing, explained: "In India, it takes a long time to train and educate suppliers so that they can reliably deliver the right quality."

Recent production changes, influenced by the technical agreement with Kawasaki and outside consultants, were based on Japanese manufacturing models. Kamath described the production organization in 1993: "Our goal is continuous improvement." Throughout the Akurdi plant, large posters bearing the slogans "Zero Defects"

Exhibit 2   *Examples of BAL Two-Wheeler Vehicles*

SUPER

CHETAK

SUNNY

M-80
MOTORCYCLE

KB100 RTZ

Exhibit 3   *Examples of BAL Three-Wheeler Vehicles*

and "Think Quality" were in evidence. "We have worker quality circles and pay our workers much higher than the average wage. We have practically no turnover and there's virtually lifetime employment at BAL." Due to the large volumes, cost benefits were achieved by dedicating certain equipment, thereby reducing downtime from changeovers. The use of CAD/CAM (computer-aided design/computer-aided manufacturing) and CNC (computer numerically controlled) equipment was widespread.

INDUSTRY STRUCTURE

Between the 1950s and the 1980s, India's industrial development policy was characterized by excessive regulation. Initially set up to avoid overcapacity in a capital-scarce economy, it spawned a maze of regulations governing product, capacity, technology, and foreign exchange availability. In the 1980s, inflows of foreign technology and equity were permitted and manufacturing capacity constraints lifted. This gradual opening of the Indian economy resulted in the entry of foreign competitors and expanded production by domestic manufacturers. By the 1990s, the Indian economy was undergoing structural change, and imports were largely unregulated. Though in recession in the early 1990s, the economy was expected to recover and grow at 5% per year during the latter half of the decade. Since 1990, consumers had felt the pinch of recession; inflation had averaged 13%, interest

rates had shot up, and consumer purchasing power had dropped considerably.

The Indian market for two- and three-wheelers was the second-largest in the world, with 1.53 million new units sold in 1992, including 66,000 three-wheelers. (China was the largest market with 2.4 million unit sales in 1992.) Scooters represented 47% of these unit sales, motorcycles 24%, mopeds 27%, and three-wheelers 2%. (Table B summarizes key characteristics of the personal transport market in India in 1992.) Due to the economic recession and the increase in the range and volume of consumer goods available to Indian consumers (such as televisions, VCRs, and washing machines), demand for two-wheelers had declined substantially, and in 1993, the Indian two-wheeler vehicle industry suffered from chronic overcapacity.

Consumers and Market Segments

Of 844 million Indians in 1991, 250 million lived below the poverty line (defined as 3,000 rupees per person per year), 52% were literate, and 74% lived in rural areas. Consumer research undertaken in 1990 segmented households by earnings and identified those groups more likely to purchase two-wheeler products. These data are summarized in Table C.

In India, two-wheelers were used for daily commuting, as opposed to the leisure/fun use common in developed countries. Public transport in India was inadequate and, as housing

Table B   The Personal Transport Market in India, 1992 (Figures in Thousands)

Means of Personal Transport	Total Units in Use in 1992	Unit Purchases in 1992	Projected Unit Purchases in 1995
Cars	3,000	165	200
Motorcycles	3,900	380	500
Scooters	7,500	690	900
Mopeds	4,600	407	500
Bicycles	69,000	7,000	7,500

Table C   Distribution of Indian Households by Income Groups and Related Purchases of Two-Wheelers in 1990

Annual Household Income*	Percentage of Households	Percentage of Scooters Owned by Income Group	Percentage of Motorcycles Owned by Income Group	Percentage of Mopeds Owned by Income Group
Up to 12.5	58%	8%	8%	10%
12.5–25	27	26	27	41
25–40	10	36	34	35
40–56	3	17	18	8
Above 56	2	13	13	6

*Rupees, in thousands.

costs in the cities increased, larger numbers of people moved to the suburbs. A major priority for many individuals entering the work force after school or college was to obtain means of personal transport.

The early 1990s witnessed a saturation of the market, excess production capacity, and increased competition. BAL executives believed that pent-up demand for two-wheelers had subsided by 1993, and that the proportion of consumers replacing their current vehicles, as opposed to first-time buyers, would increase. Concurrently, the secondary or resale market for two-wheelers was increasingly strong. Although this cannibalized BAL's new product sales, it also enabled existing BAL owners to change models regularly since they could recapture a good portion of their purchase costs by reselling in the secondary market. In 1992, the resale value of a five-year-old BAL scooter averaged 60% of the current retail price of a new BAL scooter. (By comparison, the resale value of a five-year-old Kinetic Honda scooter averaged 40% of the current retail price.) By 1993, it was estimated that 6.5 million BAL two-wheelers were on the road and that all brands of two-wheelers combined had penetrated 20% of the potential Indian market.

In 1992, 40% of BAL's domestic sales (and 30% of its scooters, 45% of mopeds, and 55% of motorcycles) were made to rural consumers. Rural consumers were concerned primarily with value for money, whereas urban customers were driven by a concept of value that included the visual appeal of the product. Although rural consumers tended to have lower incomes than urban consumers, housing and food were less costly in rural areas and the rural consumer had a higher proportion of disposable income. Some BAL executives believed that during the next decade most domestic sales growth would come from the rural segment. Major regional differences existed within India. In the north and east, consumers were more traditional. Women did not typically drive and men usually made the major household purchase decisions. In the major cities of the south and west, women played a more active role in the economy and society, and many women could be seen driving scooters and mopeds.

BAL executives described the target consumer groups for each two-wheeler product as follows:

- *Scooters* targeted the "family man," aged between 27 and 38 years. The scooter was a family vehicle that could be used to transport a whole family. Word-of-mouth recommendations, brand name, and features such as mileage (fuel efficiency), low maintenance, and high resale value were important to these consumers.
- *Motorcycle* consumers either lived in the countryside, where the rough road conditions

required a sturdy vehicle, or were young, single men. Seventy percent of BAL's M-80 sales were made to rural consumers concerned with fuel efficiency and product durability. Younger, single male consumers, between 21 and 30 years of age, looked for power and style, and the Kawasaki KB 100 appealed to them. Two-stroke motorcycles were more powerful and were often targeted at young males. Four-stroke motorcycles, regarded as workhorses, were more fuel efficient and gave the consumer better value for the money.

- *Mopeds* appealed to a broader customer segment, because they were the cheapest two-wheelers available. In recent years, style and features had become more important to the urban moped customer who accounted for 55% of all moped sales. Products such as the Bajaj Sunny were targeted at teenagers and women who looked for style and trendy features. Secondary targets included consumers over 55 years who wanted a low-cost means of personal transport.

In 1993, consumers sought reliable and robust products, with low maintenance needs and a long life, at a low cost. Important product features included fuel efficiency, style, and riding comfort. Indian consumers were characterized by one of BAL's dealers as being traditional, seeking to buy proven products. Peer pressure and "keeping up with the neighbors" were increasingly important. Dealers believed that an additional key success factor for two-wheeler manufacturers was service reach, as defined by spare-parts availability and number of service locations.

Competitors

Bajaj described the competitive environment in the Indian two-wheeler market in 1993: "The best of the world are here and they're here to stay." Six Indian groups dominated the domestic market, all with foreign collaborators. BAL was the only competitor manufacturing a full range of two-wheeler products and three-wheelers. It manufactured two of its motorcycles in technical collaboration with Kawasaki. Kinetic manufactured both scooters and mopeds and had an equity collaboration with Honda for scooters. Hero manufactured motorcycles and mopeds and had an equity collaboration with Honda for motorcycles. LML manufactured scooters in collaboration with Piaggio. Escorts manufactured motorcycles in a technical collaboration with Yamaha. TVS manufactured mopeds and motorcycles and had an equity collaboration with Suzuki for motorcycles. (Exhibit 4 summarizes these companies' shares of the two-wheeler market over time.)

The major Japanese brands had all been marketed in India since 1984. All production was domestic, with the percentage of imported parts varying with the number of years since local production began. Imported components could constitute up to 45% of a product's value during the first year of production, but had to fall to a maximum of 5% by the fifth year, according to local content requirements set by the Indian government. Tariffs on imported components were 30% in 1993. Japanese products were perceived by Indian consumers as being higher-tech, more modern, and better finished than domestic products. However, they also had a reputation for being less fuel efficient and more costly both to purchase and maintain, with limited spare-parts availability. In contrast, BAL products were renowned for being rugged, reliable, and fuel efficient. Perceived as reasonably priced, BAL products were also known for their low maintenance cost, good spare-parts availability, and good resale value.

Honda was BAL's most important competitor in 1993. Its scooter product, the Kinetic Honda, competed directly with BAL and held 14% of the scooter market in 1992. It had a technical advantage over the BAL scooters, with features such as electric starter and a modern automatic drive that appealed particularly to women, and was priced at a 15% premium to BAL. It took

Exhibit 4 *Competitor Market Shares by Product Type in India: 1985–1992**

	1985	1986	1987	1988	1989	1990	1991	1992
SCOOTERS								
Total Bajaj	78	83	69	73	73	73	77	74
Cub	8	11	13	9	7	6	5	2.5
Super	34	32	21	26	27	23	22	28
Super FE	NA	NA	NA	NA	NA	NA	1	
Chetak	21	25	21	27	28	36	36	41.5
Stride	NA	NA	NA	NA	NA	NA	0	2
MSL Priya	15	15	14	11	11	8	13	DIS
Total Others	22	17	31	27	27	27	23	25
Kinetic Honda	2	4	5	6	7	8	11	14
LML Vespa	17	10	21	17	17	17	11	11
Others	3	3	5	4	3	2	1	0
MOTORCYCLES								
Total Bajaj	14.5	15	20	20.5	21	26	27.5	28
M-80	14	8	12.5	12	12	16	19	19
Kawasaki RTZ	0.5	7	7.5	8.5	9	10	6	2
Kawasaki 4S	NA	NA	NA	NA	NA	NA	2.5	7
Total Others	85.5	85	79	79.5	79	74	72.5	72
Escorts RX 100	6.5	12	12	12	14	14.5	15	13
Escorts Radjoot	25	24	22	23	24	18.5	12.5	13
TVS Suzuki	20	15	14	13	9	8	8	8
Hero Honda	20	20	23	23	23	26	31	33
Enfield	8	9	6	6	6	6	6	4.5
Jawa-Yezdi	6	5	2	2.5	3	1	0	0.5
MOPEDS								
Bajaj								
Sunny	NA	NA	NA	NA	NA	NA	8	14
Total Others	100	100	100	100	100	100	92	86
Kinetic	46	41	51	55	50	45	35	32
TVS	33	38	44	41	31	28	33	31
Avanti	3	5	5	4	4	8	4	2
Hero	14	12	0	0	14	17	18	19
Enfield	4	4	0	0	1	2	2	2
BAJAJ TOTAL								
Two-wheeler	40	40	36	41	42	43	46	46.5
Three-wheeler	80	81	83	87	89	89	91	90

*Source: Company records.

Kinetic Honda five years to overcome initial consumer perceptions that it was less sturdy and safe than a Bajaj scooter. It was, however, positioned primarily as an urban product. In 1985, Honda had also launched the first four-stroke motorcycle, the Hero Honda, which resulted in substantial fuel economies for the consumer. In 1992, Hero Honda was the market leader in the motorcycle market, with a 33% share.

In 1993, Honda increased its equity in Kinetic to 51% and stated publicly that it aimed to capture 50% of the scooter market and a number one position in the Indian two-wheeler market overall. Honda's extensive line of two-wheeler products, both in scooters and motorcycles, allowed it to launch a regular stream of new products in the 50–150cc category. For example, Honda already had a proven four-stroke, 125cc scooter that could be adapted to the Indian market within two years. In addition, by 1993, Honda had gained significant experience of the Indian market through its two collaborations and had access to both Kinetic and Hero dealers throughout India. In 1993, Hero Honda was sold through 218 exclusive dealers and Kinetic Honda through 390 exclusive dealers.[1] Honda's strategy had been to increase its number of dealers and provide them with average margins of 4.5%.

Yamaha had a technical licensing agreement with Escorts, similar to the one between Kawasaki and BAL, and held 15% of the motorcycle market with the Escort RX 100. The product line was distributed through 490 exclusive Escort dealers. Although Yamaha had a good line of motorcycles and scooters that could be adapted to the Indian market, Escorts was losing market share and profitability. Yamaha and Escorts were thought likely to form an equity-

based joint venture, and the Escorts group had sufficient financial resources to do so.

Suzuki had a joint venture with the TVS group and held 8% of the motorcycle market. Products were distributed through 337 exclusive dealers. Suzuki also had appropriate scooter and motorcycle products for the Indian market and had recently acquired a controlling interest in its four-wheeler joint venture in India. Although in 1993 the TVS-Suzuki venture was not yet turning a profit, the TVS group as a whole had substantial financial resources.

Piaggio had recently acquired an increased stake in its Indian licensee, LML, and had taken complete management control. Piaggio's scooters were similar to BAL's products and held an 11% share of the scooter market. LML was in a relatively weak market position in 1992.

BAL MARKETING STRATEGY IN INDIA

For many years, BAL did not have a marketing department, since demand outstripped capacity and BAL enjoyed a protected sellers' market. As competition increased in the mid-1980s and capacity constraints were lifted, a marketing department evolved from the existing distribution and service organization. In 1993, the marketing department's objectives were to increase annual sales to 1 million units (retaining at least a 50% domestic market share) and achieve share leadership in all three two-wheeler subcategories as well as in the three-wheeler segment.

Product Line Development

In 1993, BAL's product strategy was to provide consumers with a full line of competitively priced two- and three-wheeler products. The objectives governing product development were to protect market share by (1) providing consumers with what they wanted, (2) matching competitor product features by constantly improving existing products, and (3) periodically introducing new products. In 1993, 30% of product development resources were allocated to incremental improve-

---

[1]Dealers were exclusive in the sense that they did not sell competitor products, with the exception of the Indian partner's products.

ments on current products and 70% to completely new product development. It was hoped that eventually these percentages would be reversed. Older scooter models were phased out—following a new model launch—when monthly sales volumes fell below 2,500 units and replaced by newer models that better fit customer preferences. In 1985, BAL had nine two- and three-wheeler models on the market; by 1992 this number had increased to 12 and was expected to hold constant into 1995. Ranjit Gupta, general manager for product development, described the situation: "BAL is under pressure from competitors to continuously improve existing products. However, we want to lead with new product introductions, and hold share through quality and price."

Prior to the 1990s, marketing, manufacturing, and R&D were organized along functional lines. A 1992 reorganization aimed to achieve greater cross-functional coordination and to accelerate the product development cycle. Engineering thereafter worked closely with marketing to define consumer needs and to translate these into new product prototypes that were continuously tested by dealers and consumers. In 1992, BAL employed 346 staff and 124 workmen in R&D, and R&D expenditures totaled 1% of sales, compared with 0.5% of sales in 1990. BAL's new product development program was comprehensive and ambitious, comprising both substantial technical developments and new body designs, features, and styling for all product lines. R&D resources were allocated to each product line roughly in proportion to its sales. Gupta explained that it was not that easy to build BAL's R&D capability: "The issue is not just a question of throwing money at R&D; we need to develop the necessary human resources."

For many years, BAL products were based on Piaggio's designs for the 150cc scooter and three-wheelers. When the government curtailed BAL's technical collaboration with Piaggio in 1971, BAL continued to develop scooters along the same basic design. The 1970s saw the need for a bigger wheel in response to rougher roads and driving conditions, and the Bajaj Chetak was developed. Other needs, such as a higher number of gears for better fuel efficiency and flexibility and a rear-engine three-wheeler for increased driver and taxi-passenger comfort, were also addressed during the 1970s. In the early 1980s, BAL entered the motorcycle segment with the launch of the first Indian motorcycle, the M-80, adapted from existing step-through motorcycle designs pioneered by the Japanese. The technical collaboration with Kawasaki resulted in the launch of a two-stroke motorcycle in 1984, the Kawasaki RTZ in 1986, and a four-stroke motorcycle, the Kawasaki 4S, in 1991. More recent product introductions included the Bajaj Sunny, a moped launched in 1991, that enabled BAL to enter this segment of the two-wheeler market; and the Super FE (Fuel Efficient) scooter launched in 1992, which increased fuel efficiency by 10%. Gupta described the current importance of product development for BAL: "In the past, product development was for fun; now it's for survival."

In 1993, product development efforts were focused on scooters. Fuel economy was an increasingly important consumer requirement due to a 30% increase in fuel prices in 1992. BAL was developing improvements in power and fuel efficiency, a new body styling, an improved electrical system, better lighting, an electronic ignition, and improved suspension system. The rationale behind this "scooter upgrade program" was to deliver increased value for money to the consumer with the objective of defending BAL's market share against competitor products that already offered many of these features. The retail price increase required for the "upgrade program" was estimated at 7%.

Future product development plans were influenced by further tightening of Indian emissions regulations between 1996 and 2001. These regulations would make it essential to change from two-stroke engines to more fuel-efficient four-stroke engines and/or to advanced fuel injection technology. The new four-stroke scooters would be priced at a 15% premium over the existing two-stroke models.

Despite being cost-competitive, BAL lacked design capability and the ability to translate new products from concept to commercialization as fast as its Japanese competitors. BAL's average cycle time for a new model was four to five years, compared with two to three years for the Japanese manufacturers. BAL's main constraints were a lack of sufficient skilled R&D personnel and the slow response of suppliers. The main options for developing BAL's R&D capabilities were to build in-house experience by developing and testing more products with the aid of CAD/CAM technology and/or to establish specific collaboration agreements. Bajaj believed that there was little chance of further alliances with BAL's major competitors and that R&D capabilities would have to be developed in-house, supplemented by specific research agreements and technology acquisitions involving outside organizations such as Orbital. Orbital was an Australian company working on fuel injection technology for two-stroke engines that would reduce both fuel consumption and emission levels. BAL's agreement with Orbital called for specific targets in fuel efficiency and emission levels to be reached at a predefined maximum unit cost. Some BAL executives however, believed that opportunities for technically upgrading two-wheeler vehicles were limited, that the rate of obsolescence was low, and that the technical performance gap between Honda and BAL was not large.

Distribution and Service

In February 1993, BAL had to ensure the effective distribution of its products to 330 exclusive dealers across the country. Physical distribution of BAL vehicles was subcontracted to 75 private transport companies who managed a total fleet of 1,400 trucks, each truck being capable of transporting 45 vehicles. Transport took between 3 and 21 days to reach a dealer. The distribution system was computerized with 30% of dealers connected by modem link, and orders were fed directly into BAL's production schedule. In 1992, 76 people were employed in marketing, sales, and distribution.

Forty BAL salespeople, organized geographically, helped the dealers plan product-specific sales targets, provided them with services and advertising support, and trained their staffs. BAL service engineers were deployed at dealerships to upgrade the technical capability of dealer service personnel, who were also trained at BAL factories. Spare parts sales had increased substantially through the service and dealer networks, and in 1990 an additional parts distributor channel was opened to serve the extensive independent retail parts network existing in the country. In 1992, 180 people were employed in service activities and 42 in spare parts. Pricing strategy for spare parts aimed to offer the consumer "readily available parts anywhere at reasonable prices." In 1992, 531 million rupees (at wholesale prices) of BAL spare parts were sold to service the 6.5 million BAL vehicles currently on the road. In 1992, it was estimated that 40% of all two-wheeler spare parts sold in India were made by BAL.

Dealer Network

By 1993, BAL had developed a network of 330 authorized dealerships in India—up from 184 in 1989—and 800 licensed service centers. BAL dealers sold only BAL two- and three-wheeler products and did not carry competitor brands; a few sold other automotive products, such as cars and trucks. All dealers maintained service centers and spare parts inventories in addition to vehicle inventories at their dealership locations. Dealerships were often family-run or partnerships that enjoyed a high status in their communities. Average sales were 150 vehicles a month with dealer inventories averaging 2.5 weeks of sales. On average, sales of new vehicles represented 80% of dealer revenues, while service and parts represented 20%. An average dealership would turn over its vehicle inventory 20 times a year and its spare-parts inventory four times a year. Unit margins were 3% of suggested retail prices; dealers supplemented their incomes with service and parts sales and the sale of used vehicles.

In 1993, BAL dealers were facing increasing competition, profitability pressures, more demanding and sophisticated consumers, and a drop in average sales volumes of around 20%. Dealers felt competition had intensified: the Kinetic Honda, launched in 1987, had gained acceptance by 1990 in the scooter segment; and Hero Honda's four-stroke was strong in the motorcycle segment. They felt that BAL had not kept up with competitor product introductions and that recent BAL new product launches had experienced a number of technical problems. "Consumers need a problem-free product," explained one BAL dealer in Pune. BAL provided no credit to its dealers on vehicle purchases, and BAL dealers had to finance their inventories from their own working capital. Dealer interest rates on working capital loans were in the order of 22%, and the cost associated with sending funds to BAL could be as high as 25% of the dealer's absolute margin per vehicle. To improve dealer profitability and reduce transit time, BAL began, in 1991, to set up regional depots, the management of which was subcontracted to carrying and forwarding agents. Effectively, a stock transfer was made to the depots from which dealers in the area sourced BAL vehicles, thereby cutting down their lead times to one or two days. By 1993, there were eight such depots, accounting for 40% of total vehicle sales to dealers. By 1994, it was expected that these and additional depots in high-volume markets a long way from the production plants would account for fully 50% of BAL's domestic sales. All major competitors had already established similar depot systems throughout the country.

BAL believed that its dealer network represented a key competitive advantage and that the company enjoyed considerable dealer loyalty. The key to dealer profitability and satisfaction, according to BAL, was a full range of two- and three-wheeler vehicles and rapid inventory turnover. BAL planned to expand its dealer network to 370 dealers over the next two years, particularly in rural areas. In all large towns, BAL had authorized more than one dealer. In recent years, many competitor dealers had switched to BAL but the reverse had never occurred. In 1993, BAL was also considering authorizing different dealers for sales of two- and three-wheelers.

Consumer Financing

The Indian government, which controlled the banking sector, did not encourage bank loans for two-wheeler purchases, and, in 1992, only 15% of two-wheeler purchases were financed in this way. To increase sales, BAL established Bajaj Auto Finance Ltd. (BAFL) in 1988 to provide consumer finance. By 1992, BAFL had financed over 100,000 vehicles through the BAL dealer network. Dealers were responsible for credit evaluations and collecting payments on loans and had to cover 50% of the cost of bad loans. This required substantial dealer personnel training. In February 1993, 160 of the 330 dealers operated BAFL consumer finance schemes, and BAFL executives believed that 10% of all future BAL sales could be financed in this way once all dealerships were properly trained and organized.

Advertising and Promotion

BAL's advertising expenditures had doubled in the 1990s from 54 million rupees in 1990 and 1991 to 110 million rupees in 1992, corresponding to 1% of total sales. In 1993, BAL was among the country's largest consumer durables advertisers, and Bajaj was a household name with many memorable television commercials. Advertising aimed to maintain Bajaj brand awareness and preference and also announce new product introductions. Advertising strategies were developed in collaboration with the dealers and focused on clarifying product positionings in response to consumer needs. (Exhibit 5 outlines the advertising objectives and copy strategies for selected BAL products. Table D summarizes advertising expenditures by product type and medium in 1992.)

In 1992, it was estimated that 20 million color televisions and 50 million black-and-white televisions were in use in India. Two channels existed: a national channel that broadcast in Hindi and English, and a local channel that broadcast in the language of the region. BAL television advertising represented 45% of total media costs, and each commercial focused on a single product, depicting a slice-of-life scene. A further 45% of advertising expenditures was dedicated to press advertising and the remaining 10% to magazine ads and radio commercials. Motorcycle print advertisements had a strong no-nonsense product focus and attempted to differentiate BAL products from the competition on the basis of technical features. The Kawasaki brand name was emphasized by BAL because of consumer perceptions that Japanese motorcycles were of better quality. Other print advertisements addressed the depressed economy with the slogan: "Times are bad, but, if you buy today, the high resale value of Bajaj is like a blank check. It's an investment." (Exhibit 6 reproduces a number of BAL print advertisements.)

In addition to national advertising, BAL cooperated with dealers locally, matching local advertising and promotion expenses incurred by dealers on a 1:1 basis. Dealers were broken down into four categories based on their sales volumes, and members of each group were allocated "matching" budgets for local press advertising. BAL would also match dealer expenses for approved promotions in conjunction with local festivals and special events. To maintain a consistent image across the country, all dealer point-of-sale posters and brochures were provided by BAL. However, the existence of 15 different languages in India meant that the same commercial could not always be used throughout India.

Advertising expenditures of 200 millon rupees were planned in 1993 to reinforce further the Bajaj brand equity. BAL planned to be more aggressive in its advertising, positioning its products more clearly, describing additional features and addressing competitor claims head on. New promotions planned for 1993 included two direct mail marketing campaigns: the first to companies, offering discounts for groups of employees; the second to small businesses with transport requirements that could be met by three-wheelers.

Competitor advertising expenditures for 1992 were as follows: Hero-Honda spent 36 million rupees (corresponding to 1% of sales); TVS-Suzuki spent 23 million rupees (1% of sales); and Kinetic-Honda spent 35 million rupees (3% of sales).

Pricing

In the past, BAL had maintained a pricing strategy that ensured an average manufacturer's mar-

Table D   BAL Advertising Expenditures by Product and Medium: 1992 (Million Rupees)

	Scooters	Sunny	Kawasaki 4S	M-80	Three-Wheelers	BAL Corporate	BAFL	Dealer Coop	Total
TV	21	10.0	9.0	4.5	0	2.5	1	2	50
Press	15	7.0	12.0	0.5	2	2.5	3	7	49
Radio	1	0.0	0.0	0.0	0	0.0	1	1	3
Magazine	2	1.5	1.5	0.0	0	1.0	1	1	8
TOTAL	39	18.5	22.5	5.0	2	6.0	6	11	110

Exhibit 5   *Advertising Objectives and Television Commercial Copy Strategies for BAL Product Line: 1992**

SCOOTERS

Objectives Increase awareness of dominant leadership position. Create demand in and expand rural/semi-urban markets.

Copy Strategies

1. Depict slice-of-life scenes throughout India, including all age groups, with the slogan: "This is my earth. The destiny of Bajaj and India are interwoven. Bajaj is India and India is Bajaj. Past and present."
2. A child asks his father, who comes to pick him up from school, why they don't have a scooter when all his friends' fathers do. The next day the father picks up his son from school on a Bajaj scooter.
3. The Bajaj Cub is positioned as a value-for-money product. A trader, renowned for being very careful with his money, explains his purchase of a Bajaj Cub: "I know what money means. I'm tight-fisted and Bajaj is value for money."
4. A wife scolds her husband for buying a Bajaj scooter without her advice. When the husband explains the benefits of the product, she tells him: "You've done the right thing, hand me the scooter keys."

MOTORCYCLES

Objectives Create strong product positions: M-80 as a rugged, low-cost vehicle for semi-urban/rural markets; Kawasaki 4S as highly fuel efficient with good driveability.

Copy Strategies M-80 commercials carry the slogan: "The tough one for the road." They use two characters from a popular television detective series in a variety of dangerous/criminal-chasing situations.

MOPEDS

Objectives Create a strong position for Sunny with teenagers as a stylish first-vehicle purchase.

Copy Strategies Commercials are based on youth love scenes and depict brief romantic stories.

*Source: Company records.

gin of 15%, gave dealers an adequate return, and created a reputation with consumers of "a company selling a good quality product at a reasonable price." In 1993, BAL was the industry's low-cost producer in India and aimed to maintain a price advantage in every market segment of two-wheelers. In scooters, BAL established price differences between models that reflected the value to consumers of incremental features. All BAL scooters were priced lower than comparable competitor products. The Bajaj M-80 was the only step-through motorcycle on the market and was positioned as a rugged, simple bike, priced at 50% of comparable Japanese motorcycles. However, on Kawasaki motorcycles, BAL's cost structure in 1993 did not allow for a similar lower price strategy and, in the moped category, the Bajaj Sunny was priced slightly higher than conventional mopeds because it offered consumers more features. (Exhibit 7 outlines 1992

Exhibit 6   *BAL Print Advertisements*

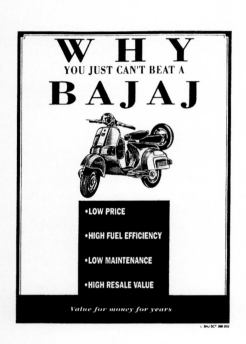

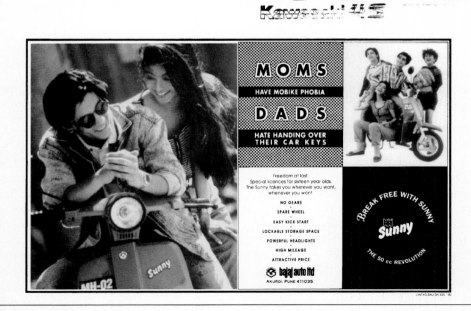

Exhibit 7   *Retail Prices and Dealer Profit Margins by Product: 1992**

	Retail Price (Rs.)[†]	Dealer Profit Margin
SCOOTERS		
Bajaj		
Chetak	20,720	650
Super FE	20,050	650
Stride	21,480	650
Cub	18,900	650
Kinetic-Honda	25,818	1,000
LML		
NV Special	22,349	775
T5 Special	24,027	850
MOTORCYCLES		
Bajaj		
Kawasaki RTZ	32,150	1,000
Kawasaki 4S	33,950	1,100
Bajaj M-80	16,200	550
Escorts		
Yamaha RX 100	35,058	1,055
Radjoot	25,157	835
Hero Honda		
Candy SS	34,354	1,130
Candy DLX	33,331	1,130
Sleek	34,821	1,130
TVS-Suzuki		
AX 100	32,800	1,400
Supra	24,061	1,400
Samurai	33,976	1,400
MOPEDS		
Bajaj Sunny	11,700	350
Kinetic		
Luna Super	10,232	650
Luna Magnum	11,335	650
Hero Puch	15,212	450
TVS		
XL	10,151	325
Champ	11,221	450

*Source: Company records.
[†]Rs.: Rupees.

retail prices and dealer margins by product for both BAL and competitors.)

In 1993, the majority of BAL's profits were generated by scooters and three-wheelers. These profits permitted the other products in the line to be priced lower in order to retain and/or gain market share. In 1993, the Kawasaki motorcycles, M-80, and Bajaj Sunny were all just about breaking even.

EXPORTS

Historical Perspective

For many years, due to high domestic demand and restricted production, BAL had not actively promoted exports. In 1975, BAL exported 1,500 three-wheeler vehicles to Bangladesh and commenced talks in other Southeast Asian countries for the first time. In the same year, the company concluded technical licensing agreements with private sector licensees in Indonesia and Taiwan. The license arrangement with the Indonesian collaborator covered assembly-cum-progressive manufacture of two scooter models, the Bajaj Chetak and the Bajaj Super, as well as a three-wheeler model.[2] The agreement with the Taiwanese licensee covered assembly-cum-progressive manufacture of Bajaj Chetak scooters. Between 1976 and 1982, over 60,000 units of CKD (completely knocked down) scooters and over 14,000 units of CKD three-wheelers were exported to Indonesia, resulting in similar unit margins to domestic product sales. Over the same period, 80,000 units of CKD Bajaj Chetak scooters were exported to Taiwan. In addition to CKD sales, BAL earned technical know-how fees for helping both licensees establish their assembly plants. The Indonesian licensee, unable to remain profitable due to the massive devalua-

tion of the Indonesian currency, combined with government pressure for more local manufacturer content, was forced to stop production in 1982. The Taiwanese licensee, under pressure from the Taiwanese government, quickly developed its own component production capabilities. A similar licensee agreement was established in Bangladesh; this was BAL's only existing licensee agreement in 1993. BAL supplied this licensee with over 2,000 units of CKD three-wheelers in 1992.

BAL's Foreign Distributors

In 1979, the first BAL foreign distributorship was established in Sri Lanka, and the export of complete vehicles was initiated. During the 1980s, distributorships were established on an opportunistic basis in the United States, Germany, Southeast Asia, and North Africa. However, BAL's attempts to export to developed countries in North America and Europe were cut short by a lawsuit instigated by Piaggio that threatened BAL dealers in those countries with legal action. Piaggio alleged that BAL was illegally copying unregistered trademarks of the exterior design and shape of the Vespa Scooter and using technology received from Piaggio before the cancellation of the technical agreement. The threat of litigation hindered the growth of exports to developed countries for a decade. Meanwhile, Japanese producers entered those markets and quickly established dominant shares. Ultimately, the lawsuits were settled to BAL's satisfaction, but, until 1985, exports were limited.

When production capacity constraints in India were lifted in the mid-1980s, BAL once again turned to developing exports. Armed with a wider product range, BAL explored new export markets and, by 1992, sold vehicles to 52 countries through 34 nonexclusive and 17 exclusive distributorships. Nineteen of the distributor agreements had been signed within the previous year. Overseas distributor selection criteria were similar to those used in India, and BAL used the help

---

[2]Assembly-cum-progressive manufacture agreements required BAL to initially supply all vehicle parts to be assembled, gradually reducing the number of parts supplied as the licensee became capable of manufacturing its own parts.

of local Indian embassies to establish short lists of potential distributors. BAL granted these distributors exclusive rights contingent on sales performance. To ensure motivation, BAL established agreements with one distributor per country at a time. Mexico was an exception with two distributors: one for two-wheeler vehicles and another for three-wheelers. BAL's foreign distributors operated essentially as wholesalers, redistributing to dealers that typically stocked a number of brands. Advertising in export markets was left to distributors. (Exhibit 8 summarizes the main points of BAL's foreign distributorship agreements.) Mr. Nulkar, head of BAL's export department, said: "Market development takes time; you need to go step-by-step and create a solid base." In 1992, export sales represented 2% of total sales, with recent export growth coming mostly from Latin America. (Exhibit 9 summarizes exports by product and geographical market in 1992.) One of BAL's corporate objectives was to increase exports to 15% of sales by 1998.

World Markets for Two- and Three-Wheelers

In 1992, the global three-wheeler market was broken down as follows: BAL held a 33% market share with 55,000 vehicles; Piaggio an 18% share; Tuck-Tuck (Thailand) a 3% share; and Chinese manufacturers a 38% share. In the three-wheeler market, BAL's exports were mostly to neighboring countries, where the vehicles were used as taxis. In 1992, Bangladesh and Sri Lanka remained BAL's major export markets for three-wheelers, importing over 4,500 BAL units in 1992. In these markets, BAL held 90% and 95% market shares respectively. The concept of three-wheelers as passenger vehicles was not well developed outside Asia.

In 1982, the world market for two-wheeler vehicles was approximately 15 million units; by 1992, this had declined to 11 million units. Seventy-five percent of the global market was dominated by five manufacturers: Honda with 31% market share in 1992, up from 25% in 1982; Yamaha with 24% in 1992, up from 17.5%; Suzuki with 7% in 1992, down from 10.5%; BAL with 7%, up from 1.5%; and Piaggio with 6%, down slightly from 6.5%. (Exhibit 10 summarizes two-wheeler unit production and sales by country over time.) Experts believed that the decline of two-wheeler sales had stabilized in mature markets and that future sales growth would occur mostly in Asia, excluding Japan, which would account for 65% of global sales by the mid-1990s. Global import figures indicated that Europe as a whole accounted for 53% of all imports in 1992, North America 21%, and the rest of the world (including Asia, Africa, South America, and Oceania) 26%. Two distinct segments existed in the inter-

---

Exhibit 8   *Principal Terms of BAL Foreign Distributorship Agreements: 1992**

- The distributor may not carry competing products.
- BAL vehicles can be sold only within the distributor's specified territory/ country.
- All products must be sold under the Bajaj brand name.
- Marketing and advertising expenses are to be borne by the distributor.
- The distributor should establish showrooms and service stations conforming to BAL standards in the main towns within its territory.
- The distributor may appoint subdealers and authorized workshops for product repairs.
- Renewal of the appointment of the distributor is not automatic.

*Source: Company records.

Exhibit 9   *BAL Unit Exports by Country and Product Line: 1992**

	Scooters	Motorcycles	Three-Wheelers	Total Units	Total Revenues (Rs. 000s)†
EUROPE					
Cyprus	2	0	0	2	17
France	0	0	0	0	0
Greece	30	29	36	95	1,775
Italy	18	0	0	18	261
Malta	18	8	0	26	342
Netherlands	3	0	1	4	55
Poland	20	3	34	57	1,667
Sweden	4	0	0	4	43
Turkey	1,100	0	0	1,100	14,072
United Kingdom	0	2	0	2	24
West Germany	666	0	0	666	6,540
Total	1,861	42	71	1,974	24,796
ASIA					
Bangladesh	136	200	1,858	2,194	37,608
Japan	6	0	1	7	94
Malaysia	0	0	1	1	37
Philippines	0	0	160	160	3,381
Sri Lanka	131	779	2,643	3,553	71,842
Singapore	6	44	0	50	1,074
Thailand	610	0	0	610	7,248
Vietnam	1	0	0	1	11
Total	890	1,023	4,663	6,576	121,295
MIDDLE EAST					
Bahrain	22	10	4	36	592
Dubai	5	70	0	75	1,166
Egypt	500	0	0	500	6,000
Iran	2	1	1	4	45
Saudi Arabia	0	0	1	1	32
Kuwait	48	14	69	131	3,251
Lebanon	18	6	0	24	330
Oman	26	15	8	49	855
Total	621	116	83	820	12,271

continued

Exhibit 9   *(continued)*

	Scooters	Motorcycles	Three-Wheelers	Total Units	Total Revenues (Rs. 000s)†
LATIN AMERICA					
Argentina	1,128	1,021	6	2,155	35,520
Belize	4	2	4	10	176
Chile	0	0	0	0	0
Colombia	6	4	0	10	134
Mexico	1,122	1,299	252	2,673	41,000
Paraguay	23	101	0	124	1,907
Peru	94	0	612	706	23,807
Venezuela	147	0	0	147	1,954
Total	2,524	2,427	874	5,825	104,498
AFRICA AND OTHER					
Angola	0	0	191	191	5,064
Benin	0	2	0	2	24
P.N. Guinea	8	0	3	11	212
Kenya	0	0	3	3	115
Mauritius	24	64	0	88	1,447
New Zealand	0	0	0	0	0
Nigeria	69	0	5	74	1,111
Rwanda	2	4	4	10	251
Sierra Leone	6	6	10	22	521
Sudan	108	0	0	108	1,448
Tanzania	0	0	1	1	33
Uganda	42	7	0	49	700
Zambia	0	46	42	88	1,924
Total	259	129	259	647	12,850
TOTAL (All Regions)	6,155	3,737	5,950	15,842	275,710

*Source: Company records.
†Rs.: Rupees, in thousands.

national market: the developed countries, comprising Europe, Japan, North America, and Australasia; and developing countries, divided further into three regions: Southeast Asia and China; Africa and the Middle East; and Latin America.

Developed Countries

In the United States, the 50cc market was dominated by Japanese competitors, and BAL had no products in the above-250cc category—the other large U.S. two-wheeler segment. In Japan, 71% of two-wheeler unit sales were of models of 50cc, characterized by fashionable, automatic, single-seater products with many plastic parts. The four main Japanese manufacturers held 80% of the Japanese market. Stringent Japanese product standards and the cost of freight made this market difficult to penetrate. In Europe, the 50cc market was also the largest segment, and recent

Exhibit 10 *Two-Wheeler Unit Production and Sales by Country: 1981–1990* *

Units (000s)	1981 Production	Sales	1985 Production	Sales	1990 Production	%	Sales	%
Japan	7,413	3,062	4,536	2,096	2,807	27%	1,619	15%
India	499	476	1,126	1,107	1,891	18	1,868	18
Taiwan	669	692	656	685	1,062	10	997	10
China	14	N/A	1,035	N/A	965	9	N/A	N/A
Italy	1,240	857	808	569	910	9	576	6
Thailand	305	284	229	202	434	4	522	5
Indonesia	503	678	227	230	409	4	415	4
Spain	188	186	168	110	385	4	430	4
Korea	124	126	171	71	283	3	254	2
Malaysia	174	170	182	159	220	2	294	3
United States	125	828	130	722	120	1	294	3
West Germany	217	451	86	215	56	1	171	2
World Total[a]	14,368	14,368	12,761	12,761	10,467	100%	10,467	100%

*Source: Company records.
[a]World total includes production and sales in countries in addition to those listed.

trends in Europe showed that mopeds were being replaced by fashionable automatic scooters. In developed countries in general, product performance requirements were exacting, and vehicles had to meet tough regulations on emissions, noise, braking, and electricals. In addition, distribution reach and after-sales service were critical. The market for three-wheelers in developed countries was virtually nonexistent; indeed, regulations often prevented their use on major roads.

Eastern European countries followed many of the product standards set in Western Europe but did not, in 1993, have adequate buying power, so their markets remained small. BAL executives believed that, with the right political and economic changes, these countries would emerge as important markets around 1997. In particular, Hungary, Poland, and the Southern CIS[3] countries might be targeted in the future.

Developing Countries

In Southeast Asia, imports of two-wheelers were restricted either by tariff barriers or import bans, and Japanese manufacturers had already established local joint-venture production facilities. China was the largest market in the world, and all the major two-wheeler manufacturers, particularly the Japanese, had set up plants in China. Competition in China was already intense. The major problem with African countries was the difficulty of access to foreign exchange and low consumer purchasing power. Some potential, however, existed for exporting CKD units to the Middle East and North Africa, where GDP per capita was higher. Latin America was an attractive market, particularly for scooter products. In general, developing countries were more price sensitive, but product performance regulations were less stringent than in developed countries.

Table E provides a summary of the consumer and product characteristics for two-wheelers in both developed and developing countries in comparison to the Indian market.

[3]Commonwealth of Independent States (the former U.S.S.R.).

Table E   Consumer Requirements and Product Characteristics by Region

Developed Countries: Europe/U.S./Japan	India/Bangladesh/Sri Lanka	Developing Countries: Latin America, Africa/Asia[a]
Mopeds, under 50cc.	Two-wheelers and three-wheelers.	Two-wheelers and three-wheelers.
Teenager market.	Scooters as the family vehicle.	Vehicle is the workhorse.
Peppy, good styling and performance.	Fuel efficient and reliable.	Low price, fuel efficient, durability of 10–15 years.
Quick model changes and latest features; auto-lube, electric start.	Up-to-date features for the same price.	Spare parts and service access critical. Model changes a negative.
Service and distribution extensive. Dealers have product liability.	Increasing product competition. Search to differentiate products.	Initial cost and ability to repair product cheaply critical.
Luxury/fun vehicle used for short distances within cities.	Personal transportation.	First and only vehicle. Essential for work and transportation.

[a]Developing countries more exposed to international products and consumer goods displayed consumer behaviors more similar to those found in developed countries.

Europe

In 1992, the total European market for two-wheelers was estimated at 2 million vehicles a year, with the under-50cc segment accounting for 60% of unit sales and the 125cc segment for 10%. Europe imported 500,000 two-wheelers a year, of which 65% were in the under-50cc moped segment. Indian vehicles imported into Western Europe benefited from the Generalized System of Preferences and did not pay import duties. Japanese vehicles, however, had to pay import duties of 9%. The 1992 regulatory harmonization of technical standards for two-wheelers in the European Community promised to reduce the need to meet diverse country regulations. However, it was estimated that complete harmonization would not take effect until 1995 at the earliest.

In 1990, BAL adapted its moped product—the Bajaj Sunny, BAL's only product in the under-50cc-segment—for the West European market. Product adaptation of the Bajaj Sunny, which consumed some 8% of total company R&D resources over the development period,

included engine and silencer modifications, the usage of approved electricals, modification of components, and brake and clutch linings. BAL initially established dealerships in Germany, Sweden, and France. The Bajaj Sunny held a considerable price advantage in the moped segment, retailing at 2,000 DM in Germany, compared with Piaggio's "Sfera" which retailed at 4,000 DM.[4] However, the Sunny had fewer features and lacked the Sfera's auto-lube, electric start, and variomatic transmission (which provided better acceleration at lower speeds). (Exhibit 11 depicts the two products.) BAL had also developed a 125cc scooter, adapted from its traditional 150cc scooter, that appealed to a limited "nostalgia" niche market of consumers with a desire for an old-fashioned-style product. By 1992, BAL had sold a total of 1,500 vehicles in the under-50cc and 200 vehicles in the 125cc segment in Europe.

---

[4]U.S. $1 = 1.6 DM, 1993.

Exhibit 11   *The Bajaj Sunny and Piaggio Sfera*

BAL's future strategy in Europe, which not everyone in the company agreed with, was to introduce the Sunny in as many European countries as possible, starting at the lower end of the moped and scooter markets and, over time, adding vehicles with more features and improved performance. However, the technical certifications necessary to export vehicles to Europe had taken BAL time and resources to understand and execute.

Latin America

In 1992, BAL exported 4,200 units to distributorships in Peru, Venezuela, Argentina, Mexico, Chile, Paraguay, and Colombia. Two-wheelers were shipped in semi-knocked down (SKD) condition to reduce freight costs. Reassembly from SKD was simple and undertaken by distributor mechanics. Three-wheelers were shipped complete on special car carrier vessels. All shipments were made directly to individual distributors from India. Both two- and three-wheeler vehicles had been in demand, and BAL believed that these markets would continue to experience strong and steady growth. There was no competition in three-wheelers, and BAL held a price advantage over Japanese two-wheeler products. (Exhibit 12 shows product-price comparisons in Mexico.) Japanese products appeared too sophisticated for these markets, requiring substantial servicing by the consumer. BAL was hoping to capture significant market shares in both Mexico and Argentina by 1995.

BAL was also evaluating the possibility of establishing technical licensing agreements and the exports of CKD units, similar to the arrangements that had been established in Taiwan and Indonesia. A licensing agreement became attractive for BAL when (1) a particular market's size and potential justified the investment required for a plant (that would follow an assembly-cum-progressive-manufacture strategy), (2) the difference in import duties on complete or SKD units and CKD units was large enough to make

Exhibit 12 *Retail Prices of BAL and Competitor Vehicles in Mexico: 1992 (U.S.$)* *

Manufacturer	Product	Retail Price
SCOOTERS		
Bajaj	Cub	$1,037
	Super	1,028
	Chetak	1,083
Honda	SA 50	1,282
	SA 50 2M	1,340
	AE R 100	1,544
	Elite 80	1,923
Suzuki	AX 100	1,784
	AG 100	2,131
	TS 185	2,268
Piaggio	STD 150	1,807
	LML 150	2,448
Yamaha	Axis 90	2,070
	Cygnus	2,800
MOTORCYCLES		
Bajaj	M-80	955
	Kawasaki RTZ	1,449
	Kawasaki 4S	1,632
Carabella[a]	Deluxe	1,555
	STD 175	1,747
Yamaha	RXZ 100	1,897
	RXZ 135	2,436
	DT 175	2,436
Kawasaki	KE 100	1,916
	KH 125	2,339
	KV 175	2,804
	GPZ 305	3,955
Honda	CG 125	2,272
	CT 125	2,535
	CB 250	3,088
	SR 250	3,321
MOPEDS		
Bajaj	Sunny	744
Carabella	Chispa-60	830
	City 60	830
	Runner 60	945
Yamaha	PW 50 CC	1,150
	MIN SH 50	1,174
Honda	SA 50	1,282
	SA 50 2 M	1,340
	C90	1,515
Suzuki	AE 50 CC	1,418

*Source: Company records.
[a]A local manufacturer of two-wheelers.

CKD imports substantially more competitive, and (3) when BAL desired to have a long-term manufacturing presence in a particular market. Possible licensee locations included Mexico.

STRATEGIC OPTIONS FOR GROWTH

Bajaj wondered how focused his company should remain in the future. Since the late 1960s, many Indian companies with the financial resources to do so had diversified into other industries. A few BAL executives believed that, given the strength of competitors in the two-wheeler market, BAL would do better to invest in other Indian consumer goods markets and focus on the future economic and industrial development of India. Other BAL executives thought that the company should diversify geographically by developing its export markets further for both two- and three-wheeler products. A third group of executives cautioned that BAL would need to focus all its resources on protecting the company's current share of the Indian two- and three-wheeler market.

BAL executives were considering three options for international markets. First, BAL could remain focused on the domestic market and export only on an opportunistic basis. Second, BAL could pursue exports in developing countries that would require minimal adaptation of the current product line. Third, BAL could try to promote exports to developed countries, initially focusing on the lower end of the moped market in Europe.

MARY KAY COSMETICS: ASIAN MARKET ENTRY

In February 1993, Curran Dandurand, senior vice president of Mary Kay Cosmetics, Inc.'s (MKC) global marketing group, was reflecting on the company's international operations. MKC products had been sold outside the United States for over 15 years, but by 1992, international sales represented only 11% of the $1 billion total. In contrast, one of MKC's U.S. competitors, Avon Products Inc., derived over 55% of its $3.6 billion sales (at wholesale prices) from international markets in 1992.

Dandurand wondered how MKC could expand international operations and which elements of MKC's culture, philosophy, product line, and marketing programs were transferable. She wanted to define the critical success factors for MKC internationally and establish a marketing strategy for future international expansion. Specifically, she was currently evaluating two market entry opportunities: Japan and China. The first was a mature but lucrative market where cosmetics marketing and direct selling were well known and accepted. The second was a rapidly growing and changing but relatively unknown market with substantially lower individual purchasing power.

THE COSMETICS AND DIRECT-SELLING INDUSTRIES

In 1992, worldwide retail sales of facial treatments and color cosmetics products exceeded $50 billion, with the United States accounting for $16 billion. The top four companies in the U.S. cosmetics market in 1992 were Procter & Gamble, with $4.3 billion cosmetics retail sales, Estée Lauder, Avon, and Revlon. L'Oréal, a subsidiary of Nestlé, dominated the world market with $5.9 billion in retail sales, followed by Procter & Gamble, Avon, Unilever, Shiseido, Revlon, Colgate-Palmolive, Estée Lauder, SmithKline Beecham, and Gillette.

Retail sales by the U.S. direct-selling cosmetics industry were estimated at $5 billion in 1992. Cosmetics companies used two approaches to direct selling: the repetitive person-to-person method, used by Avon, in which a salesperson regularly visited customers in their homes and

This case was prepared by Nathalie Laidler (under the direction of Professor John A. Quelch). Confidential data have been disguised. Copyright © 1993 by the President and Fellows of Harvard College. Harvard Business School case 594-023.

sold products one to one; and the party plan method, in which a salesperson presented and sold products to a group of customers attending a "party" or "show" in one of the customer's homes. The party plan method was used by MKC.

Other large international direct-selling organizations included Amway, which sold a variety of household and personal care products and recorded retail sales of over $3.5 billion in 1992, and Tupperware, which sold household products through the party plan method and had retail sales of over $1 billion. International sales for Amway and Tupperware accounted for 60% and 75% respectively.

MKC OPERATIONS AND PHILOSOPHY

Incorporated in Texas in 1963 by Mary Kay Ash, MKC was a direct selling cosmetics company with 1992 estimated retail sales of $1 billion, net company sales of $624 million,[1] cost of goods sold of $148 million, and earnings before interest and taxes of $110 million. (Exhibit 1 depicts the growth in MKC net revenues, operating cash flow, and number of consultants between 1986 and 1992.) MKC sold a range of skin care, personal care, and cosmetics products through approximately 275,000 independent salespeople worldwide, known as "beauty consultants," who purchased products from the company and resold them at skin care classes or facials held in homes that were attended by four to six, or one to two potential customers respectively.

The company's powerful culture was based on offering unlimited opportunities for women in business, coupled with a distinctive compensation and recognition plan. Mary Kay Ash's charismatic personality and drive had been central to the company's rapid growth and success, and, for many beauty consultants, she represented a caring and successful role model. In 1993, MKC defined its mission as promoting business opportunities for women, teaching women how to care for their skin and use cosmetics, offering skin care systems as opposed to individual products, and providing unsurpassed personal service to its customers. (Exhibit 2 outlines what the company considered to be its competitive advantages and points of difference with respect to both potential beauty consultants and cosmetics consumers.)

Product Line

In 1992, MKC manufactured a relatively narrow line of 225 SKUs (stockkeeping units), including different color shades.[2] Product policy emphasized skin care "systems" that included several related items formulated for specific skin types or skin conditions. (Table A reports the number of products—excluding different shades within color product categories—and percentage of 1992 sales for each of the eight product categories in which MKC competed.)

MKC regularly involved its sales force in product policy decisions, sending them samples of prospective new products for evaluation. Virtually all MKC products were manufactured in a single plant near Dallas, considered to be the most efficient cosmetics production facility in the world.

Sales Force

Four basic levels of independent contractors were included in the MKC sales force: beauty consultants, sales directors, senior sales directors, and national sales directors. Promotions were made from within and based entirely on performance, as defined by volume sales and recruitment of new salespeople. Virtually all MKC

---

[1] Net company sales were defined as sales of MKC products by the company to its sales consultants. Retail sales are defined as those sales made by consultants to consumers.

[2] In 1992, Avon had an estimated 1,500 SKUs.

Exhibit 1 *Mary Kay Cosmetics Net Revenues, Operating Cash Flow, and Number of Consultants, 1986–1992*

Net Revenues

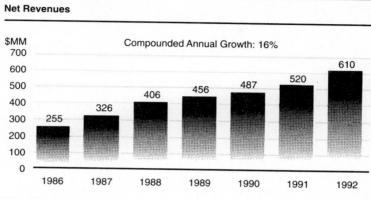

Operating Cash Flow

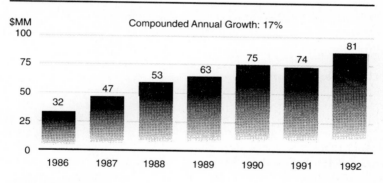

Beauty Consultants

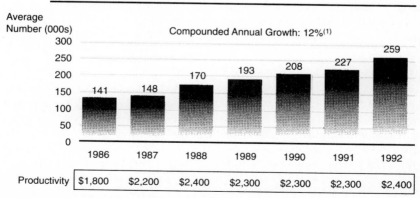

| Productivity | $1,800 | $2,200 | $2,400 | $2,300 | $2,300 | $2,300 | $2,400 |

Note: (1) Based on year-end numbers of Beauty Consultants

Exhibit 2   *The Mary Kay Cosmetics Career and Consumer Program*

The Mary Kay Career

- The Mary Kay career path allows a woman to advance into a management/training position if she so wishes. She cannot buy her way into these positions, but can earn them based on her proven ability to sell and build a team.
- The Mary Kay career path provides the opportunity to earn higher part-time and full-time compensation more quickly than other direct sales companies and most corporations.
- The company does not compete with its Consultants by offering products at retail locations, salons, or via "buying club" discounts.
- The company provides advanced training and the presentation and sales tools to allow a Consultant to offer her customers value-added services and information. "She is a teacher of skin care and glamour." In addition the Consultant receives training on leadership and aspects of running a successful business.

- The company supports a Consultant's business by offering business-building programs:
  - Direct Support (consumer direct mail program) to retain and increase current customer business.
  - Leads for new customers and recruits generated by company advertising, direct mail, and sampling programs.
- A Mary Kay Consultant is in business for herself, but never by herself. She receives ongoing training (product knowledge, business and leadership skills), recognition, and motivation from the company and her Director. The Director forms a mentorlike relationship and encourages ongoing involvement and success on the part of the Consultant.
- The unit concept of the sale force organization taps into the Japanese desire to belong to a group and compete with others based on team activities.

The Mary Kay Consumer Program

- Mary Kay Cosmetics offers women self-improvement and self-esteem enhancement through skin care and glamour education provided by a certified Beauty Consultant.
- Consumers are taught how to care for their skin and basic glamour application skills within a unique training class that provides:
  - Individualized analysis of their skin type.
  - Individual vanity tray and mirror that allows the customer to apply each product as it is explained and demonstrated.
  - The ability to try all products prior to purchase via hygienic, single-use samplers.
  - Hands-on glamour application training.
  - Fun, social interaction and entertainment aspect of a skin care class
- Consumers are offered advanced training including the ColorLogic Glamour System, Advanced Glamour, Skin Wellness, Nail Care, etc.
- On-the-spot delivery of product is provided for most products

- Enrollment in a unique gift-with-purchase program (Direct Support)
- 100% satisfaction guarantee or full refund.
- Products' packaging are designed to be as environmentally friendly as possible (refillable compacts, recycled/recyclable cartons).
- Ongoing advice and service from a trained expert.
- Skin care products designed for particular skin types and skin conditions.
- Unique glamour system designed to take the guess work out of selecting glamour shades.
- Customers have the opportunity to earn valuable product discounts or unique gifts by hostessing a skin care class.
- Value-added services and further education are provided through high-quality brochures, and newsletters given free of charge to customers

Table A

	Number of Products	% Sales (1992)
Skin care (cleansers, creams, moisturizers, foundations)	27	46%
Glamour (lipsticks, eye colors)	24	30
Fragrances	9	10
Nail care	12	5
Body care	5	3
Sun care	7	2
Hair care	5	1
Men's skin care	6	1

beauty consultants were female, and new consultants were recruited by existing salespeople, whose compensation and advancement were partly dependent on their recruiting success.

A new MKC beauty consultant had to purchase a Beauty Consultant Showcase, which cost around $100. Consultants bought MKC products at a 40% to 50% discount off the retail selling price, depending on volume. A minimum wholesale order of $180 had to be placed once every three months for a consultant to remain active. If a consultant terminated her association with MKC, the company would, if requested, buy back all her MKC inventory at 90% of the price she had paid for it.

In addition to the margins made on product sales, salespeople received a 4% to 12% commission on the wholesale prices of products purchased by those beauty consultants they had recruited. This commission, which increased with the number of recruits achieved, encouraged consultants to devote time to recruiting and training other consultants. To be promoted to sales director, a consultant had to recruit 30 active consultants; to become a senior sales direc-

tor one of the director's recruits had to become a sales director herself; and to become a national sales director, a director had to motivate at least 10 of the consultants in her group to become sales directors. Nonmonetary rewards and recognition incentives, for which MKC was renowned, included pink Cadillacs, diamonds, and furs.

Communications

MKC developed programs, manuals, and sales training aids for its sales force. Since the emphasis was on "teaching skin care and glamour" to consumers, beauty consultants had to be taught how to teach. A new recruit would attend three "classes" given by an experienced consultant, study the "Beauty Consultant's Guide," and sit through an orientation class organized by her unit director prior to her being enrolled as an MKC beauty consultant. Weekly training sessions covered product information, customer service, business organization, and money management. Each year, some 15% of the MKC sales force traveled to Dallas at their own expense for a three-day seminar where sales and recruiting achievements of top-performing consultants were recognized. Queens of Sales and Recruiting were crowned by Mary Kay Ash and well-known entertainers made guest appearances. Workshops on every aspect of building and managing the business were conducted by consultants and directors that had developed a particular expertise. In addition, many national directors held their own yearly "jamborees" patterned after the Dallas event.

MKC also supported its consultant sales force with consumer print advertising, placed in women's magazines. (Exhibit 3 reproduces some examples of recent MKC print advertisements in the United States.)

Challenges Facing MKC in 1993

In 1993, MKC was facing a mature U.S. cosmetics market, an increasing number of competing direct-selling organizations, and potentially max-

Exhibit 3   *Reproductions of Mary Kay Cosmetics Print Advertisements in the United States, 1992*

imum historical penetration in some areas of the United States. At the same time, MKC's international subsidiaries' sales growth had been modest. Given that competitors such as Avon and Amway had been very successful internationally, MKC executives could see no reason why MKC could not do the same. They believed that the MKC culture could be transferred internationally and that Mary Kay Ash's charisma, motivation, and philosophy were likely to appeal to women throughout the world.

INTERNATIONAL OPERATIONS

In early 1993, MKC products were sold in 19 countries. The company had 100%-owned subsidiaries in nine countries: Argentina (which also served Uruguay and Chile), Australia (with additional sales to New Zealand), Canada, Germany, Mexico, Taiwan, Spain, Thailand, and Russia. MKC was also planning to enter Italy, Portugal, the United Kingdom, and Japan or China in the near future. In addition, distributors existed in Costa Rica, Singapore, Malaysia, Brunei, Bermuda, Guatemala, Sweden, Norway, and Iceland.

Historically, international expansion had been opportunistic, based largely on personal contacts. The first two markets entered, Australia and Argentina, were not chosen for strategic reasons but in response to approaches to the company from local entrepreneurs. An international division with separate back-room operations, based in Dallas, had evolved to support the international businesses; this ensured the latter received adequate attention but duplicated functions and resources at headquarters.

In 1992, MKC initiated an organizational change that resulted in the formation of global resource groups to support sales subsidiaries worldwide, thereby consolidating the human resource, legal, finance, manufacturing, and marketing functions. (Exhibit 4 depicts the new organizational structure.) The global marketing group, headed by Dandurand, provided subsidiaries with product development and marketing support, advertising, public relations and consumer promotion materials, and controlled the quality, consistency, and image of the Mary Kay brand around the world. Dandurand anticipated that marketing communication strategies would gradually become more locally driven. She explained:

> Once we have firmly established consistently high quality and clearly communicated the desired image for our company and brand, the local subsidiaries will be given more autonomy to develop their own marketing communication programs.

In addition, regional sales headquarters were established for Asia/Pacific, Europe, and the Americas (excluding the United States) to support the country subsidiaries within those regions more effectively and to facilitate MKC's future international expansion.

To illustrate the challenges MKC faced internationally, the evolution of each of four MKC subsidiaries is briefly described:

Canada

The Canadian market was similar to the United States, both in product requirements and organization, and U.S. sales directors were allowed to go to Canada to recruit and build sales areas. The Canadian subsidiary had been operating for 15 years. However, in 1993, market research indicated that MKC was perceived by some Canadian consumers as out of date. A salaried country manager with a marketing and sales staff ensured local contact with the Canadian consultants and the efficient order processing and delivery of MKC products.

Australia

The Australian subsidiary began with the acquisition of an existing direct-selling company in the early 1970s. In 1992, MKC had low brand awareness and a poor image. All products were imported from the United States, and the U.S.

Exhibit 4   *Mary Kay Cosmetics Organization, 1992*

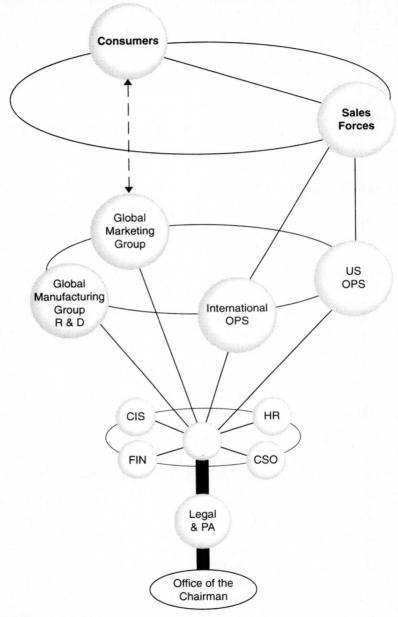

Note: CIS = Customer Information System
 CSO = Chief Scientific Officer
 OPS = Operations (incl. manufacturing)
 FIN = Finance
 HR   = Human Resources

pricing strategy had been replicated without much adaptation to local market conditions. Nutri-Metics, an Australian competitor, had successfully used a hybrid of party plan and door-to-door direct-selling methods, backed by media advertising, catalog sales, and Buying Club sales.[3] Unlike MKC, Nutri-Metics did not hold skin care classes, and salespeople could buy in and remain "active" with lower purchase commitments than were required of MKC consultants.

Mexico

In 1988, MKC established a subsidiary in Mexico, headed by a husband-and-wife team who had previously worked for the direct-selling party-plan cosmetics company Jafra. The couple became salaried employees with performance incentives. The new Mexican subsidiary also benefited initially from U.S. sales directors, who went to Mexico to recruit consultants. Three thousand new consultants joined the company in the first three months. After four years, brand awareness was high, the brand image was positive, and sales force size exceeded 6,200.

Taiwan

The Taiwan subsidiary, launched in July 1991, emphasized intensive training for new consultants. Chinese women were characterized as typically entrepreneurial, independent, and hardworking, with a strong drive to make money. The local country manager had previous experience in direct selling with both Avon and Tupperware. In 1992, rapid expansion had generated $3.3 million in sales through 1,800

consultants. Sales were expected to triple in 1993. All products were shipped from Dallas.

MKC also had established subsidiaries in Germany, with an estimated 1,500 consultants in 1993, and in Argentina which, despite periodic hyperinflation throughout the 1980s, was profitable in 1992. Poor results in the United Kingdom had resulted in the subsidiary being closed in 1985 after four years of operation, though there were plans to reopen in 1993. (Exhibit 5 presents data on MKC sales, number of directors, and number of consultants by subsidiary.)

Dandurand believed that MKC's limited international success was due partly to the direct application of the U.S. marketing strategy, products, and communications to different subsidiaries without sufficient local modifications. Other factors constraining growth included low consumer brand awareness and insufficient marketing resources to develop it. Dandurand explained:

In some countries, cultural barriers impede the use of the party plan and door-to-door selling. The size of a typical home may be smaller than in the United States, or a party for unfamiliar guests may be considered an invasion of privacy. In addition, the time required for a two-hour skin care class is sometimes an obstacle.

Future International Expansion

A strategic-planning process in early 1993 identified a "great teachers" strategy to differentiate MKC worldwide from other retail and direct-selling competitors and to build on the company's proven capabilities in this area. Greater emphasis would be placed on sales force training and on adapting MKC's positioning, the product range, and marketing communications mix to local market needs. A standard core product line would be supplemented with products developed specifically for each local market. Products would either be imported from the United States or manufacturing and/or final packaging

---

[3]Buying Clubs enabled women to purchase products such as cosmetics at a discount for their personal consumption rather than for resale. Individuals were not required to purchase a minimum level of inventory to enroll in the club. The most successful clubs offered broad product lines.

Exhibit 5   *Mary Kay Cosmetics Net Sales and Headcount, 1989 and 1992*

	Net Sales*		Consultant Count		Director Count	
	1989	1992	1989	1992	1989	1992
United States	$404,990	$559,719	171,073	232,692	4,689	5,837
Argentina	3,638	12,450	5,142	6,675	152	152
Australia	9,494	7,812	4,161	4,143	122	116
Canada	24,811	25,386	9,866	10,597	167	283
Germany	1,210	5,131	583	1,306	9	26
Mexico	4,598	8,586	2,640	6,241	25	89
Taiwan	0	3,133	0	1,064	0	13
Distributors	3,333	4,690				

*In thousands.

would be subcontracted in individual country markets, as was currently done in Mexico and Argentina. In particular, MKC was currently looking for a European manufacturing site to support its planned market entry into several European countries.

A country manager who wanted products adapted would have to seek the approval of the MKC regional president, who in turn would meet with the international marketing and manufacturing managers. MKC regional presidents were all equity holders and therefore both advocates for the interests of the countries in their region and representatives of the headquarters' perspective.[4]

MKC executives believed that the company's values were transferable. Dandurand elaborated:

Telling women they can achieve, making them believe in themselves and giving them caring and respect, is an international message. However, the message needs to be tailored to each market and communicated effectively, and I'm not sure whether or not additional role models are needed in each foreign market for the company to be successful.

---

[4]As a private company, MKC had a compensation plan for senior executives that worked like a partnership.

It was recognized that one or two charismatic leaders could generate massive growth in number of consultants and product sales.

Avon's International Strategy

Avon had become a successful international cosmetics company. Each country subsidiary was run by a country manager who had considerable decision-making authority so long as agreed-upon performance objectives were achieved. On average, 60% of the Avon products sold by a foreign subsidiary came from a common core line, while 40% were adapted to local markets. The company placed a heavy emphasis on merchandising, with 18 three-week marketing campaigns used to promote specific consumer events such as Mother's Day, and 26 two-week drive periods supported by specific sales brochures each year. Avon sales consultants had to deal with the complexity of a product line of 1,500 SKUs. In contrast to MKC, Avon employed salaried sales managers who oversaw the company's independent salespeople.

In 1992, Avon eliminated its regional headquarters in favor of a single global support group based in New York. Many Avon subsidiaries were large enough to afford their own strong functional staffs and therefore no longer needed backup from regional headquarters. MKC executives believed that their lower product line turnover ought to permit a more streamlined and lower-cost central support group than Avon's.

Avon had been more willing than MKC to adapt its marketing programs internationally, adjusting prices according to the level of consumer buying power in individual countries. Avon hired strong local nationals as country managers, giving them specific strategic direction, generous resource allocations, and clear profit-and-loss responsibility. The Avon culture was considered "hard-nosed" and numbers-driven—return on equity and return on assets being especially important—but local country managers who delivered enjoyed considerable autonomy. According to some MKC executives, MKC had a more caring orientation and placed greater emphasis on support systems, mentoring, training, and recognition of consultants.

MKC IN ASIA

MKC's Taiwanese subsidiary had, by 1992, become profitable and promised good future sales growth. As part of the recent reorganization, an Asia/Pacific regional manager would shortly establish a base in Hong Kong from which to build MKC sales in Asia.

Asia was evolving as one of the fastest-growing and most dynamic regions of the world. Its share of world GDP was scheduled to reach 32% by the year 2000, up from 24% in 1988. The choice between a Japanese or Chinese market entry would, Dandurand believed, impact MKC's long-term market position in Asia. She began to compare the two countries on some key characteristics to help make the decision (Table B). She wanted to build on MKC's past interna-

Table B   Key Characteristics of Japanese and Chinese Markets

	Japan	China
Population, 1992	124 million	1,139 million
Estimated population, 2020	137 million	1,541 million
Population distribution (0–24; 25–49; 50+):		
1993	32%; 37%; 31%	42%; 39%; 19%
2000	29%; 35%; 36%	40%; 39%; 21%
Urban population, 1992	77%	27%
Population/square mile	865	315
Gross domestic product (US $ billion)	3,370	371[a]
1993 GDP growth % (estimated)	2.3%	10.1%
1994 GDP growth % (estimated)	3.2%	9.5%
1990 per capita GNP	$14,311	$325
Average hourly compensation (US $)	$14.41	$0.24
Penetration of:		
Televisions	1 per 1.8 persons	1 per 8 persons
Radios	1 per 1.3	1 per 9
Telephones	1 per 2.3	1 per 66
1992 advertising expenditure per capita	$220	$0.86

[a]In early 1993, China's GDP was reestimated at $1,700 billion by the International Monetary Fund on the basis of purchasing power parity. This meant the Chinese economy was the third largest in the world.

tional experience and current competitive advantages to develop a market entry strategy that fit with the MKC culture and the local market environment and that would enable MKC to establish a firm base from which to build its Asian operations.

JAPAN

The Cosmetics Industry

In 1992, there were 1,100 cosmetics manufacturers in Japan, but five companies accounted for 69% of domestic sales. Domestic production exceeded $9 billion in factory sales in 1991 and included local production by foreign firms, estimated at 18% of total domestic production. Imports represented 5% of total sales in 1991, up from 3% in 1989; over 45% of imports came from France, of which 27% consisted of fragrances and cologne. In addition, Japanese tourists purchased around $500 million of cosmetics at duty-free shops each year. Table C summarizes the size of the Japanese cosmetics market and the sources of product.

Table C   Japanese Cosmetics Market Size and Sources of Shipments

$ Millions (manufacturer shipments)	1989	1990	1991
Imports:	265	318	460
From the United States	41	57	89
Local production	8,983	8,433	9,072
Exports	128	147	214
Total market	9,119	8,603	9,319

The Japanese cosmetics market was mature, recording average annual value growth of 3% between 1988 and 1992, compared with a growth rate of 4.4% in the United States. Major consumers of cosmetics were women in their twenties and thirties. Foreign-made cosmetics were considered high-status products. Issues impacting the industry in 1992 included the end of manufacturers' control over the prices at which their products were resold by retailers and a continuing decrease in the number of independent cosmetics retailers. Strict Ministry of Health regulations governing imports and the manufacture of cosmetics involved lengthy approval processes. In many cases, common ingredients approved for use in cosmetics outside Japan were prohibited by the Ministry of Health, requiring reformulations of most products.

The Direct-Selling Industry

In 1992, Japan was the largest direct-selling market in the world, with an estimated $19.2 billion in retail sales. Direct selling enabled consumers to bypass wholesale and retail distribution systems, which some viewed as inefficient and non-price competitive. Japanese women who left business in order to have children came back into a company with no tenure and had to start up the corporate ladder from scratch. Consequently, direct selling, which could be done part time, was an attractive second career for mothers seeking to reenter the work force. According to the Japan Direct Selling Association, 1,120,000 women engaged in direct selling in 1992.[5]

Amway had been in Japan since 1977 and, by 1991, recorded sales of US $1.2 billion, with a product line that included home care, personal care and food products, housewares, cosmetics, and gifts. The company had an extensive sales force of over 100,000 people, developed primarily through word-of-mouth. Training was conducted by direct distributors who sponsored new distributors. Compensation consisted of a 30% commission and a bonus based on the sales of sponsored distributors. Conventions were held every year for training purposes and to recognize outstanding performance. In 1990, only seven other foreign companies generated more

---

[5]In 1992, the total Japanese population was 124 million, of whom 41% were women over 15 years of age.

revenues in Japan than Amway. Reasons for this success were: an effective distribution system based on company-owned warehouses; high-quality, value-oriented products; good relations with dedicated distributors; and a philosophy that emphasized human relationships, fulfillment of dreams, and financial freedom.

Consumer Behavior

In the 1990s, an increasing percentage of Japanese women were going on to further education and working outside the home. In 1992, over 50% of the 51.8 million Japanese women aged over 15 years were employed, predominantly on a part-time basis. They earned lower salaries than men and preferred more flexible work schedules. Women's activities outside the home were increasing as were their expectations of equality. Many women were marrying later and having fewer children. (Exhibit 6 summarizes the results of a 1990 attitude study of 1,000 Japanese women.)

In 1992, Japanese women over 15 years old spent, on average, $400 on cosmetics (including skin care products and makeup). Forty percent of all cosmetics sales were to women in their twenties and thirties (26% of all Japanese women over the age of 15). The heaviest users were 8.8 million women aged between 20 and 29 (14% of all Japanese women over the age of 15). These heavy users were less price sensitive and more interested in high-quality cosmetics. Working women spent, on average, 25% more on cosmetic purchases than women who did not work outside the home. A fair complexion and fine-textured skin were considered hallmarks of beauty in Japan, so skin care products accounted for 40% of all cosmetic sales. The growing sales of skin care products were also fueled by the increasing average age of the Japanese population; 23% of the population would be aged over 65 years by the year 2010, compared with 14% in 1992.

Fifty-four percent of facial skin care users and 40% of shaded-makeup users purchased all or some of their products from direct-sales companies. Corresponding figures in the United States were 25% and 22% respectively. Nineteen percent of Japanese skin care users and 20% of shaded-makeup product users purchased only from direct salespeople. The average Japanese

Exhibit 6   *1990 Survey of Japanese Women* *

Age Group	Important Job Attributes	Points of Dissatifaction at Work
19–24	Realize own potential and develop own capabilities.	Low bonus, too much overtime, inability to display or develop one's capabilities.
25–29	Able to continue after marriage and children, availability of nursery facilities, flexible time schedule to take care of children.	Feel job has no value.
30–39	Availability of nursing facilities, flexible time schedule, contributes to local community.	Low bonuses, too many trivial duties.
40–43	Job encourages and promotes women.	Inadequate social benefits.
44–49	Close to home.	

*Source: Adapted from a survey by *Pola Cultural Center,* 1990. Note: Data based on a study of 1,000 Japanese women between 15 and 65 years of age.

woman spent almost three times more on skin care than the average American woman. In the area of shaded makeup, Japanese women made half the number of purchases per year compared to women in the United States, but price differentials between the two countries resulted in almost equal annual expenditures. (Exhibit 7 summarizes Japanese consumer-buying behavior for skin care and shaded-makeup products.) In addition to functional product benefits, Japanese consumers placed a special emphasis on the visual appeal of product packaging.

Japanese consumers believed that they had sensitive skin, as MKC confirmed when it ran extensive trials with Japanese women who had recently arrived in the United States. Pink was seen as a color more appropriate for children and teenagers, so the classic MKC pink was muted on potential packaging and caps retooled to present a more upscale image. It was felt that redesigned packages might also appeal to U.S. consumers and that the potential existed for a global packaging redesign.

Products

Skin care products accounted for 40% of all cosmetics sales in Japan in 1992. (Exhibit 8 details sales of major cosmetics product categories over time.) In the skin care category, sales of skin lotion increased by 12% and face wash and cleansing products by 4%, while cold cream, moisture cream, and milky lotion decreased by 1%. Makeup accounted for 23% of cosmetics sales, but its share had been declining since 1986. Foundation products accounted for more than 50% of makeup sales.

In 1992, Kao and Shiseido dominated the Japanese skin care market. Foreign manufacturers were more successful selling makeup than skin care products while the reverse was true for domestic companies. Dandurand explained:

In Japan, makeup products are associated with status, image, and dreams. Japanese women tend to aspire to look like the Western women on the cosmetics ads and so foreign brands, *with the attached status, are more popular for color cosmetics. When it comes to skin care products, Japanese women tend to be more pragmatic. They believe that they have very delicate skins that require highly scientific products especially made for them by Japanese manufacturers who understand their needs better.*

Distribution

Cosmetics were distributed in Japan through three main channels: franchise systems, general distributorships, and door-to-door sales.

Franchise systems were based on contracts between manufacturers and retailers, also known as chain stores, in which a manufacturer's affiliated distribution company provided retailers with a full range of products, marketing support, and product promotions. In addition, trained beauty consultants were provided by manufacturers at each outlet. This enabled manufacturers to maintain control over the selling process and to provide consumers with individualized service. Franchise systems accounted for 40% of cosmetics sales in 1992 but were expected to decline. A variation of the franchise system was the direct-selling franchise system whereby manufacturers dealt directly with retail accounts without going through a distribution company. This method was used by many foreign manufacturers who focused their marketing efforts, supported by face-to-face counseling, on a limited number of prestige shops and department stores.

General distributorships were the conventional channels, in which products flowed from manufacturer to wholesaler to retailer and the manufacturer and retailer were not connected directly. The manufacturer provided full marketing support via advertising and promotion for products that tended to be lower-priced and less sophisticated. The volume share of cosmetics sold through this channel was estimated at 30% in 1992 and expected to increase.

Door-to-door sales or home-visiting systems enabled manufacturers to bypass the costly, com-

Exhibit 7 *Japanese Cosmetics Consumer Buying Behavior**

Product Category	Penetration: Percentage Purchasing	Market Share (Unit)	Market Share (Value)	Distribution Share (Retail)	Distribution Share (Direct)	Average $ Spent per Purchaser	Average Number of Purchases per Year
Skin Care							
Cleansing	41.7	10.5	7.2	58.0	42.0	39.13	2.2
Cold and massage	19.1	3.2	3.1	43.1	56.9	36.40	1.6
Clear lotion	81.5	29.5	25.3	53.6	46.1	70.54	2.9
Milky lotion	52.9	10.9	9.9	57.4	42.6	42.29	1.7
Moisture cream	40.4	8.7	14.0	45.2	54.8	78.49	1.7
Mask	23.2	4.5	4.8	50.5	49.5	47.27	1.7
Whitening powder	2.1	0.4	0.6	73.4	26.6	64.72	NA
Essence	31.6	7.4	12.6	56.0	44.0	90.80	1.9
Foundation	78.9	24.8	22.5	66.1	33.9	64.59	2.5
Glamour							
Lipstick	68.9	38.8	47.3	65.5	34.5	33.93	1.7
Eye shadow	21.3	9.8	9.9	76.7	23.3	23.05	1.4
Eyeliner	11.6	4.9	3.9	65.3	34.7	16.58	1.7
Mascara	11.9	4.8	4.8	79.8	20.2	19.99	1.7
Eyebrow	20.6	8.7	6.3	70.7	29.3	20.00	1.5
Blusher	21.5	8.7	9.3	61.4	38.6	21.26	1.4
Manicure	25.9	16.0	6.1	75.6	24.4	11.72	1.9
Fragrance	16.8	8.3	12.4	63.2	36.8	36.38	1.8

*Source: Adapted from *Cosmetics and Toiletries Marketing Strategies, Fuji Keizai,* 1992.

Exhibit 8   *Japanese Cosmetics Market: Growth by Subcategory (billion yen)* *

Value of Factory Shipments	1986	1987	1988	1989	1990	1990/89
Skin Care Products	452.5	430.0	455.2	484.4	500.8	3.4%
Face wash cream/foam	41.4	42.7	46.8	51.0	53.0	
Cleansing cream/foam/gel	27.7	28.7	32.9	35.6	37.2	
Cold cream	22.5	18.2	18.4	16.8	16.7	
Moisture cream	87.9	68.7	79.0	75.9	75.3	
Milky lotion	64.6	60.6	63.0	64.6	62.1	
Skin lotion (freshener)	134.0	142.1	142.5	159.1	178.4	
Face mask	26.1	22.3	22.3	23.2	24.3	
Men's	10.2	10.2	11.6	11.8	10.7	
Other	38.1	36.5	38.7	46.4	43.1	
Makeup Products	306.8	308.8	300.3	301.9	295.8	(2.0)
Foundation	154.3	157.1	160.0	161.8	158.3	
Powder	19.6	18.2	18.9	18.8	18.5	
Lipstick	44.2	49.3	48.3	46.4	48.2	
Lip cream	9.7	9.2	10.0	8.6	9.1	
Blush	15.5	14.1	11.9	11.4	11.2	
Eye shadow	26.0	27.5	22.3	22.7	19.9	
Eyebrow/eyelash	15.2	15.0	15.1	16.9	15.8	
Nail care	17.8	15.4	11.8	13.5	13.0	
Other	4.5	3.0	2.0	1.8	1.8	
Hair Care Products	335.5	362.2	392.1	403.5	413.4	2.5
Fragrances	22.1	21.1	18.7	18.8	20.9	11.1
Special Use (Suncare, shaving, bath products)	27.3	27.9	30.2	31.1	33.7	8.6
Total	1,144.0	1,146.6	1,196.2	1,239.6	1,263.9	2.0

*Source: Adapted from *The Complete Handbook of Cosmetics Marketing 1992, Shukan Shogyo.*

plex retailing network. This direct-selling system, which had worked well in the past, was facing problems in 1992: fewer women were staying at home, and direct selling companies were finding it increasingly difficult to attract sales personnel. In 1982, this channel had represented 25% of cosmetic sales; by 1992, it represented 19%. Some direct-selling companies were diversifying into other ways of reaching the consumer. For example, Pola, a major Japanese direct-selling cosmetics company, had started marketing its products in variety stores, aesthetic salons, and by mail order. Noevir, another large Japanese direct-selling cosmetics company, Avon, and Menard had opened retail stores and salons. Other channels included beauty parlors and hairdressers. (Shares of cosmetics sales in Japan by distribution channel and by consumer age group are given in Exhibit 9.)

Competitors

The top five domestic cosmetics manufacturers in 1992 were Shiseido with 27% of the market; Kao with 16%; Kanebo with 11%; Pola with 8%; and Kobayashi Kose with 7%. These com-

Exhibit 9   *Japanese Cosmetic Sales by Distribution Channel and Consumer Age Group, 1990**

	Percentage Women 1985	Percentage Women 1990	Change 1985–1990	1990 Teens	1990 20s	1990 30s	1990 40s	1990 50s
Department store	22.8	25.2	2.4	37	30	19	19	24
Cosmetic store	44.6	37.5	(7.1)	26	48	33	37	43
Drug/pharmacy	12.7	22.3	9.6	25	20	29	18	18
Door-to-door	19.6	12.0	(7.6)	1	7	19	16	12
Supermarket	15.6	18.1	2.5	22	11	21	22	15
Beauty salon	3.7	6.1	2.4	3	7	4	7	9
Convenience store	NA	2.9		12	2	1	1	1
Variety shop	NA	1.7		5	2	2		
Others	NA	8.4		2	9	13	10	5

*Source: Adapted from a survey by Marketing Intelligence Corp.

panies spent, on average, 4% of sales on research and development, double the level spent by the major foreign manufacturers. Shiseido, founded in 1872 as Shiseido Pharmacy, entered the cosmetics business in 1902. Ninety years later, Shiseido products were sold through 25,000 chain stores and 9,000 retail beauty consultants. Kao, Kanebo, and Kobayashi Kose also operated nationwide networks. Foreign companies such as Max Factor, Revlon, and Clinique entered the Japanese market in the early 1980s and pursued selective distribution through a limited number of prestigious department stores. (Exhibit 10 summarizes sales data for the major Japanese and foreign cosmetics manufacturers, and Table D profiles the major direct-selling cosmetics companies.)

Pola was established in 1946 and had $740 million in sales in 1991. With 180,000 "Pola Ladies," 20,000 salespeople, and 6,500 retail outlets, Pola ranked third in cosmetics sales and first in direct sales of cosmetics in Japan. Originally targeted at older women, Pola had begun recently to focus on younger women with its moderately priced product line. Pola provided in-depth training for its staff, ranging from one month for a "Pola Lady" to over a year for sales research staff at company headquarters. The compensation structure for Pola Ladies had 21 levels: "Class 1" salespeople who sold up to $370 monthly made a 25% margin and no commission. A "Super Million Lady" salesperson, with monthly sales over $37,000, earned a 35% margin, a $400 jewel allowance, and $800 in bonus. In 1991, Pola spent $28.5 million on media advertising, of which newspaper ads accounted for 9%, magazine ads for 28%, and television commercials for 63%.

Nippon Menard was established in 1959 and had $373 million in sales in 1990, of which 67% was derived from skin care products and 23% from makeup. Organized into 33 sales companies and sold through over 12,000 retail outlets and 160,000 beauty specialists, it ranked eighth among cosmetics companies and second among direct-selling cosmetics companies. Main brands included Entals, Delphia, and Ires, positioned at lower price points and targeted at women in their twenties and thirties, and Eporea, positioned at a high price point and targeted at older women. Beauty specialists followed a series of four training classes and could advance through seven levels, from "beginner" to "special," depending on their monthly sales. A beginner beauty specialist, who achieved monthly sales of $300 to $450, earned a commission of

Exhibit 10 *Major Cosmetics Companies in Japan, 1990**

Company	Total Sales $ Million	Skin Care	Makeup	Hair Care	Fragrances	Men's Cosmetics
Top 5 Cosmetics Companies						
Shiseido	$1,963.3	49%	31%	3%	3%	10%
Kanebo	1,331.2	39	36	5	3	12
Pola	704.1	54	28	2	3	2
Kose	553.8	51	36	5	1	3
Kao	470.8	46	42	2	0	10
Top 5 Foreign Cosmetics Companies						
Max Factor	440.8	37	54	1	2	1
Avon	303.8	35	30	4	0	1
Revlon	92.3	25	52	10	7	0
Clinique	80.7	72	25	1	0	0
Chanel	76.1	21	21	0	58	0

*Source: Adapted from *Cosmetics and Toiletries Marketing Strategies, Fuji Keizai; 1992.*

Table D   Manufacturer Sales of Major Direct-selling Cosmetics Companies in Japan—1990

	Sales Growth 1989–1990	Total Sales 1990 ($ million)[a]	Facial Skin Care (%)	Makeup (%)	Hair Care (%)	Fragrances (%)	Men's Cosmetics (%)
Pola	2.4%	$704	54%	28%	2%	3%	2%
Nippon Menard	(2.3)	373	67	23	1	1	2
Avon[b]	1.9	304	35	30	4		
Noevir	2.8	292	64	24	4	4	4
Oppen	0.0	213	64	24	3	1	1
Aistar	0.0	185	100				
Naris	12.0	110	58	26		1	2
Yakult	1.7	50	56	22	4	2	2

[a]Total company figures. Some companies were engaged in other businesses in addition to cosmetics; therefore, percentages of cosmetic sales do not add to 100%.
[b]Avon percentages total 69% because Avon also sold jewelry and lingerie.

30% but no bonus. At the other extreme, a "special" beauty specialist sold over $23,000 per month and earned a 38% commission plus between $350 and $1,000 in bonus. In 1991, Menard spent a total of $25 million on advertising, of which 6% was on newspaper ads, 11% on magazine advertising, and 83% on television commercials.

Noevir was established in 1978 and had $292 million in sales in 1990, of which 64% was derived from skin care products and 24% from makeup. It operated on a consignment basis, with 580 sales companies selling to two levels of 109,000 agencies, through 200,000 sales people. It ranked ninth among cosmetics companies and third among direct-selling cosmetics companies. In 1992, Noevir had two subsidiaries, Sana and Nov; Sana sold through 5,000 skin care retail outlets and 400 makeup retail outlets, and Nov sold through 2,000 pharmaceutical outlets. Sana targeted younger women, while the Nov product line included hypoallergenic cosmetics recommended by dermatologists. In 1991, Noevir spent $8 million on advertising—13% on magazine ads and the remainder on television commercials.

Avon was established in Japan in 1973 and had $325 million in sales in 1991, of which 69% was derived from cosmetics. Avon sold through mail-order catalogs and 350,000 Avon Ladies. In 1992, Avon had successfully floated 40% of the subsidiary's equity on the Tokyo stock exchange. It ranked thirteenth among cosmetics companies and fourth among direct-selling cosmetics companies. The company targeted women in their thirties and forties. Unlike other direct-selling companies, Avon's products were not regularly demonstrated to consumers by Avon Ladies.

Avon, Menard, Pola, Noevir, and Amway also offered "buying club" programs. Most recruited salespeople on the basis of providing an opportunity to make extra income, but only Amway heavily stressed advancement into management based on recruiting and sales performance. Most competitors offered thorough product training at little or no cost; the training was more extensive than that provided by most U.S. direct-selling organizations. Sales presentations typically were made one-to-one, but other than through catalogs and brochures, little instruction was provided to consumers. (Exhibit 11 profiles the characteristics of consumers using the principal brands, and Exhibit 12 reproduces competitor print advertisements.)

MKC in Japan

MKC began assessing the Japanese market in 1988 with a comparative study of products and competition. It was determined that the typical Japanese woman's skin care regimen involved a seven-stage process, as opposed to three steps in the United States,[6] and that whitening products, not widely available in the United States, were very popular in Japan. In 1989, a comparative-pricing study was undertaken, and relationships were established with an ingredient supplier and a private label manufacturer who might produce an estimated 20% of the product line, tailored to the Japanese market, including whitening products and wet/dry foundation cake. In 1992, MKC proceeded with lengthy product approval processes involving the Japanese Ministry of Health. By year end, over $1 million had been invested in preparing to enter the Japanese market.

There was concern that MKC would be a late entrant in a mature, complex, fragmented, and highly competitive market. Dandurand believed that it would take three to five years before MKC would turn a profit and take share from competitors. On the other hand, 1993 might be an opportune time for MKC to launch in Japan since, increasingly, women wished both to raise children and be involved in activities outside the

---

[6]In the United States, a typical skin care regimen involved a cleanser, a toner, and a moisturizer. In Japan, several different cleansers and moisturizers were typically used in a single skin care regimen.

Exhibit 11 *Customer Profiles of MKC's Principal Potential Competitors in Japan, 1992**

	Menard	**Pola**	**Noevir**	**Avon**	**Amway**
Educational Background					
Current student	0.0	2.7	2.0	1.1	2.1
College	11.1	17.3	14.3	32.6	27.7
Senior high school	63.9	62.7	63.3	53.7	63.3
Junior high school	25.0	17.3	20.4	12.6	6.4
Marital and Employment Status					
Married—not working	27.8	32.9	22.9	44.2	39.1
Married—working	69.4	53.4	70.9	40.0	36.7
Unmarried	2.8	13.7	6.2	15.8	23.9
Age					
15–19	0.0	2.7	0.0	2.1	0.0
20–29	8.3	18.7	14.3	15.8	38.3
30–39	11.1	17.3	30.6	28.4	17.0
40–49	41.7	25.3	30.6	32.6	25.5
50–59	38.9	36.0	24.5	21.1	19.1
Occupation					
Not employed	27.8	32.0	22.4	43.2	38.3
Employed	72.2	65.3	75.5	55.8	59.6

*Source: Company reports.

home, and an economic recession created more demand for part-time employment to supplement household incomes. Some MKC executives believed that success in Japan was essential to the company's future in the countries of the Pacific Rim.

CHINA

China covered 3.7 million square miles and was divided into 22 provinces, three municipalities (Beijing, Shanghai, and Tianjin), and five autonomous regions (Guangxi, Zhuang, Nei Mongol, Ningxia Hui, Xinjiang Uygur, and Tibet). The population was estimated at 1.1 billion in 1992 and was predicted to grow to 1.5 billion by the year 2020. Eighty percent lived in the eastern half of the country depicted in Exhibit 13. Thirty percent lived in urban areas. Thirty

percent was under 15 years old. In the second half of the twentieth century, China experienced one of the fastest demographic transitions in history. Mortality rates decreased and average life expectancy rose from 42 years in 1950 to 70 in 1992. Fertility rates fell from an average of six children per woman in 1950 to 2.3 in 1992. Trends towards urbanization and a shift in population from the agricultural to the service sector were expected to continue in the 1990s.

In 1979, the "Open Door Policy" heralded a series of wide-ranging economic reforms: agriculture was decollectivized; the development of private and semiprivate enterprises to produce goods was permitted; free market pricing and more liberal foreign exchange conversion were introduced; and foreign investment became more acceptable. These economic reforms had the greatest impact on the coastal provinces where

Exhibit 12   *Competitor Print Advertisements, Japan, 1993*

Exhibit 13 *Map of Eastern China*

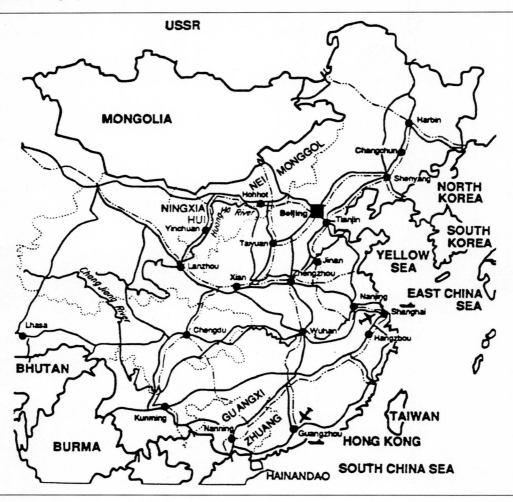

economic free zones were established to facilitate foreign investment. Guandong province, for example, had experienced the fastest growth in East Asia in the 1980s. Overall, China's GNP had increased by 9% annually during the 1980s, while consumption had increased by 6.6%. In 1990, 70% of industrial growth was attributed to private, cooperative, and foreign ventures.

Since 1988, a higher-income, urban middle class had emerged, with household earnings over $125 a month and saving rates estimated at 35%.

By the year 2000, it was estimated that 41 million households would have incomes of over $18,000 per annum. Retail sales had increased nearly fivefold since 1980. The number of retail outlets increased from 2 million in 1980 to 12 million in 1992. Most of these were private enterprises. All types of goods were available in the major cities, and the adoption rate of new products was rapid. In 1992, China was viewed as a sellers' market, but experts believed that more sophisticated marketing skills and product differentiation would become increasingly important.

In assessing the political and economic risks of investing in China, multinational companies had three main concerns. First, some thought political instability was likely to follow the retirement or death of China's long-standing premier, Deng Xiaoping. Political struggles between conservatives and reformers might delay further economic reforms. Second, the Chinese government was not granting its people political freedom commensurate with their increasing economic freedom. Progress on human rights was essential to China maintaining most-favored nation status as a trading partner with the United States. Third, multinationals importing finished goods into China faced not only high tariffs but also the likely devaluation of the Chinese currency, which would further increase the retail prices of their goods.

During the 1980s, cosmetics and toiletries became an important branch of China's light industry, and the number of cosmetics factories in China increased sixfold between 1982 and 1990. In 1992, the cosmetics market was estimated at $825 million (manufacturer sales), with skin care products dominant. There were approximately 3,000 cosmetics producers in China manufacturing limited product lines; about half were located in Shanghai. Many local brands were available as import tariffs on cosmetics averaged 100%. In 1991, the Chinese Ministry of Commerce initiated a professional training program for two million cosmetics managers, purchasers, and sales clerks. The objective was to teach them how to appraise the quality of cosmetics and skin conditions of consumers.

Consumers

There was a growing difference in purchasing power and consumer behavior between the urban and rural populations in China, with the urban population becoming increasingly prosperous and demanding and the rural consumer evolving less quickly. Eighty-seven percent of Chinese women worked, and many held two jobs: one state job and one independent job. Urban workers were generally employed in factories or workshops, employment assignments being allocated by local labor bureaus. Safety standards in factories were poor, but compensation was adequate. The wage range from lowest grade to highest grade was a factor of three, and a sum equal to 10% of total wages was typically available for bonuses. Virtually all housing, medical, and transportation costs and midday meals were subsidized by Chinese government work units. Around 25% of the household income of a two-income urban household was typically spent on food and housing; the remainder was disposable income.

Government-subsidized housing units were small; 200 square feet was the typical size of a one-bedroom urban apartment. A workers' committee still managed each apartment building. A few apartments were also available for purchase; U.S. $5,000 could purchase a two-bedroom apartment in Guangzhou in early 1993. Housing conditions were better in Guangzhou and Beijing than in Shanghai. Young workers, especially women, tended to live with their parents until they married. Once married, they would live with the husbands' parents or take their own apartments.

Female workers were entitled to 56 days of pregnancy leave and most factories had nurseries and kindergarten facilities. The Chinese government wished to encourage women to spend more time at home and therefore established the "Period Employment" system in which women could elect to take three months of maternity leave at 100% pay and/or up to seven years off at 70% of basic pay to aid in childraising. In 1992, an estimated 66% of Chinese women over the age of 25 were married.

A 1991 consumer study concluded that the average Chinese female urban consumer was 32 years old, married with one child, worked in a state factory, and earned the equivalent of $50 a month. She typically controlled the family budget and was concerned about the rising cost of living. Attracted to foreign brands, she considered skin care and cosmetics important, particularly those that prevented freckles and promoted cleanliness.

Chinese women were greatly interested in learning; education was held in very high esteem in Chinese culture. Chinese colleges and universities were increasingly asserting their independence; MKC might be able to sponsor skin care courses and sell products to the enrolled students and/or secure product endorsements from medical schools.

By 1992, differences in buying power and buyer behavior were evident across the various regions of China. The three most important regional markets were Guangzhou, Beijing, and Shanghai. (Table E summarizes key characteristics of these three metropolitan markets.)

Guangzhou

Hong Kong's influence was strongly felt in Guangzhou, whose economy was driven by the private sector. More interested in spending their disposable incomes on food, drink, eating out, and entertaining, Guangzhou consumers were wealthier but characterized as less cosmopolitan and sophisticated than other urban Chinese consumers. Described as flashy and ostentatious, Guangzhou consumers were also known as generous and free-spending. Many companies viewed

Table E   Characteristics of Three Principal Regional Markets in China: 1992

	Guangzhou	**Beijing**	**Shanghai**
Location	South (100 miles north of Hong Kong)	North (China's capital)	East Coast by Yangtze River
Population	6 million = city 25 million = province	4 million = city 11 million = province	13.5 million = city 60 million = province
Region characteristics	Low-cost manufacturing base for Hong Kong. Most flexible for business approvals and hiring.	Government ministries. Second-largest retail center and strong industrial base.	8.5% of China's industrial output. Cultural and commercial capital.
Foreign companies	Avon, Colgate, P&G, and Amway.	Shiseido, L'Oréal	Johnson & Johnson, Unilever
Consumer characteristics	Unrefined. Main interest is food and family, but more interested in glamor.	Rigid, bureaucratic; more cerebral.	Elegant, vain, tough negotiators; seek quality.
Typical wage level	$200/month, highest consumer goods spending in China. Flooded by foreign consumer goods.	$80/month but rising level of affluence in the last two years.	Over $100/month. Highest spending on clothing, cosmetics, jewelry. (Estimates = 30% disposable income.)

the Guangzhou consumer market as very similar to Hong Kong's and believed that consumer characteristics of the two markets would continue to converge.

Beijing

Beijing consumers were generally characterized as conservative and serious. Less concerned with appearances than Shanghai consumers, they spent less on clothing and personal-care products. However, Beijing, being the home of senior government and party officials, had an elite group of consumers interested in luxury goods and designer labels. Consumers were also characterized as straightforward and honest; advertisements based on fact and information were well received. Before making a major purchase, Beijing consumers would be well versed on the technical aspects of the product. On the other hand, these consumers also appeared to be more willing to try new products, and new brand launches were often initially more successful than in Shanghai.

Shanghai

As the largest city, Shanghai was the commercial and cultural center of China. Shanghai consumers were characterized as proud and very concerned about their appearances. While not the wealthiest consumers in China, they were known as the best dressed and smartest looking. Shanghai consumers spent a significantly greater proportion of their disposable income on clothing, jewelry, and personal-care products than their counterparts elsewhere in China, and premium-priced products and brands moved better in Shanghai than anywhere else. Shanghainese acknowledged and even took pride in the historical European and Western influences on their city and personal habits. Housing conditions however, were distinctly worse in Shanghai than in most other cities in China.

Shanghai was also the manufacturing center of China, and Shanghai goods were recognized as among the best in the country. As a result, Shanghai consumers were more loyal to their local brands than other Chinese consumers were. Considered the most influential market in China, it was believed that a successful launch in Shanghai was likely to be able to be extended to the rest of China, whereas a marketing program which worked in Beijing or Guangzhou would not necessarily work in Shanghai.

Products

Within the skin care category of the Chinese cosmetics market, the main product claims being made were prevention and removal of wrinkles; reduction of premature aging; absorption into and the effect upon functions of the skin; environmental protection; making skin snow-white, smooth, and more elastic; healing acne; and purifying pores. Within the makeup category, Avon's Cake Foundation claimed to complement oily skins and give complexions a smooth, matte finish.

Packaging was much more basic than in the United States or Japan. Skin care products were mainly marketed in plastic or glass jars with decorated or colored caps. Labels were applied or jar screened (stamped directly onto the jar) and carried both English and Chinese copy. Outer packaging was less common and varied widely in the quality of carton and liners used. Inserts ranged from instructions on thin paper in Chinese only to color brochures with pictures and illustrations in both English and Chinese.

Distribution

State-owned department stores with 280,000 outlets accounted for 40% of all consumer product retail sales. Collectively owned stores, of which there were 1.2 million, accounted for 32%, while 8 million individually owned stores accounted for 20% of retail sales. The remaining sales were made through 330 joint venture stores (5% of sales) and direct-selling companies (3%). Some observers argued that the Chinese distribution system was more accessible to U.S. companies than the Japanese system. However, it was even more fragmented.

Cosmetics displays in stores tended to be confusing and cluttered with many brands. In department stores however, imported brands were sold in separate cases from domestic products. Three price tiers existed: imported brands such as Dior retailed at eight times the retail prices of China-manufactured brands of Western/Chinese joint ventures and at 15 times those of local brands. Cosmetic companies rented cosmetic cases and shelf space from the department stores and paid the wages of the department store clerks.

Advertising

In 1992, per capita advertising spending in China was less than $1.00 but was expected to increase by 174% between 1992 and 1995. Newspapers were small and fragmented and rarely used for print advertising. Regional or provincial television channels were more popular than the single national channel, and advertising on the national television channel was more liable to censorship. A satellite television channel broadcast from Hong Kong, Star TV, could be accessed by 4.8 million households in China, and advertising costs through this channel averaged $0.50 per 1,000 people.

The cost of television advertising varied according to the status of the advertiser. The cost of a 30-second prime-time advertisement on provincial television in Guangzhou province in May 1993 was $200 for a local company, $500 for a joint-venture partnership, and $2,000 for a foreign importer. In Guangzhou City, these costs were about 40% of those for advertising to the entire province. For a foreign importer, the cost of a 30-second prime-time advertisement on Chinese national television was $4,000, compared to $9,000 on Hong Kong television.

Competitors

Foreign competitors in China in 1992 included Avon, Johnson & Johnson, Kao, Unilever, L'Oréal, Procter & Gamble, Revlon, and Shiseido. However, their combined sales accounted for only 3% of the market. (Exhibit 14 lists the main cosmetics products and brands available in China in 1992; Exhibit 15 provides comparative-pricing data for the major cosmetics product segments.)

In 1992, Avon was the first and only direct-selling cosmetics company in China. Avon had established a joint venture with the Guangzhou Cosmetics Factory (GCF) in which it owned 60% of the equity. GCF owned 35%, with the remaining 5% split between two Hong Kong business partners who had provided introductions to Chinese government officials. Avon operated only in the southern province of Guangdong. Sales in 1991 were about $4 million and rose to $8 million in 1992. Avon offered a full product line of 170 items (including a product that was a skin toner, moisturizer, and cleanser all in one), selling for an average of $4.00 each. Sales of skin-whitening products were especially strong. It was estimated that half the items were imported.

In 1993, Avon used television advertising to promote product benefits and print advertising to recruit salespeople. Products were sold by about 15,000 Avon Ladies, mostly part-timers, who kept their regular state jobs to retain their housing subsidies, medical benefits, and pensions. Salespeople sold Avon products for whatever markup they could achieve. On average, they were believed to earn a 30% margin on product sales. Avon distributed its products through 10 branch depots located throughout Guangdong. Two hundred sales managers, who were salaried employees, oversaw 4,500 franchise dealers, who in turn managed the sales representatives. A training program for the franchise dealers included classes on product benefits, cosmetics and skin care, and general business management.

Avon positioned itself as offering consumers service, quality, reliability, and product guarantees; the latter, in particular, was a new concept for the Chinese consumer. Typical Avon consumers were urban women, aged between 20

Exhibit 14 *Partial Listing of Skin Care Cosmetics Products Sold in China, 1992**

Brand/Product	Manufacturer
Avon Rich Moisture Face Cream	Avon (joint venture)
Avon Skinplicity	Avon (joint venture)
Ballet Pearl Beautifying Cream	Cosmetic Factory of Nanjing China
Ballet Pearl Cream	China Light Industrial Products Import and Export
Ballet Silk Peptide UV Defense Cream	Nanjing Golden Ballet Cosmetic Co. Ltd.
Bong Bao Maifanite Face-Beautifying Honey	Dongyang Mun Cosmetics Works, Zhejiang Provence
Bong Bao Maifanite Pearl Cream	Dongyang Mun Cosmetics Works, Zhejiang Provence
Dabao Instant Anti-Wrinkle Cream	Beijing Sanlu Factory
Lan Normolee Moisturizing Cream	International Gottin Cosmetics
Lorensa U.S.A. Retin-A Nourish Cream	Lorensa Cosmetics U.S.A.
Lychee Brand Pianzihuang Pearl Cream	Made in chemical factory for domestic use, Zhangzhou, Fujian, China
	Supervised by Pharmacy Industry Corporation, Fujian, China
Maxam Cleansing Lotion	Maxam Cosmetics (joint venture with S.C. Johnson)
Maxam	Maxam Cosmetics (joint venture with S.C. Johnson)
Meidi Beautiful Youth Nourish Cream	Grand Blom Co. Ltd., Hong Kong
Monica Beauty Skin Cleanser	Formulated in France
Montana Anti-Wrinkle Cream	Concord Group U.S.A. (joint venture)
Montana Bleaching Cream	Concord Group U.S.A. (joint venture)
Qinxiang Day Cream	Guangzhou Cosmetic Factory
Rhoure Ulan Cream	Guangzhou First Lab Cosmetics Industry
	Thailand First Lab Chemical Products Co. Ltd.
Ruby Nourishing Cream	S.C. Johnson (joint venture)
Swiss Natural Silk Cream	Wuxi Novel Daily Chemical Co. Ltd.
Ximi	—
Yue-Sai Protective Moisturizer	—
Ying Fong	Nan Yuan Ying Fong Group Co.

*Source: Company research.

and 35 years. Many were thought to live with their parents and spend their disposable incomes on Western goods. Compared with other imported brands, Avon was thought to be popular with younger women because Avon products were reasonably priced, and purchase—either at work or at home—was considered convenient. In addition, Avon Ladies gave their good cus- tomers a 10% to 20% discount on volume purchases and received "finder's fees" for recruiting salespeople.

By 1993, Avon had achieved a beachhead in China, but several problems were evident. Inflation was forcing frequent pay increases for Avon's trained, salaried employees, many of whom were receiving attractive job offers from

Exhibit 15 *Indexed Retail Prices of Domestic Joint-Venture and Imported Cosmetics in China by Product Category, 1992* *

Product	Domestic Joint-Venture Products			Imported Products		
	Shanghai	Guangzhou	Beijing	Shanghai	Guangzhou	Beijing
Moisturizer	100	45	121	703	341	418
Cleanser	163	57	70	459	354	366
Toner	43	72	NA	340	368	NA
Mask	NA	104	NA	NA	400	NA
Day cream	48	55	76	345	351	373
Night cream	57	100	88	354	397	385
Pearl cream	45	84	NA	341	381	NA
Nourishing cream	55	58	83	352	354	380
Hand/body lotion/cream	37	43	68	333	340	364
Eye cream	NA	69	88	NA	366	385
Anti-aging cream	18	23	53	315	320	350
Whitening lotion	39	22	80	335	318	377
Lipstick	85	59	41	381	356	337
Cheek color	NA	72	NA	NA	368	NA
Foundation	71	128	NA	367	425	NA
Nail polish	40	72	32	337	368	328
Perfume	117	98	NA	413	394	NA

*Source: Company reports.

other direct-marketing firms. Avon's salaried employees were also demanding that the company provide housing, as state-owned enterprises had traditionally done. In addition, Avon had not received the permanent discount off of the standard 30%–40% retail turnover tax and the temporary exclusivity for the direct marketing of cosmetics in Guangzhou that executives believed they had negotiated with the provincial government.[7]

Shiseido had established a joint-venture company, Shiseido Liyuan Cosmetics Co., with Beijing Liyuan in 1987. Products were sold under the brand name Huazi, and cumulative sales during the first five years after the launch were estimated at $80 million. Shiseido positioned itself as offering high-quality, technologically sophisticated products. The company offered 15 items, at prices ranging from $4 to $6, in four product categories: eye makeup; hair care; nail care; and skin care.

MKC in China

In addition to choosing a location, MKC could choose to enter the Chinese market either by designating a licensed distributor or negotiating a joint-venture agreement with a Chinese partner. Joint ventures were the most common structures Western companies used for entering China. Negotiations always involved government bodies and took an average of two years to complete. Successful joint ventures, such as those set up by Pepsi and Colgate-Palmolive, emphasized a careful search for the right partner, an in-depth market feasibility study, patience and a long-term

[7]"Avon Calling," *Business China,* Economist Intelligence Unit, July 12, 1993, pp. 1–2.

commitment to the investment, and a strong focus on training and developing local management. MKC could also choose to build a manufacturing facility as Gillette and Amway had, to expand and upgrade an existing production facility as Avon had, to subcontract manufacturing, or simply to import products from the United States. It was estimated that the construction of a one-million-square-foot manufacturing plant would take two years and cost over $20 million.

Timing was considered critical in the decision to enter the Chinese market: Avon was still marketing only in the South; the number of cosmetics competitors was increasing; and the retail infrastructure was expected to continue to improve.

MARKET ENTRY DECISION

One critical issue in deciding which markets to enter, and in what order, was the acceptability and potential success of MKC's party plan approach to sales in the two markets. In Japan, Tupperware had pioneered the use of party plans, which were then successfully used by a number of companies. By 1992, party plans had become an established and accepted sales technique in Japan. On the other hand, to date, no company had attempted the party plan approach in China. In 1992, MKC conducted a number of focus groups to help determine the acceptability and potential success of this sales approach. Initial findings suggested that the party plan method would be well-received in China. However, most homes were small, and living conditions in Shanghai were particularly difficult, and people did not, as a rule, entertain in their homes. In terms of consultant recruiting, results indicated that some Chinese women were entrepreneurial, placed an emphasis on learning and self-development, and were strongly attracted to a flexible financial opportunity that would enable them to supplement their state salaries. The focus group results indicated that Chinese women were interested in cosmetics and very eager to learn more about products and how best to use them. Dandurand believed that MKC could implement a successful party plan operation in China but that resources would be needed to explain and communicate the concept to both potential consultants and consumers.

Marketing Mix Options
Product Line

Dandurand believed that it was essential for MKC to enter any market with both skin care and makeup products. She explained: "The two product groups both depend on consumer education. First, we teach consumers how to care for their skin and demonstrate the available treatments, then how to use glamour products to enhance their natural beauty."

Individual products in both lines would require local adaptation. Developing a product line to meet the exacting government regulations and demanding consumers of Japan would require roughly three times as much time and resources as developing a line for the Chinese market. Some MKC executives argued that the product line should be adapted as little as necessary. They believed that, with the exception of certain shades of makeup, the current product line was already global in appeal.

Positioning

Assuming MKC would be marketing both the skin care and makeup products, Dandurand had to decide whether the company should be positioned as a "glamour provider," offering makeup products and expertise combined with some skin care products, or as a "skin treatment" expert that also provided makeup products. Other decisions would include the level of emphasis to place in MKC communications on the career opportunities and consumer-training aspects of the MKC organization and what messages to use to communicate them. To help with the latter, MKC conducted recruitment research in Taiwan, Japan, and China in early 1993. The results of this study are given in Exhibit 16.

In Japan, Dandurand believed that competitive differentiation was key to success but was

Exhibit 16 *Recruitment Study in Taiwan, Japan, and China, 1993* *

	Taiwan	**Japan**	**China**
Ideal Life Aspirations	Would like to work as long as they can take care of their family.	Key aspiration is to get married and be a good mother/wife.	Most women have government-sponsored jobs.
	Personal fulfillment and increased knowledge are important.	Lead fulfilling and satisfying personal lives and enjoy themselves.	Would like to reduce the number of nonproductive hours of work, expand their knowledge and feel more productive.
Jobs and Careers	Career: perceived as involving risk, long-term commitment and higher financial rewards.	Career: image of independence not positive.	Career: Sounded far-fetched, an alien concept.
	Job: no risk, short-term way to make money.	Do not feel that it is possible to combine career and family.	Job: Only vehicle to earn money. Earning money perceived as a way to become independent, gain social acceptance and self-esteem.
	To work is to gain self-confidence.	Job: Should be enjoyable and flexible, a hobby to pass time.	
		Interest was not in earning an income.	
Role Model Images	Self-confident, independent but not tough. Good relationship with family. Nice environment and surroundings.	Good mother figure. Happy family. Children playing. Husband and wife.	Pretty, youthful, well dressed. Romantic and relaxing life.
			Nice environment and surroundings.
			Career women type only prominent among younger, white-collar workers.

*Source: Based on in-depth focus groups.

unsure what the basis of differentiation should be and which age group to target. One proposed modification of MKC's U.S. strategy was a buying club, similar to those offered by Avon, Menard, and Noevir. This would accelerate the recruitment of consultants, would be more consistent with competition, and would offer women the discounts on products and purchase convenience that they wanted. However, some MKC executives argued that this approach was inconsistent with MKC's emphasis on offering consultants a career opportunity and professional consumer training, and that it would not differentiate MKC from other direct-selling companies operating in Japan.

Pricing

Even taking product development costs into account, it was estimated that unit margins obtained on products sold in Japan would be at least twice as high as for corresponding products sold in China. Dandurand, however, pointed out that startup costs, office overheads, and advertising expenditures could be somewhat lower in China and that a Chinese market entry was expected to break even within 24 months as opposed to three to five years for Japan.

Dandurand wondered how MKC products should be priced in relation to both domestic and foreign competitors, particularly Avon, to support her positioning decision, and whether to replicate the U.S. consultant compensation scheme or to adopt consultant compensation that matched competitors' programs and local economics.

Promotion

In either market, consultant recruitment programs would have to be developed, backed by print advertising, public relations, and public service workshops on women's issues. In Japan, MKC was considering establishing a toll-free number, distributing videos, organizing career opportunity seminars, and/or developing a traveling showroom to target consumers in the suburbs. Dandurand wondered what the best ways to reach potential consultants and consumers in China might be.

Building the necessary level of MKC brand awareness among consumers in Japan would require at least $3 million per year in advertising. To create comparative brand awareness levels in one region of China might require $400,000 in advertising per year for the first three years.

In order to compare the economics of the two market entry options, Dandurand made the preliminary calculations summarized in Exhibit 17.

Exhibit 17   *Preliminary Estimates of the First Year Economics of Market Entry: Japan and China*

	Japan	China
Average retail unit price U.S. $	$25.00	$9.00
Average MKC wholesale unit price	$12.50	$4.50
Cost of goods	$ 2.30	$1.20
Freight and duty	$ 0.75	$1.28
Gross margin	$ 9.45	$2.02
Product development costs/year	$ 0.9 million	$0.1 million
Promotion and advertising costs/year	$ 3.0 million	$0.4 million
Management overhead/year	$ 0.4 million	$0.25 million
Start-up investment costs	$10.0 million	$2.0 million

VIETNAM: MARKET ENTRY DECISIONS

In May 1996, three U.S.-based multinational corporations (MNCs) were considering whether to enter Vietnam, and, if so, how. The world's twelfth most populous nation, Vietnam was being widely discussed as a future "Asian dragon" because of the rapid economic growth and substantial inbound foreign direct investment (FDI) which had been stimulated by an ongoing series of liberalizing economic reforms in the previous 10 years. Opinion was divided, however, on the political and economic future of the country, which remained a one-party Communist state.

A number of U.S.-based MNCs were already operating in Vietnam, having entered immediately after the lifting of the U.S. trade embargo by President Clinton in February 1994. First to market, amid much publicity, had been PepsiCo. Only seven hours after the embargo was lifted, it had started production in a bottling plant in which it had invested with Vietnamese and Singaporean partners, and the following evening PepsiCo placed advertisements featuring Miss Vietnam on national TV. Other early entrants, which had also been poised to enter at the earliest opportunity, included Motorola, Boeing, and several banks and accounting firms. These U.S.-based MNCs faced competition from many Asian and European corporations attracted by the potential growth in the Vietnamese market. A recent survey identified Vietnam as one of the most promising countries for future Japanese investment (see Exhibit 1).

The three MNCs had each had been approached, both in their Asian offices and in the United States, by numerous potential distributors, joint-venture partners, and consultants offering advice on market entry. The decision they faced was summarized by one consultant as follows:

It's a very difficult call. Vietnam is a large market in its own right, and it has a plentiful, well-educated, and low-cost workforce. Because it was one of the last countries to open its doors, it has been able to cherry-pick what it considers best practice from the emerging markets which have preceded it. What it has achieved so far is remarkable, especially when you remember that it's still run by the Communist Party. That's partly due to the Vietnamese, who are generally hard-working, and, especially in the south, entrepreneurial. But the government does seem genuinely commit-

---

Assistant Professor David J. Arnold and Professor John A. Quelch prepared this case. Company names have been disguised. Copyright © 1996 by the President and Fellows of Harvard College. Harvard Business School case 597-020.

Exhibit 1 *Survey of Japanese Corporations: Most Promising Countries for Future Investment* *

During the Next Three Years	Ranking in 1995 Survey	No. of 336 Respondents Citings	Ranking in 1994 Survey	No. of 238 Respondents Citings
China	1	248	1	169
Thailand	2	122	2	75
Indonesia	3	110	4	58
U.S.	4	108	3	72
Vietnam	5	95	6	34
Malaysia	6	73	5	57
India	7	57	10	14
Philippines	8	52	10	14
Singapore	9	32	7	33
U.K.	10	24	9	19

During the Next 10 Years	Ranking in 1995 Survey	No. of 274 Respondents Citings	Ranking in 1994 Survey	No. of 284 Respondents Citings
China	1	215	1	265
Vietnam	2	113	2	114
India	3	98	7	38
U.S.	4	83	4	85
Indonesia	5	66	5	83
Thailand	6	66	3	92
Burma	7	40	-	-
Malaysia	8	35	6	44
Philippines	9	31	10	19
U.K.	10	16	-	-

*Source: Adapted from Export-Import Bank of Japan data.

ted to reform, and so far the transition has been remarkably smooth.

At the same time, there are still plenty of things about Vietnam that worry Western firms. Top of everyone's list are the corruption, the bureaucracy, and the lack of infrastructure. Also, the Communist Party has every intention of keeping firm control and retains some unnerving powers, such as the right to buy into foreign companies or to decide the level of profits on which it will collect taxes. The pessimists had a field day in February, when the government dismantled all foreign-language billboards and painted out all foreign brand names *on signs in Hanoi and Ho Chi Minh City, as part of its campaign against "social evils."*

It's early days yet. When you visit Vietnam, it still looks mostly undeveloped. The airports haven't been fully rehabilitated from the war, the roads are awful, and there's little sign of industrial development. But get into the city, and you'll find your hotel full of business visitors, you'll see the first tower blocks going up, the place is full of energy, and the streets are lined with small shops piled high with Western products. I've spoken to quite a few American managers who were sent here to assess the market entry situation, only to find their products already on sale all over the city. Some of it was counterfeit product, but some was genuine and had found its way here from other Asian markets.

Many companies I've spoken to are playing wait-and-see, but the market is open for business, and other firms are hoping for rich returns from getting in early.

COUNTRY PROFILE

The Socialist Republic of Vietnam was established in 1975 when, following decades of war, the country was reunified under the Communist leadership of Ho Chi Minh. Vietnam had been partitioned into a Communist north and a French-backed south by the 1955 Geneva Accords, following the defeat of the French colonial forces by Ho Chi Minh's army at Dien Bien Phu. Continuing tensions and the increasing support of both Cold War military alliances soon led to renewed war, which ended in 1975 with the withdrawal of American forces from the southern capital of Saigon (subsequently renamed Ho Chi Minh City). In 1996, all aspects of government were still controlled by the Vietnamese Communist Party and its Politbureau from the capital, Hanoi, in the north of the country. Ho Chi Minh City, the country's largest city, was regaining its former status as the commercial center of the nation. (See Exhibit 2 for a map of Vietnam.)

Doi moi ("economic renovation") was officially launched at the Vietnamese Communist Party's 1986 Congress, and the subsequent reforms included deregulation of prices, reduction of subsidies to state enterprises, ending of the collective agricultural system, new commercial-ownership laws to encourage private enterprise, new foreign investment laws, and policies directed toward the stabilization and convertibility of the Vietnamese currency, the *dong*. These reforms transformed a previously distressed economy (in 1986, inflation averaged 775%) into one of the fastest-growing in the world. Economic indicators and comparative data for the principal Asian economies are reported in Exhibits 3 and 4. In 1996, the legislative program was continuing within the government's policy framework of "market socialism," which aimed to create a market-oriented economy under the control of the state.

This economic growth had been fueled principally by foreign direct investment (FDI) and the establishment of new private Vietnamese-owned organizations. The state-owned sector accounted for 40% of GDP in 1995 and comprised approximately 6,000 state-owned enterprises (SOEs), half the number that had existed in 1990. To date only three of these SOEs had been privatized ("equitized"). Government policy was to encourage foreign joint ventures with SOEs and to establish conglomerates in key industries following the model of the South Korean *chaebols*. By 1995, 17 such conglomerates had been established in industries such as telecommunications, electricity, cement, steel, and garment manufacture. A Vietnamese government trade official described the objectives of this policy:

We are changing regulations and reducing tariffs to attract sufficient foreign investment to stimulate industrial growth, but not so much that it stifles the growth of Vietnamese industry. The number of licenses granted in each industrial sector will be limited, and tariffs will be managed to balance imports and local production in line with this policy.

Exhibit 2 *Map of Southeast Asia*

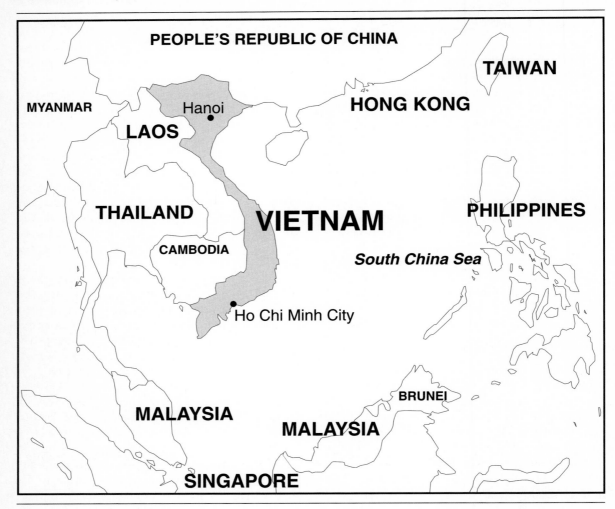

Foreign investment commitments worth almost $8 billion were made in 1995, twice the level of the previous year, bringing the total cumulative commitment since the launch of *doi moi* to approximately $20 billion for over 1,300 approved projects. The total GDP of Vietnam in 1995 was $19 billion. FDI projects in Vietnam averaged $14 million to $15 million of investment, compared with a $1 million average in the People's Republic of China. Approximately $8 billion of these commitments had been realized, of which $4 billion had been realized during 1995. The four largest sources of FDI were Taiwan (total cumulative commitment, $3.3 billion), Hong Kong ($2.2 billion), Japan ($2 billion), and Singapore ($1.6 billion), followed in rank order by South Korea, Australia, Malaysia, and France. U.S.-sourced FDI totaled approximately

Exhibit 3   *Vietnam—Economic Data**

	1995	1994	1993	1992
GDP (U.S. $ millions)	19,100	13,900	12,800	9,900
Real GDP growth (%)	9.5%	8.5%	8.1%	7.8%
Exports (U.S. $ millions)	5,200	4,250	3,010	2,600
Imports (U.S .$ millions)	7,520	5,850	3,900	2,550
Retail price inflation	14.2%	15.5%	6.5%	17.8%

*Source: Adapted from Economist Intelligence Unit data.

$1 billion since the lifting of the trade embargo in February 1994, making the United States the tenth-largest source of foreign investment, and was increasing sharply. The major investment sectors were oil and gas, hotels and commercial real estate, telecommunications, services, and light manufacturing. In addition, Vietnam was pledged international aid worth $2.3 billion for 1996, a 15% increase on the previous year, although many previous pledges had never materialized. The largest donor of foreign aid, which was intended primarily for infrastructure projects, was Japan.

Local private investment was running at approximately the same level as FDI, with some 20,000 private firms registered by the end of 1995. Local entrepreneurs faced a shortage of capital, given the country's low saving rate and underdeveloped banking sector. A significant contributor of both capital and human resources was the Vietnamese diaspora. The majority of the two million ethnic Vietnamese living abroad (the *Viet Kieu*) had fled from the south as the war ended in 1975 and had found refuge in North America, Western Europe, or Australasia. It was estimated that in 1994, 250,000 Vietnamese families had received a total of $500 million from relatives living abroad. In 1994, the Vietnamese government reversed its previous policy and instituted preferential terms for

Exhibit 4   *Comparative Performance Data for Asian Countries**

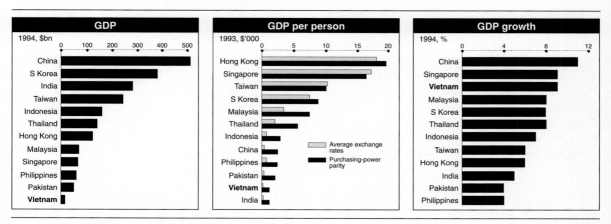

*Source: Adapted from Deutsche Bank data.

Viet Kieu returning to their homeland, including classification as domestic residents for the purposes of taxation and the establishment of joint ventures. The greatest concentration of repatriated *Viet Kieu* was found in Ho Chi Minh City, where their entrepreneurial activities and taste for Western products contributed to that city's status as the commercial center of the nation.

Vietnam's population of 74 million, growing at 2% per annum, was the world's twelfth largest and one of its most youthful: in 1995, approximately 50% of the population was aged 21 or younger. With a national literacy rate of 90%, the Vietnamese workforce was also one of the best educated among emerging markets in Asia. The recent economic growth had yet to change the living standards of the majority of the population, however. A 1994 World Bank report which praised the country's "impressive economic progress" also pointed out that 51% of the population lived in poverty. GDP per capita was $235 in 1995, compared to $2,000 in neighboring Thailand, with four televisions per 100 population (11 in Thailand) and 0.3 telephones per 100 population (3.1 in Thailand). These averages disguised wide variation between the major cities, where economic growth had been concentrated, and the countryside, still home to 80% of the population. This discrepancy, along with increasing pressure on agricultural land caused by population growth, was leading to significant migration to the cities. About 13% of Vietnamese lived in Ho Chi Minh City and Hanoi. Unemployment was estimated at 12%.

Vietnam joined the Association of South East Asia Nations (ASEAN) in July, 1995.[1] Membership entailed participation in the ASEAN Free Trade Area (AFTA), one of the targets of which was to reduce tariffs on trade between member countries to a maximum of 5% by 2003, a dead-

line extended to 2006 for Vietnam. In the same month, Vietnam signed a cooperation agreement with the European Union (EU), which gave Vietnamese goods Most Favored Nation (MFN)[2] status in the 15 EU countries and vice versa, and included a schedule of increased European aid to Vietnam. The restoration of full diplomatic relations with the United States, also in July 1995, allowed the opening two months later of negotiations regarding trade normalization between the countries, including MFN status. American officials demanded as preconditions for granting of MFN status agreement, on the issue of American military personnel unaccounted for after the end of the war, and clarification of "the legal framework, intellectual property rights, trade practices, foreign exchange controls, human and labor rights."

Forms of Market Participation

A number of entry modes were possible for an international firm seeking to do business in Vietnam. All had to be agreed by the State Committee for Co-operation and Investment (SCCI).

The simplest arrangement was for an MNC to appoint a Vietnamese import agency and export finished product to that agent from outside Vietnam. Formerly, this would have required an international firm to deal with one of nine state-owned import organizations, but recent reforms had extended the granting of import licenses to privately owned Vietnamese firms, and an increasing number of such small distributors were eagerly seeking to represent foreign MNCs. Imported products were subject to tariffs, which had been introduced to replace import quotas as part of the *doi moi* reforms. In early 1996 these tariffs ranged from 5% to 100% and averaged

---

[1]The other members of ASEAN were Brunei, Indonesia, Malaysia, Philippines, Singapore, and Thailand.

[2]In a trade treaty between two countries, agreement upon an MFN clause required that each country would trade with the other on terms at least as favorable as those agreed upon with any other country.

25%, but were subject to frequent government revision and were inconsistently applied by customs officials. In addition to a license granting importer status, a separate product-specific license was required for the import or export of any item, however small, which had to be applied for with the bill of lading at least a week before the item was expected to arrive at the Vietnamese port of entry. Open licenses valid for six months for specified items could be granted to joint ventures, BCCs, or foreign-owned ventures; otherwise, a license had to be obtained for each consignment.

MNCs wishing to invest in Vietnam had a variety of options. The government policy encouraged *joint ventures* between local SOEs and international organizations, and, in order to attract inbound investment, regulations permitted up to 70% ownership by foreign partners. The Vietnamese partner usually contributed its workforce, premises, equipment, and land use rights, the valuation of which could be problematic. The Foreign Investment Law included a buy-in stipulation, under which local parties could be granted the right to acquire an increasing share of foreign-owned ventures. In any joint venture designated by the government as an "important economic establishment" (mostly infrastructure development and energy industry projects), there was a legal requirement for the local partner to increase periodically its capital stake (and therefore equity share) in the project. A majority equity share did not bestow managerial control, however, as the law required unanimous voting by directors.

Government approval for *wholly foreign-owned* organizations was granted only in rare cases, typically large and complex projects, where joint ventures were not feasible. Like joint ventures, these organizations were limited to a 70-year life.

A *processing contract* allowed a foreign corporation to use a Vietnamese factory for production or assembly. If the products were intended for export, the foreign company could import necessary raw materials, could provide some of the equipment in the factory, and then re-export. To attract this type of venture, five Export Processing Zones (EPZs) had been created, offering reduced taxation levels and ongoing investment in infrastructure. Their reputation had suffered, however, from problems with power supply and water shortages, and the EPZ in Haiphong collapsed in late 1995 after the 70% owner, based in Hong Kong, declared bankruptcy. The most successful EPZ, Tan Thuan near Ho Chi Minh City, had attracted 60 projects. More recently, more projects had been established in new Industrial Processing Zones (IPZs), intended as centers for both domestic and export production. A number of consumer goods firms, including producers of cigarettes, soft drinks and beer, had licensed manufacturers for small-scale production while awaiting approval of their joint-venture applications for larger new production facilities.

A *business cooperation contract* allowed a private Vietnamese enterprise and a foreign partner freedom to design their own contract, and no legal entity was established. Such an arrangement required submission to the SCCI of annual accounts, from which the SCCI calculated the profit it deemed the venture to have made, and levied taxes on the two partners at differential rates.

In 1995, the Vietnamese government published a list of major infrastructure projects which qualified for *build-operate-transfer* ventures. Under such an arrangement, a foreign organization would be allowed to build a property, such as a power station or a toll road, and then retain the profit from its operation for a specified time period, at the end of which it would be transferred to Vietnamese ownership without further compensation.

Finally, foreign companies could be granted a license to establish a *representative office* in Vietnam. The role of such offices was restricted to promotion of international trade or technical support for local importers or exporters, and such offices were prohibited from engaging in investment, trading, or marketing.

All forms of market participation were subject to approval by the SCCI and in many cases also required separate approval by additional government ministries or by people's committees at the regional or city level. Consultants all warned that the granting of licenses was not only complex and time-consuming but also unpredictable, as procedures were often improvised because of the incomplete regulatory framework. One MNC, seeking to obtain a 70% stake in a joint venture, was reported to have been required to pay 120 separate fees over three years to obtain the necessary licenses, of which only 40 were required by regulations.

Doing Business in Vietnam

A number of additional factors were highlighted by consultants and managers experienced in Southeast Asia as critical to any market entry strategy.

Distribution

Potential distribution partners were plentiful but tended to concentrate only on a specified area, often as small as a few blocks in one of the major cities. The choice facing any MNC was often between a distribution organization partly or wholly owned by the government, and a young but small privately owned distributor. The former would probably boast better connections with officials but might prove less aggressive in selling, while the latter would probably be more entrepreneurial but had yet to establish a customer base. National distribution required an extensive network of distribution partners; the Castrol oil company had to establish its own fleet of trucks to deliver motor oil to its many distribution points. The principal difficulty was described by one consultant as "telling the difference between the aggressive but competent distributor and the cowboys who will be knocking at your door as soon as you check into your hotel." He also warned that Vietnamese business tended to be based upon a "trading culture":

> *Traditionally, goods have been scarce, and consumer demand could be taken for granted if you managed to get your product to the market. . . . The emphasis is still on moving product quickly and negotiating over price, rather than what Western firms know as marketing or positioning. Honda has excelled at playing this game in selling motor scooters: the company appoints a large number of distributors, who then compete with each other to achieve the sales volumes they need to retain their agencies the following year. The result is that the cities are swarming with Honda motor scooters.*

Corruption

Despite a government campaign and an increase in criminal convictions, corruption was prevalent at all levels in both industrial and government sectors. One experienced Asian MNC executive described Vietnam as "the worst country in Asia" in this regard, and attributed the problem to the generally low salary levels and the lack of an official schedule of fees for licenses and permits. One Vietnamese-American owner of a small Ho Chi Minh City distribution company indicated that U.S. corporations were especially challenged by this problem: "Their legislation[3] means that, if one of their managers gets caught, the liability can spread back up through the corporation. It scares them stiff, and it can put them at a real competitive disadvantage alongside Asian and European companies."

Vietnam's long coastline and mountainous frontiers facilitated smuggling of goods into the country. Around 40% to 60% of the consumer electronics piled high at streetside stores in Ho Chi Minh City were said to be smuggled, as were 100% of the highly visible foreign cigarette brands (because they were formally prohibited).

---

[3]The Foreign Corrupt Practices Act.

U.S. products had been widely available in the major cities before the lifting of the trade embargo in 1994, including brands as varied as Kleenex (at three times the price of local brands) and Kodak (a number of Kodak processing outlets were in operation in Ho Chi Minh City as early as 1992). Executives from Castrol had reported competition from competitive brands of brake fluid that had been illegally imported as "motor oil" and thus charged only a 1% tariff instead of 35%.

Infrastructure

Years of war and economic hardship had left Vietnam with little infrastructure to support its ambitious economic reforms. The 1,000-mile trip between Hanoi and Ho Chi Minh City required five to eight days by Highway 1—the only road linking the north and south of the country—or two days by rail. Vietnam's two major ports, Ho Chi Minh City and Hai Phong, were both shallow-water harbors upriver from the sea, so large shipments had to be offloaded into smaller feeder ships at either Singapore, Hong Kong, or Kao Siung, Taiwan. Both ports also lacked capacity and equipment to cope with booming imports, as did the country's main airports. Delays were exacerbated by product loss or damage in transit running at rates as high as 25% to 50%. Office and production premises could be subject to periodic power outages and telecommunications blackouts.

Costs

One of the major attractions of Vietnam for foreign investors was the low level of labor costs. Typical monthly compensation in Ho Chi Minh City and Hanoi was $40 for an unskilled laborer (the legal minimum wage), $100 for a secretary, and $200 for an engineer or manager. Additional employment costs were typically 50% of compensation. Rates were one-third lower outside the two major cities. Although the level of basic education was good, managerial talent was

scarce. Foreign investors also faced high office rents, and the process of establishing an office was slowed by the need for land-use permits for all premises. Telecommunications costs were also high, up to $20 per minute for calls to the United States, for example. Both property and telecommunications costs were expected to fall with continued market development.

PROFILES OF THREE MULTINATIONAL CORPORATIONS

The three U.S. MNCs considering entry into Vietnam were all experienced in international operations, and all aspired to global leadership in their industries. Exhibit 5 summarizes their international distribution arrangements.

Chemical Corporation

Chemical was the world leader in chemical adhesives and sealants for industrial applications. The company's core product range, which always formed the introductory line when entering new markets, was positioned as a replacement technology, offering superior performance cost relative to more traditional mechanical fastenings and seals. The range of potential applications was wide, including virtually all manufacturing operations, after-market applications such as automotive servicing, and even some consumer applications. The firm marketed its specialty chemicals as low-volume, premium-priced, branded products and expected to have a diverse and fragmented customer base. This marketing strategy was built upon two major thrusts. First, sales personnel were trained to tailor their offering to the individual applications of customers. Most important, this entailed "pricing to value," which required an analysis of the long-term savings to the customer of performance improvements gained by switching from traditional and ostensibly cheaper technologies. Second, the firm strived to maintain technological leadership by requiring that 30% of revenues should flow from products introduced in the previous five years.

Exhibit 5 *International Distribution Organization of Multinational Corporations*

	Chemical Corp.	**Sports Corp.**	**Children Corp.**
Total Global Network:			
Independent distributors	11	30	5
Joint ventures	0	11	1
Direct distribution subsidiaries	45	17	30
Asia/Pacific Region:			
Independent distributors	Indonesia New Zealand	Australia Indonesia New Zealand	Philippines South Korea Taiwan Thailand
Joint ventures (MNC ownership 50% or less)		Philippines (33%) Hong Kong (33%) Singapore (33%) Malaysia (33%) Thailand (28%) Taiwan (25%)	
Direct distribution subsidiaries (100% unless shown)	Australia Hong Kong Indonesia Japan Malaysia People's Republic of China(75%) Philippines Singapore South Korea Taiwan Thailand	Hong Kong India (60%) South Korea (80%) People's Republic of China (66%) Japan (51%)	Australia Hong Kong Indonesia Japan Singapore

In support of these two strategies, Chemical, which enjoyed a 61% gross margin, invested 32% of its 1995 revenues in sales and marketing and 7% in R&D laboratories in the United States, Ireland and Japan. Chemical's executives, who estimated their market share as high as 80% in the domestic U.S. market, viewed their major challenge as market expansion.

International distribution was a strength. From its foundation, the firm had been approached by numerous distributors wishing to carry its products, and it was part of company lore that its products were crossing the Atlantic Ocean before they crossed the Mississippi River. The global distribution network had evolved independently of manufacturing operations, because of the low bulk-to-value nature of its products. By 1995, the company's manufacturing operations were located in the United States, Puerto Rico, Ireland, Costa Rica, Japan, and Brazil, with additional operations (to meet local regulatory requirements) in India and the People's Republic of China. This logistics network could supply new markets at short notice: the ex-Soviet-bloc countries of Eastern Europe, for instance, were supplied from Ireland via a warehouse in Vienna within three days of a new distributor being appointed and/or placing an order.

Chemical favored independent distributors for market entry because of their existing product ranges and customer base, which provided both economies of scope for the initial low-volume business, and access to industrial customers who felt no obvious need for this replacement technology. The firm emphasized training and support to distributors in the difficult selling challenge posed by its product range, and the higher margins it offered to the general industrial supply houses who made up the majority of its distributors. To encourage investment in business development, distributors were generally granted territorial exclusivity. In many cases, however, sales had reached a plateau after several years in market, and Chemical had switched to a direct distribution subsidiary. The slowdown in sales growth was variously attributed to the lack of marketing capability by the distributor or a lack of ambition to dominate the market (distributors were often small, privately owned organizations). In the words of the head of the firm's operations in China, "Our own people always outperform even the best distributors. They run out of steam because they don't immerse themselves in our technology and the benefits it can deliver to customers." All of Chemical's 45 national distribution subsidiaries had evolved from independent national distributors.

Chemical's vice-president for Asia/Pacific, based in Hong Kong, had been with the company for 30 years, the last 16 in Asia. The region accounted for 13% of corporate sales revenues in 1995 and had grown 21% since 1994. Over the previous two years, Chemical's Asian operations had been restructured in response to their growing size, and, by 1995, there were four mar-

keting subregions reporting to Hong Kong: Eastern Asia, which included Japan and South Korea; Greater China, comprising the People's Republic of China, Taiwan and Hong Kong; Central Asia, including India; and Southeast Asia, including Singapore, Malaysia, Indonesia, Philippines, and Thailand, along with Australia and New Zealand. The regional Hong Kong office comprised five executives and two support staff. Chemical's products would be subject to a 30% import tariff in Vietnam. The regional vice-president commented:

> A lot of our attention is focused on Asia these days because of slower growth in America and Europe and because so many of our U.S. manufacturing customers are setting up here. We have an established operation here in Hong Kong, and I know we can serve Vietnam well enough from our new logistics base in Singapore. If we exported into Vietnam, using a representative office to provide technical support, our products would be three or four times the price of the local or Chinese adhesives they are using at the moment.
>
> We have received six approaches from distributors wanting to represent us—four from Ho Chi Minh City, one from Hanoi, and one from a Viet Kieu working with our products in a major customer in California. Frankly, I don't know how to evaluate these potential distributors. I doubt if any of them have the sense of quality and service needed to represent Chemical and sell its products effectively. I suppose we could set up a representative office to provide technical support. We have also been approached by an SOE seeking to establish a manufacturing joint venture, but we're in India and the PRC already.

Sports Corporation

Sports Corporation, founded in 1978, enjoyed explosive growth in its youth- and fashion-oriented market for sports footwear and apparel. Still under the leadership of its founder, Sports ranked second in global market share in most of its product markets. The company contracted out virtually all its manufacturing to independent suppliers in Asia and viewed its core competences as product design and marketing expertise. Sports's success depended on the ability to deliver innovative products to a fast-changing and segmented market. As a result, brand building, advertising and promotion, endorsements by sports teams and celebrities, and retail channel relations were all especially important.

The majority of Sports's products would face a 40% import tariff on entering Vietnam, although for some the rate would be only 20%. Maintaining normal margins, Sports's cheapest pair of sneakers could retail for $35 a pair. In 1995, Sports's major competitor had established production in Vietnam under a processing contract. Although product from this plant was intended for re-export, it was thought that investment in production facilities would have a beneficial effect on the brand's market development in Vietnam. Sports executives commented that demand might prove stronger than in other emerging markets because of the high brand awareness spread by *Viet Kieu* returning from the United States and other countries.

Reflecting the values of its founder, Sports sought as its international distributors "entrepreneurs with their own money on the line and a fortune to be made from rapid growth." Distributors were given territorial exclusivity and considerable autonomy as incentives to invest in growing their business and responding to local market conditions.

Like Chemical, Sports Corporation had in several cases bought back its distribution rights from independent distributors and established a direct distribution subsidiary. The usual catalysts for this move were financial problems in the distributor, the limited capacity of the distributor to support the business once it had grown beyond a certain size, or the desire of the distributor principals to realize profits from the agency. In general, however, Sports preferred to "leave the business in the hands of the people who know the market best."

An alternative arrangement was a minority equity position in the distributor organization. Sports did not involve itself in operational decision making, but used its access to financial and market performance figures to exercise control on a "by-exception" basis. In addition, this arrangement enabled Sports to participate in the incremental revenue stream from any brand premium the distributor was able to extract above the cost-plus price at which the product was purchased from Sports.

The Asia/Pacific region accounted for 7% of Sports Corporation's sales in 1995. The firm's Asian marketing organization had been restructured in early 1996. The regional vice-president, who had previously led a single team in Hong Kong, relocated to Tokyo to head a North Asia unit and was replaced in Hong Kong by a vice president switched from Europe to take charge of the South Asia region.

The new regional vice-president commented:

Asian markets represent our biggest growth opportunity, but we've had a number of problems in the region, in particular the logistics of moving product around the markets and creating the right sort of retail environment for our brand. Vietnam embodies all these issues. It's a huge, booming, young market, but it's underdeveloped as yet. If we wait, and one of our major competitors gets in first, we may never catch up. But our results have been a little sluggish recently, and we must avoid too much exposure in high-risk markets.

So far, our U.S. headquarters has received seven letters of enquiry from potential distributors, and we have identified five additional candidates. One of these is a company which manufactures and exports jeans and also runs a chain of four modern sports equipment

stores in Ho Chi Minh City; they are also talk-
ing to our competitors. Right now, there are
only about 20 retail outlets where athletic
footwear is being sold in a half-decent manner.
There are a lot of counterfeits on the streets.

Children Corporation

Children Corporation, founded in 1945, was
the global leader in the manufacturing and marketing of branded toys. Against all industry
trends, Children integrated almost all its manufacturing, enabling it to reap economies of scale
and achieve new quality levels in a product range
of which 80% was new every year. By 1996, the
firm's 15 manufacturing plants were located in
the United States, Canada, Mexico, UK, Italy,
Malaysia, Indonesia, and the People's Republic
of China. Children used consumer packaged
goods marketing practices, such as co-promotions, in-store merchandising and, above all,
television advertising to expand its market. The
company had developed several well-known
brands within its product line, which provided a
backdrop of continuity to the annual seasonal
launch of its new products at the toy industry's
buying fairs. In addition, it had benefited in a
number of countries from a shake-up in the retail sector, with "category killer" hypermarkets
and new entrants such as Toys 'R' Us often transforming what the firm's senior executives claimed
had been a "cottage industry of mom-and-pop
stores."

The president of the international division
identified three key success factors:

First, we're the best at understanding chil-
dren's play patterns, which are pretty similar
around the world. Second, our manufactur-
ing operations can deliver good-quality inno-
vative product at the competitive price points
needed to open up the mass market. Third,
we communicate well with our market through
advertising, co-promotions with other enter-

tainment companies, and cooperation with
retailers in merchandising.

Children's early international growth had been
spearheaded by its business as a supplier of components to local toy manufacturers. Over time,
many of these OEM customers became assemblers, as manufacture became concentrated in a
small number of low-cost centers, principally
Hong Kong, and many took on distribution
agencies for Children's full line of toys. Major
growth outside North America had only been
achieved since the early 1980s, when Children
began switching to direct distribution subsidiaries. This era also saw an easing of the tariff
and advertising restrictions, which the firm argued had hindered its international development,
and an opening of previously specialist and protected distribution trades. Children's policy when
reacquiring an international distribution franchise was to install a new management team of
local managers headhunted from local subsidiaries of MNCs operating in other consumer
goods sectors. As described by one of the firm's
country managers: "Wholesalers, distributors,
and retailers are typically all servants of many
masters. They never want one player to grow
too strong. To gain market leadership, we have
to get control of our own business and inno-
vate." Despite this, Children recognized the value
of independent distributors as market entry
partners, given the closed character of distribution systems in many country markets, and had
never entered a new country market by establishing a wholly owned subsidiary at the outset.

Asia/Pacific was the firm's smallest region in
terms of sales revenue, accounting for 11% of
1995 sales, but was regarded as having the greatest long-term potential. Children's manufacturing operations, recently expanded by the installation of substantial new capacity in Indonesia,
were run as a stand-alone global division which
supplied the company's marketing organizations. The firm faced uneven demand due to the

seasonality of gift-giving, and therefore its coordinated production schedules were inevitably skewed to suit its largest markets at the expense of the smaller ones.

Children's vice-president for Asia/Pacific was located at U.S. corporate headquarters. A small team of four regional staff in Hong Kong aided Children's country managers. After an uneven history in Asia, attributed to the "complex and protectionist" distribution systems in the region, recent sales growth was strong, especially in Japan, where several previous ventures had ended in failure. The regional vice-president commented:

> *Some of my colleagues say it's far too early to enter Vietnam, because of the undeveloped retail sector. We need the right retail environment to support our brands, which despite our best efforts will be more expensive than the toys currently on offer. But I believe that we should appoint a distributor to start selling in Vietnam now. In fact, our best-selling products are already available in the airport duty-free shops in Ho Chi Minh City and Hanoi. Demand would be very concentrated in the two largest cities, so we could easily identify the special gift-oriented distribution channels. Also, television broadcasting is relatively advanced, so advertising would be possible from day one.[4]*
>
> *We have been approached by two SOEs that make toys. Their products are low quality and retail on average for $3 a unit, compared to our $15. However, these SOEs claim to have access to over 1,000 retail distribution points throughout the country, and the top managers in one of them seem young and aggressive. But I'd be concerned about our molds being duplicated without our knowledge. We have also been asked whether we'd be interested in a processing contract, using excess capacity at one of these SOEs to assemble our toys for export. Given current labor rates, we could save $1 a unit if we assembled some of our more labor-intensive toys in Vietnam.*

---

[4]Total advertising spending was $100 million in Vietnam in 1995, up from $31 million in 1994.

AIR MILES®

In December 1991, Keith Mills, founder and CEO of AIR MILES® Travel Promotions Limited (AMTP), headquartered in the United Kingdom, was considering the decisions that had to be made at the upcoming year-end board meeting. During 1991, he and his management team had been preparing an entry strategy for establishing their promotions company in North America. The launch, in both Canada and the United States, was planned for the spring of 1992; however, several critical decisions remained. These included determining (1) which elements of the U.K. marketing program could be transferred directly and which required adaptation; (2) whether the same marketing programs could be used in the United States and Canada; and (3) whether the programs should be driven by an association with grocery product manufacturers or grocery chain retailers. These strategy decisions would have implications for the introductory marketing mix.

COMPANY BACKGROUND

AMTP introduced an entirely new concept in the U.K. in 1988: a *frequent buyer* program that enabled customers to earn free air travel on British Airways (BA) for purchasing products and services from participating retailers, manufacturers, and service companies (known as sponsors). Mills conceived of AIR MILES while working with both airlines and gasoline retailers in his London advertising agency. His airline client, British Caledonian, was concerned about the hundreds of empty seats on its daily flights out of London's Gatwick airport. It was searching for a promotion that would increase passenger volume without diluting the core business. Meanwhile, other clients were looking for ways to differentiate their businesses from competitors in markets that were quickly becoming commoditized. On a train journey from Liverpool to London, Mills came up with the AIR MILES concept to solve these clients' problems. After several revisions, Mills was able to convince BA (British Caledonian had since been taken over by BA) to become a 51% partner in the venture.

On November 1, 1988, AIR MILES was launched in the U.K. The concept was positioned as a mass-market sales promotion program designed to reinforce consumer brand loyalty. As explained by Mills, the program was based on a

---

This case was prepared by Michele Calpin (under the direction of Professor John A. Quelch). Certain numerical data have been disguised. Copyright © 1993 by the President and Fellows of Harvard College. Harvard Business School case 593-102.

win-win-win philosophy. Participating sponsors (such as Shell) were able to reward their loyal customers and differentiate themselves from competitors by having the exclusive right in their product categories to offer AIR MILES vouchers. BA, the program's participating airline, gained incremental revenues on its excess low-variable-cost seats by providing them to AMTP at reduced rates. Finally, consumers were rewarded with credit vouchers redeemable for free flights when they purchased everyday products and services.

AMTP, as the program coordinator, gained its profits by charging sponsors for credit vouchers to distribute to their ultimate customers and by paying BA reduced rates for airline seats.

PROGRAM MARKETING

The product "AIR MILES" had two primary customers—the collector and the sponsor.

Collectors could earn free air travel on BA or discounts on packaged tour vacations if they enrolled in AMTP and collected miles when they purchased products and services from multiple participating sponsors. Participation in the program was free. (Table A summarizes some of the collection offers available.)

Each AIR MILES travel credit (AMTC) was worth one free mile of air travel. There was no

expiration date on the vouchers. Table B estimates the miles that households with different income levels might save.

Table B   Estimate of U.K. Household Collection Activity

Annual Household Income	Miles Saved per Year for Participating Households
£13,000	1,200
£20,000	2,000
£30,000	3,000

An average family could collect enough AMTC for one round-trip flight from London to Paris (450 miles) every three or four months. BA flight restrictions applied during peak travel periods, and trips had to be booked at least two weeks in advance. Collectors could book their free flights through appointed travel agents or by calling the AMTP Reservation Center.

The "other customer," the sponsor, was given the exclusive right in its category to distribute AIR MILES vouchers to its end consumers. Categories were defined as products or services of-

Table A   Selected U.K. AIR MILES Offers

Product/Service	Company	Miles
Life insurance policy	Royal Life Insurance	500
£40 Sports equipment	Champion Sports	20
£10 Credit card purchases	National Westminster Bank Access card	1
Men's suit	Burton's	200
£6 Gas	Shell	1
£5 Dry cleaning	Sketchley	1
Woman's dress	Dorothy Perkins	50
£30 DIY supplies	Texas Homecare	15
£119 Car rental	Hertz	90

fered for the same general purpose in the same geographic region. Contracts were signed for one-year periods, after which time sponsors could drop out without penalty. This category exclusivity motivated sponsors; they expected to increase their revenues from 3% to 30% per year from increased purchases by loyal shoppers and from the switchers attracted by the promotion program. In return, sponsors paid AMTP between 5 and 10 pence per AMTC,[1] depending on the volume of AMTC purchased and the strategic value of their category to the program. (An economic model for a typical sponsor is shown in Exhibit 1.) For many sponsors, the AIR MILES voucher was the ideal frequency reward. Unlike cash or merchandise, it represented a marginal cost to the sponsor that was a fraction of its value to the consumer (sponsors collectively paid for 25% to 80% of the consumer value of an airline ticket, depending on the flight distance). As a result, sponsors were able to offer a benefit to consumers for less than its market value. Further, no single sponsor needed to fund an entire airline ticket by itself.

By 1991, over 100 sponsors were participating in the program. They included consumer sector companies such as Shell Oil, Holiday Inn, Hertz, Toshiba, NatWest credit cards,[2] and Comet electronic stores. Business-to-business sponsors and employee motivation sponsors were also involved in the program, contributing about 20% of revenues. Business-to-business sponsors included Arthur Bell Distillers, Singer, and P.A. Consulting. This group used vouchers to generate trade interest in their products or to encourage increased purchases from their business customers. Employee motivational sponsors, such as IBM and Trust House Forte Hotels, used

vouchers as an employee incentive by offering AMTC to top performers.

AIR MILES' 1988 launch was designed to create awareness, educate the consumer about this new promotional vehicle, and stimulate mass enrollment. The U.K. consumer had to be educated on the concept of getting free air travel for buying goods and services. To launch the program, a £100,000 laser and firework spectacular was orchestrated in London's Docklands on November 1. The next day, a £6 million communications campaign began, incorporating television advertising, full-page national newspaper advertising, direct mailings to 10 million households, and intensive public relations. The 40-second television ads showed shoppers boarding a 747 plane parked in the main street of a small country town and encouraged viewers to "Stop dreaming. Start collecting." A hotline number and direct-response coupon were placed in print media to encourage enrollment. Two-thirds of the £6 million budget was spent in the first six weeks. The remainder was spread across the year.

Sponsors backed AMTP's activities by distributing 10 million point-of-sale leaflets in the first six weeks after launch and an additional 5 million in the first year. These detailed the program, informed consumers how to register, and listed the participating sponsors that were distributing vouchers. Window displays in the 10,000 storefronts of participating retail sponsors further publicized the program. Several sponsors ran their own promotions that incorporated AIR MILES; for example, *The Daily Express* national newspaper held a contest in February 1989 in which more than 10 entrants each won 22,000 mile trips while, in 1990, Shell Oil ran a half-million AMTC prize draw. Many sponsors supported the AMTP campaign with short television spots. With the added sponsor activity, a total of £24 million in media advertising and direct marketing supported AMTP in the first year after launch.

The initial communications program proved successful. After 8 weeks, 1.25 million households were registered and 300 million AMTC

---

[1] One U.K. pound (100 pence) was equivalent to $1.77 U.S.
[2] The National Westminster Bank was the principal issuer in the United Kingdom of Master-Card credit cards under the brand name Access.

Exhibit 1   *Economic Model for a Typical U.K. Sponsor*

AIR MILES Promotion Offer:

£0–39 in purchases	0 AMTC
£40–79 in purchases	10 AMTC
£80+ in purchases	20 AMTC

Model Assumptions:

% of current customers collecting AMTC[a]	40.00%
% increase in visits through new customer activity	1.62%

Current Customers—no behavior change:

Total customer visits/yr	649,064
• % of visits over £40 (eligible for AMTC)	23.1%
• % of customers collecting AMTC	40.0%
Visits in which AMTC collected	59,974
Average number AMTC collected/visit	12
AMTC distributed—current customers	721,136

Current Customers—increased spending:

% of customers increasing their spending	1.25%
Number of visits affected	8,113
Average spending increase	£14.75
Total incremental revenues	£119,617
Average AMTC collected/visit	12
AMTC distributed—incremental	93,125

New Customers:

% increase in visits through new customer activity	1.62%
Number of new customer visits	10,490
Average spending per visit	£63.50
Total incremental revenues	£665,477
Average AMTC collected/visit	12
AMTC distributed—new customers	126,199

Totals:

Total incremental revenues	£785,094
Contribution margin	*25%
Incremental contribution	£196,273
Total number of AMTC distributed	940,460
Cost per AMTC (to sponsor)	11 pence
Total cost	(£103,451)
Total gain from AIR MILES promotion	**£ 92,823**

---

[a]AMTC: AIR MILES travel credits.

were distributed to sponsors. After 16 weeks, 1.8 million households were registered and 400 million AMTC were distributed.

AMTP's success began to wane in 1989. Of the 17 sponsors participating in the program at the launch date, only two—NatWest credit cards and Shell Oil gasoline—were still using AMTP as an ongoing customer loyalty tool by 1989 and 1990. Many sponsors terminated their involvement or ended up using the program as a one-time sales promotion because of pressure to reduce marketing expenditures in response to the U.K. recession, which depressed retail sales. During 1990, the AIR MILES program was effectively carried by NatWest and Shell, as well as business-to-business and employee motivation sponsors.

The program was effectively relaunched in early 1991 when British Airways signed on as a program sponsor. This allowed collectors not only to redeem AMTC on BA but also to accumulate AMTC for flying BA. In effect, AIR MILES became BA's frequent-flier program, with the added consumer benefit of additional sponsor offers. Electronic statements were introduced, permitting a database of collectors and their account activity to be developed. Collectors joining through BA—predominantly business travelers—were initially referred to as AIR MILES Latitudes collectors. BA's addition as a sponsor spawned renewed interest among potential consumer sector sponsors. Major new sponsors, such as Clydesdale Electrical Stores and Whitbread Pubs, provided collectors with attractive new offers. By mid-1991, the original AIR MILES program collector database was merged with the new Latitudes group database, and the "Latitudes" designation was dropped.

CONSUMER RESEARCH

In December 1990, a representative sample of 2,000 British adults were asked about their awareness and interest in AMTP. Awareness and collection rates were greatest at higher income levels and among professionals. Those aware of AMTP but not collecting offered a variety of explanations, including apathy, lack of interest in traveling abroad, and fear of flying. (Survey results are reported in Exhibit 2.)

A second survey in late 1990 polled 3,400 AMTP flight redeemers to explore their satisfaction. Survey results, reported in Exhibit 3, showed that 79% of free-flight earners rated their experience with AMTP as either excellent or very good. NatWest and Shell were clearly the main sponsors used to collect vouchers, and 55% of the round trips taken were less than 1,000 miles.

Market research profiling the attitudes and characteristics of original AIR MILES collectors and the AIR MILES Latitudes subgroup was undertaken in September 1991. Most collectors were outgoing and cosmopolitan members of the U.K. middle and upper classes. However, there were demographic differences between AIR MILES collectors and the Latitudes subgroup. Most AIR MILES collectors earned less than £25,000, and 60% were male. The collectors in the Latitudes subgroup typically earned over £25,000, and 94% were male. (Full survey results are reported in Exhibits 4 and 5.)

By the end of 1991, over 70% of U.K. households were aware of AIR MILES and 10% (2.3 million) had signed on as collectors, including 600,000 households in the Latitudes subgroup. Of all collectors, 120,000 had taken free flights.

COMPETITORS

AMTP's high awareness was partly a function of the program's uniqueness. There were no frequent-flier programs or cross-category promotion programs in the U.K. at the time of the AIR MILES launch. Single-company frequent-buyer reward programs, such as Texaco's (gasoline) Star Collection and Embassy's (cigarettes) Gift Tokens, were uncommon and unfulfilling to many consumers. They offered frequent purchasers gifts chosen from special catalogs, but most consumers did not buy enough to qualify for attractive rewards within a reasonable time period.

Exhibit 2   *U.K. Market Research Findings**

Awareness and Activation Levels

In a 1991 survey, prompted awareness of the AIR MILES program was 70%. Of those people aware, 12% were collecting AMTC.

Intention to Collect

Those people who were aware of AIR MILES but were not currently collecting were asked whether they would consider collecting AIR MILES travel credits (AMTC) in the future; 23% said that they would.

Objections to AIR MILES

Respondents who were aware of AIR MILES but had no intention to start collecting them were asked their reasons.

Respondents (%)	Reason
35%	Not interested/Doesn't appeal/Not bothered.
2	Don't travel/Don't holiday abroad/Don't like flying.
1	Would take too long to collect (a free flight).
9	Need too many AMTC to collect (a free flight).
7	Not widely available/Not all shops give them.
6	Would have to spend a lot of money.
5	Don't know enough about it.
4	It's a rip-off, con, gimmick/There is a catch in it.
4	Lack of money.
3	Prefer cheaper goods/Money off.
2	I'm too old.
9	Other/Don't know.

*Source: 1990 NOP Omnibus Tracking survey of a representative sample of 2,000 British adults.

AMTP's success spawned me-too competitors such as Holiday Points. This cross-category promotions company was backed by Thomson Holidays, the largest packaged holiday travel company in the world. AMTP preempted the Holiday Points launch by offering Thomson Holidays a place in the AIR MILES program. From September 1989, collectors were able to redeem their AMTC for packaged holidays from Thomson as well as for air travel.

A similar cross-category promotions program named "Miles Better" was announced in 1988 by Virgin Atlantic Airways, a small but important competitor of BA. However, this program never materialized. Instead, in 1990, Virgin launched Freeway, a traditional airline frequent-flier program.

Exhibit 6 shows AMTP awareness levels compared with those of its direct and indirect competitors in 1989.

ECONOMICS

By 1991, AMTP was still not at a break-even level. Voucher sales were £5.4 million for the year ended March 31, 1989; £18.3 million for 1990; and £10.5 million for 1991. Net losses of £7.5 million in 1989, £2.1 million in 1990, and £5.6 million in 1991 were realized mainly due to the high initial costs of sales, marketing, and

Exhibit 3   *1990 U.K. Passenger Questionnaire Analysis**

1. How long have you been collecting AIR MILE travel credits (AMTC)?			5. What distance did you fly with AIR MILES?	
0–3 months	2%		0–499 miles	65%
3–6 months	4		500–1999 miles	30
6–9 months	4		2000–4499 miles	4
9–12 months	14		4500+ miles	0
12–18 months	34		6. How long before the start of your trip did you book?	
18+ months	42		Less than 4 weeks	38%
2. Which are the main companies and services you collect AMTC from?			1–2 months	40
NatWest	62%		2–6 months	20
Shell	56		over 6 months	2
Toshiba	10		7. Overall, how would you rate your experience with Air Miles?	
Comet	8		Excellent	42%
Burtons/Principles	5		Very good	37
Debenhams	3		Good	15
3. How many AMTC have you redeemed for your free flight?			Fair	3
0–500	17%		Poor	1
501–1000	38		Very poor	1
1001–1500	15		8. Will you continue collecting AIR MILES?	
1501–2000	11		Yes	96%
2001–3000	10		No	2
3000+	9		Not stated	1
4. How many AMTC, if any, do you have left now?				
0–100	20%			
101–300	19			
301–600	18			
601–1000	15			
1001–2000	16			
2001+	13			

*Source: Based on 1,900 questionnaires completed by AIR MILES flight redeemers in late 1990.

database management. Breaking even on these fixed costs required annual revenues from sponsor companies of £20 million, which represented approximately £3 billion of consumer purchases. The program was projected to break even in the year ending March 31, 1992. Revenues of £49.5 million and earnings before interest and taxes of £2.5 million were expected.

AMTP derived revenues from voucher payments by program sponsors ranging from 5 to 10 pence per AMTC; these payments were made up front when sponsors received vouchers from AIR MILES. Minimum AMTC purchase commitments of up to £1 million were written into some sponsor contracts, guaranteeing a base level of revenues for the company. Consumers

Exhibit 4   *1991 U.K. Collector Demographics**

	Latitudes Collectors		AIR MILES Collectors	
	%	Index	%	Index
Male	93.9%	194	59.6%	123
Female	6.0	11	40.4	78
18–34	15.6	65	22.6	95
35–54	68.2	210	46.1	142
55–64	12.2	93	16.7	127
65+	3.3	16	14.4	70
>£20K	8.0	11	57.8	76
£20–25K	9.9	98	15.1	150
£25–30K	12.9	230	9.4	167
£30K+	69.2	843	17.7	216
Professional/manager	94.2	428	42.6	194
American Express/Diners Club Cardholders	57.6	1,646	8.5	243

*Source: September 1991 AIR MILES collector research. Note: The index compares collectors with the U.K. population as a whole. An index of 100 indicates a subgroup is represented in the sample in the same proportion as in the total U.K. population.

had to send in their collected vouchers to the AMTP customer service center (either directly or through a representative travel agent) to receive credit towards free flights. Automatic account crediting was possible for BA and NatWest collection activity.

AMTP's cost of goods sold consisted of the charges levied by BA for the airline seats and the costs of processing collector redemptions. The airline seat charges were payable to BA when collectors made flight bookings using their AMTC. By 1991, AIR MILES was operating with cost of goods of 45%.[3]

THE NORTH AMERICAN ENTRY

Mills had always envisioned AIR MILES as an international program. Before the U.K. launch, AMTP had established a Dutch international holding company to facilitate future expansion. Mills decided to enter the North American market in 1992 as a defensive strategy to preempt competitors, knowing that doing so would probably strain his young company's resources.

North America (NA) offered significant potential; there were 245 million people in the United States and 27 million in Canada. These markets were characterized by high participation in promotional programs. For example, U.S. consumers redeemed $4 billion worth of coupons representing $16 per person in 1991 compared with an estimated $5 of coupon redemptions per person in the U.K. In addition,

---

[3]The U.K. voucher redemption rate was 50%.

Exhibit 5 *1991 U.K. Collector Profiling and Database Analysis**

Selected Findings

- Residents of affluent suburbia are six times as likely to collect AIR MILES travel credits (AMTC) as those who live on poorer public housing estates.
- Family households are twice as likely to collect AMTC as those which comprise only a single adult.
- AIR MILES collectors are twice as likely as the population as a whole to read the quality press rather than the tabloids.
- Singles feature slightly more strongly among AIR MILES travelers than among AIR MILES collectors (not surprising, as it takes fewer AMTC for one to travel than for two).
- AIR MILES collectors are sporty and active (skiing, squash, and golf frequently mentioned).
- AIR MILES collectors are more likely to live in London and the South East.

*Source: AIR MILES September 1991 collector research.

the win-win-win combination present in the U.K., aligning airline, sponsor, and consumer interests, also seemed to apply in NA. Mills was able to form exclusive partnerships[4] with four major NA airlines, which accounted for more than 50% of passenger miles flown in the United States and Canada: American Airlines, United Airlines, USAir, and Air Canada. This ensured that AMTP would be able to offer collectors access to air travel on large, well-established airlines with extensive route networks. The exclusive long-term (up to 25 years) airline contracts also established a competitive barrier to entry.

[4]The airlines were contractually committed to providing a certain level of seat capacity to LMG at fixed, discounted prices; they were unable to provide reduced-rate airline seats to any other cross-category promotional program.

The airline contracts allowed AIR MILES collectors to redeem their AMTC for flights on these four carriers. However, the agreements did not allow collectors to combine AMTC with airline frequent-flier miles, nor did they allow collectors to earn AMTC for flights on these airlines.

At the same time, the risks of entering NA were daunting. AMTP was still refining its strategies and tactics in the U.K. Too precipitous a move into NA without sufficient research could be risky. Financing on the scale required to break into the NA market was difficult to obtain. The U.K. program was not yet profitable, and Mills had to sell his unproven idea to new investors. Finally, differences between NA and the U.K. could require adjustments in the program's strategy. There were already many well-established frequent-flier programs in NA.

Aside from the business risks, Mills faced personal challenges. He would have to move his family to Boston, open a new market on a shoestring budget, and essentially start all over again. Mills commented: "Once you start something you've got to see it through. I saw the huge potential in North America and I was determined to make the AIR MILES program work there."

Mills put together management teams in the United States and Canada to conduct consumer and competitive research and to make recommendations on the NA entry strategy. The AIR MILES trademark was registered, and companies formed in both countries with Mills as chairman. The U.S. company was named Loyalty Management Group, Inc., and Mike Beaumont and Mike Miles were recruited to spearhead its operations and marketing efforts, respectively. The Canadian company, Loyalty Management Group Canada, Inc., was headed by Craig Underwood and Sam Duboc. (Both the U.S. and Canadian companies are referred to as LMG.)

Consumer Research

LMG management first set out to develop an understanding of the similarities and differences

Exhibit 6   *Research International Study Results**

	Total	Taken Overseas Holiday in Past Two Years?	
	%	Yes %	No %
Prompted Awareness of Collecting Schemes			
Promotion			
AIR MILES	73%	80%	62%
Esso Gift Tokens[a]	49	51	45
Embassy Gift Tokens[a]	37	37	37
Texaco Star Collection[a]	34	37	29
Barclaycard Profile Points[a]	29	32	23
Holiday Points[b]	11	11	9
None	13	9	19
Collection of AMTC			
Whether Collecting			
Yes	8%	10%	4%
No	91	89	95
Don't know	1	1	1
Consideration of Collecting AMTC (asked of those *not currently collecting*)			
Would Consider Collecting			
Yes	24%	27%	20%
No	68	65	72
Don't know	8	8	8

*Source: Adapted from a 1990 Research International survey of a representative sample of British adults.
[a]Single company, stand-alone frequent-buyer reward programs.
[b]A cross-category frequency promotion that had publicized its launch in early 1990.

among the U.K., U.S., and Canadian consumers. Given the slim resources available, management relied on entry market research and insights provided by experienced promotional agencies.

In NA, 80%–90% of the adult population was aware of frequent-flier mileage and 10%–15% were enrolled in one or more airline programs. As a result, consumers had sophisticated knowledge of air travel reward programs. Business travelers were already heavily involved in collecting frequent flier miles through flying and/or charging expenses on airline affinity credit cards in which purchases qualified for mileage credits. Most business travelers were already committed to accumulating mileage in the frequent flier programs of the one or two airlines that they used most often.

Research also highlighted some cynicism and disenchantment with frequent-flier programs among less-frequent travelers who could not earn enough mileage points to qualify for a free flight. When NA consumers were presented with a description of the AIR MILES program, they frequently asked, "What's the catch?" For many consumers, the multiple-sponsor aspect of the AIR MILES concept offered a greater prospect of earning free air travel because of the ability to collect AMTC on everyday purchases.

Another important consideration was the greater average travel distances in NA versus the U.K. A free, round-trip flight from London to Paris was both attainable (450 miles) and exciting for the U.K. AIR MILES collector. Short-haul flights with as much appeal were less evident in NA. This meant that the NA program had to include a broad base of popular sponsors that would enable collectors to earn quickly sufficient mileage to qualify for exciting free trips before they became disenchanted.

The demographics of U.S. and Canadian consumers were similar (see Exhibit 7). However, some cultural differences were apparent. U.S. consumers spent more and saved less than Canadians. They would be motivated primarily by the excitement of the final travel reward AIR MILES would provide. Canadians, it seemed, might be more patient collectors. They would be motivated by the ability to obtain something of value (free flights) by collecting and saving AMTC. Regional differences were also evident within each national market. Canada could be divided into four regions—Ontario, Quebec, the western provinces, and the Atlantic provinces. In the United States, on the other hand, the distinction between large-city clusters and the rest of the country meant that population density varied widely across the country; the top 10 metropolitan areas accounted for over 30% of the population. (Table C and Exhibit 8 outline the population densities and regional population concentrations in the two countries.)

Focus groups and mall surveys were undertaken in the United States and Canada in late 1991. In the mall surveys, the program was described to 303 target Canadians and 600 target Americans, with representative sponsors and collection offers provided for illustration. In Canada, 47% of those surveyed said that they definitely or probably would join the program described. The figure in the United States was 65%. Respondents were then asked what they would do

Exhibit 7   *U.S. and Canadian Demographic Data, 1991**

	United States		Canada	
	Millions	**%**	**Millions**	**%**
Gender				
Male	119.7	48.7%	13.5	49.3%
Female	126.1	51.3	13.8	50.7
Age				
<25	90.5	36.8%	9.5	34.9%
25–34	43.7	17.8	4.9	17.8
35–44	35.3	14.3	4.4	16.0
45–54	24.2	9.8	3.0	10.9
55–64	21.8	8.9	2.4	8.8
65+	30.4	12.4	3.2	11.6
HH[a] Income				
<$35K		55.0%		43.1%
$35–75K		35.0		42.8
$75K+		10.0		14.1
HH Size				
1		12.8%		22.9%
2		32.6		31.4
3		20.5		17.4
4		8.9		17.7
5+		25.2		10.6

*Source: Adapted from U.S. Census data 1991 and Statistics Canada Census data 1991.
[a]HH denotes household.

Table C   Population and Area Statistics

	U.S.	Canada	U.K.
Area (sq. mi.)	3,615,123	3,851,809	94,399
Population (millions)	246	27	56
Population density (ppl./sq. mi.)	68	7	593

Exhibit 8   *Regional Population Concentrations in NA, 1991* *

United States—Top 10 ADIs[a]		
ADI Name	**Total Number of Households**	**Percent of U.S. Households**
1. New York, NY	6,858,221	7.2%
2. Los Angeles, CA	5,130,540	5.4
3. Chicago, IL	3,068,012	3.2
4. Philadelphia, PA	2,674,618	2.8
5. San Francisco/Oakland/San Jose, CA	2,234,069	2.4
6. Boston, MA	2,139,262	2.3
7. Washington, DC	1,830,797	1.9
8. Dallas/Ft. Worth, TX	1,824,765	1.9
9. Detroit, MI	1,743,755	1.8
10. Houston, TX	1,500,482	1.6
Top 10 ADIs	29,004,521	30.5%
Total United States	94,720,000	100.0%
Canada—Four Major Regions		
Region	**Total Population**	**% of Total**
Ontario	10,098,000	36.8%
Quebec	6,925,500	25.3
Western Provinces	8,044,800	29.4
Atlantic Provinces	2,341,200	8.5
Total Canada	27,409,500	100.0%

*Source: Adapted from *Progressive Grocer* Market Source and *Canadian Grocer* Market Survey.
[a]An ADI or Area of Dominant Influence denotes a geographic region reached by broadcast signals from the television stations in the principal town of the region.

if they had extra disposable income. The most frequently selected response in both countries was travel. This finding confirmed the attractiveness of free travel as a reward; travel industry data indicated that 75% of all Americans planned on taking a pleasure vacation every other year. The market research also underlined the need to have the program associated with reputable sponsors with whom consumers would normally do business. Interviewees were also asked to indicate how long they felt it was reasonable to wait before an average spender would be able to earn a free flight. Canadian respon-

dents expected, on average, to wait one to two years. U.S. respondents expected, on average, to wait one year or less. (Selected findings from this research are reported in Exhibit 9.)

Exhibit 10 profiles the demographic characteristics of four groups of the U.S. population (not mutually exclusive): the American Express cardholder, the frequent-flier, the heavy coupon user, and the consumer with a strong vacation/travel orientation. The results of this research suggested to LMG executives that they should target, in both the United States and Canada, adults aged 25–54 with household incomes over

Exhibit 9 *U.S. and Canadian 1991 Entry Market Research**

U.S. Selected Findings

1. How likely would you be to participate in AIR MILES?

Definitely	16%
Probably	49
Somewhat	29
Unlikely	5
Would not	1

2. If you had greater disposable income, what do you think you would spend it on?

Travel	69%
House	16
Clothing	7
Car	3
Jewelry	1
Other	4

3. Would you change the brands of products/services you buy?

Definitely	6%
Probably	29
Somewhat	44
Unlikely	17
Would not	4

4. Have you ever used a grocery coupon from a newspaper?

Yes	90%
No	10

5. Would you rather have a coupon for 5 miles or 50 cents off?

5 miles	80%
50 cents off	20

6. Compared to cents off coupons, how willing would you be to use air mileage coupons?

Much more	20%
Slightly more	27
The same	44
Less	7
Much less	2

7. Do you belong to a frequent flier program?

Yes	40%
No	60

8. If *yes* to Q. 7-have you ever received a free ticket?

Yes	45%
No	55

Canadian Selected Findings

1. How likely would you be to participate in a program like the one described?

Definitely would/probably would	47%
Might or might not	30
Definitely would not/probably would not	23

The following responses are based only on the respondents who definitely would/probably would participate:

2. If you had some extra disposable income, which one of the following would you be most likely to spend it on?

Travel/vacation	50%
Home improvement	27
Automobile	18
Other	5

3. Have you ever used a coupon from a newspaper?

Yes	76%
No	24

4. If you purchased a $5.00 item, would you be more willing to use a 75 cents-off coupon or a 3 AIR MILES coupon on this purchase?

75 cents off	25%
3 AIR MILES coupon	75

5. How willing would you be to collect and send in AIR MILES coupons, or proofs of purchase that were packed inside a purchase that you made?

Definitely would	40%
Probably would	40
Might or might not	14
Probably would not	3
Definitely would not	3

6. Do you belong to any frequent flier programs?

Yes	15%
No	85

7. If *yes* to Q. 6-have you ever received a free ticket from a frequent-flier program?

Yes	22%
No	78

*Source: Mall intercepts and retail area interviews—303 Canadian interviews conducted in Calgary, Toronto, and Montreal, and 600 American interviews conducted in New England.

Exhibit 10   *U.S. Target Market Analysis**

	American Express Cardholder		Frequent Flier		Heavy Coupon User		Consumer with Vacation/ Travel Preference	
	%	Index*	%	Index*	%	Index*	%	Index*
Men	55%	116	52%	108	NA	NA	46%	97
Women	45	85	48	92	100%	100	54	102
18–24	10%	76	8%	60	7%	76	14%	98
25–34	16	110	28	117	25	103	24	101
35–44	26	130	25	127	22	106	21	108
45–54	18	132	18	128	17	114	15	111
55–64	12	96	10	81	14	109	12	101
65+	7	46	11	67	16	84	13	78
<$10K	2%	18	4%	31	9%	58	6%	52
$10–19.9K	4	21	5	28	17	88	12	68
$20–29.9K	10	58	10	57	17	105	16	95
$30–39.9K	17	105	12	75	17	110	18	110
$40–49.9K	15	119	15	119	13	114	16	129
$50–59.9K	15	174	13	146	10	131	11	124
$60–74.9K	15	207	16	213	8	123	10	131
$75K+	22	264	26	318	8	114	11	131
Professional	16%	186	21%	235	10%	116	12%	134
Executive/administrator/ manager	19	228	23	280	5	76	11	129
Clerk/salesperson/technician	25	128	22	114	25	106	22	114
Craftsperson/repairperson	6	81	4	58	2	112	8	101
Not employed	19	54	22	61	45	98	31	85

*Note: The index compares respondents with the U.S. population as a whole. An index of 100 indicates typical representation of a subgroup in the sample in the same proportion as in the U.S. population.

$35,000. Lower-income households were excluded based on the level of spending needed to earn a free flight within the time period considered reasonable by consumers.

Competition

There were many frequency marketing programs in NA vying for the consumer's attention but, as a national cross-category frequent buyer program, AIR MILES would be unique.

There was a regional cross-category player called Club Multi-Point operating in Quebec, which awarded points that consumers could redeem for gifts chosen from a catalog. Its principal sponsors were Banque Nationale, Steinbergs (a grocery retailer), and Videotron (a cable-TV service). It was estimated that over 100,000 Quebecers had joined since the May 1990 launch. In the United States, two cross-category programs—START and Tuition Access—were planning launches in 1992. START enabled consumers to build retirement savings dollars based on a percentage of their spending on sponsors' products. Likewise, Tuition Access enabled consumers to save for college tuition. The main weakness of these programs was thought to be the high level of consumer spending necessary to receive a reward. (Exhibit 11 outlines these competitive programs in more detail.)

A competitive consortium was possible, operating regionally across categories and organized by a travel or airline group. Such a consortium might involve two or more airlines not involved with AIR MILES, such as Continental, Northwest, Delta, or Canadian Airlines. LMG executives believed that the launch of a competitive program would depend on the initial popularity of AIR MILES, its impact on their businesses, and their resulting need to take retaliatory action.

Other programs that competed for the consumers' attention and loyalty included frequent-flier programs, frequent-lodger programs, frequent-car rental programs, credit card affinity programs, and retailer frequent-buyer programs. (Exhibit 12 outlines these competitive programs and lists the most prominent players.) These programs differed from AIR MILES in that they were proprietary, stand-alone frequency offers in which a single company was responsible for funding the entire program. The most serious competitors on the basis of their popularity and their involvement of multiple partners were the American Airlines AAdvantage program and American Express Membership Miles.

American Airlines initiated its AAdvantage frequent-flier program in 1981. Originally intended as a short-term promotion, frequent-flier miles proved so popular that nearly every major airline, as well as many other companies, followed suit. By the end of 1991, over 20 million members had enrolled in the AAdvantage program, and the frequent-flier programs of United, American, and USAir combined were still growing at a rate of 4 million consumers annually. In Canada, Air Canada's Aeroplan and Canadian Airlines' Plus program, introduced after 1984, each had an estimated 1 million members. All these programs generated useful databases of business travelers—the airlines' most profitable customers. The larger programs all had affinity relationships with credit card companies, car rental agencies, and other services commonly purchased by business travelers; mileage was credited for the use of these services. Industry experts estimated that American Airlines realized over $200 million annually by selling frequent-flier miles to its AAdvantage partners, including Citibank, MCI, and Hilton Hotels. However, the popularity and proliferation of frequent-flier programs had reduced the competitive advantage enjoyed by any single airline.

Credit card programs such as American Express Membership Miles had developed partnerships with one or more major airlines. They allowed the consumer to collect points for credit card charges (usually $1 charged earned 1 point). These points could be converted into the frequent-flier points of the airline partners. These

Exhibit 11 *North American Competitive Cross-Category Frequency Programs*

Program	Participating Companies	Award Structure	Redemption Requirements	Restrictions
AIR MILES (U.S. and Canada)	Sponsors not yet determined. Could include gas retailers, credit card companies, car rental agencies, department stores, etc.	Established by participating companies.	Each AIR MILES travel credit equals one actual mile of air travel. Minimum award redemption: 500 AMTC.	Saturday night stay is required. Travel must be round trip. Tickets must be requested two weeks in advance. Some airline blackout dates. Redeemed on: • American • United • USAir • Air Canada
START INC. (SAVE TODAY AND RETIRE TOMORROW) (U.S.)	Sponsors not yet determined. Could include similar sponsors to AIR MILES.	If you contribute over $100 each quarter, sponsors will contribute a percentage of the purchase cost to a non-interest-bearing escrow account.	Receive deposits as cash or have deposits invested in a METLife STARTPlus Annuity	$25 membership fees for first year. Minimum contribution of $100 before collection can begin. Requires high purchase activity (estimated at $1,667 per quarter).
TUITION ACCESS/ TRUST FUND (U.S.)	Sponsors not yet determined.	Similar to AIR MILES. Sponsors will award credits for product/ service purchases.	None yet established. Credit dollars earned could be withdrawn by the student when going to college.	Credit dollars only redeemable for college tuition.
CLUB MULTI-POINT (Canada)	Steinbergs, Banque Nationale, Videotron, TVA, Telemedia.	Receive points purchasing products from sponsors.	Redeem points through a special gift catalog.	Gifts often require some cash payment as well.

Exhibit 12 *Indirect Competitors in North America*

Frequent Flier Programs	Frequent Lodger Programs	Frequent Car Rental Programs	Credit Card Affinity Programs	Retailer Frequent Buyer Programs
United States:				
American AAdvantage; Delta Frequent Flyer; Northwest WorldPerks; Southwest The Co. Club; TWA Frequent Flight Bonus; United Mileage Plus; USAir Frequent Traveler; Continental OnePass	Best Western Gold Crown; Hilton Hotels HHonors; Holiday Inn Priority; Hyatt Hotels Gold Passport; Sheraton Club International; Marriott Honored Guest; Westin Premier	Avis Corporate; Budget Awards; National Privilege; Payless Passport	American Express Membership Miles; Citicorp Diners; Citibank AAdvantage; Chase TWA Visa	Sears; Neiman Marcus
Canada:				
Air Canada Aeroplan; Canadian Plus	Same as above	Same as above	CIBC Aerogold Visa; Canadian Plus Royal Trust MasterCard; American Express Membership Miles	Sears Canada; Zellers Club Z; Canadian Tire $

credit card programs had varying restrictions. For example, American Express Membership Miles required an annual $25 membership fee and $5,000 in charges before mileage could be earned. Like frequent-flier programs, these programs also required that thousands of points be accumulated before a free trip could be obtained. Other credit cards, particularly "gold" cards, gave consumers dollar rebates on a percentage of their charges.

Though not used as widely as frequent-flier programs, retailer frequent-buyer programs were increasingly common and represented indirect competition to AIR MILES. In the United States, some retail chains, such as Sears Roebuck and Neiman Marcus, offered purchasers points that could be applied toward the purchase of other products in their stores. In Canada, retailer loyalty programs were more developed. Consumers had been collecting Club Z points from Zellers, a national department store chain, and store dollars from Canadian Tire, an automotive goods/hardware retailer, for over five years. Sears Canada also offered store credits for purchases. These Canadian programs enjoyed high consumer awareness partly because of their high annual advertising spending, estimated at $5 million for Sears Canada and $10 million for Zellers's Club Z. It was estimated that 34% of Canadian households included a Club Z member and 26% included a Sears Club member.

Final sources of competition were the emerging "product" and "corporate" cards that offered frequent purchasers of a specific company's products or services such incentives as discounts on products and/or purchase credits toward prizes. One recent example was Pepsi's "Gotta Have It" Card that offered consumers the ability to purchase specific products at discounted prices. Awareness of the Pepsi product card was estimated at 30% in the United States.

Sponsors

To succeed, LMG management knew that the NA program had to be both attractive to con-sumers and cost-effective for the sponsor companies. The right sponsors were essential. Sponsor selection was based on the following criteria: visibility and market presence; lack of product differentiation; frequency of purchase; and likely ability of collectors to attain rewards.

First, high-visibility sponsors would give AIR MILES consumer credibility and could serve as valuable allies in persuading consumers to enroll. Second, the purchase-frequency criterion was based on the notion that collecting AMTC had to become part of the consumer's lifestyle. This required that collectors have frequent opportunities to collect AMTC while buying everyday products and services. Third, sponsors also had to offer large enough travel credit awards per purchase to attract the interest of the collector.

Exhibit 13 illustrates a hypothetical collector's yearly AMTC statement. While seeking generous offers from sponsors, AIR MILES recognized that the economics had to ensure that a sponsor remain committed to AIR MILES as an ongoing loyalty program. Sponsors had to pay LMG for each AMTC credited on their behalf to a collector's account. The price per AMTC ranged from 10 cents to 25 cents, the variation depend-

Exhibit 13 *North American Collector: Typical Annual AMTC Collection Pattern*

Activity	AMTC
Spending of $5,000 on AIR MILES— affiliated credit card	500
Switch long distance service to AIR MILES' affiliate	150
Subscription to sponsor's magazine	100
Grocery purchases of $65/week from sponsoring retailer or manufacturer	250
Clothing purchases of $35/week from sponsoring department store	100
Three car rentals per year from sponsor	75
Total collected in one year	**1,175**

ing on the volume purchased and other contractual considerations, such as the strategic nature of the sponsor category. Minimum revenue commitments of about $1 million would be negotiated with several sponsors. Some sponsors would also pay LMG one-time fees of up to $5 million for product category exclusivity and marketing support.

To pursue sponsor partners, 350 different categories were identified, ranging from department stores to gasoline retailers. Among all these categories, LMG management knew that those involving grocery products were the most important "to get right." Grocery products were frequent, everyday purchases on which consumers consistently spent a significant percentage of their disposable incomes. Five AMTC could reasonably be collected on weekly household grocery purchases of $65. This translated into at least 250 AMTC per year toward a free flight. In addition, the ability to collect AMTC on groceries would set AIR MILES apart from other collection schemes.

There were two possible approaches to grocery products. AIR MILES could partner with grocery product manufacturers, such as Frito-Lay and Clorox, allowing collectors to earn AMTC for purchasing specific sponsor brands at any grocery store. The other option was to partner with grocery retailers such as Safeway and Star Market, to allow collectors to earn AMTC on their total grocery purchases at a specific chain. Partnering directly with both manufacturers and retailers was viewed by LMG executives as impossible. In past dual promotions of this nature, nonparticipating grocery retailers felt that participating manufacturers were subsidizing the efforts of participating retailers and were, therefore, helping their competitors. These retailers sometimes demanded additional trade promotions from participating manufacturers and/or threatened to delist their brands or certain items in their lines.

Fueling the uncertainty was AIR MILES' lack of experience with grocery sponsors. AIR MILES

had been unable to penetrate the grocery category in the U.K. Grocery retailing in the U.K. was dominated by five supermarket chains, collectively representing 60% of total sales. All enjoyed high profit margins (one chain, Tesco, had a 4.5% after-tax margin in 1991) and stable or increasing market shares. None had an incentive to upset the stable oligopoly by affiliating with the AIR MILES program. Grocery manufacturers had also proved unwilling to participate in the program because of the difficulties they perceived with executing the promotion. Product couponing was relatively undeveloped in the U.K. market, and manufacturers thought that consumers would be unwilling to clip and mail in product codes for AMTC redemption. Relying on grocery retailers to distribute AIR MILES vouchers for manufacturer purchases was also deemed unfeasible, given the lack of leverage packaged goods manufacturers had with the grocery trade. Over 50% of grocery store products sold in the U.K. were private-label and generic brands, compared with fewer than 20% in the United States.

In June 1991, Mills decided to form separate teams in both the United States and Canada to pursue both grocery manufacturers and retailers. The teams were asked to formulate a list of pros and cons and to scope out the interests of both manufacturers and retailers. Mills was especially sensitive to the differences between the U.S. and Canadian marketplaces.

Grocery Product Manufacturers versus Retailers

The grocery manufacturer team expressed economic and operational concerns about signing up retailer sponsors. Grocery retailers in NA—especially in the United States—operated on razor-thin after-tax margins, averaging 1.2% in 1990. When approached, many stated that they could not afford AIR MILES as a long-term program, especially given the recessionary pressures felt by the entire grocery industry in 1991.

Participation would also require investment in adapting sophisticated point-of-sale scanner equipment to assign collectors their AMTC at the checkout. There was concern that entering AMTC would hold up the checkout lines.

Many packaged goods manufacturers, on the other hand, indicated a strong desire to participate. Signing two national contracts by the end of 1991 seemed likely. Manufacturers were more used to allocating a significant percentage of their sales to promotions. By 1990, it was estimated that promotions accounted for 75% of branded manufacturers' marketing budgets, up from 50% in 1985. Manufacturers enjoyed better profit margins than retailers. This gave them the flexibility to consider offering generous awards to AIR MILES collectors, enabling them to earn free flights faster. The category exclusivity AIR MILES offered was also appealing as a source of competitive differentiation, especially as brand loyalty toward grocery products was deteriorating due to competitive price promotions and the revival of private label sales during the recession. A long-term exclusive relationship with AIR MILES promised to motivate consumers to remain loyal to the participating manufacturers' brands week after week.

Manufacturers' participation would give collectors access to AMTC regardless of the distribution channels through which they bought products. Many grocery products were distributed not only in supermarkets but in drugstores, convenience stores, and mass merchandisers. Collectors would not need to go out of their way to shop at a specific participating retailer in an area. In addition, the willingness of consumers to participate in manufacturer couponing schemes was well established. Finally, in the critical launch stage, when both sponsors and consumers had to be sold on AIR MILES, signing a few large, well-known packaged goods manufacturers might give AIR MILES the momentum needed to sell the program in other sponsor categories.

The grocery retailer team felt that having manufacturers as sponsors would be too complicated for the collector. Collectors would need to remember the brand names participating in the program, switch to the participating brands, and then clip and mail the UPC codes from product packages to credit their AIR MILES accounts. If grocery retailers were sponsors, a collector would simply have to switch to the participating grocery retailer in their area and be credited electronically for his/her entire grocery bill at the checkout.

Grocery retailers could also publicize AIR MILES in retail advertising and through in-store displays, enabling consumers to learn about and enroll in the program. Packaged goods manufacturers were one step removed from the ultimate consumer and, as such, could not be as helpful in promoting the AIR MILES concept.

Finally, participating grocery retailers would gain sales from the incentive AIR MILES provided consumers to concentrate their purchases with one retailer. AIR MILES offered the grocery retailer a long-term competitive advantage to defend its customer sales against emerging price-oriented retail formats, such as warehouse clubs and mass merchants. A few grocery store chains had expressed strong interest in participating in the program, particularly the Safeway chain in Western Canada.

The United States and Canadian Grocery Markets

In 1991, U.S. grocery retailers had revenues of $376 billion. Although the top 10 supermarket chains represented 30% of national sales, they were regional rather than national in market coverage. In contrast, the $38 billion Canadian grocery-retailing market consisted of only four regions and therefore, major retail chains enjoyed high visibility with a greater percentage of the country's population. (Exhibit 14 lists the top grocery retailers in the seven largest U.S. metro markets and in Canada's four regions.)

LMG management wanted to provide collectors with the opportunity to earn AMTC in the grocery category on a national basis. Gaining national U.S. coverage with grocery retailers

Exhibit 14 *North American Grocery Retailer Sales Concentration, 1991**

Region		Canada		
	Ontario	Quebec[a]	Western Provinces	Atlantic Provinces
% of Canadian Food Store Sales	**32%**	**28%**	**30%**	**10%**
Top chains (market share)	1. Loblaw (28%)	1. Provigo (31%)	1. Safeway (23%)	1. Sobeys (28%)
	2. A&P (21%)	2. Metro-Richelieu (25%)	2. Loblaw (10%)	2. Atlantic Cooperative (18%)
	3. Oshawa (15%)	3. Hudon et Deaudelin (15%)	3. Federated Cooperative (10%)	3. Save Easy (12%)
	4. Loeb (15%)		4. Overwaitea (7%)	4. IGA (9%)
	5. Knob Hill Farm (4%)		5. IGA (5%)	5. Loblaw (8%)

continued

*Source: Adapted from *Progressive Grocer* Market Source, *Canadian Grocer* Market Survey and information provided by the Canadian Council of Grocery Distributors.
[a]The grocery stores of the Steinberg chain were either closed down or sold to other retailers.

Exhibit 14 *(continued)*

	United States			
ADI D.C.	**New York**	**Los Angeles**	**Chicago**	**Philadelphia**
% of U.S. Supermarket Sales	**5.7%**	**6.3%**	**3.4%**	**2.4%**
Top chains (market share)	1. Shop Rite (16%) 2. Pathmark (13.6%) 3. A&P (10.4%) 4. Twin County (10.4%) 5. Waldbaum (8.8%)	1. Certified Grocers-CA (24.1%) 2. Vons (18.5%) 3. Lucky Stores (14.6%) 4. Ralphs (12.7%) 5. Quality Foods (9.1%)	1. Jewel (35.2%) 2. Dominick (21.9%) 3. Certified Grocers-MW (10.3%) 4. Central Grocers (9.4%) 5. Eagle Food (5.7%)	1. Acme Markets (24%) 2. Fleming (19.2%) 3. Pathmark (11%) 4. Shop Rite (10.2%) 5. A&P (9.8%)

ADI D.C.	**San Francisco/ Oakland/San Jose**	**Boston**	**Washington, D.C.**
% of U.S. Supermarket Sales	**3.7%**	**3.5%**	**2.7%**
Top chains (market share)	1. Safeway (32.4%) 2. Lucky Stores (26.9%) 3. Certified Grocers-CA (12%) 4. Western Pacific (6.5%) 5. Fleming (6.4%)	1. C&S (19.5%) 2. Shaws (15.5%) 3. Demoulas (13.7%) 4. Stop & Shop (11.8%) 5. Star Market (10.5%)	1. Giant Foods (33.3%) 2. Safeway (22.8%) 3. Super Rite (14.9%) 4. Richfood (5.3%) 5. A&P (4.8%)

*Source: Adapted from *Progressive Grocer* Market Source, *Canadian Grocer* Market Survey and information provided by the Canadian Council of Grocery Distributors.
[a]The grocery stores of the Steinberg chain were either closed down or sold to other retailers.

would require signing contracts with 25 different chains and ensuring no market overlap (given the geographical-exclusivity contract provision). This process might take two to three years, during which time consumers in some areas would lack the opportunity to collect on grocery purchases. In Canada, national coverage of retail grocery sales could be obtained by signing four exclusive retailer contracts, one covering each region of the country.

In either country, national distribution could be achieved in a matter of months by signing on large grocery manufacturers. Signing manufacturers had the benefit in the United States of adding recognizable national brand names to the program. Regional U.S. grocery retailers, such as Star Market in New England, did not have national name recognition, and their addition to the program would not necessarily entice key national sponsors to join.

National versus Regional Strategy

LMG executives were also debating whether to launch nationally or regionally. If successful, a regional program could be rolled out nationally.

Launching nationally at the outset would appeal to major national sponsors, such as car rental agencies and telephone service companies. A regional launch posed the challenge of organizing a group of sponsors who were interested in targeting the same region; it seemed likely that each sponsor might draw the boundaries of its target region differently. A regional approach could cause customer confusion, and advertising costs would be proportionally higher because of the need to buy media time on a regional rather than national basis. A national launch would preempt competition, whereas a regional launch might raise awareness of the concept and give new competitors time to make preemptive launches in other regions. Finally, LMG management was unsure whether a regional strategy would generate the volume of business needed to cover the high cost of launching and administering the program.

The costs of launching a regional program in New York and Toronto were estimated at $15.5 million.

Other executives favored the regional roll-out approach. There were obvious regional differences in both countries—the most striking example being Quebec, the bilingual Canadian province. Marketing and collector communications could be more effective if tailored by region. They also noted that many potential sponsor categories included strong regional players who would be interested in a deal involving regional exclusivity. This phenomenon was less evident in the smaller Canadian market, where a few national players dominated most categories, than in the United States, where regional players were stronger and the market shares of national players often varied widely by region. For example, Canada was served by five major national banks, whereas, in the United States, due to government regulations, hundreds of state-based players competed in the retail banking industry. Canada was served by three main department store chains, compared with 25 chains, none of them national, in the United States. This Canadian concentration and corresponding U.S. fragmentation occurred across many other categories, ranging from gasoline retailers to hardware stores.

Economics

LMG management estimated the fixed costs of a full NA launch at around $75 million in the first year (75% covering U.S. costs and 25% Canadian costs). These costs included marketing expenditures, administrative overhead, database management, property costs, and the staffing of a customer service center to assist collectors and to handle travel requests. The program's variable costs, including AMTC payments to the airlines and collector processing, were expected to be 40% of the 10-to-25-cent AMTC revenue AIR MILES would receive from sponsors. (Exhibit 15 outlines these costs, under different NA market entry strategies, in more detail.)

Exhibit 15 *Economic Projections Under Various North American Market Entry Scenarios*

	National Launch		Regional Launch[a]	
A: Enter U.S. Only	**Year 1**	**Year 2**	**Year 1**	**Year 2**
Grocery Manufacturers				
Number of people enrolled	3,000,000	5,000,000	500,000	800,000
Weighted average AMTC collection	150	200	150	200
Revenue per AMTC	15¢	15¢	15¢	15¢
Sales of AMTC ($000s)	67,500	150,000	11,250	24,000
Other revenues[b]	53	357	0	0
Total revenues ($000s)	67,553	150,357	11,250	24,000
Cost of goods %	40%	40%	40%	40%
Total cost of goods sold ($000s)	27,021	60,143	4,500	9,600
Gross margin ($000s)	40,532	90,214	6,750	14,400
Fulfillment	9,900	12,876	3,200	3,700
Advertising	19,730	22,000	1,000	1,700
Other marketing	895	1,000	0	0
Sales	4,264	4,800	500	800
Information systems	6,091	6,051	2,200	2,000
Operations	5,050	4,209	2,000	1,600
General and administrative	7,648	5,021	2,000	1,700
Total fixed costs ($000s)	53,578	55,957	10,900	11,500
EBIT ($000s)[b]	(13,046)	34,257	(4,150)	2,900
Grocery Retailers				
Added revenues	1,600	13,000	500	1,000
Cost of goods sold %	40%	40%	40%	40%
Added EBIT ($000s)	960	7,800	300	600

continued

[a]Regional launch in one large region in the United States, such as New York, and one in Canada, such as Toronto.
[b]EBIT: Denotes earnings before interest and taxes.

For LMG to become profitable, two conditions had to be met. First, the number of AMTC collected by each collector had to be more than sufficient to cover the cost of carrying that collector in the program. Second, the program had to attract enough profitable collectors to cover the fixed costs of the business. The business required an investment in each collector before any revenue was generated. This investment, involving enrollment costs and periodic statements, could be recouped only if the collector became sufficiently active in collecting AMTC since each AMTC collected represented, in effect, a cash payment to LMG from the corresponding sponsor. (Table D gives estimates of collection activity rates for an established program.)

Program Objectives

Mills had raised $15 million by selling shares in the NA start-up to a strategic investor. This capital, along with the up-front exclusivity pay-

Exhibit 15 *(continued)*

B. Enter Canada Only	National Launch		Regional Launch[a]	
	Year 1	Year 2	Year 1	Year 2
Grocery Manufacturers				
Number of people enrolled	900,000	1,500,000	300,000	550,000
Weighted average AMTC collection	150	200	150	200
Revenue per AMTC	15¢	15¢	15¢	15¢
Sales of AMTC	20,250	45,000	6,750	16,500
Other revenues[c]	47	416	0	0
Total revenues ($000s)	20,297	45,416	6,750	16,500
Cost of goods %	40%	40%	40%	40%
Total cost of goods sold ($000s)	8,119	18,166	2,700	6,600
Gross margin ($000s)	12,178	27,250	4,050	9,900
Fulfillment	7,699	8,353	3,000	3,200
Advertising	1,511	2,778	700	1,400
Other marketing	0	0	0	0
Sales	1,101	1,869	400	700
Information systems	5,191	4,320	2,000	1,800
Operations	4,022	3,610	1,750	1,500
General and administrative	4,439	3,371	1,750	1,250
Total fixed costs ($000s)	23,963	24,300	9,600	9,850
EBIT ($000s)	(11,785)	2,950	(5,550)	50
Grocery Retailers				
Added revenues	750	2,000	500	1,000
Cost of goods sold %	40%	40%	40%	40%
Added EBIT ($000s)	450	1,200	300	600

continued

[a]Regional launch in one large region in the United States, such as New York, and one in Canada, such as Toronto.
[c]Does not include exclusivity payments from sponsors, which could add revenues of up to 7 million.

ments of participating sponsors, was expected to fund the program through the first year, after which time it would need to be self-financing. The first-year NA marketing budget was $23 million. Based on the U.K. experience, management was counting on receiving advertising and direct marketing support from sponsors that could be equivalent to an additional $15 million in the first year.

Working off the U.K. results and the information gathered on likely sponsor, consumer, and competitive responses to an AIR MILES launch in NA, LMG management had formulated preliminary market entry objectives. First-year objectives included aided awareness levels of 80% among target consumers, high consumer knowledge of the program concept, and the enrollment of 3 million Americans and 1 million

(continued on page 209)

Exhibit 15 *(continued)*

C: Enter U.S. and Canada	National Launch		Regional Launch[a]	
	Year 1	**Year 2**	**Year 1**	**Year 2**
Grocery Manufacturers				
Number of people enrolled	4,000,000	6,500,000	800,000	1,350,000
Weighted average AMTC collection	150	200	150	200
Revenue per AMTC	15¢	15¢	15¢	15¢
Sales of AMTC ($000s)	90,000	195,000	18,000	40,500
Other revenues[b]	100	773	0	0
Total revenues ($000s)	90,100	195,773	18,000	40,500
Cost of goods %	40%	40%	40%	40%
Total cost of goods sold ($000s)	36,040	78,309	7,200	16,200
Gross margin ($000s)	54,060	117,464	10,800	24,300
Fulfillment	16,400	20,700	6,200	6,900
Advertising	22,000	25,000	1,700	3,100
Other marketing	895	1,000	0	0
Sales	5,100	6,369	900	1,500
Information systems	10,100	9,950	4,200	3,800
Operations	8,450	7,819	3,750	3,100
General and administrative	11,200	8,415	3,750	2,950
Total fixed costs ($000s)	74,145	79,253	20,500	21,350
EBIT ($000s)	(20,085)	38,211	(9,700)	2,950
Grocery Retailers				
Added revenues	2,350	15,000	1,000	2,000
Cost of goods sold %	40%	40%	40%	40%
Added EBIT ($000s)	1,410	9,000	600	1,200

[a]Regional launch in one large region in the United States, such as New York, and one in Canada, such as Toronto.
[b]EBIT: Denotes earnings before interest and taxes.

Table D Expected AMTC Collected by Segment for an Established Program*

Collector Segment	%	AMTC Collected per Household per Year
Avid	12%	1,300
Active	23%	600
Passive	40%	150
Never active	25%	0
Weighted average		355

*Source: Management estimates.

Exhibit 16   *U. S. and Canadian Proposed Launch Advertisements*

U.S. Advertisement

Buy Smart. Fly Free.

For years, business travelers have earned frequent flyer miles and have flown free. The rest of us paid for our airline tickets. Free air travel was just a dream. The *Air Miles* idea changes all that.

FREE MILES FOR THE THINGS YOU BUY EVERY DAY.

With the *Air Miles* program, you get free air travel by simply doing what you regularly do: buying things. Like long distance phone service, magazines, eye glasses, and snack foods. For our sponsors, a group of America's most prestigious companies, free miles are simply a way of saying "thank you" for buying their products.

JOINING IS FREE, TOO.

To start earning free miles, the first thing you do is join. It doesn't cost a penny. We'll set up an account for your family to keep track of your miles.

Then simply buy the kinds of products and services you would regularly buy and watch the miles pile up. Some sponsors, like your credit card or long distance company, will credit your *Air Miles* account automatically. Others, like restaurants and retailers, will give you vouchers which you send to us.

In either case, you'll regularly get a statement of exactly how many miles you've accumulated. And you'll also learn about all the new sponsors joining the *Air Miles* program every day.

YOUR SEAT IS WAITING ON AMERICAN AIRLINES, UNITED AIRLINES, USAIR, AIR CANADA.

You can use your *Air Miles* travel credits to fly to any of their destinations. Which means just about anywhere. They fly to over 280 cities around the world, with 7,000 departures a day. You could be on any one of them.

A MILE IS A MILE.

In the *Air Miles* program, each mile you collect is worth one mile of free air travel. So if grandma is 300 miles away, you need just 600 *Air Miles* travel credits to get there and back. If it's a 2,000-mile round trip to the beach, that's how many you'll need. You don't need tens of thousands of points. And since your family can collect in one account, your miles pile up fast.

When you have enough, just call the *Air Miles* reservation center more than 14 days in advance and we'll issue you airline tickets like any normal paying passenger. There are a few restrictions. You will have to stay over a Saturday. And there are some black-out dates.

ENROLL NOW. THIS MINUTE.

To join the *Air Miles* program, just send us the attached card or call us at 1-800-446-0120. We'll send you your membership card and a package that gives you all the details, tells you who all the participating sponsors are, and lists all the special offers available to members.

In the months to come there will be so many opportunities to buy a little smarter with *Air Miles*.

Don't miss one of them.   This program is void where prohibited by law.

continued

Exhibit 16 *(continued)*

Canadian Advertisement

AS OF MARCH 30, 1992, YOU CAN

SHOP LIKE ALWAYS
AND NOT EARN
FREE* AIR TRAVEL.

SHOP LIKE ALWAYS
AND EARN
FREE* AIR TRAVEL.

IF YOU PICKED <u>b</u>, READ ON.

INTRODUCING AIR MILES.

THE FREE* AIR TRAVEL REWARD PROGRAM THAT LETS YOU
SHOP LIKE ALWAYS AND FLY LIKE NEVER BEFORE.

SHOP LIKE ALWAYS. FLY LIKE NEVER BEFORE.

Canadian Advertisement

Exhibit 17 *Potential Sponsors: November 1991**

	1991 Revenue (estimated $ billions)	Probability of Signing
Grocery Retailers		
Lead Candidates		
• Safeway-U.S. (Denver)	$11.3	50%
• Safeway-Canada (Western provinces)	3.8	70
• Vons (Southern California)	5.3	40
• Purity Supreme (New England)	1.3	60
• Price Chopper (upstate New York)	1.0	70
Packaged Goods Manufacturers		
Lead Candidates		
• Coca-Cola	$4.1	25–75%[a]
• Frito-Lay	3.7	70
• Procter & Gamble	15.3	50
• Clorox	1.6	70
Other Sponsors		
• AT&T	$57.6	90%
• Citibank[b]	8.7	50
• Time Inc.[c]	3.0	75

*Source: LMG management estimates.
[a]The probability estimates for Coca-Cola varied widely from meeting to meeting.
[b]U.S. revenues for Citicorp.
[c]Time Warner Inc. publishing revenues.

Canadians. (Exhibit 16 shows proposed print ads for the U.S. and Canadian launches.)

CONCLUSION

A conference was held on November 7, 1991, in New York to sell prospective sponsors on the program. Representatives from 70 leading consumer product and service companies were present, including senior executives of several grocery retailers and grocery manufacturers.

Following the presentation, potential sponsors that expressed a strong interest in joining the program included AT&T, Citibank, Time Inc., Coca-Cola, Clorox, Procter & Gamble, Frito-Lay, Safeway, Vons, Purity Supreme, and Price Chopper. (Exhibit 17 provides estimates of their interest levels.) As a result, there was a need to finalize the NA market entry strategy. At a board meeting scheduled four weeks later, Mills would have to present his recommendations to the directors.

ORBITAL SCIENCES CORPORATION: ORBCOMM

It has the potential to transform the company from a space-technology product enterprise to a major communications and information services business.

David Thompson, president and chief executive officer of Orbital Sciences Corporation (OSC), was commenting on the importance of the company's satellite-based mobile data communications system being developed by its subsidiary, Orbital Communications Corporation (OCC). In October 1993, he was reviewing the agenda for a forthcoming day-long review of OCC's international strategy. Major areas to cover included an assessment of ORBCOMM's international potential based in part on industry-by-industry demand forecasts and the timing and sequence of ORBCOMM's international market entry in relation to the buildup of U.S. demand. Thompson wondered whether marketing efforts in the United States should proceed, follow, or occur simultaneously to marketing overseas.

Also on the agenda were individual presentations by OCC staff. Martin Deckett, vice-president of OCC's international business devel-opment, would describe the latest version of this international forecasting model. Don Thoma, director of transportation industry services and a 1992 graduate of Harvard Business School, would discuss possible ORBCOMM applications for the trucking industry in the United States and in foreign markets, with a focus on China as an example. He and Deckett were currently work-ing on estimating ORBCOMM demand for that country's trucking industry.

COMPANY BACKGROUND

Three young entrepreneurs—David Thompson, Scott Webster, and Bruce Ferguson—met at Har-vard Business School in 1981 while working on a marketing field study on the commercialization of outer space, sponsored by the National Aero-nautics and Space Administration (NASA). In-spired by their findings, the three incorporated OSC in April 1982—the year after graduation.

The founders developed a strategy for OSC that consisted of identifying market opportunities early and leveraging existing NASA technology

---

This case was prepared by Professors Das Narayandas and John A. Quelch. The original version, with the same title, was written by Jamie Harper under the direction of Professor John A. Quelch. Copyright © 1997 by the President and Fellows of Harvard College. Harvard Business School case 598-027.

to create lower-cost products that would complement government-developed systems and address the needs of specific customers. By combining engineering, marketing, and finance operations within one firm, they believed OSC could fill a special niche in an industry characterized by large organizations, enormous capital investment, high risks, and protracted and unpredictable development cycles.

OSC began producing a steady stream of innovations based on the central concept of building and servicing low-cost, unmanned launch vehicles and satellites, concentrating on two major space transportation projects. The Transfer Orbit Stage (TOS®) vehicle was developed for NASA and other customers of the Space Shuttle. A medium-sized rocket-propulsion system, TOS could deliver 3,000- to 7,000-pound payloads, typically large communications satellites, from relatively low-altitude orbits to a variety of higher-altitude orbits once they were delivered to low orbit by the Space Shuttle.

OSC's second project, the Pegasus® satellite launcher, incorporated innovations in rocket design, manufacturing, and operations. Launched from beneath a high-flying carrier aircraft, Pegasus was capable of placing 500- to 1,000-pound "minisatellites" into a range of low-Earth orbits (LEOs).[1] This new launching concept had many advantages over traditional ground-based launches—it was far less expensive, could be executed in bad weather, and launched from anywhere. OSC's success rate, across all vehicle types, was impressive: of the 21 rockets launched from January 1992 through October 1993, 20 had succeeded.

OSC grew rapidly in 1992, earning $3.8 million on revenues of $174.6 million—up 36% and 29%, respectively, from 1991. Roughly two-thirds of OSC's operating profits were re-

---

[1]Low Earth orbit (LEO): a low-altitude orbit, approximately 300 to 500 miles above the Earth's surface, with ninety- to 100-minute orbital periods.

invested in research and development. Capital expenditures increased nearly tenfold to $27 million. At the end of 1992, OSC's firm order backlog was valued at $230 million and its total backlog (including both firm and option orders) was estimated at slightly over $1 billion.

By 1993, OSC had become the recognized worldwide leader in the design, manufacture, and operation of advanced small space transportation systems and satellite products for scientific, defense, and commercial users. The company's competitive strengths included its ability to carry out small projects faster and cheaper than the typical space contractor. OSC was ready to capture an increasing share of the rapidly growing worldwide space industry. However, Thompson was looking ahead when he commented:

> *The future growth in this business will be in satellite services. While the launch business was our engine of growth in the past, we will have to get into satellite-based services for future growth.*

Exhibit 1 provides a detailed breakdown of industry revenues by market segment in the U.S. commercial space industry.

SATELLITE-BASED SERVICES

The satellite-based services market could be broken up into two distinct markets based on whether the transmission of information between users of satellite services was through fixed earth stations or mobile earth stations. Fixed Satellite Services (FSS) that used fixed earth stations included broadcasting, data transmission, and telephony. Video transmission by cable television companies and national television broadcasters contributed about 65% of overall FSS revenues. New and emerging FSS services included direct-broadcast satellite (DBS) services—television services delivered via satellite directly to the home—and narrowcasting services, such as teleconferencing and business television.

Exhibit 1   *Estimates of U.S. Space Commercial Revenues ($MM)**

Industry	1989	1990	1991	1992[a]	1993[b]
Satellite Communications:					
Satellite services					
Fixed (FSS)	700	735	1,115	1,275	1,520
MOBILE (MSS)	50	65	85	225	380
Satellite ground equipment	790	860	1,350	1,400	1,560
Space Transportation:					
Commercial launches	150	570	380	450	450
Satellite Remote Sensing:					
Remote sensing data and services	125	155	190	215	250
Other:					
Space-based research lab (Spacehab)	—	—	—	—	60

*Sources: Estimates for satellite industry by U.S. Department of Commerce, International Trade Administration (ITA), Office of Telecommunications. Commercial launch estimates by ITA, Office of Aerospace. Remote sensing estimates by U.S. Department of Commerce, Economic and Statistics Administration, Office of Business Analysis.
[a]Revised
[b]Forecast

Compared to FSS, Mobile Satellite Services (MSS) that used mobile earth stations were newer and faster growing. Land Mobile Satellite Services (LMSS) were the largest MSS application, representing 85% of the market.[2] Service offerings in this market included satellite-delivered cellular telephony, vehicle tracking and positioning, and navigational services. Recently, there had been a spate of developments in this segment. For example, there was increasing demand among commercial users for access to the Global Positioning System (GPS), a satellite constellation developed and operated by the Department of Defense (DoD) that provided positioning services for trucking, air traffic control, delivery services, and nautical navigation. In the United States, several companies had announced new technologies based on constellations of small satellites in low orbits that would provide worldwide personal, portable, and mobile data and

[2]Marine services accounted for 15% of the MSS market.

telephony services. Internationally, INMARSAT, a consortium of 64 countries, was also developing its own small satellite proposal, Project 21, which would offer portable, hand-held communications by the early 2000s.

In early 1990, OSC had established Orbital Communications Corporation (OCC) to develop and launch a constellation of 26 LEO satellites to provide a low-cost, two-way messaging and data communications MSS system worldwide (ORBCOMM). Using pocket-sized, pager-like devices, subscribers could send and receive short messages, emergency alerts, and other critical information and obtain data concerning the location and condition of cars, boats, and other valuable assets.

When fully deployed, ORBCOMM would offer the world's first global two-way wireless data and message communications. The ORBCOMM project was expected to cost $150 million, including the construction, launch, and start-up costs of the 26-satellite LEO network. Also included were the cost of four ground stations in the United States, one central network computer hub, and related software. Initial revenue and profit forecasts indicated that ORBCOMM could be profitable on the basis of projected U.S. market penetration alone.

Keeping in mind the global opportunity in this field, in April 1993, OCC had also formed a joint venture with Teleglobe Inc. of Canada (1 billion [$U.S.]revenue in 1992) to develop, operate, and market the ORBCOMM system and services worldwide. Teleglobe would manage ORBCOMM's international operations and fund roughly 60% of ORBCOMM's development costs. As the world's fifth-largest telecommunications service provider, Montreal-based Teleglobe provided all international communications services for Canada except for those with the United States.

ORBCOMM

Until the early 1990s, cellular telephones, terrestrial radio systems, and geostationary satellites had served the mobile data communications needs of a broad range of users. However, these approaches were typically very expensive and provided only limited geographic coverage. ORBCOMM addressed the shortcomings of these existing wide-area mobile data communications in many different ways. Exhibit 2 highlights ORBCOMM's capabilities.

Given its features, ORBCOMM was well positioned for use in large areas without existing terrestrial (or fixed) facilities, as a complement to terrestrial coverage in low-traffic density areas and/or to support wide-area roaming.[3] However, due to regulatory and system design constraints, ORBCOMM services would be limited to the transmission of small packets of data sent

on an infrequent basis (as opposed to voice and video, which involved much larger file transfers). In addition, ORBCOMM could not reliably penetrate large buildings, so service was generally restricted to outdoor applications in either urban or rural areas.

The System

ORBCOMM's design reflected the latest advances in small-satellite technology. (See Exhibit 3 for a diagram of the ORBCOMM communications system, which included both space and ground elements.) ORBCOMM satellites each incorporated 17 data processors and seven antennas, enabling them to transmit and receive roughly 75,000 messages every hour. ORBCOMM's satellite constellation would be placed in LEO, 425 miles from the Earth, which would provide subscribers with near-continuous communications availability and permit extensive frequency reuse around the world.[4]

Like other LEO based systems, ORBCOMM offered numerous advantages over the more traditional, large, and high-cost GEO-based satellite systems (Exhibit 4 gives more details of ORBCOMM competitors). Given their closer proximity to Earth and use of VHF technology, LEO systems had lower energy requirements, needed smaller ground terminals (communicators), and could be designed to employ existing high-volume, low-cost VHF and UHF components enabling lower equipment prices.

The satellites would be used as relays between ORBCOMM subscribers and the worldwide telecommunications network. On the ground, Gateway Earth Stations (GESs) would link the satellites with one Network Control Center (NCC)—the nerve center of the ORBCOMM

---

[3]Wide-area roaming: ORBCOMM's ability to provide 100% geographic coverage as opposed to cellular technology, which limited service to specified, typically metropolitan geographical areas.

[4]Because each ORBCOMM spacecraft served only a limited geographic area at any given time, multiple spacecraft of the ORBCOMM system could share the same spectrum. The efficiency of such frequency reuse was highly valued by regulators.

Exhibit 2   *Highlights of the ORBCOMM System*

Ubiquitous coverage	• 26-satellite constellation provided global coverage in areas not covered by any reliable MSS system at affordable cost
Two-way	• Inbound and outbound communications
	• Acknowledgment of message receipt
Low-cost	• Subscriber equipment at one-tenth the cost of alternative satellite-based systems
	• Usage charges comparable to existing national terrestrial-based systems
Mobile	• Hand-held, portable, subscriber communicators with small, inexpensive antennas and long battery life
	• Easy to use
	• Intrinsic position determination capability
Packet data[a]	• Reliable data transmission
	• Complete connectivity to other networks

[a]Packet data was an architecture for transmitting data digitally that was both efficient and highly reliable.

system. The United States network, for example, required four GESs and one NCC (these requirements would vary by country). In February 1993, OSC launched an ORBCOMM "pathfinder" satellite to conduct initial tests of the system. This satellite provided important information on the system's assigned global frequencies and also confirmed OSC's satellite and network software design.

Subscriber Equipment

The ORBCOMM system would be accessible through a variety of data processing devices ("communications" or "terminals") designed to be user-friendly, small-sized, lightweight, and have a long battery life. (Exhibit 5 shows a picture of a prototype ORBCOMM communicator.). OCC signed agreements with Panasonic, Samsung, and other manufacturers to design, build, and market ORBCOMM communicators. By early 1993, some communicator prototypes that had been developed and tested with the ORBCOMM experimental satellite included:

• a stand-alone, 10-ounce pocket-size, two-way communicator with LCD screen and alphanumeric keypad for messaging;

• a pager-size communicator for integration with data collection and monitoring devices and for stand-alone use as an emergency transmitter;

• plug-in "PCMCIA"[5] cards (credit-card-sized electronic modules) for palmtop and laptop computers to provide convenient two-way wireless e-mail capability.

By October 1994, roughly 5,000 units would be ready for commercial sale. They were expected to be priced between $50 and $400 depending on the range of features offered.

Services

With its current specification, ORBCOMM could offer a broad range of emergency, data acquisition, and messaging services, including (see Exhibit 6 for more details):

• **Data acquisition services** Two-way transfer of digital data between a central control facil-

(continued on page 219)

[5]Personal Computer Memory Card International Association (PCMCIA) was a trade association which set the standards for credit-card-sized devices that functioned as modems, for example.

Exhibit 3   *ORBCOMM Communications System* *

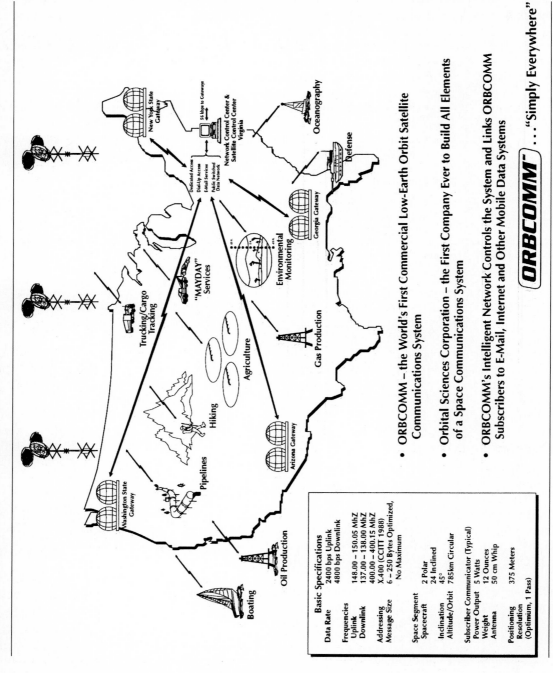

Basic Specifications

Data Rate	2400 bps Uplink
	4800 bps Downlink
Frequencies	
Uplink	148.00 – 150.05 MhZ
Downlink	137.00 – 138.00 MhZ
	400.00 – 400.15 MhZ
Addressing	X.400 (CCITT 1988)
Message Size	6 – 250 Bytes Optimized,
	No Maximum
Space Segment	
Spacecraft	2 Polar
	24 Inclined
Inclination	45°
Altitude/Orbit	785km Circular
Subscriber Communicator (Typical)	
Power Output	5 Watts
Weight	12 Ounces
Antenna	50 cm Whip
Positioning	375 Meters
Resolution	
(Optimum, 1 Pass)	

- ORBCOMM – the World's First Commercial Low-Earth Orbit Satellite Communications System

- Orbital Sciences Corporation – the First Company Ever to Build All Elements of a Space Communications System

- ORBCOMM's Intelligent Network Controls the System and Links ORBCOMM Subscribers to E-Mail, Internet and Other Mobile Data Systems

ORBCOMM™ . . . "Simply Everywhere"

*Source: Company records.

Exhibit 4   *ORBCOMM's Competition*

OCC identified two types of competition for its ORBCOMM system. The first was satellite-based, including other LEO and GEO satellite systems, while the second was terrestrial-based and included primarily Special Mobile Radio (SMR) systems and cellular technology.

Satellite-based Communications Systems

Little LEO Systems

Two other U.S. companies were also developing small satellite communications systems ("Little LEOs"). The Volunteers in Technical Assistance (VITA) was a nonprofit organization based in Arlington, Virginia, that provided technical information and assistance to developing countries. Since 1990, VITA had operated one experimental satellite. Technically different from ORBCOMM, the VITA system (VITACOMM) would provide data transfer services to developing countries, allowing users to transfer technical information as well as provide disaster relief services. Target users were scientific and humanitarian agencies. VITA planned to launch two operational satellites by 1995. Each VITA satellite was expected to cost $1 million to $1.5 million and the ground stations were estimated to cost $4,000 to $10,000. The retail price for a VITACOMM communicator was estimated at $300.

Starsys Global Positioning ("Starsys"), headquartered in Virginia, was jointly owned by ST Systems and North American CLS, a wholly owned subsidiary of CLS of France. In 1991, ST Systems was acquired by Hughes Aircraft Company, although Hughes had not exercised its option to acquire ST Systems' interest in Starsys. The Starsys TAOS system would provide similar services to ORBCOMM. In August 1992, Starsys began operating an experimental system and announced full operations by 1997. The cost of a subscriber communicator varied from $50 to $100 depending on the application and features; annual charges were estimated at $150 per subscriber in addition to usage charges. Because a majority of Starsys equity was French-owned, a debate existed as to whether it was a legitimate candidate for a U.S. FCC license.

Big LEO Systems

Big LEO satellite communications systems involved up to 66 satellites and operated in frequencies above 1 GHz. In addition to providing the data and positioning services offered by Little LEOs, Big LEO systems could provide global wireless telephone service to international travelers, users not served by cellular systems, and those in remote areas with no telephone service. As of 1993, there were five Big LEO projects under study by Motorola (Iridium), TRW (Odyssey), Loral Aerospace (GlobalStar), Mobile Communication's Holding (Ellipsat), and Constellation Communications (Aries). These companies hoped to exploit the trend towards voice communications increasingly being substituted for data communications. Service was not expected until at least 1998. Larger and more complex, these satellite systems were more expensive to build than Little LEOs, costing roughly $10 million to $20 million per satellite. Motorola's Iridium project, for example, was estimated to cost more than $4 billion. While Little Leo services could be initially less expensive than similar services provided by Big LEOs, it was possible that Big LEOs would be able to match Little LEO service prices since the cost of providing data services—in addition to their core voice service—would

continued

Exhibit 4   *(continued)*

likely be nominal. However, because of their higher frequency operations, Big LEO communicators were expected to be considerably more expensive than Little LEO equipment.

Outside of the United States, others—France, Mexico, and the CIS—were also proposing Little LEO systems. Smolsat, a Russian space consortium, had already launched six small satellites for its planned 36-satellite constellation for global data and telephony.

GEO Systems

GEO satellite systems were larger, more complicated systems in more distant orbits that resulted in higher subscriber equipment costs and service charges. Qualcomm and AMSC were the primary competitors in this segment. These systems, unlike ORBCOMM, had no restrictions on the amount of data that could be transmitted. Therefore, Qualcomm's cost per byte was much lower than ORBCOMM's, although its inbound data rate of 150 bytes per second (bps) limited message capacity. Qualcomm operated the only MSS fleet truck management system via its small mobile receivers ("OmniTracs"). The cost of OmniTracs hardware and software per truck was roughly $4,000. Qualcomm had an estimated installed base of 42,000 units, primarily with interstate trucking fleets. Using leased satellite transponders, Qualcomm offered digital data messaging and position services. Qualcomm could not offer hand-held receivers using its current technology. AMSC, on the other hand, was scheduled to launch its own GEO satellite in late 1994, which would provide seamless[1] digital mobile telephone, data, facsimile, E-mail, and position services. AMSC was planning to complement terrestrial cellular services with combined (terrestrial and satellite) cellular product offerings in 1994. AMSC would use cellular carriers, such as SNET Cellular, to sell its services. Subscriber equipment costs were estimated to start at $2,700 per truck. Big and bulky, AMSC subscribers had limited portability.

Terrestrial-based Communications Systems

Ground-based, or tower-based, mobile communications technologies were additional competition for ORBCOMM.[2] In the United States, RAM Mobile Data (RAM) and Ardis were pioneers in the SMR industry, providing data messaging services in most large urban markets. They dominated the market for mobile communications services in trucks doing local pickup and delivery. RAM, a joint venture between Ram Broadcasting and BellSouth, invested $400 million to $500 million to build 800 tower sites in the largest U.S. cities. RAM, which targeted taxi, delivery, and field services in major metropolitan areas, had over 50,000 installed units by early 1993.[3] Subscriber equipment costs were $700 per installation. System service costs per byte were below ORBCOMM's. Ardis, a joint venture between IBM and Motorola, was initially established in the early 1970s as a troubleshooting system for IBM's field operations. In 1992, Ardis, which was comparable to RAM, had 15,000 units installed outside of IBM.

Although currently limited to voice communications, cellular systems were also emerging as a threat to ORBCOMM. Cellular Digital Packet Data (CDPD), a service to convert existing cell sites

continued

---

[1]Service with 100% geographic coverage of North America.
[2]Special mobile radio services were tower-based, concentrated in metropolitan areas, involved digital and analog data transmission, and could handle high data rates.
[3]Field services included mobile work forces, such as insurance brokers or car rental sales and service staffs.

Exhibit 4   *(continued)*

for data transmission, was currently being developed by McCaw Cellular, IBM, GTE Mobile, Contel Cellular, and others. The cost of converting an existing cell was $75,000 to $125,000. By the end of 1995, digital voice and data cell networks would be operational in the United States. Compared with MSS and packet-switched data, these second-generation cellular services would provide significant advantages in the size, weight, and power demands of user equipment. These advantages were made possible by the rapidly growing number of cell sites and subscribers. In 1992, there were an estimated 10,000 cell sites and over 10 million subscribers.

Paging services offered by firms like SkyTel could also be considered ORBCOMM competition given their relatively lower cost and superior ability to penetrate buildings. The cost of a pager was $50 to $350 and service prices were $70 to $80 per month for nationwide coverage and as low as $20 per month for regional coverage. There were an estimated 14 million users of paging services in 1992. Paging, however, had a number of drawbacks. It was only one-way and confined to high-density population environments.

---

ity and a remote, unattended sensor that could be configured to collect data or control other equipment. Control applications would require the integration of ORBCOMM unit hardware with other remote equipment.

- **Tracking services** Transmission of a mobile remote-subscriber unit's position. Terminal units could be mounted in cars and connected to standard entertainment radio antennae. In the event of a theft, they could be remotely instructed to transmit position information without the perpetrator being aware of their existence.
- **Message services** Combination of the full spectrum of ORBCOMM capabilities into a single, powerful service offering. Subscribers would have the flexibility, convenience, and safety of two-way messaging, data communications, emergency alert, and position determination in one package. For example, a long-haul trucking company could send and receive messages to and from drivers, know the location of a truck at any given time, monitor critical performance indicators of the truck, and receive instantaneous notification in the event of an accident.

- **Emergency messaging services** Providing emergency alerts. By sensing an external switch closure, the remote communicator would send a short emergency message inbound to the user's home location. The unit would continue to send the alert until it received conformation of its receipt.

OCC's Marketing Strategy

There had to be three stages to OCC's marketing strategy. Phase I from 1992 to mid-1994 was the preoperational period, when no OCC satellites were in orbit; Phase II from mid-1994 to mid-1996 with intermittent service capability, when the first two satellites were in orbit; and Phase III from mid-1996 and beyond with full service capability, when full satellite capability would be offered to the United States and licensed foreign markets. Thompson commented:

This is a very tough market to manage. Internationally, we have markets that are at different stages of evolution. Not all are as evolved as the U.S. market. Further, even in the United States, not all opportunities are in the same stage of evolution. Some markets are primed

(continued on page 222)

Exhibit 5   *Prototype ORBCOMM Communicator*

Exhibit 6 *ORBCOMM Services*[*]

ORBCOMM Service Capabilities Meet the Needs of Diverse Commercial and Civil Government Markets...

ORBCOMM[sm]

Data Communications

Data Acquisition and Monitoring	Tracking

Environmental Monitoring

Boxcars and Containers

Industrial & Utilities Monitoring

Stolen Property Recovery
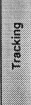

Remote Asset Monitoring
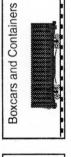

Customs and Law Enforcement

SCADA

Animal Tracking

Message Communications

Messaging	Emergency Service

Personal/ Business
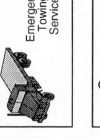

Emergency Towing Services

Communications for the Disabled

Search and Rescue

Trucking

Hazardous Materials Transport

Emergency Medical

*Source: Company records.

to receive these services, others need a lot of education and support before they will even consider using satellite-based services for their needs.

The key to success in this business is to understand customer needs, develop your technology base, identify market niches that can be best served with your technology, and then go after the best opportunities at full speed. The last part is very critical. In this business, like in the case of any other high-technology products, it can take a long time to develop the infrastructure and the market. But once things fall into place, these markets can explode in potential very, very quickly. The last thing you want to do is to educate and develop the market, and then lose it to your competition.

OCC's objective was to rapidly penetrate specifically targeted markets that would allow for efficient use of system capacity. Product and market development were at the core of OCC's marketing strategy, along with sales and distribution, although marketing to regulators, pricing, and applications development were also important. The first step in OCC's marketing strategy was to get a viable product specification accepted on a global basis. This meant that OCC had to first market to regulators.

Marketing to Regulators

OCC's early marketing efforts were initiated overseas. The initial challenge was to secure a portion of the radio frequency spectrum to provide truly global coverage for its new mobile communications system. This required OCC to obtain a spectrum allocation from international regulators. In early 1990, OCC applied to the FCC for permission to rezone the radio spectrum in the United States to accommodate Little LEO systems. Before the FCC could give the necessary permits, OCC was asked to obtain a worldwide spectrum allocation at the 1992 World Administrative Radio Conference (WARC-92),

the apex body that would address frequency allocations for a wide range of existing and emerging radio services and define the regulations that governed them.

Prior to WARC-92, OCC executives traveled to many countries to build global support for the Little LEO proposal. Countries that were influential at WARC-92 were targeted first. OCC made presentations to potential end users and governments in countries such as Japan, Venezuela, Canada, Brazil, India, Mexico, and Indonesia, emphasizing ORBCOMM's usefulness to developing countries given its low cost and ability to operate in all types of terrain. Prior to the WARC-92, OCC had memoranda of understanding (MOUs) with prospective operators in 15 countries.

In February 1992, OCC executive attended WARC-92 in Spain, joining the more than 1,400 delegates that represented 127 of the 166 member countries of the International Telecommunications Union (ITU). OCC's aim was to secure a worldwide spectrum allocation below 1 GHz for the Little LEO satellite systems. However, during the conference, OCC faced opposition. Most European countries opposed the allocations because they wanted to protect their investments in INMARSAT, which offered competing mobile satellite services. In addition, countries with high population densities favored terrestrial communications over satellite-based systems.

Nevertheless, in March 1992, worldwide spectrum allocations were granted for both Little LEO and Big LEO systems, clearing the way for individual countries to authorize the new services. In January 1993, the FCC approved the WARC-92 allocations for Little LEO communications systems in the United States. A major step in the regulatory process included the FCC's adoption of service rules that would govern the licensing and operation of LEO systems in the United States. Deckett commented:

Although we were rivals at WARC-92 negotiations, OCC, Starsys, and VITA—the three pending U.S. applicants for Little LEO li-

censes—worked together to propose service rules and sharing arrangements that would ensure that no one system was favored over the other. In fact, the Big LEO allocations that were being decided at the same time were significantly delayed due to disputes among the applicants.

In October 1993, the FCC formally adopted the U.S. service rules. Internationally, most countries were expected to follow them. OCC expected to receive its final operating license from the FCC in early 1994. The FCC was considering only the three applications from OCC, VITA, and Starsys; additional license applications would not be reviewed for one to three more years. OCC also needed to obtain licenses for its Ground Earth Stations (GESs) and subscriber transceivers, and needed to coordinate with the federal government regarding the locations of, and frequencies to be used by, the GESs.

U.S. Sales and Distribution

OCC's distribution strategy focused on rapid acquisition of customers in the most lucrative segments of the market through targeted distribution. In order to achieve this, OCC sought to develop a distribution network of Value Added Resellers (VARs). OCC planned a direct-selling approach in only the consumer messaging and emergency services. VARs would purchase ORBCOMM service directly from OCC, and then resell it to end users as part of a package that included other products or services, such as related applications software and hardware. OCC's plan was to combine its expertise in satellite-based communications with the VARs' extensive market knowledge and their large customer bases to achieve increased market access.

VARs would be responsible for developing OCC's products and marketing them to end users, with OCC lending technical and marketing support, and would also be responsible for customer billing and service functions. VARs would be selected according to their reputation, position, and strength in a target market, as well as their ability to meet a unique customer need. OCC budgeted over $100 million for marketing and distribution over the first five years of operation in the United States. A majority of OCC's sales organization was going to be set up to develop business plans, maintain competitive intelligence, and deliver merchandising programs designed to help VARs build an increasing base for ORBCOMM business.

International Sales and Distribution

Internationally, ORBCOMM services would be distributed through a network of country licensees and three or four regional "super" licensees, each of whom would oversee ORBCOMM service for several countries within a region. The license agreements were exclusive for a country or region and were renewable, contingent on meeting sales targets. OCC International (OI) was established to run the entire licensing operation outside of the United States. Teleglobe would be responsible for managing OI. After obtaining the necessary national operating approvals, country licensees would construct the ground facilities (GESs and NCC), operate the ORBCOMM system, and market ORBCOMM services. OCC managers believed that this licensing strategy would expedite country-by-country regulatory approvals and take advantage of existing local distribution channel access, customer relationships, and marketing expertise of those selected as OCC's licensees in each country.

Selecting licensees was a long and detailed process. First, OCC targeted countries with the largest expected revenues. Then, within selected countries, OCC created lists of candidate licensees by researching existing business directories and consulting government officials to identify candidates to grant operating licenses. OCC's preferred-licensee profile was a private company that might allow a minority foreign ownership with telecommunications expertise, domestic radio frequency knowledge, financial strength, and a good chance of receiving operating approvals from their governments. As of October, 1993, 20 country operators had signed MOUs with OCC and were seeking national regulatory approvals.[6] About 35 operational licenses were expected to be granted by 1996 or 1997. Candidates were being sought in a total of 47 countries. OCC's obligations under the license agreements were to operate and maintain the satellite constellation, provide access to licensees, assist licensees in planning and implementing operations, coordinate with licensees in new product development, assure worldwide quality standards were maintained, assist in arranging financing, and provide training. The startup costs to provide complete ORBCOMM geographic coverage in a country were estimated at between $1.5 million and $5 million, depending on the country's size, population, and other factors.

Pricing

One of the important issues in the negotiations with VARs in the United States and the international licensees was pricing. OCC's pricing strategy in both the United States and foreign markets was designed to encourage broad service availability and rapid subscriber growth.

In the United States, service pricing would be based on a number of variables, including the cost of providing service, the availability and cost of substitute services, and the nature of the subscriber application. Service pricing would include a monthly ORBCOMM access charge, subscriber usage charges, and a one-time registration fee. Equipment pricing would depend upon the application, features, and the sophistication of the subscriber communicator purchased.

---

[6]Countries that had signed MOUs as of October 1993 were the following: Argentina, Bolivia, Brazil, Canada, Chile, China, Colombia, Ecuador, Guatemala, Honduras, Hungary, Indonesia, Israel, Japan, Korea, Mexico, Panama, Peru, Uruguay, and Venezuela.

Internationally, the licensee agreements envisioned four distinct fees to be paid by country operators to regional distributors or OI: a one-time service license fee, usage fees, technical assistance, and software. The license fee would be at least $500,000, and would be based on the number of GESs and country-specific statistics, including population, gross national product (GNP), and telephone density. For country operators signing prior to December 31, 1992, this fee had been waived. OCC's usage fees from country operators were expected to amount to 30% of country operator revenues. Standard list prices were also developed for any technical assistance or software development that international licensees would request from OI.

Applications Development

Mobile data applications, particularly their software, were paramount to ORBCOMM's success. As Alan Parker, president of OCC, explained: "Because the service is completely transparent, it will succeed only if it can create value to both the sender and receiver." While some subscribers would develop their own applications, most would need tailored software and systems integration. OCC planned to spend $30 million for applications development over the first five years of ORBCOMM's operation. A dedicated team of in-house engineers and software developers would create applications for large subscribers, assist all subscribers in system integration, and provide technical support to VARs.

FORECASTING ORBCOMM DEMAND

The process of forecasting demand for ORBCOMM service in the United States involved three steps: vertical market definition, aggregate market forecasts, and detailed market forecasts.

In the first stage of the analysis, OCC used a top-down approach to define various segments and develop aggregate market forecasts that could be used to measure the attractiveness of each market segment. To start with, OCC's marketing department interviewed over 300 potential end users for ORBCOMM. Using this information, they defined 11 vertical market segments (VMSs): environmental, agricultural, energy, oceanography, government, cargo tracking, long-haul trucking, marine messaging, commercial messaging, consumer messaging, and emergency.

Next, from the research data collected, the marketing department constructed a U.S. demand forecast for each VMS, in order to prioritize these 11 VMSs. Demand forecasts were computed for the average number of subscriber communicators that would be connected to the ORBCOMM system each year, beginning in 1994 (with intermittent service) through 2001. Based on this analysis, the long-haul-trucking and cargo-tracking markets appeared to be most attractive in the United States. Experts also believed that this would be a major market internationally. OCC then decided to develop two applications for the trucking market. The first application was a device for the truck tractor (cab of the truck) that would allow the driver to send and receive short text messages as well as to indicate the truck's position. This information could be used by a company dispatcher to help better schedule the movements of its trucking fleet and optimize its trucking capacity. The second application was a tracking device for the truck trailer that would trace shipments, identify a cargo's location, monitor the cargo's temperature, and even indicate if the trailer doors were open.

The next step taken by OCC was to develop a more precise demand for the long-haul trucking and cargo-tracking VMS. In order to do this, Don Thoma, OCC's trucking specialist, followed four-step, bottom-up approach:

1. **Verify application fit:** Confirmed that the two ORBCOMM applications identified for trucking satisfied four criteria used to identify the most promising applications: the requirement was for small, packet-sized data only, the usage was infrequent, and it was in remote, mobile areas where no cost-effective alternative existed.

2. **Identify ideal customers:** Targeted truck tractors traveling long distances—greater than 100 miles per haul. There were 3.2 million such tractors in the United States in 1992.

3. **Perform competitive analysis:** Evaluated all other mobile data service and paging providers in the trucking market, such as Qualcomm. Evaluated the price, performance, geographic coverage, and market penetration of each competitive service offering. (Exhibit 7 shows projected penetration for key ORBCOMM competitors.)

4. **Estimate size of U.S. market:** Predicted ORBCOMM market penetration based on ORBCOMM system capabilities, competitors' penetration, and size of the U.S. trucking fleet. A range of penetration rates from 1% to 5% was estimated to be achieved by 1999.

Thoma then initiated a more in-depth, six-step, bottom-up market study of the industry:

5. **Work with trade associations:** Conducted interviews, phone surveys, and other qualitative research to understand the industry structure and trends within the industry.[7] A list of major industry participants, including potential end-users and VARs, was compiled from these meetings.

6. **Contact industry participants:** Talked to trucking companies ("carriers") and shippers to identify existing communication needs. Spoke with VARs to understand

---

[7]The three major industry participants were carriers, shippers, and consignees. Carriers owned the trucks; shippers owned the cargo being shipped, paid for the service, and were responsible for scheduling; consignees received the cargo.

Exhibit 7   *Competitors' Subscriber Estimates in the United States (in thousands)* *

	Base Year[a]	Year 1	Year 2	Year 3	Year 4	Year 5	Year 6	CAGR (%/year)
ORBCOMM[b]	1996	3	36	116	264	473	652	195%
Qualcomm	1988	1	2	10	18	24	50	151%
AMSC	1991	1	5	9	55	157	289	211%
All cellular	1984	92	340	682	1,240	2,069	3,509	107%
SkyTel (paging)	1989	53	97	134	200	—	—	56%

*Source: Company records. Note: Competitor subscriber estimates adjusted to ORBCOMM's start-up date to show relative subscriber ramp-up.
[a]Base year is the year in which services began.
[b]Total subscriber estimates are for United States only.

how they packaged such products and who their customers were.

7. **Contact competitors:** Talked to selected competitors to identify those that could possibly serve as VARs.
8. **Contact software developers:** Talked to software developers for the trucking industry to collect information on their products and to gauge their interest in developing interfaces with ORBCOMM. A majority of applications were designed to automate back-office operations, including scheduling/dispatching as well as linking the truck's cab to the home office.
9. **Refine strategy:** Synthesized the data (highlights of which are provided in Exhibit 8) to narrow OCC's marketing strategy in the trucking market. In the near term, OCC would target carriers operating large, heavy-duty trucks[8] which typically transported full loads long distances—normally interstate. To date, no single affordable communications infra-

[8]There were eight classes of trucks segmented into three groups (heavy, medium, and light duty) based on the maximum allowable fully laden weight of the truck and its payload. Classes VI–VIII, OCC's target, were heavy-duty trucks weighing from 19,500 to over 33,000 pounds.

structure had been designed to support such long-distance operations. Applications for the trailer would be emphasized initially over those for the tractor because they could be available earlier (with ORBCOMM intermittent service) and because few competing services already existed. In the longer term, OCC would focus on carriers with smaller fleets who could not currently afford existing fleet management service offerings.

10. **Determine product definition/specifications:** Talked to truckers, shippers, and VARs to identify necessary product specifications in terms of equipment, service, and price. Focus groups provided information on price, the design and features of the trailer equipment, and different formats for presenting the data.

As of September 1993, Thoma was continuing to refine the product definition. He planned to identify six trucking companies that would serve as beta sites to assist OCC in further refining its product.

International Projections

Given OCC's strategy to appoint licensees in each country, Deckett developed a model to get a preliminary demand forecast for each vertical

Exhibit 8   *Selected Key Findings of Initial Market Research on the U.S. Trucking Industry* *

I. Industry Trends
- There was a growing demand by shippers for speed, sophistication, and reliability in logistics services. Where shippers were increasingly faced with more stringent delivery requirements, they were adopting Just-In-Time (JIT) techniques that placed tremendous logistical pressures on trucking companies.
- Trucking operators and suppliers were consolidating further as the continuing profit squeeze and escalating shipper demands forced the industry to become more capital-intensive and efficient.
- Increasingly, carriers were using technologies to identify and track vehicles, shipments, and drivers. These technologies would bring significant benefits to shippers and trucking companies, but they would also enable governments to collect tolls and weight-distance taxes more easily.

II. Existing Fleet Management Systems
- As of 1993, all the major carriers were using some form of mobile communications services to coordinate their operations and ultimately improve customer service and lower operating costs. Typically, these services were used for engine and systems maintenance, for communications between driver and dispatcher to schedule and better manage the trucking fleet, and for managing back-office paperwork flow and fuel purchasing. Big carriers had larger data requirements and were typically more advanced than smaller companies.
- The majority of existing mobile communications applications were designed for the truck tractor to facilitate truck drivers communicating with the dispatcher. Applications for the trailer, for tracking and monitoring cargo, were minimal. While Qualcomm's OmniTrac was used with the trailer, service was not available if the cab and trailer were detached. ORBCOMM applications designed for the trailer could be available with the first two satellites in orbit, whereas tractor applications would require the full 26-constellation system. Tracking trailers would require less use of the ORBCOMM system (about once a day) than tractors, which would generate larger, more frequent communication between the truck and its home office throughout a given day.
- Carriers would purchase ORBCOMM and other similar products based on price first, their individual data needs second, and the associated value-added software third. The decision-making unit would be different according to the size of the carrier:
  - (a) For smaller carriers, the president (typically the owner) would make the decision
  - (b) For larger carriers, decisions would be made by the president (typically the owner), chief financial officer, head of Management Information Systems (MIS), and/or the dispatcher.

III. 1992 Truck Statistics (in thousands)[a]

Fleet Size	Trucking Companies	Class I–V[a] Truck Tractors	Class VI–VIII Truck Tractors	Trailers
500+ trucks	3.5	1,255	1,155	1,410
100–499	14.5	710	715	770
25–99	32.0	560	605	510
5–24	75.0	400	400	350
1–4	250.0	200	275	160
Total	375.0	3,125	3,150	3,200

*Sources: Adapted from company records and American Trucking Association (ATA), *1994 Marketing Databook*, pp. 3–16.
[a]Data of total U.S. commercial truck fleet market, adapted from ATA data.
[b]Class I–V trucks were typically straight trucks without trailers.

market in each country. Each forecast was computed by modifying the U.S. demand forecasts by certain factors that were derived from selected economic and other statistics for that particular country.[9] International demand forecasts were for the number of new subscribers connected to the ORBCOMM system each year, as opposed to the U.S. demand forecast that was based on the average number of subscribers during each year. More specifically, in calculating demand for a particular country, Deckett used a five-step process including:

1. Assigning the vertical markets to three groups according to the type of applications designed for each market. (This division applied to *all* countries.) For example, communications from remotely located sensors would be the dominant application in Group A markets, while mobile services would be common to Group B markets, such as the trucking industry. Group C markets would all use messaging services.

2. Determining which country statistics would affect the estimates of new connects in each group. For Group A, Deckett chose GNP and area; for Group B, he selected geographical area, size of vehicle fleet, and phone density; and for Group C, he chose population, GNP per capita, area, telephone density, and ORB-COMM system availability. Other statistics considered included miles of road and number of boats, but they were discarded for lack of comparable data across countries.

3. Computing the ratios on each statistic of the target country to the U.S. statistic (for example, the population ratio in China [4.56] was derived by dividing China's population [1.15 million] by the U.S. population [252 million]).

4. Computing a score for each group by taking the geometric average of the correlated ratios and then multiplying them by the uncorrelated ratios.[10]

5. Estimating the number of new connects in the country by applying the group factor to the adjusted U.S. demand estimates.

Deckett's methodology for calculating demand in China is demonstrated in Exhibit 9. Chinese demand estimates for the first eight years of service are provided in Exhibit 10. Deckett expected individual country licensees to develop more accurate demand estimates by revising the preliminary connect estimates based on detailed local market studies.

TRUCKING DEMAND IN CHINA

Deckett and Thoma were in the process of responding to an inquiry from China's Ministry of Transportation (MOT). MOT was currently reviewing the pending ORBCOMM license agreement with a telecommunications company headquartered in Hong Kong that was already heavily involved in the paging market. Included in MOT's review was an estimate of the potential market for ORBCOMM in China's trucking industry.

Although very underdeveloped, the Chinese trucking industry was evolving quickly. Historically, the Chinese relied on railways to ship their

(continued on page 231)

---

[9]In his model, Deckett made two adjustments to the U.S. demand forecasts. First, the government market was omitted and absorbed into each of the other 10 sectors, and second, the estimates were adjusted to reflect ORBCOMM's later service introduction (1995 or 1996) in international markets when the full 26-satellite system would be operational.

[10]It was argued that the phone density ratio and the availability ratio were uncorrelated, whereas all the other ratios were correlated. In deriving the group factors, the correlated statistical ratios were averaged together, using the geometric averaging technique. This average and the uncorrelated statistical ratios were then multiplied together to obtain the group factors. For example, Group B factor = (phone density ratio) $\times$ ((area ratio) $\times$ (vehicle ratio)) $\div$ (1/2).

Exhibit 9 *Derivation of Group Factors for China**

Group	Markets	Relevant Statistics	China Statistics	U.S. Statistics	Ratios[a]	Group Factors[b]
A	Environmental					
A	Agricultural	• GNP ($ billions)	$424	$5,686	0.075	0.276
A	Energy	• Area (sq. miles)	3,692	3,619	1.020	
A	Oceanography					
B	Cargo Tracking	• Area	3,692	3,619	1.020	0.337
B	Long-haul trucking	• Vehicles (thousands)	4,172	45,106	0.093	
		• Phone density (no. lines/100 people)	2	50	1.096	
C	Marine messaging	• Area	3,692	3,619	1.020	0.434
C	Commercial messaging	• GNP/capita ($)	$370	$22,563	0.016	
C	Consumer messaging	• Population (millions)	1,150	252	4.563	
C	Emergency	• Availability (%)	86%	92%	0.935	
		• Phone density	2	50	1.096	

*Source: Company records

[a]Calculated by dividing U.S. statistics by China statistics, except for the phone density ratio which was calculated as $1.1 - 0.1 *$ (country phone density/U.S. phone density). The ORBCOMM availability ratio reflected the "average" system availability in a target country to that in the United States.

[b]Calculated by taking the geometric average of the correlated ratios and then multiplying them by the uncorrelated ratios (phone density and ORBCOMM availability). For example, Group B factor = (phone density ratio) $\times$ SQRT ((area ratio) $\times$ (vehicle ratio)).

Exhibit 10 *Projected Numbers for New Connects for China, Based on U.S. Estimates* *

Group	Markets	U.S.[a] Year 2	China[b] Year 2	Year 3	Year 4	Year 5	Year 6	Year 7	Year 8
A	Environmental	2,180	601	1,203	1,804	1,506	1,655	2,317	2,317
A	Agricultural	8,500	2,344	4,689	7,033	9,185	7,943	7,447	7,447
A	Energy	4,650	1,283	2,565	5,130	5,130	4,137	4,137	4,137
A	Oceanography	2,640	728	1,456	2,184	1,291	331	331	331
B	Cargo Tracking	4,800	1,618	3,235	4,853	3,640	3,033	3,033	3,033
B	Long-haul trucking	9,000	3,033	6,066	9,099	12,132	14,558	16,176	20,220
C	Marine messaging	2,160	937	1,875	2,812	3,750	4,166	4,166	4,166
C	Commercial messaging	7,650	3,320	6,640	9,949	13,280	15,624	18,228	20,832
C	Consumer messaging	4,140	1,797	3,594	5,390	7,187	13,020	18,228	26,040
C	Emergency	4,200	1,823	3,646	5,468	6,250	7,812	10,416	11,718
	Total	49,920	17,484	34,969	53,722	63,351	72,279	84,479	100,241

*Source: Company records.

[a] Adjusted U.S. demand estimates for Year 2 to demonstrate how China estimates were derived.

[b] China demand estimates for Years 2 through 8 calculated by multiplying group factors and adjusted U.S. numbers of new connects for the corresponding years.

cargo. Under a centrally planned economy, it was much less expensive to transport cargo on trains as opposed to trucks. The per-mile cost of transporting a 2,000-pound cargo was 10 times greater by truck than by train. In addition, roads in China were in poor condition and most were not suitable for large tractor/trailers.

Shipping by train, however, had several disadvantages. Shippers had difficulty reserving space quickly and at short notice. It could take up to 10 to 15 days to transport cargo 600 miles by train, as opposed to two days by truck. Door-to-door service was not included, so shippers had to arrange for additional transportation to and from the train. In the late 1970s, China's economic reform and market economy forced the shipping industry to keep pace with the developing economy. Shippers needed timely and efficient transportation, and many were willing to sacrifice price for faster delivery. After 1978, trucking routes were no longer centrally controlled by the state, and therefore shippers were free to make decisions regarding how, when, and by whom their cargo would be transported. This, therefore, promised to revive the trucking industry.

Trucking carriers were owned and operated by MOT, by other ministries, by collective enterprises, and by private companies and individual owner/operators. Only 10% of trucks were privately owned, although this percentage was expected to grow in the future. In 1993, the industry was focused on improving roadways and increasing the production of trucks weighing more than 16,000 pounds. Currently, there was a very short supply of larger-sized trucks. Between 1993 and 1997, annual domestic demand for medium and heavy-duty trucks approximated 50,000 units.

Chinese trucks were classified into three types according to their weight and corresponding carrying capacity: light/small (less than 4,000-pound weight; 8,000-pound carrying capacity), medium (5,000- to 16,000-pound weight; 10,000- to 18,000-pound carrying capacity), and heavy/large (greater than 16,000-pound weight; over 20,000-pound carrying capacity). The average truck weight was 8,200 pounds.

In China in 1993, there were 3.7 million trucks, of which 20% were light/small, 75% were medium, and 5% were heavy/large. Roughly half were on the road on any given day and many trucks made return trips from their destinations without any cargo. On average, a truck traveled 90 to 120 miles per day. Four Chinese companies competed in truck manufacturing, particularly of medium-sized trucks. They could each produce 2,000 to 3,000 trucks per year.

In China, mobile communications and/or tracking services were currently provided to military, fire, and bank trucks only. All other carriers used additional manpower instead. For example, two drivers were often assigned on long-distance trips. In the event of an accident or mechanical failure, one would go to the nearest town to telephone company headquarters, while the other remained with the truck to protect the cargo.

CONCLUSION

Deckett and Thoma reviewed the U.S. trucking strategy as well as the model for forecasting the number of new connects in cargo tracking and long-haul trucking. Given the forecasting techniques already in practice and the new data on China, they wondered how best to advise the Chinese MOT in projecting ORBCOMM demand in the trucking market. Thoma expected to incorporate his analysis in his presentation at the ORBCOMM international strategy review meeting.

PART III

GLOBAL MARKETING PROGRAMS

Managers responsible for marketing in a multi-national or global enterprise must design appropriate marketing programs for each national market. To some extent, each country must be treated as a separate marketplace, because each has its own currency, legal requirements, and business methods. However, by coordinating operations on a regional or global scale, multi-nationals can gain important advantages.

The most important issue in the development of multinational marketing programs is the extent to which elements of the marketing mix are standardized regionally or globally, as opposed to being customized to each country market. The degree of customization typically varies from one mix element to another, and often varies from product to product and from country to country within the same multinational. Three generalizations may be made in this regard.

- Strategic elements of the marketing mix (see Figure 1), such as brand name and positioning are more likely to be standardized than

execution-intensive elements, such as distribution, sales promotion and customer service.
- Marketing program standardization is more feasible in the case of higher technology and non-culture-bound products marketed to a younger customer base (e.g., personal computers and software) than in the case of traditional, culture-bound products used in the home (e.g., soups).
- Standardized programs are more readily accepted in smaller country markets, in which the local organization has fewer skills and resources, than in larger, older operating subsidiaries, which can assert their independence against headquarters more easily.

Customization of the marketing mix should be guided by a simple principle. The additional costs of marketing program adaptation to meet the needs of a national segment should be exceeded by the resulting extra margin generated through higher unit sales and/or higher unit margins.

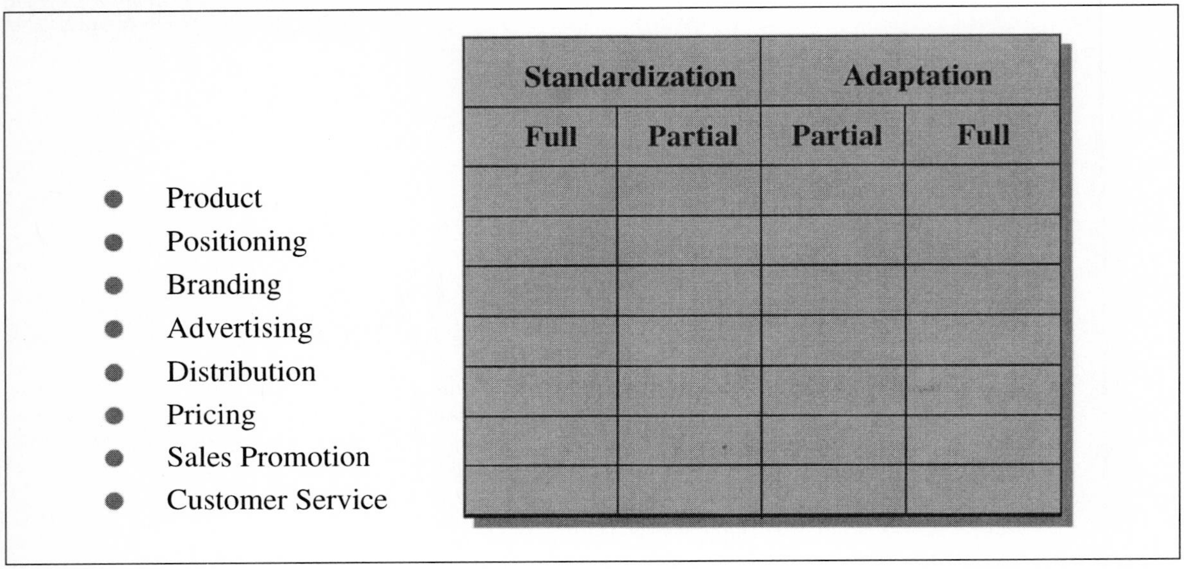

	Standardization		Adaptation	
	Full	**Partial**	**Partial**	**Full**
● Product				
● Positioning				
● Branding				
● Advertising				
● Distribution				
● Pricing				
● Sales Promotion				
● Customer Service				

Figure 3.1   Marketing Mix: Standardization versus Customization.

When customization occurs, it is essential that the country-specific programs, although different, be in harmony. Given increased consumer mobility, global communications, and the cross-border spillover of media advertising, it may be unwise for a multinational to permit radically different positionings of the same brand. To do so may underleverage the advantages that being a multinational affords, including the cross-border transfer of best marketing practices. On the other hand, the argument is often made that a customer in Paris does not obtain any added value from knowing that the exact same marketing program is being deployed in New York—and that marketing mix adaptation does not, therefore, detract from the appeal of global brands.

There are, it happens, relatively few global brands deploying the same marketing programs worldwide. Different country markets are invariably at different stages of category and/or brand development, even for global brands. For example, Heineken deploys one marketing mix in high-share markets with well-developed beer consumption and another mix in low-share markets with low per capita consumption. However, there are commonalities: outside the Netherlands, where Heineken is a mass-market beer, the brand is positioned worldwide as a premium beer consumed in social settings by good friends.

Like many other global brands, the Heineken brand name is the same as the company name. The mere fact that the brand is recognized worldwide enables Heineken to command a price premium and superior distribution. A segment of consumers in every country wants to enjoy the perceived status associated with using global brands. In addition, the commonalities in a global brand's marketing mix permit marketing investments to be amortized over a worldwide base of sales. Moreover, only global brands have the marketing muscle to participate in global sports sponsorships that are an increasingly important component of the marketing communications mix. Finally, global brands can attract and retain outstanding managers, instill pride among employees and facilitate greater headquarters control of far-flung subsidiaries.

Indeed, the issue of marketing program standardization versus customization cannot be separated from the management process issue of centralization versus decentralization. Although it is conceivable that an enlightened headquarters might decide in favor of customization, there is an ongoing tension in most multinationals between headquarters advocacy of standardization, motivated primarily by cost and control considerations, and the field operations that seem to respond to differences in customer behavior from one market to another. A weak headquarters will permit an excessive proliferation of country-specific adaptations; after all, if country managers cannot identify differences requiring adaptations, they might as well resign. On the other hand, an excessively controlling headquarters will leave money on the table by not permitting low-cost, yet potentially highly profitable, customization.

GALLO RICE

In March 1992, Cesare Preve, managing director of F&P Gruppo, marketer of the Gallo brand of rice, was reviewing his company's current market position. Specifically, he was evaluating how to further penetrate the retail rice markets in three countries: Italy, where the Gallo brand had been present for over a century and held a 21% volume share; Argentina, where Gallo had been established in 1905 and held a 17.5% volume share; and Poland, where Gallo had been distributed in small quantities for three years and held less than a 1% volume share.

Preve wondered what experience, information, and insights gained in one market could be transferred to other markets and where to focus management time and effort. Should the company attempt to consolidate its position in large, mature, slow-growth markets, or should the newer, high-growth potential markets receive a higher proportion of managerial time and marketing effort in the future? To assess the marketing requirements of each country and the potential sharing of experience across markets, Preve compiled a summary of the comparative country data (see Table A).

COMPANY BACKGROUND

Focused on the production of value-added rice, F&P Gruppo described itself as "the rice specialist" and was one of only a few companies in the world involved in the entire process, from growing and milling to the packaging and marketing of branded rice. The company added value through research and development of new and improved strains of high-quality rice, proprietary manufacturing processes, and packaging. Gallo had resisted the temptation to manufacture or market any food products other than rice. The goal of the company was to achieve market share leadership by bringing differentiated, higher-margin products to an increasingly segmented marketplace. A higher percentage of the resulting profits were, in turn, reinvested in research and development. It was a company objective to ensure that 35% to 40% of total gross margin was derived from products that were not in the product line five years before.

F&P Gruppo was a private, family-owned company dating back five generations. It owned production facilities in Italy, Germany, Argentina,

This case was prepared by Nathalie Laidler (under the direction of John Quelch). Copyright © 1993 by the President and Fellows of Harvard College. Harvard Business School case 593-018.

Table A   Market Characteristics of Italy, Argentina, and Poland (1990)

	Italy	Argentina	Poland
Population (millions)	57.7	32.3	38.4
Age distribution: 0–14, 15–59, 60+	18%, 63%, 19%	30%, 57%, 13%	26%, 60%, 14%
Percentage urban population	67%	85%	60%
Annual population growth	0.1%	1.0%	0.4%
GNP per capita (U.S. $)	15,652	2,134	2,500
Per capita expenditures on food (U.S. $)	2,170	465	256
GDP breakdown: agricultural, industrial, services	4%, 33%, 63%	13%, 41%, 45%	14%, 36%, 50%
Inflation rate	6.5%	17%[a]	600%
Cereal imports (tons)	6,699	4	1,550
Rice is a major crop	Yes	Yes	No
Television set penetration	1 per 3.9 persons	1 per 4 persons	1 per 3.9 persons
Radio penetration	1 per 3.9 persons	1 per person	1 per 3.6 persons
Literacy rate	98%	92%	98%
Advertising expenditures per capita (U.S. $)	116	13	N/A
Advertising expenditures: percentage breakdown by medium	Print = 59%	Print = 45%	N/A
	TV = 35%	TV = 31.3%	
	Radio = 2.5%	Radio = 8.8%	
	Cinema = 0.2%	Cinema = 0.8%	
	Outdoor = 3.3%	Outdoor = 14.1%	
Number of consumers per retail food outlet	182	1,318	724
Distribution concentration: percentage of retail sales through supermarkets	56%	36%	15%

[a]Argentina's inflation rate estimated for first quarter 1992, down from 3,000% in 1989.

and Uruguay and sold throughout Europe and South America. The group comprised wholly owned subsidiaries in the above four countries as well as Switzerland and Brazil, plus a joint venture in the United Kingdom.

The Gallo brand name and Gallo rooster logo were used consistently across geographic markets and product lines ("Gallo" meant rooster in both Spanish and Italian). In 1991, Gallo marketed white rice, parboiled (partly boiled) rice, and brown rice. The company had also recently introduced dehydrated, quick-cooking rice and dehydrated mixes in many of its more developed markets. These branded, top-of-the-line products delivered to the company as much as 50 times the profit margin achievable through the sale of the same quantity of bulk white rice.

THE RICE INDUSTRY

In 1991, world production of rice was around 500 million metric tons, and consumption, which

Exhibit 1   *Distributuion of Milled Rice Volume in the U.S.A. and Italy, 1992*

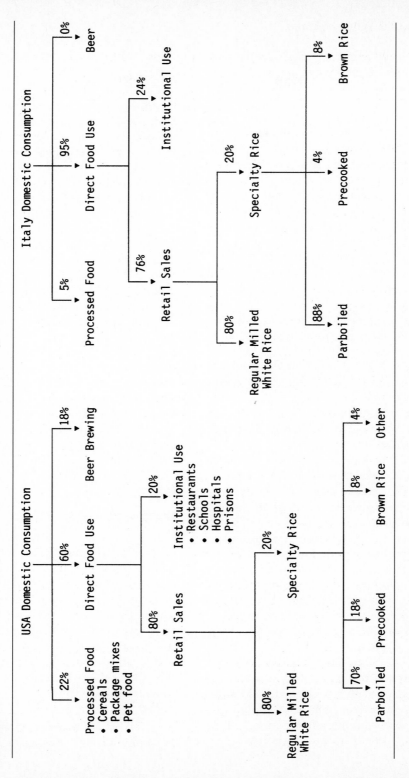

varied significantly by geographic area, was around 350 million metric tons on a milled basis. Only 12 million tons were traded internationally.

There were two main strains of rice: Indica grains, which were long and thin, fluffy when cooked, and more popular in northern Europe; and Japonica grains, which were shorter and more absorbent, creamier when cooked, and more popular in southern Europe. In recent years, Spain and Italy had increased their production of Indica rice; as a result, imports of rice into Europe had decreased.

Rice reached the consumer in many forms:

- Paddy rice was the raw material harvested from the field, with only primary cleaning and drying.
- Cargo rice resulted from an initial milling process, whereby the hulls (accounting for 20% of the raw rice weight) were removed.
- White rice was the product of the final milling process and could be refined to varying degrees.
- Brown rice was similarly milled, but the bran layer was retained on the kernel during the milling process.
- Parboiled rice was a response to the consumer's desire for more convenience. Its production involved a special milling process, whereby paddy rice was soaked in hot water, cooked with steam pressure, and then dried. During this process, the starch was gelatinized such that the vitamins migrated into the interior of the grain. This made the rice grains harder and almost impossible to overcook, resulting in a nonsticking final product. There were 40 steps in Gallo's parboiled rice production process.
- Precooked or quick-cooking rice was an increasingly popular niche product, processed by a freeze-thaw method. Regular milled rice was soaked in water to increase moisture content, boiled, cooled quickly with cold water, then allowed to freeze and thaw slowly. The end result was a rice kernel that absorbed wa-

ter more readily, thereby reducing the necessary cooking time.

Exhibit 1 shows the breakdown of rice consumption by end use and type in both the United States and Italy. Domestic consumption, calculated from domestic production plus imports minus exports, included three primary use categories: processed food production (e.g., for breakfast cereals); beer production; and direct food use. Of direct-food-use volume, most was eaten at home after purchase through food retailers. It was in this channel that branding of rice played an important role. Most retail rice sales were of basic milled white rice, with parboiled white rice being the second most important subcategory.

Gallo-milled rice consistently earned the highest of six quality grades. In 1991, Gallo handled 200,000 tons of milled rice worldwide, valued at six times the average world crop price of cargo rice. In the 1980s, many other companies tried to enter the market for value-added, branded rice products. Although this caused some price pressure, price-insensitive consumer segments were identified for certain higher-value products such as brown rice and dehydrated risotto mixes (rice mixed with dehydrated ingredients such as peppers, mushroom, chicken, and spices).

ITALY

Market Characteristics

Rice was a staple of the Italian diet. Used by 98% of the Italian population in 1991, per capita consumption averaged 5 kg[1] per annum. Some regional differences existed, with consumption being closer to 8 kg in the north (Italian rice production was concentrated in the Po valley, in the north of the country) and 3 kg in the south.

Of the 320,000 tons of rice sold in Italy in 1991, approximately 70,000 tons were sold through food service establishments, and 250,000 tons were sold through grocery stores. Retail

---

[1] 1 kg = 2.2 lbs. and 1 ton = 2,000 lbs.

sales in 1991 were 85% white rice and 15% parboiled by volume and 70% white rice and 30% parboiled by value. Sales of both parboiled rice and special rices (less than 5% of the market by value) were growing at 8% and 12% per annum respectively. White rice was losing share at 1% to 3% per annum.

Rice was seen as quick and easy to prepare, versatile, healthy, easily digested, and an alternative to pasta. Brand choices were based on quality, habit, availability, and packaging. Typically, rice was sold through stores in 1-kg cardboard boxes, although a small percentage was sold from bulk bins and in 5-kg plastic bags. Legal restrictions in Italy required each variety of rice to be sold separately; the result was extended product lines since different rice varieties could not be mixed.

Gallo in Italy

Present in Italy since the nineteenth century as a rice miller, Gallo products accounted for 21% of Italian retail rice volume in 1991, 2% higher than in 1990. The Gallo logo, a cheerful rooster, was widely recognized and symbolized a trustworthy, good-quality, albeit somewhat traditional brand. As the overall market share leader, Gallo offered three product lines:

- The basic *Riso Gran Gallo* white rice line was offered in nine varieties (ranging from simple white rice to super-fine white rice), reflecting regional preferences and different recipe requirements. For example, Gallo *Padano*, popular in Milan, was used mainly in soups. Six of the nine varieties were long-grain, more absorbent rice suitable for risotto dishes.[2] In 1991, this line accounted for 64.4% of Gallo's total Italian sales volume and 51% of its total lire sales. Gallo's volume share of white rice

sales in Italy was 17.3% in 1991. (Product package illustrations appear in Exhibit 2.)

- The *Blond* line of parboiled rice included three parboiled nonstick products and one dehydrated, quick-cooking rice (also parboiled). The three parboiled products were (1) *Orientale,* a white rice that cooked light and fluffy; (2) *Risotti,* a larger-grain rice suitable for risotto recipes; and (3) *Integro,* a "natural" brown rice that retained important ingredients and fiber sometimes depleted in the milling process. A dehydrated, quick-cooking product, *Meta'Tempo* (half time), was included in the line in 1990 and cooked in five to seven minutes. In 1991, this line accounted for 34.4% of Gallo's Italian volume sales and 48% of its lire sales. Gallo's volume share of parboiled rice sales in Italy was 35.4% in 1991. (Product package illustrations appear in Exhibit 2.)

- The *Grandi Risi del Mondo* (great rices of the world) was a super-premium line introduced in 1989 in five varieties (*Long and Wild, Bismati, Arborio, Carnaroli,* and *Patna*). Although this line carried the familiar Gallo chicken logo on the front package panels, the line was marketed through a separate sales force and specialty store distribution. In 1991, this line accounted for just 1.2% of volume sales and 1.5% of lire sales. (Product package illustrations appear in Exhibit 2.)

Most Gallo products were sold to retailers through a network of 60 agents and brokers, not by a company sales force. These agents carried other food products but no other rice brands. Due to its brand strength, Gallo received excellent push-marketing efforts from its agents. A sales incentive program rewarded those who grew the Gallo business. In 1991, Gallo was carried in stores accounting for 80% of Italian grocery sales, more than any other brand. A typical supermarket carried two of Gallo's white rice varieties and three of the four parboiled items; the higher-priced Orientale was least widely distributed.

---

[2]Risotto dishes were rice-based meals that included meat and/or vegetables.

Exhibit 2   *Product Package Illustration for the Gallo Product Lines in Italy*

Competition

The Italian retail rice market was fragmented, with many local and regional millers selling under their own brand names. Grocery retailing was also fragmented but rapidly consolidating. In 1991, supermarkets and hypermarkets accounted for 60% of all rice value sales and 64% of Gallo's value sales, up from 57% and 59% in 1989. In 1991, private labels held a 17% share of rice retail sales volume, up from 13% in 1990. Gallo also competed against three major national brands:

- *Flora,* a subsidiary of BSN, the French food conglomerate, marketed only parboiled rice and competed directly with Gallo's *Blond* line.[3] Flora offered four varieties: *Integral, Orientale, Risotti Blond,* and *Rapido.* Combined, these items held a 41% volume and a 46% value share of the Italian parboiled market in 1991.

  Flora television advertising was upbeat and depicted the lifestyles of four target segments, one for each item in the line. For example, the *Integral* commercial showed a health-conscious woman working out, while the *Rapido* commercial featured a successful businesswoman. The "lifestyle" commercials were modern, light, and appeared to be targeted at younger women. Flora also used five-minute television "infomercials" which included viewer call-in games to promote the brand. In 1990, Flora spent 20% more on advertising than did Gallo. A recent consulting study estimated that manufacturer gross margins on Flora were 30%, compared with Gallo's margins on the *Blond* line of 35%.

- *Curti-Buitoni* was acquired in 1985 by Nestlé, the Swiss food company. The Nestlé sales force provided the *Curti* brand with excellent distribution, but the brand was not heavily advertised. *Curti-Buitoni* offered both basic white rice and parboiled products and held a

10.2% and 5.6% volume share of these markets, respectively.

- *Scotti* was a family-owned, regional firm. Its product line was restricted to basic white rice. Scotti held a 7.5% volume share and had been approached by F&P Gruppo and others as a possible acquisition target.

Exhibit 3 summarizes market shares and brand awareness data for the four principal national brands in 1990 and 1991. Exhibits 4 and 5 compare Gallo and competitor market shares for white and parboiled rice and their relative retail prices.

Communication Strategy

Gallo's marketing expenditures increased from 13% of sales in 1988 to a planned 15% in 1992. (Actual promotional and advertising expenditures for 1991 and planned expenditures for 1992 are detailed in Exhibit 6.) In 1991, Gallo's television advertising was divided evenly between spot commercials and five-minute promotional infomercials. Television commercials for the *Blond* line depicted different consumers winning cooking competitions thanks to Gallo rice. Each commercial depicted a nervous individual holding a dish of rice, waiting in the wings, being called to the stage to receive an award, then being congratulated and applauded. The commercial cut back to the product, and an announcer explained that the award was won thanks to the Gallo brand of rice. Print advertisements in magazines often included a recipe, a photograph of the product, and detailed information on the differences of rice varieties. (Exhibit 7 shows a typical print advertisement, and Exhibits 8 and 9 show other Gallo magazine print advertisements.) Consumer promotions included in-store sampling and continuity programs, advertised on packages and in magazines, whereby consumers could redeem Gallo box tops for pottery and other merchandise. Gallo accounted for 33% of total category media advertising in 1991.

In 1992, television advertising planned for the *Blond* line would focus on the nonstick

---

[3]In Italy, BSN was also a strong player in branded pasta.

Exhibit 3   *Market Shares and Brand Awareness Levels for Gallo and Competitors in Italy, 1990 and 1991**

	Volume Market Shares (%)		1991 Awareness Levels (%)		
	1990	**1991**	**First Mention**	**Unaided**	**Aided**
Gallo	19.1%	21.1%	37%	62%	91%
Flora	8.1	8.8	14	28	82
Curti-Buitoni	10.5	9.2	15	30	79
Scotti	5.9	6.1	8	14	64

*Source: Company records.

benefit. Specific print advertising for *Integro* and *Meta'Tempo* products would communicate nutritional value and quick cooking time. An umbrella print advertising program, in both national and regional newspapers and magazines, would portray Gallo as serious and reliable and focus on the brand's tradition and culture.

Issues

In considering how to further penetrate the branded rice retail market, Preve was considering whether to create an entire new dehydrated line around the *Meta'Tempo* sub-brand. Consumers perceived *Meta'Tempo* to be superior to simple parboiled rice, and some thought that the product could be the base of a whole new dehydrated-product line, particularly since Gallo had a competitive advantage, being further down the

learning curve in dehydrated technology than competitors. Sales of *Meta'Tempo* were growing rapidly, and dry rice mixes (such as risottos) were selling at three to four times the retail price of normal white rice.

Gallo's Naturis company produced dehydrated, quick-cooking rice and supplied both BSN's *Flora Rapido* and Gallo's *Blond Meta'Tempo*. Flora's *Rapido* had been the only brand of quick-cooking rice on the market between 1988 and 1990. Gallo's *Meta'Tempo* was launched as a freestanding product in 1990, but had to be withdrawn due to poor sales and the high cost of promotional support. It was quickly repositioned within the *Blond* line and, by 1992, sales of *Meta'Tempo* equaled those of *Rapido*.

Preve also wrestled with several questions regarding the 1992 communications budget. First, he wondered if the competitive situation called for a substantially higher budget than in 1991.

Exhibit 4   *White Rice in Italy: Gallo and Competitor Market Shares and Relative Retail Prices, 1990 and 1991**

	Volume Market Shares (%)		Relative Retail Prices ($)	
	1990	**1991**	**1990**	**1991**
Riso-Gallo	16.4%	17.3%	1.00	1.00
Curti-Buitoni	11.1	10.2	0.98	0.97
Scotti	7.0	7.5	0.98	0.98
Private Label	15.5	17.3	0.78	0.78

*Source: Company records.

Exhibit 5   *Parboiled Rice in Italy: Gallo and Competitor Market Shares and Relative Retail Prices, 1990 and 1991**

	Volume Market Shares (%)		Relative Retail Prices ($)	
	1990	1991	1990	1991
Riso-Gallo	31.3%	35.4%	1.00	1.00
Curti-Buitoni	7.8	5.6	1.03	0.98
Flora	43.3	40.9	1.05	1.04
Private Label	14.2	12.2	0.74	0.69

*Source: Company records.

Second, he wondered whether Gallo should continue to put all its advertising behind the parboiled Blond line or allocate more support to the core white rice line.

There was also some concern that Gallo was not as strong as Flora in the growing supermarket/hypermarket retail segment. Actual retail trade margins were around 7% on Flora, compared with 1% on Gallo's *Blond* line. Preve believed that the Gallo brand was often used as a traffic builder and that consumers who purchased Gallo branded rice were also more likely to purchase higher-value products, with greater retailer margins. In addition, Preve argued that Gallo products had a higher turnover than many other food products and that F&P Gruppo allowed retailers generous payment terms. Despite this, Preve was concerned that chains would be motivated to develop their own private label lines of rice products.

Exhibit 6   *Gallo Advertising and Promotion Expenditures in Italy**

	Millions of Lira[a]	
	1991 (actual)	1992 (planned)
Media advertising:	9,466	9,210
TV ads for Blond		6,000
Gallo umbrella ads in magazines		1,150
Magazine ads for Blond Integro		200
Magazine ads for Blond Meta'Tempo		700
Supermarket magazines		180
Fees and production costs		980
Consumer promotion	3,039	2,300
Regional marketing	300	265
New product launch	789	350
Trade and sales force incentives	6,047	7,950
Total	19,641	20,075

*Source: Company records and estimates.
[a]U.S. $1 = 1,272 Lira.

Exhibit 7 *Gallo Italy: Typical Print Advertisement*

LO SPECIALISTA DEL RISO

Il "riso bianco" non è tutto uguale. Comprende molte varietà che si differenziano tra loro per grandezza e forma del chicco, per trasparenza, contenuto in amido, tenuta in cottura, capacità di assorbimento dei condimenti. Conoscerle significa sfruttare al meglio le caratteristiche di ognuna per avere in cucina risultati eccezionali.

La gamma più completa presente sul mercato è firmata Riso Gallo che, con le due linee Gallo e Gran Gallo, propone nove varietà di riso bianco tra le quali troviamo: Gran Gallo Roma, con una grana lunga e grossa che assorbe molto bene i condimenti; dà grandi soddisfazioni se usato per risotti "ricchi" di ingredienti.

Gran Gallo Arborio, nato ad Arborio nel 1946 è il riso italiano con i chicchi più grandi e perfetti: ideale per i risotti più classici e raffinati.

Gran Gallo Baldo, è il riso con la struttura più cristallina e compatta, molto resistente in cottura, va benissimo per i risotti, ma è perfetto per le insalate di riso, i timballi, il riso in teglia.

Il segreto: per ogni piatto saper scegliere il riso bianco adatto e, con Riso Gallo, il migliore.

• • • • • • • • • • • • *Ricettario* • • • • • • • • • • • •

RISOTTO CON FUNGHI PORCINI E ANIMELLE

Ingredienti per 4 persone. 250 gr di Riso Gran Gallo Arborio - 200 gr di animelle 100 gr di funghi porcini - 1,2 l di brodo di pollo leggero - 25 gr di cipolla - 10 gr di scalogno - 2 dl di vino bianco - 1 cucchiaio di estratto di carne - 10 gr di dragoncello - 50 gr di burro 50 gr di parmigiano grattugiato - olio di semi sale e pepe q.b.

Lasciare spurgare le animelle per 5 ore sotto acqua corrente fredda. Sbianchirle per 5 minuti in acqua bollente salata e asciarvele raffreddare. Una volta fredde sgranarle, liberandole dalla pellicina e spezzettarle. Pulire i funghi porcini e tagliarli a cubetti. Farli saltare, con 10 gr di burro, in una pentola antiaderente, salarli e peparli. Aggiungere e far dorare le animelle. A parte fare ridurre 2 dl di vino bianco con lo scalogno finemente tritato, l'estratto di carne un po' di burro. Per il risotto far sudare la cipolla tritata con 10 gr di burro, aggiungere il riso e farlo tostare fino a quando non inizierà a scoppiettare. Bagnare con vino bianco, farlo evaporare e portare il riso a cottura bagnandolo a poco a poco con il brodo bollente. Togliere il riso dal fuoco e mantecarlo con burro e parmigiano grattugiato: disporlo sui piatti e guarnirlo con le animelle, i funghi porcini e il dragoncello tritato. Macchiare la superficie del piatto con il fondo, di consistenza sciropposa, ottenuto con l'estratto di carne.

RISOTTO DEL DI' DI FESTA

Ingredienti per 4 persone: 250 gr di Riso Gran Gallo Roma - 1 litro di brodo - 1 cipolla - 2 peperoni gialli - 2 peperoni rossi - 1 ciuffo di basilico - 200 gr di pomodori pelati - 5 cosce di pollo - 1 bicchiere di vino bianco secco - prezzemolo tritato - olio, burro, sale q.b. - 1 foglia di alloro

Rosolare la cipolla tagliata sottile e aggiungere le cosce di pollo tagliate in tre pezzi. Far colorire, aggiungere il vino bianco secco e lasciarlo evaporare. Mettere i peperoni tagliati a listarelle e i pelati, dopo 10 minuti versare il brodo bollente e cuocere per 50 minuti. Aggiungere il riso e finire di cuocere. Completare con prezzemolo e basilico tritati e una foglia di alloro.

TRACCE DI RISO.

Quanta strada da fare in cucina, con "I grandi risi

del mondo". Seguire le loro tracce, sarà un'av-

ventura. Dall'India il Basmati, quasi una leg-

genda. In Thailandia è il Patna, l'orgoglio na-

zionale. Dal Nord America, il Long & Wild: chic-

co bianco e chicco nero. Dall'Italia infine il fio-

re. Fiore di Arborio per i risotti di grande tradizio-

ne, Fiore di Carnaroli, il re dei risi, per ricette d'au-

tore. Sono loro "I grandi risi del mondo". L'avventu-

ra da portare a tavola. La ricetta per girare il mondo.

DA GALLO, LO SPECIALISTA DEL RISO.

ARGENTINA

Market Characteristics

In 1991, an estimated 140,000 tons of rice were sold through retail stores and a further 40,000 tons through food service establishments. Per capita consumption approached 5 kg per annum, with 92% of Argentine households consuming rice at least once a week and 30% consuming rice at least three times a week. Sales of branded rice had decreased from 85,000 tons in 1990 to 81,000 tons in 1991, due to the increasing price of paddy rice relative to other food products such as meat. In July 1989, the retail price of 1 kg of meat was equal to the retail price of 5.4 kg of rice. By November 1991, the equivalent was only 2.7 kg of rice. Parboiled rice accounted for 18.2% retail sales volume in 1991, compared with 16.1% in 1990; the remaining sales were of white rice, with brown rice accounting for an estimated 2% of sales volume. (Exhibit 10 gives an estimated breakdown of rice consumption by volume.)

During the 1980s, the Argentine economy had suffered from cycles of strong growth and consumption, followed by ever-longer periods of recession. A new economic plan launched in 1991 aimed to tame inflation, initiate deregulation, privatize public enterprises, and liberalize trade restrictions and import duties. In 1992, inflation was estimated at 17%.

Rice was distributed primarily through supermarkets, which accounted for 63% of all retail rice sales in 1990; large, medium, and small stores

Exhibit 10 *Distribution of Argentina Milled Rice Volume, 1991*

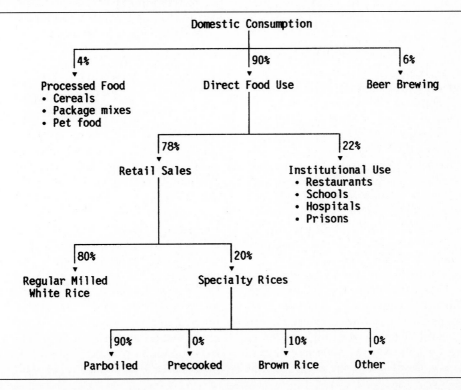

accounted for 10%, 14%, and 13%, respectively. The volume of rice sold in different packages was 72% for plastic pillows, 19% for cardboard boxes, and 9% for triangle-shaped packages. Most packages were either 1 kg or 500 grams in weight.

Gallo in Argentina

The first rice mill in Argentina was established by Arrocera Argentina, a subsidiary of F&P Gruppo, in 1905. In 1991, the Arrocera Argentina mills were running at 85% capacity, milling rice grown in Argentina. All of the output was processed into Gallo-branded products. Sales of Gallo-branded rice were U.S. $30 million in the fiscal year April 1991 to March 1992. In 1991, Gallo held a 17.5% volume share and a 23.7% value share of the total retail rice market, up from 15.7% and 22.8% respectively in 1990. In addition, Gallo held a 48% share in greater Buenos Aires, which accounted for 30% of the country's population. Solely focused on the rice market, Gallo was both the market share and product innovation leader.

The Gallo line included the following items:

- Gallo *Grano Largo Fino* and Gallo *Doble,* long-grain and European long-grain rice, were long, wide types of rice known as *doble* because each grain was double the length of an ordinary grain of rice. They were the original products in Gallo's Argentine product line and were targeted at traditional homemakers who enjoyed the art of cooking and described themselves as "knowing how to cook" and "using the brand that my mother used." Packaged in 1-kg and 1/2-kg cartons, this line accounted for 28% of Gallo's sales by volume in 1991, compared with 32% in 1989.

- Gallo *Oro,* long-grain and European long-grain parboiled rice, was positioned as a quality rice that did not stick or overcook and was easy to prepare. The line was targeted at the modern, middle-income working consumer, aged 25 years and over, who wanted ease of preparation without sacrificing taste. The line

included doble and boil-in-the-bag products in both 1-kg and 1/2-kg carton packages. The first parboiled product had been introduced in Argentina in 1963, and by 1991 this line accounted for 59% of Gallo's sales volume, compared with 62% in 1989.

- Gallo *Integral,* a long-grain parboiled brown rice, was positioned as a health and fitness product with a high nutritional value, levels of fiber, vitamins, and minerals. It was targeted at middle-income men and women, 18 years and older, who led a healthy, natural, and sporty lifestyle and wanted a balanced diet without sacrificing good taste. It was sold in 500-gram and boil-in-the-bag formats as well as the standard 1-kg box. Sales of this product represented 5% of Gallo's volume in 1991, the same percentage as in 1989.

- Gallo *Risotto* dry mixes, made of European long-grain parboiled rice, came in four flavor varieties. The rice was mixed with dehydrated ingredients such as peppers, mushroom, chicken, and spices and was targeted at middle-income consumers aged 25 and over, who were seeking tasty, easy-to-prepare meals. Launched in 1984 and sold in 300-gram boxes, it represented 1% of Gallo's sales volume in 1991 as in 1989 and held an 87% share of the Argentine risotto market in 1991.

Exhibit 11 reports shipments, manufacturer gross margins, and package sizes for each item in the product line. Gallo was one of the only companies selling rice packaged in cardboard boxes (only two other minor competitors also packaged in boxes). Product packages for the four lines are depicted in Exhibit 12.

Three-quarters of Gallo's retail sales were through supermarkets. There was a trend toward consolidation in food retailing in Argentina, with the large supermarkets (of 350 square meters or more) increasing their market share from 34% in 1989 to 38% in 1991. Gallo was weaker in the medium and smaller stores, which represented 27% of retail volume rice sales but accounted for only 15% of Gallo's retail sales volume. Ap-

Exhibit 11 *Arrocera Argentina Product Line, Shipments, Margins, and Package Sizes, 1991* *

	Shipment (tons)	Manufacturer Margin (%)	Package Sizes
Gallo Grano Largo Fino (long-grain)	1,875	35%	1 kg
Gallo Doble (European long-grain)	3,891	44	1 kg
			½-kg pillow
Gallo Oro (long-grain parboiled):			
Regular	11,173	38	1 kg
Boil-in-bag	361	41	½ kg
Gallo Doble Oro (European long-grain			
parboiled)	761	45	1 kg
Gallo Integral (long-grain brown)	786	51	1 kg
			½ kg
			boil-in-bag
Gallo Risotto (European long-grain			
parboiled dry mixes)	104	0	300 gm
Nobleza Gaucha:			
Long-grain	711	21	1 kg
European long-grain	256	35	
Long-grain parboiled	575	29	
Integral	44	43	

*Source: Company records.

proximately 90% of sales were made through a company sales force, while 10% was sold through agents serving remote areas. In 1991, the Gallo line included 28 items and was present in stores representing 77% of the country's retail food sales, with an average of seven items per retail outlet. On average, large supermarkets carried between five and seven different brands of rice.

Competition

The Argentine retail rice market was fragmented and regional. The four major national brands accounted for only 45% of total retail sales volume in 1991. Gallo faced one major and two minor competitors:

- *Molinos* food products, a subsidiary of Bunge Corporation, a large Argentine conglomerate, held 10.1% of the rice retail market by volume in 1991, up from 8.8% in 1990. It seri-

ously challenged Gallo in 1990 with its *Maximo* brand of parboiled long-grain rice.

Maximo, sold in triangle packages, held a 5.3% volume share of retail sales in 1990 and was the only Molinos brand that was not the market leader in its category. In 1991, Molinos spent twice as much as Gallo on advertising Maximo, despite the fact that the Argentine economy was depressed, promoting the brand as "*oro puro* of Molinos" on radio and television and in magazines. To gain market share, Maximo was priced 12% under equivalent Gallo products and, by the end of 1991, Maximo had increased its retail volume market share to 7.5%. Molinos had difficulty achieving quality control on its doble and brown rice entries and these were marketed under the brand name *Condor*. Distribution coverage for Molinos was still lower than for Gallo, and the company was not particularly strong in any one region.

Exhibit 12   *Product Package Illustrations for the Gallo Product Lines in Argentina*

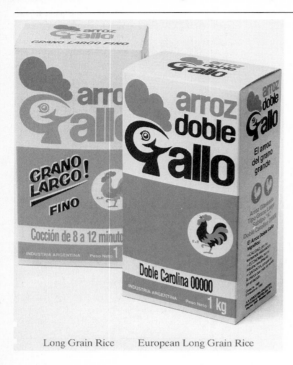

Long Grain Rice   European Long Grain Rice

Dry mixes with European Long Grain Parboiled Rice
Four flavor varieties

Long Grain Parboiled Rice

European Long Grain
Parboiled Rice

Long Grain Brown Rice, in Boil-in-Bags
Quick cooking

Exhibit 13 *Rice Brand Market Shares in Argentina, 1989–1991**

	Percentage of Total Retail Volume		
	1989	**1990**	**1991**
Arrocera (Gallo and Nobleza Gaucha)	17.7%	15.7%	17.5%
Molinos (Maximo)	8.2	8.8	10.1
Moneda	4.3	4.7	4.4
Mocovi	7.2	5.4	74.2

*Source: Company records.

Gallo had responded to Maximo with a fighting brand called *Nobleza Gaucha*. Also sold in triangle-shaped packages, it came in four varieties: long-grain, long-grain parboiled, European long-grain, and integral. In 1991, this line was priced around 25% below equivalent Gallo-branded products and around 12% below Maximo. Within one year the *Nobleza Gaucha* brand accounted for 7.7% of Gallo's sales volume and held a 1.3% share of total retail rice sales by volume in 1991. The brand was sold by Gallo sales force but supermarkets accounted for 65% of sales compared with the 75% for the Gallo brand.

- *Mocovi* and *Moneda* were smaller, regional players in the long-grain and doble market segments, with shares of 4.2% and 4.4% respectively. Mocovi, a family- owned company, successfully focused on marketing its Mocovi *Doble* brand and was the leader in the doble market segment. Moneda's products included both the *Moneda* and *Doble Moneda* brands.

Exhibits 13 and 14 summarize overall market shares for the four brands from 1989 to 1991 and the volume and value shares of their specific product lines in 1991. Exhibit 15 compares the relative retail prices and percentage distribution penetration of these brands in 1991.

Communication Strategy

Advertising expenditures on the Gallo brand in 1991 were the equivalent of U.S. $562,000, only 50% that of Maximo, and were used exclusively

Exhibit 14 *Rice Brand Market Shares in Argentina by Product Line, 1991**

	Percentage of Total Rice Market	
	Retail Volume Share (%)	Retail Value Share (%)
Dobles and Long-grain		
Arrocera:		
Gallo	5.2%	7.6%
Nobleza Gaucha	0.7	0.7
Molinos:		
Condor	2.6	3.3
Mocovi	4.2	6.9
Moneda	4.4	5.9
Parboiled		
Arrocera:		
Gallo	9.8	12.5
Nobleza Gaucha	0.4	0.4
Molinos:		
Maximo	7.5	10.3
Integral		
Arrocera:		
Gallo	1.2	2.0
Risottos		
Arrocera:		
Gallo	0.2	0.5

*Source: Company records.

Exhibit 15   *Relative Retail Prices and Distribution Penetration of Argentine Rice Brands, 1991**

	Retail Price ($ per kg.)	Index	% Distribution Penetration
Long-grain:			
Arrocera:			
Gallo Grano Largo Fino	$1.30	1.00	32%
Nobleza Gaucha long-grain	1.07	0.82	12
Molinos:			
Condor long-grain	1.26	0.95	35
Mocovi:			
Long-grain	0.98	0.75	10
Moneda:			
Long-grain	1.20	0.92	15
Doble:			
Arrocera:			
Gallo Doble	2.54	1.95	51
Nobleza Gaucha European long-grain	1.61	1.24	8
Molinos:			
Condor Doble	2.06	1.58	37
Mocovi:			
Doble	2.05	1.58	47
Moneda:			
Doble	1.82	1.40	29
Parboiled			
Arrocera:			
Gallo Oro	1.68	1.29	75
Gallo Doble	2.30	1.77	40
Nobleza Gaucha	1.30	1.00	26
Molinos:			
Maximo	1.48	1.14	59
Integral			
Arrocera:			
Gallo	2.16	1.66	45
Risottos			
Arrocera:			
Gallo	6.70	5.15	42

*Source: Company records.

to back Gallo Oro. Television commercials included demonstrations of how to prepare and serve rice (particularly boil-in-the-bag products) and "slice-of-life" depictions of family scenes. For example, one commercial showed children sneaking into a kitchen to eat the rice their mother just prepared, while a second depicted a daughter making the same dish for her mother that her mother used to make for her when she was a child. Other promotional programs in 1991 included consumer promotions and sales force incentives.

Exhibit 16 summarizes marketing expenditures for Arrocera Argentina in 1991 and planned expenditures for 1992. The budget for 1992 was $1.9 million, to be divided as follows: $762,000 on a new Gallo *Oro* television campaign; $400,000 on print advertising for the whole Gallo line; $220,000 on Gallo *Oro* radio advertising; $57,000 on consumer promotions; and $173,000 on sales force incentives.

Competitive television commercials focused on displaying the cooked product in different forms. A typical Maximo television commercial stressed quality, price, and ease of preparation. The commercial was fast-paced with a musical background and depicted a number of meals that could be prepared with Maximo rice. A *Moneda* television commercial depicted a woman hosting a dinner party, explaining that, when she used to cook rice, "nothing happened," but that with *Moneda,* she was able to serve flavorful meals. (Exhibits 17 and 18 show examples of Gallo print advertisements in Argentina, and Exhibit 19 gives an example of a Maximo print advertisement.)

Issues

First, Arrocera Argentina managers were debating how to respond to a market that was eroding due to a difficult economic climate and high product prices relative to other food products. Preve was hesitant, however, to implement price reductions on the high-end products, despite a

Exhibit 16   *Advertising and Promotion Expenditures for Arrocera Argentina, 1991–1992* *

	U.S. $†	
	1991 (actual)	1992 (budget)
Media Advertising		
Television commercials:		
Gallo Oro	$342	$762
Doble Gallo		194
Risotto		
Others		84
Print advertising:		
Gallo Oro		
Doble Gallo		
Risotto		80
Others		320
Radio advertising:		
Gallo Oro		220
Doble Gallo		52
Promotions		
Consumer promotions:		
Gallo Oro	35	
Doble Gallo	25	26
Others	60	31
Trade promotions		25
Sales force incentives	100	173
Total	$562	$1,967

*Source: Company records.
†In thousands

drop in raw material costs of approximately 63% between 1988 and 1991. Second, the issue as to whether Gallo should attempt to match Maximo's level of advertising was raised. Third, Gallo was committed to introducing new products and planned to launch *Meta'Tempo* quick-cooking rice under the brand name Gallo *Quick* in 1992. A key question was how the brand should be positioned and priced in the Argentine market, and what proportion of total marketing expenditures should be allocated to its launch.

(continued on page 259)

Exhibit 17   *Gallo Argentina: Print Advertisement for the Risotto Line*

Risottos Cremosos... Deliciosos...

Disfrute de los mejores risottos
con *Gallo Todo Resuelto.*
En cualquiera de sus 4 variedades: a la Normanda,
a la Piamontesa, a la Española y Primavera.
Su exquisito sabor proviene de la utilización
de verduras frescas deshidratadas de primera calidad
(sin el agregado de sustancias químicas ni conservantes)
y de la utilización del mejor arroz: Doble Gallo Oro.

Exhibit 18 *Gallo Argentina: Two Separate Print Advertisements for Gallo Integro*

EN 25 MINUTOS
USTED PUEDE MEJORAR SU VIDA.

El tiempo en el que se cocina
Arroz Gallo Integral.
La elección más natural para su vida.
La base de una dieta equilibrada.
Sana. Rica.
25 minutos en punto.
Prepárese. Y mejore su vida.

- Retiene la película de salvado.
- No contiene colesterol.
- Bajo contenido de sodio.
- Sin preservantes ni ingredientes artificiales.
- Con vitaminas B1, B2, y E.
- Posee Calcio, Hierro y Fósforo.

ARROZ GALLO INTEGRAL. EL PUNTO DE PARTIDA DE UNA VIDA SANA.

Comer sano es el mejor camino
para su cuerpo.
Con Arroz Gallo Integral usted puede
disfrutar de todo el sabor a partir de
una alimentación más equilibrada.
Más natural. Más rica en todo sentido.
Haga la prueba.
Arroz Gallo Integral lo pondrá en
carrera de una vida más saludable.

- Retiene la película de salvado.
- No contiene colesterol.
- Bajo contenido de sodio.
- Sin preservantes ni ingredientes artificiales.
- Con vitaminas B1, B2, y E.
- Posee Calcio, Hierro y Fósforo.

ARROZ GALLO INTEGRAL.
EL PUNTO DE PARTIDA DE UNA VIDA SANA.

Exhibit 19   *Gallo Argentina: Print Advertisement for the Maximo Competitor Brand*

Since it would be the first brand in the pre-cooked segment of the Argentine market, Arrocera Argentina executives believed that Gallo *Quick* could be positioned to enhance Gallo's product leadership and market share. They suggested pricing the product at a 60% premium to Gallo *Oro*.

POLAND

Market Characteristics

With the demise of Communist control, Poland underwent rapid cultural and political change in the late 1980s. After 1989, Poland was flooded by imported goods of all kinds, mainly from Germany, Italy, and France. To deal with these imports, private wholesale and retail chains emerged in 1991 to replace the state-owned stores. Although the Polish economy was still suffering from inflation and low wages in 1992, consumers were becoming increasingly sophisticated in the quality of products they demanded. With the advent of advertising and private companies, Poland was believed to be evolving from a market dominated by commodities to one where branding would become important.

Prior to 1989, rice had been imported in bulk by the state from Vietnam, Thailand, China, and Indonesia. It was of variable quality, often dirty and broken, and was sold in low-quality paper bags. Traditionally used as a substitute to potatoes, as a booster in soups, in cabbage rolls, or for rice pudding, rice had a low-quality image. Traditionally, imported food such as rice had been subsidized by the state. The end of these subsidies in 1989 resulted in price increases on imported food of around 1100%.

In the 1980s, distribution of branded Western products, including branded rice, had been controlled by a state-owned company called Pewex with a network of around 800 stores. Purchases could be made only in U.S. dollars. The stores enabled the state to obtain hard currency from consumers who received it from family members living outside Poland. In 1989, the Polish currency (the zloty) was tied to the U.S. dollar. An additional 800 private exchange stores and markets sprung up to distribute imported foods. Sales of such products by entrepreneurs through makeshift street stalls and open-air car-trunk markets also became common. These were later organized into covered market halls. In 1991, private food retail outlets began to emerge although there were no dominant supermarket chains as yet. In 1992, 70% of retail food sales were made at open markets and market halls, 15% at supermarkets, and 15% at small grocery stores.

In 1988, total rice consumption in Poland was 64,000 tons or 1.5 kg per capita. By 1991, per capita consumption reached 2.3 kg per annum. Used by 65% of the population, 80,000 tons were sold through retail stores in 1991. Of this volume, 90% was standard white rice; parboiled rice was a novel product for Polish consumers. (Exhibit 20 shows the breakdown of rice volume in Poland in 1991.)

Gallo in Poland

In 1988, Arrocera Argentina started exporting to the Polish market through an agent who received a commission on sales to Pewex. Gallo rice was sold in 200 Pewex shops in packages with both Argentine and Polish labeling at an average retail price of $1 per kg. In 1991, with Pewex in decline, Arrocera's agent established a private distribution company, Argentyna Ltd., to import and distribute the products he had previously handled for Pewex. In addition to rice, Argentyna Ltd. imported and distributed tea, beverages, and soups. Argentyna did not handle other brands of rice.

Between March 1990 and January 1991, 59 tons of Gallo *Oro* (parboiled) and 9 tons of Gallo risottos, both imported from Argentina, were sold through Pewex. Initial package labels carried Spanish text to which a Polish sticker had been added; subsequent packages carried bilingual Spanish-Polish labeling. From February 1991

Exhibit 20   *Distribution of Milled Rice Volume in Poland, 1992*

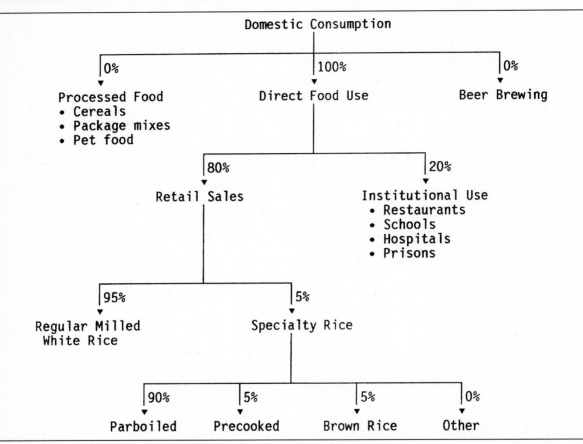

to February 1992, 70.5 tons of Gallo *Oro* parboiled white rice were imported exclusively through Argentyna Ltd. from Gallo's German factory, P&L Rickmers. Prior to 1991, P&L Rickmers had experienced excess capacity. These 1-kg carton box packages carried the bilingual label. In 1992, Gallo expected to sell 100 tons of Gallo *Oro* in 1-kg cartons, less than one-quarter of 1% of the retail market volume.

In 1992, Argentyna Ltd. had a central warehouse in Warsaw and distributed 65% of Gallo's product volume directly to retailers in the War-

saw area. The remaining 35% of sales were made through four secondary distributors that served the major cities of Krakow, Sczeczin, Poznan, and Lodz. The Gallo brand was available in 200 supermarkets and upscale grocery stores, which accounted for 30% of all grocery sales volume in Warsaw and 5% in Poland. In 1992, Rickmers' gross margin averaged 21% of its selling price. The Argentyna Ltd. margin averaged 40%, while secondary distributors made about 20% margin on Gallo products. Retailer margins were 15%. Exhibit 21 shows photographs of three food

Exhibit 21 *Store display of rice in Poland*

stores, at the high, medium, and lower range, retailing rice in Poland in September 1992.

Competition

Gallo's main competitor was the *Uncle Ben's* brand owned by Mars Company, distributed in Poland since 1991. In addition, several German and Belgian brands of both white and parboiled rice had entered the market at lower price points. In mid-1992, it was estimated that 95% of the market was unbranded, white rice, packaged in paper bags, which retailed at an average price of 8,000 zlotys (U.S. $0.58).

Uncle Ben's sold long-grain parboiled rice and brown rice in 1-kg cartons, 1/2-kg cartons, and boil-in-the-bag packages. In just over a year, Uncle Ben's had penetrated 90% of the supermarket and grocery outlets in Warsaw. Initially, the company had supplied its products to retailers on credit and accepted returns of unsold product. The launch was supported with U.S. $500,000 of expenditures on television commercials, print advertising, and point-of-sale displays.

Uncle Ben's used a North American television commercial translated into Polish. It depicted a rural picnic in the southern United States, where an African-American community was preparing to welcome home a young soldier. Considerable consumer confusion existed between the Gallo and Uncle Ben's brands; increased advertising by Uncle Ben's resulted in increase in sales for Gallo and other imported brands. In 1992, Uncle Ben's was expected to sell over 200 tons of rice. It was believed that Uncle Ben's was losing money in Poland but that the company's strategy was to increase brand awareness and build long-term market share.

Britta, Doris, and *La Belle Caroline* were other major foreign rice brands distributed in Poland. Usually priced lower than Uncle Ben's or Gallo, these brands were not advertised. (Exhibit 22 summarizes the relative prices of different brands in February 1992.)

Consumer Research

A consumer research study in September 1990 indicated that a basic meal in Poland consisted of meat, potatoes, and a vegetable. Rice was seen as an occasional substitute for potatoes. There was little knowledge of different types of rice and rice recipes, little understanding of nutrition, and little exposure to foreign foods. Homemakers were used to buying what was available, preparing meals every two or three days that could be stored in refrigerators; most Polish households had access to refrigerators in 1990.

Exhibit 22 *Relative Retail Prices of Major Rice Brands in Poland, February and September 1992**

	February 1992		September 1992	
	U.S. $/kg	Index	U.S. $/kg	Index
Parboiled				
Gallo Oro	2.28	1.00	1.78	1.00
Uncle Ben's	3.50	1.54	2.24	1.26
Doris (Belgian)	1.27	0.56	1.23	0.69
White Rice				
Local brand (in plastic bags)	0.72	0.32	0.56	0.33
Local brand (instant rice flakes)	1.50	0.65	1.32	0.75
Britta (German)	1.50	0.65	1.31	0.73
La Belle Caroline (French)	NA	NA	1.23	0.69

*Source: Company records.

In product trials of Gallo products, parboiled rice was enthusiastically received. Ease of cooking (aided by clear cooking instructions), taste, and ability to store once cooked, were cited as the main benefits of Gallo *Oro*. One drawback, however, was that consumers found the rice too firm for use in soups. Savory rice (with mushrooms added) was not well received; it had an unfamiliar taste and smell, had to be watched when being prepared, and was higher in price. Brown rice was viewed negatively; most consumers felt that a good-quality rice should be long-grained and white and, lacking in nutritional awareness, were unwilling to pay a price premium. Consumers suspected the boil-in-the-bag concept because it involved cooking in plastic. Cartons were the preferred form of packaging and Polish labels were deemed necessary. Gallo managers wondered whether all these perceptions would continue or whether an investment in consumer education by Gallo and other foreign brands would change them.

Communication Strategy

Gallo's initial plan was to superimpose a Polish voice on an Argentine television commercial of a Chinese cook demonstrating how to prepare Gallo *Oro*. A variety of dishes that included rice were shown during the commercial, and the nonstick properties and taste of the rice were stressed. Testing revealed that the pace of the commercial was too quick and that the central message and product benefits were not well understood. The commercial was never aired. In addition, television advertising was becoming increasingly expensive and radio was therefore considered as an alternative medium.

From February 1991 to February 1992, Gallo spent U.S. $5,000 on promotional support and point-of-sale displays. In September 1992, $6,000 was spent on print advertising in women's magazines. A full-page advertisement, to be placed in one magazine for three consecutive months, pictured a Gallo *Oro* carton and included a description of the product and a suggested cooking

Exhibit 23 *Proposed Gallo Communication Budget in Poland, 1992**

	U.S. $
Advertising	
Newspaper ads	4,000
Women's magazines	6,000
Promotion	
Point-of-purchase material	5,000
Three promotion reps	2,500
Other	2,500
Total	20,000

*Source: Company records.

recipe. A total of U.S. $20,000 was budgeted for 1992, and Exhibit 23 outlines the proposed breakdown of expenditures.

Gallo's agent believed increased advertising expenditures were essential. He explained:

> Gallo's product quality is better than the other, cheaper brands, but consumers don't know this. We are caught between Uncle Ben's, perceived as a premium product, and brands such as Britta and Doris that compete on price. People do not know that Gallo is high quality and we need to create this perception of the brand.

Issues

Preve wondered how to establish the Gallo brand in Poland. Specifically, which lines should be introduced and in which order? How should the products be positioned and priced? What level and types of advertising and promotion would be needed? Could the Polish market be expected to evolve like Argentina and, subsequently, like Italy? If so, how rapidly would this evolution take place? To assess the potential transfer of products and expertise from one country to another, Preve reviewed the Gallo line in the three countries (see Exhibit 24).

Exhibit 24 *Gallo Product Line by Country**

	Italy	Argentina	Poland
White Rice			
Round, short grain	Riso Gallo Originario		
Semi-long, "pearl"	Riso Gallo Padano		
Round, fat grain	Riso Gallo Vialone Nano		
Long-grain Italpatna	Riso Gran Gallo Europa		
Long-grain	Riso Gran Gallo Ribe	Gallo Doble + Nobleza Gaucha	
American long-grain	Riso Gran Gallo S. Andrea	Gallo Grano Largo Fino + Nobleza Gaucha	
Semi-round Japanese	Riso Gran Gallo Roma		
Crystalline	Riso Gran Gallo Baldo		
Large grain Italian	Riso Gran Gallo Arborio		
Brown		Gallo Integral + Nobleza Gaucha	
Parboiled			
Long-grain	Blond Risotti	Gallo Oro + Nobleza Gaucha Gallo Oro	Gallo Oro
Long-grain brown	Blond Integro		
Long-grain Patna	Blond Orientale	Gallo Doble Oro	
Dehydrated long-grain	Blond Meta'Tempo	Gallo Quick	
Risottos			
Parboiled dry mixes		Gallo Risotto	

*Source: Company records.

SONY CORPORATION: CAR NAVIGATION SYSTEMS

In April 1996, Masao Morita, President of the Sony Personal and Mobile Communication Company, a division of the Sony Corporation, pondered how to recover Sony's initial leadership in car navigation systems in Japan. As the first company to launch a reasonably priced (around $2,000) after-market model in 1993, Sony could claim to have created the world's largest car navigation systems market in Japan. Since the late 1980s, Sony had led a group of 40 companies in establishing an industry standard (called NaviKen) which enabled consumers to benefit from mutually compatible digital map software, while manufacturers reduced their risk by sharing development costs. Sony's efforts grew the Japanese market from 58,000 units in 1992 to 160,000 in 1993. Sony held a 60% market share in 1993. Exhibit 1 reports unit sales of car navigation systems in Japan through 1995 and forecasts from 1996 through 2005.

Market growth fueled intense competition in Japan, leading to many new product launches and lower prices. The average retail price per unit decreased from $4,000 in 1990 to $2,500 in 1995.[1] Ironically, competitors not in the NaviKen group were able to introduce new and improved products more often and more rapidly by developing or acquiring proprietary digital map technologies. Increasingly sophisticated consumers sought out differentiated products with the latest features. In contrast, NaviKen member companies, including Sony, lost time while trying to agree on standard software upgrades. Sony's unit sales increased but at a slower growth rate than the market: Sony's market share fell from 60% in 1993 to 23% in 1994 and 17% in 1995,

---

[1]$2,500 was the retail price with a monitor. A system retailed at around $1,500 in 1995 if a monitor was sold separately as shown in Exhibit 1.

This case was prepared by Yoshinori Fujikawa (under the direction of John A. Quelch). Confidential data have been disguised. Copyright © 1996 by the President and Fellows of Harvard College. Harvard Business School case 597-032.

Exhibit 1 *Market Development and Forecasts in Japan**

	1990	1991	1992	1993	1994	1995
			Actual			
Entire Market						
1. Unit Sales	16,400	27,600	57,800	160,400	343,500	578,500
Growth Rate Year-on-Year (%)		168%	209%	278%	214%	168%
2. Retail Sales (¥ million)	6,430	10,290	15,470	25,020	51,530	83,880
Growth Rate Year-on-Year (%)		160%	150%	162%	206%	163%
3. Retail Price/Unit (¥)	392,073	372,826	267,647	155,985	150,015	144,996
4. % Penetration of New Cars	0.27%	0.46%	0.96%	2.67%	5.73%	9.64%
5. Cumulative Number of Car Navigation Systems Installed	16,400	44,000	101,800	262,200	605,700	1,167,800
6. % Penetration of All Cars	0.03%	0.07%	0.17%	0.44%	1.01%	1.95%
After-Market						
7. Unit Sales			39,000	139,016	297,900	462,500
Growth Rate Year-on-Year (%)				356%	214%	155%
% of Entire Market (%)			67%	87%	87%	80%
OEM Market						
8. Unit Sales			18,800	21,350	45,600	116,000
Growth Rate Year-on-Year (%)				114%	214%	254%
% of Entire Market (%)			33%	13%	13%	20%

	Estimate	Forecast				
	1996E	**1997E**	**1998E**	**1999E**	**2000E**	**2005E**
Entire Market						
1. Unit Sales	850,000	1,200,000	1,500,000	1,800,000	2,000,000	2,800,000
Growth Rate Year-on-Year (%)	147%	141%	125%	120%	111%	107%
2. Retail Sales (¥ million)	114,080	150,000	170,000	190,000	200,000	230,000
Growth Rate Year-on-Year (%)	136%	131%	113%	112%	105%	103%
3. Retail Price/Unit (¥)	134,212	125,000	113,333	105,556	100,000	82,143
4. % Penetration of New Cars	14.17%	20.00%	25.00%	30.00%	33.33%	46.67%
5. Cumulative Number of Car Navigation Systems Installed	1,990,200	3,132,400	4,472,000	5,928,500	7,350,000	12,385,000
6. % Penetration of All Cars	3.32%	5.22%	7.45%	9.88%	12.25%	20.64%
After-Market						
7. Unit Sales	550,000	700,000	800,000	850,000	900,000	1,100,000
Growth Rate Year-on-Year (%)	119%	127%	114%	106%	106%	104%
% of Entire Market (%)	65%	58%	53%	47%	45%	39%
OEM Market						
8. Unit Sales	300,000	500,000	700,000	950,000	1,100,000	1,700,000
Growth Rate Year-on-Year (%)	259%	167%	140%	136%	116%	109%
% of Entire Market (%)	35%	42%	47%	53%	55%	61%

*Source: 1990-1995 figures are actuals drawn from Yano Keizai Kenkyusho, *1996 Car Navigation Systems: Market Forecast and Corporate Strategy* (Tokyo, Japan) 1996–2005 figures are forecasts of the case writers, based on research interviews (E = estimated).

Notes: 1. Manufacturer unit sales.
2. Retail sales levels do not include monitors, adapters, or software, sold separately from the navigation systems.
3. = category 2 ÷ category 1.
4. Assuming that annual new car sales in Japan were approximately 6 million (i.e., category 4 = category 1 ÷ 6 million).
5. Assuming that the car navigation system will be renewed every five years. (i.e., 1992 figure = 90–92 total, 1997 figure = 93–97 total, etc.)
6. Assuming that there were approximately 60 million cars in Japan. (i.e., category 6 ÷ 60 million).

Exhibit 2   *Major Competitors' Unit Sales and Market Shares in Japan: 1994–1996E**

Company/Brand	Unit Sales, Total Market (% Market Share)							
	1994		**1995**		**1996E**		**Three Years**	
Pioneer	82,000	(24%)	112,000	(19%)	157,000	(19%)	351,000	(20%)
Sony	80,000	(23%)	98,000	(17%)	124,000	(15%)	302,000	(17%)
Matsushita	50,000	(15%)	90,000	(16%)	149,000	(18%)	289,000	(16%)
Alpine	36,000	(10%)	87,000	(15%)	127,000	(15%)	250,000	(14%)
Mitsubishi	4,600	(1%)	30,000	(5%)	41,000	(5%)	75,600	(4%)
Kenwood	19,000	(6%)	27,000	(5%)	38,000	(4%)	84,000	(5%)
Zanavi	—	(0%)	24,000	(4%)	45,000	(5%)	69,000	(4%)
Clarion	17,000	(5%)	24,000	(4%)	39,000	(5%)	80,000	(5%)
Fujitsu Ten	18,000	(5%)	20,000	(3%)	37,000	(4%)	75,000	(4%)
Nippon Denso	6,500	(2%)	15,000	(3%)	26,000	(3%)	47,500	(3%)
Sharp	7,000	(2%)	11,000	(2%)	13,000	(2%)	31,000	(2%)
Casio	5,000	(1%)	10,500	(2%)	11,000	(1%)	26,500	(1%)
Sumitomo Denko	11,900	(3%)	7,800	(1%)	10,000	(1%)	29,700	(2%)
Toshiba	3,500	(1%)	6,000	(1%)	8,000	(1%)	17,500	(1%)
Citizen	—	(0%)	6,000	(1%)	8,000	(1%)	14,000	(1%)
Calsonic	500	(0%)	2,800	(0%)	4,000	(0%)	7,300	(0%)
NEC	1,500	(0%)	2,000	(0%)	3,000	(0%)	6,500	(0%)
Chuo Jidosha	—	(0%)	2,000	(0%)	2,000	(0%)	4,000	(0%)
Maspro	700	(0%)	1,500	(0%)	1,000	(0%)	3,200	(0%)
Sanyo	300	(0%)	1,200	(0%)	2,000	(0%)	3,500	(0%)
Nakamichi	—	(0%)	700	(0%)	—	(0%)	700	(0%)
Total	343,500	(100%)	578,500	(100%)	845,000	(100%)	1,767,000	(100%)

Company/Brand	1996E Unit Sales (% Market Share)				1996E Unit Sales (% Sales Composition)	
	After-Market		**OEM**		**After-Market**	**OEM**
Pioneer	140,000	(21%)	17,000	(9%)	(89%)	(11%)
Sony	121,000	(19%)	3,000	(2%)	(98%)	(2%)
Matsushita	119,000	(18%)	30,000	(16%)	(80%)	(20%)
Alpine	70,000	(11%)	57,000	(30%)	(55%)	(45%)
Mitsubishi	25,000	(4%)	16,000	(8%)	(61%)	(39%)
Kenwood	38,000	(6%)	—	(0%)	(100%)	(0%)
Zanavi	9,000	(1%)	36,000	(19%)	(20%)	(80%)
Clarion	32,000	(5%)	7,000	(4%)	(82%)	(18%)
Fujitsu Ten	37,000	(6%)	—	(0%)	(100%)	(0%)
Nippon Denso	4,000	(1%)	22,000	(12%)	(15%)	(85%)
Sharp	13,000	(2%)	—	(0%)	(100%)	(0%)
Casio	11,000	(2%)	—	(0%)	(100%)	(0%)
Sumitomo Denko	7,000	(1%)	3,000	(2%)	(70%)	(30%)
Toshiba	8,000	(1%)	—	(0%)	(100%)	(0%)
Citizen	8,000	(1%)	—	(0%)	(100%)	(0%)
Calsonic	4,000	(1%)	—	(0%)	(100%)	(0%)
NEC	3,000	(0%)	—	(0%)	(100%)	(0%)
Chuo Jidosha	2,000	(0%)	—	(0%)	(100%)	(0%)
Maspro	1,000	(0%)	—	(0%)	(100%)	(0%)
Sanyo	2,000	(0%)	—	(0%)	(100%)	(0%)
Nakamichi	—	(0%)	—	(0%)	—	—
Total	654,000	(100%)	191,000	(100%)	(77%)	(23%)

*Source: Adapted from Yano Keizai Kenkyusho, op cit.

Exhibit 3   *Sales Comparison: NaviKen Group versus Non-NaviKen Groups: 1994–1996E**

	NaviKen Format Group	Proprietary Format (Can Read NaviKen)[a]	Proprietary Format (Cannot Read NaviKen)[a]
Companies			
	Sony	Matsushita	Pioneer
	Mitsubishi	Alpine	Clarion
	Zanavi	Kenwood	Nippon Denso
	Sharp	Fujitsu	Sumitomo Denko
	Casio		Nakamichi
	Toshiba		
	Citizen		
	Calsonic		
	NEC		
	Chuo Jidosha		
	Maspro		
	Sanyo		

	NaviKen Format Group		Proprietary Format (Can Read NaviKen)[a]		Proprietary Format (Cannot Read NaviKen)[a]	
Group Unit Sales (% Share)						
1994	103,100	(30%)	123,000	(35%)	117,400	(34%)
1995	200,000	(35%)	216,000	(37%)	162,500	(28%)
1996E	262,000	(31%)	361,000	(43%)	222,000	(26%)

	NaviKen Format Group		Proprietary Format (Can Read NaviKen)[a]		Proprietary Format (Cannot Read NaviKen)[a]	
1996E Group Unit Sales (% Composition)						
After-Market	246,000	(78%)	225,000	(73%)	173,000	(78%)
OEM	70,000	(22%)	82,000	(27%)	49,000	(22%)

*Source: Calculation of the case writers, based on the figures in Exhibit 2.
Note: [a]The second group's car navigation systems can read both proprietary and NaviKen software, while the first group's
systems can only read NaviKen CD-ROMs. The third group's systems can only read their respective original software.

and was estimated to drop to 15% in 1996. Exhibit 2 summarizes the major competitors' market shares. Exhibit 3 compares sales performance of NaviKen and non-NaviKen companies.

In Europe and the United States, Sony was also the first to launch car navigation systems in the automobile after-market. Fewer than 1,000 units had sold in test markets to gather informa-

tion in each region by the summer of 1996. In Europe, local manufacturers such as Philips and Bosch started to market competing products aggressively. Other Japanese competitors such as Alpine, Matsushita, and Pioneer were expected to enter Europe and the US by 1997. Exhibit 4 summarizes market forecasts for car navigation systems by geographic region.

Exhibit 4 *Market Forecasts for Japan, Europe, and the United States**

	Estimate		Forecast			
	1996E	1997E	1998E	1999E	2000E	2005E
Japan						
1. After Market (Unit)	550,000	700,000	800,000	850,000	900,000	1,100,000
2. OEM Market (Unit)	300,000	500,000	700,000	950,000	1,100,000	1,700,000
3. Entire Market (Unit)	850,000	1,200,000	1,500,000	1,800,000	2,000,000	2,800,000
4. Entire Market (Retail ¥ mil.)	¥114,080	¥150,000	¥170,000	¥190,000	¥200,000	¥230,000
5. Entire Market (Retail $ mil.)	$1,141	$1,500	$1,700	$1,900	$2,000	$2,300
6. Retail Price/Unit ($)	$1,342	$1,250	$1,133	$1,056	$1,000	$821
7. % Penetration of New Cars	14.17%	20.00%	25.00%	30.00%	33.33%	46.67%
8. Cumulative Number of Installed Units	1,990,200	3,132,400	4,472,000	5,928,500	7,350,000	12,385,000
9. % Penetration of All Cars	3.32%	5.22%	7.45%	9.88%	12.25%	20.64%
Europe[a]						
1. After Market (Unit)	10,000	50,000	100,000	200,000	400,000	900,000
2. OEM Market (Unit)	20,000	50,000	100,000	150,000	200,000	900,000
3. Entire Market (Unit)	30,000	100,000	200,000	350,000	600,000	1,800,000
4. Entire Market (Retail ¥ mil.)	—	—	—	—	—	—
5. Entire Market (Retail $ mil.)	$60	$170	$300	$455	$600	$1,440
6. Retail Price/Unit ($)	$2,000	$1,700	$1,500	$1,300	$1,000	$800
7. % Penetration of New Cars	0.33%	1.11%	2.22%	3.89%	6.67%	20.00%
8. Cumulative Number of Installed Units	30,000	130,000	330,000	680,000	1,280,000	3,752,000
9. % Penetration of All Cars	0.02%	0.10%	0.25%	0.52%	0.98%	2.89%
United States						
1. After Market (Unit)	10,000	50,000	100,000	250,000	400,000	1,000,000
2. OEM Market (Unit)	10,000	50,000	100,000	300,000	500,000	1,400,000
3. Entire Market (Unit)	20,000	100,000	200,000	550,000	900,000	2,400,000
4. Entire Market (Retail ¥ mil.)	—	—	—	—	—	—
5. Entire Market (Retail $ mil.)	$34	$150	$260	$550	$720	$1,200
6. Retail Price/Unit ($)	$1,700	$1,500	$1,300	$1,000	$800	$500
7. % Penetration of New Cars	0.13%	0.67%	1.33%	3.67%	6.00%	16.00%
8. Cumulative Number of Installed Units	20,000	120,000	320,000	870,000	1,770,000	4,720,000
9. % Penetration of All Cars	0.01%	0.06%	0.16%	0.44%	0.89%	2.36%

	Estimate		Forecast			
	1996E	1997E	1998E	1999E	2000E	2005E
TOTAL (Japan, Europe, **United States)**[a]						
1. After Market (Unit)	570,000	800,000	1,000,000	1,300,000	1,700,000	3,000,000
2. OEM Market (Unit)	330,000	600,000	900,000	1,400,000	1,800,000	4,000,000
3. Entire Market (Unit)	900,000	1,400,000	1,900,000	2,700,000	3,500,000	7,000,000
4. Entire Market (Retail ¥ mil)	—	—	—	—	—	—
5. Entire Market (Retail $ mil.)	$1,235	$1,820	$2,260	$2,905	$3,320	$4,940
6. Retail Price/Unit ($)	$1,372	$1,300	$1,189	$1,076	$949	$706

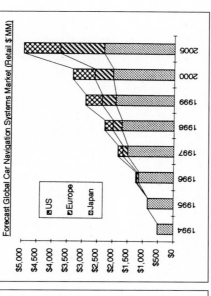

Forecast Global Car Navigation Systems Market (Retail $ MM)

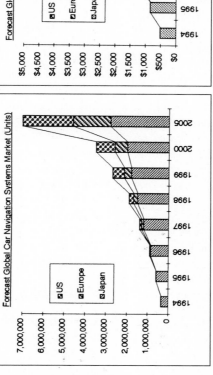

Forecast Global Car Navigation Systems Market (Units)

*Source: Forecasts of the cast writers, based on research interviews.

Notes: [a]Europe figures include France, Germany, Italy, and U.K.

Categories 1, 2, and 3: Manufacturer unit sales.

3. Category 3 = Category 1 + 2.

4. The Figures are for the value of retail sales.

5. Assuming an exchange rate = ¥100/$1 from 1996 throughout the year 2005.

6. Category 5 ÷ Category 3.

7. Assuming that annual new car sales in Japan, Europe, and the U.S. were approximately 6 million, 9 million, and 15 million, respectively. (i.e., Category 7 = Category 6 ÷ 6 million)

8. Assuming that the car navigation system will be renewed every five years. (i.e., 1992 figure = 1990–1992 total, 2000 figure = 1996–2000 total, etc.)

9. Assuming that there were approximately 60 million cars in Japan, 130 million in Europe, and 200 million in the U.S. (i.e., Category 9 = Category 8 ÷ 60 million)

Sony Corporation: Company Background

The Sony Corporation was founded in 1946 in the remains of a bombed department store as the Tokyo Tsushin Kogyo (Tokyo Telecommunications Engineering) by Akio Morita (Masao's father) and Masaru Ibuka. As a young company, Sony did not have a *network* of affiliated companies and lacked the strong domestic sales base and the distribution networks that supported the other companies.

With only $500 in capital, the founders realized they would have to differentiate themselves from their larger competitors by developing more innovative products. And from the failure of their first new product—a tape recorder that customers deemed expensive and flimsy—they learned the importance of paying close attention to consumer needs. Throughout its history, Sony pursued the innovation of commercially appealing products, maintaining a large research organization and vesting unusual decision-making authority in its engineers. The company's first breakthrough occurred after Ibuka acquired a patent license for transistors. Morita and Ibuka began mass production of transistor radios in 1954, and dubbed their new product Sony, after *sonus,* the Latin word for sound. Soon thereafter, the pair renamed the company.

Internationally as well as in Japan, Sony was often first to market with technological innovations that set industry standards. In 1968, Sony's sophisticated Trinitron technology expanded the color television market. In 1979, it launched the legendary Walkman, a lightweight portable tape player with headphones. In the mid-1980s, Sony developed a compact-size camcorder video camera. Such innovations turned Sony into a leader in consumer electronics with FY 1995 worldwide sales of over $43 billion.

Sony's only significant failure came in the early 1980s, when its Betamax-format VCR lost out to VHS. Sony had developed the videocassette recorder as early as 1975, but motion picture studios protested that the new machine would encourage widespread copyright infringement of movies and television programs. Discussions of this matter gave Sony's competitors such as Matsushita and JVC time to develop a different VCR format, VHS, which permitted an additional three hours of playing time and was incompatible with Sony's Betamax. Although Betamax was generally considered technically superior, VHS soon became the industry standard, and Sony lost its early lead in the lucrative VCR market.

The Betamax VCR experience in the early 1980s convinced Sony that technological innovation alone could not insure market dominance, and that the match between hardware and software was critical. Subsequently, Sony began to cooperate more with competitors to develop industry standards. In the 1980s, for example, Sony joined the Dutch electronic firm Philips to pioneer compact-disc (CD) technology.

In the mid-1990s, Sony Corporation reorganized to keep the company market-driven and to increase autonomy. Sony organized its businesses into 10 divisions, including Display, Home AV, Information Technology, Personal AV, Personal and Mobile Communications, Broadcast Products, Image and Sound Communication, Semiconductors, Components and Computer Peripherals, and Recording Media and Energy. To develop future top managers, Sony appointed promising young executives as presidents of each company with substantial autonomy. Masao Morita was appointed president of the Personal and Mobile Communication Company.

Car Navigation Systems

Evolving Products

A car navigation system plotted a driver's current location on a dashboard-mounted LCD monitor by calculating signals received from satellites and/or utilizing a dead reckoning system fed by speed and gyro sensors. The system also told the driver the best way to his or her destination by employing a digital map database stored on either a CD-ROM, a computer hard disk, or an IC card. Unlike VCRs and personal computers, car navigation systems hardware and software were not standardized as of 1995, but a typical model consisted of hardware such as a satellite signal receiver, a CD-ROM player, an LCD monitor mounted in or on a car dashboard, and digital map software in the form of a CD-ROM. See Exhibit 5 for a picture of a typical car navigation system. Exhibit 6 summarizes the cost and margin structure of the system.

In the late 1980s, the earliest car navigation systems could only report where a driver was, his/her desired destination, and whether or not the car was headed in the right direction. By the mid-1990s, however, the systems had become more intelligent. Recent models could inform a driver of his/her current location at all times and deduce the best route to a destination automatically by taking into account current traffic conditions. Some systems could even communicate verbally with the driver and provide turn-by-turn instructions on the LCD map or through voice.

Enabling Hardware

Car navigation systems were facilitated by the Global Positioning Satellite (GPS) system, a constellation of 24 satellites operated by the U.S. Department of Defense. GPS was originally developed at a cost of $10 billion for military applications during the Cold War, but became available for civilian use at no charge in the late 1980s.

The central concept behind GPS was triangulation. If a car's exact distance from a satellite was known, the car's location had to lie somewhere on the sphere defined by that radius. If the driver's distance from a second satellite were also known, the car's position had to lie along the circumference of the circle where the two spheres intersected. Knowing the distance from a third satellite would result in two points where all three spheres intersected. GPS in fact used four signals from four different satellites to locate the position of the antenna.

Triangulation on GPS could result in accuracy as close as 30 meters. Worrying that GPS could be used by an enemy to guide missiles or smart bombs, Department of Defense engineers intentionally built errors into the system for civilian use. The civilian signal could deliver 95% accuracy within 100 meters of the actual location. The GPS signal could also be blocked by tall buildings, trees, or overpasses, a common problem in large cities.

In order to improve the precision in identifying the car's location on the earth, the car navigation systems were equipped with a few supporting technologies. When GPS did not function accurately, a backup dead-reckoning system of speed and gyro sensors typically installed in the car trunk could take over seamlessly and relay the car's speed and direction to the navigation system. Aided by the dead-reckoning system, map-matching technologies enabled the car navigation system to pinpoint the car's position on the digital map.

In car navigation hardware, there was no dominant product standard. Some products utilized both GPS signals and dead-reckoning systems, but others employed only one of the two. Product interfaces were also diverse. Some displayed a colorful digital map on an LCD monitor. On a typical LCD screen, a small, red circle sign, representing the car, moved along a highlighted street leading the driver to his/her desired destination. Some other models' monitors showed only right or left arrow signs and the street name to signal the next appropriate turn. Others did not have display devices but provided directions verbally.

Diverse Software Formats

The software database technology used in car navigation systems was the offspring of GIS, or Geographic Information Systems. GIS was originally developed by the U.S. Department of Defense for guiding missiles. In essence, GIS software turned a conventional map into a digital database.

Exhibit 5 *Typical Car Navigation System Model (Sony NVX-F160)* *

**Sony Puts You on the Map:
Introducing the Sony
Mobile Navigation System.**

Have you ever missed a freeway exit? Or searched in vain for a campground? Or stayed in a traffic jam because you didn't know the neighborhood? Are you ever reluctant to roll down your window and ask for directions from a stranger? Do you ever want to map out a day of sales calls in advance? If you answered "yes" even once, you're a candidate for the Sony NVX-F160 Mobile Navigation System.

This technological breakthrough helps you find your destination faster and more efficiently than you ever thought possible. How? Our Global Positioning System (GPS) **Satellite Receiver** calculates your vehicle's current location with incredible accuracy. As you drive, your location is displayed on a **CD-ROM-based Digital Map** which constantly updates you on where you are, what highway you're on and what's ahead. And the NVX-F160 helps get you there faster, by pointing out the general direction and straight line distance to your destination.

The USA Guide includes newly expanded coverage of Interstate, state and county roads in the 48 states, plus street-by-street detail in 32 major cities. Regional Guides cover every street

and road in each region! All map discs include an **Information system** that can find just about anything, right down to the nearest sculpture garden, RV campground with laundromat or inside-looping roller coaster. With **Address Finder**, you "type in" an address on available streets and the digital map will display the block you're looking for. It's a great time saver whether you're making sales calls or planning a coast-to-coast vacation. Sony's **5-inch Color LCD Monitor** displays everything

brilliantly, while Sony's **Wireless Remote Control** runs the whole show. And when you arrive, simply pop the Monitor and Remote into your glove compartment or take it with you. So there's nothing to entice would-be thieves.

Satellite navigation may sound futuristic. But it's waiting for you now in the Sony NVX-F160.

The USA Guide can locate places, calculate driving distances, even give you the phone number for local road conditions!

"Type in" a city name, place name, or even an address on available streets to find its location instantly!

Satellite navigation means no more time wasted driving in circles

Looking for attractions? Searching for sports? The NVX-F160 puts it all at your fingertips.

The NVX-F160 provides travel advice that's detailed, informative and smart.

Regional map discs provide detailed information on hotels and restaurants.

*Source: Company materials.

Exhibit 6   *Typical Cost and Margin Structure for Car Navigation Systems* *

Typical Cost and Margin Structure for Car Navigation Systems:	
Retail Price	100%
less Dealer Margin	35%
Manufacturer Selling Price	65%
less Manufacturer Margin	5%
Manufacturer Total Cost	60%
Indirect Cost (SGA)	10%
Direct Cost	50%
(LCD Monitor	30%)
(CD-ROM Player	8%)
(CPU	7%)
(GPS Receiver	3%)
(Other Components	2%)
Japanese Model (e.g., Sony NVX-F16):	
Retail selling price	$2,000
less Dealer margin[a]	$700
Manufacturer selling price	$1,300
less Manufacturer total costs	$1,200
Manufacturer margin	$100
Overseas Model (e.g., Sony NVX-F160):	
Overseas retail selling price	$3,000
less Overseas dealer margin[a]	$1,000
Manufacturer selling price	$2,000
less Manufacturer total costs[b]	$1,800
Manufacturer margin	$200

*Source: Estimation of the case writers, based on research interviews.
Notes: [a]Dealer charged separate fee for product installation. Japanese dealers charged around $200. U.S. and European
    dealers charged around $300.
    [b]Manufacturer total costs of overseas model included applicable transportation costs and import duties.

For accurate navigation, a digital map had to contain correct details of every street. Every sign, every painted line, every relevant piece of information along the road had to be included. For example, the database had to note whether there was a concrete divider along a highway, whether two streets intersected or one was on an overpass, and so forth. Consequently, each street corner required three to four dozen items of data.

As many data layers as desired could be added to the digitized map. Postal zip codes and phone numbers could be stored in the database so that a driver could find a destination by entering an address and/or phone number. Information on "points of interest," such as banks, restaurants, and gas stations, could also be digitized on the map. One could analyze these data in hundreds of different ways and, in conjunction with a GPS receiver, could interact with the data at real-time basis. In real life, for instance, an ordinary stranger was not likely to know the ATM closest to any given spot. However, with a points-of-interest database, a car navigation system could sort through ATMs by distance, find the nearest one operated by the driver's preferred bank, and provide route guidance to this ATM.

Collecting and digitizing all the road-related information and the point-of-interest data were labor-intensive tasks. Government geological surveys and commercially published maps were often old and inaccurate. Hence, digital map companies had to send out research teams to take aerial and ground photos to fill in gaps and update the old information. Collecting and digitizing the necessary information on the city of Boston, for example, required 20 engineers to work for one year. Given continuous change due to road construction and store openings and closings, digital map companies had to retain local staff to update the data.

The cost of digitizing the cartography of the United States was estimated at $1 billion, with an additional $100 million a year for updating. A single company starting this task in 1995 could not achieve payback before 2005. There were two major digital map companies in the United States competing independently. As of early 1996, Etak, a Silicon Valley division of Rupert Murdoch's News Corporation, had covered cities represent-

ing 80% of the U.S. population. NavTech, another Silicon Valley startup, had covered 90% of the U.S. population.

There were three digital map companies working in Europe. Etak had focused its European operation on the United Kingdom and had so far covered cities accounting for 80% of the population. EGT, NavTech's European subsidiary, had covered 80% of Germany and 70% of France. A third company, TeleAtlas, was digitizing Italian maps. These companies had developed independently noncompatible digital map software.

In Japan, 40 companies, including car companies, electronic firms, and digital-map developers, had formed the Japan Navigation Research Association, known as NaviKen, in the early 1980s, and completed 100% digitization of the entire country by 1988. The NaviKen format was consistently applied in the navigation systems produced by the NaviKen member companies, such as Sony and Mitsubishi. However, other incompatible formats had been developed independently, by Pioneer and Matsushita, respectively, which did not join NaviKen. Exhibit 7 compares the number of

(continued on page 280)

Exhibit 7   *Number of CD-ROMs by Car Navigation System Producer: 1995**

Company Software Format	Sony NaviKen	Alpine Proprietary + NaviKen[a]		Matsushita Proprietary + NaviKen[a]		Pioneer Proprietary
General Road Maps	5	7	(2)	6	(1)	2
Sports (golf, ski, camping, etc.)	6	6	(0)	6	(0)	3
Travel (hotels, parks, etc.)	4	4	(0)	4	(0)	1
Shops/Restaurants	1	1	(0)	1	(0)	1
Radar Detection	0	0	(0)	0	(0)	1
Games/Quizzes	4	4	(0)	4	(0)	6
Karaoke	0	0	(0)	0	(0)	56
Total	20	22	(2)	21	(1)	70

*Source: Adapted from various product catalogues.
Note: [a]Numbers include both original and NaviKen CD-ROMs, since Alpine and Matsushita's systems can read NaviKen software.
Numbers in parentheses are proprietary CD-ROMs developed by Alpine and Matsushita.

Exhibit 8   *Channels for Car Navigation Systems**

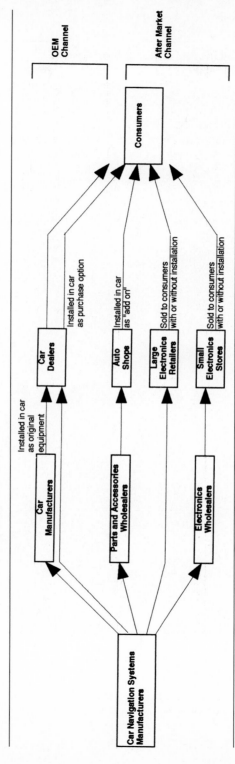

*Source: Analysis of the case writers, based on research interviews.

Exhibit 9   *OEM and After-Market Car Navigation Systems** *

OEM Model (Nissan)

*Source: Company materials.

Exhibit 9   *(continued)*

After-Market Model (Sony NVX-F16)

CD-ROMs available for different competitors' car navigation systems.

The data storage media also varied. Some devices used the digital map stored on a CD-ROM, while others on computer hard disk or IC card. CD-ROM based navigation systems were popular in Japan and Europe, but hard disk and IC card were believed equally acceptable in the United States, especially for low-end products.

Distribution Channels

Car navigation systems could be sold either on an OEM basis or through after-market retail channels. Exhibit 8 summarizes the distribution alternatives.

In the OEM channel, car navigation system producers contracted with car assemblers to supply car navigation systems to the automaker's specifications. The systems were either pre-installed by the car manufacturers or installed later by dealers as a purchase option on new cars.

After-market models were usually designed and marketed by car navigation system makers and distributed through wholesalers to auto parts retailers and electronics outlets. Sales to end consumers were either made on a cash-and-carry basis or involved dealer installation and other after-sales services.

All components of OEM models, including LCD monitors, were neatly installed together with audio equipment such as radio, cassettes, and CD players in the car dashboard. In contrast, after-market systems usually had to be installed as "add-ons" to the dashboard. Exhibit 9 compares OEM and after-market car navigation systems. Volume contracts with the car manufacturers meant that Japanese OEM products were technically one to two years behind and more expensive than after-market models.

In the Japanese market, 80% of the systems were sold through after-market channels while 20% were sold on an OEM basis. However, as the technological innovation diffused and products became more standardized, the percentages were forecast to be even by the year 2000 and to be reversed by 2005. The fledgling European

markets mainly involved OEM sales in 1995, but the proportion of after-market sales was expected to increase. The U.S. market was still undeveloped, but OEM models were expected to exceed after-market sales, especially if the price decreased substantially.

In Japan, major auto parts chains, such as AUTOBACS and Yellow Hat, accounted for 60% of after-market unit sales. Hybrid models based on both GPS and dead-reckoning sensor were distributed though these auto parts retailers since they required professional installation and maintenance. These auto parts retailers carried at most five brands on their shelves. GPS-based systems that did not require complicated installation were channeled mainly through large electronics discount chains and were more subject to price competition.

MULTINATIONAL MARKETS

Advanced Japanese Market

The Japanese market for car navigation systems was the world's largest in 1995 with sales of 580,000 units and $840 million.[2] Car navigation systems were installed in 10 percent of new Japanese cars in 1995. The penetration rate for all cars registered in Japan was 2 percent. With competition among 30 companies, the average retail price

---

[2]The concept of the car navigation system had been around in Japan since the early 1980s. Honda claimed to be the first company to put a navigation system on the road. However, the dead-reckoning system, which required a driver to replace a slidelike map at each town boundary, did not attract consumers. The Japanese market remained small during the 1980s, although electronic car component producers, such as Alpine and Nippon Denso, did supply car navigation systems on an OEM basis to the automobile assemblers. They offered the navigation systems as optional accessories on a limited number of their luxury models, such as the Honda Legend and the Toyota Crown. The navigation systems at that time were priced at around U.S. $6,000.

per unit decreased dramatically from $4,000 in 1990 to $2,500 in 1995. As competitors vied to introduce new models with the latest technological features, market shares fluctuated wildly.

The popularity of car navigation systems reflected the uniqueness of the Japanese car driving environment. First, the Japanese road system was more complicated than its European and U.S. counterparts. Since not all the streets had names and road signs were few and far between, people relied heavily on maps and landmarks for finding their way. Caught on narrow roads without the benefit of a highly developed highway system, drivers were always looking for a way to bypass heavily congested arteries, especially in major metropolitan areas.

Given serious traffic jams and well-developed train systems, most Japanese used their cars for weekend joy-riding rather than daily commuting.[3] Many therefore welcomed car navigation systems as a means of finding their way around in unfamiliar cities and towns.

Japanese car drivers, especially young people, were willing to spend heavily on cars and electronic accessories. Many drivers would readily invest over $2,000; few U.S. drivers would invest more than $1,000. Outside Japan, higher auto theft rates discouraged heavy investments in expensive electronic options. Exhibit 10 summarizes results of Japanese consumer and dealer research.

The Japanese car navigation market was boosted further by Japanese government investment in improving the efficiency of the Japanese road system. A real-time traffic information system called VICS (Vehicle Information and Communication System), would be launched in Tokyo and Osaka in 1996.[4] With VICS information, the next generation of navigation systems would be able to incorporate real-time traffic and weather alerts so that drivers could avoid gridlock, accidents, or washed-out roads.

Emerging European Market

The European market lagged behind Japan by some five years. However, once major electronics manufacturers, such as Bosch and Philips, introduced products in Germany, the market began to develop. The market was expected to grow from annual sales of 30,000 units and $60 million in 1995 to 600,000 units and $600 million by 2000 (See Exhibit 4).

European road systems were complex, especially in historic inner cities. However, most streets had names and road signage was good. As a result, opinions differed on whether a car navigation system needed to show a digital map on an LCD monitor or if right/left arrow signs and voice guidance were sufficient.

European drivers frequently drove across borders. Car navigation systems therefore needed to provide multilingual guidance. Digital map software also had to correspond to different traffic rules and road regulations from country to country.

European governments collaborated on efforts to improve the highway system. For example, the European Union's DRIVE program analyzed how the car should relate to the road infrastructure, while the PROMETHEUS project involving all major European manufacturers examined how cars could communicate with each other. The technologies developed through these projects contributed to Philips's and Bosch's development of navigation technologies, such as route calculation and guidance.[5]

Untapped U.S. Market

The U.S. market lagged both Europe and Japan. Car navigation systems were not widely known.

---

[3]If all the cars registered in Japan were to be on the road at the same time, the distance between each would be only four feet.

[4]The ATIS (Advanced Traffic Information System) was launched earlier in 1995. The system allowed a driver to retrieve real-time traffic information by using a car cellular phone.

---

[5]"Smart Cars," *TelecomWorld,* August 1992, pages 44–45

Exhibit 10 *Results of Japanese Consumer and Dealer Surveys: 1992–1995* *

1992 Consumer Survey[a]

- Forty-five percent expressed their interest in buying a car navigation system in one or two years; two percent had already purchased one.
- Those who would buy a system were willing to spend $500–$1,000 (50%), $1,000–$2,000 (40%) and $2,000+ (10%).
- Seventy-five percent of those who would buy a system rated "accuracy of road map" as an important factor for their purchase decision, followed by "detailed traffic information" (56%), "number of CD-ROMs" (52%) and "up-to-date point-of-interest information" (43%).
- Benefits mentioned in order of frequency: can enjoy weekend drive better (90%); can drive in unfamiliar area (80%); can use landmarks for finding a route (75%).

1994 Dealer Survey[b]

- Eighty percent of respondents stated that the price of car navigation systems was too high. Among these, 80% believed $1,500 was appropriate and 20% said $1,000.
- The most frequently asked question by customers to retailers was: "Can I use NaviKen format CD-ROMs?"
- Ninety-two percent of dealer salespeople preferred selling systems with NaviKen compatible software.

1995 Customer Survey[c]

- Customer demographic was as follows:
  - 20–24 years (15%), 25–29 years (30%), 30–39 years (40%), and 40 years and older (15%);
  - married (44%) and not-married (56%);
  - male (95%) and female (5%).
  - 75% owned new cars and 25% used cars
  - Average price of their cars was $33,000.
- Respondents used car navigation systems: when driving in unfamiliar area (95%); when enjoying weekend drive (85%); not during regular commute (70%); all the time (15%).
- Ninety percent stated that a map display was essential for route guidance while 10% said arrow signs and voice guidance were sufficient.
- Important factors influencing the purchase decision in order of frequency of mention: accuracy of map and map-matching; automatic route calculation; easy-to-set-up destination; speed of route calculation.
- Respondents wished to have the following information: "real time traffic jam" (100%), "one-ways" (85%), "real-time parking space" (80%), "alternative bypass route" (80%), "expected arrival time to the destination" (75%).

---

*Source: Compiled from the following surveys conducted by one of the car navigation systems producers:
[a]Survey of 550 high-potential purchasers, sampled from car audio magazine readers in October 1992.
[b]Survey of dealer salespeople in 20 largest auto parts chain stores, conducted in May 1994.
[c]Survey of 600 owners of car navigation systems, sampled from car audio magazine readers in October 1995.

However, one forecast predicted the U.S. market would surpass the European market by 2000, with annual sales of 900,000 units and $720 million, and approach the size of the Japanese market by 2005, with sales of 2.4 million units valued at $1.2 billion a year (See Exhibit 4).

The United States was well organized with street names, traffic signs, and highly developed highway systems. The value of car navigation systems, which pinpointed a car's current location, was not so obvious to the U.S. driver. For car navigation systems to be attractive, they had to provide turn-by-turn route guidance and other more sophisticated functions.

As of 1995, few U.S. consumers were familiar with car navigation systems. A manager at one digital-map maker explained:

> *If it were described to you before you experienced it, you might not understand. But after testing the system, most drivers come around. All it takes, after all, is the admission that a map database knows more about the road than you do.*[6]

Consumer research studies indicated rising interest among U.S. consumers. One study reported that 58% of the consumers had heard about vehicle navigation systems, primarily through television (37%) or published material (36%). Among those aware, most could recall the system's purpose and basic features, but relatively few understood what "GPS" meant, knew about voice prompts, or about systems being available in rental cars.

The same research reported that 70% of respondents were interested in purchasing a car navigation system. Among those, 26% were interested in buying an OEM, preinstalled, in-dash model with display, 57% voted for an after-market, on-dash model with a monitor, while 17% indicated preference for a lower-end voice navigation model with no display. Respondents were willing to pay $700 to $1,000 for a preinstalled OEM model, $600 to $700 for the second type, and $500 to $600 for the third type. Exhibit 11 summarizes the detailed research results.

Another survey, conducted by J.D. Power and Associates, focused on potential purchasers. The study involved 170 consumers taking two-day test drives of navigation system-equipped automobiles and completing three questionnaires: one prior to driving the system-equipped cars (to assess awareness and image of the navigation systems); one following a ten-minute test drive (to simulate consumer impressions after a dealership test drive); and one after driving the car for two days (to simulate impressions following an experience driving a system-equipped rental car). Exhibit 12 summarizes the research results.

The survey revealed that both the ten-minute and the two-day test drives enhanced respondents' understanding of the system's features, benefits, and ease of use. After the initial test drive, participants noted several key advantages including convenience, the ability to save time and money, the ability to replace maps, and less of a need to ask for directions. The extended two-day test led to lower stress and improved driving confidence. The longer test drive increased the likelihood of respondents recommending the system to family and friends.

In 1992, five years after Japan, the federal U.S. government began a six-year program of investing in smart highway technologies, including sensors, television cameras, and radars to monitor city traffic and relay traffic conditions to central computers. From workstations at command headquarters, technicians would be able to alter freeway signals and stoplights to reroute traffic and relay advisories to cars equipped with more sophisticated navigation systems. On the other hand, safety regulations in thirteen major states, including California and New York, prohibited any in-car visual devices, except for security purposes.

---

[6] *Wired,* Winter 1995

Exhibit 11 *Survey of California Car Renters: January 1996**

- Drivers were willing to pay, on average, $5 more per day to rent a car with a navigation system.
- Drivers who would purchase or lease a car with a navigation system (70% of the sample) were willing to spend, on average, an extra $550. Eleven drivers were willing to spend over $1,000.
- Drivers who would buy navigation systems and install them in their current cars (35% of the sample) were willing to spend, on average, $1,100.
- 20% said they would buy the navigation system if it cost $1,200.
- 20% stated they used the system "all the time." Another 30% used it "a lot."
- Benefits mentioned in order of frequency: prevents you from getting lost in a new city; helps you find your destination; eliminates the need for maps; increases driving safety; you don't have to stop and ask directions; takes you via best route; gives feeling of confidence when driving.
- Problems mentioned in order of frequency: took time to figure out how to use it; destination not in computer; not able to calibrate alternate route; out of range error; directions unclear and/or hard to hear; monitor hard to read.
- 60% found the navigation system worked better than they expected.
- 60% used the system for guidance in getting to a destination. 20% used it for finding points of interest, for experimenting with different routes and for determining current location.
- Two-thirds of respondents stated the device was easier to use when the car was parked. 40% believed it was distracting to use while driving.

*Source: Compiled from survey of 53 frequent Avis car renters in California, conducted by Center for Strategy Research, January 1996.

SONY IN INTERNATIONAL COMPETITION

Competition in Japan

In November 1990, the first GPS-based after-market car navigation system was introduced by Pioneer Electronic Corporation, a Japanese leader in car stereo and laser disc players. Since the GPS signal was not yet available around the clock and was easily interrupted by high-rise buildings in Tokyo, Pioneer defined the product as a "Satellite Cruising System," emphasizing the innovative and entertainment aspects of the product rather than its practical capabilities as a navigation device.[7] Pioneer had developed its own digital map software and stressed the variety of point-of-interest information its system could provide, ranging from hotels to restaurants. In addition, to distract drivers from Japan's endless traffic jams, Pioneer included entertainment software containing games, quizzes, horoscopes, and karaoke. Pioneer distributed the products through the same channels used for conventional car stereos, principally auto parts shops, since the product required professional installation. Despite a high retail price over $5,000, Pioneer sold 20,000 units annually in the early 1990s.

The market changed dramatically in June 1993, when Sony entered the after-market segment with the NVX-F10 including a 4-inch LCD monitor at a low price of $2,000. Six months later, Sony introduced NVX-15 with a larger 5-inch display at $2,500. Unlike Pioneer, Sony emphasized the product's practical benefits and named it "Digital Map Car Navigation System." Sony advertised the product as a problem-solving device for drivers who did not want to face traf-

---

[7]With only 12 satellites until 1992, GPS did not provide the signals necessary for 24-hour coverage. The system became complete with 24 satellites in 1993.

Exhibit 12 *Results of J.D. Power Consumer Survey: August 1995**

- Using a ten-point scale for satisfaction, where ten is "extremely satisfied," 80% of respondents rated their overall satisfaction as a "nine" or "ten," resulting in a mean of 8.43.
- 60% were "very likely" to recommend the system to family and friends after the ten-minute test drive. The percentage increased to 70% after the two-day test drive.
- Respondents preferred an in-dash OEM system to an on-dash after-market model by a margin of four to one, due to perceived better quality and system reliability resulting from more professional installation and better integration with the vehicle's electrical system.
- Those who would buy an after-market system mentioned perceived transferability/portability and lower price as reasons for their preference. The average expected price for an after-market model was $900, versus $1,000 for an OEM system.
- Those preferring an after-market model expected to purchase it at "specialty store" (41%), "electronic store" (17%), "discount store" (13%) and "department store" (6%). "Specialty store" included outlets specializing in selling and installing alarms, audio systems, and vehicle cellular phones.
- Over 80% said that availability of a car navigation system would be an important factor in deciding which vehicle to purchase next time.
- Regarding the value of different point-of-interest information, "emergency assistance/hospital/police" was rated highest (9.03), followed by "auto care/gas" (8.23), "travel points" (8.13), "entertainment/tourist attractions" (8.04), "business facilities" (7.50) and "ATM/banks" (7.39).
- Focus group discussions revealed high interest in point-of-interest listings of new and different entertainment and dining options, particularly in unfamiliar areas. Said one New York participant:
  "We went to Connecticut to visit relatives and arrived early and decided to get something to eat." "We just looked through point-of-interest listings and selected a restaurant."
  A participant from Los Angeles noted:
  "The system opens up your world; it lists theaters and restaurants and places you haven't heard of."

*Source: Adapted from J.D. Power and Associates, *The Power Report*, November 1995.
Notes: Survey of 170 high-potential purchasers by J.D. Power and Associates, July and August 1995.
     Respondents participated in a two-day test drive of a vehicle equipped with an Avis car navigation system.
     They were screened for the following criteria:
- Household income of at least $50,000.
- Cellular phone ownership and monthly cellular phone bill of $50 or more.
- Average of 2 or more hours per day in vehicle on business travel (excluding normal commute).
- Ages 25–59.

fic jams, get lost in unfamiliar towns, or be late for appointments. These GPS-based products showed only the driver's current position on the digital map screen, but did not provide route guidance toward the destination. However, sharply lower prices attracted many consumers. Aiming at rapid market expansion, Sony distributed almost 50% of its units through consumer electronics chan 1993, achieving a 60% market share.

To develop the market further, Sony set out to establish an industry standard for digital map software. Sony was the most active member of the Navigation Research Association to set the NaviKen format for CD-ROM based digital

Exhibit 13 *Number and Timing of New Product Introductions in Japan: After-Market Models**

Company/Brand	1990	1991	1992	1993	1994	1995	Total	1995 Product Line[a]
Pioneer	2	0	1	4	4	3	14	7
Sony	0	0	1	3	5	5	14	8
Matsushita	0	0	0	1	3	3	7	4
Alpine	0	0	0	3	2	2	7	2
Mitsubishi	0	0	1	1	3	4	9	6
Kenwood	0	0	1	0	3	2	6	3
Zanavi	0	0	0	0	0	4	4	4
Clarion	0	0	0	2	1	2	5	3
Fujitsu Ten	0	0	0	0	1	3	4	3
Nippon Denso	0	0	0	0	0	2	2	2
Sharp	0	0	0	0	3	0	3	2
Casio	0	0	0	0	1	1	2	2
Sumitomo Denko	0	0	0	1	3	1	5	3
Toshiba	0	0	0	2	2	3	7	5
Citizen	0	0	0	0	0	3	3	3
Calsonic	0	0	0	0	2	3	5	4
NEC	0	0	0	0	1	1	2	1
Chuo Jidosha	0	0	0	0	1	1	2	1
Maspro	0	0	1	0	1	1	3	2
Sanyo	0	0	0	1	0	3	4	3
Nakamichi	0	0	0	0	1	0	1	1
Total	2	0	5	18	37	47	109	69

*Source: Analysis of the case writers, based on research interviews.
Note: [a]After adjusting for discontinued products.

Exhibit 14 *Unit Market Shares of Advanced Models in Japan: 1993–1995**

	Turn-by-Turn Route Guidance			Automatic Route Calculation	
	No (GPS)	**Yes (Hybrid)**		**No (Manual)**	**Yes (Automatic)**
1993	98%	2%	1993	97%	3%
1994	56%	44%	1994	50%	50%
1995	20%	80%	1995	30%	70%

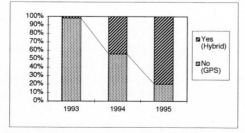

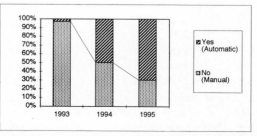

*Source: Analysis of the case writers, based on research interviews.

Exhibit 15 *Sony Product Introduction Chronology: 1992–1995* *

General Information						
Product	**Retail Price**	**Launch Date**	**Cumulative Unit Sales**[a]	**(%)**	**1995 Unit Sales**[a]	**(%)**
NVX-1	$4,700	92/06	7,000	(3%)	—	(0%)
NVX-F10	$2,100	93/06	100,000	(41%)	—	(0%)
NVX-F15	$2,800	93/10	15,000	(6%)	—	(0%)
NVX-F1	$1,600	93/10	4,000	(2%)	—	(0%)
NVX-2	open price	94/02	3,000	(1%)	—	(0%)
NVX-F16	$2,500	94/06	15,000	(6%)	7,000	(7%)
NVX-3	$1,400	94/06	4,000	(2%)	—	(0%)
NVX-B50	$1,800	94/10	9,000	(4%)	4,000	(4%)
NVX-4	$1,500	94/10	9,000	(4%)	4,000	(4%)
NVX-F16MK2	$2,500	95/02	10,000	(4%)	10,000	(10%)
NVX-A1	$1,300	95/04	4,000	(2%)	10,000	(10%)
NVX-S1	$1,500	95/07	40,000	(16%)	40,000	(41%)
NVX-F30	$2,300	95/07	20,000	(8%)	20,000	(20%)
GPX-5	$2,100	95/12	3,000	(1%)	3,000	(3%)
Total			243,000	(100%)	98,000	(100%)

	Hardware		**Functions**			
Product	**GPS or Hybrid**	**w/ or w/o Monitor**[b]	**Route Guidance**	**Route Calculation**	**Auto Route Re-Calculation**	**Voice Recognition**
NVX-1	GPS	w/	No	No	No	No
NVX-F10	GPS	w/	No	No	No	No
NVX-F15	GPS	w/	No	No	No	No
NVX-F1	GPS	w/	No	No	No	No
NVX-2	GPS	w/o	No	No	No	No
NVX-F16	GPS	w/	No	No	No	No
NVX-3	GPS	w/o	No	No	No	No
NVX-B50	Hybrid	w/o	No	No	No	No
NVX-4	Hybrid	w/o	No	No	No	No
NVX-F16MK2	GPS (w/ Hybrid Option)	w/	No	No	No	No
NVX-A1	GPS	w/o	No	Yes	No	No
NVX-S1	Hybrid	w/o	Yes	Yes	No	Optional
NVX-F30	GPS	w/	Yes	Yes	No	Optional
GPX-5	GPS (w/ Hybrid Option)	w/	Yes	Yes	No	Optional

*Source: Analysis of the case writers, based on research interviews.
Notes: [a]All sales were made in Japan in the after-market. All products used the NaviKen format.
    [b] "w/o monitor" means that the product was sold without a monitor. A customer needed to buy a monitor (which cost $500–$1,000) to complete the system.

Exhibit 16   *Top 10 Brand Product Comparisons: 1995**

Company	Product[a]	Retail Price	Launch Date	1995 Unit Sales[a]	Hardware	
					GPS or Hybrid	w/ or w/o Monitor[b]
Pioneer	AVIC-XA1	$2,630	95/11	30,000	Hybrid	w/
Sony	NVX-S1	$1,500	95/07	40,000	Hybrid	w/o
Matsushita	CN-V700	$1,570	95/07	50,000	Hybrid	w/o
Alpine	NTV-W055V	$2,480	95/11	40,000	Hybrid	w/
Mitsubishi	CU-9510	$1,490	95/05	15,000	Hybrid	w/o
Kenwood	GPR-03EX	$1,450	95/10	15,000	Hybrid	w/o
Zanavi	XA-N1	$1,480	95/06	5,000	Hybrid	w/o
Clarion	NAX9100	$1,470	95/11	10,000	Hybrid	w/o
Fujitsu Ten	E500NCU	$1,650	95/11	10,000	Hybrid	w/o
Nippon Denso	MV-1000S	$2,580	95/01	3,000	Hybrid	w/

Company	Software	Functions			
	Digital Map Format	Route Guidance	Route Calculation	Auto Route Re-Calculation	Voice Recognition
Pioneer	Original Only	Yes	Yes	No	No
Sony	NaviKen Only	Yes	Yes	No	Optional
Matsushita	Both	Yes	Yes	Yes	No
Alpine	Both	Yes	Yes	Yes	No
Mitsubishi	NaviKen Only	Yes	Yes	No	No
Kenwood	Both	Yes	Yes	No	Yes
Zanavi	NaviKen Only	Yes	Yes	No	No
Clarion	Original Only	Yes	Yes	No	No
Fujitsu Ten	Both	Yes	Yes	Yes	No
Nippon Denso	Original Only	Yes	Yes	No	No

*Source: Adapted from *1996 New and Improved Car Navigation Systems,* Naigai Shuppan Publishing, 1995.
Notes: [a]For each brand, this exhibit reports sales of the best selling after-market model in 1995.
   [b]"w/o monitor" means that the product sold without a monitor. A customer needed to buy a monitor (which cost $500–$1,000) to complete the system.

maps. The standard-setting effort lowered entry barriers, resulting in 10 new entrants in 1994 and another five in 1995. Competition fueled market growth from 160,000 units in 1993, to 340,000 units in 1994, and to 580,000 units in 1995.

Market growth encouraged intense competition and faster new-product development. Ex-

hibit 13 reports the timing of product introductions by different competitors. Once every six months during 1994 and 1995, competitors introduced progressively more advanced product. In April 1994, Matsushita, which had not joined NaviKen, was the first to develop a hybrid system employing both GPS and dead-

Exhibit 16   *(continued)*

| Company | Product[a] | User Test Result (5 = excellent, 1 = poor) | | |
		Easy to Use Command	Easy to Read Monitor	Easy to Find Destination
Pioneer	AVIC-XA1	2	3	3
Sony	NVX-S1	2	3	3
Matsushita	CN-V700	5	5	4
Alpine	NTV-W055V	4	4	5
Mitsubishi	CU-9510	3	3	2
Kenwood	GPR-03EX	3	3	2
Zanavi	XA-N1	4	3	4
Clarion	NAX9100	3	5	3
Fujitsu Ten	E500NCU	3	4	2
Nippon Denso	MV-1000S	5	4	5
Average		3.4	3.7	3.3

| Company | Product[a] | User Test Result (5 = excellent, 1 = poor) | | |
		Speed of Route Calculation (Seconds)	Accuracy of Route Guidance	Total Score
Pioneer	AVIC-XA1	2 (141)	3	13
Sony	NVX-S1	2 (121)	2	12
Matsushita	CN-V700	3 (58)	5	22
Alpine	NTV-W055V	5 (16)	5	23
Mitsubishi	CU-9510	2 (110)	4	14
Kenwood	GPR-03EX	3 (57)	2	13
Zanavi	XA-N1	4 (43)	3	18
Clarion	NAX9100	4 (46)	4	19
Fujitsu Ten	E500NCU	2 (110)	3	14
Nippon Denso	MV-1000S	4 (42)	4	22
Average		3.1 (74)	3.5	17

[a]For each brand, this exhibit reports sales of the best selling after-market model in 1995.

reckoning sensors. The Matsushita model was also the first to be able to calculate and communicate the best route to a destination. In October 1994, Alpine, which was originally a NaviKen member but later became an independent developer, introduced the first hybrid model that could provide turn-by-turn route guidance. In early 1995, Pioneer introduced a new hybrid model with a flash memory chip in its CPU; this enabled the entire system to be upgraded by simply installing a new CD-ROM. As shown in Exhibit 14, these more sophisticated hybrid models began to outsell the simpler GPS-based products by 1995.

NaviKen member companies, including Sony, did not respond quickly enough. It took the 40 NaviKen members more than a year to agree on a standardized software upgrade. In addition, NaviKen members saw little room to differentiate their products from each other. As shown in Exhibit 15, Sony introduced new products almost every six months, but all were modified versions of the original GPS-based products, which did not provide automatic route calculation or turn-by-turn route guidance. In May 1994, Sony introduced NVX-F16, an extended version of the NVX-F15, but sold only 15,000 units by April 1996. In October 1994, Sony introduced NVX-B50, which employed a CD-ROM changer in which a driver could place six different CD-ROMs. The product sold only 9,000 units by April 1996. Sony had perhaps introduced the product too early, because the average navigation system owner had only 1.5 CD-ROMs as of 1995.

In July 1995, Sony finally introduced NVX-S1, a hybrid system with a route guidance function. However, the market did not respond well to this late entry. According to a trade magazine, NVX-S1, which still employed the NaviKen standard in its digital map database, calculated a route too slowly and provided turn-by-turn guidance too infrequently compared to competitive products. See Exhibit 16 for a summary of the magazine's product comparison.

By 1995, competition focused on the richness of the digital-map databases. In October 1995, Alpine introduced another new product with a database of 11 million phone numbers built into its digital map software, which a driver could use to identify his/her destination. The product sold well, giving Alpine market-share leadership, as shown in Exhibit 17. Other competitors followed suit, building more advanced databases filled with large numbers of phone numbers, landmarks, and other point-of-interest information.

Fighting against heavy odds in the main models, Sony turned its product strategy back to the GPS-based model by introducing portable navigation systems. In December 1995, Sony introduced Handy Navigation System GPX-5, the world's first detachable model. It could be used both inside and outside an automobile, targeting customers who wanted to use the system for outdoor camping, bike touring, and marine sports. The GPS-based device alone retailed for $2,000, with an option to purchase a gyroscopic sensor to convert the system into a hybrid for an additional $300. A customer could also add a home station kit for $200; this could connect a navigation system to a home television and enable a consumer to plan a route before going out to drive. See Exhibit 18 for pictures of Sony's portable navigation system.

European Competition

In Europe, car navigation systems were first installed on an OEM basis in luxury automobiles in late 1994. Philips developed its first system as an optional accessory to BMW's 7- and 5-series models in October 1994. Philips's model employed a hybrid system with GPS and dead-reckoning sensors, provided route guidance by either map, arrows, or voice, and used the CD-ROM-based digital-map software developed by EGT, a subsidiary of NavTech in the United States. Retailing for DM 6,900 ($4,600), the first model sold 10,000 units in 1995. In September 1995, Philips started marketing the same product at the same price through after-market channels in Germany and France, but sold only 400 units in the last three months of 1995.

In October 1994, Bosch began supplying car navigation systems for Mercedes S-Class models. Bosch's product was similar to Philips's except that it provided route guidance only with arrow signs and voice direction, with no map on the display. Bosch employed the CD-ROM-based map database developed by Etak. Retailing for DM 4,000 ($2,700), the product sold 8,000 units in 1995. Bosch also developed a model with a map on the monitor for the after-

Exhibit 17 *Unit Market Share Changes in After-Market/Auto Parts Store Channel in Japan: 1994–1995**

1994 January–June		1994 July–December		1995 January–June		1995 July–December	
Pioneer	24%	Pioneer	29%	Alpine	24%	Alpine	29%
Sony	24%	Alpine	16%	Pioneer	21%	Pioneer	20%
Matsushita	15%	Sony	13%	Matsushita	14%	Matsushita	15%
Kenwood	9%	Matsushita	11%	Sony	8%	Clarion	10%
Fujitsu	7%	Fujitsu	8%	Clarion	7%	Kenwood	9%
Clarion	6%	Kenwood	7%	Kenwood	6%	Sony	7%
Alpine	5%	Clarion	6%	Fujitsu	6%	Fujitsu	4%
Sumitomo Denko	4%	Sumitomo Denko	6%	Sumitomo Denko	3%	Sumitomo Denko	3%
Others	4%	Others	4%	Others	10%	Others	3%

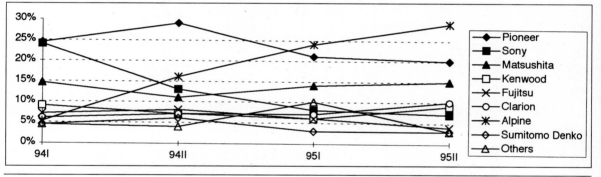

*Source: Analysis of the case writers, based on research interviews.
Note: This exhibit reports unit market shares in the auto parts chain channel, which represented 60% of after-market unit sales in Japan.

market segment in Germany and France, introducing it in June 1995, three months earlier than Philips. Retailing for DM 6,500 ($4,300), the after-market model sold 1,800 units by December 1995.

Besides the two European companies, only Sony competed in the after-market segment. Sony started test marketing its GPS-based model in France in late 1995, but sold only 300 units by April 1996. The product specification was similar to Sony's NVX-F16 and used Etak software. The GPS system pinpointed the car's current position on an LCD monitor, but it did not give route guidance to the destination. It showed a driver where the destination was located, but the driver had to plan the route. It was unclear whether Sony would continue marketing the tested model in Europe.

Some other companies, including Alpine, Matsushita, and Pioneer, were said to be planning to enter the European market in 1997 and 1998. Luxury car manufacturers such as Jaguar and Volvo were reportedly considering OEM installation of car navigation systems. Volkswagen, Audi, and Opel were rumored to be seeking OEM suppliers of low-end models offering voice navigation with no monitor for around DM 600 ($400). Exhibit 19 summarizes current and prospective competitors in Europe and the characteristics of their products.

Exhibit 18   *Sony Handy Navigation System GPX-5*

*Source: Company materials.

Exhibit 18 *(continued)*

車で Car Navigation

外で Field Navigation

家で Home Navigation

Exhibit 19 *Current and Prospective Competitors in Europe**

| | General Information | | | | Hardware | | Software | |
	Company	Auto Maker	Retail Price	Launch Date	Cumulative Unit Sales	GPS or Hybrid	Interface: map, arrow, voice	Digital Map Format	Software Media
					Current Competitors				
OEM	Bosch	Mercedes	DM 4,025	10/94	8,000	Hybrid	arrow, voice	Etak	CD-ROM
	Philips	BMW	DM 6,900	10/94	10,000	Hybrid	map, arrow, voice	NavTech	CD-ROM
After-Market	Bosch	Travel Pilot	DM 6,500	06/95	1,800	Hybrid	map, arrow, voice	Etak	CD-ROM
	Philips	Carin	DM 6,900	09/95	400	Hybrid	map, arrow, voice	NavTech	CD-ROM
	Sony	NVX-160	DM 5,500	10/95	300	GPS	map	Etak	CD-ROM
					Prospective Competitors				
OEM	Mitsubishi	Volvo	—	Early 97	—	Hybrid	map, arrow, voice	TeleAtlas	CD-ROM
	Bosch	VW	DM 600	Early 97	—	GPS	voice	Etak	CD-ROM
	Bosch	Audi	DM 600	Early 97	—	GPS	voice	Etak	CD-ROM
After-Market	Alpine	NTV-W055V	DM 6,000	Mid 96	—	Hybrid	map, arrow, voice	NavTech	CD-ROM
	Matsushita	—	—	Early 97	—	Hybrid	map, arrow, voice	—	—
	Pioneer	—	—	Early 97	—	Hybrid	map, arrow, voice	—	—

*Source: Analysis of the case writers, based on research interviews.

U.S. Competition

As shown in **Exhibit 4**, sales of 1 million units per year were expected in the United States by 2000. On the other hand, none of the models introduced to date had sold more than a few thousand units as of 1995. Car navigation systems were not yet widely known among U.S. consumers.

Industry observers believed price reductions would be critical before demand for car navigation systems would take off in the United States. Market research revealed that few U.S. consumers would pay over $1,000 for car navigation systems. Auto manufacturers had told the car navigation makers that they needed prices to drop to as low as $500, which was not expected until 2005, after further investments in mapping, data storage, and route guidance were completed.

Zexel, a Japanese auto parts supplier, was the first to bring car navigation systems to the United States.[8] As an OEM, Zexel began supplying systems for GM's Oldsmobile Eighty-eight in summer 1994. Zexel's navigation products employed hybrid systems with GPS and dead-reckoning sensors and provided route guidance by either map, arrows, or voice. The digital map database was stored in a 170 MB hard disk drive located in a car trunk. With the price tag of $1,995, however, the product was expensive. In 1994, the most expensive car accessory in the United States was a European-branded premium hi-fi speaker system for $1,200. Due to a lack of marketing expertise at Zexel and Oldsmobile and due to the fact that digital maps were only available for a few major cities, only 2,500 units were sold by the end of 1995.

Zexel licensed its product technology to Rockwell for after-market sales. Rockwell sold the product to rental car companies such as Avis and Hertz. The rental car companies purchased a few thousand units in total and rented the systems for a $5 to $7 daily upcharge. However, neither Rockwell nor the rental car companies had aggressively marketed the product.

Sony began marketing the NVX-F160, the U.S. version of the Japanese model NVX-F16, in California and Florida in late 1994. Despite its lack of route guidance capability, Sony launched the NVX-160, the most advanced model in Sony's product line as of 1994, in order to be the first to market an after-market model. At a price of $2,995, only 800 units were sold by the end of 1995.

A low-end product priced under $1,000 was introduced in December 1995 by Amerigon, a Silicon Valley startup known for its voice recognition technology. The system was bundled with car stereos and sold under car audio brand names by manufacturers such as Alpine, Clarion, and Kenwood. The price was about $600, although when the stereo and installation were included, the price was more like $1,000 to $1,500. This CD-ROM based system, named AudioNav, did not employ GPS, relying instead on a dead-reckoning sensor alone. There was no monitor, only a voice system that used a microphone similar to one used in a cellular phone. The driver had to spell out the destination for route calculation. It was hands free, but the driver had to find a street sign or local landmark if he/she became lost. Unit sales to date were unknown.

Within a year or two, Alpine and Nippon Denso were expected to supply OEM models to Honda and Toyota factories in the United States. Pioneer, Alpine, and Matsushita were expected to enter the U.S. after-market segment, introducing modified versions of their latest domestic-market models. Exhibit 20 lists current and prospective competitors in the United States and characteristics of their products.

SUMMER 1996: RECONSTRUCT THE GLOBAL STRATEGY

Masao Morita, the son of the legendary founder Akio Morita, contemplated how to formulate its multinational marketing strategy for the fast-

---

[8]Zexel did not sell car navigation systems either on an OEM basis or through after-market channels in Japan as of 1996.

Exhibit 20 *Current and Prospective Competitors in the United States**

	Company	Auto Maker	Retail Price	Launch Date	Cumulative Unit Sales	GPS or Hybrid	Interface: map, arrow, voice	Digital Map Format	Software Media
		General Information				Hardware		Software	
Current Competitors									
OEM	Zexel	GM/Olds-mobile	$1,995	08/94	2,500	Hybrid	map,arrow, voice	NavTech	Hard Disk (170 MB)
After-Market	Sony	NVX-160	$2,995	10/94	800	GPS	map	Etak	CD-ROM
	Rockwell	GuideStar	$1,995	01/95	7,000	Hybrid	map, arrow, voice	NavTech	Hard Disk (170 MB)
	Amerigon	AudioNav	$600	12/95	—	Dead Reckoning voice, No GPS		NavTech	CD-ROM
Prospective Competitors									
OEM	Alpine	Honda	$2,000	Mid 96	—	Hybrid	map, arrow, voice	NavTech	Hard Disk (170 MB)
	Nippon Denso	Toyota	—	Late 96	—	Hybrid	map, arrow, voice	NavTech	Hard Disk (170 MB)
	Bosch	Mercedes	—	Early 99	—	Hybrid	map, arrow, voice	Etak	CD-ROM
After-Market	Delco (US)	Telepath 100	$500	Mid 96	—	Dead Reckoning voice, No GPS		NavTech	CD-ROM
	Pioneer	—	—	Early 97	—	Hybrid	map, arrow, voice	NavTech	CD-ROM
	Matsushita	—	—	Early 97	—	Hybrid	map, arrow, voice	—	CD-ROM
	Clarion	—	—	Early 97	—	Hybrid	map, arrow, voice	NavTech	CD-ROM
	Kenwood	—	—	Early 97	—	Hybrid	map, arrow, voice	NavTech	CD-ROM

*Source: Analysis of the case writers, based on research interviews.

changing car navigation systems market for the next five years. Given the different market conditions from one region to another and Sony's unsatisfactory position in each market, Morita resolved to reevaluate the company's marketing strategy for car navigation systems and the benefits Sony could and should provide drivers around the world. Morita needed to resolve the conflicting views within his company regarding several key issues.

Geographical Focus Issue

Some managers believed it was time to focus much more effort on markets outside Japan. One international marketing manager said:

> Both the European and U.S. markets are expected to grow as large as the Japanese market within 10 years. We should preempt competitors with our own after-market models. We will be too late if we wait until these overseas markets take off. We should be the company that creates these markets as we did at home.

In contrast, a marketing manager in Tokyo insisted that Sony should focus on reestablishing its competitive position in Japan:

> Our share is down because we have lagged behind our competitors in developing more accurate hybrid models and more sophisticated route guidance technology. The fact is, in 1996, 98% of our car navigation sales come from Japan. The growth forecasts for markets overseas are totally speculative.

The allocation of R&D resources depended in part on Sony's geographical priorities. In 1996, Sony employed 200 highly skilled engineers dedicated to car navigation systems development, all of whom were stationed in Japan, except for only one each in Europe and the United States.

Product Choice

Given the poor performance of the current overseas model NVX-F160, it seemed that a simple GPS-based model at a price of $3,000 was un-

likely to appeal to drivers in Europe and the United States. There were at least three product options for Sony: (1) launch the Handy Navigation System GPX-5, the portable GPS model most recently introduced in Japan, as a global product; (2) modify the hybrid NVX-S1 for Europe and/or the United States; and (3) develop a new low-priced model for overseas markets.

A marketing manager in Tokyo emphasized the advantage of the GPX-5 as a global product:

> The portable nature of the GPX-5 should appeal to a much broader population, including consumers interested in outdoor camping, bike touring, and marine sports. Users can also use it to enjoy regular TV channels while traveling. Since the product is detachable, it is not strictly an automobile device so auto safety regulation and product liability issues may not apply. Portability also reduces the risk of theft.

The U.S. country manager, however, questioned the product's potential:

> For the product to succeed in the United States, we need software with geocoded information specifically for camping sites, fishing locations, mountain skiing routes, and the like, all of which currently do not exist. It will cost at least $1 million and take nine months to develop software for each recreation activity. By the time we have a variety of CD-ROMs, competition could be on different basis. In addition, if the product is priced around $3,000 again, it will flop. Finally, modifying the GPX-5 for the United States would require five engineers working for six months.

Another manager in Tokyo proposed to modify the NVX-S1, the hybrid model with turn-by-turn route guidance capability, for overseas markets:

> In the countries where street names are clearly signed and road systems are straightforward, the current GPS-based model, which only shows the driver's position on the map, adds little value to drivers. We need a more sophisticated hybrid model, which can be upgraded

to accommodate future advances such as a real-time traffic information service and a traffic emergency warning system.

However, there were also pessimistic views regarding this product modification:

In turn-by-turn route guidance technology, Sony lags far behind its competitors overseas. The product modification option requires Sony to reinvent its digital map software for the U.S. and European markets. When competitors launch more sophisticated route guidance systems, the present system will quickly become obsolete. Moreover, this option will incur substantial time and cost. It will take two years for our software vendor Etak to digitize U.S. and European maps for turn-by-turn route guidance. This will cost $100 million in initial development costs and $30 million for annual maintenance and content upgrades. This option will require 50 engineers to work with Etak in the U.S. and Europe. NavTech, Etak's competitor, will have soon digitized 100% of the U.S. and European maps for turn-by-turn guidance. We can switch from Etak to NavTech, but we are not sure how much competitive advantage we will lose by using the same database as our main competitors.

Rejecting the above product modification options, some sales managers in the United States argued for developing low-end models from scratch, solely for the overseas market:

As consumer research has shown, it is obvious nobody here will buy a $3,000 gadget for his/her car. If we want to create a market here, we need a product designed to meet local needs. European and US drivers don't need a fancy digital map nor an expensive LCD monitor and will be happy with some simple arrow-and-voice guidance at a price of $1,000 or less.

The international marketing manager in Tokyo, however, strongly opposed this low-end product strategy:

Even if a low-end, stripped-down product stimulates the market in the short run, Sony will gain little in the long run. It will precipitate price competition and may shrink the market, at least in value terms. The product will not be adaptable to future developments in road infrastructure. It will diminish Sony's leadership image in car navigation systems. Furthermore, this option will need 60 of our engineers to work for a year on developing this new product. Given the competition we face at home, we cannot afford to divert them.

Standard-Setting Issue

There was wide debate over continuation of the NaviKen consortium. Some managers contended that Sony should leave NaviKen or at least develop proprietary digital map technology in parallel in order to compete head-to-head with other companies. A young manager in charge of product development stated:

The NaviKen format was helpful early on. However, product introductions are now so frequent that we need our own digital map technology to respond quickly to the market's evolving needs. Customers appreciate a differentiated database to standardized ones. As one survey says, an average consumer owns only 1.5 CD-ROMs, and most do not use CD-ROM maps across different hardware anyway. Car navigation systems are not the same as personal computers.

In contrast, several of the digital map engineers who were heavily involved in establishing NaviKen format in the 1980s opposed such a radical move. As one senior engineer stated:

Such a myopic and opportunistic action may bring some market share in the short run, but hinder market development for the future. Standardized software will always benefit the consumer as well as the industry, as has been shown in the cases of CD players and VCRs. Our market research shows 80% of our customers care about software compatibility. As a market leader, Sony always tries to grow the market pie. Sony does not pursue a larger share of a shrinking market. After all we've put into establishing the NaviKen standard, why should we quit now? Now it is time for us to extend our effort overseas and to stimulate consumer demand as we have done in Japan.

Other managers took a compromise view. While supporting NaviKen in Japan, they proposed to establish different digital map formats for Europe and the United States. One manager explained:

To boost the market overseas, especially early on, we need a variety of compatible software. However, the NaviKen standard was developed for the unique Japanese road system, and is not extendible to other markets. Since the traffic infrastructures are very different from country to country, we should try to establish new product standards region by region.

AB SANDVIK SAWS AND TOOLS: THE ERGO STRATEGY

"Fifteen years ago we competed with price. Today we compete with quality. Tomorrow it will be design."

Robert Hayes, 1991

Göran Gezelius, the president of the Sandvik Saws and Tools Business Area, looked out his office window at the serene waters of Lake Storsjön. It was early spring and the trees had not yet taken on their summer foliage. He had just returned from a two-week trip to North America a day early and had some free time in his normally hectic schedule. He thought that overall Saws and Tools business results for 1995 had been adequate. Early operating results suggested that 1996 would be a challenging year. But from a strategic perspective, he was not entirely satisfied with what was being accomplished with the recently introduced Ergo hand tools, especially in North America. There was a meeting of the Ergo Steering Committee later in the week, and

he needed to review the performance of ergonomic hand tools strategy. He reached for his Ergo file.

OVERVIEW

Over the last three years, beginning in 1993, ergonomically designed hand tools had become an increasingly important part of the strategy for the hand tools component of the Saws and Tools Business Unit. Ergonomics, the science of optimizing the interaction of the person and their work environment, had always been considered in the design process. But in 1991 Sandvik acquired Bahco Verktyg AB, a maker of spanners[1] and wrenches. Bahco had been working with an industrial design firm, and they had developed an intensive methodology that set new standards for ergonomic design. In mid-1993, the Ergo Project Group was formed within Saws and Tools and created a common design philosophy and

---

[1]Called an adjustable wrench in North America. The spanner had been invented by Bahco's founder.

This case was prepared by Roderick White and Julian Birkinshaw. The authors may have disguised certain names and other identifying information to protect confidentiality. Copyright © 1997, Richard Ivey School of Business at The University of Western Ontario. Version: 1997-04-24.

marketing statement across the range of hand tools, from handsaws to screwdrivers. A sequence was established for the conversion of existing tools to the new ergonomic standard and the change over began. By early 1996 the process was about half completed. A considerable investment had already been made in redesign, retooling production processes and repositioning products in the marketplace. More would be required to complete the conversion.

Even though the complete line of ergonomic tools would not be available for another two to three years, Göran was concerned that the initial sales of Ergo tools already introduced were not as strong as hoped. Personally he still felt very committed to the Ergo concept. However, he wondered whether the Ergo Committee should reexamine the strategy and consider alternative courses of action.

COMPANY BACKGROUND

AB Sandvik Saws and Tools was one of six global business areas within Sandvik AB. The others were: cutting tools, rock tools, hard materials, steel, and process systems. Exhibit 1 provides a brief description and overview of each business area. Each operated as an autonomous business. Group management provided a few support activities (finance, legal, international sales/trading companies for less-developed markets) that were drawn on by the business areas as needed.

With headquarters in Sandviken, Sweden, about 150 kilometers (km) north of Stockholm, Sandvik began in 1862 as a manufacturer of high-quality steel. Never a volume producer of steel, Sandvik specialized in applications where quality, uniformity, hardness, and sharpness were important. Initially steel was used for things like saws, fish hooks, drills for rock mining, and razors. In 1886 the company started making saws. As expertise accumulated it led into other related businesses like steel tubing and cutting tools.

Although the company had evolved into different businesses, there were several themes common to all Sandvik's businesses. Sandvik products were functional. They provided the customer maximum value in terms of performance, quality, speed, productivity, and flexibility. Sandvik's products usually sold at a premium price (on a per unit basis) but had higher performance and overall lower costs to the customer. The performance advantages incorporated into Sandvik's products originated with its engineering and R&D efforts. Partly as a consequence of its attention to customer functionality Sandvik tended to focus on niche markets. For example, Sandvik supplied the steel used by a leading compass manufacturer to make their magnetic compass needles (1,000 kg per year) or the balls for ballpoint pens (2 billion annually). In order to maintain direct contact with the customers and ensure that they understood the value of its products, Sandvik forward integrated, as far as feasible, into sales and distribution. Sandvik also manufactured most of what it sold.

The Sandvik Group's activities were global in scope. The group was active in over 60 countries. Over 90% of sales were to customers outside Sweden (see Exhibit 2) and two-thirds of Sandvik's almost 30,000 employees were located outside Sweden. At the same time, Sandvik was the quintessential Swedish company: conservative, understated, and traditional in style, with a strong work ethic and a homogeneous corporate culture. As stated by chairman of the board, Percy Barnevik, "Sandvik cannot be described as a company given to excesses . . . put simply, the company does a darn fine job without a lot of fuss and without any particular recognition for it."

Most of the group's businesses were industrial. Thus, sales, and profits even more so, tended to follow the business cycle. (See Exhibit 3.) Partly as a consequence of this exposure Sandvik had a very conservative financial structure. Long-term liabilities were just 14% of total capital and the company had 6.9 billion SEK (Swedish kronor) in cash and short-term investments (22.5% of total assets) at the end of 1995. This liquidity al-

Exhibit 1   *AB Sandvik: Results by Business Area, 1995*

Business Area	Sales		Operating Profits[a]		Return on Sales (%)
	SEK m.[c]	%	SEK m.[c]	%	
Tooling	9,576	32%	2,436	47%	25.4%
Rock tools	2,015	7	219	4	10.9
Hard materials	1,224	4	185	4	15.1
Steel	9,807	33	1,623	31	16.5
Saws and tools	2,674	9	184	4	6.9
Process systems	1,810	6	101	2	5.6
Seco tools[b]	2,555	9	542	10	21.2
Intra group	39	—	(96)	—	
Group total	29,700	100	5,194	100	17.5

Description of Business Areas

Business Area	No. of Employees	Description
Tooling	11,010	Sandvik Coromat as the global leader in cemented carbide inserts used for the machining of metal. Inserts were the cutting edge in machine tools, like lathes. CTT Tools produced principally high-speed steel tools like drills, threading tools, and reamers.
Rock tools	1,877	This business was a leading supplier of cemented-carbide-tipped rock-drilling tools (and tool systems) used in mining, civil engineering, and water-well drilling.
Hard materials	1,447	This business manufactured and marketed unmachined carbide blanks, as well as customized wear parts (e.g., seal rings). Sandvik was the largest competitor in this business, and the only one with global scope.
Steel	7,257	Steel manufactured tube, strip, wire and bar for demanding applications. Products were produced in stainless and high alloy steels and in titanium, nickel, and zirconium alloys.
Saws and tools	2,998	Used mainly by professionals, S&T products included hand saws and saw blades, wrenches, spanners, pliers, files, and pruning tools, as well as guide bars and saw chains.
Process systems	888	Manufactured the steel belts and engineers the complete systems used in automated sorting and chemical and food-processing.

[a]After depreciation, before financial charges.
[b]A separately listed public company. Sandvik owned 61%.
[c]SEK m.: Swedish kronor, in millions. 1 SEK was equal to approximately $0.15 U.S.

Exhibit 2   *Sandvik AB: Sales by Region*

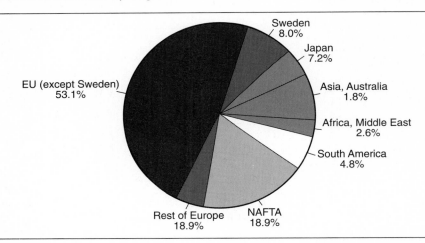

*Source: Company annual reports.

Exhibit 3   *Sandvik AB: Financial Performance**

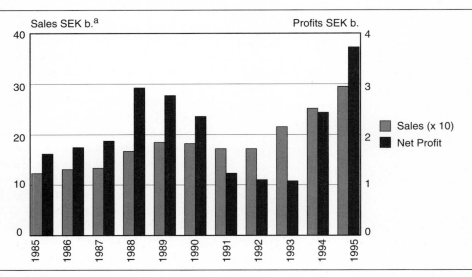

*Source: Company annual reports.
[a]SEK b. = billions

lowed Sandvik to make selective acquisitions to develop and strengthen selected business areas, and the company had been active in this way.

SAWS AND TOOLS GROUP: PERFORMANCE TOOLS— ALWAYS AVAILABLE

Sandvik Saws and Tools, with invoiced sales of 2674 MSEK[2], accounted for 9% of Sandvik AB's turnover. Historical information on sales and profit for this business area are presented in Table A.

Table A

Millions of SEK	1991	1992	1993	1994	1995
Sales	1437	2049	2363	2583	2674
Profit before financial items	(16)	(82)	(3)	185	184
No. of Employees	3676	3275	3060	3050	2998

Saws and Tools had 40 sales units around the world and 16 production units in eight countries. Saws and Tools made and marketed a wide range of hand tools, including pliers, wrenches, ratchets, screwdrivers, hammers, chisels, scrapers, files, hand saws, bow saws, hacksaws and blades; as well as gardening/agricultural hand tools (pruners, loppers, sécateurs, or pruning shears). It also manufactured and sold forestry products (chainsaw bar and chain) and industrial bandsaw blades. Sales for 1995 by major product centers are shown in Table B.

Saws and Tools' hand-tool product range included more than 8,000 items.[3] Over the last five years, product offerings had been globally

Table B

Product Center	% of 1995 sales	
Gardening	10%	
Hand tools (carpentry)	16%	
Mechanics hand tools (forged)	27%	
Files and handles	6%	
Metal cutting saws (excluding bandsaws)	19%	
Hand tools and associated products		78%
Bandsaws	13%	
Forestry products	9%	
Total	2674 MSEK[a]	

[a]Swedish kronor, in millions.

rationalized. All products were the same in all markets and available on a global basis. With its wide range of products, customers could meet their needs in hand tools and machine saw accessories from a single source, almost anywhere in the world.

Manufacturing was globally rationalized. Most products were made at one facility, and for those products made in more than one place the assortment was usually rationalized between the facilities. Exhibit 4 provides the location of major manufacturing facilities. Direct labor costs per hour differed by country. Germany had the highest cost, followed closely by Sweden. Costs at facilities in the southern United States and England were about 60% of those in Sweden. Portugal and Argentina were even lower labor cost areas. Overall, labor accounted for about 20% of hand-tool costs.

The business unit's products were designed to appeal to professional users in many different markets. The following statement made this focus clear.

---

[2]MSEK: Swedish kronor, in millions.
[3]This included all SKUs. It was estimated that only about 400 SKUs were amenable to Ergo design.

Exhibit 4   *Location of Saws and Tools Manufacturing Facilities*

Location	Product Center	No. of Employees
Edsbyn, Sweden	Forestry tools	147
Bollnäs, Sweden	Hand tools (hand saws)	160
Sveg, Sweden	Hand tools (bow saws)	40
Enköping, Sweden	Pliers (pliers and adjustables)	336
Lidköping, Sweden	Metal saws (hack)	242
	Bandsaws	23
Hasborn, Germany	Wrenches	90
Wuppertal, Germany	Wrenches	80
Maltby, England	Metal saws	37
	Bandsaws	23
Vila do Conde, Portugal	Files	243
Branford, CT, USA	Bandsaws	140
Milan, TN, USA	Forestry (chainsaw bars)	51
Dyer, TN, USA	Forestry (saw chain)	97
Santo Tome, Argentina	Wrenches	312

More than 80 percent of everything we sell is bought by professionals. Professionals will be our most important customers for a long time, even though nonprofessional use is expanding. If our products are accepted by the professionals and discerning users who often buy their tools privately, then we don't have to worry about the nonprofessionals. Our reputation will induce them to buy our tools.[4]

Of course, quality and performance were very important to professional users. Saws and Tools management felt their "do-it-ourselves" approach was important to delivering value to their customers.

A main reason why we manage to maintain a high standard of quality is that we control the entire cycle, from basic research through product development and manufacturing to distribution. The Sandvik Group is a world leader in materials technology. We regularly introduce innovations that put us ahead of competitors. Ergonomic design, hard pointing of hand saws, bimetal hacksaws and roll-top guide bars are just a few examples.[5]

Whenever possible Saws and Tools sold through resellers into each local market. However, its own distribution was increasingly centralized. There were only two distribution points for all of Europe. A new state-of-the-art distribution center in the Netherlands serviced the European Union. Nordic countries were served from Sandviken. This approach was a dramatic change from a few years earlier when each country sales unit held its own inventory and ran its own distribution system. With the new system, delivery was promised anywhere within Europe in 72 hours and to major cities within 48 hours. Many resellers were linked by EDI to Sandvik's computers. North American distribution was

[4]We're determined to become the best supplier in the hand-tool industry, company publication, May 1994, page 16.

[5]We're determined . . . , May 1994, page 24.

not yet as rationalized. But it had never been as fragmented. Currently it was done from facilities in Scranton, Pennsylvania, and Mississauga, Ontario. Other regions of the world tended to have local, country-based distribution.

Hand tools were distributed through a number of channels. Consumers (non-professional users) generally bought their tools through hardware stores or mass merchandisers. Most hardware stores were members of large buying groups. Professional users either brought their tools personally, or had them supplied by their employers. In either case they tended to buy from industrial or agricultural supply companies. Distributors tended to work on a regional basis and often carried competing products from different manufacturers.

In most of Europe, Saws and Tools had strong distribution for its hand tools. In North America, the distribution system had been built around bandsaw blades. The general mill supply distributors carried an assortment of products including bandsaw blades and hand tools. But in almost all instances, these distributors already carried the product assortment of one of the major U.S.-based competitors, such as Cooper and Stanley products.

A sales force of 22 Sandvik people (16 in the United States and six in Canada) and nine manufacturers' representatives[6] serviced industrial distributors. Other channels, like electrical and plumbing supply houses, retail "big box" stores, and hardware chains, were served by agencies and manufacturers' representatives. Altogether they had about 40 field sales people. Saws and Tools had one manager coordinating this channel.

Saws and Tools did not sell hand tools directly to the end user. They had a policy of not bypassing resellers. Sales people would, however, often do joint sales calls on industrial customers

---

[6]Manufacturers' representatives were not employs of the company. They worked on commission and usually represented several noncompeting manufacturers.

with the reseller's representative. Saws and Tools participated in all the major trade shows.

Sandvik was organized with sales units in each major country responsible for local sales and distribution. Global product centers (PCs) were responsible for manufacturing of the product, and with input from the sales units for marketing and pricing. Product profit responsibility was with the product centers. The management for most hand-tool PCs was located in Sweden.

SANDVIK BRAND: THE FISH-AND-HOOK

The Sandvik brand, represented by the fish-and-hook symbol, was well recognized by many professional users within Europe. It did not have the same degree of recognition in North America or Asia/Pacific. As one manager explained:

> In Europe we have strong brand recognition among industrial distributors (the trade) and professional end users. However, our brand recognition does vary between countries and product lines. The trade knows us everywhere (in Europe); the end users primarily in Scandinavia, U.K., Switzerland, and Holland; less in Germany; and very little in France and southern Europe. Overall we have strong brand recognition for hand saws, adjustable wrenches, and electronic pliers.
>
> In the U.S.A., our brand recognition with the end user is weak, or even nonexistent, except for bandsaw blades and electronic pliers. In Latin America, Sandvik has very strong brand recognition in Argentina; in the remaining parts we are mainly known for Sandflex™ hand hacksaw blades. In Asia we are recognized for handsaw blades and to some extent for adjustable wrenches.

Among casual users, Sandvik was widely known in Scandinavia and the Netherlands for hand saws and adjustable wrenches, in the U.K. for hand saws, in Switzerland for chisels and hand saws, and in France for pruning tools and hand

Table C

	USA				Europe		
Category	**Market MUSD 1994**	**Sandvik Share**		**Category**	**Market MUSD 1994**	**Sandvik Share**	
Screwdrivers	218	~0		Screwdrivers	~200	3	
Adjustable and pipe wrenches	116	~0		Adjustable wrenches	~50	~15	
Pliers	140	~0		Pliers	250	4	
				Hand saws (carpenter)	100	25	
Hand saws	150	10		Hacksaws and blades	100	20	
Hacksaw blades	17	5		Mechanics' tools	2000	6	
Mechanics' tools	~1200	~0		Other	2000	6	
Other	1000	3					

saws. In the Americas and Asia, Sandvik was not known to casual users.

These differences in brand recognition were reflected in different market shares by region. As shown in Table C, Saws and Tools had larger shares in Europe.

In the United States, Saws and Tools did have a more substantial presence in forestry (chainsaws, bars, and chains) and industrial bandsaw blades. But these products were not amenable to ergonomic design.

Sandvik sought to have the customer associate Sandvik with "performance tools, always available." High performance had always been a Sandvik hallmark. With the new distribution strategy, availability was improving.

Sandvik's pricing policy was related to its business strategy. Its prices were based upon the market leader for that professional product line in that region. The policy stated, "Our price should stay within a range of 90% to 105% of the market leader. We never undercut the leader by more than 10%."[7] Saws and Tools also tried to keep prices consistent between countries in a region (although not necessarily between regions).

ACQUISITIONS

Many of Saws and Tools' markets were highly fragmented, but restructuring was occurring: a situation the company recognized:

> *The hand-tool industry in Europe is ripe for restructuring. Sandvik Saws and Tools has taken the initiative in this process. . . . We've acquired competent tool manufacturers and added strong brands. We've gained economies of sale in production, marketing, and distribution. We've improved customer service and will continue to do so.*[8]

During the last few years Saws and Tools had acquired Bahco (spanners and pliers) Belzer (screwdrivers and ratchets), Lindstrom (electronic pliers), and Milford (industrial bandsaw blades).

---

[7]We're determined . . . , May 1994, page 49.

[8]We're determined . . . , May 1994, page 6.

STRUCTURE OF THE HAND TOOL MARKETS

In general, the hand tool industry had been fragmented, with many small, local companies making one or two types of tools. (For example, fifty companies made screwdrivers.) Sandvik was the only European-based manufacturer with a wide range of products for professional users. In Europe the 50 largest companies accounted for 50% of the market. However, the industry was less fragmented in the United States, where five firms accounted for 50% of the industry.[9] Larger players like Cooper Industries and Stanley produced and sold a range of branded tools. But retailers like Sears, with their Craftsman™ tool line, also had a strong position, particularly in the consumer market.

Both Craftsman and Stanley brands were more oriented to the home market, less towards the professional user. Stanley claimed to be the "largest manufacturer of consumer hand tools in the world."[10] Stanley also had a line of products oriented to the professional user. Stanley's tool business included consumer, industrial, and engineered segments. The first two segments were most directly competitive with Sandvik. Consumer tools included hand tools, such as measuring instruments, planes, hammers, knives and blades, wrenches, sockets, screwdrivers, saws, chisels, boring tools, masonry, tile and drywall tools, and paint preparation and application tools. Industrial tools included industrial and mechanics hand tools, as well as high-density industrial storage and retrieval systems. The consumer segment had 1995 sales of $739 million (U.S.) and industrial sales of $552 million. Seventy-two % of Stanley total sales were in the United States, 16% in Europe. The United States accounted for 79% of operating profits.

Professionally oriented products were generally produced by specialized, single-product-line

firms of limited geographic scope: single-product, single-market companies. Of course Sandvik with a broad product line and wide geographic scope was an exception to this rule, as was Cooper Industries in the United States. Cooper had 1995 tools and hardware sales of $962 million (U.S.). It competed directly with Sandvik in pliers, conventional and adjustable wrenches, files, saws, hammers, and screwdrivers. Cooper also had other products within its tools and hardware segment, including drapery hardware, power tools, chains, soldering equipment torches, and cutting products. Cooper had many identifiable brands, e.g., Crescent™ in adjustable wrenches and Kirsch™ in drapery hardware. However, Cooper itself was a holding company with no strong brand identity. Sales outside the United States were 37% of total sales, up from 31% two years earlier. Some niche players were attempting to grow geographically. Adjustable wrenches from Top, a Japanese company, had recently been appearing outside its home market.

Distribution of hand tools was also changing. An interesting North American phenomenon was the emergence of big-box specialty retailers, like Home Depot and Builder's Square. With their large stores and wide product assortment, these outlets targeted both the professional and do-it-yourself markets.

THE ERGO STRATEGY

The awareness of ergonomics is growing and it is going to continue to grow. The cost of NOT addressing ergonomics is also going to continue to grow.

Professor Thomas Armstrong
Center for Ergonomics,
The University of Michigan

Saws and Tools had an ongoing interest in ergonomic design. This interest was enhanced when in early 1992 Sandvik acquired the Bahco Tool Group, headquartered in Enköping, Sweden. Bahco, working with an industrial design firm, Ergonomi Design Gruppen, had developed a

---

[9]We're determined . . . , May 1994, page 6.
[10]Stanley Works, 10-K, 1995.

Exhibit 5 *Development of Ergonomically Designed Hand Tools**

---

11 Points, in Chronological Order
 1. Specification of demands
 2. Analysis of competitors—tools and markets
 3. Background material
 4. Production of functioning model
 5. User tests I
 6. Evaluation and modification of models
 7. User tests II
 8. Design proposal
 9. Product specification
10. User test III and preparation before launching
11. Follow up on statistics

---

*Approved by: The Scientific Committee of Musculoskeletal Disorders of the International Commission on Occupational Health (ICOH).

---

methodology for designing ergonomic tools. (See Exhibit 5.) Prior to the Sandvik acquisition, Bahco had used this process to develop ergonomic screwdrivers (1983), adjustable wrenches (1984), wood chisels (1985), slipjoint pliers (1986), side cutters (1989), combination pliers (1991), and a combination adjustable wrench (1991).

The ergonomic approach to hand-tool design fit well with Sandvik's basic strategy and appealed to Saws and Tools management. The 11-point Ergo process became the standard for the Saws and Tools group and the formal Ergo strategy came into being in mid-1993, when the Ergo Project Committee was formed.

The Ergo Project Committee was asked to build, direct and coordinate the Ergo Concept across the group, specifically to:

- ensure that all products designated as Ergo had followed the 11-point process.
- identify products to add to the Ergo range.
- establish guidelines for pricing Ergo products.
- product documentation and promotional materials.

The committee had eight members, six from different Saws and Tools units and two from EDG. It was chaired by Connie Jansson, R&D manager for Sandvik Bahco.

One of the first tasks of the committee was to identify those products most amenable to the Ergo concept and establish priorities for conversion to the Ergo standard. Major considerations were existing and potential volume and the prospects for global sales, as well as recognizable benefits and the potential to enhance Sandvik's market position. Exhibit 6 provides a list of Ergo products done to date or immediately pending. Each Ergo product had undergone the 11-point process and was done in collaboration with Ergonomi Design Gruppen (EDG).

ERGONOMI DESIGN GRUPPEN (EDG)

EDG was an independent industrial design firm located in an old, converted church on the outskirts of Stockholm. Sweden was asserted to have a comparative advantage in design, and EDG was one of the best midsized independent industrial design firms in Sweden. EDG assumed a major role in the initial ergonomic design process. Olle Bobjer was the senior ergonomist at EDG and Hans Himberg was the principal of the firm. Both played an active role with the Sandvik account. The firm employed 16 professionals, mostly industrial designers.

Exhibit 6   *Ergo Tools since 1992*

Type of Tool (by Product Center)	Launch Date
Sandvik Bahco	
Combination adjustable	1993 (2nd generation)
Gripping pliers	1994
Electronic pliers	1995
Pipe wrenches	pending
Sandvik Belzer	
Screwdrivers	pending (2nd generation)
Ratchet wrench	1994
Sandvik gardening	
Sécateurs	pending
Plate shears	pending
Sandvik hand tools	
Paint scrapers	pending
Hand saw	1995
Sandvik files	
File handles	1995
Metal saws	
Hacksaw frame	pending

The relationship with EDG was very close. EDG did work on a wide range of products for many different companies but had agreed to do hand tool design only for Sandvik. A portion of their fees was tied to the sales volume of the finished product. Sandvik felt the relationship gave them the benefits of an in-house design group, but with a much higher level of expertise.

EDG managed the 11-point development and certification process. Ergonomics was an applied science. The process was based upon feedback from sophisticated professional users of the tool under development. The process began with studies of how end-users worked. Work sites were visited, people interviewed, and videos of the tools in use were made. Multiple prototypes were built, tested, and assessed by end-users. (See Exhibit 7.)

If sufficiently unique, aspects of an Ergo product could be patented by Sandvik. But this type of protection was unusual. Most often, design patents were applicable when Ergo tools differed from traditional tools in appearance. Saws and Tools used both types of protection whenever possible. Several competitors had been stopped from copying Sandvik products.

The combined capabilities of EDG and Sandvik provided Saws and Tools with an area of distinctive competence. They felt no competitor could match their ability to design, develop, and manufacture ergonomic hand tools. But from the beginning, the Ergo Committee had recognized that "a product can successfully combine all the right things but stumble in the marketplace because of failure to communicate effectively about the product to potential purchasers."[11]

[11]A Research Approach to Ergonomic Hand Tools, April 1994, page 3.

Exhibit 7 *Prototypes of Electronics Nippers*

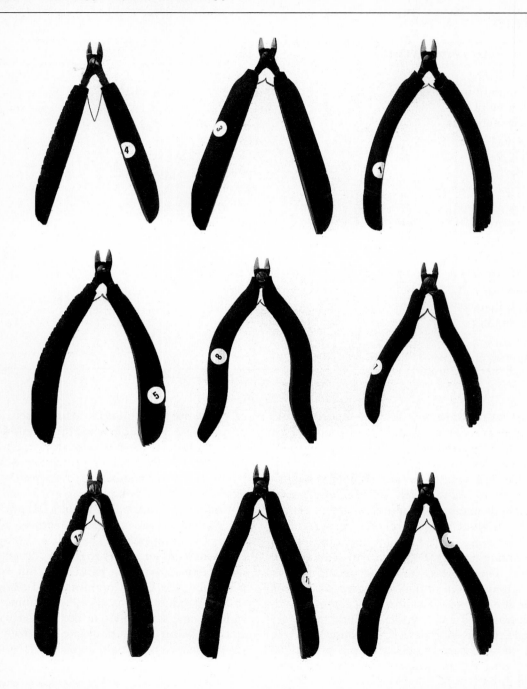

ERGO BENEFITS

Designing and manufacturing ergonomic hand tools was one thing; selling them was another. Hand tools had been used for centuries. Many of these tools had incorporated local norms and evolved into effective instruments; others remained largely unchanged since the industrial revolution. A better understanding of how the human body functioned in relation to work, the science of ergonomy, and the ongoing development of new materials presented opportunities for significant improvements in most hand tools.

The specific benefits of ergonomic design varied by tool (see Exhibit 8). But generally there were two principle benefits of ergonomic hand tools that were in fact both related to reduced physical stress on the worker:

- reduction in work-related physical disorders
- increases in productivity

Work-related disorders, more properly called cumulative trauma disorders (CTD) or repetitive motion injuries (RMI), were recognized as the number-one occupational hazard of the 1990s by experts in the field. Carpal tunnel syndrome was one such work-related injury. Nerves and tendons to the hand pass through the carpal tunnel, inside the wrist. Repetitive, stressful hand motions can cause the tendons to become inflamed, putting pressure on the nerves in this area, resulting in pain and numbness.

The highest risks for CTD were encountered when a job or tool required a combination of force and precision used repeatedly, without sufficient rest time for the body to recover. For example, a vineyard worker pruning grape vines and making up to 10,000 cuts per day would be at high risk.

Properly designed ergonomic tools reduced musculoskeletal stresses and strains and provided sensory feedback to the user for accuracy and optimum control. They were proportioned to the dimensions of the user and were efficient in the use of human energy. While good styling and ergonomic design often went hand-in-hand, there was a difference. Styling looks at the superficial aesthetics of the object; ergonomic goes deeper. Shapes, materials, and textures are selected for their functionality.

Ergonomics had also caught the attention of governmental health and safety agencies. Legislation had been proposed in the United States that would make employers liable for damages if they were not using ergonomic best practice. This proposed legislation had been shelved and was not under active consideration.

There were sound economic reasons for a company to use ergonomic tools. These included: fewer on-the-job accidents and worker sick days; reduction in injuries that sometimes result in disability claims, lawsuits, and higher insurance costs; and improved worker morale and job satisfaction.

Naturally, workers using well-designed tools could be more productive. While this benefit was recognized within Saws and Tools, it was not explicitly mentioned in any of the marketing materials. Groups concerned with worker health and safety, like unions, were seen as key opinion leaders in getting the Ergo concept accepted. Generally, they were more concerned with the health benefits than the possible productivity improvements.

It was recognized from the outset that "there is a latent demand within the professional hand tool users for ergonomic products. Many people need them, but few ask or know anything about them."[12] The report went on to say, "It is our job to educate the users/ dealers about real ergonomic tools. This will be difficult, as many competitors claim to have ergonomic tools."

Indeed, although the user may prefer one type of tool, it was difficult to conclusively demonstrate the ergonomic benefits of one tool over another. Because most CTD was caused by re-

---

[12]A Research Approach to Ergonomic Hand Tools, April 20, 1994, page 23.

Exhibit 8   *Typical Benefits of Ergo Hand Tools*

1. Hexagonal nut, so you can use a wrench if you need to pull hard.

2. Small diameter lets you tighten or loosen the screw quickly.

3. Plenty of room for precision control with thumb and index finger.

4. Completely rounded handle, so you avoid pressure points on your hand.

5. Fits your hand well – the right diameter provides maximum power. Ridged surface increases friction even when the handle is oily.

6. The handle is designed for both power and precision.

7. Large, rounded end minimizes pressure in your hand.

1. Long, narrow jaws make it easy to reach the places you need to.

2. Jaws grip tightly in three places, so you don't have to squeeze the handles so hard.

3. Larger jaw opening than other slip joint pliers. Can be adjusted with parallel jaws in 11 different positions.

4. Unique thumb grip lets you adjust jaw opening without letting go or losing control of the pliers.

5. Long, softly rounded grip that doesn't end in the middle of your hand.

6. The handles can't close, so your hand won't get caught between them.

petitive motions, it took weeks if not months to emerge. Comparative testing, a technique used to demonstrate the value of many other Sandvik products, was difficult under these circumstances. Thus, while Sandvik believed its Ergo tools were better than those produced by its competitors, they could not easily prove this claim. Instead, the initial marketing program relied on Sandvik's reputation for quality and explained the 11-point development program for Ergo tools.

INTRODUCTION OF ERGO TOOLS

When Sandvik acquired Bahco, their product line included a number of Ergo tools. With Sandvik's resources, distribution of these tools was broadened and the application of the Ergo concept to other products was accelerated.

When first introduced, Ergo products were additions to the top end of Sandvik's product range; they did not immediately replace an existing product. As a consequence, a product range, such as screwdrivers, included both Ergo and non-Ergo products. However, the adjustable-wrench category had evolved to the point that it included only Ergo products (first and second generation). Ergo products were positioned as the premium product within the Sandvik assortment and priced to reflect this positioning.

After Sandvik launched the Ergo strategy, the initial marketing/communication program targeted opinion leaders who could influence the tool purchase decision: ergonomists, health and safety engineers, safety (union) representatives, human resource managers, etc. Sales unit staff were trained in the benefits of ergonomic hand tools and provided with aids such as brochures and videos to help them communicate the concept.

Sandvik had not had significant hand tools sales in the United States prior to Ergo. It was hoped that Saws and Tools could expand its position in the U.S. hand-tools market using the Ergo products. Because of the investment required and the lack of warehouse space, only about 2,000 hand-tool SKUs (stockkeeping units) were currently available in the United States (compared to 8,000 in Europe). Because of this limited assortment, Sandvik could not offer to replace a distributor's other hand-tool suppliers. They positioned themselves as innovative product specialist targeted on niche markets. Ergo was introduced into the United States during the spring of 1995. As part of the introduction, Dr. Thomas Armstrong, a well-known U.S. ergonomist, and Sandvik personnel explained the Ergo concept to interested health and safety professionals, mostly from large automotive and aerospace manufacturers.

COST OF ERGO TOOLS

The increased costs of the Ergo strategy were difficult to ascertain precisely. Sandvik periodically redesigned its hand tools, and the added cost of employing the Ergo methodology were hard to calculate. Upfront design costs paid to EDG for an Ergo tool and associated with the 11-point program ranged from 200,000 to 1,500,000 SEK, depending on the complexity of the project. A typical project would be about 600,000 SEK. In addition to this amount, EDG also received a royalty. For a successful product, EDG design costs would account for 1% to 2% of sales[13] during its first 10 years.

Any design change, ergonomic or otherwise, required the retooling of the manufacturing process. The Ergo strategy had accelerated the number of design changes, but it was not necessarily much more expensive. These costs differed. The new Ergo screwdrivers had cost about a million dollars (U.S.) and the Ergo ratchet about $200,000. The Ergo loper saw had required a new injection mold for the handle at $100,000 and a new grinding technique for the blade that

---

[13]Internal transfer price from the product center to the sales unit.

required an investment of $400,000 in equipment. Generally, retooling costs ranged from $500,000 to $1,000,000 (U.S.), assuming the equipment for producing the same type of non-Ergo tool was available.

Ergo products were sometimes more difficult and costly to manufacture. Most often this was the result of a more complex shape and/or a special gripping surface being incorporated into the product. As one manager observed:

> *Any increase in costs has to be seen in light of the previous state of the tool. Ergo tools incorporate a higher level of enduser input and preference. The cost change, from our experience, and as a rule of thumb, is +10%.*

While some of the manufacturing processes were more challenging, none were proprietary. Smaller companies might have difficulty replicating some Ergo products, but larger manufacturers willing to expend the effort would be able to do so.

PRICE PREMIUM

Sandvik tried to adhere to its normal pricing policy with Ergo products. Because of the unique Ergo design, it was often difficult to find a comparable product, but in most instances there was a somewhat similar competitive offering to serve as a benchmark. This product, however, was most likely a niche product and not the market leader, at least in terms of volume. Ergo products were priced at a zero to 20% premium over competitive products. The amount of the premium took into account the cost of the product, the additional value it offered the user, and the pricing of competitor products. The price premium over low-end, nonprofessional products could be much greater. The latest generation of Ergo adjustable wrench was five times the retail price of the cheapest product available in the Scandinavian marketplace. In North America, the premiums tended to be even greater.

GOING GLOBAL

The Ergo strategy also reinforced Sandvik's global approach to the hand-tool business:

> *In the past, the hand-tool business was local. Customer preferences varied widely, even within one country. Patterns of tool choice and use were passed on from one generation of craftsmen to the next. Local manufacturers and small-town businesses, which were often family-owned, served local customers.*
>
> *Now . . . the hand-tool business has gone from local to regional to global. The industry still leans toward tradition. There are still local preferences and idiosyncrasies that we will have to deal with for some time to come. . . . The market as a whole is moving toward universal acceptance of tool types and ranges. It's increasingly feasible to sell the same product design in many countries.*[14]

Of course, Ergo tools were designed for optimal function with the human hand—something that did not differ between countries, or cultures. When required, Ergo products came in a range of sizes to accommodate different-sized hands.

Tariffs were not judged to be a significant factor. On hand tools shipped between the EU to the United States tariffs ranged from 5 to 9%; from the United States to the EU, tariffs tended to be slightly lower, from 3 to 4%. Adjustable wrenches were an extreme case, with tariffs from the EU to the United States of 9% and from the United States to the EU of 3%.

SITUATION IN EARLY 1996

By 1995, there were seven categories of Ergo products, with numerous variations within each category. (See Exhibit 9.) As shown in Exhibit 10, sales were 224 million SEK, or 8.4% of the group's overall sales, and about 6.4% of hand-tool sales.

---

[14]We're determined . . . , May 1994, page 8.

Exhibit 9   *Ergo Product Categories, 1996*

Sandvik ERGO Products

Accompanying this brochure you will find literature on many of the products that Sandvik is proud to include in their Ergo range. The tools are one important part of the work process which can be improved by the application of ergonomics. Other important factors are the work-stations, posture and rest.

The durability, strength, availability and diversity of the Sandvik tool range is an established fact, as are the fast delivery and service we offer. Ergonomic design adds a whole new dimension of cost-saving through health awareness to our tools. Since the potential benefits to our customers are clear, Sandvik is looking positively and "ergonomically" at the future.

How about you?

An expanding range
A selection from the increasing range of Sandvik "Ergo" hand tools. All of these tools meet the exacting criteria of the Sandvik 11 Point Ergo Program.

Exhibit 10   *ERGO Branded Products 1995 External Invoicing*

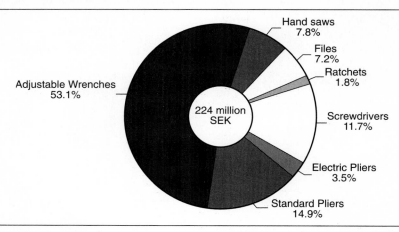

*Source: Company records.
ªSEK b. = billions

These sales were not evenly distributed, however. As shown in Table D, Europe accounted for most of the Ergo sales.

Table D

Unit Sales* of Ergo Product 1995	Europe	North America	Rest of World
Adjustable wrenches	1300	8	200
Standard pliers	300	4	60
Screwdrivers	996	25	16
Handsaws f/c 1996	177	9	28
Files, handles	587	15	38
Electronic pliers	—	20	—
f/c 1996	10	30	—
Ratchet wrenches	16	1.1	0.1
f/c 1996	22	0.1	0.4

*In thousands.

Of course, the Ergo hand tools had just been introduced in a limited range to North America during 1995.

It was difficult to assess the precise impact of the Ergo strategy. As Per Tornell, the Nordic Sale Unit manager, explained:

We dominate certain product categories in the Nordic countries. In adjustable wrenches, we have 50 to 60% share of the unit volume and 90% of the value for professional users. And, we've (Bahco) had this position for a long time. Ergo has helped us to maintain our strong position. But in ratchets, we are one of ten competitors, with about a 20% share. I feel that the new Ergo ratchet will help us to improve our position, but it is too early to tell. It takes years for this type of thing to have a noticeable impact.

Screwdrivers are a good example. Over ten years ago, Bahco introduced the Ergo screwdriver. At that time it was a radical redesign; very different from the traditional product. The difference in the product was obvious to the user. We are now the market leader in Sweden and Finland. But it took ten years.

In North America the situation was different. Sandvik Saws and Tools was known in the United States for its forestry products, and industrial bandsaws. The only hand tools for which it had even limited recognition were hand saws and electronic pliers. Ergo had been launched in February 1995 in the United States. The concept had been well-received by health and safety professionals. But their endorsements had not yet materialized as significant orders. Saws and Tools was targeting large industrial users such as Ford and GM. It was hoped these users could appreciate the benefits of the Ergo product and pull it through the distribution channels.

As one U.S. manager observed:

Distributors will not really push a product. They stock what their customers ask for. Since we have a limited assortment and not much brand recognition, and our prices are at or above the top end, it's a difficult sell. The availability of our hand-tool products through distributors is not as extensive as we would like. We would like to use Ergo to develop, expand, and strengthen our channels.

Another manager went further:

The health and safety people have not been able to convince the purchasing people to specify our product. They'll look at our product, but it usually comes back to an issue of price. Most hand tools are only used occasionally, and repetitive motion injuries are not considered to be a major factor. Naturally we try to sell the advantage—the prevention of one lost-time accident will more than pay for the tool. And where RMI is a factor, like in trimming

electronic circuit boards with snippers, we have done well. For the same reason, we expect our Ergo metal shears, when they are developed, will be well accepted. But again, this is a niche where the benefit is clear.

Meanwhile the ergonomic idea seemed to be gaining popularity with other competitors. Stanley had recently distributed marketing literature stating that their products were ergonomically tested by an independent testing firm. However, there was no evidence that Stanley employed a rigorous process for incorporating ergonomic into the design of their hand tools. It was also known that Cooper had formed an ergonomic working group, including customers and ergonomists as well as company personnel. Nothing had yet emerged from this group.

CONCLUSION

Göran Gezelius observed:

Interest and recognition in Ergo from our own salespeople as well as distributors has been excellent. We have not succeeded yet in turning this recognition into big sales figures in markets where we were not previously known with our hand tools. In markets where we are known—Scandinavia, U.K., Netherlands—it appears as if Ergo helps us to increase our market share. However, if we are to become a truly global, professional hand tool company, we need to improve our position where we are less well known, especially North America. It is not clear whether Ergo will help us in a significant way to accomplish this objective, or what more needs to be done.

PLANET REEBOK

In March 1993, David Ropes, Reebok's vice president of worldwide marketing services, was about to meet with the director of marketing communications for Europe to discuss the international rollout of *Planet Reebok* (PR), the company's first global advertising campaign. The campaign had been launched in the United States in January 1993, where initial reactions were positive. As part of the international rollout, and at the explicit direction of corporate headquarters, PR was scheduled to be introduced soon in Reebok's three most important international markets: France, Germany, and the United Kingdom. Existing national television advertising campaigns in these three markets would have to be phased out as a result.

Prior to the meeting, Ropes reviewed PR copy research results from the three European countries. He wished to reassure himself that the PR campaign would be effective. He also wanted to determine whether he should encourage, permit, or initiate any further adjustments to the PR executions prior to the European rollout.

COMPANY AND INDUSTRY BACKGROUND

Reebok International Ltd., headquartered in Stoughton, Massachusetts, was a leading worldwide designer, marketer, and distributor of sports, fitness, and lifestyle products, principally footwear and apparel. Reebok's U.K. ancestor company was founded in the 1890s by Joseph William Foster, who made the first running shoes with spikes for top runners. In 1958, two of the founders' grandsons started a companion company that came to be known as Reebok, named for an African gazelle. In 1979, Paul Fireman negotiated for the North American distribution license for Reebok U.S.A. In 1984, in a reverse acquisition, Fireman and his backers, principally Pentland Industries Plc., acquired the U.K. licensor.

In 1981, Reebok introduced the first athletic shoe designed for women. With the Freestyle aerobic shoe, Reebok supported three trends that transformed the athletic industry: the aero-

This case was prepared by Jamie Harper (under the direction of Professor John A. Quelch). Copyright © 1994 by the President and Fellows of Harvard College. Harvard Business School case 594-074.

bic exercise movement, the influx of women into sports, and the acceptance of well-designed athletic footwear by adults for street and casual wear. By 1992, the Freestyle had become the best-selling athletic shoe of all time. Reebok sales soared from $13 million in 1983 to over $3 billion by 1992. After-tax profits in 1992, before restructuring charges, were $232 million. Gross margins were 42% in 1992; selling expenses were 18% of sales. Around 80% of the company's sales and profits were generated by Reebok-branded footwear; the remainder were accounted for by the Avia and Rockport brands and by sales of branded apparel. Reebok employed 4,600 people in 1992, 21% of whom worked at company headquarters. Three hundred employees managed relations and ensured quality control with independent manufacturers of Reebok shoes in 50 factories located in six Far East countries.

In 1992, Reebok held a 20% unit share and a 24% dollar share of the U.S. branded athletic sports shoe market. Its primary competitor, Nike, held a 20% unit share and a 28% dollar share. Both companies held a 15% dollar share and a 13% unit share of the non-U.S. branded athletic shoe market. Adidas, a long-standing German manufacturer of athletic footwear, was thought to hold only a 3% unit share in the United States but held a 16% unit share outside the United States.

Reebok's rapid growth was driven by its introduction in 1982 of the first aerobic/dance shoe specifically targeted at women. The aerobics shoe established Reebok as a fitness brand. Even though Reebok soon produced shoes for men and women, the brand always remained particularly strong among women buyers and developed a more fashion-oriented image than Nike, which continued to emphasize performance sports and to appeal primarily to male athletes. In 1991, Reebok management consciously set out to broaden the brand image to establish its leadership in sports as well as fitness. Reebok's

new goal was to become the number-one performance sports and fitness brand in the world by the end of 1995.

To achieve this goal, Reebok first reorganized in early 1992 around three product groups:

- **Sports** (44% of 1992 sales) included running, basketball, tennis, football, baseball, soccer, rugby, lacrosse, volleyball, and indoor court shoes.
- **Fitness** (52%) included aerobics, cross training, walking and Preseason™ shoes; Step Reebok™ equipment; Reebok's Classic shoe lines; and Weebok™ shoes for infants.
- **Casual** (4%) included the Boks™line of casual footwear and Reebok's line of golf shoes.

Second, Reebok placed renewed emphasis on research and development to bring to market new, performance-driven, shoe technologies such as Graphlite, a lightweight and high-strength composite material that created a lightweight shoe without any sacrifice in stability or strength. Reebok also continued to leverage the success of the "Pump" technology, an integrated system of one or more inflatable chambers that could be adjusted to provide custom fit and support in footwear. New product lines were also established for a variety of sports, such as cleated footwear for soccer and baseball. Introduced in 1992, Reebok's Outdoor line of hiking, mountain biking, and surfing shoe wear promised to become one of the company's fastest-growing shoe categories in 1993. The company also launched new athletic concepts, such as Preseason footwear, a special line of training shoes for athletes who played competitive sports.

Third, Reebok invested a higher proportion of its marketing budget in securing individual athlete and team endorsements. Most notable among Reebok's new signings was Shaquille O'Neal (SHAQ), a basketball player who later signed with the Orlando Magics.

Fourth, Reebok developed a distinctive logo to reinforce the brand's performance orientation in the sports arena and compete against Nike's "swoosh" and Adidas's three-stripes logo. In January 1993, Reebok launched its new "Vector" logo to replace the company's Union Jack flag logo. By fall 1993, all Reebok performance athletic footwear products, except its Classic product lines, were scheduled to carry the Vector logo.

International Development

Reebok's entry into international markets began in earnest in 1987. The company first established distributors and later, as the distributors reached critical mass, sought to acquire controlling interests in them. By 1993, the company was seeking to develop a global identity for the Reebok brand. Between 1988 and 1992, Reebok's international sales of footwear grew from $180 million to $1 billion. Reebok held the number-one market share position in the United Kingdom, Canada, Australia, New Zealand, Denmark, Sweden, Hong Kong, and Singapore. The international branded athletic footwear market outside the United States was estimated at $7.2 billion and 221 million pairs of shoes in 1992.

The company's International Operations group, headquartered in London, England, was responsible for Reebok sales outside of the United States and Canada. A regional office in Hong Kong managed all operations in Asia/Pacific, while another in Chile oversaw Latin American operations. The group marketed Reebok products in 140 countries worldwide through a network of wholly owned subsidiaries,[1] joint ventures, and independent distributors[2] (see Table A):

---

[1]Reebok's wholly owned subsidiaries were located in Austria, Chile, France, Germany, The Netherlands, Italy, Russia, and the United Kingdom; its majority-owned subsidiaries were located in Japan and Spain.
[2]Many of Reebok's 45 subsidiaries, joint ventures, and distributors also handled sales in smaller, neighboring countries.

Table A   Reebok's International Distribution Network

	Latin America	Europe	Asia/ Pacific	Total
Subsidiaries	1	8	1	10
Joint ventures	3	2	6	11
Distributors	1	18	5	24
Total	5	28	12	45

Europe was Reebok's largest regional market outside North America, representing 65% of 1992 international sales. Reebok's subsidiaries in France, Germany, and the United Kingdom were the company's largest in sales and profitability. (See Exhibit 1 for selected sales data by region and Exhibit 2 for information on the European market.) An assessment of Reebok's overall competitive position in 1992 revealed the following:

- Worldwide market share was concentrated in the Big Three (Reebok, Nike, and Adidas), although Adidas's share was in decline due to changes in ownership;
- Reebok was growing faster than Nike;
- Nike was increasing its advertising spending;[3]
- Overall market growth was sluggish due to the economic recession;
- Demand for casual shoes was increasing faster than for athletic shoes;
- New market opportunities were evident in Eastern and Central Europe.

Reebok established the following six strategic objectives for its European markets in 1993:

1. Prevent Nike from taking ownership of the 15- to 25-year-old consumer

---

[3]Outside of the United States, Reebok's 1992 media expenditures were about $35 million and Nike's were about $45 million, up 10% and 51%, respectively, from 1991.

Exhibit 1   *Branded Athletic Footwear Sales by Region, 1992 ($ millions)* *

	Europe	North America[a]	Latin America	Asia/Pacific
Athletic footwear market				
Sales (at wholesale prices)	$4,300	$6,500	$1,200	$1,700
Pairs of shoes (millions)	124	391	44	53
Reebok sales (at wholesale prices)	$643[b]	$1,558	$137	$192

*Source: Company records.
Note: Numbers for all international markets are approximations only, and include estimates of the wholesale value of products sold by unowned distributors.
[a]United States and Canada only.
[b]Includes "other," such as Africa, Middle East, etc.

2. Replace Adidas as the European performance brand
3. Win in Germany
4. Strengthen management support systems
5. Take "ownership" of the retail shelf
6. Lead, not follow, the market

Competitive Position

Nike, founded in 1964, was an Oregon-based manufacturer and distributor of performance athletic footwear and apparel and was Reebok's principal competitor. In the mid-1980s, Nike temporarily lost share leadership in the United States to Reebok, as it was late responding to the aerobics movement and the increased interest of women in fitness and sports. However, Nike recovered U.S. share leadership, aided by the endorsement of Michael Jordan, a highly successful basketball player with the Chicago Bulls, who endorsed Nike products in advertising. Nike dominated the basketball, football, and baseball shoe categories, because the Air Jordan line of basketball shoes and apparel cast a performance

Exhibit 2   *Reebok Data on Selected European Markets, 1992* *

	France	Germany	United Kingdom
Reebok sales[a] ($MM)	171	116	186
Advertising expenditures ($MM)	9.8	6.7	7.4
Other marketing expenditures[b] ($MM)	8.4	6.7	7.0
Brand unit share (%)			
Reebok	19%	11%	25%
Nike	22	16	18
Adidas	28	40	12
Unaided brand awareness (%)			
Reebok	73%	56%	75%
Nike	76	80	71
Adidas	95	97	75

*Source: Company records.
[a]At factory prices.
[b]Includes sales promotion, merchandising, public relations, sponsorships, market research.

halo over the rest of Nike's product lines. Beginning in 1991, Nike attempted to broaden its appeal to women, increase its share of the fitness shoe category, and displace Reebok as the leading brand in tennis footwear.

Throughout its history, Nike advertising consistently targeted athletic performance messages primarily at teens and young men active in sports. Since 1987, Nike's highly successful "Just Do It" campaign served as an umbrella for a variety of performance-based messages. Beginning in 1991, Nike softened its hard-driving performance message with more emphasis on humor and entertainment. For example, Nike's "Air/Hare Jordan" television ad featured Michael Jordan and Bugs Bunny working together in outer space to rescue millions of Nike shoes that had been stolen by Martians.

In the United States, Nike's relative brand position was stronger than in overseas markets. Nike had tended to control its international subsidiaries more tightly than Reebok. Advertisements developed in the United States were typically run in overseas markets with minimal adaptation.

REEBOK ADVERTISING STRATEGY

Reebok Campaigns 1986 to 1992

In the early 1980s, Reebok advertising appeared primarily in print media. Ads targeted at serious athletes and "weekend warriors" emphasized functional product attributes in sports contexts. The company also retained famous athletes to endorse its products. Beginning in 1986, however, Reebok started to introduce new advertising themes. "Because Life Is Not A Spectator Sport" was an eighteen-month-long umbrella campaign[4] that associated the Reebok brand with an active lifestyle. The campaign highlighted everyday sports participants rather than shoes, technical features, or high-profile athletes.

In 1987, as its brand franchise and product line expanded, Reebok marketing managers developed television, radio, and print ads for each athletic footwear category. These ads focused on one or more of the following four themes: performance, new technology, "classic" styling, and fashion. The proportion of the budget allocated to Reebok umbrella brand advertising diminished in favor of product category specific advertising.

In 1988, Reebok, lacking exciting new products to launch, commissioned a fresh and provocative umbrella to revitalize the Reebok name. The campaign, "Reeboks Let U.B.U.," focused on the freedom of expression and individuality that one could achieve by wearing a pair of Reebok shoes. Television and print ads, targeted primarily at young women, showcased everyday people performing humorous and wacky acts. One television ad, for example, featured a bride emerging from a subway escalator wearing Reebok shoes and showed a group of pregnant women aerobic dancing.[5]

During the two years that followed the "Reeboks Let U.B.U." campaign, Reebok advertising struggled to achieve the appropriate balance between a serious performance and a lifestyle/fashion orientation. The 1989 "Physics Behind the Physiques" campaign was based on the premise that men and women work out in sports to look good as well as to stay fit. This theme was replaced in 1990 by the less-performance-driven "It's Time To Play" campaign, which stressed that the pursuit of sports and fitness should be "fun," not just a competitive battle.

Early in 1991, Reebok launched the "Pump" technology, which permitted athletes to inflate

---

[4]An umbrella advertising campaign aimed to establish a common brand image across all product categories within the brand franchise and was often tied together by a common tag line and logo.

[5]For further information on Reebok's advertising through 1988, see Tammy Bunn Hiller and John A. Quelch, "Reebok International Ltd.," HBS Case No. 589–027.

chambers built into Reebok shoes to achieve a customized fit. Reebok placed most of its advertising dollars into the "Pump Up and Air Out" campaign to launch the line head-on-head with Nike's Air technology.

The "Life Is Short. Play Hard." (LISPH) umbrella campaign, introduced in the second half of 1991, reflected Reebok's new effort to position itself as the number-one sports and fitness brand worldwide. The copy themes were: "be the best you can be," "compete with yourself," "get the most out of life," and "in the striving lies the achievement." The campaign targeted 15- to 44-year-old branded athletic shoe buyers. Executions included:

- "Sky Surfer": A sky diver wearing the Pump Cross-Trainers, attached to a surfboard performing stunt maneuvers at 10,000 feet.
- "Talking Tennis Balls": A woman wearing the Pump Tennis shoes aggressively hit tennis balls with animated faces of an angry boss, a yapping poodle, and a slick pick-up guy.
- "STEP": A couple wearing Reebok Step Aerobic shoes raced up an Aztec pyramid, interspersed with shots of men and women doing step aerobics in a gym.
- "Fence": A tennis player wearing the Pump Tennis shoes hit tennis balls into a wire fence until the fence was covered with yellow balls that spelled the word "Pump."

These executions were developed to meet the following criteria: originality, impact, correct brand/product balance, and performance with a human face. Copy tests in the United States indicated very high unaided and aided brand and copy recall.

The "Dan and Dave" campaign was developed under the LISPH umbrella. It was created to challenge Nike's sponsorship of the 1992 Olympics basketball "Dream Team" and high-profile athletes. The "Dan and Dave" executions, which included humorous interactions between two leading United States decathletes, ran for eight months. Reebok was the exclusive athletic footwear and apparel sponsor of the NBC Network telecast of the 1992 Summer Olympic Games.

Also running in 1992 was a Reebok campaign specifically targeting women under the tag line "I Believe." This campaign focused on the self-esteem that women could achieve through pursuit of sports and fitness. It was designed to counter Nike's increasing efforts to penetrate the women's market.

Advertising Challenges in 1993

The company's 1993 marketing strategy was to position Reebok as the number-one sports and fitness brand worldwide. Nike's recent move to softer advertising messages created an opening for Reebok to emphasize pure athletics, but with a tone of humanity. According to one Reebok manager, "Sports are won with skill and not with an attitude." All Reebok executions were developed to communicate the message: "Pure athletics plus humanity."

This theme was reflected in the 1993 *SHAQ* campaign that featured Shaquille O'Neal, aged 21, of the Orlando Magics, a highly rated young basketball star whom Reebok executives hoped would assume the mantle of Michael Jordan, who endorsed Nike. The campaign was targeted at males, aged 12 to 34. The television executions portrayed a young superstar in the making, emphasizing O'Neal's basketball prowess and agility, his passion and commitment to the game, and youthful zest for life.

A continuing advertising challenge at Reebok was the lack of internal support for umbrella campaigns. Although they all shared a single brand name, Reebok's product categories operated as independent business units. Category managers were judged on the sales and profits of their product lines; they were not specifically responsible for building the Reebok brand. Because each of the category managers faced a different set of competitors, and because Reebok's market share differed across categories, they all wanted to develop their own category-specific advertising. Category managers were habitually concerned about the percentage of the total advertising budget that was siphoned off to fund umbrella campaigns that promoted the Reebok image.

International Advertising

Due to the speed of Reebok's international expansion, headquarters had not developed guidelines for the advertising used by international subsidiaries and distributorships. During the 1980s, individual country managers had appointed their own agencies and developed their own advertising copy and tag lines, while occasionally borrowing executions made for the United States and other country markets. For example, "Sky Surfer" was the principal Reebok television ad running in France and Germany, but without the LISPH tag line. In fact, this tag line was not used in any advertisements in Europe (except in print ads in Switzerland), because it was variously regarded by local managers as too harsh or too hard to understand.

By 1991, international sales accounted for a third of Reebok's total revenues. Several headquarters executives believed that greater message consistency around the world would help develop the brand image and improve the cost effectiveness of Reebok advertising. The company selected a single advertising agency to work with each of Reebok's three regional offices covering Asia/Pacific, the Americas, and Europe. In Europe, the Euro RSCG agency was appointed to work with Reebok's European headquarters in London to establish advertising and brand image guidelines; to approve local adaptations of standard ad copy; to ensure the efficiency of

Exhibit 3 *Reebok Media Advertising Budget Breakdowns: 1992–1993 ($MM) ***

	1992		1993 (Proposed)	
	United States	**International**	**United States**	**International**
By Category Type				
Product category specific	$30	$35	$30	$15
Planet Reebok	—	—	30	30
SHAQ	—	—	15	—
Dan and Dave	18	—	—	—
Dan and Dave (Olympics)	12	—	—	—
I Believe	25	—	—	—
	$85	$35	$75	$45.0
By Media Vehicle				
Television	$60	$10	$52	$22.5
Print	25	25	23	22.5
	$85	$35	$75	$45.0
By Geographic Area				
Asia	—	$25	—	$13
Europe	—	10	—	30
Latin America	—	—	—	2
		$35		$45

*Source: Company records.

Reebok's media purchases throughout Europe; and to place advertising on European satellite television networks, such as EuroSport and MTV, which reached countries where the Reebok subsidiaries were too small to afford their own television advertising.

After 1991, the marketing directors of Reebok's European country subsidiaries began to meet more often to exchange ideas and to provide input to regional and worldwide headquarters as new campaigns were developed. However, achieving agreement on a single pan-European campaign proved difficult because Reebok's advertising and positioning had evolved differently in each country. As one European country manager said:

> We have had to go to our own way on advertising. Even if Reebok's U.S. advertising were applicable in our market, which it usually is not, the campaigns change so often that to follow the United States would leave us and our customers confused about what the brand stands for.

Advertising objectives in foreign markets were often different from those in the United States; because the Reebok brand was at an earlier stage of development overseas, the company's market shares were usually lower, and the product line was typically narrower. Because the Reebok advertising budget in each international market was much smaller than in the United States, country managers typically allocated 80% to umbrella campaigns that built Reebok's image. In the United States, where Reebok brand recognition was already high, category managers argued for spending at least 80% of the budget on product category-specific advertising and the remainder on umbrella campaigns.

Reebok's 1992 and 1993 advertising budgets for the United States and for international markets are summarized in Exhibit 3. Advertising accounted for 60% of Reebok's U.S. marketing budget in 1992, followed by public relations (5%), promotions (10%), merchandising (10%), and sponsorships (10%). Reebok marketing budgets in its larger international subsidiaries were allocated similarly.

PLANET REEBOK

Planet Reebok (PR) was conceived as a global brand campaign that would help define Reebok as the number-one sports and fitness brand worldwide. It was believed that PR could finesse the divergent perceptions of Reebok that existed internationally by tapping into the universal values of sports and fitness. Perhaps an American spin could be added to the extent that the United States was widely perceived as the world leader in athletic culture.

PR advertising would hopefully ensure that Reebok was the desired brand badge—something that was worn not just because it worked functionally but because it evoked the following strong and appealing image:

> Reebok is the brand for individuals all over the world who play at the peak of their potential and live life to the fullest.

People who lived on or visited PR would not only excel physically but would also become mentally able to achieve a broader set of goals. As a result, the PR campaign platform, described in Exhibit 4, was highly versatile. The style, tone, and feel of PR advertising executions would convey a Reebok personality that was athletic, human, honest, self-confident, aspirational, occasionally outrageous, and one that could range from being soul-stirring to thrilling and aggressive.

The PR campaign's broad target would be men and women aged 18 to 49 who participated in sports and fitness activities. The core target, however, would be men and women aged 18 to 29 who worked out or played sports two or more times a week. The PR umbrella campaign was intended to work in all media from television and print to outdoor and cinema. Advo-

Exhibit 4   *Planet Reebok Campaign Platform**

In Sport	In Life
Freedom	Losing the negative controls or limitations in life from parents, to school, to bad legislation, to too many lawyers.
No Drugs/Stimulants	Environmentalism, better air, less waste, no more products or services that we don't need and can no longer afford. No more false vanities or implants.
Pain	Suffering for the things in which you believe. Caring enough to endure discomfort.
Determination	Desire for a better, freer, more equal society; the ability to speak out against anything from racism to pollution.
Learning	Being open-minded, having freedom of action and spirit, not caring about race or creed. Having a cross-cultural view.
Confidence	Feeling empowered to change and achieve things that you desire; feeling that there are others like you, politically, emotionally, sexually—any way.
Training	Making yourself a better, stronger, more positive and valuable human being for the Planet to nurture.
Self-respect	Looking and feeling better, respecting the desires, rights and freedom of others.
Competition	Achieving what you want, not what others tell you that you can have.
Mental Agility	Better education for you and all. Being smart and able to cope.
Camaraderie	Feeling connected in a world intent upon finding differences and alienation.
Success/Winning	Achieving what you want and enabling others to have what they need.
Losing	Being capable of understanding your own weaknesses and those of others.

*Source: Company records.

cates believed it could also be the basis for exciting point-of-sale merchandising materials.

Creative Development

PR was developed originally as a creative concept for Reebok's Outdoor shoe category. In spring 1992, John Andreliunas, the Outdoor brand manager, recognized the trend toward action sports that was best reflected in Reebok's "Sky Surfer" ad. The fast cuts and provocative, daring outdoor shots suggested a world of sports and fitness where there were no limits to what could be attempted or achieved. Planet Reebok would be a place where such novel sports could be born and grow and where Reebok's outdoor shoes would be totally appropriate.

Ropes quickly realized the potential of PR as a broader global campaign and asked Reebok's U.S. agency, Chiat/Day/Mojo, to explore PR as a single-brand identity for Reebok worldwide. Four challenges soon became evident. First, PR had to be integrated with the overall strategy of positioning Reebok as the number-one sports and fitness brand worldwide. Second, the use of the word *planet* generated debate. Some executives were wary of its close connection with the environmental movement. Others believed it had no association with health, fitness, and sports. A third group objected that PR was not sufficiently innovative, given the existence of the Planet Hollywood chain of restaurants. Third, the U.S. category managers expressed their customary concerns about siphoning off funds from category-specific advertising. Fourth, by mid-1992, the "Life Is Short. Play Hard." campaign had earned a loyal following among several marketing managers, country managers, and the trade.

Ropes presented preliminary PR television ads (known as "rip-o-matics") to all Reebok country managers at an offsite meeting in Scotland in August 1992. These executions, prepared in the United States without input from overseas managers, featured teenagers playing extreme sports and heavy metal music played in the background. Throughout the television commercials, "negative" captions such as "No Slogans," "No Meetings," "No Faxes," and "No Phones" flashed on the screen. Many of the country managers expressed concern that the preliminary PR commercials were too youth-oriented. The quick cuts and action sports would be less appealing to audiences over 24 years old. The marketing directors from countries where Reebok was a relatively new brand and/or in close competition with Nike for market share leadership wanted Reebok to be more broadly positioned. However,

Reebok managers from the United States, where Nike held a clear lead over Reebok in market share, especially among teenaged males, welcomed the brand being positioned against a younger audience.

After the offsite meeting, the PR creative was reworked to have a broader appeal, particularly among women, by blending more everyday sports, such as women's aerobics, with the action sports. International settings and outdoor sports specific to foreign countries were also incorporated, based on input from country managers. At the same time, a new copy approach was considered for the PR campaign. Instead of the original negative positioning ("No Slogans," "No Meetings," etc.), Chiat/Day/Mojo proposed an approach that emphasized the positive attributes of life on Planet Reebok. The "No" captions were eventually adopted after the two versions were tested internationally in November 1992.

The final PR creative was completed by early 1993. Chiat/Day/Mojo prepared creative briefs that outlined the campaign's advertising objectives, target audiences, and intended consumer take-aways.

United States Executions

Five television commercials (summarized in Table B) formed the core of the U.S. PR campaign. Each began with an image of the Earth moving

Table B Planet Reebok Executions

Execution	Length (seconds)	Target Audience	Content
"Planet Brand"	60	Men 12–24	Professional athletes and "real" people playing a variety of sports.
"Planet Sports"	30	Men 12–24	Professional athletes playing a variety of sports.
"Women's Sports"	30	Women 12–24	Female professional athletes excelling at their individual sports.
"Women's Fitness"	30	Women 12–24	"Real" women walking and doing step aerobics.
"Planet Outdoor"	30	All 12–24	"Real" people playing action sports.

Exhibit 5 *Storyboard for "Planet Brand" Television Ad**

Exhibit 6 *PR Print Ad for United States**

IF YOU'RE LOOKING FOR A PLACE WHERE THE ONLY THING CLEARER THAN THE SKY IS YOUR HEAD, YOU SEEK PLANET REEBOK. SO TO GO FAR FROM WHERE YOU'RE SITTING RIGHT NOW, TRY THE TELOS (ON TOP). IT'S A LIGHT HIKING SHOE WITH A CARBON RUBBER OUTSOLE. GOOD FOR TRAILS AND A WEEKEND TRIP TO THE LAKE. THE AMAZONE (JUST BELOW) HAS A DIAMOND LUG OUTSOLE AND A MOLDED FOOTBED. THINK OF IT

AS A COMBINATION OTTER/SANDAL. THE TOUGHEST OF ALL IS THE PUMP™ MASSIF (BOTTOM). AN ITALIAN-MADE SHOE WITH THE PUMP™ TECHNOLOGY FOR A CUSTOM FIT. 3-BAR KNIT LINING AND WATER-PROOF FULL-GRAIN LEATHER. IT'S A HEAVY-DUTY MOUNTAIN BOOT GOOD FOR MAJOR HIKES AND MULTIDAY TRIPS. SO TRY ON A PAIR. AND GET LOST. FOR MORE INFORMATION ON REEBOK OUTDOOR PRODUCTS, CALL 1-800-843-4444.

HOW DO YOU

GET TO

PLANET REEBOK?

GO OUT YOUR DOOR,

TAKE A RIGHT,

THEN JUST KEEP

GOING.

*Source: Company records.

toward the viewer and the caption: "What is life like on Planet Reebok?" Quick cuts of exhilarating sports and fitness action followed, accompanied by fast-paced music and the "negative" captions. Exhibit 5 presents a storyboard of the "Planet Brand" television advertisement. Exhibit 6 shows a PR print ad for Reebok's Outdoor line of footwear.

PR was launched in the United States at the end of January 1993 during the Super Bowl. Reebok purchased two minutes of commercial time for $3.4 million. One 60-second execution from both the SHAQ and PR campaigns was shown during the second and third quarters of the game.

The PR campaign in the United States included only a modest level of print advertising and point-of-sale materials. The U.S. sales force was preoccupied with placing point-of-sale materials that supported the new SHAQ product line and Reebok's new Vector logo.

Of the $75 million Reebok planned to spend in 1993 in the United States on media advertising, around $30 million would be devoted to PR, $15 million to SHAQ (which focused on basketball), and $30 million to other category-specific advertising.

Communications Tests

After launch, Reebok management was interested in measuring consumer awareness, understanding, and perceptions of the PR and SHAQ campaigns. In March 1993, the company conducted communications tests of PR and SHAQ executions that targeted men and women against two Nike campaigns that also targeted men and women. The test structure is shown in Table C.

Around 1,000 respondents were interviewed in 30 U.S. markets. Respondents were divided into five groups of 200. Each was exposed to two representative executions from one of the five advertising campaigns included in the test. Each respondent, therefore, viewed only one campaign. Qualified respondents were female and

Table C   Communications Tests (1993)

Campaign and Executions	Gender and Age of Respondents
SHAQ ("Legends," "Elders")	Men aged 12–34
PR ("Womens Sports and Fitness")	Women aged 12–34
PR ("Planet Sports," "Planet Outdoor")	Men aged 12–34
Nike Women's ("Stretcher," "Runner")	Women aged 12–34
Nike Men's ("Barkley," "Majerle")	Men aged 12–34

male athletic shoe consumers, between the ages of 12 and 34, who spent at least $25 on a pair of athletic shoes.

Both the PR and SHAQ campaigns were received positively by respondents. Positive reactions to SHAQ were especially strong among young males, thanks to the charismatic personality of Shaquille O'Neal who was becoming an increasingly prominent role model for this group. Positive reactions to PR were also strong, particularly among women. However, PR's message seemed more diffuse and less tangible. Exhibit 7 summarizes the research findings.

INTERNATIONAL ROLLOUT OF PLANET REEBOK

PR was scheduled to be rolled out internationally in March 1993. Prior to PR, Reebok subsidiaries and their advertising agencies had developed separate campaigns with different themes. In France, Germany, and the United Kingdom, for example, the tag lines for their 1992 umbrella campaigns were "Break The Rules," "Get The Feeling!" and "The Edge," respectively. Examples of print ads from each campaign are shown in Exhibits 8 through 10.

Exhibit 7 *Selected Findings of Communications Tests of PR, SHAQ, and Current Nike Advertising Conducted in the United States, March 1993**

- Among men, *Planet* and *SHAQ* were well received (top-two box likability scores of 83% and 80%, respectively), more so (in general) than the Nike ads tested (75%). *SHAQ* likability among younger men was higher than that of *Planet* (64% to 41% top-box likability).
- *Planet* far exceeded the Nike women's ads on top-box likability ("like them a lot") among women, although women awarded *Planet* and *Nike* similar top-two box scores (77% and 79%, respectively). A higher percentage of women than men reacted positively to *Planet*.
- Consumers believed that both *Planet* and *SHAQ* fit well with their overall image of the Reebok brand; the Nike commercials tested did not fit as well in consumers' minds with their overall image of Nike, particularly among women.
- *Planet Reebok* was most often described as exciting, fun, upbeat, fast-paced, and different/unique; women tended to feed back health and energy associations, while men focused on excitement/fun descriptors. Consumers appeared to be entertained by viewing the experiences on Planet, but were in some cases overwhelmed by the visuals and so less likely to translate these into a strong performance message. Athletics and performance-type messages appeared to be secondary to "fun," although consumers *did* tend to describe people living on *Planet Reebok* as "athletes/those who like athletics" while women described them as "fit/in good shape." In addition, performance enhancement (among women) and performance edge (among men) were communicated more often by *Planet* than by either *SHAQ* or the Nike ads.
- Unaided recall of Shaquille O'Neal as the spokesperson in the *SHAQ* series was nearly perfect, as was also the case for the Barkley execution; Majerle's recognition was much lower. Kareem Abdul-Jabbar also received 56% recognition in the *SHAQ* spot, followed distantly by Wilt Chamberlain, John Wooden, and Bill Walton in that order.
- Shaquille O'Neal was extremely well liked by the 12- to 34-year-old male audience who viewed the spots, particularly in comparison to Barkley and Majerle. He was widely viewed as an appropriate spokesperson for Reebok, top in his field, and an interesting person; additionally, he received higher scores for "someone I like" and "a good role model" than either of the two Nike athletes.
- The *SHAQ* campaign did a better job communicating performance to its male viewers than *Planet*, and registered high recall of "using a rookie to sell shoes" as the perceived main point of the commercial. The *SHAQ* ads were received more favorably among the younger male audience (12–18) than the older (19–34).
- However, *SHAQ* generated some confusion among viewers (27%), particularly the "Elders" execution. Many respondents could not understand the words (and/or meaning of the words) being spoken; however, this did not detract from the likability of the ad or its performance message. Additionally, the Nike Barkley/Majerle ads generated substantial confusion; questioning the executions' relevance to shoes.
  - Notably, the Nike ads generated stronger brand imagery for Nike among men than the Reebok ads (*SHAQ* and *Planet*) did for Reebok, particularly for
  - best brand for sports,
  - comfortable shoes,
  - "in" with me and my friends,
  - more technologically advanced, and
  - appropriate for me.

Exhibit 7   *(continued)*

These results were more a function of the images cumulatively resulting from previous campaigns than the executions tested. Among women, the Reebok and Nike images were equally strong for most attributes.

- **The Nike ads appeared to appeal to a broader user profile than the Reebok ads.** All ads were successful at communicating a "competitive," "serious sports" profile; however, Nike also communicated dimensions such as "winner," "attractive," and "street smart."
- **Of concern was the relatively low top-two box (excellent, extremely good) overall brand rating for *Planet* (26%) compared with *SHAQ* (57%) or the Nike ads (50%).** The overall Reebok brand rating for those women exposed to *Planet* (52%) was comparable to the rating for Nike (55%) among those women exposed to Nike ads.

*Source: Company records.
Note: Based on a five-cell (200 respondents per cell) exposure test of five advertising campaigns (three Reebok and two Nike) conducted in 30 U.S. markets. Respondents were female and male athletic shoe wearers, aged 12 to 34.

PR represented the first effort of Reebok headquarters to require worldwide adoption of an advertising campaign. As a result, the introduction of PR would require the phasing out of the existing individual country campaigns, no matter how successful. In the first quarter of 1993, Reebok marketing directors in the European subsidiaries had spent little on television advertising in anticipation of the arrival of finished PR commercials from the United States. While some Reebok country managers resented losing control over their advertising, others welcomed the flexibility PR allowed to show different sports under one campaign umbrella. The 1993 advertising media budget for PR outside the United States was $30 million, two-thirds of which would be spent in the United Kingdom, France, and Germany. Some Reebok country managers argued that European headquarters should contribute to the launch expenditures of PR in European markets. Executives at Reebok's European headquarters were willing to explore spending an additional $3 million to advertise PR on MTV, EuroSport, and other satellite-based networks that delivered programming across Europe.

Both television and print advertising were included in the European PR budget in a 70:30 ratio. International television and print adaptations of the PR executions had to follow the guidelines summarized in Exhibit 11. The adaptations were paid for by Reebok's three regional organizations that covered Latin America, Europe, and Asia/Pacific. Reebok subsidiaries could modify PR print ads but only at their expense and subject to the approval of the communications director at Reebok's European headquarters. For example, they could choose the athletes, shots, and shoes they wanted to feature and write their own headlines and body/copy. Exhibits 12 through 14 present proposed PR print ads for France, Germany, and the United Kingdom. In the case of PR television ads, Reebok subsidiaries could translate the supers (captions) and voice-overs and suggest rough edits (e.g., the substitution of locally popular sports) to regional headquarters.

European Sports Shoe Market

Research on sports shoe markets outside the United States was limited to individual country-specific studies that included noncomparable data. Reebok therefore commissioned two multicountry studies to provide more comprehensive market research.

(continued on page 343)

Exhibit 8   *1992 Print Ad from "Break The Rules" Campaign in France*

*Source: Company records.

Exhibit 9   *Print Ad from "Get The Feeling!" Campaign in Germany**

*Source: Company records.

Exhibit 10 *1992 Print Ad from "The Edge" Campaign in United Kingdom**

BEST OF LUCK IF YOU'RE RUNNING FOR PARLIAMENT THIS SUNDAY.

Exhibit 11 *Reebok Guidelines for International Television and Print Adaptations**

	Global Agency	**Regional Agency**	**Local Agency**
Television			
Initial Cuts	To supply		
Footage Shot	To supply		
European Adaptation		Adapt and present to markets	
Local Market Interpretation			Review footage shot; supply rough edit to Regional Agency; supply translated supers
Local Market Adaptation		Approve supers Edit films	
Local Market Material		Supply to format required	
Local Market Broadcast			Send to TV stations
Pan-European Material		Supply to satellite stations	
Billing	Negotiate global usage costs	Editing/film costs to RIL; courier costs to local agency	
Review	Review European reel with regional agency	Compile European reel	
Print			
Initial Executions	To present		Decide local market requirements
European Adaptation			
a) Photography			Source material from regional agency or locally
b) Copy	Supply copy briefs	Agree on European copy briefs; supply to local agency	Write copy; supply translated copy to regional agency for approval
c) Production			Develop mechanicals
European Implementation Billing	Negotiate usage for stock		Negotiate usage for local shots; fund all production costs
Review		Review with global agency	Supply proofs to regional agency

*Source: Company records.

Exhibit 12 *Proposed PR Print Ad for France**

*Source: Company records.

Exhibit 13   *Proposed PR Print Ad for Germany**

Exhibit 14 *Proposed PR Print Ad for United Kingdom**

PLANET REEBOK

ON PLANET REEBOK YOUR PERSONAL BEST IS SUDDENLY A LITTLE BIT BETTER.

THE GREAT IRONY FOR THE RUNNER IS THAT THE BETTER YOU GET, THE HARDER IT IS TO GET EVEN BETTER. IMPROVEMENTS IN PERFORMANCE BECOME MARGINAL AFFAIRS. THAT'S WHY WE'VE INTRODUCED THE PUMP GRAPHLITE HXL. THE GRAPHLITE ARCH BRIDGE IN THE MIDSOLE MEANS YOU HAVE LESS SHOE TO CARRY WITH YOU. SO YOU GET EXTRA LIGHTNESS WITH NO LOSS IN STABILITY. IT HAS THE PUMP™ AIR CHAMBER SYSTEM IN ITS COLLAR, TO GIVE YOU A MORE COMFORTABLE, SNUG FIT. AND IT HAS A HEEL CUSHIONED WITH HEXALITE TO GIVE YOU GREATER SHOCK ABSORPTION. IT WILL HELP YOU MAKE YOUR PERSONAL BEST JUST A LITTLE BIT BETTER.

PUMP GRAPHLITE HXL

Reebok

*Source: Company records.

In 1992, 1,000 consumers in France, Germany, and the United Kingdom were interviewed to profile sports shoe purchasers in each country. Respondents were 15 to 55 years of age and had purchased a pair of sports shoes within the previous six months for themselves or other members of their households. Selected results of the study are presented in Exhibit 15.

In January and February 1993, focus group interviews were conducted in France, Germany, and the United Kingdom. The study was sponsored by Euro RSCG, in advance of the PR campaign rollout, to understand the factors that influenced consumer attitudes, needs, and motivations for athletic footwear purchases and brand selections. Ten focus groups, with 8 to 10 respondents in each group, segmented by gender, age, and level of athletic participation, were conducted in each country. Participants played a variety of sports, had purchased a pair of sports shoes in the past six months, and owned more than one brand. The most important findings addressed consumer perceptions of the Reebok and Nike brands across the three countries. These results are provided in Exhibit 16.

Pre-launch Research Studies

Qualitative research to pretest consumer responses to PR advertising executions in Reebok's three principal European markets was conducted in two rounds. In November 1992, the first study researched PR rip-o-matics. In February 1993, a second research project elicited consumers' responses to three completed executions.

The November 1992 study was based on four focus groups conducted in France, Germany, and the United Kingdom. Qualified group members were males and females, aged 15 to 35, who participated in sports and/or fitness activities at least once a week, had purchased branded sports footwear in the previous six months, and intended to make their next purchase within 12 months. Two rip-o-matics were tested—one with the positive PR copy and the other with the neg-

ative copy. The objectives of the focus groups were:

- to assess what consumers understood PR to represent from the advertising
- to evaluate how well the advertising built the desired brand "badge" or image
- to gauge interest, identification with, and liking for the advertising
- to establish how the advertising could be made to work even harder

Reactions to the advertising executions in each of the three countries are presented in Exhibit 17. The results indicated consistently positive findings regarding the notion of "planet," the positioning of Reebok, product and user imagery, and the motivational impact of the ads. However, respondents in the three countries differed in their identification with and emotional connection to PR. Reebok executives explained these cross-border variations in terms of differences in cultural background, attitudes toward and participation in sports and fitness, and current brand perceptions. The most positive response appeared to be in the United Kingdom, but some executives thought this was due to Reebok's higher brand share in this market and/or to the fact that the commercials were tested in English in all three countries.

The second study also involved focus group discussions in France, Germany, and the United Kingdom. Four focus groups were conducted in each country with males and females, aged 16 to 24. In each group there were three Reebok owners, two Nike owners, and three owners of major local brands. Half the members of each group were serious athletes who played sports at least two times a week and selected their shoes based on their sports needs. The remainder were casual users who wore athletic footwear in nonsport situations. Respondents were exposed to three PR executions, one of which had been recently introduced in the United States and two of which were new executions developed just for Europe that included softer sport and lifestyle

(continued on page 350)

Exhibit 15 *Selected Findings of 1992 Sports Shoe Tracking Study in France, Germany, and United Kingdom**

	France			West Germany			East Germany	United Kingdom		
	1990	**1991**	**1992**	**1990**	**1991**	**1992**	**1992**	**1990**	**1991**	**1992**
Profile of Sports Shoe Purchaser										
Male	50%	50%	55%	51%	50%	54%	50%	52%	50%	52%
Female	50	50	45	49	49	46	50	48	50	48
15–24	32	31	28	27	26	28	27	34	31	31
24–34	30	29	29	27	27	25	24	25	28	28
35–44	21	26	28	25	24	28	26	27	28	27
45–55	18	14	15	21	23	19	23	14	13	13
Profile of Reebok Brand Purchaser										
Male	53%	55%	54%	48%	54%	59%	NA	47%	43%	50%
Female	47	45	45	52	46	41	NA	53	57	50
15–24	36	38	36	33	33	37	25	40	36	29
24–34	27	21	29	30	27	22	—	26	24	28
35–44	18	27	23	19	18	24	25	21	26	31
45–55	18	14	13	16	23	17	50	13	15	12
Brand Share										
Reebok	12%	13%	19%	6%	8%	11%	2%	18%	19%	25%
Nike	18	22	22	14	16	16	12	13	13	18
Adidas	38	35	28	49	42	40	41	15	12	12
Puma	—	—	—	21	21	20	19	6	5	4
Brand Loyalty (% of owners likely to buy same brand next time)										
Reebok	48%	65%	58%	75%	81%	75%	75%	81%	76%	68%
Nike	54	50	48	81	75	73	67	71	54	59
Adidas	59	55	54	85	78	80	55	67	61	66
Puma	—	—	—	79	73	62	49	64	58	43
Brand Awareness—Unaided										
Reebok	49%	63%	73%	35%	49%	56%	33%	64%	75%	75%
Nike	61	78	76	68	69	80	65	64	66	71

Adidas	96	96	95	98	91	97	97	77	76	75
Puma	—	—	—	92	85	89	84	48	44	47
Brand Awareness—Aided										
Reebok	67%	82%	88%	63%	77%	85%	50%	94%	98%	99%
Nike	81	91	91	89	90	95	86	95	98	99
Adidas	95	98	98	100	100	100	100	98	99	100
Puma	—	—	—	99	99	98	96	93	97	97
Advertising Awareness—Unaided										
Reebok	27%	31%	46%	9%	20%	23%	15%	22%	46%	45%
Nike	42	48	50	33	34	41	40	26	33	41
Adidas	45	35	38	28	30	23	34	19	19	12
Puma	—	—	—	22	26	25	31	7	5	8
Advertising Awareness—Aided										
Reebok	34%	37%	54%	10%	20%	28%	17%	32%	60%	60%
Nike	47	55	61	36	34	44	45	36	47	55
Adidas	51	48	52	29	32	29	40	30	32	25
Puma	—	—	—	23	27	30	38	12	13	19
Sports Shoe Usage										
Only sport	23%	19%	23%	27%	21%	23%	10%	9%	9%	8%
Mainly sport, casual too	24	27	25	25	24	25	16	14	13	14
Mainly casual, sport too	17	16	13	24	24	22	35	19	19	20
Only casual	11	14	10	13	16	17	25	36	42	43
Work and casual	22	18	24	10	14	11	11	21	15	13
Other	3	4	5	—	1	1	1	1	2	2
Association of Brands with Technical Benefits										
Reebok Hexalite	3%	10%	11%	1%	5%	6%	2%	7%	13%	16%
Reebok Pump	8	25	42	2	23	29	15	19	42	45
Reebok ERS	12	17	15	4	11	9	2	20	21	23
Nike Air System	31	42	41	20	30	30	24	29	45	51
Adidas Torsion	30	38	38	27	31	29	18	16	28	29
Puma Disc	—	—	7	—	—	24	16	—	—	25

*Source: Adapted from 1992 Sports Shoe Tracking Study, prepared by Marketing Focus U.K. Ltd, January 1993.
Note: Responses based upon interviews with approximately 1,000 respondents in each country in each year.

Exhibit 16 *Perceived Brand Personalities of Reebok and Nike in France, Germany, and United Kingdom**

	Gender	Commitment	Appearance	Technology	Nationality	Disposition
Reebok						
France	• Feminine		• Subtle • Elegant	• Precise • Technological[a] • Leading edge[a]	• British • Cosmopolitan • American[a]	• Extrovert[a] • Sporty • Trendy • Exciting[a]
Germany	• Feminine	• Passive	• Plain • Discreet		• British • American(?)	• Sociable • Harmless • Serious
United Kingdom	• Feminine	• Passive • Safe	• Discreet • Subtle • Crafted	• Broad	• British • American(?)	• Inoffensive • Acceptable • Defendable • Down to earth
European Synthesis	• Feminine	• Passive	• Stylish • Classic • Elegant • Discreet • Subtle		• British • American(?)	• Serious • Sociable • Inoffensive
Nike						
European Synthesis	• Masculine • Muscular	• Vigorous • Competitive • Aggressive • Performer • Player	• Complicated • Gaudy • Bulky	• Innovative • Technological • Specialist • Gimmicky	• American	• Exciting[a] • Young • Energetic • Hyped • Extrovert[a]

*Source: Adapted from *Project Genesis*: European Qualitative Research on Reebok and the Sport Shoe Market, prepared for Reebok by Euro RSCG, March 1993.
[a]In France, there was overlap in the attributes associated with the two brands.

Exhibit 17 *Selected Findings of Focus Group Research to Pretest Planet Reebok Concept and Execution, November 1992**

	France	Germany	United Kingdom
First Impressions	Dynamic, showed wide range of sports Visually rich Violent and macho Spoke to everyone wanting to play sports	Showed diversity of brand Difficult to understand, exposures too short Imitation of Nike PR idea was unique and fast	Made you sit up and watch Liked fast change to different sports No everyday people, just sports professionals Recalled "no" declarations
PR Perceptions PR Is...	An exclusive atmosphere Where one landed almost inadvertently	Stage for success-oriented, athletic people Place for people who loved sports Place for people who sought personal goals	World of sports Land of opportunity America A place to escape to
People on PR	Like machines Soulless Only played sports Didn't even eat	Young Conscious about body Sensation-seeking Risk-takers	Physically fit individuals into many sports False and competitive Perfect, figure glamorous The elite
Life on PR	Sports Where being in shape was valued Where men and women never met Only sports and action mattered	The American way of life Sports were everything Sports were fun as long as you were successful	Not easy, had to do things for yourself Where you could achieve the impossible Where everything was wonderful (not reality)
Attitudes toward PR Motivation	NA	NA	Most males were highly motivated by ads Most females felt intimidated
Appeal	Disliked focus on individualistic values in sports Overall absence of humanism	Disliked watching ads too fast, music unpleasant Unclear intended meaning, captions confusing	Most females felt on the outside looking in They disliked youth and sports professional focus
Relevance	Relate better if more brotherhood, team focus Relate better with more humanist sporting values	Couldn't relate played sports for fun, not danger Couldn't identify with 'struggle' in ads	Most males related well and became really involved

continued

Exhibit 17 *(continued)*

	France	Germany	United Kingdom
PR Brand Positioning			
Reebok	Performance and technology oriented	Performance brand, but low credibility	Performance brand, not for casual wear
	Accessible	Reebok seen as leisure/casual oriented	Brand for the 1990s
	Modern		Reebok covered the world
User	Serious and young athletes that were hand-picked	Individuals	Individuals that were young and athletic
		Pushing, testing limits	The elite
	Combative	Achiever of personal goals	Achievers, competitive
	Superhuman		
Product	Broad range of shoes	NA	Shoes for multiple sports, ages, and fitness levels
	Sturdy		
	Resistant		Durable
Other	Didn't believe Reebok had so many products	Didn't communicate fun, human factor, empathy	
Execution			
Music	Disliked change in music type and rhythm in ads	Similar to Nike's ads	Intriguing, catchy, and inspiring
		Reinforced restless feel	Caught attention, but too slow
Captions	Fairly well understood by all	English words cool, but crucial meaning missed	Liked captions, but flashed by too quickly
	Preferred "No" version because it was funny	Too much information	Many difficult to read
Pace	Aggressive	Short exposures provoked curiosity and fear	Liked fast and exciting rhythm
	Breathless		Too fast for older females

Sports Shots	Liked diversity of sports, but too many geared to performance Superhuman sports	Liked soccer most Also football, free-climbing, basketball and rafting	Liked all sports, but wanted more English-specific sports
Product Shots	Barely noticed shoes	Didn't even notice shoes initially Wanted more technical information	Wanted more on shoes so could study them More information would make shopping easier
Suggestions	Alternate violent with calm sports More women, less violence Inject enjoyment, comaraderie	Shots of tennis, volleyball, outdoor soccer	Shorter; bigger-sized captions on screen longer More "nos"[a] with better phrases
"No" Version	Preferred by most for humor and humanism	Couldn't relate; play sports for fun, not danger Couldn't identify with 'struggle' in ads	Preferred by males about sports and competition Women felt intimidated
Positive Version	Less preferred and understood Too complicated, philosophical, demanding	NA	Females really understood what PR life was like Males found less relevant and too philosophical

*Source: Adapted from *Planet Reebok TV Advertising Test (France)*, prepared by Research International, November 1992; and *Presentation on Planet Reebok (U.K.)*, prepared by Marketing Focus Ltd, November 1992. October 1992; and *Project No. 02384 (Germany)*, October 1992.
[a]Executions that included the "no" captions, such as "No Meetings," "No Faxes," "No Phones."

Exhibit 18 *Conclusions of Research on New Executions of Planet Reebok in France, Germany, and United Kingdom, February 1993*

I. Of the three executions, the ad developed in the United States was the most appealing in all three countries, although it had less appeal among women over 20 years old and among casual athletes.

II. The PR ads communicated effectively that Reebok was "the brand for all people all over the world," but the attitude that Reebok desired to have associated with the brand name were not nearly as well communicated:
  - The brand personality that emerged was not "empathetic" or "human";
  - The advertising message was interpreted in a confusing way, particularly in France and Germany, and was not seen to differentiate Reebok from Nike in either style or content.

III. The advertising appealed strongly to sports and/or fitness enthusiasts, both male and female, aged 18 to 30 years old. However, the large portion of the market that purchased sports shoes for casual rather than sports use was not so motivated.

IV. The effects of the ads, especially the ad developed in the United States, if run in the United Kingdom, could include:
  - Reduced affinity of women toward Reebok;
  - Weak motivation toward purchase of Reebok;
  - Presentation of Reebok as a me-too to Nike, a concept that was neither credible currently nor desirable for Reebok in the longer term;
  - Building stronger empathy toward the brand among 14- to 17-year-olds.

V. In Germany and France—and probably in other non-English speaking countries—PR was not expected to have a strong effect. It might be ignored by some due to comprehension problems or it might encourage perceptions of Reebok as a copycat of Nike.

---

*Source: Adapted from *Planet Reebok: Advertising Creative Development Research*, prepared by Strategic Research Group, February 1993.

---

cues. Translations of the English captions were given in the French and German focus groups. Translations of the campaign platform concept were also provided to ensure comprehension of the PR strategy.

The study revealed that the appeal of the PR executions depended on the level of understanding achieved. Comprehension of the PR concept was strongest in the United Kingdom, followed by France and then Germany. Respondents in all countries were consistent in their views of the pace and visual appeal of the PR advertising. However, interest in the use of "planet" as a creative concept was modest. While some respondents found the PR philosophy to be interesting,

the majority could not understand it. The researchers explored further the following three issues:

1. *The complexity of the advertising message delivered.* The PR campaign attempted to express Reebok's vision of life through a series of sports metaphors. Respondents had difficulty understanding how an individual's approach to sports was necessarily a metaphor for his or her approach to life. They were used to seeing sports and high performance in sports as a signal of product quality and technical features. The PR executions covered a lot of ground and did not clearly com-

municate the central concept. So, while they were exciting to watch, although too aggressive in tone for some respondents, they did not convey the complete message to many viewers.

2. *The inability of the creative vehicle to deliver the intended message.* Usually, advertising messages were thought to work as follows:
Creative vehicle → comprehension of the central creative idea → take-away of the intended message.

The PR executions, however, were assimilated differently:

Secondary cues → estimate of central creative idea → received message take-away different from what was intended

In the case of the PR ads, the sports activity depicted rather than sports as a metaphor for life was regarded as the central creative idea. Viewers played back observations on how sports were performed to achieve a winning competitive advantage. Only Reebok's attitude toward sports—not its approach to life—was communicated by the advertising, and this attitude was frequently interpreted as hard-edged and aggressive. Serious athletes tended to relate best to PR, whereas casual athletes felt alienated and less comfortable. Viewers who played sports primarily for personal satisfaction also had trouble relating to PR. Although they might be committed athletes, PR showed an attitude they did not all want to be associated with.

3. *The dissonance between the PR advertising and existing brand perceptions.* In the United Kingdom, PR advertising was seen as positioning Reebok as American and similar to Nike; this contradicted current perceptions of the brand as British. In Germany, respondents were confused when the brand was presented as performance-oriented, since they associated it with a softer and more feminine image. There was a risk that those consumers unable to relate to the advertising would be distanced from the brand and might then see Reebok as just another global sports shoe company. The researchers were concerned that the brand personality depicted by the current PR advertising would not be credible or motivating or differentiate Reebok. Exhibit 18 summarizes the conclusions of the research.

CONCLUSION

Following the campaign's March, 1993 launch in Europe, Planet Reebok would be introduced in Asia/Pacific and Latin America. On his way to the staff meeting, Ropes considered the challenges that he and his colleagues faced with the European launch just a few weeks away. How much emphasis, he wondered, could Reebok management at world headquarters expect the three subsidiaries in Europe to place on Planet Reebok in 1993 and in the future? What more, if anything, could Ropes and his staff do to ensure the success of the global PR campaign in Europe?

DHL WORLDWIDE EXPRESS

In July 1991, in Jakarta, Indonesia, the shouts of the *kaki lima* (street vendors) outside did little to soothe Ali Sarrafzadeh's concerns. Sarrafzadeh, DHL's Worldwide sales and marketing manager, had spent the previous three days chairing the Worldwide Pricing Committee workshop at DHL's annual directors' meeting. On the following day, he was to present his recommendations on pricing to the conference's 300 attendees.

Some of the statements made during the workshop meetings were still ringing in his head:

If I have P&L [profit and loss] responsibility for my region, then I better be able to set my own prices. If not, how am I supposed to impact profits? By managing my travel and entertainment account?

—*Jurgsen Beckenbauer*
Regional Director, Central Europe

Many of our large multinational customers have come to us and told us that they want a consistent worldwide pricing structure. . . . If we don't offer worldwide prices and our competitors do, are we going to lose some of our largest accounts?
—*Christine Platine*
Account Manager, Brussels headquarters

If our pricing structures were consistent across regions, it would be much easier to consolidate regional reports. With better reporting, we could gain valuable information about our costs. . . . The simpler our pricing structure, the easier it is to manage hardware and software around the world.
—*Adelina Rossi*
VP Systems, Brussels headquarters

We are the only company which services some regions of Africa. Thus, we charge premium prices in these markets. If we are forced to charge the same rates as in other regions, we will only lose profits. Sales will not grow with lower prices.
—*Aziz Milla, Country Manager*
Cameroon, Africa

Our prices have always been 20%–40% higher than the competition's prices. We can command these premium prices by continuing to give more value to our customers. . . . Our pricing must not encourage "cherry picking." We don't want customers to just ship with us on routes that are difficult to serve, such as those to and from Africa.
—*Bobby Jones, Regional Director, U.S.A.*

Sarrafzadeh wanted to make recommendations on pricing strategy, structure, and decision

---

This case was prepared by Greg Conley (under the direction of Professor John A. Quelch). Confidential company data have been disguised. Copyright © 1992 by the President and Fellows of Harvard College. Harvard Business School case 593-011.

making. On strategy, he viewed his options as recommending either a price leadership strategy or a market response strategy. The former meant DHL would charge premium prices and aim to deliver superior value-added services in all markets. The latter meant DHL would set prices independently in each country, according to customer usage patterns and competitive pressures.

If the principle of standardized worldwide pricing was pursued, what were the pricing structure implications? For example, should DHL charge a weekly or monthly handling fee (a set fee in return for automatically visiting a customer each business day) in all countries? Should the same price be charged for shipments between any two cities, regardless of which was the origin and which the destination?

Regarding pricing structure, Sarrafzadeh had to address several additional questions. Should DHL have different pricing schedules for documents and parcels? Should DHL set different prices for different industries? For example, should prices be different for banking and manufacturing customers? Should DHL offer special prices to multinational corporations seeking to cut deals with individual shippers to handle all their express document and parcel delivery needs worldwide?

Another issue was the DHL discount program. Sarrafzadeh had to decide whether DHL should continue to offer volume discounts. If so, should they be based on units, weight, or revenue?

In addition, Sarrafzadeh wanted to recommend who should hold primary price-setting responsibility. He considered his three options to be a centralized, decentralized, or hybrid approach. A decentralized approach would continue the present policy in which country/region managers set all prices and headquarters offered counsel and support. Under a centralized approach, a headquarters management committee would set all prices around the world. Country managers would be responsible for collecting data and making suggestions to headquarters. A third option was to establish multiple pricing committees, each including managers from both headquarters and the regions and each responsible for setting prices for one or more specific industries.

Company Background and Organization

DHL legally comprised two companies: DHL Airways and DHL International. DHL Airways was based in San Francisco and managed all U.S. operations. DHL International was based in Brussels and managed all operations outside the United States. Each company was the exclusive delivery agent of the other. Revenues for 1990 were split: $600 million for DHL Airways, and $1.4 billion for DHL International. One DHL executive commented, "The main reason DHL is involved in domestic shipping within the United States is to lower the costs and increase the reliability of our international shipments. If not for our domestic business, we would be at the mercy of the domestic airlines bringing our packages to the international gateways." In 1990, DHL accounted for only 3% of intra-U.S. air express shipments but 20% of overseas shipments from the United States.

DHL was the world's leading international express delivery network. It was privately held and headquartered in Brussels, Belgium. The company was formed in San Francisco in September 1969 by Adrian Dalsey, Larry Hillblom, and Robert Lynn. The three were involved in shipping and discovered that, by forwarding the shipping documents by air with an on-board courier, they could significantly reduce the turnaround time of ships in port. DHL grew rapidly and, by 1990, serviced 189 countries. In 1990, revenues were approximately $2 billion. Profits before taxes were 4% to 6% of revenues. (Exhibit 1 summarizes the growth of DHL operations from 1973 to 1990; Exhibit 2 displays DHL's revenues by industry.)

DHL used a hub system to transport shipments around the world. In 1991 the company

Exhibit 1   *DHL Operations Statistics, 1973–1990*

	1973	**1978**	**1983**	**1990**
Shipments[a]	2,000,000	5,400,000	12,400,000	60,000,000
Customers	30,500	35,000	250,000	900,000
Personnel	400	6,500	11,300	25,000
Countries served	20	65	120	189
Hubs[b]	0	2	5	12
Flights/day	14	303	792	1,466
Aircraft[c]	0	5	27	150
Vehicles[c]	300	2,235	5,940	7,209

[a]Shipments included both documents and parcels.
[b]Hubs were major shipment sorting centers.
[c]Aircraft and vehicle data included both owned and leased equipment.

operated 12 hubs (as shown in Exhibit 3). Within Europe, the United States, and the Middle East, DHL generally used owned or leased aircraft to carry its shipments, while on most intercontinental routes it used scheduled airlines. In 1991, approximately 65% of DHL shipments were sent via scheduled airlines and 35% via owned or leased aircraft. The other leading shippers also utilized scheduled airlines, but to a lesser extent than DHL. Federal Express relied on its own fleet of planes to transport all its shipments. Pierre Madec, DHL's operations director, noted:

> FedEx has a dedicated airfleet, which ties up capital and limits the flexibility of its operation: express packages are forced to wait until the FedEx plane's takeoff slot, which at major international airports frequently does not tie in with the end-of-the-day courier pickups. By using a variety of scheduled international carriers, DHL is able to optimize its transport network to minimize delivery times.

DHL was organized into nine geographic regions. Region managers oversaw the relevant country managers and/or DHL agents in their regions and held profit-and-loss responsibility for performance within their territories. Revenues and profits were recognized at the location where

a shipment originated. Only 70 people worked at DHL's world headquarters in Brussels. The main functions of the worldwide marketing services group, of which Sarrafzadeh was a member, were business development, information transfer, communication of best-practice ideas, and sales coordination among the country operating units.

Exhibit 2   *DHL Worldwide Revenues by Industry, January–June 1991*

Industry	Revenues (%)
Conglomerates	10%
High technology	8
Import-export	8
Banking	7
Transport	7
Heavy engineering	6
Chemicals	5
Precision manufacturing	5
Professional services	4
Foodstuffs	4
Textiles/leather	4
Other	32

Exhibit 3   *DHL Hub System*

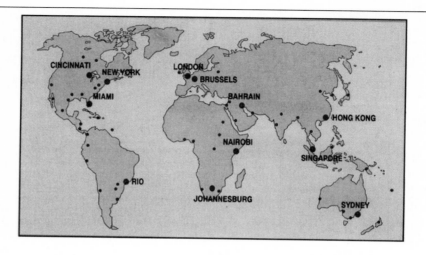

The word "Hub" derives from the image of a wheel with the spokes, the Hub is a sorting and redistribution centre and the spokes are flights in and out.

DHL routes material via Hubs, we do not use direct flights to every destination around the world. There are Hubs in every area of the world:

USA (Cincinnati, New York);   **AFRICA** (Johannesburg, Nairobi);

MIDDLE EAST (Bahrain);   **FAR EAST** (Hong Kong, Singapore);

AUSTRALIA (Sydney);   **EUROPE** (London, Brussels);

The routing of material through the Hubs passes on a saving of both time and cost for the customer.

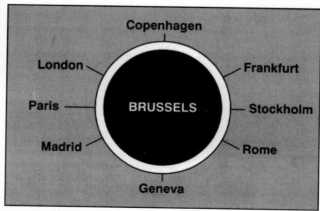

Of DHL's 60 million shipments in 1990, 50 million were cross-border shipments. DHL's worldwide mission statement, included in its 1990 annual report, read:

DHL will become the acknowledged global leader in the express delivery of documents and packages. Leadership will be achieved by establishing the industry standards of excellence for quality of care and by maintaining the lowest cost position relative to our service commitment in all markets of the world.

DHL management believed that achievement of this mission required the following:

- Absolute dedication to understanding and fulfilling DHL's customers' needs with the appropriate mix of service, products, and price for each customer.
- Ensuring the long-term success of the business through profitable growth and reinvestment of earnings.
- An environment that rewards achievement, enthusiasm, and team spirit, and that offers each person in DHL superior opportunities for personal development and growth.
- A state-of-the-art worldwide information network for customer billing, tracking, tracing, and management information/communications.
- Allocation of resources consistent with the recognition that DHL is one worldwide business.
- A professional organization able to maintain local initiative and local decision making while working together within a centrally managed network.

DHL's annual report also stated: "The evolution of our business into new services, markets or products will be completely driven by our single-minded commitment to anticipating and meeting the changing needs of our customers."

The International Air Express Industry

Total revenues for the international air express industry were approximately $3.4 billion in 1989 and $4.3 billion in 1990. The air express industry offered two main products: document delivery and parcel delivery. Industry revenues were split roughly 75:25 between parcels and documents. In 1989, the parcel sector grew by 40%, while the document sector grew by 15%. The growth of parcel and document express delivery was at the expense of the air cargo market and other traditional modes of shipping.

The growth of the air express industry was expected to continue. One optimistic forecast for 1992 is presented in Table A. Other observers were concerned that shipping capacity would expand faster than shipments, particularly if economic growth slowed.

Table A   Worldwide International (Cross-Border) Air Express 1992 Estimated Revenue Growth Rates

Market	1992 Estimated Growth Rate
Europe	28%
Asia/Pacific	30
United States	25
Rest of the world	9
Total	25%

Note: Growth rates for time-sensitive documents/packages under 30 kilograms.

Acknowledging continuing progress toward completion of the European market integration program by the end of 1992, an article on the air express industry in Europe in *Forbes* (April, 1991) noted:

The express-delivery business in Europe is booming. . . . Measured by revenues, the European express-delivery business is growing at a 28% compound annual rate. Big European companies are stocking products and parts in central locations and moving them by

Exhibit 4   *Major Air Express Competitors, 1988*

	DHL	FedEx	TNT	UPS
International Air Express revenues (in $ millions)	$1,200	$200	$500	$100
International Air Express employees	23,000	5,000	10,000	3,000
Countries covered	184	118	184	175
Total service outlets	1,427	1,135	800	1,700
Service outlets outside United States	1,207	278	750	465
Ratio of Owned: Agent country operations	2.00:1	0.53:1	0.77:1	0.36:1
Owned aircraft	49	38	17	3
Years of international experience	20	5	17	3
Document: Parcel revenues	65:35	20:80[a]	50:50	20:80

[a]After FedEx's 1989 acquisition of Tiger International, Inc., its document:parcel revenue ratio remained relatively unchanged as Tiger concentrated on heavy air freight. However, post-acquisition, document and parcel combined revenues represented a smaller portion of total revenues.

overnight express, instead of running warehouses in each country.

Competitors

Air express companies serviced a geographic region either by using their own personnel or by hiring agents. Building a comprehensive international network of owned operations and/or reliable agents required considerable time and investment and, therefore, acted as a significant barrier to entry.

DHL's principal competitors in door-to-door international air express delivery were Federal Express, Thomas Nationwide Transport (TNT), and United Parcel Service (UPS). (Exhibit 4 provides operational data for the top four competitors; Table B summarizes their 1988 market shares.)

Founded in 1973, FedEx focused for many years on the U.S. domestic market. During the late 1980s, the company began to expand internationally through acquisitions and competitive pricing, sometimes undercutting DHL's published prices by as much as 50%. Between 1987 and 1991, FedEx invested over $1 billion in 14 acquisitions in nine countries: the United Kingdom, Holland, West Germany, Italy, Japan, Aus-

tralia, United Arab Emirates, Canada, and the United States. FedEx also entered the international air freight business through the acquisition of Tiger International (Flying Tigers), which expanded further FedEx's global reach in document as well as parcel delivery, particularly in Asia. However, the challenge of integrating so many acquisitions meant that FedEx's international operations lost $43 million in 1989 and $194 million in 1990. Nevertheless, with 45%

Table B   International Air Express Market Shares by Revenue (1988, U.S. $)

Company	Market Share (%)
DHL	44%
FedEx	7
TNT	18
UPS	4
Others	27
Total	100%

of the U.S. air express market, 7% of the European market, and leadership in value-added services based on information systems technology, FedEx remained a formidable competitor.

TNT was a publicly owned Australian transport group that had historically concentrated on air express delivery of documents. TNT focused mainly on Europe and had a low profile in North America. To participate in the North American market, TNT held a 15% stake in an American shipper, Airborne Freight Corporation. This stake could be increased to a maximum holding of only 25% under U.S. aviation laws. During the late 1980s, TNT began to target heavier shipments and bulk consolidations to fuel its growth.

UPS was a privately held U.S. company, most of whose equity was owned by its employees. UPS had traditionally been known as a parcel shipper that emphasized everyday low prices rather than the fastest delivery. Unlike DHL, UPS sometimes held a package back to consolidate several shipments to the same destination in the interest of saving on costs. UPS had historically tried to avoid offering discounts from its published prices.

UPS's 1990 annual report proclaimed the company's strategy as follows:

> UPS *will achieve worldwide leadership in package distribution by developing and delivering solutions that best meet our customers' distribution needs at competitive rates. To do so, we will build upon our extensive and efficient distribution network, the legacy and dedication of our people to operational and service excellence, and our commitment to anticipate and respond rapidly to changing market conditions and requirements.*

In addition to the industry giants, there were many small shipping forwarders that concentrated on a specific geographic area or industry sector. In the late 1980s, many of these small companies were acquired by larger firms trying to increase their market share. National post of-

fices were also competitors in air express, but they could not offer the same service and reliability because they were not integrated across borders (that is, no national post office could control the shipment of a package from one country to another). One industry executive commented: "When we have internal competitive discussions on international business, the post offices just don't come up."

Finally, the regular airlines were minor competitors in door-to-door express delivery. British Airways operated a wholesale airport-to-door courier service called Speedbird in cooperation with smaller couriers that did not have international networks. Swissair serviced 50 countries through its Skyracer service in cooperation with local agents. In the heavy cargo sector, most airlines were allied with freight forwarders who consolidated cargo from different sources and booked space in aircraft. These alliances represented significant competition as DHL expanded into delivery of heavier shipments. Some airlines were reluctant to upset their freight forwarder customers by dealing with integrated shippers such as DHL.

Competition in the air express industry, aggravated by excess capacity, had resulted in intense price competition during the late 1980s.[1] DHL's chairman and CEO, L. Patrick Lupo, estimated that prices had dropped, on average, 5% each year from 1985 to 1990, with extreme price drops in some markets. For example, in Great Britain, DHL's list prices for shipments to the United States fell approximately 40% from 1987 to 1990. Some of the price reductions were offset, in part, by rising volume and productivity, yet Lupo noted, "There's no question that margins have been squeezed."

---

[1]DHL planes flew, on average, 85% full in 1990. FedEx and UPS planes on international routes were thought to be achieving only 60% capacity utilization.

DHL Services

DHL offered two services: Worldwide Document Express (DOX) and Worldwide Parcel Express (WPX). DOX offered document delivery to locations around the world within the DHL network. DOX was DHL's first product and featured door-to-door service at an all-inclusive price for nondutiable/nondeclarable items. Typical items handled by DOX included interoffice correspondence, computer printouts, and contracts. The number of documents sent to and from each DHL location was, in most cases, evenly balanced.

WPX was a parcel transport service for nondocument items that had a commercial value or needed to be declared to customs authorities. Like DOX, WPX offered door-to-door service at an all-inclusive price that covered DHL's handling of both the exporting and importing of the shipment. Typical items handled by WPX included prototype samples, spare parts, diskettes, and videotapes.

DHL imposed size, weight, and content restrictions for all parcels. The size of a package could not exceed 175 centimeters in exterior dimensions (length + width + height), and the gross weight could not exceed 50 kilograms. Further, DHL would not ship items such as firearms, hazardous material, jewelry, and pornographic material.

Table C compares DHL's parcel and document businesses for 1990.

DHL offered numerous value-added services, including computerized tracking (LASERNET),

24-hour customer service every day of the year, and proof-of-delivery service. Customers could also tap the assistance of specialized industry consultants based in DHL regional offices. Such value-added services could enhance customer loyalty and increase DHL's share of a customer's international shipping requirements. However, such services were expensive to provide and customers using them were often not always charged extra, particularly since those services were also offered by key competitors such as FedEx.

DHL had 20 years of experience in dealing with customs procedures and, by 1990, was electronically linked into an international customs network. All shipments were bar-coded, which facilitated computerized sorting and tracking. Thanks to a direct computer link between DHL and customs authorities in five European countries, customs clearance could occur while shipments were en route. In addition, DHL's staff included licensed customs brokers in 80 countries.

DHL had been cautious about differentiating itself on the basis of speed of service, and arrival times were not guaranteed. However, DHL executives believed that their extensive network meant that they could deliver packages faster than their competitors. Hence, in 1991, DHL commissioned an independent research company to send on the same day five documents and five dutiable packages from three U.S. origin cities via each of five air express companies to 21 international destinations (three cities in each of seven regions). Exhibit 5 reports the percentages of first place deliveries (i.e., fastest deliveries) achieved by each competitor in each re-

Table C   DHL's Document and Parcel Business, 1990

	Total Revenues	Revenues Growth (1989–1990)	Total Shipments	Total Weight	Gross Profits
Document	60%	+14%	70%	50%	53%
Parcel	40%	+28%	30%	50%	47%

Exhibit 5   *Shipment Delivery Speed Tracking Study: Fastest Delivery, 1991*

	DHL	TNT	FedEx	UPS	Airborne
Western Europe	39%[a]	34%	4%	26%	NA
Eastern Europe	42	16	14	28	1%
Southeast Asia	34	16	18	6	27
Far East	56	11	21	3	9
Middle East	70	6	16	2	7
South America	28	10	32	9	21
Africa	62	9	13	10	7
All documents[b]	55	15	13	13	6
All parcels	40	14	21	11	14

Notes: [a]To be read, for example: Of the packages shipped on the five carriers to Western Europe, 39% of the packages that arrived first at their destination were shipped by DHL.
[b]Some rows do not sum to 100% due to ties.

gion. DHL had the highest percentage of first place results in six of the seven regions. The research also indicated that DHL was consistently able to deliver more dutiable items through customs in time for earliest business district delivery (before 10:30 A.M.) than any of its rivals. A similar intra-European study found that DHL also achieved the highest percentage of first place deliveries on packages shipped between cities within Europe.

DHL also commissioned the independent research company to ascertain how it was rated by customers against its key competitors. Table D reports the ratings on the two attributes—reliability and value—considered by customers to be the most important in choosing an international air express service.

Table D   Ratings of Air Express Carriers

	DHL	TNT	FedEx	UPS
Reliability	8.4	7.7	7.8	8.1
Value for money	8.0	7.3	7.5	8.0

Source: Triangle Management Services Ltd. and IRB International Research, 1991.
Note: Respondents rated each carrier on a 10-point scale (10 = high).

The study also asked the customer sample which air express carrier they would turn to first when sending both a document and a parcel to destinations in each of four geographic regions. Results are presented in Exhibit 6. The results of a comparative study of unaided brand awareness

Exhibit 6   *Sample Customers' First Choice of Air Express Carrier by Final Destination, 1991* *

	DHL	TNT	FedEx	UPS
Documents				
Europe	32%	7%	8%	5%
North America	38	10	10	4
Middle East	35	14	6	5
Australia	38	10	7	5
Other	40	14	6	6
Parcels				
Europe	28%	5%	7%	7%
North America	32	7	12	8
Middle East	33	13	6	7
Australia	27	9	10	9
Other	32	10	4	9

*Source: Triangle Management Services Ltd., and IRB International Research, 1991.

Exhibit 7   *Sample Customers' Unaided Brand Awareness for International Carriers of Documents and Parcels, 1991* *

	DHL	TNT	FedEx	UPS
Documents				
All countries	87%	50%	23%	16%
France	77	27	20	20
Germany	90	71	25	20
Italy	91	45	19	15
United Kingdom	85	67	37	22
Parcels				
All countries	72%	58%	28%	29%
France	58	40	14	10
Germany	67	76	28	46
Italy	75	62	23	27
United Kingdom	72	58	43	35

*Source: Company records.

for the major international air express companies are summarized in Exhibit 7.

Customers

In the early years of air express, banks and finance houses were the major customers. For financial institutions, delays in delivery of checks and promissory notes could cause considerable financial losses. During the 1970s, most air express shipments were "emergency" in nature. Examples included an urgent contract, a check or note that sealed a financial transaction, a computer tape, a replacement part, and a mining sample which had to be studied before drilling could begin. During the 1980s, many customers began to use air express more systematically. For example, companies which operated "just-in-time" inventory systems began to use express delivery services to deliver components.

In 1990, DHL had 900,000 accounts, of which the top 250 accounts represented 10% of revenues and 15% of shipments. DHL had only about 10 global contracts with customers (representing 1% of revenues), as few multinational corporation (MNC) headquarters had expressed interest in negotiating such agreements. Like DHL, most MNCs were decentralized. However, DHL did have many regional agreements with MNCs as well as contracts in individual country markets.

Exhibit 8 shows how DHL segmented its U.S. customers in 1990 by level of monthly billings and provides profile information on each segment. Tony Messuri, DHL New England area sales manager, noted:

> There are two principal types of customers. First, there are the people who know where they're shipping. They know where their international offices are located and will ask overseas offices for feedback about shippers. These customers select a carrier that's well received and well respected by their own customers, both internal and external.
>
> Second, there are customers who cannot forecast where their future shipments will be going. They are more price-sensitive, but they can't give us enough information to enable us to set their discounts properly on the basis of anticipated volume. We are at more risk here of making a poor pricing decision. Sometimes, a few months after we and the customer agree on a price and discount, the customer will conclude that it's overpaying, then seek more discounts from us or switch shippers.
>
> Customers are very service-sensitive. The small customers tend to switch shippers more readily. Often it only depends on which company's sales rep visited most recently.

The parcel market was typically more price-sensitive than the document market. For most companies, the total cost of shipping parcels was a much larger line item than the total cost of shipping documents. Further, the decision-making unit was often different for the two services. The decision on how to ship a document was fre-

Exhibit 8   *Profile of DHL's U.S.A. Customer Base (1990)* *

Customer Segment: Level of Monthly Billing, International	Percent of Total Accounts	Percent Typical Sales	Percent DHL Profits	Percent Using Discount[a]	Penetration[b]	DHL Only[c]
$ 0–$ 2,000	15%	5%	45%	10–35%	70%	95%
$ 2,001–$ 5,000	40	15	20	30–40	70	80
$ 5,001–$15,000	35	30	25	40–50	60	60
$15,000+	10	50	10	45–60	35	35
		100%	100%	100%		

*Source: Company records.

[a]The exact discount was negotiated between DHL and the account. Percentages represent discounts off the published DHL tariff.

[b]Penetration means the percentage of all accounts in the segment that used DHL for at least some of their international shipping needs.

[c]To be read, percent of DHL customers who use only DHL for international shipping.

quently made by an individual manager or secretary. As one shipper stated, "Documents go out the front door, whereas parcels go out the back door." Parcels were shipped from the loading dock by the traffic manager, who typically could select from a list of carriers approved by the purchasing department. In some companies, parcel shipment decisions were being consolidated, often under the vice-president of logistics. As one European auto-parts supplier stated: "We view parts delivery as a key component of our customer service."

As a result, many customers split their air express business among several firms. For example, all documents might be shipped via DHL, while parcels might be assigned to another carrier. Alternatively, the customer's business might be split by geographic region; a multinational company might assign its North American business to Federal Express and its intercontinental shipments to DHL. For the sake of convenience and price leverage, most large customers were increasingly inclined to concentrate their air express shipments worldwide with two or three preferred suppliers.

Pricing
Evolution of Pricing Policy

As DHL expanded service into new countries throughout the 1970s and 1980s, it developed many different pricing strategies and structures. DHL country managers had almost total control of pricing. They typically set prices based on four factors: what the market could bear, prices charged by competition (which was often initially the national post office), DHL's initial entry pricing in other countries, and DHL's then-current pricing around the world.

DHL's prices were historically 20% to 40% higher than those of competitors. (Exhibit 9 provides sample prices for DHL, TNT, FedEx, and UPS.) In most countries, DHL published a tariff book that was updated yearly. Competitors who followed DHL into new markets often patterned their pricing structures after DHL's.

DHL had developed a sophisticated, proprietary software package called PRISM to analyze profitability. A PRISM staff officer at each regional office advised and trained country operating units on use of the software. The program

Exhibit 9   *Sample Published List Prices on Selected Routes (1990)*

Service	DHL	TNT	FedEx	UPS
1 kilogram document London–New York	$51	$47	$50	$44
2 kilogram document Brussels–Hong Kong	131	143	118	97
2 kilogram parcel Singapore–Sidney	120	120	39	34

could calculate profitability by route or by customer in a given country. However, PRISM could not consolidate the profits of a given customer across countries. (Exhibit 10 provides a fuller description of PRISM.) All profitability analyses had to be based on average costs due to the variability in costs associated with transporting a shipment. For example, a package from Perth, Australia, to Tucson, Arizona, might be consolidated seven to eight times in transit and travel on five to six planes. Further, every package from Perth to Tucson did not necessarily travel the same route. (Exhibit 11 shows the revenues and costs associated with two sample lanes to illustrate the significant impact of geographical differences on costs and profitability.)

PRISM was not used extensively by all DHL offices. As one country manager put it: "We and the customer both want a simple pricing structure. PRISM just provides more information, adds to complexity, and takes time away from selling."

Base Prices and Options

DHL's base prices were calculated according to product (service), weight, origin, and destination. Prices were often higher for parcels than for documents of equivalent weight, due to extra costs for customs clearance, handling, packaging, and additional paperwork. FedEx charged the same for parcels and documents. shipment weights were computed in pounds in the United States and in kilograms in all other countries.

Moreover, weight breaks varied among countries. For example, in Hong Kong breaks were every half kilogram and in Spain every two kilograms. Some DHL executives believed that, for the sake of simplicity, DHL's weight breaks should be the same worldwide. (Table E gives examples of base prices on routes from London.)

Table E   DHL Sample Prices, 1990

From London	First 1/2 Kilo	Each Additional 1/2 Kilo
Document:		
to New York	£24.50	£1.60
to Switzerland	£26.00	£2.20
to Japan	£26.50	£2.50
Parcel:		
to New York	£27.00	£1.60
to Switzerland	£32.00	£2.20
to Japan	£34.00	£2.50

Pricing Structures

In all country markets served, DHL followed one of three pricing approaches: monthly handling fee, frequency discount, and loaded half-kilo.

Under the first approach, DHL charged a flat monthly fee to customers who wanted to be in-

Exhibit 10   *Development and Description of PRISM (Pricing Implementation Strategy Model)* *

DHL local management was judged on revenue and controllable costs. The contribution of each local operation was calculated by subtracting local costs from revenue. This measure of performance did not, however, consider the costs to other country operations of delivery and whether the selling price was sufficient to cover the cost of pickup, line haul, hub transfer, delivery, and headquarters overhead and management costs.

In 1987, all countries and regions analyzed their costs and provided DHL headquarters with detailed delivery, pickup, hub, and line haul costs. Using these data, headquarters developed the PRISM (Pricing Implementation Strategy Model) software package. The inputs to the model were cost data along with competitive price information. PRISM costs were based on historical data which had been consolidated and averaged.

Country organizations were provided with the PRISM software which enabled them to analyze their profitability at the country, customer segment, and individual customer levels. The methodology was refined further to take into account the scale economies large shippers provided to DHL.

PRISM was used for the following purposes:

- Analyzing the profit impacts of possible tariff adjustments, taking into account the competitive intensity of the route.
- Identifying low- or negative-margin customers whose yields should be managed upwards.
- Settling price strategy for different customer segments.

Country and regional managers were still measured on local contribution (local revenues minus local costs). They were, however, encouraged to analyze profitability by account when developing their annual budgets and use PRISM when considering price revisions. The level of use of PRISM varied by region and country.

*Source: Company records.

cluded on its regular pickup route. DHL automatically visited such customers once each business day without the customer having to contact DHL for pickup. The purpose was to motivate customer usage of DHL's services and encourage customers to process all their shipments through DHL. Customers who elected not to be on DHL's regular route could either call for shipment pickup or drop off a shipment at a DHL office. Customers who called for pickup were charged a nominal pickup fee. Under the monthly fee structure, customers did not receive volume discounts.

Sarrafzadeh summarized his views on the problems with this approach:

The monthly fee can work but only if it is properly marketed. Because it does not relate to a unit of value, customers resent it and salespeople can't defend it. As a result, it has often proved hard to raise the monthly fees as fast as the per-shipment charges.

In some markets, including the United Kingdom, DHL offered a frequency discount structure under which a discount was provided based on number of units shipped. The more often a customer used DHL during a given month, the cheaper the unit shipment cost.

The frequency discount was based on the total number of documents and parcels shipped. For example, if a customer purchased 10 document and 20 parcel shipments in a given month, it received a discount of £10 per shipment. Under the frequency discount structure, a customer

Exhibit 11 *Revenue and Cost Lane Examples: DOX and WPX*

	DOX (Document)	WPX (Parcel)
U.K. to United States (1990)		
Revenue	$5,723,000	$2,342,000
Outbound cost	2,392,915	667,712
Hub cost	596,608	490,436
Line haul[a]	1,121,882	647,915
Delivery	1,376,953	386,049
Margin	234,642	149,888
Margin (%)	4.1%	6.4%
Shipments	231,139	68,580
Revenue/shipment	$24.76	$34.15
Belgium to Hong Kong (1990)		
Revenue	$13,800,000	$6,660,000
Outbound cost	6,341,100	1,837,733
Hub cost	1,138,146	1,181,400
Line haul	2,926,662	1,767,733
Delivery	2,276,292	1,180,134
Margin	1,117,800	693,00
Margin (%)	8.1%	10.5%
Shipments	456,802	109,544
Revenue/shipment	$30.21	$60.25

[a]Line haul refers to the air segment of the shipment.

did not pay a standard monthly route fee and DHL visited the account only upon request.

The per-shipment frequency discount was retroactive and was computed for each customer at the end of the calendar month. Conversely, FedEx's discounts were based on forecast demand rather than past performance and on revenues rather than unit shipments. FedEx monitored a new account's actual shipments for six months before the account qualified for a discount, and then adjusted the discount upward or downward based on quarterly shipment data and shipment density.[2]

[2]Shipment density referred to the number of items picked up per stop. The more items collected per stop, the lower the pickup cost per unit. DHL's information systems did not permit it to award discounts based on shipment density.

Sarrafzadeh noted:

Once you publish your frequency discounts, they're no longer discounts. They're expected. Though they may sometimes attract the small routine shipper, it's easy for competitors to discover what the discounts are and undercut them. Better to publish only the book prices and apply discounts as needed on a case-by-case basis.

The loaded half-kilo structure used in the United States resembled the frequency discount structure, except that discounts were based on total weight shipped during a given month rather than on the number of shipments.

Price Negotiations

The largest customers sought one- or two-year deals with shippers to handle their transport needs. Typically, when a current agreement was nearing its end, the customer put its business up for bid and solicited proposals from interested shippers. Proposals incorporated the following information: transit times, overhead rate structures, rates for specified countries, tracking capabilities, sample tracking reports, sample annual activity report, and a list of international stations (indicating which were company-owned stations versus those run by agents). Most bid requests were made by the purchasing manager, yet the decision-making unit was often a committee comprising managers from the traffic, sales and marketing, customer service, and purchasing departments. The decision was complicated because the major shippers were organized into different regions and lanes, thereby hindering direct comparisons among proposals. Sophisticated accounts typically calculated the bottom-line cost of each proposal, while unsophisticated accounts based their decisions on comparisons on a few "reference prices" (e.g., New York to London).

The average term of shipping agreements was two years, with almost all ranging between one and three years. Fifteen percent of DHL agreements involved formal contracts, while the other 85% were "handshake" agreements. Some customers tried to renegotiate prices in the middle of an agreement, though most *Fortune* 2000 companies abided by their deals.

DHL sales reps had significant flexibility when negotiating proposals. For example, the rep could tailor discount rates by lane such that an account would obtain large discounts on its most frequently used routes. DHL senior management typically gave only general direction to sales reps on negotiating discounts. For example, senior management might advise, "Hold price on Asia, yet you can give some on the United States and Europe." Most proposals associated a monthly minimum level of billings (adjusted, if necessary, for seasonality of the business) with the offer of any discounts.

DHL sales reps could negotiate discounts from book prices up to 35%. District sales managers could approve discounts up to 50%, while dis-

counts above 50% required the approval of a regional sales director. Further, discounts over 60% required approval from the vice president of sales. For all discounts over 35%, a sales rep had to submit a Preferred Status Account (PSA) report, which included a detailed analysis of the profitability of the account. As shown in Exhibit 12, the PSA used a computer model to calculate fixed and variable costs, net profits by geographic lane and product line, and overall contribution margins. When deciding on the discount, management considered not only the financial implications of the discount but also competitive and capacity factors.

Tony Messuri, DHL New England area sales manager, stated:

> It is good to have pricing flexibility. Managers at most companies are just looking for justification to use us. But they and DHL upper managers both know that we're not the only game in town. . . . We can sit down with a customer and build our own rate table leaving the book prices aside. We can customize the table to the customer's needs. This customization really helps negotiations.

Sales and Advertising

DHL had a single sales force that sold both document and parcel services. Sales reps were organized geographically and were evaluated primarily on monthly sales. Typically, sales reps had separate monthly sales objectives for international, domestic, and total sales and received a bonus whenever they exceeded any one of the three. Sales managers were evaluated against profit as well as revenue objectives.

When a new account called for a pickup, that account was assigned an account number the next day and was called upon by a DHL sales rep within a week.[3] At large companies, sales reps

---

[3]In the United States, prospective accounts with less than $500 in annual express shipment expenditures were handled by DHL's telemarketing center in Phoenix.

Exhibit 12   *Sample DHL Preferred Status Account Report*

PSA Analysis for:	Plasmo Systems
No. of Pickup Sites:	1
Stops per Month:	20
Origin Station:	Bowston
Model Date:	1/31/90
Costs Date:	4/7/89

Margin by Lane (Note: not all lanes included)

Service	Lane	Revenue	Pickup Costs	Ship Costs	Weight Costs	Net Profit	% Profit
DOC	A Europe	45.89	3.12	24.02	7.62	11.13	24.3%
DOC	B Europe	48.02	3.12	28.72	7.66	8.70	18.0
DOC	C Europe	31.99	3.12	24.59	4.94	−0.66	−2.1
DOC	D Europe	23.17	3.12	20.46	2.34	−2.75	−11.9
DOC	E Latin Am	38.01	3.12	20.92	4.32	9.65	25.4
DOC	F MidEast	40.79	3.12	22.08	7.26	8.33	20.4
DOC	G Caribbean	31.32	3.12	21.29	3.76	3.15	10.1
WPX	A Europe	44.95	3.12	38.61	4.44	−1.22	−2.7
WPX	B Europe	73.25	3.12	47.36	5.49	17.28	23.6
WPX	D Canada	25.49	3.12	29.24	3.51	−10.38	−40.7

Margin by Product Line

Service	Revenue	Pickup Cost	Ship Cost	Weight Cost	New Profit	% Profit
DOC	743	46	535	90	72	9.7%
WPX	214	12	196	21	−15	−7.0

Fixed/Variable Cost Report

Service	Revenue	Variable Cost	Gross Margin	Fixed Cost	U.S. Cost	Int'l Cost	Net Profit	% Profit
DOC	743	476	267	195	494	177	72	9.7%
WPX	214	173	41	56	180	49	−15	−7.0

targeted the traffic, shipping and receiving, and purchasing departments, while at small companies, they focused their efforts on line managers, such as the vice-president of marketing or vice-president of international.

Prior to 1984, DHL headquarters developed global advertising campaigns that the regions and countries could adopt or not as they saw fit. After 1984, each country operation could contract with its own local advertising agency. Headquarters approval of locally developed commercials was not required, though standard guidelines on presentation of the DHL name and logo had to be followed worldwide. In addition, headquarters marketing staff disseminated to all DHL offices commercials that had worked espe-

Exhibit 13 *Portion of a Sample U. S. Advertising Flying Van*

Our business took off 21 years ago, and we're flying higher than ever.

It's significant that the letters DHL stand for the names of three people (Dalsey, Hillblom and Lynn).

Significant, because it took their personal entrepreneurial vision to recognise a business need, and their personal energy to get the solution off the ground.

Today, however, it's even more significant that the letters DHL stand for over 23,700 names: the highly trained, highly motivated employees

DHL is as international as the United Nations. Our network spans 186 countries, states, territories and protectorates.

And from Ouagadougou to Wagga Wagga. Jakarta to Jeddah, there is not likely to be any city or town that you might wish to send something to, that does not feature on our list of 70,000 destinations served.

Most of all, however, the letters DHL have come to stand for two key words which mean so

If you're a major company you cannot afford anything less than total reliability when you air express your important documents and packages.

And as the world's largest international air express company, it is DHL's mission to provide it. Which we do.

It may be that your own company has an equally impressive growth story to tell. But old or new, large or small, please consider this.

and wouldn't you be better able to concentrate on your own job, if you allowed DHL to apply its expertise to your international air express needs?

DHL WORLDWIDE EXPRESS®

Exhibit 14 *Part of a Sample Advertisement: Europe*

Sixty million deliveries a year around the world and around the clock.

London to Ouagadougou, Wagga Wagga, Yucatan, Kiribati — wherever. Take it from us that, with 70,000 cities and towns on our list, your air express destination is not likely to faze us.

Every 58 seconds, a plane takes off somewhere in the world carrying some of those 60,000,000 shipments.

190 of those planes are our own. Plus over 7,200 vehicles. Plus more owned-and-operated service centres in more countries than any of

Plus, above all, over 25,000 DHL employees. Trained in over 100 languages. But trained in the same company philosophy.

To think globally and act locally. To apply our global and group resources to each customer's advantage. To go that further mile which shows a customer that we're not just going through the motions — we care.

That care is demonstrated by the fact that we never use agents. We believe that if you want a

So if your concern is on-time delivery of your important documents and packages, you are unlikely to do better with any other operator.

But where you *definitely* will not be able to do better is with the total reliability which DHL provides.

From oil wells in Alaska to clinics in Africa, farms in South America to factories in China, people turn to DHL when they have to be sure. In some places, indeed, DHL is just about the

So please consider the implications of this for you and your business.

After all, such total reliability is hard to find these days.

cially well in a particular market and that might be worth extending to others.

DHL spent roughly 4% of worldwide sales on advertising. In 1990, DHL launched a new advertising campaign in the United States based on the slogan: "Faster to More of the World." This campaign, inspired by the fighter pilot movie "Top Gun," featured flying DHL delivery vans. (See Exhibit 13.) In the United States, the objectives of DHL's advertising campaign were threefold. First, DHL wanted to raise brand awareness. Second, DHL aimed to explain that shipping overseas required different capabilities than shipping within the continental United States. Third, DHL sought to convince consumers that DHL was the best at shipping overseas because of its experience, network, worldwide scope, and people.

DHL advertising in Europe used the slogan: "You know it's arrived the moment it's sent." (See Exhibit 14.)

Conclusion

As he pondered DHL's pricing options, Sarrafzadeh recalled the old adage: "The value of a thing is the price it will bring." Perhaps DHL's profits would be maximized if each country manager simply charged each customer "whatever the market could bear." However, from a headquarter's perspective, Sarrafzadeh believed a degree of order and consistency was necessary in DHL's pricing strategy, structure, and decision-making process. In particular, he wondered how pricing policy could enhance customer relationships, help to retain customers, and minimize their tendency to split their shipments among several air express carriers. Further penetration of existing accounts where DHL carriers were already making pickups and deliveries would, he was convinced, result in increased profits.

PART IV

MARKETING IN EMERGING MARKETS

Prior to the fall of the Berlin Wall in 1989, emerging markets were a mere asterisk in the revenue base of most multinational corporations. Capital budgeting and marketing investment discussions at world headquarters focused invariably on the so-called Triad—Western Europe, North America, and Japan. The rest of the world was an afterthought. Ten years later, resource allocation decisions in the boardroom are increasingly complicated. The countries of the so-called Triad still account for around 70% of world trade flows and equity market capitalization, so they can hardly be ignored, but future growth appears to lie in the emerging yet more volatile markets of Asia, Latin America, and Central Europe.

Paradoxically, in the era of globalization, more new nations have achieved independence than in any other decade of modern human history, as a result of the breakup of the U.S.S.R., Yugoslavia, and Czechoslovakia. The nomenclature has shifted from "Third World countries" that did little more than supply cheap raw materials to the better-off nations, to "emerging markets," implying a demand as well as a supply role.

Emerging markets are attractive for two reasons. First, population and economic growth is outstripping the so-called developed world (which will soon represent no more than 15% of the world's population). Second, the developed markets are more complicated to serve, often requiring clever segmentation. Needs in the emerging markets are more basic. In many cases, the simple mass market that existed in the United States in the 1960s is mirrored in the emerging markets of the 1990s.

Not all emerging markets are created equal. Some, such as Hong Kong and Singapore, enjoy per capital incomes higher than many countries in the developed world. At the other extreme are so-called trailing markets, many in Africa, characterized by pervasive poverty.

Conventional wisdom in international marketing would have emerging markets follow—with an appropriate time lag—the patterns of market evolution established earlier in the developed world. Where per capita income constraints influence heavily a product's market penetration, this may be so. However, there are many examples of leapfrogging, whereby emerging markets move swiftly to adopt the latest technology, skipping over intermediate technologies used previously in the developed world; cellular and wireless communications are one example. In addition, the speed with which urban consumers in emerging markets have embraced "Western" brands of low-priced consumables has surprised many marketers. In some cases, steady-state market penetration rates comparable to those in developed countries have been reached within three years after launch.

Astute multinationals understand that marketing innovations in emerging markets can often inform and improve marketing practices in the developed world. Traditionally, idea transfers have involved one-way traffic from developed to emerging markets, with little emphasis on reverse learning. Recently, however, Motorola has uncovered important insights into the future of cellular telephones from consumer research in China. Similarly, Kentucky Fried Chicken (KFC) has learned how to design and operate large eat-in restaurants in China, where a visit to a KFC outlet is a special treat, as opposed to the convenient fast-food experience it is in the United States.

While marketing programs often need to be adapted to emerging market cultures, the level of customization required is often surprisingly modest. For example, the functional benefits addressed by Gillette blades are the same worldwide, though the frequency of shaving and the areas shaved vary considerably across cultures. Gillette's sales mix also varies, with more expensive Sensor systems accounting for a higher percentage of sales in developed markets, while basic double-edge blades, often sold singly, account for the bulk of sales in poorer emerging markets. The brand name and the product quality remain consistent worldwide. Prices of some Gillette products may be lower in emerging markets to encourage brand trail, but not to the point of encouraging widespread diversion of products from lower- to-higher-priced markets.

Consumers in emerging markets are as savvy as those in developed markets when evaluating product quality. The notion that obsolete product or surplus inventory can be dumped in emerging markets is naive. Indeed, in some trailing markets, harsh climactic conditions may require more robust product formulations and packaging, and narrower product lines may be appropriate when distribution is fragmented among many undercapitalized vendors.

Distribution systems are modernizing in the cities of emerging markets with surprising rapidity. For example, in São Paulo, Buenos Aires, and Mexico City, retail distribution has consolidated to the point that multinational marketers are having to deal with supermarket chains as powerful as any in the developed world. Falling tariff barriers and the arrival of Carrefour and Wal-Mart have prompted local retailers to consolidate and/or enter into strategic alliances with their global counterparts.

Beyond the cities, however, distribution in emerging markets remains uneven and fragmented. Bicycle vendors and mobile-delivery vans are often necessary to reach rural communities in India, for example. Multinationals entering emerging markets with poor transportation infrastructure are often surprised at how much they have to invest (for example, in their own delivery trucks) to achieve widespread distribution. Such investments must be calibrated against the long-term potential of these markets.

BRAAS GMBH

In mid-February, 1990, at 5:15 P.M., rush hour had started in the comfortable, forested suburbs of Frankfurt, the region that symbolized West Germany's postwar economic resurgence and home to the West German roofing-materials market leader, Braas GmbH. Three months before, on November 9, 1989, the Berlin Wall had fallen.[1] Crowds in East Germany warned that they would come to the deutsche mark (DM) if it did not come to them. Faced with the prospect of massive immigration into West Germany from the East, political and business leaders needed to decide whether, when, and how the two countries' legal, financial, legislative and social structures should merge.

While BMWs and Mercedes crowded onto West Germany's highways, Braas executives were debating whether to produce in East Germany and how to sell there. Braas had three options to supply East Germany: ship high-quality Braas products from West Germany, enter a joint venture providing Braas with a local manufacturing capability, or build new greenfield plants. In each case, the participants needed to decide whether to hire and train local salespeople, or use existing or additional West German salespeople. Because Braas attributed its West German market leadership in part to its salesforce management, the company's decision regarding the East German sales organization could be key to its success in the new market.

COMPANY BACKGROUND

In 1948 Rudolf H. Braas became the first person to manufacture roof tiles from concrete on an industrial scale. This event revolutionized the country's roofing materials market. In postwar Germany, most pitched roofs[2] were covered

---

[1] In 1949, Germany was officially split into two countries: the Federal Republic of Germany (FRG or "West Germany") and the German Democratic Republic (GDR or "East Germany"). The Berlin Wall, erected by East Germany in 1961, divided the country's former capital. On November 9, 1989 East German authorities announced their decision to open the border with the West, signaling the end of the Berlin Wall.

[2] A pitched roof had a slope of at least 17 to 18 degrees.

This case was prepared by Carin-Isabel Knoop (under the direction of John A. Quelch). Confidential data have been disguised. Copyright © 1995 by the President and Fellows of Harvard College. Harvard Business School case 595-041.

with lozenge-shaped clay tiles, which were not frost resistant and were produced manually. The cheaper and more resilient concrete roof tiles progressively displaced clay tiles. By 1989, 60% of all tiles sold in Germany were made of concrete, 30% were made of clay, and 10% were made of slate. This split was the same for individual housing as well as commercial buildings with pitched roofs. In 1990, the market for building materials in West Germany amounted to around DM 35 billion. Roofing materials accounted for about 5% of this volume. Around half of all new roofs were flat; the other half were pitched.

Successive Braas executives had been inspired by Rudolf Braas's innovative and pioneering spirit. In 1953, Braas GmbH was incorporated as one of the first Anglo-German joint ventures after World War II.[3] Braas launched the first proprietary branded building material in Germany, a tile called the "Frankfurter Pfanne." In 1990, it was still Braas's leading product. Braas was also the first construction materials manufacturer to offer a 30-year guarantee on its tiles' quality and frost resistance.

Braas's 1989 sales were DM 877 million, and the company generated a DM 54.3 million after tax profit.[4] Four-fifths of the company's sales were realized in West Germany. Braas products were sold in Austria, Switzerland, France, Italy, Sweden, Denmark, Norway, and Hungary. Throughout its international expansion, Braas remained committed to local production and decentralization. Exports accounted for only 7% of Braas's international turnover and were mostly materials for flat roofs and roofing accessories. Braas executives attributed the company's success to a commitment to technological leadership and innovation, customer service, market proximity, and good relations with its employees, half of whom in Germany were Braas shareholders.

Success in the tile business encouraged Braas to broaden its product range to include complementary products. Braas's strategy was to acquire flat roofing and chimney manufacturers that were first or second in their markets. In the late 1960s, Braas entered the plastic-systems components market. Plastic components included fixtures designed to seal or ventilate ridges, hips and eaves, skylights, and vent pipe outlets. In the 1970s, Braas began offering several types of roofing membranes, used to guarantee good, flat roofing and impermeability. In the 1980s, Braas added roof windows and skylights, and in 1990, it acquired one of Germany's leading manufacturers of chimney and ventilation systems. Braas was able to offer an "integrated roofing solution" for pitched as well as flat roofs. The company's 3,590 employees produced and sold roofing materials for flat and pitched roofs (86% of sales), chimney systems (9%), and other building materials (5%).

Building materials for pitched roofs remained Braas's core business and, in 1989, still accounted for 75% of sales. Pitched roofs could be covered with tiles, metal sheets, bitumen, or asphalt. Tiles were considered more aesthetic. Concrete tiles were the most frequently used material for pitched roofs in West Germany. The pitched roof market segment amounted to 75 million square meters.[5] In 1989, Braas sold only tiles made of concrete. The main competitors in this segment were Eternit and Nelskamp. However, after competing against clay tiles for 25 years, Braas decided to enter the clay tile segment in 1990. There were over 30 clay tile sup-

---

[3]The joint venture was established with the British Redland PLC group, which had been manufacturing concrete roof tiles in Great Britain since 1919. By the late 1980s Redland had become one of the world's leading producers of construction materials, with manufacturing operations in over 30 countries.
[4]In July 1989, U.S. $1 = DM 1.85.

---

[5]Ten concrete tiles = 1 square meter (approximately 10 square feet).

pliers, the largest of which had a turnover of DM 120 million.

Braas's concrete tiles were produced, marketed, and sold by Braas Dachsysteme GmbH, a subsidiary within Braas GmbH.[6] Braas had 16 concrete tile plants in West Germany. The company designed its plants and manufactured its own production equipment. Concrete tiles were made of a cement, sand, water, and iron oxide mixture which was extruded into shape using tile molds. After passing through a dryer, they were packaged and stored at the plant, where they were picked up by customers. The standard size of a tile was 0.1 square meter and the average tile lasted more than 30 years. Braas's more modern plants could produce up to 25 million tiles per year. Braas estimated its break-even capacity utilization at 8 to 10 million tiles.

The ability to run one to three shifts, add overtime, or accelerate the production process provided output flexibility in tile production. Output flexibility could be important because the demand for pitched-roofing materials tracked housing starts, which in turn reflected the economic cycle. In the spring of 1990, Braas's plants were operating at full capacity under a two-shift regime. Half a day of set-up time was required to clear the production line and change the dies to make a different model. In 1989, Braas offered eight tile models in four to eight colors, depending on regional preferences.

Competitive Environment

Braas defended its West German market leadership in concrete tiles against two main competitors, Eternit and Nelskamp. At the end of 1989, West-Berlin-based Eternit had over 3,200 employees and sales of approximately DM 450 million, with less than one-third coming from building materials for pitched roofs. In 1990,

Eternit operated four concrete tile plants, with another one scheduled to come on line in 1991. Eternit often undercut Braas's prices significantly.

Nelskamp was a much smaller owner-operated company headquartered in the Rhine region. It did not publish an annual report. The company competed on relationships and value-added services. Nelskamp's 1989 tile sales were estimated at DM 150 million, with approximately DM 120 million coming from concrete tiles. It operated three concrete tile plants. A map of the locations of Braas, Eternit and Nelskamp concrete tile plants in West Germany is provided in Exhibit 1.

All three companies sold only through wholesalers and had their own sales forces. Braas and Eternit both sold their concrete tiles in West Berlin prior to 1989, but their products were not available in East Germany. Braas had 120 sales representatives selling tiles; Eternit and Nelskamp had approximately 25 each. Braas acted as a price leader and sold its Frankfurter Pfanne tile to wholesalers for approximately DM 1. Most of Braas's products were priced 10% to 20% above competitive products. Competitors could also be relied on to follow Braas's innovations. Most competitors' products were therefore quite comparable to Braas's.

THE CONCRETE TILE BUSINESS

In West Germany, architects usually determined the type of roof (flat or pitched) and the type of tile (concrete, clay, or slate) to be used for the roof on a particular construction project. They occasionally specified a tile "similar to the Frankfurter Pfanne," but rarely did they specify a supplier. Responsibility for the final selection of a tile model and supplier often fell on roofers. In the case of most renovations, only the roofer was involved in material selection.[7]

---

[6]Braas Dachsysteme will be subsequently referred to as Braas. Braas GmbH will be used to refer to the Braas Group.

[7]In the case of older historical buildings, public authorities and their experts were involved in the tile selection.

Exhibit 1 *Locations of Braas and Competitors' Concrete Tile Works in East and West Germany in 1989*

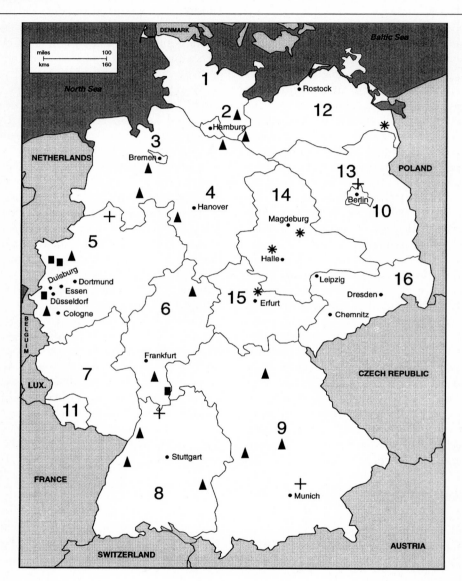

▲ Braas tile factories in West Germany

✳ Plants included in Braas joint venture in East Germany

■ Nelskamp plants

✛ Eternit plants

In 1989, there were approximately 8,000 roofers in West Germany. The majority belonged to roofers' associations, which were organized by region. The typical roofing business was a local firm with 10 employees and yearly sales of DM 1 million. Late delivery, breakage, or poor tile quality could hold up an entire construction project and hurt a roofer's reputation. For a roof of 180 square meters or 220 square yards,[8] materials costs amounted to about DM 4,000 and labor costs were another DM 5,000. Total construction costs for such a house were around DM 300,000.

Once a type of tile and supplier had been selected, roofers expected the tiles and roofing accessories to be easily accessible and readily available. Because the precise number of tiles needed for a job could only be estimated, extra tiles had to be available. Like roofers, contractors cared about product quality and supplier reliability. The contractor in charge of a construction project would occasionally recommend a tile supplier to the roofer. Usually, though, contractors solicited and followed roofers' suggestions. The same process was true for private home builders.

In 1989, there were about 2,500 construction materials wholesalers in West Germany. Most of them provided storage, delivery, credit, and product information. Wholesalers that specialized in materials for roofs and walls usually carried several lines of tiles. Tiles typically accounted for half of their sales. On the other hand, large, generalist wholesalers that also carried a whole range of construction materials, as well as plumbing and sanitation equipment, usually only carried one or two lines of tiles and a more restricted product range. Braas, like Eternit and Nelskamp, sold its concrete roof tiles only to wholesalers. Larger wholesalers carried over 200 product lines, including roofing materials and accessories. Their yearly sales ranged from DM 1 million to over DM 50 million, with an average firm

selling DM 20 million and having 35 employees. Six regional wholesaler buying groups were particularly strong. The ten largest buying groups accounted for half of Braas's concrete tile sales.

MARKETING AT BRAAS

In the late 1980s, the Frankfurter Pfanne, Braas's leading product, enjoyed over 90% aided awareness among key target groups such as roofers and architects. Among homeowners, aided awareness approached 85%. Braas executives credited these results to a mixture of push-and-pull marketing focused on four target groups: end users (contractors and home owners), architects, roofers, and wholesalers. Braas used an integrated communications mix of personal selling, direct mail, advertising, public relations, trade shows and exhibits to promote its brands and products.

At least once a year, Braas invited major wholesalers to seminars on the construction industry, business management, and selling skills. This attention paid off when an indecisive roofer took a wholesaler's advice that "you cannot go wrong with Braas." Wholesalers applied a 20% markup on Braas's price of DM 10 per square meter of concrete tile. Roofers charged an average of DM 50 per square meter of laid tiles to cover both labor and material costs.

Braas sales representatives visited wholesalers regularly to take care of product displays, provide merchandising support, and ensure adequate inventory levels. They also provided wholesalers with samples of Braas's newest products. To minimize the downtime of construction crews, Braas ensured that its tiles were carried by as many wholesalers as possible and that their inventory was complete.

To ensure a constant dialogue with its key target groups, Braas had created and regularly convened "consultation boards" with roofers, wholesalers and architects. These boards enabled Braas to gather market intelligence and client feedback. Each board in turn provided a professional and

---

[8]One square yard = 0.84 square meters.

social forum for its participants. Braas was also a major presence at trade shows, mailed its quarterly *Braas Heute* magazine to hundreds of professionals in its target groups, and used direct mail to inform roofers and architects of product innovations. Braas strove in every way to cultivate good relations with its target groups. For example, truck drivers who picked up tiles at Braas plants were encouraged to use the phones and the showers on the premises. In the morning they were greeted with hot coffee. Drivers often ate in Braas's plant cafeterias and developed friendships with Braas employees. Similarly, Braas let roofers use its conference rooms when they were not needed. A "Braas roofer" usually remained loyal. On occasion, however, a particularly tight budget might require a roofer to consider cheaper suppliers.

Eternit's sales force targeted mainly developers and architects who carried out large construction projects all over Germany. In contrast, Nelskamp had evolved into a strong regional player around its base in the Rhine region. Its sales representatives concentrated on selected roofers, wholesalers, and architects, who tended to remain very loyal to Nelskamp. In other parts of Germany, Nelskamp relied on larger wholesalers to push its products.

SALES FORCE MANAGEMENT

In 1989, Braas had 19 sales managers and 120 sales representatives. Most sales representatives covered the equivalent of two to three counties (*kreis*).[9] Sales managers covered 15 to 20 counties. The sales representative was the company's ambassador and a client's only contact with Braas. A popular saying at Braas was that "entrepreneurs were leading entrepreneurs." Sales representatives visited the company's 18 sales

---

[9]Public authorities in Germany compiled sociodemographic information and issued urban-development and construction permits at the county level.

offices to file sales reports, discuss problems, or catch up with their peers. Complaints regarding breakage were always handled by the relevant sales representative. Only stubborn cases were referred to sales managers. Sales managers and sales representatives believed that a complaint well-handled could increase loyalty.

The sales representative at Braas was called a "technical consultant" (*Fachberater*) and was a specialist in pitched roofs. Depending on the sizes of their territories, sales representatives drove 3,000 to 4,000 kilometers a month. The number of kilometers tended to decrease with experience in a territory once a sales representative had developed a portfolio of core clients. In 1989, the average sales volume for building material for pitched roofs per territory was DM 4.4 million. To organize their schedules, sales representatives categorized members of each target group (roofer, architect, contractor, wholesaler) within their territory according to potential. "A" clients or contracts were to be visited once a month, "B" clients could be visited once a quarter, and "C" clients once a year. Even though sales representatives were expected to complete seven to ten sales calls a day, they averaged six to seven calls a day, of which four or five could be considered as "good quality calls." The typical Braas sales representative was responsible for 20 wholesalers (10 in the A category), 70 roofers (50 in the A category), and 200 architects (20 in the A category). Exhibit 2 recounts a typical day of a Braas sales representative.

Every second sales call was to a roofer. Braas representatives visited nearly every roofer in West Germany. Experienced representatives stated that a strong relationship should have developed by the sixth or seventh visit. New sales representatives often had to invest a year or two developing such relationships before seeing results in the form of increased sales in their territories. Some relationships, once developed, then lasted decades. Selling at Braas was intensely personal. A sales manager pointed out:

Exhibit 2   *A Day with Mr. W., Braas Sales Representative*

7–8 A.M.	Stayed at home.* Contractor called and asked Mr. W. to come to construction site to help select roofing accessories (roof with 25,000 Braas Frankfurter Pfanne).
9:30 A.M.	On way to construction site, Mr. W. dropped off display of new tile model at B-wholesaler. Said he would return to discuss and set it up.
10 A.M.	Contractor, architect, roofer and Mr. W. met at site, briefly discussed yesterday's soccer results, and climbed on the 40-meter roof. Mr. W. recommended a Braas spire. Back at construction office, contractor mentioned aeration problems. Mr. W. described Braas' ventilation systems and new tile model. Showed group new Braas catalogue and suggested they pick up a copy at nearby wholesaler.
11:30 A.M.	Drove 5 mins. to C-roofer who always used Eternit but was turning business over to son who sometimes used Braas. Roofer had encouraged Mr. W. to pass by again when he had come six months ago. Mr. W. had coffee with family and left brochure.
Noon	Drove 15 mins. to A-roofer, loyal Braas client. Roofer complained about breakage. Mr. W. said he would investigate and left prospectus on new tile.
1 P.M.	Drove 10 mins. to local B-architect, left a brochure and his card with the secretary. On the way, took Polaroid shot of a new construction site in the town center.
1:20 P.M.	From his car Mr. W. called A-contractor who had complained because wrong tiles had been delivered. Braas had replaced tiles immediately although it turned out to be roofer's mistake. Contractor thanked Mr. W. for call.
1:30 P.M.	Drove 7 mins. to large A-wholesaler in area, whom he visited twice a week, to explain why a roofer who had received information on a project from this wholesaler purchased his tiles from another wholesaler. Wholesaler said he understood and mentioned two new projects. Chatted about family matters.
2:30 P.M.	Drove 10 mins. to a B-roofer and left brochure on new tile in the mailbox.
2:50 P.M.	Drove 20 mins to large A-wholesaler. Had coffee and cake with manager (in business over 40 years). Manager mentioned breakage. Mr. W. talked about new tile's popularity.
5 P.M.	Drove home 75 mins. Had unpacked car, prepared sales reports, completed client cards, and updated folders with information on potential projects by 7:15 P.M.

*Always held "open phone" when contacts knew he could be reached. The morning calls usually influenced the day's schedule.

The man from Braas is always welcome because he is liked as a person. I treat my clients like my friends. I am Mr. Muller talking to Mr. Schneider, not a Braas representative dealing with a wholesaler. Sometimes we do not even talk about Braas. We might talk about construction projects, which is important because the sooner I know about a construction project, the better the chances that Braas tiles will be put on the roof. So I tell my clients about construction permits being released and they tell me about new projects. Also, I am always on the road, and I keep my eyes open. When I see that a house is being torn down, I make a note of it, because eventually something will be built there.

Some sales representatives were recruited through advertisements, but word-of-mouth and Braas's reputation and visibility in the building sector guaranteed a steady supply of candidates. Recruits had to be likeable, hard-working, independent, and creative. They had to be able to handle conflict and rejection. They had to possess basic manual as well as technical skills, because sales representatives were often asked for advice by roofers. During their first month at Braas, they learned about the company's products and selling philosophy. They also received formal training in roofing techniques and perfected their selling skills through internal and external seminars. Sales representatives ranged in age from 25 to 60; half were between 35 and 45 years old. Turnover among the sales force was low at 2% per year.

Annual sales targets by product line and by region were communicated from above to sales managers. They then defined quotas with and for each of their sales representatives. A sales representative's gross salary ranged from DM 50,000 to 100,000, while sales managers' salaries ranged from DM 100,000 to 120,000, 60% to 70% of which was base salary. Base salary increases reflected seniority more than performance. Commission was not based on a percentage of net-sales invoice value but on the percentage gross margin achieved on product sold. This percentage differed by product type and was lower on a basic high-volume product than on a newly introduced lower-volume product. Finally, generous incentives focused the sales force on product introductions. Incentive packages, mostly gifts and travel, rewarded team and individual performance. In addition, sales managers each received a sales budget to cover selling and marketing expenses in their regions. They reported unit sales to headquarters every day and actual-versus-budget results were compiled and reviewed monthly. A part of their remuneration was tied to their individual regions' contributions to Braas's annual results.

Every year sales managers evaluated their representatives' ability to find new clients, keep existing clients, maintain good client records, manage clients' complaints to their satisfaction, and communicate well. Because the West German market was mature and market share in most areas had been stable for years, most sales representatives concentrated on maintaining market shares in their territories and meeting their sales objectives. In the late 1980s, the sales force had to face slowing market growth and an erosion in unit prices in some regions of West Germany.

THE EAST GERMAN OPPORTUNITY

German reunification had been both a possibility and a goal ever since the country was officially split in 1949. Regardless of its timing, reunification was expected to present a formidable economic and social challenge. The territory of West Germany would be expanded by 43%, its population by 25%, and its gross national product by no more than 10%. Per capita income in East Germany was two-fifths of that of West Germany. West Germany had twice as many cars per capita. On the other hand, more than 50% of the East German population was "employed," because full employment was guaranteed under East German Communist rule. It was unlikely that this would survive reunification. The resulting emotional and social disruption was difficult to predict.

The poor quality of East German housing highlighted the East German planned economy's inability to address its people's most basic needs. Half of East Germany's seven million dwellings pre-dated 1945. One million were considered uninhabitable and another two million were severely damaged. One-quarter of all apartments had access only to common toilets; fewer than half were centrally heated. Average living space per capita in the East German state of Mecklenburg Vorpommern was 25.6 m², compared to 39.8 m² in the West German state of Saarland.[10] Refer to Exhibit 3 for selected data on East and West Germany.

The East German ministry in charge of construction and infrastructure had communicated

---

[10]*Statistical Yearbook for Germany* (Bonn: Federal Statistical Office, 1992), p. 269.

Exhibit 3   *Basic East and West Germany—Selected Demographic and Economic Data: 1989**

	East Germany	**West Germany**
Population (in millions)	16.7	61.7
Population density (sq. km per person)	25	35
No. of cities over 500,000 inhabitants	3	12
Percent of population living in urban areas	77	86
No. of square meters of living space per capita	28.2	36.4
Percent of household income spent on housing and energy	2.4	20.3
Average working week in manufacturing (hours)	35.9	39.9
GDP/capita in U.S. $	$5,256	$19,743
Labor productivity index	49	100
Primary energy consumption per capita (in tetrajoules)	225	185
No. of individuals per car	4.5	2.1
No. of individuals per television set	5.8	2.4
No. of individuals per telephone	4.3	1.6

*Sources: Adapted from DMI, Berlin (quoted in the *Financial Times*, May 4, 1994); *Statistical Yearbook* (United Nations Press), 1990/1991; *The Economist Book of Vital World Statistics* (Times Books), 1990; *German Statistical Yearbook* (Federal Statistical Office), 1993; and *European Marketing Data and Statistics* (Euromonitor), 1994.

annual targets to ministerial groups (*kombinate*) in charge of a particular segment (e.g., building and clay materials). These *kombinate* oversaw companies in their segment and supervised their operations. These companies (*volkseigene betriebe,* or "people's companies") fulfilled the production orders they received from the *kombinate* to which they belonged. They were assigned a certain quantity of materials each year, which they picked up at predetermined plants.

The Joint Venture Proposal

When the Berlin Wall fell in November 1989, the institutional structures that governed the operations of manufacturing plants disintegrated. Supplies of raw materials and sales were no longer assured, and plant directors had trouble meeting payrolls. Entrepreneurial plant managers began to contact companies in the West. In January 1990, the director of a *Kombinate* in the construction sector and the director of a tile plant in Saxony came to Braas looking for a Western partner. Such a partnership would have given Braas a regional stronghold in Saxony and access to one-fifth of East German tile production capacity, estimated at 75 million tiles in 1989.

Braas executives did not consider a regional solution acceptable and therefore initiated contacts and negotiations at every level of the East German construction sector. In June 1990, Braas had to decide on an offer to enter into a joint venture which would organize four of the five major East German concrete tile plants and their 690 employees under one management. The joint venture was valued at DM 22 million. Braas would inject DM 11 million in capital in return for 50% of the shares, the rest being held by the people's companies in charge of building materials. Total annual production capacity at the four plants was estimated at 55 million tiles. However, the plants were old and in need of repair, so capacity utilization was less than 50%. Breakage rates exceeded 20%, or seven times the Braas average, and 18 employees were required to operate one production line, or 2.5 times as many as in Braas's West German plants. While one work hour was required to produce 8,000 tiles at Braas, five work hours were required to produce the same volume in the East German plants.

A major challenge would be to restructure the plants' work force and transform what had been a culture of waste, inefficiency, and indifference about customers and quality. Under East Germany's Communist regime, creativity, decision-making, and initiative had been discouraged. Workers referred problems to supervisors and frequently stopped production to await instructions. On the other hand, dealing with scarcity of equipment and supplies had increased East German workers' resourcefulness. They were often described as diligent, proud, and conscientious workers with good technical training. Many were motivated to work for joint ventures. They hoped for relief from poor working conditions in antiquated plants but many knew that the unravelling of the inefficient Communist production system would lead to massive unemployment.

The East German Construction Materials Market

Braas estimated that, within a few years, it would be able to sell 100 million tiles per year in East Germany. This estimate was based on the population size to which an average number of square meters of roofing material per capita could be applied. In 1989, the East German roofing market was estimated at 18 million square meters and was expected to grow at 15% a year.

However, market growth would depend on the pace of reconstruction, economic condition, and West German capital injections. Most of the construction in the first three years after reunification was expected to be publicly financed and involve projects dealing with infrastructure, large-scale housing, and the renovation of exist-

ing housing. Despite unclear land and property rights, construction was expected to boom.

Furthermore, because output plans and protectionism had determined past market shares and use of various roofing materials, the analysis of existing market information was of little use in forecasting future market demand. For example, clay tiles for pitched roofs, though once as popular as in West Germany, held only 1% of the total roofing materials market. Concrete tiles accounted for more than 50% of the market, fiber cement and bitumen shingles for more than 40%. In 1989, a low quality East German copy of the "Frankfurter Pfanne" was available for 1.10 to 1.15 East German marks in two different colors. Braas planned to apply the same prices to its products sold in East Germany to avoid transshipping or customer complaints.

Braas faced the dual challenge of locating target customers and dealing with the lack of an organized distribution structure similar to that in West Germany. Construction projects were completed by contractors and craftsmen, including roofers, who had no influence on the types of materials used. Most roofers obtained the materials set aside for a particular project directly from the plants. The roofing profession had been systematically discouraged in East Germany. Any roofer with more than 11 employees was subjected to a 90% tax. However, material scarcity had promoted collaboration and barter among roofers. An unofficial roofers' guild had developed, and lists of roofers were accessible. It was much more difficult to locate architects. Most of them had been working within the construction *Kombinate* and specialized in large public projects. Finally, there were almost no construction materials wholesalers in East Germany.

The superiority of Braas's products as well as the meaning and the importance of service would also have to be communicated. West German construction and construction materials companies were known for quality and expertise although individual company and brand awareness was low. Many roofers had heard of Braas and the Frankfurter Pfanne. Braas executives disagreed about the awareness levels among roofers for Braas products; their estimates ranged from 10% to 30%.

THE DEBATE AT BRAAS

In its assessment of the "reunification bet," the German business community, like the group assembled at Braas, was broadly split into the "wait and see" and the "act and see" camps. The discussion was led by the managing director together with the company's chief financial officer, the national sales manager for pitched roofing materials, and the marketing director for pitched roofs. After three hours, the managing director summarized the discussion.

Managing director: Because we all believe that the East and West German markets will converge, we agree that Braas's positioning as a high-service provider should be extended to East Germany and that Braas products will be sold through wholesalers. We still have to decide whether to sign the joint-venture contract, build entirely new plants, or service the market from the West. In any event, we will need a sales organization.

As I said earlier, the joint venture would signal clearly to clients and competitors that we are committed to the East German market and that we intend to be the market leader there, too. The plants are largely obsolete but the production crews are experienced. We should be able to produce and sell tiles of acceptable quality within months of signing the contract.

I agree that leaving the market open in the meantime is risky. Therefore we should inform roofers, architects and wholesalers that Braas will be producing there soon. We conduct seminars with roofers in the West, why not in the East? If we tell them now that Braas will be producing in East Germany in several months, they will be ready to buy our tiles when they come off the line.

Chief financial officer: You are forcing me to repeat the risks of the joint venture. Let's be realistic. We are unable to assess precisely the extent, cost, and complexity of the necessary investment. Some equipment is 20 years old. Only cursory due diligence has so far been performed. The land on which the plants are located can only be leased, because land cannot be purchased. Who knows what land ownership reform will bring. Renovating East German plants will subject us to the region's paradoxical combination of relatively high labor costs and low productivity. To reach Western productivity levels, the work force will have to be cut by two-thirds. This will not help our public relations. Imagine the headlines in the local papers.

Also, the plants' bad reputation could hurt us, because Braas could become associated with poor quality. Quality control is unknown, packaging rare, and handling careless. Breakage rates have always been high, which did not matter as long as clients had no alternative. Finally, although the joint venture includes four "sales offices," there is no sales force. Let's build our own modern plants in East Germany. We can locate them where we want. We will not be burdened by past reputation.

Managing director: The unclear property rights you mentioned will make it impossible to quickly find and acquire sites for one or more greenfield plants. A production work force will have to be hired and trained. Ramp-up could take over a year. As for the existing workers in the joint venture plants, a massive layoff cannot happen. Employment levels will probably have to be guaranteed as part of the joint venture agreement. Some of the employees could be retrained for selling jobs.

Sales manager: You may be right. But remember that we are dealing with production workers. We will probably have to advertise for sales representative positions in Berlin newspapers. I wonder who will respond. Who knew how to sell in Communist countries?

Assuming that enough people respond, how will we screen them? There won't be any candidates with the right mix of personality, selling skills, product knowledge and industry experience. What kind of sales representative will be needed? How will he be different from us, or will he be just the same? We must remember that the East German system suppressed the key characteristics of a Braas salesman: independence, initiative, drive, and customer friendliness. The type of training in commercial and technical skills the new recruits would need to receive would have to cover much more ground and take much longer than our classical training program.

Finally, how will we set the salary? If we pay too much, new recruits might show off, alienate the clients, and upset our people here. If we pay too little, we will not get the best candidates. We, the Braas salespeople, are living billboards. A few bad apples could hurt our image and reputation there as well as here.

Marketing director: *It seems to me that you optimists have forgotten that we are not alone. Between now and the moment Braas tiles would come off the line in East Germany, Eternit or foreign competitors could capture the market. Roofers will drink beer at Braas receptions and buy tiles from Eternit!*

Even though we have used joint ventures many times before and with success, we have to remember that East Germany is not a classical foreign market. Goods already have started flowing in, and I expect that our competitors will move in to capture market share. Letting competitors increase their overall German share will increase their power towards wholesalers and potentially hurt our core business in the West. It could interfere

with our expansion plans in Eastern Europe. One of the plants proposed in the joint venture is next to the Polish border and could be an ideal springboard into that country.

Time is even more important than money now. Our plants and sales offices located close to the border should cover regions in the East as soon as possible. Regardless of whether or not we sign the joint venture, we must establish a presence in the market immediately. Our West German plants, including the ones closest to the common border, are currently producing enough tiles to meet demand in West Germany. By adding a third shift and overtime staff, we can probably squeeze out another 100 million tiles. Transportation will be a problem, though, on the poor East German roads.

Managing director: *When we decided to enter Hungary in 1985, we did not "ship and see" until we better understood the market. We decided to produce locally, not merely because of high transportation costs but also because we did not want to seem like we were just there to make a few quick sales. Shipping from West Germany will convey the wrong message.*

Sales manager: *There is another risk. Increasing production and sales capacity by 30% will strain Braas's resources and might hamper our ability to maintain the high level of service and reliability that our customers have come to expect. Running at full capacity will make it hard to fill rush orders and satisfy last-minute client needs. This will hurt us in the West.*

Marketing director: *It's true that we do not know where the market is going. The truth is that it's tough to tell whether the label "Made in West Germany" will be an advantage or a disadvantage in East Germany, in the short and long term. Also, can we assume that people will want tiles again any time soon and how can we know which types they will prefer? We now have about 50 combina-*

tions of type and color. If we try making and selling all our models in East Germany, we may well confuse new sales representatives as well as new clients.

Sales manager: The best way to find out is to send a team of experienced Braas sales representatives over there. They are the best spokespeople for Braas's products and philosophy. They will be able to identify and contact key target groups, as well as set up a distribution system. They can hire and train East Germans to replace them. Our success depends on our relationship with wholesalers and our constant contact with target groups. We are in a position to structure the East German market. It took us 35 years to build our sales organization here, how can we expect to clone it overnight and deliver? How can you hire a new sales force and expect it to develop a distribution system it does not understand?

Our representatives in the border regions could expand their geographical coverage eastward. Another solution will have to be found for the densely populated Berlin region. One of us could go to Berlin with a small team of sales representatives and cover the city and suburbs. The less-developed and less-populated regions can be taken care of later.

Managing director: So we have at least one volunteer!

Sales manager: Well, I have two children and I'm already on the road two nights a week. My wife will not let me spend the entire week in East Germany. Besides, no one is ready to cover me at home. Some of my clients have been doing business with me for 13 years. Can I tell them that I have more urgent things to do? Actually, most of my men would probably not volunteer for the same reasons. How can I convince them to leave? If they go, they will want to be promoted to sales managers! Will we hire new sales representatives to cover their territories or will they get their territories back when or if they return?

Managing director: In fact, I am not even sure that we would do such a good job. Our style may be too pushy. Our salespeople have limited experience in new markets. There is no language barrier, but regional dialects and traditions have remained very strong. Perhaps only East Germans can communicate with East Germans.

The managing director proposed a break. He felt that German reunification was an extraordinary event that called for a bold response on the part of successful West German companies such as Braas. Before reconvening the meeting, he jotted down a few numbers outlining the economics of the principal options (Exhibit 4).

Exhibit 4   *Basic Economics of Principal Market Entry Options**

Frame: 1990 to 1994
Market volume: 100 million tiles in 1990
Market Compound annual growth rate to 1994: 15%
Braas' cost of goods sold: 40% of sales
Braas' cost of capital: 15%
Price for 1,000 Braas tiles: DM 1,000
Estimate of sales force needed: 5 sales managers and 35 sales representatives

continued

---

*Source: Company records and casewriter interviews.

Exhibit 4   *(continued)*

Option A: Tiles manufactured in East Germany. Tiles sold in East Germany using an East German salesforce.

- Salesforce salaries approximately 60% of West German levels in 1990. Expected to increase by 20% per year until 1994.
- Capital expenditures: maximum of DM 40 million per plant[a]
- 50% desired market share in the pitched roof segment in 1994
- Sales price includes warehousing and transportation costs[b]

Option B: Tiles manufactured in West Germany. Tiles sold in East Germany using West German salesforce.

- DM 270 per 1,000 tiles for additional transport costs (27 pfennigs/kilogram)
- DM 250 per 1,000 tiles for additional warehousing costsa[b]
- Sales force salaries would increase at 5% per year due to inflation
- DM 800,000 of extra selling expenses: travel, bonuses, accommodations[c]
- Operating expenses incurred by increasing production of West German plants[d]
- 35% desired market share in the pitched roof segment in 1994

*Source: Company records and casewriter interviews.
[a]Plants in the joint venture could be renovated or rebuilt at a cost of DM 40 million each when market demand so required. Maximum production capacity of a modern plant was 20–25 million tiles.
[b]Warehousing sites would be needed in East Germany to guarantee rapid order fulfillment and quick response to last-minute client needs.
[c]Training costs are not considered because training would be required in both cases.
[d]Operating expenses occasioned by adding shift and overtime, increased maintenance and machine wear. Level comparable to additional expenses required to bring East German plants up to acceptable quality levels before renovation was completed.

Option A   *Tiles Manufactured in East Germany. Tiles Sold in East Germany Using East German Sales Force.*

	1990	1991	1992	1993	1994	
Market size (index)	100	115	132	152	175	15% CAGR[a]
Market share	15%	30%	40%	50%	50%	
Units sold (millions)	15.0	34.5	52.9	76.0	87.5	
Revenues (DM millions)	18.8	43.1	66.1	95.1	109.3	
COGS[b]	7.5	17.3	26.5	38.0	43.7	40% of revenues
Transport	—	—	—	—	—	
Warehouse	—	—	—	—	—	
Sales force	1.9	2.3	2.7	3.2	3.9	20% CAGR
Additional expenses	—	—	—	—	—	
Capital expenditure[c]	40.0	0	40.0	40.0	40.0	
Cash flow	(30.6)	23.6	(3.0)	13.8	21.7	
Discounted @ 15%	(30.6)	20.5	(2.3)	9.1	12.4	
Net present value	9.13					

[a]CAGR: Annual growth rate.
[b]COGS: Cost of goods sold.
[c]Plants are renovated at a cost of DM 40 million each when existing production capacity utilization so requires.

Exhibit 4   *(continued)*

Option B   *Tiles Manufactured in West Germany. Tiles Sold in East Germany Using West German Sales Force.*

	1990	**1991**	**1992**	**1993**	**1994**	
Market size (index)	100	115	132	152	175	15% CAGR[a]
Market share	10%	15%	25%	30%	35%	
Units sold (millions)	10.0	17.3	33.1	45.6	61.2	
Revenues (DM millions)	12.5	21.6	41.3	57.0	76.5	
COGS[b]	5.0	8.6	16.5	22.8	30.6	40% of revenues
Transport	2.7	4.7	8.9	12.3	16.5	
Warehouse	2.5	4.3	8.3	11.4	15.3	
Sales force	3.2	3.4	3.5	3.7	3.9	5% CAGR
Additional expenses	0.8	0.8	0.9	0.9	1.0	
Capital expenditure[c]	0.0	0.0	0.0	0.0	0.0	
Cash flow	(1.7)	(0.2)	3.2	5.9	9.2	
Discounted @ 15%	(1.7)	(0)	2	4	5	
Net present value	10.03					

KOÇ HOLDING: ARÇELIK WHITE GOODS

In February, 1997, the top management team of Arçelik, the major appliance subsidiary of Koç Holding, Turkey's largest industrial conglomerate, assembled in Cologne, Germany for the biannual Domotechnica, the world's largest major appliances trade show. The team was led by Hasan Subasi, president of Koç Holding's durables business unit, and Mehmet Ali Berkman, general manager of the Arçelik white-goods operation, which accounted for two-thirds of the durables business unit's turnover.[1]

The Arçelik stand was in a prime location in Building 14; nearby were the booths of Bosch, Siemens, and Whirlpool. The Arçelik stand displayed 236 products carrying the Beko brand name, 35% of them refrigerators and freezers, 25% washing machines, 20% ovens, and 15% dishwashers.[2] Several innovative products were on display, including washing machines that were more water and energy efficient than competitive products, as well as refrigerators made from materials that were 80% recyclable and incorporated special insulation panels for greater operational efficiency. In 1996, Arçelik's Beko brand had received a Green Dove award from the European Community (EC) for attention to the environment in design and production.[3]

The trade show exhibit, costing $1 million to organize, reflected Arçelik's determination to become a major player in the global white-goods industry. Yet there was still debate in the company regarding how much emphasis to place on international sales; which geographical

---

[1]"White goods" was a term used to describe major kitchen appliances. The corresponding term, "brown goods," described major household appliances used outside the kitchen, such as televisions and stereo systems.

[2]Most Arçelik products sold outside Turkey carried the Beko brand name.

[3]In 1997, the European Community comprised 15 member countries with a combined population of around 350 million.

This case was prepared by Robin Root and John Quelch. Confidential data have been disguised. Copyright © 1997 by the President and Fellows of Harvard College. Harvard Business School case 598-033.

markets to concentrate on; and whether to focus on supplying appliances on an OEM basis, building the company's own Beko brand, or both.[4]

COUNTRY AND COMPANY BACKGROUND

Turkey

In 1997, Turkey, a country of 63 million people, was positioned at the historical crossroads between East and West, Communism and capitalism, Islam and Christianity. Turkey bordered Eastern Europe, the Caucasus, the Balkans, North Africa, and the Middle East—all regions in various states of political and economic flux in the 1990s. In this context, successive Turkish governments promoted domestic and foreign policies that would nurture its still-modest private sector yet promote the pursuit of global competitiveness so that Turkey would be a credible candidate for entry into the EC.

The establishment of the Republic of Turkey by Mustafa Kemal Ataturk as a secular nation state in 1923 marked the end of 600 years of sultan rule. Ataturk aimed to move Turkey quickly into the ranks of industrialized Western nations by anchoring the republic's constitution in a parliamentary democracy. From the start, a strict division between religion (Islam) and government was constitutionally guaranteed and backed by the Turkish military. To build the economy, Ataturk set up temporary state-run enterprises that would later be turned over to private sector management. Privatization, however, did not get fully underway until the mid-1980s, when the government also formally established the Istanbul Stock Exchange.

---

[4]An OEM (original equipment manufacturer) sold products to other manufacturers, distributors or retailers; these products typically carried brand names specified by the purchasing companies.

During the 1980s, the Turkish government established the convertibility of the Turkish lira and promoted exports to improve its balance of payments. Turkey's rapid growth and relative economic stability, while the envy of other developing countries, was long overlooked by Western governments, who focused instead on its strategic role as a NATO firewall against Soviet expansion. The possibility of membership in the EC changed the business mentality within Turkey. Large, family-run industrial conglomerates, the engines of Turkish modernization, started to emphasize professional management and to apply global manufacturing standards.

In 1990, the growth in Turkey's gross national product reached an all-time high of 9.2%, sparking the interest of investors from Europe and North America. After a slowdown to 0.9% growth in 1991, the Turkish government stimulated consumer demand and increased public investment; the economy grew 5.9% in 1992 and 7.5% in 1993. A major recession in 1994, which saw 5.0% negative growth, was followed by 7.3% growth in 1995 and 7.1% in 1996. Despite the political uncertainties that accompanied Turkey's first Islamic government, sustained GNP growth of 8% was forecast for 1997. The country was, however, afflicted by high inflation (80% in 1996 and 75% forecast for 1997), high interest rates, depreciation of the lira, and a deepening budget deficit. Data on the Turkish economy between 1992 and 1996 are presented in Exhibit 1.

Koç Holding

Vehbi Koç began his business in 1917 with a $100 investment from his father, who was a shopkeeper. Seven decades later, he left behind one of the world's largest private fortunes and the most advanced industrial conglomerate in Turkey, Koç Holding, which was established in 1963. Until the death of Behbi Koç in early 1996, at age 95, Koç Holding had been the only company on the Fortune 500 list of interna-

Exhibit 1   *Turkish Economic Data: 1992–1996**

	1992	**1993**	**1994**	**1995**	**1996**
GDP growth rate (%)	6.4	8.1	−5.4	7.3	7.1
GDP per capita (U.S. $ at PPPa rates)	4,991	5,562	5,271	5,411	5,634
Inflation	70%	66%	106%	94%	80%
Exchange rate (lira/U.S. $)	8,555	14,458	38,418	59,501	81,995

*Sources: Bank of America WIS Country Outlooks, November 1996; Union Bank of Switzerland New Horizon Economies, August 1995; Union Bank of Switzerland New Horizon Economies, April 1997; Statistical Yearbook of Turkey, 1996.
aPurchasing Power Parity (PPP) refers to the rates of currency conversion that equalize the purchasing power of different currencies. The GDP and PPP per capita in Istanbul were thought to be double the national average.

tional businesses to still be owned and operated by its founder.

The legacy bequeathed by Vehbi Koç was as philosophical as it was financial. Shortly after Ataturk established the Republic of Turkey in 1923, Koç became the first Turk to challenge the trading power of the republic's Greek, Armenian, and Jewish minorities. By age 22, he had discerned that the higher living standard enjoyed by these groups was a function of their dominance in commerce—a vocation which most Turks had been discouraged from entering. Koç went on to become one of the first Turkish businessmen to realize the benefits of foreign partnerships. In the late 1930s, he became a sales agent for companies such as Burroughs, Mobil Oil, and Ford. In 1948, he built his first factory to manufacture light bulbs with General Electric. Half a century later, Koç Holding controlled close to 100 companies in nearly every sector of the Turkish economy, the total output of which accounted for approximately one-tenth of the country's GNP.

As a testament to the passions and principles he cultivated over his seven-decade reign, the Koç patriarch circulated a letter among his three grandsons just three months before he passed away in 1996. In it, he exhorted them to rise to the challenge faced by most third-generation managers in family businesses: namely, to single-mindedly focus on enhancing further the company's financial and social value.

In 1996, the 36,000 employees of Koç Holding generated $12 billion in revenues. Koç was a major player in the automotive industry, household appliances, consumer goods, energy, mining, construction, international trade, finance, tourism, and services sectors. The company grew three times faster than the Turkish economy between 1985 and 1995. Its corporate logo, a red ram's head (Koç means ram in Turkish), was visible on street corners, shops and office buildings throughout Turkey. Koç Holding had a nationwide distribution network of 9,400 dealers and 23 overseas offices responsible for achieving $884 million in foreign exchange earnings. As the leading taxpayer in Turkey, Koç Holding initiated and underwrote numerous philanthropic projects in the areas of education, health, cultural heritage, and environmental conservation.

Arçelik

Arçelik was established in 1955 to produce metal office furniture.[5] In 1959, the company began manufacturing washing machines. Arçelik subsequently began manufacturing refrigerators, dishwashers, air conditioners, and vacuum cleaners in five Turkish factories. Unit sales across these five categories reached 2,110,000 in

---

[5]Arçelik (pronounced arch-e-lick) is a Turkish word meaning "clean steel."

1995, making Arçelik the sixth-largest European manufacturer of household appliances and the only significant white-goods manufacturer between Italy and India. In addition, Arçelik sourced other appliances including ovens, televisions, water heaters, and space heaters from affiliated Koç companies. Unit sales of these products reached 900,000 in 1995. Arçelik owned 63% of Ardem, a Koç company that made cooking appliances, and 23% of Bekoteknik, which made televisions and other consumer electronic products. To round out its product line, Arçelik sourced small household appliances, such as irons, from other companies outside the Koç Group. By 1996, Arçelik was the largest company within Koç Holding. Sales and earnings data for 1990 to 1996 are reported in Exhibit 2. Key dates in Arçelik's history are summarized in Exhibit 3.

Arçelik manufacturing capacity, actual production and unit sales for 1992 to 1996 in the three most important white-goods categories are summarized in Exhibit 4. Arçelik's unit market shares in Turkey in 1996 were 57% in refrigerators, 60% in washing machines and 70% in dishwashers. Competitive market share and market-size data for each category of white goods are presented in Exhibits 5 and 6. Refrigerators accounted for 38% of Arçelik sales (by value), washing machines for 32%, dishwashers for 10%, and ovens for 15%.

In 1988, the Turkish government agreed to a phased program of tariff reductions with the European Community. With respect to white goods, Turkish tariffs on imports from the EC, which ranged between 40% and 55%, would be reduced to zero between 1992 and January 1996, according to the schedule shown in Exhibit 7. A 5% Turkish tariff on imported components from the EC would also be removed. As a result, exports of Western European appliances into Turkey would become progressively more price-competitive (not least because white-goods plants in Europe were operating at only 65% capacity utilization) and possibly challenge Arçelik's dominance of the Turkish market.

In preparation for the removal of import tariffs, Arçelik invested heavily in upgrading its manufacturing quality and productivity to world-class standards. Between 1991 and 1996, capital expenditures totaled $247 million, approximately 6% of sales. By 1995, all Arçelik plants had received ISO 9001 quality certification. Through the incorporation of just-in-time and flexible manufacturing systems, Arçelik reduced raw material and labor costs, thereby increasing the productivity of its refrigerator production by 43% between 1990 and 1995. The corresponding increases for washing machines and dishwashers were 50% and 20%. Arçelik had no manufacturing plants outside of Turkey.

In addition, Arçelik also invested heavily in R&D. During the 1970s and 1980s, Arçelik licensed technology from General Electric and Bosch-Siemens. Arçelik paid unit royalties but was only permitted to sell its production in Turkey. Over time, Arçelik developed its own appliance designs, often at lower cost than the licensed technologies. Starting in 1989, Arçelik transformed itself from a manufacturer that

Exhibit 2   *Arçelik's Sales and Earnings: 1990–1996**

$U.S. million	1990	1991	1992	1993	1994	1995	1996
Sales	765	1,001	1,060	1,150	859	982	1,241
EBIT	98	134	159	148	147	144	172
Net earnings	72	91	86	97	39	60	84

*Source: Company records.

Exhibit 3   *Key Dates in Arçelik's History**

Year	Event
1955	Arçelik is founded.
1959	Arçelik produces Turkey's first washing machine.
1960	Arçelik produces Turkey's first refrigerator.
1965	JV with General Electric to produce electric motors and compressors.
	Bekoteknik is founded to operate in the "brown goods" electronics industry.
1966	Arçelik produces vacuum cleaners.
1974	Bekoteknik manufactures TV sets.
	Arçelik produces Turkey's first automatic washing machine.
1975	Arçelik receives General Electric technology licenses for white goods.
1977	Ardem joins the Koç group to produce kitchen ranges.
1980	Arçelik exports refrigerators.
1985	Arçelik licenses washing machine technology (2 models) from Bosch-Siemens. (Production ceased in 1994.)
1986	Arçelik licenses dishwasher technology (1 model) from Bosch-Siemens. No exports are permitted. (Still in production in 1996.)
1989	Arçelik establishes its Beko sales office in the United Kingdom.
1991	Bekoteknik and Arçelik receive ISO 9001 certification.
	Research and development center is established.
	Arçelik launches first toll-free customer call center in Turkey.
1993	Arçelik opens a new dishwasher plant in Ankara.
1994	Bekoteknik receives the EU Green Dove Award.
1996	Arçelik agrees to supply 100,000 OEM dishwashers to Whirlpool each year for five years.
	Çayirova, Eskirsehir, and Ankara plants receive ISO 14000 certification.

*Source: Company records.

used licensed technologies to one of the leaders in white-goods research and development. The company sponsored master's theses at Turkish engineering schools on subjects relevant to its research agenda and secured World Bank funding to research how to eliminate CFCs from refrigerators. Between 1990 and 1995, $69 million or 1.5% of sales was allocated by Arçelik to R&D. The fruits of these investments were evident in the innovative, technology-based features on display in the Arçelik booth at Domotechnica in 1997.

In the area of human resources, Arçelik prided itself on lean management, with only four levels in the organization. The work force was highly educated and many Arçelik managers had attended business schools in North America and Europe.

WHITE-GOODS MARKETING IN TURKEY

Demand

As of 1996, 99% of Turkey's 13 million households owned refrigerators, the same percentage as in the EC. The corresponding percentages for other major appliances were 47% for automatic washing machines (90%), 15% for dishwashers (31%) and 56% for ovens (70%).

Exhibit 4   *Arçelik Capacity, Production, and Sales (in thousands) by Major Appliance: 1992–1996**

	Capacity	Production	Change	Capacity Utilization
Refrigerators				
1992	1,050	569.2	2.7%	54%
1993	1,050	709.6	24.6	67
1994	1,050	630.4	−11.1	60
1995	1,050	900.6	42.8	85
1996	1,050	990.8	10.1	94
Washing Machines				
1992	760	551.8	−7.2	72
1993	800	653.7	18.4	81
1994	800	500.4	−23.4	62
1995	900	625.6	25.0	70
1996	1,100	750.8	20.0	68
Dishwashers				
1992	200	180.0	36.9	90
1993	300	244.5	35.8	81
1994	300	217.3	−11.1	72
1995	300	205.3	−5.5	68
1996	500	301.6	46.9	60

*Source: Company records.

Demand for white goods in Turkey was influenced by the pace of household formations and urbanization, interest rates, retail price levels and the rate of economic growth. Sensitivity analyses estimating the effects of changes in some of these variables on unit sales of appliances in Turkey are presented in Exhibit 8. Consumer purchases of appliances increased dramatically in the first half of 1996 as shown in Exhibit 9. Arçelik sales increased 21% in this period. Berkman commented:

Domestic demand is strong and will remain so. Annual population growth is 1.7% and the number of households increases by 2.5% each year. Around 50% of the population is under 30 and an increasing percentage (currently 63%) live in cities and towns, which makes it easier for us to reach them.

Imports satisfied some of the increase in domestic demand, reaching 3% of white-goods sales in Turkey in 1993. When, in 1994, the Turkish lira devalued sharply and the economy went into recession, imports of white goods declined while exports increased. In January, 1996, with the import tariffs cut to zero and the economy strengthening, imports increased. For example, between January and July of 1996, 20% of dishwashers sold in Turkey were imported. Analysts estimated the sustainable import penetration rate at 5% for refrigerators, 10% for washing machines, and 15% for dishwashers.

Exhibit 5 *Turkish Market Share and Unit Sales for White Goods**

	Refrigerators		Washing Machines		Dishwashers		Ovens	
	1995	1996	1995	1996	1995	1996	1995	1996
Koç	54.6%	56.5%	64.2%	59.7%	75.8%	70.4%	68.0%	67.6%
Peg	38.2	30.9	23.5	23.5	17.0	20.5	25.9	23.0
Merloni	4.3	4.1	4.0	5.5	1.9	2.6	—	—
Others	2.9	8.5	8.3	11.3	5.3	6.5	6.1	9.4
Unit Sales[a]	868,197	1,039,519	856,890	1,135,669	263,570	331,030	446,591	509,493

*Source: Company records.
[a]Unit sales include imports, so Arçelik market share reported here are lower than the company's share of domestic production.

Exhibit 6   *Brand-share Breakdowns for Two Principal White Goods Marketers in Turkey: 1996**

	Refrigerators	Washing Machines	Dishwashers	Ovens
Koç Group				
Arçelik	39.2%	39.9%	53.7%	44.4%
Beko	17.3	19.8	16.7	22.9
Peg Group				
AEG	8.3	5.6	2.4	5.1
Profilo	18.9	10.6	2.8	13.1
Bosch	3.3	6.1	13.7	4.5
Siemens	0.4	1.2	1.6	0.4

*Source: Company records.

Exhibit 7   *Turkish Tariff Reduction Program for White Goods Imports from the European Community: 1992–1996*

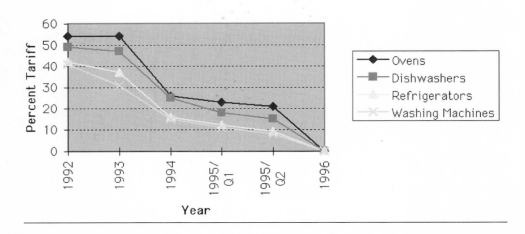

Exhibit 8   *Impact of Changes in Interest Rates, Consumer Prices and GNP Per Capita on Arçelik Sales and Profits**

Change in Arçelik's Sales and Profits	Interest rates increase by 10%	Consumer prices increase by 10%	GNP per capita increase by 10%
Refrigerator unit sales	−12.5%	−12.7%	+1.3%
Washing machine unit sales	−8.1%	−7.1%	+4.3%
Dishwasher unit sales	−10.4%	−10.1%	+21.6%
Total sales revenues	−6.9%	−8.1%	+3.7%
Total profits	−13.3%	−14.1%	+11.5%

*Source: Adapted from a Schroeders investment report, 1996.

Exhibit 9   *Change in White Goods Retail Unit Sales in Turkey**

	January–April 1995	January–April 1996
Refrigerators	−8.6%	+17.8%
Washing machines	−36%	+68%
Dishwashers	−40%	+56%
Ovens	−15%	+4.5%

*Source: Adapted from a Schroeders investment report, 1996.

Competition

Arçelik's principal white-goods competitor was Peg Profilo. Facing increasing competition, Peg Profilo had been sold to Bosch-Siemens of Germany in 1995. Peg Profilo sold its products under the Profilo and AEG brand names.[6] Imports of premium-priced Bosch and Siemens appliances began in 1996. Although penetration was limited to date, Arçelik managers noted heavy advertising behind the Bosch name, aimed at challenging Arçelik's dominance of the premium end of the white-goods market. Several Bosch shops were opened to supplement the existing network of Peg Profilo dealers. There was some evidence of strained relations, as Bosch-Siemens tried to impose formal contracts on dealers used to the handshake-style agreements of Peg Profilo.

Profilo's market shares in 1996 were 31% in refrigerators, 24% in washing machines, 23% in ovens, and 20% in dishwashers. Profilo capacity utilization was only 60%. Arçelik managers expected that Profilo would become more competitive in washing machines and dishwashers (in which the firm had not invested in new production technology) as a result of the acquisition. Units carrying the Profilo name could be imported from Bosch-Siemens' efficient German or low-cost Spanish plants. In addition, Profilo

refrigerators, which were more up-to-date, were expected to be exported through Bosch-Siemens' overseas network.

The number three competitor, Merloni, was a joint venture between the Italian consumer durables producer and Pekel, the Turkish white-goods company owned by Vestel, which was originally owned by Polly Peck International. Merloni had obtained majority control of the refrigerator factory in 1993. Arçelik managers believed that Merloni competed for market share with Peg Profilo's brand more than with the Arçelik and Beko brands.

Consumer Behavior

Relative to per capita income, the penetration of white goods in Turkish households was high. This was attributed to the desire of Turkish consumers to buy prestigious durables for their homes and to sustained marketing efforts on behalf of the Arçelik and Beko brands.

When buying a new or replacement appliance, 50% of consumers were believed to shop only one store; the remainder shopped around. Replacement purchasers were invariably triggered by the breakdown of an existing appliance and were therefore especially unlikely to shop around. High inflation also encouraged consumers to shorten their decision-making processes. In 1996, wage increases were outpacing inflation, so demand for white goods was especially strong.

A consumer's perceived risk and brand sensitivity varied according to the white goods being

---

[6]AEG was an Electrolux brand sold under license in Turkey by Peg Profilo. After the Bosch-Siemens acquisition, little effort was put into promoting the AEG brand.

purchased. As explained by Arçelik's marketing manager:

> *Refrigerators are nothing more than boxes, and consumers are familiar with them. There's little that can go wrong. Dishwashers, on the other hand, are more complex appliances, and first-time dishwasher purchasers are more risk-averse.*

ARÇELIK MARKETING IN TURKEY

Brand Building

Arçelik sold white goods under two brand names, Arçelik and Beko. A third brand, Aygaz, that Arçelik had inherited through the acquisition of an oven manufacturer, was discontinued in 1995 and its product line absorbed into the Beko brand family.

In 1996, there were 33 million Koç white-goods appliances in use in 13 million Turkish households. Arçelik was a trusted brand. However, some older consumers did not remember fondly the product quality of Arçelik' early appliances sold in the 1960s; to them, the quality of Turkish-made products was still doubtful. Though the product lines of both brands were similar, except for external design differences, Beko brand managers claimed their brand had a more "high tech" image that appealed to younger consumers. The strong penetration of Beko in brown goods (25% market share) was believed to reinforce this perception. Beko was also marketed in Turkey as a "world brand"; Beko retailers capitalized on the brand's penetration of export markets as a signal of quality to Turkish consumers.

In 1996, Arçelik and Beko advertising and promotion budgets accounted for 2% and 4%, respectively, of both brands' sales. Advertising included both television and print advertising. The print component included some cooperative advertising with the cost shared between Arçelik and its retailers on a 50/50 basis. Promotions included "trade-in" offers designed to accelerate consumers' repurchase cycles.

Pricing

Arçelik's product lines covered a full range of price points; the most expensive, fully featured item in a product line was typically double the price of the least expensive. With an inflation rate of 80% in 1996, Arçelik prices were increased that year by 9% every two months. Reductions in unit manufacturing costs, stemming from improved productivity and declines in world plastic and stainless steel prices, enabled Arçelik to take price increases below the rate of inflation. Doing so helped Arçelik retain market share.

Arçelik white goods were priced consistently nationwide. They were the highest priced among domestically manufactured white goods but retailed at prices lower than imported models. Exhibit 10 compares white-goods retail prices (including 23% value added tax) across a variety of brands.

As shown in Exhibit 11, Arçelik's average operating profit before interest and taxes was 13%. Arçelik's operating profit on exports was considerably lower. While registering strong profits on refrigerators, Arçelik unit margins on washing machines and dishwashers in 1996 were lower than competitors' margins, due to depreciation charges associated with Arçelik's heavy investments in plant modernization and the fact that several lines were still ramping up to efficient volumes of production.

Distribution and Sales

Ninety-five percent of white goods were sold to individual customers through retail stores; only 5% were sold by manufacturers directly to building contractors. Single-brand retailers accounted for 60% of retail unit sales of white goods in Turkey; the remaining 40% were sold through multibrand outlets. In addition to traditional appliance specialty stores, new channels such as Carrefour and Metro hypermarkets were opening in greater Istanbul. Selected Beko products (but no Arçelik products) were sold

Exhibit 10 *Comparative Index of Retail Prices for Turkish White Goods Brands: 1996**

Brand Name	Refrigerators	Washing Machines	Dishwashers	Ovens
Arçelik (Arçelik)	100	94	58	42
AEG (Peg)	91	89	64	38
Bosch (Peg)	112.5	102	87	—
Miele (import)	123	—	—	—
G.E. (import)	320	—	—	—
Westinghouse (import)	147.5	—	—	—
Electrolux (import)	116	127	90	—

*Source: Company records.

through these outlets. Around 28% of Turkish white goods were sold in Istanbul.

Arçelik delivered products to the Turkish market through exclusive retailers. There were 1,650 outlets carrying only the Arçelik brand, of

Exhibit 11 *Arçelik Cost and Price Structure in Turkey*

Cost Structure

Retail Selling Price[a]	125
Wholesale Price[b]	112
Advertising and Promotion	3
Selling and Distribution	5
Factory Price	100
Variable Costs	58
Direct Materials	51
Direct Labor	4
Variable Overhead	3
Research and Development	4
Depreciation	10
General and Administrative Expenses	15
Operating Profit (Before Interest and Taxes)	13

*Source: Company records.
[a]The price at which exclusive Arçelik retailers sold to the end consumer, excluding value-added tax. Retailers generally made 5–6% pretax profit.
[b]The price at which Atilim, Koç's captive marketing company, sold the product to the exclusive retail network in Turkey.

which 700 accounted for 70% of sales. Another 1,050 outlets carried only Beko products. Beko also reached consumers through a further 2,500 to 3,000 nonexclusive outlets, which accounted for 30% of Beko sales. Arçelik was not available in any multibrand outlets. Arçelik typically added 100 new outlets per year and discontinued 30. New outlets included existing multibrand appliance dealers who applied to become Arçelik dealers, stores established by the sons of existing Arçelik dealers, and stores started by sufficiently well-capitalized entrepreneurs. New outlets had to be established in new residential areas and in areas where appliance demand increased with disposable income. According to Arçelik's national sales manager:

Being the Arçelik dealer in a community is a much-sought-after position of importance. We have many applicants to choose from. Our dealers are loyal because our brand pull results in inventory turns three times faster than for our nearest competitor. As a result, our unit margins at retail can be narrower.

The product mix varied according to the size of each store and the demographics of the neighborhood in which it was located. An Arçelik store manager commented:

Consumer demand for appliances is strong. People are switching from semiautomatic to automatic washing machines. First-time pur-

chases of dishwashers are strong. Consumers living in apartments often have big families and need large refrigerators.

One hundred salespeople visited the Arçelik dealers, typically once every two weeks. Beko sold through 150 salespeople. Salesforce was a modest 5% per year.

A strong Arçelik retailer might carry $100,000 worth of inventory in the store and $500,000 in a warehouse, all on 100-day payment terms from the manufacturer. Typically, 15 sales would be made each day, including six washing machines, four refrigerators, and two dishwashers. An average dealer might make five sales per day and hold $50,000 in floor inventory.

Ninety percent of Arçelik white goods were sold to consumers on credit installment plans of between 3 and 15 months. In addition to factory-sourced finance, a newly established Koç finance company also offered credit, often at interest rates slightly below the rate of inflation.[7] Each Arçelik dealer was liable for payment on the units sold on installment. The bad-debt rate was less than 1%. Arçelik's competitors, such as Bosch, were obliged to offer the same terms. Carrefour stores in the major cities could only offer their customers bank credit at rates significantly higher than Arçelik.

Service

With the average white goods appliance in use for twelve years, the quality and availability of after-sales service was important to Turkish consumers in influencing other brand purchase decisions. Service for Arçelik and Beko white goods was provided by 500 authorized dealers who serviced only these two brands. Another 450 dealers serviced the brown goods of the two brands. There was not joint ownership of sales outlets and service dealers, though informal ties were common. Forty percent of service dealer revenues was generated by installations of newly purchased appliances; delivery and installment costs were included in the retail prices. The service organization was especially challenged when there was a surge in consumer sales, as in 1996.

INTERNATIONAL EXPANSION

Opportunistic exports of Arçelik white goods began in the 1980s through Koç Holding's export company, principally to the geographically neighboring markets of the Middle East and North Africa. Arçelik models did not have to be adapted to local requirements. In 1983, an export department was established within Arçelik. One of its tasks was to develop bid proposals on foreign government tenders and for foreign contract builders of low-income housing. In 1988, Arçelik's export department contracted to supply refrigerators on an OEM basis to Sears Roebuck for distribution in the Caribbean and Latin America under the Kenmore name. Though Arçelik's exports were a modest percentage of total sales during the 1980s, Arçelik was the largest exporter among Koç Holding companies.

In 1988, the Turkish government's tariff reduction agreement with the European Community prompted an increased interest in exports. Mr. Berkman explained:

We needed to find out more about our likely future competitors. One way to do so was to sell Arçelik products in the tough developed markets. The Americas were too far away, in terms of both transportation costs, product adaptation requirements (for 110 volt current), and our ability to understand consumers. Western Europe was much closer. We thought we would learn a great deal by competing against the best in the world on their home turf and better prepare ourselves to defend our domestic market share against the likes of Bosch and Siemens.

---

[7]Securitizing receivables and installment loans through Koç Finans reduced Arçelik's working capital needs and, therefore, its average cost of capital.

As of 1996, almost half of the 990,000 Arçelik and Beko refrigerators produced were exported. In that year, 7.6% of Arçelik's total sales (by value) were exports, up from 2.4% in 1991. A breakdown of exports by destination is presented in Table A. Arçelik exported to the countries listed in Exhibit 12, which reports 1996 unit sales of refrigerators and washing machines by market. Arçelik's most successful European market was the United Kingdom, where it had achieved 8% market penetration. In the Middle East and North Africa, Arçelik had achieved almost 20% market share in Tunisia. The firm held between 1% and 4% market share in most of the other product markets listed in Exhibit 12.

Table A Value of Arçelik Exports, by Destination: 1996

Destination	Percentage
United Kingdom	28%
France	18%
Other European Union	14%
North Africa	17%
Eastern Europe and central Asia	6%
Other	17%

In 1996, Arçelik exports of white goods were principally refrigerators and washing machines, as shown in Table B. Technology licensing agreements precluded exports of most dishwashers. In 1996, Arçelik's refrigerator plants were operating at full capacity. By 1998, an ex-

Table B Arçelik White-Goods Exports and Mix: 1996

	Export Units	% Beko	% OEM
Refrigerators	430,000	70	30
Washing machines	55,000	50	50

tra 350,000 units of capacity was expected to come on stream. Management expected to double exports of washing machines in 1997 without any addition of capacity. Dishwasher exports were expected to increase to 110,000 units in 1997, when Arçelik was to supply the first of five annual installments of at least 100,000 OEM units to Whirlpool for distribution in Europe. This was the first time Arçelik had agreed to an OEM contract with a global competitor; Arçelik was not permitted to sell similar models in Europe under its own brand names.

Arçelik in Western Europe

Starting in 1989, Arçelik opened sales offices in the U.K., then France, then Germany, reasoning that, in these larger European markets, there might be more opportunities for a new brand to establish a sufficient volume of sales to be viable. At the same time, the export effort to other markets continued. In all export markets, Arçelik focused on building the Beko name (since it was easier to pronounce than Arçelik in a wide variety of languages).

United Kingdom

A sales office was established in the U.K. in 1989. The U.K. market was selected for this initial effort because it was price sensitive and not dominated by domestic brands. By 1997, there were 1 million Beko appliances in use in the U.K., two-thirds of which were refrigerators and one-third televisions. Sales of 300,000 Beko refrigerators were expected in 1997, of which two-thirds would be tabletop-height refrigerators and one third full-size refrigerators.[8]

In addition to refrigerators, Beko was beginning to sell dishwashers, washing machines, and

[8]In contrast, the market as a whole comprised 60% full-size refrigerators and 40% tabletop-height refrigerators.

Exhibit 12 *Total Refrigerator and Washing Machine Unit Sales in Arçelik Export Markets: 1996**

	Refrigerators (1996 Unit Sales)	Automatic Washing Machines (1996 Unit Sales)
European Community (EC)		
France	2,500,000	1,600,000
Germany	3,600,000	2,600,000
United Kingdom	2,500,000	1,400,000
Benelux	1,200,000	600,000
Denmark	200,000	130,000
Spain/Portugal	2,000,000	1,300,000
Greece	NA	NA
Middle East and North Africa (MENA)		
Egypt	500,000	250,000
Lebanon	100,000	40,000
Syria	200,000	100,000
Iraq	400,000	200,000
Iran	1,000,000	250,000
Tunisia	120,000	25,000
Algeria	250,000	30,000
Morocco	110,000	20,000
Eastern and Central Europe, and Central Asia		
Albania	NA	NA
Romania	300,000	150,000
Bulgaria	130,000	70,000
Russia	2,200,000	600,000
Malta	NA	NA
Turkmenistan	100,000	15,000
Uzbekistan	100,000	15,000
Kazakstan	100,000	15,000
Azerbaijan	NA	NA
Ukraine	300,000	50,000

*Source: Company records.

ovens. Management had focused from the outset on building the Beko brand; only 10,000 of the units sold in 1996 were marketed on an OEM basis.

Melvyn Goodship, managing director, explained Beko's success in the U.K.:

We exploited an underserved niche for table-top refrigerators. Our factories in Turkey had spare capacity in the early nineties, so could promptly fill our orders and deliver consistent product quality. At first, we were accused of dumping, but lower-priced brands from Eastern and Central European countries are now criticized for that. Through patience and persistence, we have built our brand reputation and distribution.

By 1996, Beko had penetrated the three principal specialty appliance chains in the U.K.—Curry's, Comet, and Iceland. Beko appliances were also sold through the principal mail order catalogs—Empire and Littlewoods. Management believed Beko appliances were available through 65% of selling points in the U.K. Beko maintained a warehouse in the U.K. to serve its retail accounts.

In 1996, the Beko brand was supported by £600,000 of advertising, including £100,000 to launch Beko washing machines and £150,000 of cooperative advertising.[9]

The retail price of a typical Beko tabletop refrigerator was £150, including 17.5% value added tax and a 25% distribution margin. Comparable refrigerators of other brands would retail at £300 for Bosch, £200 for Hotpoint (the U.K. market share leader),and £160 for Indesit (an Italian manufacturer). Cheap brands of inconsistent quality from eastern and central European countries could be found for £120. Manufacturer prices of branded products were so competitive that large retailers saw no need to assume the inventory risk of contracting for OEM production.

France

Arçelik opened a French sales office in 1993. By 1996, annual sales were up to 75,000 units. However, according to the French sales manager:

The French market is in a recession and is cluttered with competitors. It is hard for us to break into new accounts. Nineteen ninety-seven will be a crucial year.

The French white-goods market was highly competitive. Fifteen trade accounts controlled 75% of consumer sales. Thirty percent of white goods unit sales carried store brand names. Appliance specialty stores accounted for 45% of unit sales, hypermarkets for 30%, and mail order companies and department stores for 25%. There were no dominant national brands. The long-standing French brands, Thomson and Brandt, each accounting for 20% of unit sales were, by 1997, owned by Italian manufacturers.

Arçelik pursued a two-brand strategy in France. Management believed that if the Beko brand was launched at a low price, it would be impossible to raise it later. The Beko brand was therefore positioned and priced similarly to the mainstream Candy brand from Italy. The Beko brand accounted for 25% of the company's unit sales in France in 1996. Other Koç or OEM brands were priced lower than Beko to attract volume orders.

Of 75,000 units sold in France in 1996, 68,000 were refrigerators and 7,000 were washing machines and ovens. Of the 75,000, 15% were sold to kitchenette manufacturers and 15% were sold on an OEM basis to Frigidaire. Seventy percent of the remaining units were shipped to hypermarkets, notably LeClerc (the third largest hypermarket chain in France), and 30% to appliance specialty stores. The French sales office had not yet been able to break into any department stores or mail order accounts. A two-year test, involving telemarketing Beko white goods to retailers was currently underway. The only advertising for Beko in France appeared in the LeClerc catalog.

Germany

Arçelik opened a German sales office within an existing company called Interbrucke GmbH in 1994 under a general manager who had previously been an importer of Beko televisions.

---

[9]In 1996, one U.S. dollar was equivalent to 80,000 Turkish lira (June, 1996); one British pound was equivalent to $ U.S. 1.60; and one German mark was equivalent to $ U.S. 0.65.

Well-known, premium-priced German brands such as Bosch, Siemens, AEG, and Miele held a 60% unit market share of white goods. The remaining 40% was divided among numerous lower-priced Italian and East European manufacturers, none of whom held more than a 4% share.

About 60% of white goods were sold through traditional appliance retailers, almost all of whom were members of retail-buying groups or served through regional wholesalers. Twenty percent of white goods were sold through mail order firms like Quelle, usually at prices below those in the specialty retailers. Of the remaining units, 10% were sold through mass merchandisers, 5% through hypermarkets, and 5% through traditional department stores.

In 1966, Beko sold 30,000 refrigerators in Germany, up from 10,000 in 1995, and 20,000 washing machines, up from 5,000 in the preceding year. Unit sales of refrigerators and washing machines in Germany in 1996 were 3,600,000 and 2,600,000, respectively. Management predicted sales of 70,000 and 30,000 for the two Beko lines in 1997. To date, 80% of Beko sales had been made to retail-buying groups and regional wholesalers; the remaining 20% had been made in the manufacturers of prepackaged kitchenettes which were sold to home builders. By the end of 1996, Beko white goods were being bought by 12 accounts, in all cases on an OEM basis.

Beko white goods were imported from Turkey and stored in a rented warehouse in Germany. The average retail price of a Beko refrigerator was DM 399. Comparable Bosch and Siemens refrigerators sold for DM 499 to DM 599.

Beko had no resources for a consumer advertising campaign, though some funds were available to buy advertising space in retailer catalogs.

The general manager commented on Beko's prospects in Germany as follows:

The Germany economy is weak right now and population growth is flat. Demand for appliances is soft but fairly predictable. Consumers and, therefore, distributors are more price sensitive, especially in the former East Germany. This plays to our strength as a value brand. More retailers than ever before are scrambling to sell appliances, so that's putting further pressure on margins.

In this price-sensitive climate, I believe Beko's prospects are good. Germany is Turkey's largest trading partner. The challenge is to develop relationships with the big customers and persuade them to switch to Beko. If we can build unit volume by supplying OEM (or private label) product to these customers, we may be able to make enough money to invest in building the Beko brand.

Assessing Progress

Progress in Western Europe was slower than some executives expected, leading them to question the strategy. A senior manager at headquarters in Istanbul commented:

We should not focus on breaking into Western Europe where growth is limited and where five companies control 75% of unit sales of white goods. Instead, we should focus on the emerging markets of Russia and Central Asia, where foreign brand names are not yet entrenched on consumers' minds. We are geographically well positioned to supply these markets. The fact that our products are made in Turkey will be a plus in those markets whereas, in Western Europe, we have to avoid mentioning it.

However, others supported the emphasis on Western Europe:

The former Communist markets of East and Central Europe will be important, but right now they are too volatile. Tariff rates change overnight and we have no tariff advantage over Japanese and Korean competitors in these markets like we do in Western Europe. We would have to make risky investments in local manufacturing and distribution; finding the right local partners and sufficiently skilled workers would be difficult. I would rather focus on Western Europe for the moment. The markets are tough to crack, and our unit margins are lower than in Turkey but at least our goods enter duty-free and demand is predictable.

CONCLUSION

In between hosting visitors to their Domotechnica booth in Cologne, Arçelik's managers continued to discuss informally whether or not they were placing the correct emphasis on international markets and whether their brand-building and market selection strategies were appropriate. Some of the comments at the booth included:

In 1996, we showed we could hold our own in the Turkish market against the top brands in the world. In fact, our market share in refrigerators actually increased. This means we can now push our international exports more aggressively.

Wait a minute. Capacity is tight. If the Turkish market continues to grow at the current rate, we'll need most of our planned capacity for 1997 to meet domestic demand. And we know that we make at least twice as much unit margin if we sell an appliance in Turkey than if we export it.

The current rate of economic growth is not sustainable. The government, in anticipation of a general election, is pumping money into the economy. The economy will probably slow down, maybe even go into recession in 1997. I don't think we'll have a capacity problem.

We've got to emphasize building the Beko brand worldwide. We'll never make big money on OEM business, whether we are making to order for other manufacturers—who are, in fact, our competitors—or for retail chains. Special orders add to complexity costs in our plants and we lose our R&D edge when we simply follow the customers' blueprints. Occasionally, you can build up a long-term relationship with an OEM customer through consistent, on-time deliveries but, more often than not, OEM orders are one-shot deals through which the customer is trying to exert leverage on his or her other suppliers or cover against a strike threat.

I'm not so sure. Selling OEM production is more profitable than selling the equivalent number of Beko branded units. Marketing costs per unit are lower and we don't have to invest in pull advertising support through our national distributors.

You don't understand. We're making products of outstanding quality these days. Because Turkey's reputation for quality manufactures is not well established, we've had to work doubly hard to achieve recognition. We shouldn't be wasting any more time doing OEM production of lower-priced, simple models when we have the quality to take on the best in the world at the premium end of the white-goods market.

HARLEQUIN ROMANCES—POLAND

Nina Kowalewska, managing director of Arlekin Wydawnictwo (Arlekin), the wholly owned Polish subsidiary of Harlequin Enterprises Ltd., sat at her Warsaw office in September 1992, reviewing the first year of operations. She was preparing for a meeting at Harlequin's European headquarters with Heinz Wermelinger, international executive vice-president, and with Coen Abbenhuis and Ernst Boesch, regional directors for Europe. At the meeting, she intended to present a 1993 marketing plan and pro-forma income statement for Arlekin.

Harlequin Enterprises published romance fiction novels targeted at women. The novels were love stories in a wide variety of "girl-meets-boy" settings that aimed to offer women escape and entertainment. Launched in Poland in October 1991, Harlequin novels had, in just six months, captured 90% of the Polish romance series market and achieved market penetration levels comparable to those in North America. Kowalewska had played a key role in building Harlequin's popularity in Poland and now had to determine how best to maintain and further develop this success.

COMPANY BACKGROUND

Founded in 1949, Harlequin Enterprises Limited had evolved from a small Canadian printing house into the largest romance fiction publisher in the world. In 1991, Harlequin sold 193 million books on six continents in 20 languages. Harlequin held a 13% share of U.S. mass-market paperback sales and an even higher share in overseas markets. Harlequin had introduced and developed the mass-market romance series concept and pioneered the use of packaged consumer goods marketing techniques, including branding, in bookselling. (Exhibit 1 summarizes key events in the company's development.)

The acquisition of the British publisher, Mills & Boon, in 1971 spurred Harlequin's international expansion. By 1991, 56% of unit sales came from outside North America, of which 86% came from Western Europe. The pace of Harlequin's new product launches had increased from eight new titles published each month in 1970 to 67 new titles each month in 1991. These new titles were published under 12 differ-

---

This case was prepared by Nathalie Laidler (under the direction of John A. Quelch). Proprietary data have been disguised. Copyright © 1993 by the President and Fellows of Harvard College. Harvard Business School case 594-017.

Exhibit 1   *Key Events in the Historical Development of Harlequin Enterprises Limited*

1949   Harlequin, a Canadian company, starts printing a wide variety of American and British books, ranging from mysteries and westerns to classics and cookbooks, written by authors such as Agatha Christie and Edgar Wallace.

1957   Harlequin begins buying the rights to romance novels from an English firm, Mills and Boon, the largest romance fiction publisher in the English-speaking world.

1964   Mills and Boon romances dominate Harlequin's product line.

1968   Harlequin issues a public stock offering in Canada.

1971   Harlequin purchases Mills and Boon and starts expanding internationally.

1972   Overseas acquisitions, partnerships, English-language export editions, and foreign licensee deals enhance Harlequin's international presence.

1973   Harlequin launches its North American direct mail operation, later expanded into the U.K., Australia, the Netherlands, France, and Scandinavia.

1981   Harlequin is purchased by Torstar Corporation, a large Canadian communications company.

1984   Harlequin purchases one of its major competitors, Silhouette, owned by Simon and Schuster.

1989   Harlequin celebrates its 40th anniversary by launching a novel in 18 languages in 100 countries on the same day.

---

ent series umbrellas, each with a distinct positioning and target audience.

Harlequin's parent company, Torstar Corporation, a large Canadian communications company with operating revenues of C $ 895 million[1] in 1991, had experienced both revenue and profit declines since 1989. In 1991, Harlequin Enterprises Limited represented 40% of Torstar's revenues and 58% of its profits, with international sales, particularly in Japan, Australia, and Eastern Europe, fueling revenue and profit growth.

INDUSTRY CHARACTERISTICS AND PRODUCT LINE

The U.S. Book Publishing Industry

Although 60% of the 91 million U.S. households did not buy a single book in 1991, an estimated two billion books were purchased by the other 40%; 62% of these were adult books, of which 66% were popular fiction books.[2] Mass-market paperback books accounted for 63% of all adult books sold, and romance novels accounted for 46% of mass-market paperback sales. Bookstores accounted for 29.5% of romance novel sales, grocery and food stores for 23%, discount stores for 19%, drug stores for 11.5%, and department stores and direct mail for 8.5% each. Retail spending on romance novels in 1991 totaled $700 million, 27% more than in 1990, and was expected to increase by 37% in 1992. Although romance novels were often purchased on impulse, some devoted ro-

---

[1]C $1.14 = U.S. $1.

[2]Some of the material in this section is adapted from the 1990/1991 Consumer Research Report on Book Purchasing prepared by the NPD Group, Inc., for the American Booksellers Association, the Association of American Publishers, and the Book Industry Study Group, Inc.

mance novel customers at Barnes and Noble (a large U.S. bookstore chain) were estimated to have spent $1,200 each on romance novels in 1991. For many publishers, the resilience of the romance segment provided much-needed cash during the 1991 recession.

Most publishers promoted books individually. Sales were hard to predict and returns to publishers of unsold books were permitted. While Harlequin had to compete with all mass-market paperback publishers, two forms of sales and marketing existed in the romance novel market: publishing of individual "best-seller" romances, where success was dependent on the output and reputation of a particular author; and publishing and marketing series of romance novels, as Harlequin did. Competitors included Zebra Books, Avon, Dell, and Berkley, which published both series and single titles, and combined, held a 20% share of the U.S. romance series market. Between 1990 and 1992, romance series sales stabilized while single-title, best-seller romances, such as novels by Danielle Steele, gained ground. Many U.S. publishers believed that this trend in favor of single titles that emphasized the author's name rather than the brand name of the publisher would continue.

Product Line

In 1991, Harlequin was one of the world's foremost publishers of paperback novels; 800 new titles were released and more than 6,600 foreign editions were published. The company attributed its success to its focus on romance fiction and the application of consumer packaged goods marketing principles to publishing. Marketing emphasized the Harlequin, Mills & Boon, or Silhouette brand names rather than each individual author or book title. By standardizing production and distribution methods across all titles, Harlequin achieved economies that translated into lower retail prices. Most titles retailed at U.S. $2.95. In 1992, a Harlequin book was cheaper than many women's magazines.

Harlequin sold only paperbacks and published its books in 12 different series. Every month, each series published between two and eight new titles. The consumer could identify with the heroine, meet the hero of her dreams, travel the world, and revel in romance, all in two to four hours. Plots allowed many twists and surprises, but a satisfying ending was assured. In North America, eight series were published under the Harlequin brand: Superromance, American Romance, Temptation, Intrigue, Historicals, Regency, Romance, and Presents. Four series were published under the Silhouette brand:[3] Romance, Desire, Intimate Moments, and Special Editions. Harlequin U.K. published three series under the Mills & Boon brand: Romance, Doctor/Nurse, and Masquerade/Historical. In addition to romances, Harlequin also offered an action/adventure series, targeted at male consumers, and a mystery series, targeted at women who enjoyed clue/detective-oriented mysteries.

Each romance series targeted a specific type of reader. For example, Harlequin Temptation, a more sensual line, was aimed at younger women. Books within each series were all similar in appearance. For instance, Harlequin Presents books were classical romance stories that all had the same white cover, prominent logo and cover design with a circular inset. (Exhibit 2 illustrates some of Harlequin's North American book covers.) Regular monthly titles were complemented by special seasonal collections (for example, Christmas, Valentine, and Mother's Day editions), in-line promotions, and single titles.

Harlequin editors played an important role in segmenting the romance fiction market by differentiating each series according to length, level of sensuality, degree of realism, and setting. Editorial offices in London, New York, and Toronto worked with more than 1,200 established au-

[3]Harlequin had purchased Silhouette, its major North American competitor, in 1984.

Exhibit 2   *Examples of Harlequin and Silhouette North American book covers*

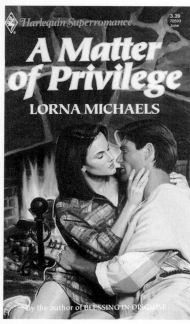

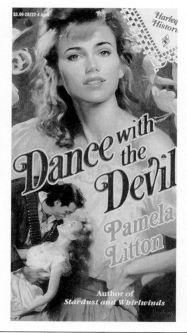

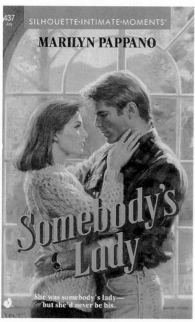

thors and, in addition, screened 14,000 unsolicited manuscripts received every year, about 30 of which were accepted for publication.

A new Harlequin book had a shelf life similar to a magazine. It might receive one month's shelf exposure before having to make room for one of the following month's releases. Unsold copies were returned by retailers. Harlequin return rates worldwide averaged 35% a month. While some returns were resold, most were shredded and destroyed. Returns were "a necessary evil"; a lower return rate would mean many retail outlets stocking a book would run out of it, resulting in lost sales for Harlequin.

Consumers

Harlequin defined its target segment as all women over the age of 15 years. In North America, this represented a market of 105 million consumers. In 1991, 11 million women in North America bought at least one Harlequin and/or Silhouette novel. A 1989 study found that 56% of women had purchased a paperback book in the previous three months, 27% had purchased a romance novel, 13% had purchased a Harlequin, and 9% had purchased a Silhouette. In a similar 1985 study, the corresponding figures were 60%, 28%, 13%, and 10%. (Exhibit 3 reports other findings of this study.) Respondents to the 1989 survey were found to be reading less than in 1985, but a higher proportion of them were reading romance fiction.

The average romance novel reader was aged 39 years, with a household income of $40,000. Forty-five percent were college graduates, and over 50% worked outside the home. Harlequin and Silhouette readers stated that relaxation, entertainment, and escape were the main reasons for purchase. Research indicated that women, many of whom worked both inside and outside the home, had less leisure time and that the "escape" offered by romance novels helped counteract the pressures they felt.

HARLEQUIN'S NORTH AMERICAN MARKETING PROGRAM

Distribution

Harlequin novels were sold in over 100,000 retail outlets in the United States and 10,000 outlets in Canada. Harlequin maintained its own sales force in Canada and was represented by Simon & Schuster Consumer Group in the United States. Harlequin placed wholesalers (accounting for approximately two-thirds of sales) and direct retail accounts on a monthly standing order system, whereby they received previously agreed-upon volumes of the 12 series each month. This reduced the need for the continuous selling of single titles.

The distribution process was constantly streamlined. Books were shrink-wrapped in various combinations of pre-packs, with dates on front covers to help consumers and retailers identify new titles at a glance. Books also carried bar codes that enabled books to be scanned at the point-of-sale for specific title and price information. In the 1970s, Harlequin North America began distributing its books through food, drug, and discount stores. By 1991, these channels accounted for the majority of Harlequin's retail sales, as they did for mass-market paperbacks in general.

Harlequin operated a direct mail system, distributing titles under the Harlequin, Silhouette, Worldwide Mystery, and Gold Eagle names. It provided advance home delivery sales of new titles to an estimated 250,000 readers. Harlequin executives believed that, as consumers became more familiar with the Harlequin product line, they tended to settle on one or two specific series, and the added convenience of receiving books by mail became increasingly attractive.

Advertising and Promotion

Harlequin enjoyed high name recognition and a consistent image. However, in 1989, unaided brand awareness for Harlequin in the United

---

Exhibit 3   *Major Findings of 1989 Usage and Attitude Study in North America**

- In 1989, 69% of women had read a paperback in the preceding year compared with 73% in 1985. Of these readers, 58% in 1989 reported having read a romance paperback compared to 56% in 1985.
- The Harlequin brand had a 77% aided brand awareness in 1989 compared to a 90% aided brand awareness in 1985. Silhouette aided brand awareness was 45% in 1989 and 56% in 1985. Corresponding unaided brand awareness figures were 27% in 1989 and 35% in 1985 for Harlequin and 5% in 1989 and 9% in 1985 for Silhouette.
- In 1989, 64% of respondents had read at least one Harlequin novel and 31% had read at least one Silhouette novel.
- Among women who read Harlequin and Silhouette books, 85% and 79%, respectively, had been reading them for over two years.
- Among women who had purchased a romance novel in the previous three months, 28% had purchased from bookstores, 27% from grocery and food stores, 22% from discount and general merchandise stores, 15% from drug stores, 12% from department stores, and 12% through direct mail. For purchasers of Harlequin and Silhouette books, the channel mix was slightly different: 31% had purchased them from grocery and food stores, 26% from bookstores, 19% from discount and general merchandise stores, 19% from drug stores, and 15% through direct mail.
- Among Harlequin purchasers, 37% bought "what looked interesting, regardless of series or publisher," 21% planned the purchase as part of the weekly shopping trip, and 20% bought a Harlequin because the product "caught my eye."
- Women read Harlequin and Silhouette novels for the following reasons, in order of importance: good, relaxing read; good entertainment value; "leaves you feeling happy and uplifted"; exciting to read; for escape reading; "for someone like me."
- Harlequin readers spent relatively more time than nonreaders reading books in general, browsing in shopping malls, and watching videos and television movies, and relatively less time participating in active sports, attending plays and cultural events.

---

*Source: Company records. Note: The 1989 survey was based on telephone interviews with 1,500 women aged over 15 years.

States was 77%, down from 90% in 1985. Harlequin in North America planned a major advertising campaign to combat the decline in awareness.

In 1991, Harlequin spent U.S. $8 million on advertising and promotion in North America. Harlequin's campaigns promoted an entire line rather than a single title. In 1991, Harlequin focused its marketing budget on print advertising, consumer promotions, retail displays, and point-of-sale merchandising materials.

In 1975, Harlequin became the first publisher to use television advertising in North America. In 1991, television and radio advertising were not used, but extensive women's press advertising was employed to build awareness and encourage trial. (Exhibit 4 shows a two-page Harlequin advertisement from *People* magazine in 1992.) In addition, trade-press advertising was used to keep booksellers up to date on new titles and series.

Consumer promotions focused on sampling nonreaders. Sixteen-page samplers were inserted in women's magazines and complemented by money-off coupons. Best-selling authors held media tours and autographing events, and the

Exhibit 4   *Two-page North American Harlequin Print Advertisement from People Magazine, 1992*

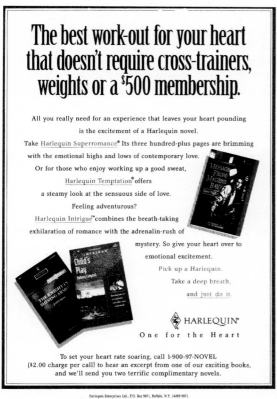

most dedicated readers were thanked for their support at lavish parties. Sales promotions, used to increase awareness and trial of Harlequin books, included (1) in-book and in-store promotions that encouraged cross-series sampling by offering gifts in return for multiple proofs-of-purchase; (2) in-line promotions with miniseries featuring special themes[4]; and (3) joint promotions with other firms selling perfume, cosmetics, lingerie, and confectionery. In 1991, a consumer sweepstakes under the banner "Fashion: A Whole New You" offered prizes such as cars, trips, and fashion wardrobes. In addition, consumer competitions with books as prizes often ran in local media.

Harlequin offered retailers display racks to accompany standing orders. These ranged from spinners,[5] wire racks, and wooden shelf systems

---

[4]In 1992, for example, a 12-title series was launched in the European Community, with one title set in each member country.

---

[5]Spinners were stand-alone rotating display racks.

to cardboard bins in which promotional titles were displayed. Colorful shelf stickers and window posters were also distributed to retailers. Trade promotions were usually linked to consumer promotions and often included prize drawings for store personnel.

Challenges

In North America, Harlequin faced several challenges in 1992. Unit sales of best-sellers were growing faster than expected, eroding Harlequin's share of the mass-market paperback category. Price increases to offset cost increases could protect profit margins, but at the expense of demand. Management was concerned that Harlequin's image among consumers and retailers as the clear innovator in the series romance subcategory might be eroding. In response, Harlequin planned several new product launches along with changes in advertising and packaging.

INTERNATIONAL OPERATIONS

In 1991, Harlequin's international sales outside North America, including sales by licensees, exceeded 108 million units and generated net revenues of U.S. $140 million. Overseas operations consisted of wholly owned subsidiaries in the United Kingdom, Australia and the Far East, Holland, Scandinavia, Japan, Spain, and Poland; joint ventures in Germany, France, Greece, Italy, and Hungary; and licensing of local publishers to publish in their native languages, in return for royalty payments, in Denmark, Iceland, South America, and Korea. Harlequin subsidiaries and joint ventures were delineated primarily on a linguistic rather than geographical basis. For example, Axel Springer, Harlequin's German joint-venture partner, had the rights to sell to the German-speaking populations of Switzerland and Austria as well as in Germany.

Once a book had been published in the U.K. or North America, it became available to the entire Harlequin network. Finished books were distrib-uted to overseas editors who chose which titles to reprint, often combining editorial products from two or more series to create ideal blends for their particular markets. Their selections were then locally translated, edited, and printed. Cover illustrations were commissioned in Toronto and London for all titles and held on file at Harlequin's European headquarters for local editors to access as needed. Series names were decided locally, and editors either borrowed from existing series or created entirely new titles to suit their local markets. For example, the Mills & Boon Romance series was known in different countries as Sabrina, Julia, Romantikkaa, Azur, Jazmin, Bianca, and Safir. Most overseas operations released a given month's title between eight months and a year after North America or the United Kingdom. To illustrate the level of local adaptation, Exhibit 5 shows the North American, Polish, and Hungarian front covers of the same title.

Eastern Europe

In 1990, Harlequin's European Headquarters were established in Baar, Switzerland, by Heinz Wermelinger, who had previously managed European operations from Toronto, Canada. The need for a European office was fueled by flattening demand in Western Europe, management's interest in adding better direct-mail operations, and the opening of the Eastern European economies, which greatly expanded the potential market for Harlequin novels. Harlequin was flooded by requests for licenses and joint ventures from publishers and private entrepreneurs in Eastern and Central Europe.

Within four months of the fall of the Berlin Wall in October, 1989, Harlequin books, under the brand name *Cora,* were for sale on newsstands throughout the former East Germany. Harlequin's German joint-venture partner, Axel Springer, simply increased production runs to meet the new demand from the former East Germany. In April 1990, a Hungarian licensee launched Harlequin and, by September 1992,

Exhibit 5   *Book Covers of a Single Title Published in North America, Poland, and Hungary*

Harlequin was firmly established in both Hungary and Poland, with plans to launch in Czechoslovakia and Bulgaria later that year. Harlequin executives estimated that in 1995, they would sell 35 million books in Eastern Europe.

Decision making was shared between the local managing directors of these country subsidiaries and the Baar executives. The local knowledge and contacts of the former combined with the operational, technical, and historical experience of the latter, made these working relationships particularly effective. Back-room operations, including standardized financial control systems, were run from Baar, which also shared experience, information, and ideas among subsidiaries.

Hungary

After initially licensing a local entrepreneur, Harlequin established a joint venture in Hungary in July, 1991 to further penetrate the market. Harlequin expanded elsewhere in Eastern Europe through wholly owned subsidiaries.

In 1992, Hungary had a population of 11 million, a gross domestic product (GDP) per capita of $4,186, and an inflation rate of 25%. A Harlequin novel retailed for $0.85. Although Harlequin dominated the romance series market in September 1992, new competitors continued to appear. Cumulative sales had reached 8 million books by September 1992, with six titles issued per month and average book returns of 25%.

Distribution of Harlequin books in Hungary was carried out by the post office. Three thousand of the country's kiosks, the traditional retail outlets for newspapers and magazines, were privatized in 1992, while 6,000 remained under post office control. To use post office distribution, the Harlequin product had to be 8 inches by 5.8 inches in size—larger than a standard paperback and more like a magazine. This magazine format precluded Harlequin novels from being distributed in bookstores. Harlequin executives wanted to convert the product line to a standard paperback format, but this might jeopardize post office distribution.

Despite frequent television commercials that explained the product and informed viewers of new titles, brand awareness remained modest. However, *Julia*, the main series name, had unaided brand awareness of 75% among adult women. The Harlequin brand name was placed on book covers after July 1992.

Harlequin executives believed that further growth depended on more intensive distribution. Two supermarket chains, with 830 stores, could be supplied by the current post office distribution system. The challenge was to convince them to stock the Harlequin line.

POLAND

Country Background

In 1992, Poland had a GDP per capita of U.S. $2,945 and an inflation rate of 45%. The population was 38 million, of whom 55% were women and 62% lived in urban areas.

Prior to 1989, Poland had suffered from persistent shortages of goods. A centrally planned economy, accompanied by price controls and limited hard currency convertibility, resulted in a market where goods were affordable but in short supply. As a result, even goods of inferior quality could find a market. In 1989, dramatic economic reforms, including the elimination of price controls, reductions in state subsidies, and free convertibility of the Polish zloty,[6] were implemented to stimulate the private sector. The country began moving rapidly toward a market economy, and a large market for foreign goods opened up. However, the transition was painful and characterized by high inflation, lack of financial resources, frustration and a black-market mentality. A common complaint was: "Before, there was nothing to buy. Now you can buy anything, but nobody has the money to do so."

---

[6]In September, 1992, U.S. $1 = 13,800 zlotys.

The Book Industry

Prior to 1989, under the Communist regime, all production and distribution of printed matter in Poland was centrally controlled. Every stage of book publishing and retailing was managed by a state monopoly. All 60 publishing houses, printing plants, and distributors were subsidized by the state, and only one advertising agency, also state-owned, existed.

Poland was a country with a strong literary tradition. However, censorship meant most people read "safe," classical literature. For 40 years, no new romance novels had been published legally in Poland. Due to subsidies, books were cheap and public libraries were supplied free-of-charge by all publishers. Authorized publishers (as opposed to black-market operators) would send their print runs to Skladnica Ksiegarska, the state-controlled book distributor, which would, in turn, sell the books to 18 wholesalers, who supplied all retail bookstores. However, by 1992, two of every five books published in Poland were shipped directly from publisher to retailer. Dozens of sidewalk vendors emerged as a growing retail channel, particularly for best-sellers. As the industry fragmented, distribution became a key challenge; publishers had to somehow inform the myriad of wholesalers and retailers about the publication and availability of each new title.

Economic restructuring in Poland impacted the book industry. Between 1989 and 1992, average book prices increased three to five times. With monthly interest rates of 12% in mid-1992, booksellers wanted to stock only books that sold out quickly. One result was an increase in the distribution of pornography and scandal stories at the expense of serious literature. As one industry expert said: "Poland no longer has money for culture." The demise of Communism created a strong demand for new books from the West, especially political fiction novels, followed by suspense novels, romances, and general-interest titles such as cookery books. For some Poles, Western novels held an appeal for

that reason alone. However, Polish intellectuals dismissed many of these books as "Western trash." In addition, many Polish consumers associated reading with learning and perceived popular literature as a waste of time. "We still have to convince people that reading can be fun," stated Arlekin's editor-in-chief. "Reading is increasingly competing with watching videos and cable television."

Consumers

In 1992, there were 15 million women in Poland over the age of 15 years; 8.4% of them had college degrees, and a majority of the rest had completed high school. Eighty-five percent of adult Polish women worked outside the home and were responsible for a second source of household income as well as for household management. Given an average salary in mid-1992 of only 2.7 million zlotys a month, few women could afford modern household appliances to help them with their chores. At the same time, benefits such as day care and maternity leave had declined since the fall of Communism.

HARLEQUIN IN POLAND

In preparing to enter the Polish market, Harlequin Baar executives sought to appoint a strong local manager who could develop a team that would work in tandem with the European headquarters. Kowalewska was appointed managing director of Arlekin in August 1991. Previously, she had managed distribution of *The Financial Times* in Poland. Kowalewska then chose her own team of four editors and operating staff.

By September 1992, Arlekin was the largest foreign publishing company in Poland. Arlekin's cumulative sales in Poland had exceeded 10 million units, and 168 titles had been released. (Average monthly sales by product line are reported in Exhibit 6.) Kowalewska attributed Arlekin's success in part to a common message in every novel: "The heroines are always active women who succeed and win. They offer positive role

Exhibit 6   *Arlekin Average Monthly Unit Sales: January–August 1992**

Product Line	Average Monthly Gross Unit Sales
Romance	550,000
Desire	400,000
Temptation	95,000
Superromance	75,000
Valentine special[a]	90,000
Best-sellers	100,000
Summer specials[a]	45,000

*Source: Company records.
[a]Sales of these two categories are annual volume sales since they are published only once a year.
Note: These figures are not net of returns. During its first three months in distribution, Arlekin had no returns. In 1992, returns increased substantially, to almost 30%.

models to our readers." The impact was evident in consumer correspondence. In the first eight months of 1992, Arlekin received over 20,000 letters, all of which were answered. To many Polish consumers, Arlekin was already more than just another company.

In the fourth quarter of 1991, Arlekin generated a margin of 5% after marketing expenses.

This margin rose to 11% during 1992. (Exhibit 7 summarizes Arlekin's income statements for the last three months of 1991 and for 1992, estimated as of September.)

The Product Line

Initial print runs were 50,000 copies per title per month, increasing, by September 1992, to between 75,000 and 150,000 copies per title per month, depending on series popularity. Arlekin had no warehouse capacity of its own; books were shipped from the printer directly to distributors' warehouses.

The initial product line was selected by the New York and Toronto editorial staffs who chose classical, successful, and representative titles. In October 1991, Harlequin entered the Polish market with a highly publicized launch of eight titles—four from the Romance and Presents lines, and four from Silhouette's Desire line, a somewhat more sensual series. This launch represented a "critical mass" of titles that permitted the promotion of multiple-unit purchases and established a base on which to later build direct sales. Translation and editing were done by Arlekin.

A Polish cover design, promoting the Harlequin brand name and logo, was created to stim-

Exhibit 7   *Arlekin Pro Forma Income Statements: 1991 and 1992**

	1991	1992E
Net units shipped (thousands)	2,500	10,200
Average retail cover price (zlotys)	10,000	15,000
Net revenue (millions zlotys)	15,600	95,000
Cost of goods[a]	10,200	53,000
Gross margin	5,400	42,000
Advertising and promotion	3,500	25,000
Selling, general and administrative overhead[b]	1,100	6,500
Operating margin	800	10,500

*Source: Company records. E: Estimated.
[a]Includes printing costs (75%), distribution costs (17%) and royalties (8%).
[b]Includes translation costs.

ulate impulse purchases. Each series had a different background cover color: Romance was white, and Desire was red. The covers included the Joey Harlequin logo, the Harlequin brand name (the largest element on the cover), the name of the series, the title, and the author's name. Standard Harlequin artwork, featuring a realistic painting, also appeared on each cover, whereas Harlequin's Polish competitors used photographs on their covers. The English series names were retained to capitalize on the product's Western origin. Titles were translated.

Following the launch, additional product series were chosen by Baar executives and individual titles selected by Arlekin. Fifteen Polish volunteer readers rated existing Harlequin novels and determined which should be translated for the Polish market. Translations were subcontracted, took approximately two months, and cost 25 million zlotys per book. Four Arlekin editors and eight proofreaders checked translations for language and style. Kowalewska was determined that the product be of the highest possible quality and stated: "You may not like the genre, but, within this market, we are the best. Our books contain no mistakes; they are perfect."

In May 1992, Harlequin moved from 8 to 14 titles per month and from two to four series. (Exhibit 8 shows sample covers for a novel in each of the four series.) The Romance line was extended to six titles, while the Superromance series was introduced with one title and the Temptation series with two titles. The basic product line was also supplemented each month by best-seller and seasonal publications (for Christmas and Valentine's Day, for example). Best-sellers, such as Penny Jordan's *Power Play*, carried the Harlequin name only on the back cover. Book cover color coding was retained, and consumers often referred to their preferred series by color rather then by name. The cover artwork further distinguished each series. For example, the Romance novels' artwork was always placed in a circle, while the Superromance novels' artwork was always in an oval. Superromance novels were twice as long as the other series and double the price.

Arlekin planned to introduce three new series in 1993: (1) an upscale Silhouette line; (2) an Intrigue line that would be a combination of mystery/paranormal with romance; and (3) a medical setting series. Existing lines would be expanded further to include each month eight titles in the Romance series, four in the Temptation series, six in the Desire series, and one best-seller title. As the product line expanded, Arlekin believed that many women would start choosing a single series rather than reading titles from multiple series, as they still did in September 1992. The best-sellers had been especially successful; they were purchased by a broader audience beyond committed Harlequin readers and were not, therefore, thought to cannibalize sales of Harlequin series novels.

Distribution

Initially, Harlequin decided to distribute its novels through two channels: the formerly state-controlled magazine and press distribution channel, run by Ruch; and the book distribution channel, dominated by Skladnica Ksiegarska. During 1991, each accounted for 50% of Harlequin sales. By September 1992, Arlekin also sold to private distributors and directly to the largest Polish bookstore chain. Kowalewska believed that high visibility and availability were necessary to stimulate purchases of Harlequin novels. Distributors and retailers had to be educated on the importance of timely display of monthly publications and on the management of returns.

Ruch, the established distributor for newspapers and magazines in Poland, operated 49 regional warehouses and, by September 1992, distributed 80% of all Harlequin novels sold in Poland to a network of 22,000 kiosks. About 12,000 of these had recently been privatized, and the new owners were seeking to increase profits by expanding the range of goods they

Exhibit 8   *Sample Covers for Novels in Each of the Four Polish Series*

carried. Ruch earned a retail margin of 30% on Harlequin novels, of which 2% went to the company-owned kiosk operators. To motivate the privatized kiosk operators required an extra 5% margin. However, many independent, privatized kiosks obtained Harlequin novels not from Ruch but from independent distributors, earned higher margins, and then returned unsold Harlequin product through Ruch.

Because Skladnica Ksiegarska, Poland's largest state-owned wholesale book distributor, went bankrupt in 1992, Arlekin decided to sell direct to Poland's largest bookstore chain, Dom Skiazki (The House of the Book) with 660 stores throughout the country. This chain represented 5% of Arlekin's sales and earned a retail margin of 35%.

Fifteen percent of Harlequin sales were made through five private distributors that, together, served 3,000 to 5,000 private bookstores. The distributors earned a margin of 10% to 15%, while the bookstores earned 20% to 25%. These distributors did not yet fully understand the rationale for Harlequin's returns policy and therefore did not always comply with it.[7] In addition, they were thought likely to shift quickly to distributing other products if they became more profitable than books. Other "serious" book distributors regarded Harlequin products as frivolous and declined to carry them.

Arlekin enjoyed a competitive advantage due to its strong retail distribution. "We have an image of a solid, reliable company and we can get our books stocked by the trade because we do not request cash up front," explained Kowalewska. Arlekin believed that distribution costs would increase as more publishers sought to push their products through the established channels. Arlekin was therefore exploring two other distribution options in September 1992: the post office and subscriptions.

---

[7]Returns were supposed to be destroyed but some found their way back to retail outlets, especially independent kiosk operators.

Post Office

The post office served as a savings bank for many Polish consumers due to the underdevelopment of the banking sector. In September 1992, Arlekin began testing the use of post offices as retail outlets on a six-month trial basis. The central post office warehouse would be supplied each month with 16,000 copies of each title. After one month, Harlequin novels were available in 2,000 out of 8,000 post offices. The post office earned a retail margin of 30% on Arlekin sales.

Subscription

Arlekin was considering offering consumers quarterly pay-in-advance subscriptions to receive Harlequin novels. The subscription plan would target rural consumers, who had difficulty finding the product, and current Harlequin readers. Subscription applications would be placed in magazines and inside the back covers of Harlequin novels. In addition, invitations to join the subscription service would be mailed to 60,000 consumers that had responded to Arlekin promotional competitions and questionnaires. Administration of the subscription program could be subcontracted to a large Polish magazine publisher who serviced one million subscribers each month. Arlekin was hoping to register 30,000 to 40,000 subscribers by the end of 1992, increasing to 100,000 by the end of 1993. After the costs of postage and handling, Kowalewska expected initial margins to be comparable or slightly lower than on retail sales. She wanted to establish the direct sales channel as soon as possible, since she believed that sales through this channel would eventually improve margins for the company.

Competition

In October 1991, Arlekin's two main competitors were Amber and Phantom Press. Both were private Polish companies publishing a variety of paperback best-sellers in the areas of suspense, crime, and romance. Phantom Press published two titles per month in four romance series, including translations of the Bantam series, Loveswept. Amber concentrated on best-sellers, but Kowalewska considered its translations to be of poorer quality. Both companies were, by origin, printers rather than publishers, and their print runs averaged 150,000 copies per title in October 1991.

Alfa, a Polish company which had published unauthorized translations of Harlequin novels prior to Harlequin's entry, was sued in 1992 and exited the market. Another local company, Aramis, which entered the market in March 1992 with the same "Garden of Love" slogan that Arlekin used and similar book covers and typeface, was threatened with litigation and subsequently changed its marketing approach. (Table A summarizes competitor market shares between September 1991 and September 1992.) Competitors' average print runs for new titles had declined significantly, and their return rates were reportedly as high as 85%.

In September, 1992, the market was still growing and more new entrants were rumored. Some publishers regarded romance novels as an easy market in which to score quick sales because Arlekin had promoted the genre so successfully through its own heavy advertising.

Table A   Arlekin and Competitor Market Shares

	Sept. 1991	Jan. 1992	Sept. 1992
Harlequin	0%	50%	90%
Phantom Press	50%	30%	5%
Alfa	30%	0%	0%
Amber	10%	5%	3%
Others (including Aramis)	10%	15%	2%

Arlekin's introductory retail prices aimed to stimulate multiple, impulse purchases and yet position the product as the "Rolls Royce" of romance fiction. In October, 1991, the product was launched with a retail cover price of 15,000 zlotys, but an initial 33% promotion resulted in an actual retail price of 10,000 zlotys. Competitive products were priced at 12,000 zlotys. Arlekin's launch strategy emphasized rapid market penetration ahead of short-term profits.

After three months, Arlekin ceased its special promotion, allowing a retail price per unit of 15,000 zlotys to take effect on January 1, 1992. By September 1992, the principal competitive products were all retailing at 15,000 to 16,000 zlotys. Arlekin intended to hold its price at 15,000 zlotys until at least the end of the year, despite increases in production costs. Kowalewska explained her pricing policy: "Our consumers need to feel that they can depend on Harlequin. Prices on everything else are so volatile that holding the price of a Harlequin novel constant goes a long way to creating loyalty among our consumers."

Promotion and Advertising

Prior to 1989, advertising in Poland was rare, and many consumers suspected that an advertised product was inferior to one selling without advertising. However, by 1992, television and radio commercials and print advertisements were widespread and accepted.

The Harlequin product line was launched as offering escape for women, with the slogan "Escape into the world of Dreams . . . Harlequin books are a garden of love." Harlequin consumer research indicated that romance novels were read most often in three situations: during travel; before going to sleep; and during vacations. Thus, three television commercials were created for the launch, one for each usage situation. The commercials opened with a monochromatic picture of a young woman on a tram, lying next to a sleeping husband, or sitting alone at a cafe table. The woman's expression was slightly melancholic, a man's voice whispered, "Escape into the world of dreams. . . ." At this point the scene changed and full color was restored; the woman was seen traveling in a limousine, in a luxury bedroom, or on a yacht, each time accompanied by a handsome man. The commercial ended with the man's voice stating, "Harlequin is a garden of love." Kowalewska explained the objective of the commercials: "We wanted to show an average woman, tired and grey, who was transformed by the books into a happy, beautiful woman, adored by a wonderful man." During the launch the television commercials were aired three times a day in 10-day cycles with 10 days off between cycles. The television campaign cost 2.3 billion zlotys in the first three months.

In addition to the television commercials, Arlekin held press receptions and ran advertisements, based on the television commercials and book cover artwork, both on radio stations (six exposures a day in 10-day cycles with 10 days off between cycles) and in all major women's magazines. Exhibit 9 reproduces a print advertisement, based on one of the television commercials used during the launch. Exhibit 10 reproduces a later print advertisement, based on book cover artwork, used in response to competition from Aramis. During the first three months following the launch, magazine advertising expenditures were 300 million zlotys.

Trade promotions during the first three months following the launch included free display racks to retail outlets to increase the product's accessibility and visibility. (Display racks used in bookstores and street kiosks are illustrated in Exhibit 11.)

Arlekin quickly achieved high brand awareness. Kowalewska believed the appeal of Western products for their own sake would be short-lived so she was determined that consumers perceive Arlekin as a Polish company selling an international product. In 1992, Arlekin budgeted 25 billion zlotys for advertising and promotion, allocated as shown in Exhibit 12.

Following the launch, Arlekin developed eleven 10-second television spots to serve as "reminders." During 1992, Arlekin aired 50 spots per month on the two national television channels and sponsored Polish reruns of American television programs such as *Dynasty* and *Bill Cosby,* as well as local programs and talk shows. As a result of media price increases, Kowalewska planned to reduce the frequency of television spots. Radio commercials were also run three times a day, for two ten-day periods a month, on both Polish national radio and three private local radio stations. In addition, a Harlequin Club radio talk show was aired twice a month, in which women discussed their personal problems.

Full-page Harlequin advertisements appeared on the back covers of women's magazines. After Aramis attempted to use the slogan "Garden of Love," Arlekin responded with "There are many romances but only one true love, Harlequin." In September 1992, Arlekin was planning its first test of outdoor advertising, placing posters of book cover artwork in bus shelters throughout central Warsaw. Arlekin also planned to publish a "Letter to Consumers" in a print advertisement that would describe Arlekin's charitable donations to a children's hospital. Arlekin gave to charity, sponsoring cultural events, donating to hospitals, and financing student scholarships. As a result, Arlekin enjoyed excellent media coverage.

Special events were an increasingly important element in Arlekin's communication strategy, especially as media advertising costs escalated. These included the creation and celebration of Valentine's Day in Poland in 1992, accompanied by special commercials and publicity stunts, such as the hanging of a huge heart from the top of the Palace of Culture (the largest and oldest building in central Warsaw) and Kowalewska's televised "speech to the nation," an infomercial in which she described both Harlequin products and the Arlekin company. In 1992, Arlekin also held its first "Readers Party," at which 100

(continued on page 429)

Exhibit 9   *Arlekin Print Advertisement: "Don't waste time! Every month, Harlequin offers you 8 new, fascinating stories about great love! With two series. Ask for them in bookstores and Ruch kiosks."*

Exhibit 10   *Arlekin Print Advertisement: "There are many romances but only one true love. . ."*

Exhibit 11   *Harlequin Retail Display Racks in Poland*

1. A Harlequin free-standing book display rack in the corner of a Polish bookstore. The rack displays only Harlequin novels.
2. A Harlequin flat-shelf book display rack in a street vendor book-stall. The rack displays a variety of non-Harlequin books.

Exhibit 12   *Arlekin Advertising and Promotion Budget Allocation: 1991 and 1992* *

	1991 (3 months)	1992 (8 months)
Advertising:		
Television commercials	60%	50%
Radio commercials	4%	8%
Women's magazine advertising	7%	4%
Production costs	15%	4%
Promotions:		
Point-of-sale displays—racks, plastic bags, stickers	8%	2%
Promotional incentives—cocktail parties, competitions	5%	5%
Market research	1%	2%
Other/Reserve[a]		25%

*Source: Company records.
[a]Includes percentage of the budget that had not, as of September 1992, been used. The mix of expenditures would be similar to that during the first eight months.

randomly selected readers were invited to draw prizes, and a celebrity cocktail party when Arlekin's cumulative sales in Poland passed one million units. Kowalewska explained her strategy for deciding which special events to promote: "We want to be the experts on love. We want to be called upon to judge the best love songs and the beauty contests."

In developing her proposed 1993 communication plan, Kowalewska was especially concerned about how to overcome the prejudices of some Polish consumers against the romance genre and convince them to reach for a Harlequin novel. Some executives felt that the artwork in Arlekin advertising was incompatible with the images found in the more sophisticated, fashion magazines that appealed to some non-Harlequin readers. A new series of magazine print advertisements was developed to reach these consumers (see Exhibit 13 for a sample proposed print advertisement). The first ad showed a black-and-white modern photograph of a young boy with the headline "I can't recognize my mother." This would be followed the next month by a similar photograph of a middle-aged man with the caption "I can't recognize

my wife." The third ad in the series would show a photograph of the same woman with a dreamy expression, holding a Harlequin novel in her arms. Kowalewska wondered whether the proposed advertising would, in fact, appeal to current nonreaders and whether it would confuse or alienate current readers.

Consumer Research

Three months after the launch, a questionnaire was placed inside the back covers of Harlequin books. The resulting 10,000 responses gave Arlekin the following consumer profile information:

- 39% of readers were younger than 19, 30% were between 19 and 26 years old; 25% were 27 to 40 years old; and 6% were older than 40.
- 67% lived in cities and towns.
- 52% purchased Harlequin novels in bookstores and 56% from "Ruch" kiosks.

A further market research study was conducted in June 1992 with 660 Polish women aged 15 and above. The purpose was to explore familiarity with and readership patterns for

Exhibit 13   *Proposed Print Advertisement: "What's Happening to My Mother?"*

Harlequin books. Results are summarized in Exhibit 14.

Consumer panels were conducted in September 1992 to profile Harlequin readers and Harlequin nonreaders. Nonreaders expressed contempt for the romance genre and described Harlequin television commercials as unrealistic, difficult to relate to, and targeted at teenagers. Some nonreaders suggested that Harlequin novels should include suspense and horror series, others that the commercials should be more humorous. Many of these nonreaders had, however, either read or were interested in reading best-sellers, such as novels by Penny Jordan. Harlequin novels were read as time fillers and as a means of escape. Committed users were emotionally attached to Harlequin and did not want the product changed in any way. There was, however, little attachment to a particular series; avid readers not only read all Harlequin novels but also read competitors' books. What nonreaders considered unrealistic and in poor taste, readers considered beautiful, particularly the book cover artwork. Readers could be divided into three categories: those that bought and collected the product, those that read the product but borrowed it rather than bought it, and those that bought some but not all of the products they read and exchanged these with friends. A majority of readers stated that 10 titles published each month was sufficient and that they would purchase more books more often if the unit price was lower.

Challenges for 1993

By September 1992, Harlequin had sold over 10 million books but to fewer than 2 million consumers. To increase sales revenues in 1993, Kowalewska could raise unit prices, sell more books to current purchasers, and/or attract new purchasers and readers. As she prepared a 1993 marketing plan to present to Harlequin Baar executives, Kowalewska was considering how to adjust to the evolving distribution channels in Poland, whether to proceed with a subscription service, and whether to launch a new advertising campaign. She also wondered what additional consumer research and marketplace information she should gather to decide these issues.

Exhibit 14   *Harlequin Market Research in Poland: June 1992**

- 37% of respondents were not familiar with Harlequin books (but more than half of these were over 58 years of age); 39% were familiar with them but had never read them; 8% had read one or a few Harlequin books but no longer did so; 11% claimed to read Harlequin books; 69% of Harlequin readers had been reading the novels for over six months.
- 40% of respondents did not read books at all. Reasons given included lack of time (28%); inability to afford books (20%); lack of interest in reading (15%); and poor health/eyesight (9%).
- Among respondents who did not read Harlequin books, 46% did not read romance novels; 22% could not afford the books; 22% did not have the time, and 10% read competitive products.
- Among Harlequin readers, 35% bought the books themselves; 46% borrowed them from friends; 13% received them from relatives; and 7% borrowed them from the library.
- Respondents who read Harlequin books were influenced by family and friends (38%); bookstores and newsstand displays (15%); and television commercials (29%).
- 64% of Harlequin readers passed their books on to others once they had read them, while 26% collected them.

---

*Source: Company records

EMDICO

On August 2, 1990, Iraqi forces invaded Kuwait. Fortunately, D. Srinivasan, marketing manager with Fuji Film's distributor in Kuwait, was visiting the United States at the time. However, when he returned to Kuwait in March 1991 after the end of Gulf War, he found his house ransacked. After several months visiting with his family in India, Srinivasan returned to the region late in 1991 as general manager of EMDICO (Emam Distribution Co. Ltd.) in Jeddah, Kingdom of Saudi Arabia (KSA). EMDICO was Fuji's newly appointed KSA distributor.

In his new role, Srinivasan had to develop a marketing strategy to relaunch the Fuji film and camera product lines among others in KSA. Srinivasan set out to convince management in Tokyo that they had made the right decision in appointing EMDICO. Their confidence would, he hoped, result in some monetary support to subsidize his marketing strategy and in the timeliness and availability of Fuji product shipments from Japan to KSA.

THE KINGDOM OF SAUDI ARABIA

Founded in 1932 by King Abd Al-Aziz, KSA was a country one-third of the size of the United States with a population of 17 million in 1991.[1] The population had been only 3.2 million in 1950 and was expected to double by 2010. As shown in Exhibit 1, KSA dominated the Arabian peninsula. Around 75% of the population lived in urban areas: the most important cities were Riyadh (2 million) and Jeddah (2 million). A quarter of the population were expatriates, principally Egyptians, citizens of other Arab countries, and nationals from the Indian subcontinent. Only one quarter of the expatriates were accompanied by other family members, though the percentage was increasing. Arabic was the official language, but English was widely used in business circles.

The age distribution of the 13 million native Saudis who lived in 3.8 million households is shown in Table A. Of Saudi households, 2.8 million included a husband, wife and children.

---

[1]The combined population of the countries in the Middle East region, as defined by Fuji, was about 100 million in 1991.

This case was prepared by Yoshinori Fujikawa (under the direction of John A. Quelch). Confidential data have been disguised. Copyright © 1996 by the President and Fellows of Harvard College. Harvard Business School case 597-029.

Exhibit 1 *Map of the Arabian Peninsula*

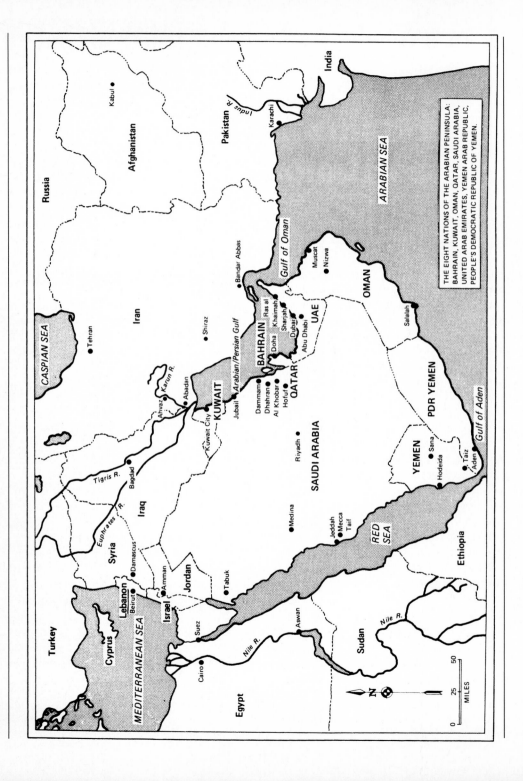

Table A   Age Distribution of Native Saudis*

Age Group	Percentage
0–15	49%
16–30	20%
31–45	14%
46–60	10%
Over 60	7%

*Source: *Arab News,* December 15, 1992.

The KSA gross domestic product (GDP) was SR 427.5 billion (U.S. $114 billion) in 1992.[2] KSA per capita income was higher than in all other Middle Eastern countries, except Bahrain, Kuwait, and the United Arab Emirates (UAE). The petroleum sector, with a quarter of the world's proven oil reserves, accounted for 35% of GDP and most export earnings. Almost every Saudi household had a television, refrigerator, cooker, and washing machine. Ninety-two percent of households owned a car. Two-thirds of households owned stereo and video equipment. This level of affluence reflected the absence of any personal income tax and KSA government subsidies of utilities and public transportation, as well as the availability of free education and health care.

The value of brand building, advertising, and market research was increasingly understood. International brands were sold freely through increasingly modern retail outlets (including 100 supermarkets among 17,000 food stores). However, media advertising expenditures were only SR 40 per capita in 1990, compared to almost $300 in the U.S. As a result of the Gulf War, subscriptions to satellite television channels increased greatly.

The KSA constitution and government were based firmly on the teachings of the Islamic Koran. Alcohol was banned. KSA was home to the pilgrimage centers of Mecca and Medina. The faithful prayed toward Mecca five times daily. Every business had to close for half an hour at each of these prayer times. In accordance with the Muslim calendar, commerce was conducted from Saturday through Wednesday; Thursday and Friday were weekends.

Consumer behavior in KSA was influenced heavily by Muslim prescripts. In a culture where family honor was defined by adherence to strict codes of conduct, women could not appear in public unveiled and they were not permitted to drive. Market research indicated that one-third of daily shopping decisions were made solely by Saudi husbands, one-third solely by Saudi wives, and one-third jointly. However, husbands made two-thirds of the actual purchases and only one in seven Saudi wives actually visited stores to purchase goods.

Cultural norms affected the prevalence of photography. Women could not normally have their pictures taken or take pictures themselves. Weddings, however, would almost always be recorded, but only by women. Family portraits might also be taken at photo studios. However, concern that a stranger in a film processing laboratory might see a woman unveiled or, worse, duplicate a photo being processed, limited this practice. For these reasons, a family that visited a photo studio for a portrait often preferred to wait until the pictures were developed.[3] Consumer surveys in KSA and the U.S. found the following differences in speed of film-processing service requested (see Table B):

---

[2]One U.S. dollar was equivalent to 3.75 Saudi riyals (SR).

[3]Partly as a consequence, there were only 28 wholesale labs in KSA in 1991, compared to 3,400 in the United States. Wholesale labs collected films from retail sites such as photo studios and camera shops, developed and printed them at a lab, then redistributed the finished photographs to the retailers for customer pickup. The time between customer dropoff and pickup was typically two to three days.

Table B   Film-Processing Speed
              Requested

Speed	KSA	USA
1 Hour	85%	35%
7 Hours	10%	40%
Overnight	5%	25%

On the other hand, the mix of subjects which consumers chose to photograph was similar in the two countries, as shown in Table C:

Table C   Selected Photo Subjects

Subjects	KSA	USA
People	60%	70%
Nature/Landscape	15%	15%
Buildings	10%	14%

FUJI FILM BACKGROUND

Fuji Photo Film Co, Ltd., headquartered in Tokyo, Japan, was one of the world's leading manufacturers and marketers of photographic film, cameras, photo papers, and magnetic tapes. Net sales in 1990 were $8 billion.

Fuji organized its product lines into three groups: imaging systems (37% of worldwide sales), photofinishing systems (23%), and information systems (40%). The most important single product line was the Fujicolor series of color negative films, and the biggest-selling item was the Fujicolor Super HR 100, ideal for everyday photography. Fujicolor Super film was available in other speeds (HG 200, HG 400 and HG 1600). Fuji REALA was a color negative film that delivered colors as seen by the human eye. Fuji Chrome VELVIA color reversal film was for professional use. NEOPAN black and white film, used especially for sports and press photography, was available in three speeds.

The imaging systems group also offered a broad selection of cameras, from simple point-and-shoot compact cameras such as the FZ-5 and DL-25, to the FZ-3000 with its binocular-style body and dynamic 38mm to 115mm zoom lens. The range also included sophisticated professional models. Fujicolor Quicksnap disposable cameras were launched in 1985, followed in 1987 by Quicksnap Flash and Quicksnap Marine. Also included in the product line was the FOTORAMA instant ID photo camera.

The photofinishing systems group sold photographic paper in a wide variety of surfaces and sheet sizes, photofinishing equipment, and chemicals. Fuji pioneered the development of a compact and durable minilab, the FA Compact II.[4] Although slower than the minilabs made by Kodak and Konica, it was more compact, better designed and easier to service.

The information systems group sold materials and equipment for printing industries, medical-imaging products, office automation systems, floppy disks, and computer tapes. Fuji was especially strong in digital medical X-ray imaging systems, which it sold to large and midsized hospitals worldwide.

In Japan, Fuji's bright green packages were as ubiquitous as Kodak's yellow packages were in the United States. In 1990, Fuji accounted for 70% of film sales, 20% of camera sales, and 15% of magnetic tape sales in Japan.

Around 25% of Fuji's sales were generated outside Japan. Fuji's sales in the Middle East were around $150 million, 2% of Fuji's total revenues and 8% of Fuji's overseas sales.

Fuji typically entered new consumer markets with its film product line, followed by its cam-

---

[4]A minilab consisted of a film processor for developing the film and a printer which transmitted the images to photo paper. The word "minilab" was used interchangeably for a machine itself as well as for a store using a minilab machine on site. By 1991, there was one minilab for every 12,000 people in the United States.

eras. Fuji often offered its basic products first, adding the more expensive and specialized items in its lines as demand increased. In KSA, for example, 80% of Fuji film sales were of the popular 100-film speed, compared to 45% in the United States. Recently, sales of the FA Compact II minilab to photo studios and other outlets had helped Fuji penetrate the major cities of several developing markets, where Fuji often found itself playing catch-up to Kodak.

KSA Market Structure

As shown in Exhibit 2, around 6 million rolls of color film were imported annually into KSA between 1984 and 1989. At 6 million rolls per year, the KSA film market was 2% the size of the U.S. market while KSA's population was 7% that of the United States. The disparity was attributed to lower per capita disposable income and cultural constraints on picture taking. In 1990, the Iraqi invasion of Kuwait disrupted shipping in the Gulf and only 2.9 million rolls were imported. As part of the postwar recovery process, some 4 million rolls of film were expected to be imported into KSA in 1991, up 35% fro 1990. This figure partly reflected the high level of inventories already held by distributors and retailers in KSA.

No film or cameras were manufactured in KSA. All were imported by Saudi distributors who each exclusively represented a single brand. They marketed the imported products to a variety of channels, typically taking a 15% margin on the selling price. In 1991, the KSA import tariff on film and cameras was 12%.

As shown in Exhibit 3, Kodak and Konica were locked in a tight competition for market leadership in film sales. Konica was also the number five brand in unit camera sales. Of the 2,400 outlets in KSA through which film was sold, only 30 sold Kodak exclusively and 30 Konica. The remaining outlets were not tied to any one brand; few outlets, however, carried more than two brands of film. Cameras were sold by about 700 of the 2,400 outlets selling film.

As indicated in Exhibit 4, photographic studios accounted for 25% of film sales but only 5% of cameras. Camera and electronic stores retailed 65% of cameras and 30% of film. One third of film was sold by minilabs which provided on-premise processing in less than an hour. In addition, a few supermarkets served as convenient collection points for used films, which were then sent to wholesale labs for processing.

There were 216 minilabs in KSA in October 1991. The Konica distributor in KSA had sold the most minilabs to date. The smallest Konica minilab sold for SR 250,000 and required the retailer to make a 50% down payment. Minilab models varied in the speed and quantity of film they could process at any one time. Most minilabs could process any brand of film and many sold two or more brands of film, not just the brand associated with the minilab. Profile information from a market research study on minilabs in KSA is presented in Exhibit 5. Srinivasan also developed the economic projections shown in Exhibit 6 for dealer interested in buying the Fuji FA Compact II minilab. Srinivasan believed that the break-even point on the cheapest Konica minilab required the processing of 20 films per day versus 13 for the Fuji machine.

Fuji's Market Position in KSA

Because Fuji film was sold in Israel, Fuji was blocked from doing business in the Middle East until the Arab boycott was lifted in March 1983. Meanwhile, Kodak had been selling in KSA since the 1960s and Konica since the 1970s.

Once the boycott was lifted, Fuji asked Mitsui Corporation, a Japanese trading company, to identify exclusive distributors in all Middle Eastern countries. In 1984, Fuji itself appointed an exclusive distributor to represent its product line in KSA. The selected firm already distributed several

Exhibit 2 *KSA Film and Camera Markets: Industry and Fuji Imports, 1985–1995E*

KSA Market[a]	1985	1986	1987	1988	1989	1990
Color Film Rolls (units)	6,200,000	6,135,000	6,170,000	5,760,000	6,060,000	2,900,000
Color Paper (sq. m.)	3,700,000	4,040,000	3,900,000	3,800,000	2,000,000	2,025,000
Cameras (units)[b]	200,000	81,500	143,000	54,200	98,300	80,000
Minilabs (installations)	100	115	140	170	190	214

KSA Market[a]	1991E	1992E	1993E	1994E	1995E
Color Film Rolls (units)	4,000,000	5,500,000	5,600,000	5,800,000	6,000,000
Color Paper (sq. m.)	2,500,000	3,000,000	3,100,000	3,200,000	3,300,000
Cameras (units)[b]	60,000	115,000	120,000	130,000	136,000
Minilabs (installations)	230	250	300	380	460

Fuji Unit Sales[a, c, d]	1985	1986	1987	1988	1989	1990
Color Film Rolls (units)	560,000 (9%)	368,000 (6%)	555,300 (9%)	518,400 (9%)	545,000 (9%)	232,000 (8%)
Color Paper (sq. m.)	110,000 (3%)	202,000 (5%)	78,000 (2%)	80,000 (2%)	20,000 (1%)	20,250 (1%)
Cameras (units)[b]	2,000 (1%)	1,200 (1%)	1,300 (1%)	400 (1%)	900 (1%)	800 (1%)
Minilabs (installations)	8 (8%)	10 (9%)	12 (9%)	14 (8%)	15 (8%)	15 (7%)

Fuji Unit Sales[a, c, d]	1991E	1992E	1993E	1994E	1995E
Color Film Rolls (units)	320,000 (8%)	700,000 (13%)	800,000 (14%)	1,000,000 (17%)	1,200,000 (20%)
Color Paper (sq. m.)	25,000 (1%)	300,000 (10%)	400,000 (13%)	500,000 (16%)	660,000 (20%)
Cameras (units)[b]	1,000 (2%)	10,000 (9%)	15,000 (13%)	20,000 (15%)	22,000 (16%)
Minilabs (installations)	16 (7%)	36 (14%)	60 (20%)	86 (23%)	110 (24%)

Notes: [a]Estimates of imports by distributors into KSA, based on the export figures in Japan Ministry of Finance, *Japan Export-Import Statistics 1991*. These are not estimates of retail sales.
[b]Volatility partly due to entry and withdrawal of foreign camera manufacturers.
[c]Percentage figures in parentheses are Fuji market shares.
[d]Target figures for 1992E–1995E were sales goals set jointly by Fuji management and EMDICO.

Exhibit 3   *Brand Unit Market Shares in KSA: 1991*

	Fuji	Kodak	Konica	AGFA	Others
Color Film Rolls	8%	43%	44%	5%	0%
Color Paper	9	46	43	2	0
Cameras[a]	2	2	5	0	91
Minilabs	7	43	40	3	7
Medical X-ray	60	20	5	10	5

[a]The leading camera brands in KSA were Yashica (27% of unit sales), Canon (17%), Olympus (8%), Nikon (7%), and Konica (5%).

Exhibit 4   *KSA Distribution Channels for Film and Cameras: 1991*

	% Film Sales (Units)	% Camera Sales (Units)	Total Number of Dealers	Number of Fuji Dealers	Fuji Dealer Penetration
Studios	25%	5%	1,542	308	20%
Minilabs	35	20	216	66	30
Camera/Electronics Stores	30	65	218	22	10
Supermarkets	5	—	284	48	17
Industrial/Hospital	—	—	460	46	10
Others	5	10	100	6	6
Total	100	100	2,820	496	18

multinational company brands, including the Japanese camera brands Olympus and Pentax. However, according to one industry observer:

Fuji's distributor never gave great emphasis to the Fuji line. It accounted for only 10% of their sales at most. They focused mainly on camera stores. Also, dealer service was not that great, stockouts and late deliveries were common, and several dealers switched to competitive brands.

By the middle of 1991, Fuji's market shares in film, cameras and minilabs in KSA were estimated at 8%, 2% and 7% respectively, as shown in Exhibit 3. Fuji penetration of distribution outlets was correspondingly low, as shown in Exhibit 4. The product mix of Fuji's KSA sales in 1991 is summarized in Exhibit 7.

Fuji management was concerned that the KSA distributor's performance was lagging distributor performance in other Middle Eastern countries. For example, Fuji had placed its equipment in only 16 out of 216 minilabs in KSA, compared to 35 out of 183 in the neighboring United Arab Emirates (UAE) which had a population of only 2 million. Although the higher penetration of minilabs in UAE could be explained by higher per capita income and a more open society, the difference in Fuji's market shares was attributed to the relative competence of the distributors. In Iran, Syria, and Qatar, Fuji's share of minilab installations exceeded 30%. Exhibit 8 reports minilab installations in Middle Eastern countries by brand.

Early in 1991, Fuji management decided to change its distributor in KSA. The market dis-

---

Exhibit 5   *Profile of Minilabs in KSA: October 1991*

- Of the 216 minilabs in KSA, 85% were in stand-alone retail outlets and 15% were in supermarkets.
- In 20% of the retail outlets with minilabs, more than one minilab was installed.
- 70% of KSA minilabs were in photo studios, which typically derived 20% of their revenues from portrait photography.
- On average, 75% of a minilab's revenues were derived from photofinishing and 25% from retail sales. Of retail sales, 60% were from film, 20% from cameras, 10% from batteries, and 10% from album, frames, videotapes, etc.
- 80% of all KSA minilabs were concentrated in Jeddah and Riyadh.

---

ruption caused by the Gulf War afforded a good opportunity. As one executive said:

> Our existing distributor did not respond well to the marketing challenges caused by the war. It seemed like a good time to start over, especially since a surge of economic growth was expected in the aftermath of the war.

Fuji's distributor in UAE recommended to the general manager of Fuji's international marketing division that he contact Sheik Hani S. Emam, whose distribution companies held exclusive sales and service contracts for several multinationals selling furniture, clocks, and other consumer products.

Fuji planned to publicly announce the appointment of EMDICO on December 7, 1991. Fuji management was concerned that the former distributor would launch a media campaign and file a breach of contract complaint with the Saudi government. Although Fuji management believed they had sufficient evidence of missed sales targets and poor service, BMW, in a recent similar case, had been required to pay compensation to its former distributor and its operations in KSA had been frozen for several months while the dispute was resolved.

The situation was complicated by the fact that the existing distributor was holding SR 3 million of inventory (at distributor selling prices), 90% in film and 10% in other products. About 30% of this inventory had not been paid for. Retail outlets supplied by the distributor were believed to be holding SR 5 million of inventories purchased from the distributor, which would retail for SR 9 million. However, 20% of the Fuji film inventory in retail channels was believed to have passed its expiration date and a further 30% was set to expire within three months.[5] Some dealers had suggested privately to Srinivasan that they would appreciate EMDICO replacing the expired film with new stock at no charge.

THE 1992 MARKETING PLAN

Negotiations between EMDICO and Fuji management resulted in the market growth assumptions and sales goals for 1992 through 1995, summarized in Exhibit 2. Should these goals not be reached, Fuji reserved the right to reassign the distributorship after a minimum period of two years. Srinivasan's mission was to develop a marketing plan that would meet Fuji's objectives yet, at the same time, make money for EMDICO. Srinivasan estimated EMDICO's minimum 1992 general and administrative overhead associated with the Fuji distributorship at SR 400,000. He believed that EMDICO was well-placed to complete for two-year government contracts to supply medical X-ray film to hospitals. His focus, therefore, was on improving Fuji sales to consumers which he expected would account for 80% of EMDICO's Fuji-related revenues over the next five years. He turned to resolving the following issues:

---

[5]Fuji applied an expiration date two years from date of production to all its film packages. Beyond the expiration date, the quality of the film could not be guaranteed.

Exhibit 6   *Sample Profit Planning for Prospective Minilab Owner*

Assumptions
(X) Model: FA Compact

(A) EMIDICO's Selling Price	SR[b]	180,000	per unit
(B) Paper Price	SR	12	per sqm dealer net
(1) Processing Rolls[a]		20	rolls/day
(2) Working Day		26	days
(3) Processing Fee	SR	6	per roll
(4) Printing Fee	SR	1.00	per print, 1 print = 10.2 cm * 15.2 cm = 0.0155 sqm
(5) Production Ratio		90%	

Profit and Loss Calculation
Monthly Revenue

(6) Film Processing	SR	3,120	= (1) * (2) * (3)
(7) Printing	SR	18,720	= (1) * (2) * 36 prints * (4)
(8) Total Revenue	SR	21,840	= (6) + (7)

Monthly Expense

(9) Paper	SR	3,869	= (1) * (2) * 36 prints * 0.0155 * (B) / (5)
(10) Chemical	SR	874	= 4% on total revenue
(11) Free Film, Album, and Envelope	SR	4,680	= (1) * (2) * SR 9.00
(12) Total Expense	SR	9,422	= (9) + (10) + (11)

Margin

(13) Gross Margin (SR)	SR	12,418	= (8) − (12)
(14) Gross Margin (%)		57%	= (13) / (8) * 100

Fixed Cost

(15) Salaries	SR	2,500	Assumed
(16) Rent and Utilities	SR	2,500	Assumed
(17) Minilab Depreciation	SR	3,000	= (A) / 60 months (5 years)

Profit

(18) Net Profit (SR)	SR	4,418	= (13) − (15) − (16) − (17)
(19) Net Profit (%)		20%	= (18) / (8) *100

[a]Break-even film unit sales = 13 rolls/day.
[b]SR: Saudi riyals.

The Announcement

Opinions differed about how intensively the December 7 public announcement of EMDICO's appointment should be leveraged. A local agency proposed a press conference in Jeddah, to which journalists and 300 top dealers would be welcomed by Srinivasan, his new management team, and senior Fuji managers from Japan.[6] Fuji's relaunch strategy would be announced at this event. The cost estimate was SR 120,000, plus a further SR 30,000 if advertisements were placed in the major national news-

[6]It was estimated that half of these dealers would be among those already carrying Fuji and half would not.

Exhibit 7   *Fuji Sales Mix by Product Line (Pre-EMDICO): 1991E*

Product Line	1991E* (Pre-EMDICO)	
Color film rolls	SR 2,080,000	(62%)
Color paper	500,000	(15%)
Cameras	90,000	(3%)
Minilabs	180,000	(5%)
Medical X-ray	500,000	(15%)
Total	3,350,000	(100%)

*E: Estimated.

papers. The proposed newspaper advertisement is presented in Exhibit 9. Alternatively, the announcement of EMDICO's appointment could simply be mailed to all dealers in KSA at a cost of SR 10,000.

Geographical Coverage

Srinivasan had to decide where to focus his initial relaunch efforts and how rapidly to roll out nationwide, if at all. The three options he considered were to concentrate on Jeddah (which accounted for 23% of KSA film and camera sales and 18% of retail outlets selling film and cameras); to focus on the ten largest cities in KSA, including Jeddah with a combined population of 13 million (and which accounted for 90% of KSA film and camera sales and 85% of retail outlets selling these products); or to launch nationwide. To meet the sales targets set by Fuji management, he was inclined to go national as soon as possible.

Communications

The 1992 communications budget depended on the geographical coverage and aggressiveness of the roll out plan. Srinivasan believed his first priority should be to reestablish awareness of the Fuji brand. He therefore planned to use roadside signs (known as mupi boards) and billboards in the first half of 1992 and possibly to supplement these with television and/or radio advertising in the second half of the year. He estimated the monthly costs shown in Table D:

Table D   Monthly Advertising Costs by Medium, Depending on Geographic Coverage

Media	Jeddah	Ten Cities	National
Roadside signs[a]	SR 8,000	SR 35,000	SR 40,000
Billboards	10,000	46,000	56,000
Television	15,000	75,000	100,000
Radio	8,000	40,000	60,000

[a]Monthly costs for each medium to achieve 200 gross rating points (frequency times reach) under each geographic option.

Organization

Srinivasan had already begun to recruit an entirely new sales and service organization. There was no shortage of qualified personnel and no inclination to hire any of the staff who worked for the former distributor. Srinivasan estimated the manpower requirements and monthly costs shown in Table E:

Table E   Monthly Salaries and Number of Employees, Depending on Geographic Coverage

Manpower (Monthly Salary)	Jeddah	Ten Cities	National
Sales Staff (SR 2,000)	3	8	12
Regional Sales Managers (SR 6,000)	1	3	4

Exhibit 8 *Minilab Installations in the Middle East: 1991*

Country	Fuji		Konica		Kodak		AGFA		Others		TOTAL	Population	Population per Minilab
Bahrain	4	(11%)	7	(20%)	6	(17%)	10	(29%)	8	(23%)	35	550,000	15,714
Iran	30	(38%)	7	(9%)	28	(35%)	12	(15%)	2	(3%)	79	56,000,000	708,861
Jordan	5	(12%)	7	(17%)	28	(68%)	0	(0%)	1	(2%)	41	3,000,000	73,171
Kuwait	1	(2%)	3	(7%)	20	(48%)	8	(19%)	10	(24%)	42	2,000000	47,619
Lebanon	8	(14%)	4	(7%)	29	(51%)	14	(25%)	2	(4%)	57	3,000,000	52,632
Oman	3	(6%)	9	(18%)	13	(26%)	8	(16%)	17	(34%)	50	2,100,000	42,000
Qatar	10	(38%)	10	(38%)	5	(19%)	0	(0%)	1	(4%)	26	500,000	19,231
Saudi Arabia	16	(7%)	89	(41%)	57	(26%)	31	(14%)	23	(11%)	216	17,000,000	78,704
Syria	25	(34%)	22	(30%)	23	(31%)	0	(0%)	4	(5%)	74	12,500,000	168,919
United Arab Emirates	35	(19%)	44	(24%)	49	(27%)	45	(25%)	10	(5%)	183	2,000,000	10,929
Total	137	(17%)	202	(25%)	258	(32%)	128	(16%)	78	(10%)	803		

Note: Countries listed are those included in Fuji's definition of the Middle East region.
Percentage figures in parentheses represent each brand's share in each country.

Exhibit 9 *Proposed Newspaper Advertisement for Relaunch*

The technology that went into space and back is back.

FUJI FILM TECHNOLOGY, PROVEN IN SPACE, IS NOW BACK IN THE STORES.

FUJI is in the forefront of space exploration. Fuji films chosen by high science to vividly capture the mysterious beauty of deep space. Always with impeccable results.

Now, the same high technology that is being proven in space is made available to you - FUJI Films.

FUJI has a wide range of films for various applications to meet amateur or professional photography requirements. Each one guaranteed to provide sharp, clear and colorful reproduction always.

So, the next time you buy a roll of film, specify space-proven FUJI Films. And get pictures with a world of difference.

Sole distributor of Fuji products for the Kingdom of Saudi Arabia

EMDICO
EMAM DISTRIBUTION CO. LTD. w.l.l.
Kilo 11, Madinah Road, P.O. Box 1716, Jeddah 21441
Saudi Arabia, Tel: 691-7036/682-4294
Fax; 691-7036/691-8227.

Exhibit 9   *(continued)*

SAUDI GAZETTE

Thursday, December 12, 1991

Important Announcement

_____ Stores want to inform their esteemed clients that contrary to what has been published in some local papers they are still the accredited agent of Japanese Fuji **FUJI** Foto-film and the sole distributor of its products in the Kingdom as per a franchise contract signed with the company and registered at the Ministry of Commerce under Reg. No. 2544.

Consequently _____ Stores consider themselves the accredited agent and sole distributor of Fuji products in the Kingdom and in this capacity preserve the legal right to initiate legal action against whoever claims to be an agent of the above mentioned company.

_____ Stores are pleased to inform their clients that Fuji films, cameras and other products are available at their stores and at very reasonable prices.

Costs included expenses and transportation. Sales managers would spend half their time selling and half their time supervising.

Srinivasan planned to place special emphasis on customer service. A computerized inventory management system was being installed to insure timely and accurate deliveries of dealer orders. In addition, service engineers were needed to maintain and repair the minilabs that Fuji sold or leased to dealers. One service engineer (costing SR 2,000 per month) could typically cover 12 minilabs. The number of service engineers required would depend on how aggressively Fuji set out to install its minilabs at retail outlets. Fuji management offered to train EMDICO service engineers at no charge to the distributor.

Distribution

Srinivasan knew he had to correct Fuji's current low dealer penetration, but he had to decide on which dealers and channels to focus his sales efforts. He estimated that a salesperson could make five solid sales calls per day and that at least two calls would be necessary to persuade a dealer to carry the Fuji brand. The length of a sales call depended in part on the breadth of the product line to be presented. He was hopeful that the loyalty of all Fuji's current dealers could be reinforced and that some of the 100 dealers who had dropped the brand in the previous two years could be persuaded to sign up again.

Srinivasan believed strongly in point-of-sale signage. He planned to offer current Fuji dealers and new dealers outdoor store signs that would feature the dealer name and the Fuji name in the green, red, and white colors associated with the Fuji brand. Srinivasan estimated the average cost of these signs at SR 2,000. In addition, the annual cost of supplying each dealer with point-of-sale materials, brochures, and ceiling danglers for inside the stores, and Fuji tape for the perimeters of shop windows and display cabinets, would be SR 600. Srinivasan planned to use the slogan "You can see it's Fuji" in Arabic and English on the in-store ceiling danglers. He also wanted to print special envelopes for Fuji film processed in Fuji minilabs with the slogan "Quality prints in record time." In addition, EMDICO delivery vehicles carry prominently the Fuji logo.

As part of the communications and distribution strategy, Srinivasan had all but decided to establish a flagship, company-run retail outlet to be called Fuji Image Plaza in the forecourt of the Safestway supermarket, the most modern, high traffic store in downtown Jeddah. The space would cost SR 15,000 per month and operating costs would be SR 5,000. The store would be run as a photographic studio, the full Fuji product line would be displayed and sold, and a Fuji minilab would process film and be available for dealer demonstrations. The initial investment in fixtures and equipment would be SR 180,000. A perspective view of the proposed store is presented in Exhibit 10.

Product Mix

Srinivasan had to decide whether the sales targets required him to launch the complete line of Fuji films (some 15 items) and cameras (12 models) as soon as possible or whether he should focus, at least initially, on selected, higher-volume items (say four types of color film and three camera models). The latter approach might ease inventory management but send a negative signal that Fuji was not a full-line supplier.

Srinivasan was also considering three alternative product rollout strategies. The first was to simultaneously relaunch both film and cameras, given that purchase of one typically stimulated purchase of the other. Advocates argued that promotions on cameras could be used to persuade dealers to stock Fuji film. The second option was to focus initially on rejuvenating film sales and to delay promoting cameras until at least the second half of 1992. A third option was

Exhibit 10 *Fuji Image Plaza*

Exhibit 11 *Typical Margin Structure for Fuji Products Sold in KSA*

Film Retail (e.g., Fujicolor HR100)	
Retail selling price	SR 10.00
less Dealer margin	3.50
EMDICO selling price	6.50
less EMDICO promotion	0.40
less EMDICO margin	0.50
Fuji selling price[a]	5.60
less Fuji variable costs	3.08
Fuji margin	2.52
Color paper (per one film development = per 36 prints = per 0.6 sqm color paper)	
Retail selling price[b]	SR 42.00
less Dealer margin	25.65
EMDICO selling price[c]	16.35
less EMDICO margin	1.64
Fuji selling price[c]	14.71
less Fuji variable costs	8.09
Fuji margin	6.62
Camera (e.g., FZ-5)	
Retail selling price	SR 133.00
less Dealer margin	43.00
EMDICO selling price	90.00
less EMDICO promotion[d]	12.50
less EMDICO margin	14.50
Fuji selling price[a]	63.00
less Fuji variable costs	34.00
Fuji margin	29.00
Minilab (e.g., FA Compact II)	
EMDICO selling price	SR 180,000
less Finance charge[e]	14,300
less EMDICO margin	25,700
Fuji selling price[a]	140,000
less Fuji variable costs	97,000
Fuji margin	43,000

[a]Fuji selling prices to EMDICO include applicable transportation costs and import duties.
[b]Retail selling price of color paper includes processing fee (SR 6.00/film) and development fee (SR 1.00/print—36 prints).
[c]Photo paper and chemicals
[d]A camera promotion such as a free Fuji film and/or camera batteries would typically be offered with each purchase.
[e]Finance charge was paid by EMDICO, not by a minilab owner. EMDICO planned to offer a bank leasing program to prospective minilab owners. Under the program, EMDICO would receive full amount initially from a bank when a minilab sales was made. EMDICO would charge a minilab owner on monthly basis and pay back to the bank with appropriate finance charge.

to build the relaunch around minilabs sales on the grounds that dealers who installed Fuji mini-labs would be inclined to stock and push Fuji film and cameras. The FA Compact II seemed like a marketable product, but Kodak and Kon-ica might respond to any Fuji sales initiative by offering more attractive terms on their minilabs.

Pricing

The anticipated margin structure for Fuji film, cameras, processing and minilabs are shown in Exhibit 11. Srinivasan was contemplating retail prices on Fuji film at about 5% below Kodak and 5% above Konica. Srinivasan had to take into account Fuji's current image in the market, the need to signal the brand's true quality, and the importance of not provoking a price war.

CONCLUSION

As December 7, the date set for the public an-nouncement of EMDICO's appointment, ap-proached, Srinivasan pondered his options. As indicated in Exhibit 2, Fuji management had set some ambitious sales goals for EMDICO from 1992 to 1995. This suggested the need for an aggressive relaunch of the brand begin-ning with a high profile press conference. On the other hand, the possible reactions of the previous distributor and of Kodak and Konica were a source of concern. Perhaps a lower pro-file relaunch and a gradual rollout were prefer-able. In either case, details of the marketing program for the relaunch had to be deter-mined.

GILLETTE INDONESIA

In October 1995, Chester Allan, Gillette's country manager in Indonesia, was developing his unit's 1996 marketing plan. Once completed, it would be forwarded to Rigoberto Effio, business director in Gillette's Asia/Pacific group based in Singapore. Each year Effio received and approved marketing plans for the 12 countries in his region, which reached from Australia to China. Once approved by Ian Jackson, Asia/Pacific group vice-president, the overall marketing plan for the region would be reviewed subsequently, along with other regional plans, by Robert King, executive vice-president of Gillette's International Group.

Allan's plan projected a 19% increase in blade sales in Indonesia in 1996, from 115 million to 136 million. This seemed reasonable given a 17% increase in 1995 over the previous year. With a population of almost 200 million, Indonesia represented an important country in the portfolio of markets for which Effio and Jackson were responsible. Effio wondered whether investment spending in marketing beyond the 1995 level of 12% of sales might further accelerate market development. Given the growth rates of Gillette's business in other Asia/Pacific countries, Effio believed that a 25 to 30% increase in blade sales could be achieved in Indonesia in 1996.

THE COMPANY

Founded in 1901, Boston-based Gillette was the world leader in blades and razors and in nine other consumer product categories—writing instruments (Paper Mate, Parker and Waterman), correction products (Liquid Paper), men's electric razors (Braun), toothbrushes (Oral-B), shaving preparations, oral care appliances (Braun Oral-B plaque remover), pistol-grip hair dryers (Braun), hair epilators (Braun), and hand blenders (Braun).

Gillette manufacturing operations were conducted at 50 facilities in 24 countries. A London office had been opened in 1905, and a blade factory opened in Paris the following year. The company's products were distributed through wholesalers, retailers and agents in over 200 countries and territories.

This case was prepared by Diane E. Long (under the direction of John Quelch). Confidential data have been disguised. Copyright © 1996 by the President and Fellows of Harvard College. Harvard Business School case 597-009.

Gillette managed its worldwide business through a combination of business and regional operational units. The North Atlantic Group manufactured and marketed Gillette's shaving and personal care products in North America and Western Europe. The Stationery Products Group, part of the Diversified Group, produced and sold Gillette's stationery products in North America and Western Europe. The Diversified Group also included Braun, Oral-B, and Jafra, each managed by a worldwide unit. The International Group, headed by Robert King, produced and marketed the shaving, stationery, and personal care products everywhere, except for North America and Western Europe. The International Group comprised three geographic divisions: Latin America; Africa, Middle East and Eastern Europe; and Asia/Pacific. Ian Jackson, group vice-president based in Singapore, oversaw operations in 12 Asia/Pacific countries.

Of Gillette's 1995 sales of $6.8 billion, blades and razors accounted for $2.6 billion (40%). Blade and razor sales in the Asia/Pacific region were more than $600 million. The company had consistently maintained profitable growth over the previous five years. Between 1990 and 1995, sales grew by 9% annually, net income by 17%, and earnings per share by 18%. Gillette's mission was to achieve worldwide leadership in its core product categories. In 1995, three-quarters of sales came from product categories in which Gillette held worldwide share leadership. The company emphasized geographic expansion along with research and development, advertising, and capital spending as drivers of growth. New product activity and entry into and development of new markets were considered essential.

Geographic expansion required the company management to "think global, act local." Eduardo Kello, International Group business manager, explained:

> *Headquarters develops new products. They are usually launched first in the U.S. or Western European markets, but quickly introduced in every market worldwide. We start in a new emerging market with simple blades, we introduce the shaving concept. Later, we upgrade the market to higher value products and shaving systems. The country management in each market usually decides the mix of products to push and how to allocate marketing resources against them.*

Robert King further emphasized the importance of persuading Gillette's country managers to take initiative:

> *Trying to drive new product activity from headquarters is like pushing on a string. The string moves much more easily if a country manager is pulling on it than if headquarters is pushing on it.*

While headquarters in Boston emphasized increasing worldwide sales and distribution of higher-margin shaving systems such as Sensor, this was not feasible in many Asian markets. Only a few consumers were sophisticated and wealthy enough to be potential customers for the Sensor. In Indonesia, for example, the focus was still on introducing the concept of shaving with basic Gillette products.

INDONESIA IN 1996

The Republic of Indonesia was an archipelago of more than 15,000 islands and 196 million people who spoke over 250 regional languages and dialects. (See Exhibit 1 for a map of the country.) Approximately 3,000 miles separated Sigli on Sumatra to the west from Sarmi on Irian Jaya to the east. In 1995, President Suharto had led the country for thirty years. Major economic development programs, legal reforms, and changes in domestic policies could only be enacted if supported by the president. Although rumors of his pending retirement circulated, there was no sign of any change in the political power structure in 1996.

By 1995, Indonesia's population had reached 196 million, with 35% living in towns and 65% in rural areas. Indonesia had averaged annual gross domestic product (GDP) growth of over

Exhibit 1   *Map of Indonesia*

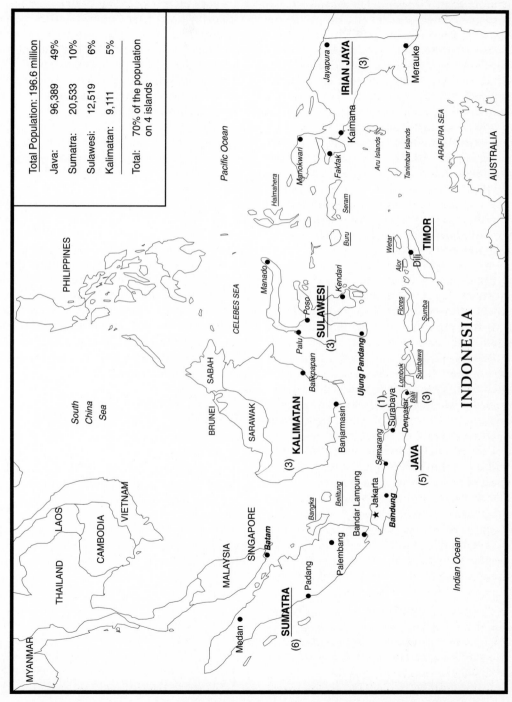

Note: Numbers in parentheses indicate number of Gillette distributors in a particular region.

7% for more than 20 years. The country traditionally exported agricultural and oil petroleum products, but economic development plans since the oil crisis of 1988 had encouraged growth in non–oil-related industries. Economic policy was laid out in five-year plans known as Replita.[1] The goals of Replita VI, applicable in 1996, were to maintain annual GDP growth of 6.2%, expand the manufacturing sector by 9.4% a year, and expand the non–oil/gas component of manufacturing by 10.3% a year. Inflation in 1996 was expected to be 12%. Over the years, the liberalization of foreign investment policy had increased private sector involvement in the economy; the central government focused on developing infrastructure in the poorer regions and on human resources.

Economic progress was manifested in increased per-capita incomes and improved standards of living for most of the population. The government stressed export-oriented industrialization to fuel growth and a demand for labor that would keep pace with population growth. During Replita VI, it was expected that more than two million Indonesians would enter the workforce each year. The rupiah[2] had depreciated in order to maintain Indonesia's export competitiveness. The value of committed foreign investment reportedly increased from $826 million in 1986 to $10.3 billion in 1992 and to $23.7 billion by June 1994.[3] In 1996, Indonesia was expected to have the highest foreign direct-investment/export ratio (74%) of any major emerging market. However, only around one-half of approved foreign direct-investment projects had been implemented.

Economic growth had not been consistent throughout the archipelago. Java and Bali had grown much faster than poorer regions, such as Irian Jaya and East Timor; contribution of these poorer regions to the country's economy was minimal. Java and Bali accounted for 7% of the land, 60% of the population, and 75% of the gross domestic product. Four of the five major urban centers (Jakarta, Bandung, Surabaya, and Semarang) were on Java.

The average standard of living on Java and Bali was much higher than in the rest of Indonesia. An improving education system ensured that foreign companies would be attracted to the major urban areas, fueling further growth. Market research showed that consumer marketers launched their campaigns in and expected most of their sales from the top five cities (the four in Java plus Medan on Sumatra) which together accounted for 35 million of the population. About 60% of Gillette's 1995 sales were made in these five metropolitan areas.

Table A shows the percentages of households falling into each of several income classes in 1995 and projections for 2000. Also shown is the percentage of each income group who shopped regularly in supermarkets in 1995.

Indonesian Shaving Practices

Gillette traditionally entered a market with the basic double-edge blade. Effio explained, "We lead with our strength—the shaving business. Later we leverage the distribution established for our blades on behalf of our other product lines."

Shaving was still underdeveloped in Indonesia, but the incidence of shaving was increasing (see Table B). A 1995 survey of urban men over 18 years (of whom there were 40 million) indicated that 80% shaved. Those who did shaved on average 5.5 times per month, compared to 12 times per month in Hong Kong and 26 times per month in the United States. Tracking data indicated that, in 1993, 66% of urban adult men had been shaving with an average incidence of 4.5 times per month.

---

[1]Replita was the shortened form for the Indonesian name *Rencana pembangunan lima tahun,* which meant five-year development plans.
[2]Rupiah exchange rate in 1995 was U.S. $1 = 2,200 rupiah.
[3]*EIU Country Profile 1995,* p. 19.

Table A   Percentages of Households by Income Sector and Supermarket Shopping Incidence: 1995 and 2000E

| | Percentage of Population | | Percentage Shopping |
Income Segment	1995	2000E*	in Supermarkets: 1995
>$10,000	15.9%	20.6%	40%
$5,000–$10,000	17.0	19.6	25
$2,000–$5,000	32.7	33.8	10
<$2,000	34.4	25.9	2

*Estimated.

Shaving incidence was influenced by several factors. There was increasing awareness of Western grooming practices, especially in urban areas, as a result of exposure to foreign media and the increasing presence of multinational companies and their overseas personnel. College students and graduates entering the workforce were especially important trendsetters. On the other hand, grooming products were still regarded as luxury items by many. In addition, Asian beards did not grow as fast as Caucasian or Latino beards, so shaving incidence would be lower, even in a fully developed market.

Forty percent of men who shaved used store-bought blades all or part of the time. The remainder used dry or wet knives. The average number of blades used in a year by the 20% of shavers who always used blades was fifteen. The average number of blades used by occasional users was four. Only 4% of men used shaving foam or lotion; 25% used soap and water, 12% used water alone, and 58% shaved dry.

Gillette's Operation

Gillette entered Indonesia in 1971 with majority ownership of a joint venture with a local company. Gillette's razor blade plant, built in 1972, was located about one hour from Jakarta. Gillette manufactured 75 stockkeeping units (SKUs) in the factory, of which 65 were shaving items. The major product was the double-edge blade for razors and cartridges. Double-edge blades accounted for 60% of the value of products manufactured. Oral-B products were a small portion of the plant's operations; the plant had just begun to "tuft" or put the bristles on the brush handles. The plant was highly automated and run by 68 full-time employees. In addition, 75 casual workers were employed on one- to two-year contracts. In 1995, the plant produced 150 million blades, of which 46 million were exported. The 1996 production plan called for output of 168 million blades, of which 50 million would be exported. Production manager Eko Margo Suhartono said:

> We are looking to import new equipment and expand the line capacity to 230 million double-edge blades per year, which we hope will be sufficient to meet demand for the next five years. We needed this extra capacity by 1996

Table B   Shaving Incidence Per Month

Shaving Incidence per Month	Percentage of Surveyed
10 times or more	15%
5–9 times	34
4 times	26
3 times	10
2 times	7
1 time	8

but implementation has been delayed to 1997. This means, in 1996, we will have more overtime and must continue to improve plant productivity.

The manufacturing team had improved business processes as well as production efficiencies. They cut the cycle time from placement of order to product out the door from 50 to 43 days. Effio explained, "Before, it would take us seven days to make almost 3 million blades; now we only need three days on the floor. This is an incredible response to sales demand." Due to the demand of other MNCs for experienced workers, there was a need for continuous staff recruiting and training and increasingly upward pressure on worker wages.

In addition, the production team carefully planned the timing of materials inputs. Due to distribution and transportation inefficiencies, the need for buffer inventories was substantial. Cartridges and handles for the razors were imported. The Gillette's women's razor was launched in 1995. The razor was imported, but packaged in the country. Problems with customs clearances could impact the entire manufacturing cycle.

The plant obtained electricity from the local grid, supplemented by two backup generators. Water was drawn from a well on the property. Gillette purchased ammonia and other basic raw materials from local suppliers.

Gillette and Competitive Product Lines

The Gillette brand name was synonymous with high-quality double-edge blades. In fact, the Bahasa Indonesian word for blade sounded similar to the name Gillette. In 1993 Gillette held 28% of the blade market by volume. By 1995 Gillette's unit share had grown to 48% and was expected to increase to 50% in 1996.

Gillette's policy was to make all of its products available to all of its country subsidiaries. Headquarters persuasion and successful launches of new products in other countries were often helpful in motivating country managers to adopt new products.

Gillette's product line in Indonesia included the following:

- Three types of double-edge blades: the basic Gillette blue stainless blade, a premium double-edge blade (Gillette Goal Red), and an improved blue blade (Gillette Goal Blue).
- Disposables. In the United States and Europe, Bic dominated the market for disposable razors with plastic handles as a result of aggressive pricing. In other markets, Gillette had been able to position its disposable as a system, rather than a low-priced convenience product. In Indonesia, Gillette sold two types of disposables, the Goal II and the more advanced Blue II.
- The GII (named Trac II in the United States) was the earliest shaving system from Gillette to incorporate twin-blade technology, whereby the first blade lifted the hair out of the follicle for the second blade to then cut it off.
- The Contour system (named Atra in the United States) added a pivoting head (as opposed to the fixed head on the GII) which enabled the twin blades to stay on the face more consistently.
- The Sensor system added an improved pivoting action and independently sprung twin blades.

Exhibit 2 provides a detailed breakdown of Gillette sales by product. Information on Gillette's gross margin as well as manufacturer, distributor, and retailer selling prices by product line is also provided. Gillette sold 115 million blades in Indonesia in 1995, of which 100 million (87%) were double-edge. In contrast, double-edge blades accounted for 70% of sales in Malaysia and only 20% in Australia. Sales of systems and disposables accounted for 30% and 50% of units sold in Australia, and 25% and 5% of units sold in Malaysia. The share of Gillette Indonesia sales accounted for by the higher-margin disposables and systems was projected to increase in 1996 to around 20% of units.

Exhibit 2 *Gillette Indonesia Product Line and Margin Structure: 1995*

Products	Unit Sales (millions)		% of Units Sold Made Locally	Manufacturer Selling Price/Unit[a]	Manufacturer Gross Margin %	Distributor Selling Price/ Unit[b]	Retail Selling Price/Unit
	1995	1996E					
Double-edge Blades	100	108					
Gillette Blue Blade	5	5	100	0.06	47	0.08	0.11
Gillette Goal Red	80	90	100	0.11	50	0.15	0.20
Gillette Goal Blue	15	13	100	0.08	48	0.11	0.15
Disposables	5	10					
Goal II	4	8	100	0.21	32	0.31	0.40
Blue II	1	2	0	0.35	52[c]	0.49	0.64
System Blades	10	18					
Gillette GII	2	3	20	0.45	52	0.68	0.82
Gillette Contour	5	7	20	0.55	52	0.77	1.00
Gillette Sensor	3	8	0	0.65	40[c]	0.91	1.19

[a]In U.S. dollar equivalent. E: Estimated.
[b]Distributors often sold (at an average 8% markup) to subdistributors or wholesalers, who in turn (at an average 12% markup) sold on to mom-and-pop retailers, who took (on average) a further 20% markup.
[c]Represents, in the case of imported products, the difference between Gillette Indonesia's selling price and the landed transfer price.

As indicated in Exhibit 3, Gillette Indonesia's 1995 sales from shaving products were valued at $19.6 million. Through a combination of volume increases (19%) and price increases (20%), Gillette Indonesian management projected that this number would increase to $27.6 million in 1996. Gillette's overall gross margin on shaving products was 46% of gross revenues (or 55% of net revenues after discounts). An income statement for Gillette Indonesia's shaving products business is presented in Exhibit 4.

Gillette's main competitors were imported, low-end, double-edge blades from eastern Europe and China. Based on market research conducted in the four major cities, Tatra, Super Nacet, and Tiger were the most often mentioned competing brands on the market. Gillette's retail prices were sometimes four times those of competitive products. Chester Allan in Jakarta explained, "Currently most of the poorer rural shavers cannot afford Gillette products and buy low-price, low-quality brands, such as Tiger and Tatra. However, with rising incomes and improved Gillette distribution and display, consumers are moving to Gillette."

Exhibit 3 *Gillette Indonesia Sales Breakdowns: 1995 and 1996*

Sales Revenues in 1995	1995	1996E
1995 Total Revenues	$23.0	$32.2
Revenues from export sales	1.4	2.3
Revenues from in-country sales	21.6	29.9
In-country Sales:		
Shaving products total sales	$19.6	$27.6
Blades	10.3	11.2
Disposables	1.2	2.5
Sensor	5.6	10.4
Razors	2.0	3.0
Prep products	0.5	0.5
Nonshave products	$2.0	$2.3

Exhibit 4 *Gillette Indonesia: Percentage Income Statement for Shaving Products, 1995*

Gross revenues from shaving products	100%
Less: Trade discounts	10
= Net revenues	90%
Less: Variable manufacturing costs	36%
Variable selling costs (sales commissions)	2
Variable distribution costs	6
= Gross margin	46%
Less: Advertising	9%
Consumer promotions and merchandising	3
General sales and administrative costs	14
= Profit from operations	20%

Gillette's disposables faced two competitors: Bic, from the United States and Bagus, a locally manufactured brand. Neither of these sold in high volumes, so the competition was not keen. The Schick division of Warner Lambert imported its higher-end products, but sales were minimal. According to Allan, "Gillette has 90% of the premium-priced segment of the market which we developed."

Gillette brand blades commanded high awareness in the Indonesian market. Market research conducted in 1995 among Indonesian male shavers, reported in Exhibit 5, showed 97% brand awareness and 55% brand used most often ratings for Gillette's Goal Red blade.

Distribution and Sales

Indonesian regulations prohibited a foreign company from directly importing or distributing its products. These regulations protected Indonesian distributors and resulted in inefficien-

cies. The American Chamber of Commerce in Jakarta estimated that 45% of retail prices in Indonesia covered distribution services.

To ensure distribution of products in the face of weak communications, poor traffic conditions, and lack of distribution service technology, Gillette managers and those in other MNCs had to focus on the basics of distribution over which they had little control and from which they extracted no direct profit.

Gillette had originally appointed a single national distributor, but by 1993, it was apparent the arrangement was not working satisfactorily. No single distributor could provide an even depth of coverage in every district throughout the entire country. Mohammad Slamet, Gillette's national sales manager in the early 1990s, explained:

There are many distribution issues which require on-the-spot responses. A distributor who is headquartered hundreds of miles away can-

Exhibit 5   *Indonesian Male Consumer Awareness and Usage of Blades: 1995**

Products in Survey	Brand Awareness	Ever Used	Brand Used Most Often
A. Double-edge Blades:			
Gillette:			
Gillette Goal Red	97	85	55
Gillette Goal Blue	49	18	5
Gillette Blue Blade	14	5	1
Competitors:			
Tatra	42	21	4
Super Nacet	16	4	—
Tiger/Cap Macan	59	44	11
B. Disposable Blades:			
Goal II	41	16	4
Blue II	9	3	—
C. System Blades:			
Gillette GII	12	4	1
Gillette Contour	9	4	3
Gillette Sensor	12	4	1

*Source: Company records. Note: Based on a sample of 300 male adult consumers.

not provide a quick enough response. In addition, there often arise sensitive, purely local issues which can only be resolved by someone familiar with the relationships, customs, and dialects of each area.

In 1993, Gillette appointed 23 distributors dispersed across the country. The new distributors were previously known to Slamet or were identified through referrals. In the year following implementation of the new system, sales rose by 60%.

A good distributor had the working capital and/or bank credit line to stock sufficient inventory and to bridge the time gap between paying Gillette and receiving payments from its customers. Second, a good distributor also had sufficient salespeople, warehouses, and reliable transportation equipment. Third, strong local connections with government officials and the trade were critical to success.

A typical distributor represented different manufacturers and product lines. Gillette's distributors were encouraged to hire people to handle only the Gillette business, in the belief that such focus would result in the greater push. Gillette itself expanded its internal sales and trade relations staff to work with the new distributors.

In 1995, Nyoman Samsu Prabata was Gillette's national sales manager. Nyoman's organization comprised three regional managers (covering western, central, and eastern Indonesia) who supervised a total of 12 area managers and supervisors. These managers were well-compensated but were often tempted away by better offers from other multinationals; such was the shortage of general-management talent in Indonesia. Nyoman's group coordinated the efforts of 23 geographically based independent distributors and their 260 salespeople. While Gillette's distributors hired many of the sales staff and paid their base salaries, Gillette covered their commissions and other incentives for reaching targets, which averaged 20% of their total compensation.

Nyoman explained:

The number one job of the Gillette sales team is educating the distributors and their salespeople. We have to train them how our products work so they can demonstrate the products on their own. We have to educate them on the benefits of our products compared to both traditional shaving methods and to competitive products. We also educate them on warehousing and handling methods to reduce damage to the product.

For example one distributor's warehouse was located in an area of Jakarta with poor transportation and prone to flooding. "A few days ago, the warehouse roof fell in under pressure from the rain. The actual damage was minimal but the operation had to stop for a day. He just would not listen to us," explained Nyoman.

In Indonesia, direct verbal confrontation was socially unacceptable. This sometimes resulted in strained relations between a distributor and an area manager festering for months without being solved. Another challenge was the different degree to which employees and consumers observed Muslim religious practices. Nyoman commented:

In Jakarta, while people are faithful followers, the attitude is a bit more casual and there is an understanding that not everyone is practicing to the same degree. However, outside Jakarta, religious practices are more closely observed. In Aceh on Sumatra, it would be an insult to wave good-bye with your left hand. In Bali, the Hindu religion is dominant so, for the "Galungan" holiday, Hindus fast for two days . For Nyepi, complete silence must be observed for one day, so any devout Hindu stays home and does not even turn on the electricity. Not only does this affect our business, but I must plan ahead for holiday staffing.

Gillette gave its distributors 45 days' credit. In return, the distributors would give their customers anywhere from 30 to 60 days' credit. Nyoman said:

While we try to insist on timely payments via bank transfer, there are many times when receivables are overdue. Though the sales staff and area mangers are responsible for receivables, I often have to get involved, and it is important to be tough on the issue. As you move further away from Jakarta, the legal system does not provide much support, so ensuring distributors have the working capital to cover the spread between payables and receivables is critical to their selection.

In addition to the distributors who supplied wholesalers and, in turn, the extensive network of small retailers in Indonesia, Nyoman also supervised a national accounts team who negotiated sales to the major Indonesian supermarket chains, often shipping to them direct. Supermarket chains included Hero, which had 54 outlets, Metro with five outlets, and others located in the large, urban centers. These chains purchased directly from manufacturers and could handle products efficiently. In 1995, supermarkets accounted for 5% of Gillette's shaving products sales in units and 8% in value; corresponding 1993 figures were 2% and 4%. Market research showed that higher income, urban consumers were increasingly shopping in supermarkets. Most sales of Gillette's higher-priced shaving products were sold through these outlets. Competition for shelf space was intensifying. Some supermarkets were imposing slotting allowances on suppliers of up to 80% of a new product's cost to provide shelf space.

Traditional wholesalers and distributors came under pressure as a result of these trends. Many wholesalers had poor facilities, traditional goods-handling methods, and antiquated accounting—some still used an abacus to track the business. They tended to focus on turnover alone rather than in conjunction with profit margin. They were also slow to see the potential of upgrading their customers to higher unit margin products.

Distribution coverage in Indonesia required consumer goods manufacturers like Gillette to reach more than 60,000 small kiosks and mom-and-pop shops. Gillette did not distribute through the many itinerant salespeople who traveled with their wares on bicycles from village to village. The entrepreneurial owners of the small retail outlets would respond to requests from consumers and, in turn, demand the product from their wholesalers. "Pull marketing can be effective," Slamet said. "Once the mom-and-pops start getting requests for a new product, they are willing to stock it. This is how market testing takes place," Effio explained.

Communications

As indicated in Exhibit 4, Gillette Indonesia spent 9% of gross sales on advertising and 3% on consumer promotions and merchandising. Ten percent of gross sales was accounted for by off-invoice allowances to the trade and other forms of trade deals. The advertising budget for shaving products in 1995 was around $2 million.

Media advertising was targeted principally at urban male consumers. About half the advertising budget was spent on television (there were five private channels and one government-owned) and half on print. Television advertising included some program sponsorships. The adult literacy rate in Indonesia was 77%, and half of Indonesian adult males read a newspaper at least once a week. The allocation of Gillette advertising was weighted towards systems and disposables to encourage consumers to trade up.

Gillette headquarters developed television advertisements for use worldwide, with the intent that local voiceovers and local package shots would be superimposed. (A sample Gillette print leaflet [with translation] is shown in Exhibit 6). Gillette Indonesia's marketing manager explained:

We are still in the early stages of educating consumers about shaving. An ad made in Boston for the U.S. market may not have sufficient details about the basics. Nothing can

Exhibit 6A *Gillette Indonesia Print Leaflet*

Tahukah Anda ?

- Jumlah rambut yang tumbuh di wajah pria bisa mencapai 30.000 helai.
- Pertumbuhan rambut tersebut per hari rata-rata 0,38 milimeter.
- Panjang maksimum yang bisa dicapai seumur hidup sekitar **80 sentimeter.**
- Dalam keadaan kering, janggut sama kakunya dengan seal lembaga yang berdiameter sama.

- **18.000 SEBELUM MASEHI** Manusia primitif mengerik rambut pada wajah mereka dengan batu dan tulang yang dipertajam, sebagaimana tergambar pada lukisan-lukisan di goa purba.

- **336 SEBELUM MASEHI** Iskandar Zulkarnaen memerintahkan para prajuritnya untuk bercukur, sehingga tentara Persia tak dapat menjambak janggut mereka dalam pertempuran.

- **1698.** Kaisar Rusia, Peter Yang Agung, mengenakan Pajak atas janggut, untuk membiasakan rakyatnya mengikuti tradisi bercukur yang dilakukan masyarakat Barat.

- **1895.** King C. Gillette, asal Amerika, menemukan pisau cukur modern yang mengubah total kebiasaan bercukur pria di seluruh dunia. Dimana-mana orang meninggalkan pisau cukur tradisional dan menggantinya dengan pisau cukur bermata ganda yang dapat diganti-ganti.

ENAM LANGKAH MENCUKUR LEBIH LICIN, LEBIH LEMBUT DAN LEBIH NYAMAN

1. Bersihkan Wajah

Cucilah muka dengan air hangat dan sabun, lalu bilas hingga bersih. Tak perlu dikeringkan, biarkan kulit wajah dan rambut dalam keadaan basah.

2. Usapkan Gillette Foamy

Usapkan Gillette Foamy secara merata di atas permukaan yang akan dicukur.

Mencegah penguapan air dan mengurangi gesekan antara kulit dengan mata pisau. Sekaligus melembutkan kumis atau janggut yang akan dicukur.

3. Mulailah dari tempat yang Tepat.

Cukur rambut cambang, pipi, dan leher terlebih dulu. Rambut yang paling koku tumbuh di dagu dan sekeliling bibir dan memerlukan waktu lebih lama untuk menyerap air untuk menjadi lembut.

4. Bercukurlah Secara Benar.

Bercukurlah dengan tarikan yang lembut dan ringan. Usahakan untuk sesedikit mungkin melakukan tarikan. Pisau cukur Gillette dirancang untuk menghasilkan cukuran yang lebih licin, lebih lembut dan nyaman.

5. Bilaslah Mata Pisau

Di tengah kegiatan mencukur, sesekali bilaslah mata pisau cukur dengan air yang deras (misalnya dari keran) guna membuang limbah cukuran. Usai bercukur, mata pisau harus langsung dibilas dan dihentak - hentakkan sampai airnya kering.

6. Jangan Mengusap Mata Pisau.

Jangan sekalikali mengusap mata pisau dengan apa pun, karena akan merusak ketajamannya.

<u>Gunakan cartridge yang sesuai dengan pisau cukur Gillette Anda.</u>

Exhibit 6B: *English Translation of Gillette Indonesia Print Leaflet*

Do you know?

- Up to 30,000 hairs can grow on a man's face.
- The hairs grow at an average rate of 0.38 millimeters per day.
- They can reach a maximum length of approximately 80 centimeters (32") over a lifetime.
- When it is dry, a beard is as stiff as copper fibers of the same diameter.

- **18,000 B.C.** Primitive men scraped the hair off their faces with sharpened stones and bones, as depicted in drawings in ancient caves.
- **336 B.C.** Alexander the Great ordered his soldiers to shave so that the Persian army would not be able to grab their beards in battle.
- **1698.** Peter the Great, Czar of Russia, imposed a tax on beards to get his people used to following the shaving practices of Western societies.
- **King C. Gillette**, an American, invented the modern razor, which totally changed men's shaving habits all over the world. People everywhere gave up traditional razors and replaced them with replaceable double-edged razors.

SIX STEPS TO A SMOOTHER, GENTLER AND MORE COMFORTABLE SHAVE

1. Clean your face

Wash your face with hot water and soap, then rinse it until it is clean. You don't have to dry it, leave your face and hair wet.

2. Apply Gillette Foamy

Apply Gillette Foamy evenly over the surface to be shaved. It prevents water evaporation and reduces friction between the skin and the razor blade. At the same time it softens the mustache or beard which you are going to shave.

3. Start at the Right Place

First shave the sideburns, cheeks and neck. The stiffest hairs grow on the chin and around the lips and need more time to absorb water in order to become soft.

4. Shave Correctly

Shave with gentle and light strokes. Try to make as few strokes as possible. The Gillette razor is designed to produce a smoother, gentler, more comfortable shave.

5. Rinse the Razor Blade

While shaving, rinse the razor blade once in a while under running water (for example from the tap) to get rid of the whiskers. After shaving, the razor blade must be rinsed right away and shaken until dry.

6. Don't Wipe the Razor Blade

Don't ever wipe the razor blade with anything, because it will destroy its sharpness. *Use the cartridge that is right for your Gillette razor.*

be taken for granted here, especially when it comes to advertising the entry-level products, the double-edge blades.

Gillette Indonesia managers differed over the relative emphasis that advertising should place on persuading consumers to shave for the first time, increasing the incidence of shaving among existing shavers, and trading existing shavers up to higher-margin, more sophisticated shaving systems. As a compromise, the 1995 advertising budget was split equally among these three objectives. One-third of the total budget was allocated to advertising Sensor.

Special promotions were run in 1995 on the Sensor and Contour systems. Gift-with-purchase promotions (involving an Oral-B travel toothbrush, a toilet bag, or a trial sample of Foamy shaving cream) were targeted at upper- to middle-income urban males. Promotional efforts were sometimes focused on the members of executive clubs, attendees at golf tournaments, or workers in specific office buildings.

Coupons were not used in Indonesia; redemption systems through retailers were not yet in place. However, Gillette found that lucky draws with entry forms inside product packages worked well; consumers had to mail in entry forms to be included in the draws.

Gillette used similar packaging in Indonesia as in the United States for its more expensive systems products. The Goal II, the cheaper of Gillette's disposables, was advertised on radio. The number of blades per pack varied by outlet; twice as many were included in the pack for supermarkets as in the pack for mom-and-pop stores.

SETTING THE COURSE

As Allan reviewed his initial projections for 1996 (see Exhibit 3), he wondered how rapidly the Indonesian market for blades and razors could or would expand. Should the Indonesian market be allowed to just move along at its own pace? If so, what would that pace be? Alternatively, should Gillette Indonesia invest additional resources either in advertising and promotion or in sales and distribution, to accelerate the process of market development? If so, which products should be emphasized? Would further investment be wasted if it were on concepts and products that were beyond consumers' understanding or willingness to pay?

Allan resolved to set out his objectives for Gillette Indonesia in 1996 and to develop a detailed marketing plan, including an income statement projection. He knew his plan would have to satisfy Effio's objectives for Gillette's growth in the Asia/Pacific region.

PART V

MANAGING INTERNATIONAL PARTNERS AND ALLIANCES

In the early 1980s, Professor Michael Porter's "five forces" analysis depicted companies in a value appropriation battle with their customers, suppliers, and competitors; today, we see them focused more on value creation by working in mutually advantageous partnerships with these same groups. Similarly, Professor Raymond Vernon's seminal analysis of business-government relationships described MNCs holding "sovereignty at bay"; but today we see the same companies pursuing cooperative relationships with host governments worldwide, often becoming partners in ventures with them.

This dramatic change in strategic thinking and organizational relationships has made the boom in alliances, consortia, and strategic partnerships a worldwide phenomenon. It has been driven by some new market forces, has led to some new business forms, and has created some new strategic costs and risks.

NEW FORCES AND MOTIVATIONS

International business has long been characterized by joint ventures, but these were typically opportunistic, localized, and short-lived relationships established by companies to gain access to unfamiliar foreign markets. The more recent explosion in global alliances is much different: they typically involve much larger partners, are global in scale, and are strategic in nature.

The biggest driver of this change is the shift occurring in the critical scarce resources constraining companies' growth. Where once the constraints were imposed by the availability of capital, today the limiting resources increasingly are information, knowledge, and expertise. Although not restricted to R&D, this intellectual capital constraint is often seen clearest and earliest in a company's research labs: efficient scale of R&D is rising, the scope of relevant technologies is broadening, and the product life cycles are shrinking. Together, these forces have created a situation in which the cost of product and process development has skyrocketed. Equally problematic is the reality that few companies by themselves have all the technology and expertise they need to become (or remain) leading-edge competitors in a competitive game increasingly played on the field of innovation. More than anything else, this has become the engine driving the scramble for alliance partners.

PARTNERSHIP MOTIVATIONS AND FORMS

The motivations for forming strategic partnerships are many and varied, and their legal forms and administrative frameworks are too numerous to catalog. Among the newest alliance relationships, however, four clearly interlinked categories deserve to be highlighted:

- **Partnership for technology exchange.** The huge advances made in various scientific and technological fronts have often led to the transformation of whole industries. (Think, for example, of the impact of the transistor and the semiconductor on the consumer electronics industry.) At one level, these forces drive industry consolidation through massive mergers and acquisitions such as the ones that have swept through the pharmaceutical, banking, and professional services industries. But even such consolidation has often proven insufficient to provide the critical mass necessary to gain global scale efficiencies, and even newly merged pharmaceutical behemoths like SmithKline Beecham or Novartis are still frantically expanding their huge portfolios of distribution agreements, cross-licenses, and other strategic partnership arrangements.

- **Partnership for global competitiveness.** In the face of such industry restructuring and the emergence of dominant players, a flurry of activity has occurred, creating partnerships and alliances among smaller players uniting to gain some competitive defense against the industry giants. This is the motivation that led to Fujitsu's various worldwide partnerships in order to combat IBM. It also is the driving force behind the numerous initiatives among the small players in the software industry to unite in strength against Microsoft. For many companies in smaller countries, the chance of partnering with a dominant global player represents the most effective way in which they can gain access to the benefits of the global competitive game. It is this motivation that has driven so many companies to enter into joint-venture partnerships with Corning as that company expands into market worldwide.

- **Partnerships for industry convergence.** The technological turmoil has no respect for industry boundaries, and one of the major forces driving the growth of the cross-border partnerships and alliances has been the convergence of once-separate industries and groups of competitors. Among the clearest examples of this has been the blurring of the boundary between the computer and telecommunications industries, and more recently, software, media, and the whole field of entertainment. Another classic example has been the pharmaceutical companies' links into biotechnology. But perhaps the most interesting partnership arrangements have emerged in the field of high-definition TV (HDTV). Because HDTV involved a wide range of technologies, huge investments, and enormous risks, this development has led to the creation of several global consortia, many of which have primarily been nationally based. As a result, groups of companies in Japan are facing off against others in the United States, with a third epicenter in this emerging global battle developing in Europe.

- **Partnerships to create industry standards.** The HDTV battle is largely motivated by the recognition that a single set of global industry standards probably will emerge and the company (or more likely the consortium) that can establish the dominant format will have an enormous competitive advantage. When global markets were more fragmented, the world was able to develop multiple standards, attested to by the existence today of NTSC, PAL, and SECAM TV transmission standards. However, by the time of the videocassette recorder, global markets were converging, and competitive rules were changing. Despite the technological superiority of Philips's V 2000 system and Sony's Betamax technology, the clear winner in the VCR battle was the VHS standard sponsored by Matsushita. Supported by a vast number of partners and licensees, this format quickly emerged as the dominant world standard. Its success became a powerful lesson for many companies, and made developing industry standards a driving force for partnerships and alliances ever since.

Partnership Costs and Risks

Though there are numerous benefits to creating global partnerships, there are at least as many costs. Among the greatest risks is what has become known as the problem of the obsoleting bargain. Although most partnerships are established on the basis of mutual interdependency and joint gains, that initial balance can easily be disrupted—sometimes through the deliberate subversion of one of the partners. The critical interdependency is maintained only as long as both sides need each other, but if one partner develops the skill of the other, the basis for the partnership may be eroded. This has been the fate of many joint-venture relationships for market entry, particularly in Japan. When General Foods created a partnership with Ajinomoto, it was based on exchanging the company's technology in instant coffee manufacturing for the Japanese company's market access and management capability in that very different culture. Over several years, however, Ajinomoto learned most of General Foods' technology, while the American company learned very little about the Japanese market. Unsurprisingly, the balance that once held the partnership together began eroding and the problem of the obsoleting bargain became clear. Similar problems led to the breakup of the technology agreements between Komatsu on one side and International Harvester and Cummins on the other.

If the obsoleting bargain is the main strategic risk in most partnerships, then boundary management is the major organizational cost. Most companies entering into alliances of various kinds focus primarily on the strategic logic and spend very little of their negotiating efforts trying to understand the organizational logic of the new partnership. Yet research continually shows that it is in the organization and management of the partnerships that most of the difficulty arises. For managers in the partnership, it requires the ability to take responsibility for matters over which they do not have complete control. This classic partnership problem requires both partners to commit to careful selection of boundary-spanning managers, major integration of information systems, a realignment of incentives and rewards, and constant monitoring by top management.

If such intensive management attention comes at a cost, then it is only because these alliances offer such substantial potential benefit. For many companies, they have become the linchpin of their global competitiveness.

LOCTITE CORPORATION– INTERNATIONAL DISTRIBUTION

In December 1992, the senior management of Loctite Corporation was reviewing the company's international distribution policies in the light of a recent decision to acquire an equity interest in their Hong Kong distributor. Worldwide distribution capability had been a key element in the corporation's achievement of global leadership in the chemical-adhesives industry. Loctite had a range of relationships through which it accessed international markets, including export agents, distributors, joint ventures, and wholly owned subsidiaries.

Chairman and CEO Ken Butterworth, a 17-year Loctite veteran who had once worked for Loctite's Australian distributor, was continually looking to open up new markets with potential. With economic recession limiting growth in Loctite's core North American and European markets, expansion in the Asia/Pacific region was a key strategic goal. Butterworth was discussing the company's Hong Kong options with David Freeman, president and COO, an En-

glishman with an 18-year Loctite career, and Martin Wiley, an American who had worked for the company for 30 years and was now regional manager for the southern half of Loctite's Asia/Pacific operations.

COMPANY BACKGROUND

Founded in 1956, Loctite Corporation, headquartered in Hartford, Connecticut, had grown to become the world's leading manufacturer and marketer of adhesives, sealants, and related products. During the 1980s, it had enjoyed impressive growth; net sales had increased from $228 million in 1983 to $608 million in 1992, and net earnings had grown during the same period from $22 million to $72 million. The 1992 balance sheet showed total assets of $557 million, stockholders' equity of $383 million, and long-term liabilities of $36 million. The company had achieved Fortune 500 status in 1990, and in 1991 was ranked 477 in revenue, 190 in

---

This case was prepared by David J. Arnold (under the direction of John A. Quelch). Copyright © 1993 by the President and Fellows of Harvard College. Harvard Business School case 594-021.

Exhibit 1   *Loctite Corporation: Income Statements, 1990–1992 ($ in thousands)* *

	Year Ended December 31,		
	1990	**1991**	**1992**
Net sales	$555,185	$561,218	$607,967
Cost of sales	215,132	217,501	229,175
Gross margin	340,053	343,717	378,792
R&D expense	21,731	22,498	26,152
Selling, general, and administration expenses	222,884	222,240	239,640
Restructuring charges	0	4,434	12,740
Earnings from operations	95,438	94,545	100,260
Investment income	11,010	13,365	9,173
Interest expense	(6,790)	(5,477)	(5,593)
Other expense	(934)	(346)	(94)
Foreign exchange loss	(7,440)	(6,202)	(8,601)
Earnings before income taxes	91,284	95,885	95,145
Provision for income taxes	23,861	23,971	22,834
Net earnings	$67,423	$71,914	$72,311
Earnings per share	$1.86	$1.98	$1.99

*Source: Loctite Corporation annual reports.

profits, 24 in profit as a percentage of sales, and 18 in per share annual growth over the previous decade. (Exhibit 1 summarizes Loctite's income statements from 1990 to 1992.) By 1992, the company estimated its worldwide market share in industrial adhesives at 70 to 80%.

As stated in the 1992 annual report, Loctite's growth had been based upon a "strategy of promoting diversity in end-use markets and geographies for our core business; diversification into new businesses in which senior management has little expertise is not part of our strategy." This core business remained the sale of chemical adhesives to industrial users who had previously used mechanical fasteners such as screws and bolts; industrial chemical adhesives and sealants accounted for 50% of corporate revenues in 1992. From this base, Loctite had expanded into related markets in the 1970s, such as the automotive aftermarket, an entry built upon the acquisition of Permatex. In the mid-1970s, Loctite had also entered the consumer adhesives market and grew this business through acquisitions, principally the purchase of Woodhill Chemicals. More recently, Loctite had also expanded its technology base through the acquisition of silicone and polyurethane companies, and in 1990 had acquired a U.S. company selling hand-cleaning products, seen as a natural complement to adhesives and sealants.

Geographical expansion had begun early in the company's history. By 1992 Loctite had equity positions in operations in 33 countries outside the United States—with third-party distributors in other countries—and almost 60% of sales and 70% of earnings were derived from operations outside the United States.

ORGANIZATION

Loctite was organized into four regional groups: North America, consisting of the United States, Canada, and Mexico; Latin America, consisting of all countries south of Mexico; Europe, which included the former Communist bloc countries and was also responsible for operations in the Middle East and Africa; and Asia/Pacific, stretching from Korea to Australasia and as far west as India. Within these regions, operations were organized into three business groups: the industrial market, including original equipment manufacture (OEM) and maintenance, repair, and overhaul (MRO) customers;[1] the retail and consumer markets; and the automotive after-market.

Organization structures varied by region. The president of North America headed a functional organization with no country managers, as the United States, Mexico, and Canada were viewed as a single market and divided into 12 sales regions (one of which, for example, spanned the U.S.-Canada border). These regional sales managers reported to a vice president of sales in Hartford. In the three other regions, country managers with profit responsibility reported to regional management, who also sometimes had

---

[1]Original equipment manufacturers (OEM) made products for sale as new items, either under their own brand name or those of third parties. Maintenance, repair, and overhaul (MRO) organizations were service businesses offering after-sales support to maximize the performance of the products. The automotive after-market, an industry built around the service and maintenance of motor vehicles, was an MRO market, although it was of sufficient importance to Loctite to merit its own business group.

regionwide responsibility for a line of business. For example, the vice-presidents of northern and southern Europe, based in Munich and Milan, were also responsible, respectively, for development of Loctite's industrial products and consumer products throughout the entire European region. On a more informal basis, Loctite's two vice-presidents of Asia/Pacific, based in Hong Kong and Tokyo, had complementary sales and technical backgrounds that helped them jointly develop business in the region. A limited number of functional managers also had regional responsibilities, such as the vice-president of manufacturing in Europe, based in Dublin near the major Irish plant, and regional marketing managers, who provided guidance to and transferred best practices among marketing managers in Loctite's subsidiaries and distributors. (Exhibit 2 depicts Loctite's organization structure as in 1992, and Exhibit 3 gives a breakdown of employees by region.)

The corporation was run in a decentralized fashion, with only 56 people in the Hartford headquarters office. Direct reports to Butterworth and Freeman, besides the regional managers, included the heads of various corporate staff groups and New Business Development (NBD). The primary role of NBD was research and development, from basic chemical research through product development. There were no corporate marketing managers, as Butterworth believed that "marketing belongs at the coal face." Planning was a bottom-up process, which required national units to present their detailed plans annually to visiting corporate staff, usually either Butterworth and/or Freeman. Drawing on their years of experience at Loctite and their knowledge of other markets, they were able to challenge and refine the plans. Butterworth acknowledged that these sessions could be "brutal," but he always ensured that his visits incorporated customer meetings and social functions that ensured a strong enough relationship between headquarters and the field that the

Exhibit 2   *Loctite Corporation: Organization Structure, 1992* *

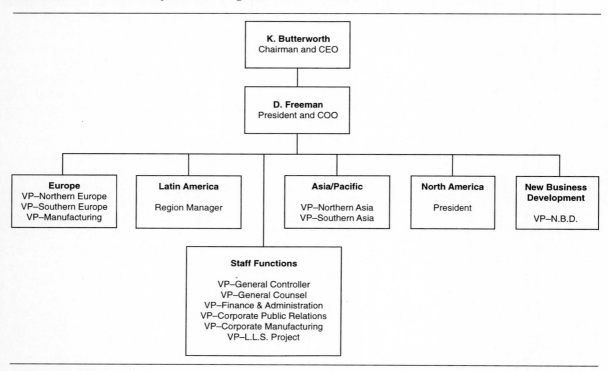

*Source: Loctite Corporation.

Exhibit 3   *Employees by Region, December 1992* *

	Total		**Regional Management**
North America	1,792	(48.6%)	2
Europe	1,095	(29.7%)	4
Asia/Pacific	278	(7.5%)	4
Latin America	524	(14.2%)	2
	3,689		
Corporate headquarters	56		

*Source: Loctite Corporation.

latter could accept his challenging management style.

PRODUCT LINE

Loctite's strategy was to offer a full range of adhesive and sealant products to meet the different needs of a broad range of customers. The 1991 annual report stated, "Loctite generally does not rely on blockbuster products. . . . We tend to have more application-sensitive products, each of which requires specific marketing focus to introduce." Technical leadership in product development was key to Loctite's success. In 1992, the company spent 4% of its revenue on R&D at facilities in Connecticut, Ireland, and Japan. Loctite sought to derive a minimum of 25% of its annual revenues from products launched within the previous five years.

Loctite sold three principal product lines: anaerobic adhesives, which accounted for 28% of corporate sales in 1992 and were sold exclusively in industrial markets; cyanoacrylates (CAs), which sold in both industrial markets (15% of sales) and consumer markets (18% of sales); and silicones (12% of sales). Loctite also sold adhesives and sealants based on other technologies, such as the epoxies used to bond microchips to circuit boards. Other revenues were derived from hand-cleaning products, which Loctite had recently introduced in several countries under the Fast Orange brand name, and a variety of dispensing equipment which Loctite had developed for its products, ranging from simple hand-held guns or rollers to complex assemblies such as screen-printing devices which could fit into computer-controlled assembly lines.

Anaerobic adhesives were the "family crown jewels," the technology on which the company had been founded in 1956. They were stored and dispensed in liquid form, but self-hardened into tough plastics as soon as they were deprived of air. Originally developed to bond cylindrical

metal parts (such as a bolt to a nut), they were later employed in a wide range of applications such as engine housings and bearings. The benefits of anaerobics compared to mechanical fixings were fourfold:

1. *Cost savings.* Unlike mechanical fixings, aerobic retention was not dependent upon the precision with which the parts were engineered, and so allowed manufacturers to achieve savings on components.
2. *Speed of assembly.* The application of the adhesive was simple and fast compared to mechanical fixings. By switching from mechanical fastenings to chemical adhesives, Westland, the U.K. helicopter manufacturer, reduced assembly time for each of the 200 bearings in its Lynx aircraft from 10 to 15 minutes to two minutes without any modification of the parts involved.
3. *Strength in service.* However fine the tolerance to which they were engineered, the two or more parts of a mechanical fixture could be in contact only at their high points, typically 25% of the surface, leaving what Loctite referred to as "inner space." The liquid anaerobic adhesive, by filling all this space, provided 100% surface contact, resulting in a stronger fitting, less wear in use, and lower maintenance requirements.
4. *Leakproofing.* Since total surface fit eliminated the leakage of liquids or gas, an anaerobic could act as a sealant and improve the performance of an assembly. Vibration and other wear caused by leakage of liquids or gas could also be eliminated, reducing maintenance requirements.

CAs set faster than anaerobics but were less tough and durable. Suitable for a wider range of applications and materials beyond metal-to-metal fixtures, they were also sold to consumers as instant general-purpose adhesives. The first CA had been introduced by a division of Eastman Kodak in 1958, and during the 1960s Eastman sold CAs to Loctite for repackaging. Loctite developed its own manufacturing technology in 1971 and, by 1978, was believed to have exceeded Eastman's share of the North American industrial CA market. Loctite's consumer CA brand, Super Glue, had grown to become a major player in selected markets around the world, although it faced tough competition from several international brands such as the world leader, Krazy Glue, manufactured by Toagosei of Japan.

Silicone products had been added to the product line in the late 1980s as part of Loctite's strategy of broadening its technology base. Sold exclusively in industrial markets, they were used for a range of applications complementary to the rigid plate fixings for which anaerobics were best suited, such as coating, sealing, lubricity, thermal conductivity, and electrical insulation. They were particularly important in "formed-in-place" gaskets (where their leakproofing qualities outperformed traditional materials such as metal or rubber) and in electronic manufacturing (for example, in the protection of electronic components on a printed circuit board).

Product formulations were, with few exceptions, identical in all markets and countries. Packaging was more variable and was customized to individual markets, with the Irish packaging plant able to print packages in 62 languages, with low changeover costs. In line with Loctite's strategy of focus in product range and diversity in markets and geography, local salespeople were encouraged to adapt their communications messages to individual customers.

SALES MIX

The sales mix of Loctite products varied from one country to another, although Loctite's business was always based upon the core industrial product lines of anaerobics and industrial CAs. Freeman commented, "We will only enter the automotive aftermarket and/or consumer mar-

kets when a base of business has been established and profitability achieved in the industrial market." In Loctite's more mature American and European operations, the sales mix covered the entire Loctite product range. A typical distributor in these mature markets carried approximately 100 stock-keeping units (SKUs), consisting of various sizes of some 30 Loctite products. Around 25% of SKUs were common to virtually all distributors, and these typically generated at least 50% of a distributor's sales. Having built its business on these core products, a mature market distributor then expanded its range of Loctite products according to the type of customer industries it served. In many less-developed markets, by contrast, Loctite was still building its core industrial business.

Loctite's sales mix was also broadly based in terms of customers, with no one end-user in the United States accounting for more than 1% of corporate sales, and no North American distributor accounting for more than 10%. While some of the sales mix variation was due to inherent differences in market potential and stage of economic development, Butterworth also believed it was due to the differing skills, experience, or contacts of distributors, which resulted in their focusing on one or two of Loctite's product lines at the expense of others. Experience gained in industrial markets, for instance, had seldom proven transferable to the building of a consumer business. In total, 18% of Loctite worldwide revenues in 1992 were from nonowned operations outside North America, consisting of 12.5% from joint ventures and 5.5% from independent distributors. Ten years earlier, independent distributors had contributed approximately one-third of revenues.

The greatest variation in sales performance was in consumer markets. In 1992, for instance, consumer product sales represented only 6% of revenues in North America, where Super Glue ranked second in market share, but were considerably higher in Europe, which accounted for over 60% of worldwide sales of Super Glue.

Loctite's worldwide market share in consumer instant adhesives was 20 to 25%. In markets where Loctite had been the first to launch consumer instant adhesives, or where a distributor had invested substantially in building a consumer business, Loctite was the market leader; Brazil and France were the primary examples. In many other countries, Loctite faced more intense competition for consumer product sales and could not easily afford the investment required to build a consumer brand franchise through advertising.

Despite its dominant worldwide share in industrial adhesives, Loctite believed its products had achieved only limited penetration of the available market. Mechanical engineers were generally untrained in the chemistry of adhesive technology and relied by a three-to-one margin on the traditional mechanical fastening approaches in which they had been educated. These prospective customers often rejected an initial Loctite sales approach by declaring that they had no need for chemical adhesives. Loctite's marketing and sales efforts, therefore, focused on educating both distributors and end-users in the properties of its products through seminars, product videos, and product demonstrations at end-user premises. Another problem was that prospective customers often regarded adhesives or fastenings as the least important components of their products. Wiley commented, "Selling industrial adhesives is like selling salt to restaurants." Butterworth believed that Loctite had to work hard on changing its image from a glue company to that of a high-technology company; in 1992 he had approved a partial three-year sponsorship of a Lotus Formula 1 racing car, which incorporated some Loctite products in its assembly.

Loctite faced few direct competitors, and none held more than a 5% share of the world market for industrial adhesives. Major competitors were National Starch, a Unilever subsidiary, which marketed under the Permabond brand name; the German chemical company Henkel; and, more recently, the Japanese Three Bond Corporation, which competed in both retail and industrial markets in Japan but in only industrial markets in North America. 3M had entered the CA market but had withdrawn in 1983. These competitors invested only a fraction of what Loctite invested in R&D. Each offered a narrower product line than Loctite, focusing either on a single adhesive technology or on products for a specific vertical market such as electronics. Most competitors simply copied Loctite products and sought to recruit employees of Loctite and its distributors.

DISTRIBUTION IN NORTH AMERICA

By 1992, Loctite products were available through approximately 1,600 outlets across North America. Distributors ranged from single-outlet distributors to Loctite's largest customer, Bearings Inc., with some 260 outlets. The value of Loctite ex-factory sales to these distributors approximated $70 million in 1992. The average distributor margin was 30 to 35%.

Loctite was represented in only a small proportion of the 50,000 potential outlets for its products in North America. Loctite believed that selective distribution allowed it to provide a superior level of service to its end customers while still achieving sufficient market coverage. Loctite devoted considerable effort to the selection of distributors. The process began with Loctite surveying the number of manufacturing plants, their sizes and lines of business in a given region, and calculating the sales potential. Selected potential end-users of Loctite products were often researched as to their preferred suppliers, and a number of potential distributors was identified. The criteria for appointment as a Loctite distributor included the mix and type of the distributor's existing customers, other lines carried, creditworthiness, and any previous contacts with Loctite. It was Loctite's policy to have two or three distributors covering any market, so that end-users had a choice of suppliers.

The low level of knowledge of adhesive technology among many end-users was reflected at the distributor level, and in its early years Loctite had to persuade potential distributors to carry its line. Although the company's success in the 1980s meant more distributors applied to carry the Loctite line than the company needed, Loctite continued to provide more support to distributors than that offered by any other competing supplier. Support included training of the distributor's inside and outside salespeople, demonstrations of new products in Loctite seminars, and extensive merchandising aids such as item selection charts and case histories of applications in different industries. A typical distributor employed one or two outside salespeople and four or five counter staff; Loctite usually targeted two of them for intensive product training. Loctite also undertook joint sales efforts with each distributor and ran seminars at end-users' premises, hoping that eventually the distributor would learn enough to be able to run such seminars independently.

Distributors could expect attractive returns. Although Loctite products represented only 2% to 5% of turnover for most distributors, their distributor margin of 30 to 35% was 50 to 100% higher than the average margin for the other products they carried. In addition, inventories of Loctite products turned over two to three times faster than most other distributors' product lines. While some of these distributors carried competitor adhesives in product lines that Loctite no longer covered—such as epoxy resins—they rarely carried directly competitive products in Loctite's categories.

These factors had resulted in a stable network of distributors. Of the 1,600 outlets, some 1,400 had been Loctite distributors for at least 10 years, with most of the growth in the 1980s coming either from additional appointments in areas that were insufficiently covered or from the acquisition of new outlets by existing Loctite distributors. It was rare for a distributor to choose to leave the Loctite network, and only occasionally did Loctite have to dismiss a distributor. The company anticipated some broadening of its distribution in North America to approximately 1,800 outlets by 1996, while maintaining its selective distribution strategy.

The two largest categories of distributors were bearing distributors, serving engineering and equipment manufacturers, and general mill suppliers, which offered a wide range of product lines to factories, from industrial clothing to nuts and bolts. Both served a broad base of customers. A few distributors served only specific vertical markets such as automotive, oil, or electronics firms (although electronics customers were increasingly served by general distributors).

The Loctite North American sales force that served these industrial distributors was organized into 12 regions. Given the differences in buying patterns across Loctite's three product-market sectors, some salespeople within each region specialized in areas such as OEM when justified by the volume of business. Direct sales to large end-users were managed by specialist sales representatives who reported to a national sales manager. In 1992, direct sales represented 40% of the industrial business in North America. This figure included some drop shipments, whereby Loctite delivered large orders direct to end-users who were established customers of a distributor and paid the relevant distributor 10% of the end-user price.

Working alongside the sales organization were six market managers, based in Connecticut and reporting to the vice-president of marketing. The six markets were automotive, electronics, other OEM, maintenance, automotive aftermarket, and consumer retail. There were plans to consolidate the North American business into a single organization in Connecticut rather than continue to have efforts directed at the consumer retail market and automotive aftermarket run separately from Cleveland, Ohio—the pre-acquisition base of Woodhill.

A more intensive distribution strategy was adopted for the maintenance market, in which applications were less complex. For this market, Loctite products were available through some 5,500 outlets under a separate brand name, Permatex. When distributors applied to represent Loctite products in geographical areas that Loctite already covered sufficiently, they were often encouraged to take on the Permatex line instead. There was minimal overlap between the two sets of distributors: the 1,600 industrial distributors could stock the more widely available Permatex products, but the 5,500 maintenance outlets could not carry Loctite-branded products. Cannibalization between the two lines was minimal.

LOCTITE'S INTERNATIONAL DEVELOPMENT

In the late 1950s, Loctite began its international growth with opportunistic export sales to Canada, Australia, and the United Kingdom. Some shipments were also made to Japan under licensing agreements. This international business soon grew to the point where Loctite had to appoint national distributors who, as principals, bought product from Loctite for resale. During the 1960s, expansion continued into Europe: a French distributor was appointed, along with two in Germany—one for anaerobics and one for CAs. All overseas sales were of exported products, until the establishment of manufacturing plants in Ireland and the Netherlands in the late 1960s. International expansion was also accelerated by acquisitions; for example, joint ventures in Australia, Chile, and Venezuela came with the Permatex acquisition.

In the early 1970s, Loctite began acquiring equity interests in its distributors. This process began in Europe, with the establishment of the corporation's first joint venture in Belgium and the acquisition of distributor companies in the United Kingdom, Spain, and Italy. By 1992, Loctite's international operations consisted of a portfolio of wholly owned subsidiaries, joint ventures, and distributorships (see Exhibit 4). In most cases, Loctite's penetration of a country market began with a relationship with a distributor, followed by an increasing stake in the business and eventual Loctite ownership. All joint ventures and wholly owned subsidiaries had evolved from Loctite's relationships with third-party national distributors. (Exhibit 5 shows Loctite's equity transactions in international operations for 1985 to 1992.)

In 1992, the North America and Europe regions each accounted for approximately 40% of sales, but Europe contributed 50% of earnings. (Exhibit 6 summarizes financial data by region.) In 1992, an economic recession across much of Europe meant that slower growth was anticipated than in the 1980s. Wholly owned Loctite subsidiaries generated 97% of the company's European sales, the balance coming from distributors and joint ventures. Asia/Pacific sales depended heavily on automotive and electronics manufacturers in Japan, where sales had declined sharply in 1992. Growth in newer markets had offset this downturn, and these were expected to be the basis for the growing importance of the region in Loctite's global strategy. In 1992, 85% of Asia/Pacific sales were derived from wholly owned Loctite companies. In Latin America, 82% of sales were from wholly owned companies, 68% of sales were made in Brazil, and economic development and market conditions varied widely among countries.

The decision to enter a country typically began with an assessment by Loctite management of the market potential. There were several ways to identify potential distributors or partners. The most important, as in North America, was discussion with potential end-users of Loctite products—typically, 10 or more manufacturers were approached and questioned about their preferred distributors for factory supplies. A second method was to obtain recommendations from Loctite distributors in neighboring countries, who often knew the major regional distributors of imported industrial supplies. Third, the distributors of complementary product lines, such as Borg Warner products, were identified.

Exhibit 4   *Loctite Corporation: Countries Served by Loctite Operating Units, 1992**

	Loctite Equity Holding (%)	Loctite Manufacturing Plant (M)	Loctite Internal Packaging Plant (P)
North America:			
Canada	100%		
Mexico	100	M	P
Puerto Rico	100	M	P
United States	100	M	P
Europe:			
Austria	100		
Belgium	100		
Czech Republic	100		
Denmark	0		
France	100		
Finland	0		
Germany	100		P
Hungary	100		
Ireland	100	M	P
Italy	100	M	P
Netherlands	100		
Norway	51		
Poland	100		
Portugal	0		
Slovenia	100		
South Africa	100	M	P
Spain	100		
Sweden	0		
Switzerland	0		
United Kingdom	100		
Asia/Pacific:			
Australia	100		
Hong Kong	0		
India	40	M	P
Indonesia	100		
Japan	100	M	P
Malaysia	100		
New Zealand	0		
People's Republic of China	50	M	P
Philippines	0		
Singapore	100		
South Korea	100		
Taiwan	51		
Thailand	51		

continued

Exhibit 4   *(continued)*

	Loctite Equity Holding (%)	Loctite Manufacturing Plant (M)	Loctite Internal Packaging Plant (P)
Latin America:			
Argentina	100		
Brazil	100	M	P
Chile	100	M	P
Colombia	100		P
Costa Rica	100	M	P
Ecuador	0		
Peru	0		
Venezuela	51	M	P

*Source: Loctite Corporation.

This three-pronged initial search would typically surface three to six potential distributors, with whom discussions would then ensue. The whole selection process from assessing a country's market potential through to appointment of a distribution partner typically took one to two years. Although Loctite preferred distributors who had previous experience of distributing imported products, there were few other criteria regarding the most suitable type of business. In Taiwan, for instance, the appointed distributor was a large conglomerate operating many businesses besides distribution, whereas the distributor in Indonesia was a smaller, family-owned business.

Loctite usually granted a new distributor exclusive rights in its territory and provided extensive support. After initial product and sales training, Loctite sales personnel continued to visit a distributorship at least monthly, while senior regional officers visited at least quarterly. Butterworth and/or Freeman also visited every international distributorship and subsidiary for a business review at least once a year. This review would also be the basis for deciding whether a distribution contract would be re-newed. Typically, contracts were open-ended rather than for fixed terms, with Loctite reserving the right to give six months' notice of severance if performance was significantly below agreed-upon sales and/or profit projections (exceptions could be made for extraneous factors such as a recession in the national market). The right to terminate a distribution contract had rarely been exercised. Freeman believed that in the past, Loctite had sometimes been too supportive of underperforming distributorships but that many of the problems encountered might have been avoided with earlier and preventive intervention by Loctite management. Freeman commented:

The prime message we convey to distributors is the importance of pricing to value. It's difficult for many international distributors to understand what they regard as high Loctite prices. Instead of assessing the value of our products to the customer, they are tempted to set margins and prices low, as they do for the other products they carry, such as bearings, where price competition is fierce. We've learned that our support is necessary early in

(continued on page 482)

Exhibit 5   *Loctite Corporation: Equity Transactions in International Operations, 1985–1992* *

	1985	1986	1987	1988
Mexico			Acquired 100% of manufacturing joint venture	
United States				
Belgium			Bought out remaining 49% of joint venture	
Czech Republic				
France		Acquired 51% of 20-year distributor		
Hungary				
Italy				
Netherlands				
Poland				
Slovenia				
Australia			Acquired 100% of joint-venture partner in automotive aftermarket venture	
India				
People's Republic of China (PRC)		Formed 50/50 joint venture with Loctite Technical Institute		
Singapore/ Malaysia				
South Korea	Formed subsidiary alongside national distributor to provide technical support			
Taiwan				
Thailand				
Argentina				Cancelled distribution contract and formed subsidiary
Chile	Bought out joint-venture partner to form subsidiary			
Colombia	Bought out 20% balance of joint venture to form subsidiary			
Venezuela				Increased joint venture holding from 49% to 51%

*Source: Loctite Corporation.

continued

Exhibit 5 *(continued)*

	1989	1990	1991	1992
Mexico				
United States	Acquired specialty silicone company	Acquired hand cleaner company		
Belgium				
Czech Republic		Opened representative office		
France				
Hungary		Opened representative office		
Italy	Acquired polyurethane company			
Netherlands		Bought out national distribution rights and formed subsidiary		
Poland		Opened representative office		
Slovenia		Opened representative office		
Australia			Merged automotive aftermarket venture into Loctite Australia subsidiary	
India		Formed 51% joint venture with seven-year national distributor		
People's Republic of China (PRC)				
Singapore/ Malaysia				Bought out national distribution rights from 23-year distributor and formed subsidiary
South Korea		Cancelled distribution contract to activate subsidiary as full marketing company		
Taiwan			Formed 51% joint venture with six-year distributor	
Thailand		Formed 51% joint venture with five-year distributor		
Argentina				
Chile				
Colombia				
Venezuela				

Exhibit 6   *Loctite Corporation: Financial Data by Region (U.S. Dollars, in Thousands)* *

	1990		1991		1992	
Sales Revenues:						
North America	242.4	43.7%	248.6	44.3%	266.7	43.9%
Europe	222.7	40.1%	220.0	39.2%	244.2	40.2%
Asia/Pacific	41.7	7.5%	47.0	8.4%	47.2	7.8%
Latin America	48.4	8.7%	45.6	8.1%	49.9	8.2%
	<u>555.2</u>		<u>561.2</u>		<u>608.0</u>	
Operating Profit:						
North America	39.8	30.0%	45.8	33.5%	56.8	36.8%
Europe	70.1	53.0%	67.9	49.7%	78.1	50.6%
Asia/Pacific	9.1	6.9%	9.6	7.0%	5.8	3.8%
Latin America	13.4	10.1%	13.3	9.7%	13.5	8.8%
New business development	−20.4		−21.7		−25.8	
Corporate headquarters	−16.5		−15.9		−15.4	
Restructuring change	0.0		−4.4		−12.7	
	<u>95.5</u>		<u>94.6</u>		<u>100.3</u>	

*Source: Loctite Corporation. Note: Operating profit by region determined based on allocations of Sales and Expenses to units which generated or are responsible for the sales or expense.

the relationship to help them adapt to this way of selling.

Loctite regarded sales growth as the most important performance measure in evaluating distributors. Freeman explained:

In most international markets the business potential is not a constraint to growth, as chemical adhesives and sealants have little or no penetration, and mechanical fixtures are still dominant. A good distributor in Asia/Pacific, for instance, might be able to grow the business by 35 to 40% annually, and we would expect a minimum of 10 to 15%. The main reason why France is our second-largest market is not because it has greater potential, but because over a long period the distributor reinvested a large proportion of his profits back into growing the business.

Once a distributor had established a profitable business in the industrial market, Loctite

regional managers would help the firm identify opportunities for growth by reviewing the range of applications for which Loctite products had been successfully employed in other countries. These case studies of vertical industry marketing programs would be introduced by regional sales management and by distributors from one country visiting another and reporting directly on successful initiatives they had undertaken. From surveys of the potential customers for these new applications and experience in other markets, Loctite managers were able to advise the distributor on potential sales volumes.

In many cases, slowing sales growth had stimulated Loctite's acquisition of equity stakes in international distributors. "Once a core business is established, it's tempting for a distributor to sit on the higher margins which Loctite products give him," commented Butterworth. Loctite also believed that many distributors found it difficult to execute the complex sales approach

LOCTITE®

We are
Multi-National Account
Managers in Japan.
If you need our help,
contact us at....

FAX No. 81-45(785)0747

Phone No. 81-45(784)2500

Loctite Japan MNA Management Team

Y. MAEDA
SONY
16 YEARS SERVICE AND 11 YEARS IN CHARGE OF SONY ACCOUNTS. LIVES IN YOKOHAMA.

N. FUJIWARA
MATSUSHITA
16 YEARS SERVICE AND 12 YEARS IN CHARGE OF MATSUSHITA ACCOUNTS. LIVES IN OSAKA.

H. KATO
HONDA
8 YEARS SERVICE AND 6 YEARS IN CHARGE OF HONDA ACCOUNTS. LIVES IN YOKOHAMA.

I. TSURUWAKA
NISSAN
11 YEARS SERVICE AND 9 YEARS IN CHARGE OF NISSAN ACCOUNTS. LIVES IN YOKOHAMA.

S. KASAMAKI
TOYOTA
ONE OF STARTING MEMBERS OF LOCTITE AND 11 YEARS IN CHARGE OF TOYOTA ACCOUNTS. LIVES IN NAGOYA.

N. KOMATSU
MAZDA
8 YEARS SALES EXPERIENCE AT MAZDA ACCOUNTS LIVES IN HIROSHIMA.

How to communicate ...

If you would like to know anything about Multi-National Accounts in Japan, Please Fax to MNAMs and copy to K.Fujii, who will interpret your English message for MNAMs and vice versa.

K. Fujii
Communications Coordinator

Applications....

Electronics

FDD	Gimbal/Carriage	326 LVUV
HDD	Shaft/Bearing	
LCD	Terminal sealing	648
		350

Speaker	Magnet bonding
	392/792
	Speaker assembly for phone
	403, 411, 424
PCB	Tacking jumper wire to PCB
	Tak Pak AD
Chip	SMT(one by one, pin transfer)
	348, 3607

Automotive

Engine	Core Plugs sealing	962T
ATX	Flange sealing	518, FMD-127
Bolt	Precoating	204
	Dri Loc	
LIS	Power steering case	PMS-10E

A,B,C. for communication with Japanese key staff at customers ---.

A – Provide Japanese catalogs and data.
B – Request a Japanese language letter of introduction from MNAM and bring it on the first call.
C – Introduce Japanese ACHs of the MNA in Japan.
D – Learn a few Japanese words and use them, for instance.

> • KON-NICHIWA (HELLO)
> • ARIGATO-GOZAIMAS (THANK YOU)
> • YOROSHIKU-ONEGASHIMAS (WE HOPE FOR YOUR POSITIVE REPLY IN THE NEAR FUTURE)
> • SHITSUREI-SHIMAS (GOOD-BY NOW)

For our timely support, what we need to know from you are ---.

A – Current business status and/or relationship between you and MNAs.
B – Applications you are developing at MNAs and ACHs.

Loctite Products Specified/used in Japan

⟨TOYOTA⟩ Loctite products are listed in the following specifications.

Spec. NO	PRODUCT
TSK6706	962T
TSK6708	572,575
TSK6709 CLASS 1	206
" " CLASS 2	204
TSH7910	PMS-10E

⟨NISSAN⟩ A lot of Loctite products are specified in Nissan Engineering Standard (NES) as Anaerobic Adhesive M8514. Please contact us for details.

⟨MAZDA⟩ D/Loc is specified in MAZDA Engineering Standard (MES) CF 530B, as follows.
  CLASS 1   202
  CLASS 2   200

⟨HONDA⟩ There is no specification for anaerobic adhesives, but their needs for pre-applied threadlockers. 206 and 204, have been growing. Design manual for Dri-Loc and liquid threadlockers will be compiled soon.

⟨MATSUSHITA⟩ Our products are mainly applied for Audio-Visual Appliances and office automation equipment.
Try to develop all potential applications in parts assembly for VCR, HDD, FDD, LCD and telephone.

⟨SONY⟩ UV products, such as 326UV Blue, 326LVUV etc., are mainly applied to motor assembly, optical devices, VCR, FDD and Audio parts assembly.
Since 348 was specified in Sony's chipbonder spec. No. 7-432-910-74 in 1992, this business is one of our most promising applications. Please try!

Profile of Accounts

TOYOTA
Date of Establishment: Aug. 1937
Sales* 8,941 Bill. Yen
Net profit* 201 Bill. Yen
Number of employees: 75,300
Number of offshore manufacturing plants 34

NISSAN
Date of Establishment: Dec. 1933
Sales* 4,271 Bill. Yen
Net profit* 54 Bill. Yen
Number of employees: 55,600
Number of offshore manufacturing plants 19

HONDA
Date of Establishment: Sept. 1948
Sales* 2,911 Bill. Yen
Net profit* 33 Bill. Yen
Number of employees: 31,500
Number of offshore manufacturing plants 26

MAZDA
Date of Establishment: Jan. 1920
Sales* 2,304 Bill. Yen
Net profit* 9.2 Bill. Yen
Number of employees: 29,800
Number of offshore manufacturing plants 13

MATSUSHITA
Date of Establishment: Dec. 1935
Sales* 4,995 Bill. Yen
Net profit* 110 Bill. Yen
Number of employees: 47,600
Number of offshore manufacturing plants 44

SONY
Date of Establishment: May. 1946
Sales* 1,979 Bill. Yen
Net profit* 21 Bill. Yen
Number of employees: 19,800
Number of offshore manufacturing plants 21

* : Annual business term(April 1991 – March 1992)

Loctite(Japan)Corporation
1-15-13, Fukiura, Kanazawa-ku,
Yokohama, Japan 236

Sales Headquarters
Phone No. 81-45(785)0747
Telefax No. 81-45(784)2500

Loctite (Japan) Corporation

required for its products. In a country where double-digit sales growth was maintained, Loctite was content to continue to serve the market through an independent distributor. Historically, however, Loctite always managed to accelerate sales growth after taking an equity interest in a distributor.

Loctite had recently introduced two mechanisms for global management. The first was the appointment of multinational account coordinators for international customers. Based in the home country of a multinational, these managers were responsible for keeping distributors worldwide informed of their customer companies' plans and operations and coordinating prices across country markets. A national distributor would be given a price range for a multinational customer by the account coordinator. This ensured that the subsidiaries of a company such as Seagate Technology, with R&D in California and manufacturing in Singapore and Malaysia, would be able to receive roughly equivalent prices no matter where Loctite products were procured, as well as a uniform worldwide service. In turn, each multinational account's profitability could be assessed worldwide. By 1992, about 25 accounts were managed in this way, representing approximately 5% of corporate sales, although the percentage was as high as 25% in markets such as Singapore and Malaysia. (Exhibit 7 shows a brochure produced by Loctite's Japanese multinational account coordinators describing their role.)

A second Loctite coordination initiative was the establishment of three global task forces, one for each business area. Each task force included vice-presidents from each of the four regions and met four times a year. Their main function was idea transfer across regions; the Industrial task force, for instance, was helping Loctite's European operations develop its electronics business, which had not grown as fast as in other regions. The task forces were also a vehicle for improving worldwide coordination of branding, packaging, and pricing of Loctite products.

EUROPE

Loctite gained most of its early experience of joint ventures and subsidiaries in Europe. Butterworth had managed Loctite's European operations in the 1970s out of a regional office in Paris that had been closed during the recession of the early 1980s. By 1992, the corporation had acquired all of its European operations except those in Switzerland, Portugal, Sweden, Denmark, and Finland, which continued as independent distributors, and in Norway, where Loctite owned 51% of a joint venture.

The evolution of the French business was typical. The French distributor had learned about Loctite products in the early 1960s as a result of an existing relationship with the company that served as Loctite's U.K. distributor. By 1979, the French distributor had grown the Loctite business to a point where it was established as a company in its own right. This opened the door for Loctite to buy the whole business, not just the franchise, but during the early 1980s the franchise plunged into loss as it attempted to develop the consumer market for instant adhesives, despite the fact that its key managers had experience serving only industrial markets. In 1986, Loctite acquired a 50% stake with an agreement to purchase the remaining 50% five years later, which it duly did according to a previously agreed-upon formula. By 1992, France was the second-biggest market after the United States, with a strong consumer business. The original French manager and most of the employees were still in place two years after the change of ownership.

The distributor relationship had a less happy ending in the Netherlands, where the local distributor of 20 to 30 years' standing refused to sell Loctite any stake in its business. Loctite wanted to establish a single company covering the three Benelux countries (Belgium, the Netherlands, and

Luxembourg). The original contract imposed stiff penalties on Loctite for withdrawing its franchise. In addition, the Loctite distributor successfully contested a noncompete clause in the Dutch courts and had it reduced from five to two years. By 1992, the former distributor was carrying a competitor's product line.

Loctite was seeking to establish itself early in the former Communist bloc countries of Eastern Europe, but was following a different approach to achieving distribution. In the 1980s, Loctite had developed export sales to these countries, working through a network of contacts ranging from the government agents who administered hard foreign currency purchases, to engineering academics involved in manufacturing process development. Following the collapse of Communism, the countries assessed as having the greatest potential were Poland, Hungary, and Czechoslovakia, since their economies relied to a greater extent on conversion or assembly technologies, whereas the economies of the former Soviet republics were based more on natural resources and raw materials. In each of these three countries, representative offices were established in 1990, headed by one of Loctite's previous contacts and typically supported by two local Loctite-trained sales engineers. All were full-time Loctite employees, able to supplement their salaries with bonuses based on sales performance. These representative offices carried minimal inventories; their orders were processed through Loctite's Vienna warehouse. Loctite planned to form full subsidiaries in these countries as soon as possible.

LATIN AMERICA

Loctite attempted to minimize its capital investment in Latin America, serving all Central American countries from its subsidiary in Costa Rica and concentrating its South American regional management staff at its Brazilian subsidiary in São Paolo. The Latin American business had been strongest in the automotive aftermarket, with more recent success in consumer markets—the same number of tubes of Loctite Super Glue were sold to consumers in Brazil as in the United States. By 1992, corporate and regional managers were pushing local distributors to develop the factory maintenance market.

Loctite's experience in Argentina reflected a problem common to more regulated, emerging economies. Though small in annual sales, the Argentinean distributor had access to Loctite's technology as a result of the establishment of a local manufacturing plant in 1975, which government regulations at that time required Loctite set-up to enter the market. When Loctite bought out the distributorship in 1988, the head of the company left and set up a plant in direct competition with his former partner.

ASIA/PACIFIC

Although Loctite had long been active in Asia/Pacific, acquiring its joint-venture distributors in Japan and Australia in the mid-1970s, penetration was still low in this region, partly because most of Loctite's investment in international expansion to date had concentrated on building business in Europe. Historically, Loctite had appointed agents in Asia/Pacific countries for whom Loctite's business typically represented a third or more of sales and a higher proportion of profit. In recent years, with more attention focused on the region, Loctite had reconsidered its approach to distribution.

In the 1980s, Thailand, Taiwan, and Korea had been identified by Loctite as especially attractive markets. After extensive search processes, distributors were appointed in each of the three countries, but sales growth over the first two years proved disappointing in all three cases. After several visits to the distributors, Butterworth concluded that the problem lay in a lack of familiarity with the sales approaches required for Loctite products and the operating policies of the company. "In North America,

Europe, and Australia, we were able to appoint real Loctite veterans to build our businesses. There simply were no Asian *Loctite Charlies.*" Loctite's customary policy of relying entirely on local principals was therefore changed in two ways: Loctite began taking equity interests in its Asian distributors earlier in the relationships and began placing its own employees in the distributorships to provide the technical and sales education required to build their businesses.

Loctite formed 51% joint ventures with the Thai distributor in 1990 and the Taiwanese distributor in 1991, basing the business valuations upon current profitability, with agreements that the remaining 49% would be purchased five years later according to an agreed-upon formula. In the intervening five years, the formula guaranteed the distributor that Loctite would grow the business by an average of 10 to 15% annually, and also guaranteed that Loctite would pay a pro rata share of any profits on sales growth above this level. In most cases, profits for the first two years were below the guaranteed minimums, as Loctite invested in business development. The "sunset" buyout price at the end of the five-year period was based upon profit levels in the fourth and fifth years.

In the years preceding the formation of the joint ventures, Loctite personnel had been appointed to work in the distributor companies, primarily to provide technical support. Wiley commented that this had met with mixed success:

> There were often control issues beneath the surface and attempts to isolate the Loctite representative because he wasn't "family." While joint ventures seemed the obvious way to run the business in Asia/Pacific—combining Loctite product expertise with local culture—it was often difficult. We certainly need local managers to front the sales effort and to cope with the idiosyncracies of local government and distribution systems, but it always

> takes several years before they really become Loctite people.

Soon after the Thai joint venture had been formed, the distributor was being run almost entirely by Loctite personnel. In Taiwan, where the joint venture partner, FTF Trading, was a large conglomerate with businesses ranging from supermarkets to the automotive aftermarket, Loctite employees again largely ran the business, with FTF contributing to management of the complex administrative requirements of doing business in Taiwan.

In Korea, the distributor resisted what he saw as Loctite's infiltration into his business and sought to retain all the cash flows generated by his Loctite distributorship. Loctite's appointment of a sales engineer only strained the relationship further. As the distributor's cooperation could not be obtained, Butterworth and Freeman decided that the market potential warranted establishing a wholly owned subsidiary alongside the distributor in 1985. Initial profitability was low, aggravated by the need to let the distributor's existing inventory sell through or be bought out by Loctite to avoid dumping of stock at low prices, but by 1988, Loctite's Korean sales had tripled. Eventually, in 1992, Loctite canceled the distributor's contract.

Wiley believed some expatriate management was necessary to grow businesses in Asia/Pacific at the rate it now required.

> Our agents in this region used to be able to make gross margins as high as 70 to 80% on our products. We are now considering cutting this margin, maybe by as much as half, and insisting on employing some local engineers, training them in Connecticut, and supporting them inside the distributorships.

He also considered it important that, in Asia/Pacific, Loctite maintain its approach of initially restricting each distributor to a few core products:

> In Asia/Pacific I start a distributor on a range of six to eight machinery adhesives. These are

our bread-and-butter products, offering good margins to the distributor, and they are also the perfect way for him to learn the Loctite approach. The ideas of selling the customer something which they didn't know they needed, and of pricing to value rather than cost, are new to many of these distributors, partly because of cultural background and partly because of the nature of the other products they carry. Only when the distributor has established this core business, which takes a year or two, do I encourage him to move into other markets and broaden his product line.

The trend toward greater Loctite involvement in its distribution operations had resulted in the number of Loctite employees in the Asia/Pacific region rising rapidly to 278 in 1992. Of these, only six were in the regional offices, the remainder being attached to Loctite's joint ventures or wholly owned subsidiaries in the region. At that time, only one Loctite employee, in Indonesia, was working inside an independent distributor company. Nevertheless, Loctite still believed in the need for local management; in cases where expatriate managers headed national distributors, they were required by Butterworth and Freeman to identify and develop local national successors within five years.

Despite this trend toward greater control of its distribution, Loctite had recently enjoyed a successful and cooperative relationship with a new independent distributor in Indonesia. Until 1991, Indonesian sales had been managed by the Singapore distributor. Loctite was unhappy with both the level and growth of sales, attributed to lack of attention by the domestically focused Singapore distributor, and decided that a separate national distributor was needed for Indonesia. The Indonesian distribution rights were reacquired with no payment to the Singapore distributor, and an initial survey of potential manufacturing customers produced a list of four potential distributors. In 1990, however, Loctite

was introduced to a fifth candidate—a general mill supplier—by a former Loctite employee of 20 years' standing, who now headed up international distribution for a spray-gun manufacturer. After the head of this family-run business had attended a Loctite regional distributors' conference where he had impressed regional management with his knowledge of the region and its network of manufacturing supplies distribution, the firm was appointed as Loctite's exclusive distributor in Indonesia, without a formal contract and with an understanding that Loctite would eventually want to buy out the business for about twice the annual gross margin.

Wiley commented that Loctite was impressed by the management policies of Kawan Lama, the Indonesian appointee, which were unusual for a manufacturing supplies distributor in Asia.

The company has a very modern approach to human resource management, with extensive training and high levels of pay. They are also prepared to invest in growing our business, even appointing about a dozen subdistributors to cover specific regions and industries better than they could themselves.

Loctite had reciprocated with extensive training support.

Two weeks after we appointed Kawan Lama as distributor, at a time when they had only about $500 worth of Loctite products on their shelves, I ran a full-day training seminar on their premises and was impressed by the high number of staff who attended, including the head of the company. Since they were appointed, we have invested almost 100 mandays in training seminars for the company's staff, customers, and subdistributors.

In India, Loctite encountered problems which it attributed to the distributor's lack of familiarity with Loctite. Indian government regulations in the 1970s dictated that Loctite could initially take only a 40% stake in the business, and that the company had to establish manufacturing operations in the country. Disagreements soon emerged over pricing levels, with the local distributor cutting them below what Loctite regarded as appropriate in order to boost sales volume. Although the original principal of the distributorship had left the business when Loctite acquired the remaining equity, the corporation was still not confident that the new manager was enough of a "Loctite man." By 1992, Loctite was moving toward its goals of acquiring the balance of the business and launching, for the first time in Asia/Pacific, a product line targeting the consumer market.

The People's Republic of China (PRC) had also long been regarded as a market with huge potential. A joint venture was required by local law, and Loctite had, in 1985, taken a 50% stake in such a business. This business was run by a Chinese manager with U.S. citizenship and extensive knowledge of Loctite. In 1992, Loctite was negotiating to increase its stake in the business, although 100% ownership was not legally feasible and not necessarily desirable. An assessment of the emerging Vietnamese market was also being conducted, so that Loctite would be able to act swiftly if and when the U.S. trade sanctions on doing business there were lifted.

HONG KONG

Loctite's distribution in Hong Kong had been managed for 10 years by a Hong Kong Chinese who had been Loctite's Asia/Pacific region manager. He had left the company to set up his own business with some modest financial assistance from Loctite. By 1990, the distributor had developed a sizable business, but was still almost entirely dependent upon Loctite products. Loctite sales to the Hong Kong distributor were $1,183,000 in 1992, and the distributor was estimated to achieve a gross margin around 50%. However, Loctite had become increasingly dissatisfied with the distributor's willingness to reinvest profits in the business and to expand its customer base. Loctite had therefore taken back

the distribution rights to several product lines outside the core of industrial adhesive products. The relationship had been further strained by the refusal of the Hong Kong distributor to accept anything other than technical support from Loctite; this insistence on independence extended to a refusal to share accounts and business plans, which Loctite expected to receive from all its distributors.

Having decided that some form of Loctite control was necessary to boost sales growth in Hong Kong, Butterworth, Freeman, and Wiley were considering their options. The trend toward acquiring 100% of a Loctite distributorship and establishing a wholly owned subsidiary was exemplified by the recent acquisition of Singapore/Malaysia rights from Asia Radio, the Singapore-based firm that had distributed Loctite products for 23 years. The benefits of working with local companies, however, were exemplified by the early success of the relationship with Kawan Lama in Indonesia. Also prominent in their thoughts was the concept of a Greater China subsidiary formed from the operations in Hong Kong, the PRC, and Taiwan. The Greater China concept was fueled by the fact that control of Hong Kong was scheduled to revert to the PRC from the United Kingdom in 1997. Wiley reported that Loctite's PRC joint venture was already competing with the Hong Kong distributor to supply factories in the booming southern Chinese province of Guandong and offering prices substantially lower than those offered by Loctite's Hong Kong distributor. He estimated that PRC customers accounted for 25% of the Hong Kong distributor's sales. Sales revenues in 1992 for the Taiwan and PRC joint venture operations were $1,613,000 and $2,277,000 respectively. Wiley estimated that, as in Hong Kong, Loctite commanded 75% to 80% of the established market in these countries. In terms of market penetration, however, the joint ventures lagged behind Hong Kong; penetration of market opportunity was estimated at less than 20% in Taiwan and less than

5% in the PRC, compared with less than 50% in Hong Kong.

Butterworth, Freeman, and Wiley concluded that Loctite had three options regarding the Hong Kong operation:

1. Buy 51% or more of the existing Hong Kong distributorship, and grow the business from its existing base.

2. Find a new distribution partner, probably an established local business, and form a second joint venture in Hong Kong.

3. Buy out 100% of the Hong Kong business and attempt to build a Greater China subsidiary.

There were no major legal issues or constraints shaping the decision.

PECHAZUR

Saliou N'Dione, the 42-year-old founder, CEO, and majority shareholder of Pechazur, sat at his desk in Abidjan, Ivory Coast, considering alternative strategies to further the growth of his company. Pechazur had been marketing frozen fish to the Ivorian market for 12 years and had been exporting frozen wild shrimp and fish fillets to France for 10 years.[1] In early 1993, N'Dione was planning to open a new processing plant in the neighboring country of Benin, effectively doubling Pechazur's production capacity of frozen shrimp and fish fillets for the export market, and expand Pechazur's fishing fleet to supply fresh fish to the local Ivorian market.

The increased competition from farm-raised shrimp in the late 1980s and early 1990s had caused world prices for wild shrimp to fall steadily. N'Dione wondered what marketing strategy would enable him to expand his shrimp exports and ensure the continued growth and profitability of his company.

COMPANY BACKGROUND

N'Dione founded Pechazur in 1980 to import and distribute frozen fish in the RCI (République de la Côte D'Ivoire). N'Dione, Senegalese by birth, had previously worked in three large fish and seafood processing companies in Senegal during the 1970s. His decision to found a company in RCI rather than Senegal had been based not only on the large RCI market demand but also on the reduced social and family obligations he would face in the RCI. In West African society, individuals faced strong social pressures to share with extended family and friends. Although positive from a social-welfare perspective, these pressures often made it difficult for individuals to reinvest business profits, since they were expected to use surplus funds to provide financial assistance to their extended families.

In 1982, a decline in the purchasing power of Ivorian households due to an economic recession prompted N'Dione to seek export markets,

---

[1]Wild shrimp were fished from the sea and/or saltwater lagoons. They were distinct from farm-raised or aquaculture shrimp grown in controlled farm environments.

This case was prepared by Nathalie Laidler (under the direction of John A. Quelch). Copyright © 1993 by the President and Fellows of Harvard College. Harvard Business School case 593-077.

Table A   Pechazur Volume Sales, 1987–1992

Tons[a]	1987	1988	1989	1990	1991	1992
Frozen fish imports sold to the RCI market	1,500	780	800	757	350	101
Pechazur fish (frozen) sold to the RCI market	0	0	283	264	1,234	1,027
Export shrimp	320	430	398	406	352	434
Export processed fish	212	98	97	108	124	221
Total volume sales	2,032	1,308	1,578	1,535	2,060	1,783

[a]1 ton = 1,000 kg = 2,222 lbs.

and Pechazur began purchasing, processing, and exporting frozen shrimp and frozen fish fillets to France. In 1987, increasing demand for these export products led to the construction of a modern processing plant—80% financed by Pechazur's retained earnings—located at Dabou, 30 miles from the capital, Abidjan. At this time, Pechazur assisted local shrimp fishermen in forming cooperatives, providing them with nets and technical assistance. In 1988, Pechazur established its own fishing subsidiary, Sari-Fish, once again largely financed by retained earnings. Sari-Fish comprised five industrial sea fishing vessels, four of which were fully equipped with on-board freezers. In 1989, N'Dione purchased a majority shareholding of ICA,[2] a French shrimp importer, thereby establishing a distribution and marketing subsidiary in France. In 1992, with the financial participation of the International Finance Corporation (IFC),[3] Pechazur was constructing a new processing plant in Benin, where shrimp were abundant and production costs lower, and developing a new fleet of fishing vessels to provide the local RCI market with fresh fish.

Pechazur was a family-run business: N'Dione's wife was the company's finance director; N'Dione's brother was the Dabou plant manager; his brother-in-law the director of Sari-Fish;

[2]ICA was the Société Internationale de Commerce Agro-Alimentaire.

[3]The IFC was part of the World Bank organization.

and his cousin was a captain on one of Sari-Fish's fishing vessels. N'Dione had a very strong work ethic and paid particular attention to the training and development of his executive staff. N'Dione both inspired and required hard work and dedication from his colleagues and employees, and an attention to excellence was evident at every level of the organization. N'Dione commented, "In Africa, ideas are not as important as who one works with."

In January 1993, Pechazur was an integrated fish and shrimp producer and marketer, fishing, purchasing, importing, processing, packaging, distributing, and marketing frozen fish to the RCI market and exporting frozen shrimp and fish fillets, principally to France. (Table A reports volume sales from 1987 to 1992; Exhibit 1 presents Pechazur's income statements from 1989 to 1992.)

RÉPUBLIQUE DE LA CÔTE D'IVOIRE

RCI, located on the coast of West Africa, flanked by Liberia and Ghana, and bordered by Guinea, Mali, and Burkina Faso, was a French protectorate between 1842 and 1960, when it became independent. From 1965 to 1975, RCI achieved real average GDP (gross domestic product) growth of 7.7% per annum based on exports of coffee, cocoa, and timber. Massive foreign bank lending occurred from 1975 to 1977, and when the price of coffee and cocoa fell dramatically in 1979, the government's current account and budget deficits grew quickly.

Exhibit 1   *Pechazur Income Statements, 1989–1992*

	1989	**1990**	**1991**	**1992**
Sales revenues (FCFA millions):	1,659	1,656	1,753	1,837
Export subsidy	123	218	144	238
Total revenues	1,782	1,874	1,897	2,075
Production costs:				
Purchases and raw material	1,057	780	954	1,137
Water and energy	95	139	163	165
Maintenance	52	87	97	109
Other direct costs	58	20	39	14
Personnel	129	96	127	153
Depreciation	57	69	66	67
Total production costs	1,448	1,191	1,446	1,645
Operating margin	334	683	451	430
Overhead and fixed costs	199	396	246	206
Profit before interest and taxes	135	287	205	224
Interest	52	57	27	25
Tax	8	10	21	17
Net profit	75	220	157	182

From 1980, the country fell into economic decline, and in 1987, the fall of the U.S. dollar, declining coffee and cocoa prices, large devaluations in neighboring Ghana and Nigeria, and inadequate controls on government spending threw the country into recession. Anticipating a recovery in commodity prices, RCI increased foreign borrowing to cover revenue shortfalls. However, commodity prices remained depressed; foreign debt rose from 37% of GDP in 1979 to 130% in 1991, and real GDP per capita fell by an average of 5% per annum from 1987 to 1990. Nevertheless, RCI's overall postindependence record of economic development was one of the best in Africa, and in 1991 the country's GDP per capita was U.S. $770. (Exhibit 2 provides key data on RCI in 1991.)

Under Prime Minister Ouattara, appointed in 1990 by President Houphouet-Boigny, a program of stabilization and structural adjustment was implemented, aimed at reducing the fiscal deficit, privatizing public-sector firms, and liberalizing the marketing of principal export crops. The RCI government also worked with foreign lenders to clear up public debt arrears and revitalize the illiquid banking system. Despite these measures, RCI in 1992 still suffered from relatively high production costs and a lack of competitiveness in international markets, due in large part to the overvaluation of the FCFA.[4] Diversification of exports and the development of import-substituting industries were hindered by high production costs and the domination of the public sector in the economy. In 1991, government investment accounted for 61% of total investment. The business sector operated under rigid job security and wage regulations and faced unfavorable fixed prices on a number of import and export commodities. In addition, as

[4]RCI, along with 13 other African countries, ex-French colonies and protectorates, shared a common currency—the FCFA—that was tied to the French franc. In 1992 1 U.S. $ = 248 FCFA.

Exhibit 2   *Ivory Coast—Demographic and Economic Data, 1991*

Population	12.4 million; 47% urban; 20% of workers come from poorer neighboring countries
Age distribution: 0–14; 15–59; 60+	45%; 50%; 5%
Ethnic and religious groups	Over 60 tribes and 5 main languages; 30% Moslem, 20% Christian, 60% indigenous
GDP per capita	U.S. $770
Real GDP and consumer prices (% change 1990–1991)	–0.5% and 1.0%
GDP breakdown: primary, secondary, and tertiary sectors[a]	35%; 20%; 45%
Central government spending (% GDP)	30%
Chief crops, minerals, and other resources	Coffee and cocoa; diamonds and manganese; timber, rubber, and petroleum
Fish catch	93,000 tons
Exports: value and main partners	U.S. $2.9 billion: Netherlands = 19%; France = 14%; United States = 11%; Italy = 8%
Imports: value and main partners	U.S. $1.6 billion: France = 31%; Japan = 5%; United States = 5%
Communications: television sets, radios, telephones, newspaper circulation	1 per 19 persons; 1 per 8 persons; 1 per 97 persons; 12 per 1,000 population

[a]Primary sector = agricultural production; secondary sector = industrial production; tertiary sector = services.

government revenues fell after 1980, taxes on established businesses rose sharply. In 1991, 94% of tax receipts came from business income taxes, payroll taxes, sales taxes, and taxes on imports and exports.

On the other hand, the RCI had invested heavily in infrastructure and education during the boom years and the land was fertile with many well-established plantations. In addition, the trade balance was generally positive.

The ownership and management of the industrial sector was largely foreign and included many Lebanese immigrants; only 17% of managing directors were Ivorian in 1992, and privatized, formerly state-run enterprises were being purchased primarily by foreign companies. The strongest sectors of industry were those with some export potential. Frozen shrimp were among RCI's major exports in 1991, and Pechazur was often cited by members of the local

business community as one of the most successful companies in the RCI. In 1992, Pechazur was the only significant private company operating profitably in RCI that was owned and managed entirely by indigenous Africans.

THE IVORIAN FISH INDUSTRY

Fish was a staple of the Ivorian diet. Per capita consumption of fish in the RCI in 1991 was 18 kg, resulting in a total demand of 216,000 tons. Domestic fishing was carried out by both industrial fishing vessels, accounting for 48,000 tons in 1991, and small, independent fishermen, accounting for an additional 45,000 tons. Imports of frozen fish were estimated at 115,000 tons in 1991, and smoked fish from Ghana and Mali at 8,000 tons.

The variety of fresh fish marketed in the RCI was impressive, ranging from "surface" fish

Exhibit 3   *Photographs of Fish Stalls in a Typical Market in Abidjan*

such as mackerel and sardines to other fish such as carp. Fresh fish, landed daily by industrial vessels at the port, were purchased in bulk by wholesalers at the "Criee"[5] and sold to distributors, who in turn ensured the link to retailers. Independent fishermen had well-established networks of intermediaries that enabled their products to quickly reach the market stands. Imports and distribution of frozen fish were dominated by a half-dozen companies that possessed the necessary refrigeration trucks and warehouses. Wholesalers would regularly collect products from these warehouses to supply their retail customers.

Although distribution was highly fragmented, relationships were well established and long standing. Fish wholesaling and retailing operations were run by women. Nearly all fish were sold in open-air markets, either fresh, thawed, or smoked. About 50% of fish consumed in the RCI was smoked. The smoking process, which gave the fish a longer shelf life, was carried out by a large number of small entrepreneurs. (Exhibit 3 shows photographs of a typical market in Abidjan.) Prices depended on supply and demand and fluctuated daily. In 1991, the average wholesale price per kilogram (kg) for small mackerel and sardines was 150 FCFA, and the average retail price to the consumer was 175 FCFA. For higher-quality fish, equivalent prices were 350 FCFA and 450 FCFA.

Pechazur in RCI

Pechazur began importing frozen fish into the RCI in 1980 to meet a level of consumer demand that was outstripping local supply. However, low prices and competition from other importers that avoided paying import duties forced Pechazur to reduce this activity, and by 1992

---

[5]The "Criee" was the daily market located at the port, where wholesalers purchased fish landed by industrial vessels.

less than 10% of Pechazur's sales to the RCI market were of imported fish—the rest being landed by the Sari-Fish subsidiary. The company owned three large freezer-warehouses in Abidjan with a total storage capacity of 400 tons.

By early 1993, stricter RCI government regulations in exacting import duties allowed Pechazur to consider importing frozen fish once again. In addition, Soviet fishing vessels, which accounted for the bulk of imports in the 1980s, no longer represented a reliable source of supply.

N'Dione was planning to purchase three additional vessels in 1993—at a cost of 800 million FCFA—to provide fresh fish to the local Ivorian market. (The Sari-Fish subsidiary had one vessel that did not have on-board freezing capacity and that was already supplying the local market with fresh fish.) The annual catch that each vessel could deliver if operating at capacity was 1,895 tons. Fundamentally different from the original four Sari-Fish vessels, the new vessels would be used exclusively for fishing for fresh fish.

THE WORLD MARKET FOR SHRIMP

In 1990, world shrimp production totaled 2.6 million tons, 75% of which was derived from farm-raised or aquaculture shrimp. Farm-raised shrimp first appeared on the world market in the 1980s, priced on average 50% below traditional wild shrimp. The major sources of farm-raised shrimp were Asia and South America: China supplied 150,000 tons in 1991; Thailand 120,000 tons; South America 150,000 tons, of which Ecuador supplied 50%. Several varieties existed: the "Black Tiger" variety, which was very popular in Japan, accounted for 46% of farm-raised shrimp volume in 1991, and the "White China" variety for 21%.

Industry experts noted that lower-priced, farm-raised shrimp expanded consumer demand but also increased consumer price sensitivity and led to industry consolidation and restructuring. Many consumers in the West did not

Table B   Characteristics of the Major Shrimp Markets, 1991

	Japan	United States	Western Europe
Consumption in tons	384,000	300,000	240,000
Consumption per capita	3.1 kg	1.2 kg	0.8 kg average
Volume of imports in tons	283,000	227,500	170,000
Origin of imports	Indonesia = 20%	Ecuador = 20%	Africa = 26%
	China = 18%	Thailand = 19%	Ecuador = 14%
	Thailand = 18%	China = 15%	Indonesia = 12%
	India = 15%	India = 7%	Thailand = 8%
	Others = 29%	Mexico = 7%	China = 6%
		Panama = 3%	India = 4%
		Others = 29%	Others = 30%

know the difference between wild and farm-raised shrimp and, therefore, readily substituted the lower-priced, farm-raised product for wild shrimp. However, some experts believed that the superior taste of wild shrimp insured that a niche market would always exist for it.

The world shrimp market was dominated by three regions of consumption: Japan, the United States, and Western Europe. (Table B summarizes consumption and import data for these three markets.)

The Japanese Market

Although Japan represented the largest market for shrimp, all products were sourced from within Asia and it was thought to be very difficult to penetrate this market. The Japanese market was an important influence on prices and product quality standards for the rest of the world.

The U.S. Market

Consumption of shrimp in the United States increased throughout the 1980s to reach 1.2 kg per capita in 1991. The early 1990s, however, saw a decline in consumption, due in part to the economic recession. Away-from-home consumption through restaurants accounted for 75% of U.S. shrimp volume. Although distribution was highly fragmented among 450 importers, a trend towards consolidation was evident. Prices varied substantially according to product type and stock levels. In 1992, shrimp retailed anywhere between $2.99/lb. and $5.99/lb. In early 1993, importers and supermarket chain buyers were increasingly seeking stable, long-term supply agreements, while large, vertically integrated companies such as Aquastar, involved in farm-raising, distribution, and retail branding, were capturing an increasing share of the market.

The domestic shrimp industry consisted of 25,000 independent shrimp fishermen, located principally in Louisiana, who harvested 70,000 tons of wild shrimp in 1992. The quality of their catch was at risk from melanosis, which resulted when the time between capture and freezing of the shrimp was too long. This had created a negative quality image for wild shrimp in the United States. Supermarket buyers preferred farm-raised shrimp for several reasons: higher perceived quality, due to a freezing process that took place immediately following harvest; a cleaner product, resulting from the starving of the shrimp prior to harvest; regular, stable supplies; and lower prices.

The U.S. shrimp retail market was dominated by products that increased the ease of preparation; shelled, headless, and cooked shrimp were the norm. In addition, lower-priced, smaller-sized shrimp (40 to 60 units per kg) were more popular. Approximately 70% of retail sales were made through the seafood counter, where shrimp were presented unbranded, loose on ice. The remaining 30% of sales were of cartons or plastic bags from the freezer case, where brands such as Neptune, Bumble Bee, and Northern King were dominant.

The European Market

In 1991, imports of shrimp into the 12-country European Economic Community (EEC) totaled 170,000 tons, of which 30% went to the Spanish market, and 22% went to both the French and British markets. Per capita consumption in 1992 varied widely among the member countries, from 0.3 kg in Germany to 2.5 kg in Denmark. Consumers in southern European countries, such as Spain, Italy, and Portugal, tended to consume pink or tropical shrimp, while consumers in northern European countries preferred grey shrimp (fished in the North Sea). Imports from many African countries, including the RCI and Benin, did not pay import duties into the EEC, due to a trade agreement between the EEC and former colonies of the member states.

Spain dominated the European fish and seafood industry as a result of high per capita consumption and a large, modern fishing fleet that supplied much of the EEC's needs. Due to overfishing in EEC waters and increased levels of pollution, Spanish fishing vessels obtained agreements to fish throughout the West African coast. Large, vertically integrated companies such as Pescanova, involved in shipbuilding to the production of fish-based, ready-to-eat meals, increasingly dominated the market.

THE FRENCH MARKET

Shrimp represented the second-largest category of seafood product imported into France. Imports in 1991 amounted to 37,400 tons, valued at FF 1.4 billion. The majority of imported product was purchased in U.S. dollars, so changes in the FF/$ exchange rate often impacted demand.[6]

Consumption

Shrimp consumption in France increased by 7.5% from 1990 to 1991. In 1991, 38.5% of French households consumed an average of 1.2 kg of shrimp at home, compared with 37.8% of households consuming an average of 1.1 kg in 1990. Retail prices increased by only 1% during this period; purchases of shrimp were believed to be price sensitive, and stable prices were thought to result in increased consumption. (Exhibit 4 summarizes data on the seasonality of consumption and prices. Exhibit 5 reports market shares by type of shrimp products, and Exhibit 6 shows differences in shrimp consumption by region.)

The French retail shrimp market in 1991 totaled 43,000 tons, comprising 11,000 tons of grey shrimp and 32,000 tons of pink shrimp, of which 30% was captured wild and 70% was farm-raised. At-home consumption accounted for 25,800 tons, or 60% of this volume, and away-from-home consumption accounted for 17,200 tons, or 40%. Shrimp were consumed at home mainly on special occasions, and because they were bought infrequently, consumers often valued the advice of a specialist fishmonger when making a purchase.

Distribution and Retailing

Attracted by an expanding market, more than 60 firms imported shrimp into France in 1992, compared with 12 in 1988. This increasing frag-

---

[6]1 U.S. $ = 5.6 FF in 1992.

Exhibit 4   *French Retail Shrimp Sales and Prices by Month, 1991*

Period	Volume (tons)	Price (FF/kg)
1 (January)	729	99.01
2	545	95.08
3	706	99.31
4	635	97.52
5	529	97.05
6	617	93.10
7	567	94.14
8	433	107.74
9	489	90.18
10	679	95.28
11	783	89.82
12	762	87.41
13 (December)	1,388	87.02

mentation fueled a price war and added to the power of distributors. Successful distributors balanced in-stock availability to ensure rapid customer service with lowering costs through operating with minimum stocks. Other important factors were product quality and consistent availability of supply. Distribution of shrimp in France was highly fragmented and complex. (Exhibit 7 describes the roles of the main players.) As the retail market for shrimp expanded, some supermarket and hypermarket chains were backward integrating to assume the role of wholesaler/distributor for their own retail outlets. In 1992, 69% of retail shrimp sales were accounted for by hypermarkets and supermarkets which had captured market share from traditional fishmongers. (Exhibit 8 shows the share of retail sales by type of outlet in 1990 and 1991 and average retail prices in 1991.)

Most supermarkets and hypermarkets had specialty fish departments staffed by fishmongers. A high-quality fish department was thought to be a source of competitive differentiation. An esti-

Exhibit 5   *French Volume Market Shares by Type of Shrimp, 1991*

	Market Shares by Type of Shrimp	
	1990	1991
Grey Shrimp:		
Cooked	23%	18%
Raw	4%	5%
Pink Shrimp:		
Cooked	35%	43%
Raw	8%	7%
Unspecified	30%	27%

mated 70% of shrimp were sold loose and unbranded on ice. A further 10% were processed for use in value-added products such as cocktail mixes and breaded shrimp, while the remaining 20% were sold frozen in the freezer case. The latter were generally packaged in 1-kg plastic bags and carried the brand names of importers or wholesalers such as Surgele des Mer, Sofimar, Adripêche, and Table Plus. (Exhibit 9 summarizes the range of products and prices of shrimp found

Exhibit 6   *Differences in Shrimp Consumption by Region, France 1991*

Region	Percentage of Volume	Consumption Index[a]
North	12.5	129
East	5.3	56
Paris	29.8	153
West	19.3	102
West-Central	6.2	79
East-Central	7.7	55
South-West	7.4	83
South-East	11.8	101

[a]Based on average consumption per capita.

Exhibit 7   *Distribution of Shrimp in France—Main Channels and Players**

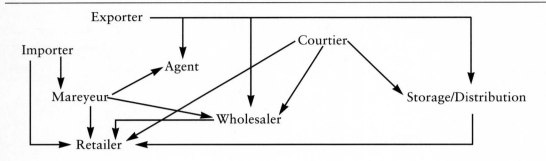

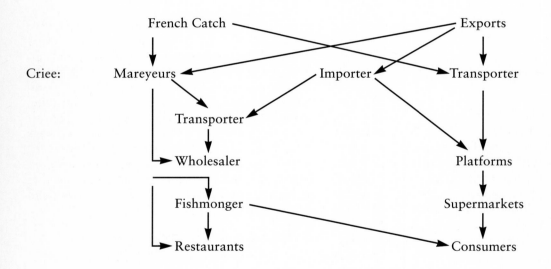

- **Criee:** The main marketplace where the individual fishermen and fishing fleets sell their catch on a bidding basis straight off their boats. Boats returning to port announce their catch to the Criee 24 hours before arriving.
- **Mareyeurs:** They bid for fish at the Criee, either as independents or on behalf of larger, more integrated players. They also prepare and clean the fish and play an important financing role, paying suppliers daily while allowing customers 30-day payment terms.
- **Wholesalers/Courtiers/Agents:** They put together extended product lines and supply their customers on a daily basis.
- **Platforms:** They exist for logistical efficiencies. They are large storage areas where products can be sorted and regrouped to improve the efficiency of transportation to the retail outlets.
- **Distributors:** They typically distribute fish and other fresh produce to the retail outlets.

*Source: FIOM.

Exhibit 8   *Share of Shrimp Retail Sales by Type of Outlet and Average Retail Prices of Shrimp,*
France 1991

| Retail Outlet | Percentage of Retail Sales | | Average Prices |
	1990	1991	(FF/kg 1991)
Hypermarkets	30%	35%	80.30
Supermarkets	17	18	83.15
Superettes	1	1	75.94
Fishmongers	26	21	107.18
Markets	20	20	102.14
Direct sales	3	3	85.73
Other	3	3	72.07

in the freezer department of a large French hypermarket in January 1993.) Increasingly, smaller package sizes (0.5 kg, 0.2 kg, and 0.1 kg) were being marketed to stimulate impulse purchases.

The French Fish-Fillet Market

At-home consumption of fish fillets was estimated at 32,933 tons in 1991—a 2% increase in volume over 1990; 42% of this volume was frozen. Consumption of breaded fish products was estimated at 31,856 tons in 1992—a 5% decline compared to 1990—while whole fish consumption at 14,956 tons registered a 19% growth over 1990. Of the fillets, 34% were cod, 19% pollack, 18% mackerel, and 29% other. More exotic fillets, such as tropical sole and red mullets, were only just starting to appear as stand-alone, frozen products in 1992.

Major brands such as Findus, Vivagel, Captain Iglo, and Servifrais dominated the market for frozen fish. Distributor brands accounted for 22% of retail frozen fish sales. Companies such as Findus were broadening their product lines with various value-added and gourmet products, and packaging of these products was becoming more sophisticated and eye-catching.

Exhibit 9   *Range of Shrimp Products and Retail Prices in the Freezer Department of Auchun, a*
Large Supermarket in France, January 1993

Brand Name	Packaging	Size	Characteristics	Price/kg
Surgele des Mers	1 kg plastic bag	#1	Raw, not shelled	137.38 FF
Camarones	1 kg plastic bag	#2	Raw, not shelled	149.92 FF
Adripêche	1 kg plastic bag	#3	Cooked, not shelled	105.90 FF
Table Plus	1 kg plastic bag	#4	Cooked, not shelled	93.80 FF
Table Plus	0.5 kg plastic bag	#5	Cooked, not shelled	63.50 FF
Sofimar	1 kg plastic bag	#7	Raw, not shelled	59.50 FF
Surgele des Mers	0.2 kg basket	#7	Cooked, and shelled	78.90 FF
SDTP	1 kg plastic bag	#8	Cooked, not shelled	64.98 FF

PECHAZUR'S OPERATIONS

Production

In 1992, Pechazur sourced 60% of its shrimp from 2,000 Ivorian fishermen, organized into eight cooperatives, all except one of which were located within 10 km of the processing plant. These traditional fishermen used "pirogues," similar to dug-out canoes, to fish by hand with nets in the lagoons or large saltwater lakes near Abidjan. Shrimp migrated to these lakes from the sea in order to reproduce; consequently, shrimp caught in the lagoons tended to be smaller than those caught at sea. The lagoon shrimp catch was highest between January and August. Pechazur owned and operated refrigerated pick-up vans that collected, weighed, and recorded the volume of shrimp supplied by each fishing cooperative. Pickups took place several times a day to ensure product freshness. Prices were agreed upon for two- to three-month periods and the fishermen were paid by weight, irrespective of shrimp size.

Pechazur had helped the fishermen form cooperatives and had initially helped supply them with fishing nets. N'Dione believed that Pechazur had managed to establish a stable, longterm relationship with the fishermen, a "moral contract" that effectively prevented potential competitors from being able to source lagoon shrimp in the RCI. A French competitor had attempted to establish a shrimp-processing operation in 1990 but had been unable to obtain a sufficient supply of shrimp to do so.

Sari-Fish, Pechazur's fishing subsidiary, supplied the remaining 40% of shrimp, as well as all the fish destined to be processed into fillets and exported. The Sari-Fish fleet consisted of five vessels, four with on-board freezing equipment and frozen-storage capacity of 30 tons each. Sari-Fish was the only company fishing shrimp out of Abidjan that had the capacity to freeze on board. The vessels fished for 30 days at a time, with five days' port maintenance between trips. The average catch was 150 kg of shrimp per vessel each day.

On average, the nets were cast six times a day and shrimp were fished at between 12 and 40 meters depth, 3 to 4 miles off the coast. The vessels were not assigned to specific areas; each captain decided where to fish based on experience, and Pechazur captains shared information to help each other's productivity. As soon as the shrimp were brought aboard, they were treated with citric acid to prevent melanosis (which blackened the product), sorted by size into two-kilogram cartons, weighed, frozen for three hours at −40°C, and stored in the freezer until the vessel returned to port. At this point the smaller-sized shrimp, representing 40% of the catch on average, were transported to the processing factory, while the larger shrimp, accounting for roughly 60% of the catch, were exported directly. These larger shrimp accounted for 25% of all Pechazur's shrimp exports. Product quality, particularly the prevention of melanosis, was highly dependent on the immediacy and precision of the freezing process on board the fishing vessels and at the processing plant. Pechazur paid particular attention to ensuring that the product was always kept on ice or frozen.

Although maximizing the shrimp catch was the goal of Pechazur's captains, the nets in fact yielded 80% fish and 20% shrimp by volume. All the fish caught in the process were frozen on board and stored. Some species such as mullet were transferred to the Dabou plant to be processed into fillets for export, but most of the fish were sold locally.

Processing

The Dabou plant could process six tons of raw shrimp a day. It employed 150 women to wash, cook, shell, fillet, freeze, sort, and package the products. Hygiene checks and sanitary precautions were stringent; workers were checked for cuts, wore masks when handling the product

Exhibit 10   *The Sorting Process at Pechazur's Dabou Processing Plant*

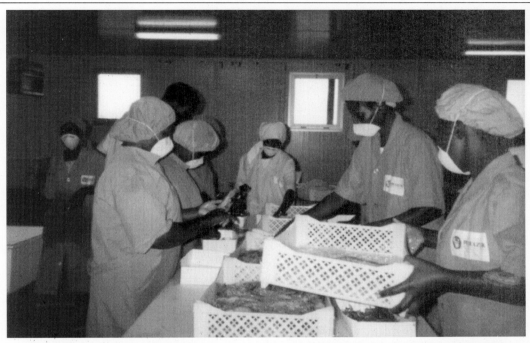

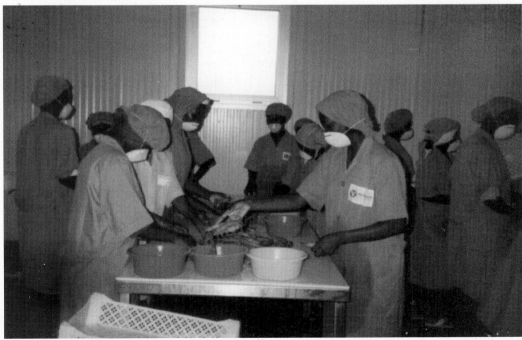

Exhibit 11 *Pechazur's Packaging Cartons for Export Shrimp, January 1993*

(see Exhibit 10), and had to disinfect both hands and feet before entering the factory. In addition, personal-hygiene messages were aired frequently over the plant's audio system. Pechazur had successfully met all EEC sanitation regulations. The plant technology was simple, with an emphasis on manual labor. Worker turnover was very low, two-thirds of the workers having been employed since the start of operations. Shelling and sorting were done in groups of 12 workers and one supervisor/worker around aluminum tables. The factory had backup water supply and electric generators so the plant could run autonomously if necessary. Due to shrimp migration patterns, when the lagoon catch was high, the sea catch was lower, and vice versa; this helped level operating capacity.

Lagoon shrimp arrived at the factory during the night and early morning, loose in plastic trays. When the factory began operations in the morning, the shrimp were washed and chemically treated to prevent blackening. Eighty percent of all shrimp passing through the factory were then cooked in boiling water, resulting in a product weight loss of about 13%. Pechazur shrimp cooked to a natural pink and did not require artificial coloring as did competitive Asian products. Following cooking, the shrimp were dipped into a frozen salt-and-sugar solution for two minutes, lowering their temperature to 2°C. This gave the shrimp a slight sheen and kept them fresh. Approximately 25 to 30% of the cooked shrimp were then shelled. The shelling process, which resulted in a further 34% weight loss, was an entirely manual process applied to those cooked shrimp that appeared slightly damaged. In addition to the cooked shrimp, 3 to 4% of the raw shrimp passing through the factory were also shelled to meet the needs of certain customers.

Following cooking and shelling, the shrimp were manually sorted by size. Shrimp of similar size were packaged into two-kilogram cartons, and the weight of each packaged carton was double-checked. (Exhibit 10 depicts the sorting process at the Dabou factory.) Packaging costs averaged 55 FCFA per kg, and Exhibit 11 shows

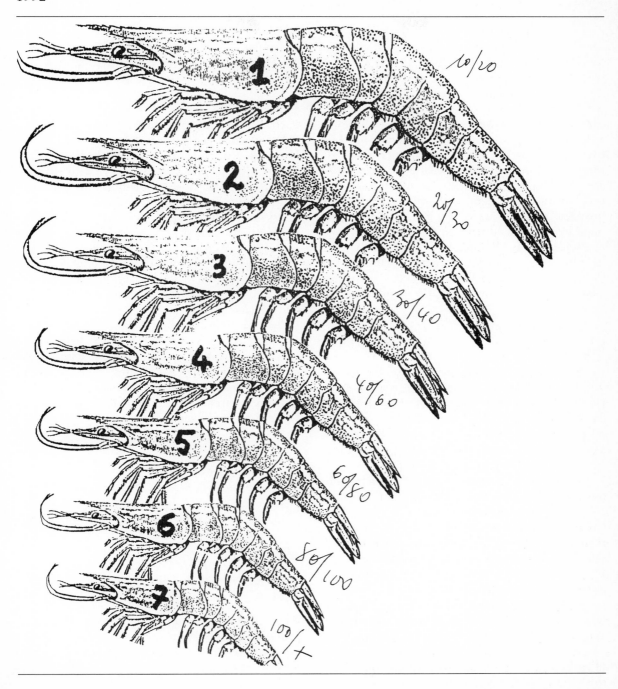

some of the packaging cartons used by Pechazur. All packaging carried the Pechazur name, a brief product description, and a sell-by date. The cartons were subsequently placed into freezers for four hours at −40°C and later stocked at −18°C in larger storage freezers. Fish fillets followed a similar cleaning process and all filleting was done manually. The freezing process for these products, however, lasted only two hours and each fillet was individually wrapped. The total frozen storage capacity of the plant was 40 tons, and Pechazur also owned additional storage capacity of 150 tons just a few miles away. Four or five containers, each holding 10 tons of product, left the factory each month for shipment by freighter directly to Europe.

Pechazur was planning to enter into an agreement to supply a local Nestlé plant with shrimp flour, produced from the byproducts of shrimp shells and heads, for use in the production of bouillon cubes.

Product Line

In 1992, 63% of Pechazur's sales by volume and 30% by value were made in the RCI. Ninety percent of these sales were of fish landed by the Sari-Fish fleet and 10% were of frozen fish imports. Exports represented 37% of Pechazur's sales by volume and 70% by value; of exports, 70% were sold in France.

Two-thirds of Pechazur's export sales by volume and 80% by value comprised wild shrimp of various sizes at various stages of processing. (Exhibit 12 depicts seven different sizes of shrimp to scale and the percentage of Pechazur's sales by volume accounted for by each size.) In 1992, of the 434 tons of frozen shrimp exported, 25% were large raw shrimp that had been frozen on board; 72% were cooked, of which 20% were also shelled; and 3% were raw and shelled.

The remaining third of Pechazur's export sales by volume and 20% by value comprised sole, red mullet, cuttle fish, and octopus fillets.

(Exhibit 13 itemizes Pechazur's export product line in 1992.) Products were shipped to France in special containers, taking 15 days to reach Marseille, and transport costs were estimated at 1.6 FF/kg, paid for by the importer.

Exports

Pechazur had been exporting wild shrimp to France for 10 years but had experienced growing competition in the late 1980s from farm-raised shrimp, priced 50% below wild shrimp. By 1992, farm-raised shrimp had captured 70% of the French market. Wild-shrimp suppliers had to drop their prices by 25% to try to hold market share. Average retail prices in France in September 1992 were 80FF/kg for farm-raised shrimp and 110FF/kg for wild shrimp. (Table C summarizes Pechazur's volume and value exports to France between 1985 and 1992.)

Société Internationale de Commerce Agro-Alimentaire (ICA) was Pechazur's distribution and marketing subsidiary in France. Established in 1989, it initially distributed both Pechazur and competitor products from Senegal. In 1990, N'Dione purchased a controlling interest in ICA. As he explained:

Pechazur needed credibility and continuity in the French market. We had to have a local operation to protect us from unethical pressures from wholesalers. For example, wholesalers sometimes complained about the quality of our product arriving in France and demanded price reductions, knowing full well that we could not take the product back. With French employees representing Pechazur in France, such pressures were less likely.

After 1990, ICA distributed only Pechazur products, and N'Dione made all major operating decisions. ICA regularly reported French market prices to Pechazur which could, in response, adjust its production mix at the Dabou

Exhibit 13   *Pechazur Export Product Line: January 1993*

Whole raw shrimp/frozen aboard:
Boxes = 2 kgs—Master carton = 18 kgs
Sizes: #1 (10/20 units per kg)
       #2 (20/30 units per kg)
       #3 (30/40 units per kg)
       #4 (40/60 units per kg)
       #5 (60/80 units per kg)
       #6 (80/100 units per kg)
       #7 (100/120 units per kg)

Shelled raw shrimp:
Boxes = 2 kgs—Master carton = 12 kgs
Sizes: SSS (40/60 units per kg)
       SS (60/100 units per kg)
       S (100/140 units per kg)
       G (140/190 units per kg)

Whole raw shrimp/day frozen:
Boxes = 2 kgs—Master carton = 18 kgs
Sizes: #5 (60/80 units per kg)
       #6 (80/100 units per kg)
       #7 (100/120 units per kg)

Whole cooked shrimp:
Boxes = 2 kgs—Master carton = 12 kgs
Sizes: SX (10/20 units per kg)
       SL (20/30 units per kg)
       S (30/40 units per kg)
       EE (40/60 units per kg)
       E (60/80 units per kg)
       G (80/100 units per kg)
       M (100/120 units per kg)
       MG (120/140 units per kg)
       ZZ (200/250 units per kg)

Shelled cooked shrimp:
Boxes = 2.5 kg—Master carton = 20 kgs
Sizes: DS 00 (up to 100 units per kg)
       DS 0 (100/150 units per kg)
       DS 1 (150/250 units per kg)
       DS 2 (250/400 units per kg)
       DS 3 (400/700 units per kg)
       DS 4 (700/800 units per kg)

Cooked shrimp tails:
Boxes = 3 kgs—Master carton = 18 kgs
Sizes: E (up to 90 units per kg)
       G (90/150 units per kg)
       M (150/250 units per kg)
       P (250/350 units per kg)

Fillets of tropical sole:
Boxes = 2 kg—Master carton = 16 kg
Sizes: Large
       Standard

Tropical sole:
IQF (individual quick frozen)
Loose—Master carton = 16 kg
Sizes: 0.15/0.2 kg per unit.
       0.2/0.25 kg per unit.

Rockling fillets:
Boxes = 2 kg—Master carton = 16 kg

Rockling medallions:
Boxes = 2 kg—Master carton = 16 kg

Whole red mullet:
Loose—Master carton = 18 kg
Sizes: #1 (4/6 units per kg)
       #2 (6/8 units per kg)
       #3 (8/12 units per kg)
       #4 (12/16 units per kg)
       #5 (16/+ units per kg)

Fillets of red mullet:
Boxes = 2 kg—Master carton = 16 kg

Cuttlefish whites:
IQF—Loose—Master carton = 20 kg
Sizes: G (2/3 units per kg)
       M (4/6 units per kg)
       P (6/9 units per kg)
       PP (9/15 units per kg)
       X (4/7 units per kg)

Cuttlefish head and legs:
Boxes = 3 kg—Master carton = 20 kg

Strips of cuttlefish:
Blocks = 1 kg—Master carton = 20 kg

Whole Squid:
Loose—Master carton = 20 kg

Table C   Volume and Value of Pechazur Export Sales to France, 1985–1992

Year	Shrimp Volume (tons)	Processed Fish Volume (tons)	Shrimp (FCFA millions)	Processed Fish (FCFA millions)
1985	45	N/A	124	N/A
1986	177	19	N/A	N/A
1987	320	212	N/A	N/A
1988	430	98	N/A	N/A
1989	398	97	1,213	130
1990	406	108	1,221	130
1991	352	124	1,075	181
1992	302	156	881	225

factory and press for better raw material prices in the RCI.

In 1992, 40% of Pechazur's export sales were made through ICA; a further 40% was distributed through SOCOPA, a large diversified food distribution group, while the remaining 20% reached the Spanish, British, and German markets through a variety of importers.

When ships transporting Pechazur product arrived in Marseille, the containers were unloaded and transferred to a refrigerated warehouse owned by an independent company called Somatref. ICA rented warehouse space from Somatref, and the ICA warehouse stock averaged 60 tons. ICA organized delivery of the product, but recently some customers, particularly large supermarket chains, elected to collect their purchases directly from the warehouse to reduce storage costs and streamline operations. ICA sold to a stable customer base of wholesalers and distributors, who invariably repackaged and branded Pechazur's products under their own brand names, with the result that the Pechazur brand was unknown to the end-consumer. Sales were made throughout France, with a focus on the south of the country. According to ICA, Pechazur had established a reputation among French distributors for consistent, high-quality products.

ICA aimed to minimize storage costs while maintaining sufficient inventory to meet customer needs. Agazzi, ICA marketing manager, noted: "Our goal is to sell our products in large quantities." In 1992, typical order sizes ranged from 500 kg to 5 tons. ICA was one of only a few importers with a single supplier, which, according to Agazzi, resulted in a predictable supply flow and consistently high product quality. The majority of ICA's competitors paid for imported shrimp in U.S. dollars, while ICA paid Pechazur in French francs. As a result, exchange rate fluctuations between the U.S. dollar and the French franc could strongly impact the relative competitiveness of Pechazur products in France.

Pricing and Margins

Costs, selling prices, and average margins for Pechazur products are given in Table D. Since prices fluctuated frequently, these figures represent yearly averages. Larger shrimp commanded higher margins than smaller shrimp, but as the captain of one of Sari-Fish's fishing vessels put it, "Unfortunately, large shrimp do not self-select themselves to be caught. We have to take the small with the large."

Table D   Costs, Prices, and Margins for Pechazur's Main Product Lines

	Raw Material Cost (FCFA/kg)	Processing (FCFA/kg)	Selling Price (FCFA/kg)	Margin (FCFA/kg)[a]	Percentage Margin
Shelled, cooked lagoon shrimp	1,163	520	2,153	470	28
Shelled, raw sea shrimp	1,992	520	2,950	438	18
Whole, cooked lagoon shrimp	1,072	460	1,890	358	23
Whole, cooked sea shrimp	1,926	400	2,893	567	24
Whole, raw sea shrimp (frozen-on-board)	1,540	103	2,176	533	32
Fish fillets	350	564	1,140	226	25
Whole fish for the local market[b]	300	0	380	80	22

[a]Margins before packaging costs.
[b]Product margins for sales to the local market were 20% of selling price for fresh fish, 11% for imported frozen fish, and 23% for frozen fish.

Exhibit 14 also details Pechazur export product prices FOB.[6] Prices in France fluctuated weekly; Pechazur had to meet market prices to achieve sales and maintain the existing customer base. ICA's margins averaged 8% in 1992. The margins obtained by the different intermediaries and retailers typically resulted in a final retail market price of two times the ICA sales price. For example, large-sized shrimp, priced at 75FF/kg by ICA, could retail for 150FF/kg in a supermarket. Recently, channel margins had come under pressure due to the consolidation and rising power of the major supermarket chains, who were backward integrating and thereby competing increasingly with seafood distributors.

The Benin Plant

Benin, with a population of 4.8 million, had traditionally been an important transit and trading center for the neighboring countries of Nigeria and Togo. Following a coup d'état in 1972, a Marxist government had maintained power until 1989. In 1993, the country was plagued with an illiquid banking system; large, bankrupt state companies; and high levels of internal and external debt. As part of a structural adjustment program initiated by the World Bank, the IFC was searching for opportunities to promote private enterprise. The majority of entrepreneurs in Benin were, however, involved in trade with neighboring countries (fueled, in part, by the overvalued FCFA and large price discrepancies between Benin and Nigeria) and were not interested in investing in productive assets. Due to Pechazur's recognized success in the RCI, the IFC proposed to N'Dione that he establish a shrimp-processing plant in Benin to be 20% financed by the IFC.

As export prices on shrimp dropped, N'Dione had been looking for ways to decrease Pechazur's production costs in order to remain competitive with farm-raised shrimp. Benin appeared to be a favorable location due to its large source of lagoon shrimp and lower labor and energy costs. Total product costs would be 15% to 20% below those for identical products processed in the RCI.

---

[6]FOB prices did not include transportation costs.

Exhibit 14 *Pechazur Export Product Prices FOB to France, January 1993*

Whole raw shrimp/frozen aboard

#1 (10/20 units per kg)	90FF
#2 (20/30 units per kg)	72FF
#3 (30/40 units per kg)	58FF
#4 (40/60 units per kg)	45FF
#5 (60/80 units per kg)	35FF
#6 (80/100 units per kg)	28FF
#7 (100/120 units per kg)	22FF

Whole cooked shrimp:

SX (10/20 units per kg)	100FF
SL (20/30 units per kg)	88FF
S (30/40 units per kg)	70FF
EE (40/60 units per kg)	58FF
E (60/80 units per kg)	46FF
G (80/100 units per kg)	34FF
M (100/120 units per kg)	29FF
MG (120/140 units per kg)	26FF
Z (140/180 units per kg)	23FF
ZZ (200/250 units per kg)	20FF

Shelled cooked shrimp:

DS00 (up to 100 units per kg)	48FF
DS 0 (100/150 units per kg)	46FF
DS 1 (150/250 units per kg)	42FF
DS 2 (250/400 units per kg)	28FF
DS 3 (400/700 units per kg)	22FF

Fillets of tropical sole:

F/S1 0.07kg–0.1kg	32FF
F/S2 0.07kg	29FF

Tropical sole:

0.15/0.2 kg per unit	21FF
0.2/0.25 kg per unit	21FF

Cuttlefish whites:

G (2/3 units per kg)	24FF
M (4/6 units per kg)	23FF
P (6/9 units per kg)	21FF

Red mullet:

Fillet/kg	32FF
Whole/kg	9FF

Société Beninoise de Pêche (SOBEP) was founded in 1992, with N'Dione holding 79% of the shares, the IFC 20%, and a local lawyer, also a personal friend of N'Dione's and a deputy in the National Assembly, 1%. The processing plant, located in the port of Cotonou, was similar to the Dabou plant in the RCI and was expected to be fully operational by February, 1993. It could process up to four tons of raw product a day and would source lagoon shrimp from local fishermen as well as sea shrimp and fish from Nigerian vessels with on-board freezing facilities. Expected annual production levels were 520 tons of shrimp, of which 75% would be sourced from lagoon fishermen, and 240 tons of fish fillets, sourced entirely from the Nigerian vessels. The SOBEP plant had a frozen storage capacity of 400 tons.

Five pickup vans would collect the output of 1,000 fishermen, located around a large lagoon, several times a day. The fishermen were not as yet organized into cooperatives but the director of SOBEP explained how this would eventually happen:

> *It's all a question of confidence. First we must work at creating a habit; once the fishermen get used to the way we work and see that we pay fairly and regularly, we will be able to help them form cooperatives and ensure a regular and stable supply of lagoon shrimp.*

Adjacent to the SOBEP plant, a large frozen warehouse with a storage capacity of 500 tons was being built in 1993 and N'Dione planned to import frozen fish to supply the local Benin market. Consumption levels and distribution channels for fish in Benin were very similar to those in the RCI. In the longer term, N'Dione was considering acquiring a fishing fleet that would operate out of Cotonou in much the same way as Sari-Fish.

OPTIONS FOR GROWTH

N'Dione reflected on the different challenges facing Pechazur and the company's opportunities for further expansion. He wanted to develop a coherent strategy that would address the balance between export and local sales; the relative importance of fish versus shrimp sales; the balance between supply generation and demand management activities; and the further development of the product line.

The Export-Local Sales Balance

N'Dione believed that maintaining a balance between export and local sales was a sensible diversification move that would not result in a lack of focus. The RCI and Benin were both large markets where fish were a major component of the daily diet. However, the local economies of both countries were depressed, and individual purchasing power had declined substantially over the past decade, resulting in increased pressures on prices and profitability. On the other hand, Pechazur was facing substantial competition from farm-raised shrimp in export markets, which had caused the company's average revenues per kg of shrimp to decline.

N'Dione perceived the export of fish fillets as "necessary, simply because they are caught along with the shrimp." Fish fillets were useful as a capacity filler in processing, shipping, and export marketing, but the fish fillet market in Europe was dominated by large, well-established brands against which it seemed difficult to compete effectively.

Supply Activities

Pechazur could expand its current supply-side activities by enlarging its fishing fleet and/or constructing additional processing plants, either in RCI or neighboring countries. However, N'Dione believed that expanding supply activities could be justified only if the demand for the output was sufficiently high and if the resulting sales were profitable.

N'Dione had evaluated the possibility of starting a shrimp aquaculture farm. However, not only were the capital requirements high, but an existing aquaculture farm in Abidjan, operated by a local division of Unilever, was experiencing serious productivity and quality control problems.

Demand and Marketing Activities

With the SOBEP factory coming on-line in early 1993, Pechazur needed to expand its sales to the French market and/or attempt to penetrate other geographic markets. N'Dione believed that improving access to export markets was one of Pechazur's key challenges. He was concerned about the perceived quality of African products in Western markets and wondered how best to build Pechazur's credibility.

France

Pechazur was known as a quality shrimp supplier in France and could continue to sell through ICA and other importers. On the other hand, due to the changing nature of the distribution structure in France, N'Dione was increasingly interested in striking a private label agreement with one or more supermarket chains. This, however, would place Pechazur in direct competition with its existing client base. Further penetration of the institutional or restaurant market was also appealing, but it was highly fragmented and could be accessed only via wholesalers and distributors.

Other Export Markets

These included other European countries and the United States, Japan being perceived as too difficult a market in terms of both competition and logistics. N'Dione wanted to initiate sales to the U.S. market but wondered what the best way of achieving this might be. He explained, "My dream would be to find a U.S. partner committed to developing Pechazur sales and sharing the risks and profit potential with us."

Product Line

Although Pechazur could not change its product mix in terms of shrimp sizes, the company could choose the proportion of shrimp that were cooked and/or shelled. To date, the volume of cooked and shelled shrimp had largely been determined by customer requirements. N'Dione wondered if Pechazur should attempt to specialize in two products: raw sea shrimp frozen on board; and shelled, cooked lagoon shrimp.

N'Dione pondered whether the long-term success of Pechazur lay in developing consumer brand recognition and applying the Pechazur brand to value-added products sold at retail, such as frozen ready-to-eat meals in which shrimp was at the "center of the plate."

MASTERCARD AND WORLD CHAMPIONSHIP SOCCER

One of our goals was to underscore MasterCard's transformation from a U.S.-oriented credit card company to a truly global brand and payment services organization.

—C. Alexander McKeveny,
Vice-President of Global Promotions,
MasterCard International

On July 17, 1994, Brazil won its fourth World Soccer Cup trophy in the Pasadena, California, Rose Bowl stadium. The four-week final round, played in the United States, was the culmination of hundreds of qualifying matches played between 1992 and 1994, and had been a resounding success. MasterCard International, one of the world's leading global payments franchises, had been one of the 11 worldwide sponsors of the event.

While the Brazilians enjoyed a national holiday honoring their team's success, the group which had orchestrated MasterCard's first global sponsorship gathered to reflect on its impact and lessons. At this stage, the team had to assess what the 1994 World Cup sponsorship had achieved for MasterCard and its member financial institutions. They needed to decide if and how the effort should be repeated. The proposal to sign on as a sponsor for the 1998 World Cup, with the final rounds to be played in France, was already on the table.

MASTERCARD INTERNATIONAL

New York-based MasterCard was a global payments franchise comprising nearly 22,000 member financial institutions. It operated as a not-for-profit association. MasterCard did not issue cards, set annual fees on cards, or determine annual percentage rates (APRs).[1] It did not solicit

---

[1] The *annual percentage rate* (APR) was the yearly interest charge applicable to outstanding credit card balances.

This case was prepared by Carin-Isabel Knoop (under the direction of John A. Quelch). Copyright © 1995 by the President and Fellows of Harvard College. Harvard Business School case 595-040.

merchants to accept cards or set their discount rates.[2] Financial institutions managed the relationships with consumers and merchants. MasterCard's mission was "to be the world's best payment franchise by enabling member banks to provide superior value and satisfaction to their customers, thereby building member profitability."

MasterCard fulfilled this mission in three ways. First, it managed a global family of brands (MasterCard, Cirrus, and Maestro)[3] and related products, including travelers checks. Like a franchiser, MasterCard developed new products and services, set and enforced policies governing the use of its brands, and created umbrella marketing programs to support them. The logos of all three brands were based on MasterCard's familiar interlocking circles. Second, MasterCard established procedures for accepting and settling transactions between MasterCard and its members on a global basis. Third, MasterCard provided a communications network for electronic authorization and subsequent clearing[4] of credit and debit card transactions, monitored member banks' compliance with interchange rules, and worked with government authorities to track and combat credit card fraud. MasterCard was funded through quarterly assessments on members for their use of the MasterCard mark and from operational service fees. The annually set assessments varied from region to region and reflected each issuer's and acquirer's volume of MasterCard sales. Each region had to be self-funding. Operational service fees were charged on a per-transaction basis for services, including card authorizations, settlements of monthly cardholder accounts, and listings of revoked or restricted cards.

MasterCard's Development

The Franklin National Bank (New York) introduced the first modern bank credit card in 1951. California-based Bank of America extended the idea throughout the country by introducing the BankAmericard (now Visa) in 1960. It franchised a single bank in each major city as a local affiliate responsible for enrolling cardholders and signing contracts with merchants to accept cards as payment. In 1966, a group of bankers who were not "franchisees" of BankAmericard created its own network, the Interbank Card Association (ICA), which became MasterCard International.

Unlike BankAmericard, ICA was not dominated by a single bank; ICA was run by member committees. In 1968, ICA formed an association

---

[2]The *discount* rate was the fee a merchant paid a member bank to process a purchase charged to a MasterCard card. The *acquirer* was a licensed MasterCard member that had an agreement to process the data from merchant transactions involving the card. The *issuer* was an institution that entered into a contractual agreement with MasterCard to issue its cards. *Interchange* referred to the exchange of transactions between acquirers and issuers. At MasterCard, a *principal* member had a direct participation in the interchange system. An *association member* was a member that was controlled by, and formed to service, one or more financial institutions, and that processed credit card transactions on behalf of the group. An *associate* member participated indirectly in interchange via a principal or association member.

[3]*Cirrus* was a wholly owned MasterCard subsidiary that operated an international automatic teller machine (ATM) sharing network. *Maestro* was a global, on-line point-of-sale debit program. Transaction amounts were immediately debited against the cardholder's bank deposit account.

---

[4]*Clearing* involved the exchange of financial transaction details between an acquirer and an issuer to facilitate posting of a cardholder's account and reconciliation of a customer's settlement position.

with the Mexican bank Banamex, with Euro-card International in Europe (later Europay International),[5] and with several Japanese members. The Bank of Montreal joined in 1969. That year ICA acquired for its member banks the rights to the Master Charge name and the interlocking circle logo. Use of the Master Charge logo on the full face of the card became mandatory in 1970. In 1973, a computerized international authorization system was set up. In 1974, the magnetic strip became a standard feature and Access Ltd., a subsidiary of the U.K.'s National Westminster Bank, signed on. In 1975, the Bank of South Africa became the first African member and, in 1979, the first Australian member joined. That year ICA became MasterCard International and its trademark was changed from Master Charge to Master-Card to reflect the association's expansion beyond charge card services.

Throughout the 1980s, MasterCard developed new products and services, including credit products, debit services, point-of-sale processing for merchants, remote banking, and cardholder services. It introduced travelers checks in 1981 and pioneered market segmentation with its Gold MasterCard card aimed at upscale consumers. In 1983, MasterCard was the first to introduce the laser hologram on its card as an anti-counterfeiting measure. In 1984, MasterCard launched the Banknet global transaction network to authorize MasterCard transactions. By this time, the MasterCard mark had been established, and the size of its logo on the card could be reduced. Card issuers were assigned 60% of the card face for their own identification, compared with 25% in the early stages of brand development. As a result, an issuer's logo and name could appear more prominently. In 1987, card is-

suers were assigned 80% of the card surface which included a hologram that was two-and-half times larger than its predecessor.

In 1988, MasterCard acquired Cirrus Systems, Inc., owner of the U.S.-Canadian ATM network, which was founded in 1982, and acquired 15% of Eurocard International. Master-Card launched MasterCard Debit,[6] followed one year later by the global MasterCard ATM network. In 1990, MasterCard updated its logo and let issuers use 85% of the card surface. The global hologram had to appear in the same place on every MasterCard card, with the MasterCard logo directly above or below it. No other local acceptance mark on the card could be larger than the MasterCard logo. In 1990, MasterCard became the official card of the 1990 World Cup and launched MasterValues, a point-of-sale discount program and the largest bank card retail promotion in the United States. MasterValues coupons offered cardholders instant savings at national and regional merchants.

MasterCard continued to enhance its interchange and clearing systems and perfected its co-branding initiatives, which facilitated the entry of major industrial corporations (such as General Motors, AT&T, and General Electric) into the credit card business.[7] In 1991, Master-Card entered a worldwide alliance with the Thomas Cook travel group, enabling Master-Card to offer a range of cardholder services at Thomas Cook locations. The 1994 World Cup sponsorship was agreed to. In 1992, Maestro completed the first-ever U.S. coast-to-coast

---

[5]*Europay International* resulted from a merger of Eurocard International, Eurocheque International, and European Payment Systems Services (EPSS).

[6]*MasterCard Debit* enhanced members' proprietary ATM cards by guaranteeing acceptance at retail and cash-access locations that accepted MasterCard cards. Instead of using a line of credit, MasterCard debit transactions were withdrawn from a deposit account much like conventional checks.

[7]A *co-branded* card was a customized card produced for a specific retailer or service provider.

national online POS debit transaction[8] and Maestro International was formed. The familiar interlocking circles were incorporated into the logos of Cirrus and Maestro. At the end of 1993, gross dollar transaction volume was U.S. $320.6 billion, cards in circulation reached 210.3 million, and acceptance locations worldwide grew to 12 million locations in more than 220 countries and territories. Maestro debit cards numbered 110.5 million, and the MasterCard/Cirrus ATM Network had grown to 162,000 ATMs in 55 countries. Exhibit 1 summarizes MasterCard's business by product and by region.

MasterCard's Organizational Structure

The President and CEO of MasterCard International was responsible for the entire MasterCard organization and its subsidiaries worldwide. Direct reports included Global Marketing, which developed and managed MasterCard products, promotions, product enhancements, and services worldwide. Its responsibilities included the World Cup sponsorship and global advertising campaign development.

Governed by a global board of directors, elected annually and representing its member financial institutions, MasterCard operations were organized into six regions : Asia/Pacific (21.9% of MasterCard's 1993 total gross dollar volume and 18.8% of all MasterCard cards in circulation worldwide), Canada (4.3% and 4.6%), Europe (24.2% and 15%[9]), Latin America (5% and 5.8%), Middle East/Africa (1.3% and 0.6%), and the United States (43.4% and 53.3%). The U.S.

---

[8]At the point of sale, the merchant swiped the Master Card and the cardholder using a Maestro Card would input his/her personal identification number (PIN). Authorization took a few seconds and the transaction would be deducted from the cardholder's associated bank account. In addition to a POS receipt, the cardholder could see a detailed listing of all transactions on his/her associated deposit account statement.
[9]Including ATMs.

region shared office space with MasterCard headquarters in New York. Historically, MasterCard's operations had been decentralized, and there had been limited contact between the United States and other regions. Except in Europe, where licensing and marketing activities were handled by Europay, regional boards reviewed and approved regional marketing plans. MasterCard headquarters also organized a network of marketing and operations committees including members from all regions. Ad hoc advisory committees were sometimes formed on an as-needed basis to provide guidance on specific projects.

THE PAYMENT SERVICES INDUSTRY

At the end of 1993, there were more than 650 million general-purpose cards in circulation worldwide (including MasterCard, Visa, Discover, American Express, Japan Credit Bureau, and Diners Club cards). The value of transactions on these cards in 1993 exceeded $1 trillion. The use of debit cards as well as ATM cash access was also rising dramatically. Several types of payment cards and services existed. The two types of general-purpose cards were bank cards (such as the MasterCard and Visa cards), issued by banks and financial institutions, and charge cards referred to as travel and entertainment (T&E) cards, which did not come with a line of credit (such as the American Express green cards and Diners Club cards). Cardholders had to pay their total monthly bills upon receipt. In contrast, proprietary credit cards, issued by stores and oil companies, could be used for purchases from the outlets of the issuer. Credit cards offered a consumer installment and/or a revolving line of credit up to a limit set by the issuer. Interest was charged on the outstanding unpaid balance. A debit card was tied directly to a consumer's demand deposit account and functioned as a paperless checking account. MasterCard members offered both credit and debit cards.

Competition varied at a regional level but four players remained constant worldwide: MasterCard, Visa, American Express, and Din-

Exhibit 1   *MasterCard Data by Product and by Region, 1993*[*]

	Cards in Circulation (in millions) 1993		Gross Dollar Volume (in billions)[b] 1993		Acceptance Locations (in millions) 1993		Acceptance ATMs (in thousands) 1993		Maestro Cards (in millions) 1993
Asia/Pacific	39.5	(12.1)%	70.1	(67.8)%	4.1	(15.4)%	2.9	(193.2)%	13.0
Canada	9.6	(11.8)	13.9	(9.6)	0.5	(1.1)	2.5	(1.1)	2.5
Europe	31.5	(8.8)[a]	77.5	(13.4)	2.9	(10)	77.8	(62.3)	70.0
Latin America	12.3	(−5.2)	15.9	(20.1)	1.3	(27.8)	4.8	(119.5)	5.0
Middle East/Africa	1.2	(6.7)	4.1	(23.1)	0.2	(16.1)	1.1	(12.9)	2.0
United States	116.3	(15.5)	139.6	(23.4)	3.0	(3.1)	73.5	(6.1)	18.0
Worldwide	210.3[a]		320.6	(28.1)	12.0	(11.3)	162.6	(31.3)	110.5

[*]Source: MasterCard 1993 Annual report. Note: Numbers in parentheses indicate percentage changes from preceding year.
[a]Includes ATMs.
[b]All volumes are reported in U.S. dollars. Regional growth rates other than in Latin America are adjusted for currency fluctuations.

Exhibit 2   *Data for MasterCard, Visa, American Express: 1993**

	MasterCard 1993	Visa 1993	American Express 1993	Total 1993
U.S. cards (millions)	116.2	168.6	24.7	309.5
Cards worldwide (millions)	215.8	335.1	35.4	586.3
U.S. volume ($ billions)	139.1	227.0	89.8	455.9
Worldwide volume ($ billions)	320.6	527.9	124.1	972.6
U.S. Merchant locations (millions)	2.9	2.8	N/A	N/A
Non-U.S. merchant locations (millions)	8.6	8.2	N/A	N/A
Total merchant locations (millions)	11.5	11.0	3.6	N/A

*Sources: Adapted from company records and Faulkner & Gray's *Credit Industry Directory* (1994 Edition).

ers Club. Exhibit 2 presents data on the United States and worldwide performance of these four competitors. At the end of 1993, Visa had the largest card base worldwide, with 335.1 million cards in circulation and access to more than 164,000 ATMs in 69 countries. Gross dollar volume, including travelers checks, was U.S. $542 billion, generated at more than 11 million acceptance locations. Unlike MasterCard, Visa was a non-stock, for-profit corporation owned by member banks. Like MasterCard, Visa did not issue cards and had no direct payment relationship with cardholders. Visa was also evolving into a payments company, offering a range of online and offline debit products in the United States and providing traveler's checks and global ATM access to its cardholders worldwide. Visa and MasterCard products from one bank were virtually indistinguishable from those of another. Duality, or the handling of both MasterCard and Visa International transactions (issuing, acquiring, or both) by a single institution, was common in the United States, but less prevalent in other regions. Exhibit 3 shows a sample credit card application for either a Citibank Visa or MasterCard.

Diner's Club introduced the first T&E card in 1950. In 1960, it was the first card issued in Japan. In 1993, Diners Club generated $7.9 billion in worldwide charge volume off a base of 1.5 million cardholders. The world's largest issuer of T&E cards was American Express (AmEx), which introduced its green card in 1958. AmEx had almost five times as many cards as Diners Club and 30% more than the Japan-based JCB card.[10] In 1993, Amex worldwide gross-dollar volume was U.S. $124.1 billion, with 35.4 million cards in circulation and 3.6 million merchant locations. Unlike MasterCard and Visa, Amex issued its own cards and maintained a direct relationship with its cardmembers and merchants. This gave the company access to specific consumer information that could be used to segment its cardholder base and offer targeted promotional and customer service programs. To compete more directly with MasterCard and Visa, AmEx introduced the Optima Card with revolving credit in 1987. Optima remained a small portion of the AmEx portfolio. The Amex gold and platinum cards, targeted at higher income consumers, also came with credit lines.

---

[10]In fiscal year 1992, JCB, established by Sanwa Bank in 1961, had 27.5 million cards in circulation and U.S. $30.9 billion in worldwide volume. It was accepted in more than 2.9 million outlets in 139 countries worldwide, and offered access to more than 160,000 ATMs in 47 countries.

Exhibit 3   *Citibank Visa and MasterCard Card Application, 1994*

Citibank Visa. Citibank MasterCard.

Some people think all MasterCard® and Visa® cards are the same. The truth is no one else puts more behind their cards than Citibank.

With Citibank Classic MasterCard and Visa, you get the kind of service only the world's largest issuer of MasterCard and Visa cards can offer.

• Citibank Photocard

For added security, you can have your picture and signature digitally imprinted on the front of your Citibank Classic card.*

• The Lowest Price On Most Card Purchases

With Citibank Price Protection, if you find the item advertised in print at a lower price within 60 days of your purchase, Citibank will refund the difference — up to $150!**

• Round-The-Clock Customer Service

Toll-free, 24-hour customer service is available 7 days a week. When you have a billing question, usually all it takes is one call. And if your card is lost or stolen, call us to receive a new one, usually within 24 hours.

• Extra Coverage For What You Buy

Buyers Security℠ covers most anything you charge on your Citibank Classic card against fire, theft or accidental damage for 90 days from the date of the purchase. Also, Extended Warranty doubles the original manufacturer's U.S. warranty period for up to one additional year on most Citibank Classic card purchases.**

If we were to tell you all the benefits our cards offer, we wouldn't have room for an application. So complete, sign and return the attached application today.

CITIBANK

* Please do not send a photo at this time. Details will be provided once you become a cardmember.
** Certain conditions and exclusions apply. Details will be provided once you become a cardmember.
The Buyers Security and Extended Warranty programs are underwritten by Zurich International (UK) Ltd.

PLEASE DETACH ALONG DOTTED LINE, FOLD, SEAL AND MAIL.

---

1 PLEASE PRINT CLEARLY WITH A BLACK OR BLUE PEN
YES! I want my Citibank Classic card.   Select One: ☐ Citibank MasterCard®   ☐ Citibank Visa®   SECTIONS 1 THRU 7 MUST BE COMPLETED

PLEASE TELL US ABOUT YOURSELF

2 Please Print Your Full Name As You Wish It To Appear On The Card (First, Middle, Last) | Your Home Address, Number And Street | Apt. #

City Or Town | State | Zip Code | Years At Address | ☐ Own Home ☐ Own Condo/Co-op | ☐ Rent ☐ Live w/ Parents | ☐ Other | Social Security Number

Date Of Birth (Month/Day/Year) | Mother's Maiden Name | Home Phone Number And Area Code | Name Home Phone Is Listed Under | Are You A Permanent U.S. Resident? ☐ Yes ☐ No

Previous Home Address, Number And Street | City Or Town | State | Zip Code | Years There

ADDITIONAL STUDENT INFORMATION (Only Current College Or Graduate Students Complete This Section)

2A College Or Graduate School Name (Do Not Abbreviate) | Your Mailing Address At School | Apt. # | City Or Town | I M P O R T A N T

State | Zip Code | Your Phone Number And Area Code At School | Official School Zip Code | Name Your Phone Is Listed Under | You must enclose in an envelope with this application a complete legible copy of your validated ID from a college/university (or paid tuition bill) for the current semester.

Your Class: ☐ Fresh ☐ Soph ☐ Junior ☐ Senior ☐ Graduate ☐ Faculty/Staff ☐ Other | Graduation Date mo./yr. | Send Card And Billing Statement To: ☐ Home ☐ School

PLEASE TELL US ABOUT YOUR JOB (Current Students: Job Not Required)

3 Business Name Or Employer At Current Job | Position | Years At Job | Employer Phone Number And Area Code

Check Here If You Are: ☐ Retired ☐ Self-Employed | If Retired Or Self-Employed, Enter Bank Name | Bank Phone Number And Area Code | Bank Account Number

ABOUT YOUR INCOME

4 You need not include your spouse's income, alimony, child support or maintenance payments paid to you if you are not relying on them to establish creditworthiness. Your total yearly income from all sources must be at least $8,000 to be considered for cardmembership. (No student minimum)

Your Total Personal Yearly Income $ | Other Yearly Household Income $

Other Yearly Income Sources

IMPORTANT ACCOUNT INFORMATION

5 Please Check Those That Apply. Be Sure To Specify Institution/Bank Name.

☐ Money Market/ NOW Account | Institution Name:

☐ Checking Account | Institution Name:

☐ Savings Account | Institution Name:

☐ Visa/MasterCard | ☐ Diners Club | ☐ American Express
☐ Dept. Store/Sears | ☐ Gasoline | ☐ Other

WOULD YOU LIKE AN ADDITIONAL CARD AT NO CHARGE?

6 If Yes, Print The Full Name Of The User (First, Middle, Last) (Students: Does Not Apply)

REV 7/94

PLEASE SIGN THIS AUTHORIZATION

7 I certify that I meet/agree to all Citibank credit terms and conditions of offer on other side. Please allow 30 days to process this application.

X
Applicant's Signature | Date

1B8WF 3149Y C7185 0000   1CBBI 31499 85088 &&Y0

Left margin: FOLD, MOISTEN HERE, SEAL AND MAIL. Have you included your ☐ Social Security Number ☐ Phone Numbers ☐ Signature?

The Competitive Challenge in the United States

With a return on assets of 2%, credit cards remained retail banking's single most profitable product in the United States from the 1960s to the 1990s.[11] By then, the U.S. region was approaching saturation. The results were heavy competition among credit card issuers, increased market segmentation, waivers of annual fees, reduced APRs, and costly value-added card features.[12] Increases in the number of cardholders now had to come at the expense of other issuers rather than through market growth. Increases in volume required penetration into merchant segments where payments were largely made by cash and/or checks. ATM access was extremely widespread and served as the forerunner of POS debit, the industry's newest battlefield. In the on- and offline arenas, MasterMoney and Visa Check offered global acceptance at all their merchants' locations, and MasterCard's Maestro competed directly with Visa's Interlink. Finally, bank mergers in the early 1990s increased the power of top member banks by linking huge card portfolios. The five largest MasterCard and Visa issuers accounted for 50% of 1991 cards in circulation in the United States, compared with 30% in 1986.

In addition, new forms of competition emerged in the mid-1980s. The Sears-owned Discover card entered the U.S. credit card market in 1986, was accepted in 1993 at more than 1.8 million U.S. merchant locations, charged no annual fee, and rebated up to 1% on cardholder purchases. It competed directly with MasterCard for the value-conscious consumer segment by offering a cash-back rebate based on charge volume. Discover also introduced tiered pricing based on spending patterns rather than payment patterns. Major banks responded only after the 1990 launch of AT&T's low-rate, no-fee Universal Card, which, three years later, claimed 20 million cardholders. Also, "nonbanks," card-issuing banks owned by corporations such as General Electric, increased their share of the general purpose card market from 19.3% to 25.2% in the two-year period ending January 1993.[13]

In 1990, MasterCard's market share had sunk to an all-time low of 26.6% of all Visa, MasterCard, Discover and Amex charges in the United States, compared with 30.6% in 1987. The brand had targeted the mass market and been described as "unfocused."[14] By 1993, MasterCard led the industry in growth for the second consecutive year. MasterCard attributed its turnaround to a new positioning emphasis on value and usefulness, replacing the prior emphasis on using the card in the pursuit of pleasure. This value positioning was adopted for all payments products in the franchise and fit with MasterCard's aggressive pursuit of co-branding whereby MasterCard, its member financial institutions and major corporations, such as American Airlines, AT&T, General Motors and Shell Oil, partnered to create credit card products with a unique and valued consumer benefit. By 1993, these "affinity" or "co-branded" cards accounted for one-third of U.S. MasterCard credit cards. Furthermore, MasterCard's aggressive effort to persuade supermarkets, government agencies, and health care organizations to accept the credit card in transactions further expanded its usefulness. The advertising campaign of the late 1980s—"MasterCard. Master the possibilities"—was replaced with the slogan, "MasterCard. It's more than a credit card. It's

---

[11]Wanda Cantrell, "Is there any gold left in credit cards?," *United States Banker* (April 1994), pp. 22–30.

[12]Examples of value-added cards: affinity cards, co-branded cards like the General Motors card that offered rebates on product purchases or frequent flyer miles, and cards tied to a retirement annuity or college tuition.

[13]The *Directory of the Card Industry* (1994 Edition), pp. 17–20, was a significant source for this section.

[14]See Peter Lucas, "The Master Plan at MasterCard," *Credit Card Management* (February 1993), pp. 41–44.

smart money," which served as an umbrella for all products and services.

Success in the U.S. card business hinged on persuading member banks to issue one's card, on getting customers to adopt and use it regularly, and on convincing retailers to accept it. This prompted the use not only of price promotions such as low APRs and no or low annual fees, but also of non-price, added-value features such as merchandise protection, ease of use, reliable and speedy approval and clearing of transactions, fraud control, and attractive merchant discount rates.

The cost of acquiring a new account was estimated at $70 to $100. Voluntary cardholder attrition was 10% to 15% until 1993 when it fell below 10%. Retention and usage frequency were key to ensuring that each cardholder was profitable. "Top-of-the-wallet" positioning was crucial with most customers carrying three or more credit cards from various issuers. As competition for the share of customer transactions increased, credit card companies stepped up advertising and promotional efforts. In 1992, AmEx's worldwide communications budget topped $1 billion, $200 million more than in 1990.[15] Television advertising represented one-third of communications spending. Direct mail campaigns and frequent-user programs were gaining in importance. Promotion moved to direct comparisons, away from themes stressing the freedom and prestige the cards offered to users.

Growth in International Markets

Slowing market growth and declining profitability[16] at home focused the attention of U.S.-based payments-services companies on growing international markets. Non-U.S. charges at both Visa

---

[15]*Business Marketing* (October 1993), p. 73.

[16]Bank card profitability as measured by return on assets (outstanding balances) declined from 2.3% in 1990 to 1.87% in 1992. (Source: Faulkner & Grey's *Card Industry Directory* [1994 Edition], p. 18.)

Exhibit 4   *MasterCard and Visa Relative Shares (%) by Region, 1993*

	MasterCard	Visa
Asia/Pacific	47%	53%
Canada	31	69
Europe and Middle East/Africa	31	69
Latin America	45	55
United States	38	62
Worldwide	37	63

*Source: Company records.

and MasterCard overtook U.S. volume in 1990. Exhibit 4 summarizes MasterCard and Visa shares per geographic region. The use of payment cards differed from country to country, depending on local banking regulations and market conditions, including economic factors such as inflation and credit costs.

After the United States, Canada was one of the world's most developed credit card markets. Customers rarely switched banks. Duality was nonexistent. Visa led MasterCard in terms of market share, thanks to a five-year head start. The Asia/Pacific region's diverse 41 countries included the well-developed Australian market; export-oriented economies such as Korea, Hong Kong, Singapore, and Taiwan; and the Indian and Chinese cash-based markets. Banking infrastructure and consumer banking behavior were as diverse as the 900 languages spoken in the region. Duality was common, which meant that many financial institutions issued both MasterCard and Visa credit cards. MasterCard and Visa were tied in terms of gross dollar volume. Diners Club and JCB were also well established. In 1990, Japan ranked fifth among countries in gross dollar volume of credit card transactions and second in cards in circulation. Japan accounted for 60% of all MasterCard cards in the region.

Western Europe, with a population of 320 million, a GDP twice that of Japan, and low payment card penetration, was particularly attractive to global payment franchises. While Americans held an average of 3.9 credit cards per person in the early 1990s, only 21% of Western Europeans held a single credit card. Where available, credit cards tended to have high APRs. Revolving credit cards, however, were common in the United Kingdom and Scandinavia, and the "pay later" phenomenon was gaining ground throughout Europe. Most European payment cards were debit cards, delayed debit cards, or charge cards tied to checking accounts. The majority of Europeans had access to overdraft lines of credit directly from their banks at much more favorable rates. The Eurocheque card was Europe's leading personal debit payment system. Around 52 million cards served as check guarantees for Eurocheques and were accepted by over 5 million merchants in 25 countries. Whether used locally, in another European country, or in North Africa, the Eurocheque functioned like an ordinary check, enabling cardholders to make purchases in local currency. In the early 1990s,

European financial institutions were enhancing their cards by joining online global debit programs such as Maestro. By the end of 1993, more than 50 million cards and 254,000 terminals were involved in the program in Europe. The first online intercontinental POS debit transactions were completed in July 1993. Eastern and Central Europe were thought to offer new growth opportunities.

In the early 1990s, household payment card penetration in Europe was in the 40% to 50% range. Visa's penetration averaged 20% while Eurocard/MasterCard's penetration averaged 12% but varied more by country. Eurocard/MasterCard household penetration ranged from 28% in Switzerland to 1% in Spain, compared with 17% and 21% respectively for Visa. Exhibit 5 provides data on payment card ownership and household penetration by brand and country in Europe. MasterCard's European partner, Europay, offered a Europackage with a full range of Pay Before, Pay Now, and Pay Later products. MasterCard's travelers checks

Exhibit 5   *Card Ownership and Household Penetration (%) by Brand and Country in Europe, 1991**

	Ownership of any Payment Card	Visa: Penetration of Households	Eurocard/ MasterCard: Penetration of Households	American Express Penetration of Households
Austria	47%	8%	13%	1%
Belgium	70	23	11	4
France	61	25	9	2
Germany	33	6	15	5
Italy	11	8	1	2
The Netherlands	31	4	19	3
Scandinavia	45	20	9	2
Spain	42	21	1	1
Switzerland	48	17	28	10
United Kingdom	63	42	26	2

*Source: Adapted from *PSI 1991 European Study Report*.

(co-branded with Thomas Cook and Eurotravelers Cheque) held a 40% share of the European market. Its Pay Now products included the Eurocheque, the European Debit Card, Maestro, and EC-ATM, which offered cash access at nearly 78,000 ATMs in Europe and more than 162,000 ATMs worldwide. Europay surpassed Visa with a 71% share of the European debit market segment. In the Pay Later category, Europay offered co-branded Eurocard/MasterCard cards that targeted higher-income consumers and competed with AmEx. AmEx had a much smaller merchant base than MasterCard but was better recognized by a large percentage of Europeans. The Eurocard/MasterCard was long perceived as a T&E card in Germany. In the United Kingdom, the Access MasterCard card was seen as a credit card. The card was referred to as Carta Si MasterCard in Italy and as Etnocard MasterCard in Greece.

Latin America encompassed a range of economies at different stages of development. In the 1990s, many nations passed reforms to counter hyperinflation and embarked on ambitious privatization and economic liberalization programs. Increased foreign investment fueled economic activity and greater consumer spending. MasterCard was the leading bank card in many markets in the region. On the debit side, capitalizing on a strong merchant network and extensive ATM network, Maestro had committed several key institutions in the region's most important markets. Amex was making inroads in the upscale and tourist markets, mostly at the expense of Diners Club. Visa had over 200 co-branded programs in Latin America, 53 in Mexico alone, but most only netted 5,000 to 10,000 cardholders. The Middle East/Africa region was characterized primarily as a destination market (i.e., most card usage was generated by visiting businesspeople and tourists) except for the well-developed South Africa market. MasterCard, Visa, and Amex had all built strong merchant networks. Both MasterCard and Visa issuers offered local-currency-only cards in a few countries

due to exchange controls. Many banks in the early 1990s expressed an interest in online POS debit services, since these products did not depend on the creditworthiness of the population.

WORLD CHAMPIONSHIP SOCCER, 1991–1994

As MasterCard International expanded its products and global presence, creating and maintaining a unified worldwide image became increasingly important. MasterCard also needed to communicate its evolution from a U.S. credit card company to an international payments system. MasterCard executives believed that, as a global payments company, MasterCard should sponsor an appropriate global "property." Soccer, the world's most widely followed sport, was an option.

The Rise of Event Sponsorships and Lifestyle Marketing

Sports sponsorships were by no means new to American corporations. Gillette continued to devote 65% of its advertising and promotional budgets to sports 80 years after it had initiated baseball sponsorship in 1910. Coca-Cola was already sponsoring the Olympic Games in 1928. Sports had been popular with sponsors because of their competitive nature, huge consumer interest and awareness, strong emotional appeal and television coverage, and perhaps most importantly, the fact that sports fans spread across the full range of demographic and psychographic types. Sports crossed national frontiers and cultural barriers, and could involve an individual, a team, or an event. Event sponsorship was most popular with large corporations because, as Mark McCormack, a pioneer in the field of sports sponsoring,[17] once remarked, an

---

[17]McCormack was the founder of IMG, one of the most powerful agencies in the marketing of sporting event rights with a 1993 turnover estimated at U.S. $800 million.

event "[did] not break a leg, sprain an ankle, fail a drug test or lose six-love, six-love."

In 1991, for the first time in 30 years, advertising spending in the United States decreased by 1.5%.[18] In contrast, *Special Events Report* estimated that corporate sponsorship in the United States for sports, arts, and cause-related events reached $1.4 billion in 1989 and topped $1.8 billion in 1991. Worldwide spending on sponsorship rights was estimated at $2.5 billion. This figure included only the sponsorship rights. Marketing and promotion-related expenses that usually accompanied sponsorships typically doubled or tripled the investment in sponsorship rights.

The Olympic Games and the World Cup were the only two truly global sporting events. The Olympics was popular with some sponsors because of its strong association with patriotism, high standards, and the product-positioning platform it offered. Visa had been an Olympic sponsor since 1988. An "Olympic product" was positioned as the "best" product of its type. The Olympics' attractiveness as a sponsorship vehicle had been impaired by what was perceived as excessive commercial exploitation and by instances of "ambush marketing," whereby competitors "ambushed" official sponsors by associating themselves with an event indirectly.[19]

The World Cup grew out of the Olympic movement. Fourteen nations sent a soccer team to the 1920 Antwerp Olympics. In 1928, the Federation Internationale de Football (FIFA) decided to run its own competition, and the first World Cup was held in 1930. By the 1980s, it was the single biggest sporting event

in the world, and the World Cup trophy was the most coveted sports trophy. Originally fixed at 16 teams, the tournament was expanded to include 24 teams in 1982 and would include 32 teams in 1998. The cumulative television audience for the 1990 games was estimated at 26 billion in over 160 countries. More than 31 billion people were expected to watch the matches leading up to and including the final rounds of World Cup '94.

What the World Cup might have lacked in imagery, it made up by offering comparative advantages to potential marketing sponsors. Qualifying matches were held over four years around the world, with the four-week finale held in multiple locations in a single country. The Olympics lasted two weeks in a single location once every two years (the Summer and Winter Olympics were held every four years on an alternating cycle). The 1992 Summer Olympics, for which Visa had been an official sponsor, had a cumulative TV audience of 16.6 billion. No advertising in the form of perimeter signage was allowed at the Olympics, in contrast to the World Cup. Market research data indicated that onscreen visibility of sponsor identities during World Cup telecasts increased brand awareness among match viewers.

The World Cup '94 Sponsorship Decision

ISL, a privately held major sports marketing company headquartered in Switzerland, with annual sales around $100 million, owned the marketing rights to the World Cup and the Olympics. ISL approached MasterCard in 1989 with the opportunity to participate as an official product in Italia '90. As "Official Card," MasterCard received no perimeter signage around the soccer fields, since this was reserved for "Official Sponsors," but it could use the event as a platform for public relations, advertising, and promotions. This experience led

---

[18]*Marketing News 1992.*

[19]A hypothetical example of ambush marketing would be: Coca-Cola sponsors an event and Pepsi buys many of the television advertising spots that run while the event is aired.

MasterCard to expand its soccer sponsorship efforts. For a reported $15 million, Master-Card became one of the eleven worldwide[20] sponsors of World Cup '94.[21] In April 1992, MasterCard signed on soccer legend Pelé as the exclusive MasterCard World Cup Spokesperson for an estimated $2 million. Pelé, who had led Brazil to three World Cup titles, would be featured on posters and in television commercials and made available to member banks for promotional appearances around the world. Separately, MasterCard signed category-exclusive sponsorship agreements for the U.S. National Team (which would compete in the World Cup as host nation) and for "gold level" sponsorship of U.S. television broadcasts of World Cup matches.

The MasterCard sponsorship program, internally referred to as World Championship Soccer (WCS), guaranteed MasterCard a presence at 269 matches to be played at 16 major international soccer events between 1991 to 1994. MasterCard had exclusivity in the payments systems category.[22] Exhibit 6 details the WCS

---

[20]The 11 worldwide sponsors were Canon, Coca-Cola (*), Energizer, Fuji, General Motors (*), Gillette, JVC, M&M/Mars (*), Master-Card (*), McDonald's (*), and Philips. The Gold Sponsors, who received priority on U.S. prime television commercial time, are marked with an asterisk.

[21]The 16 U.S. team sponsors were Adidas, American Airlines, Anheuser-Busch, Chiquita, Coca-Cola, Fuji Film, Gatorade, JVC, M&M/Mars, MasterCard, Procter & Gamble, Sheraton, Sprint, Toys 'R' Us, Transitions Optical, and Upper Deck.

[22]Exclusivity in the Payment Systems Category included: credit cards, debit cards, T&E cards, debit cards, check guarantee cards, ATM/ATM networks, traveler's checks, and non-bank wired transfers. Thus, Maestro was the official online point-of-sale debit card, and Cirrus was the official ATM network of the World Cup '94.

events, and Exhibit 7 summarizes MasterCard's sponsorship rights. Prominent among these was MasterCard's right to have two display boards on the perimeters of the soccer pitches in all 269 matches. These boards would, of course, be picked up on television coverage of the matches. The 1994 World Cup's final 52 games were played from June 17 to July 17, 1994, in nine U.S. cities: Boston, Chicago, Dallas, Detroit, Los Angeles, New York, Orlando, San Francisco, and Washington, D.C. In the United States, ABC broadcast 11 games and ESPN broadcast the other 41 games without interruptions, due to the continuous nature of soccer play. Commercials aired pre-game (1:30-second spot), at halftime (2:30), and post-game (1:30). As a "gold" sponsor, Mastercard received four 30-second ads in all U.S. telecasts, as well as an additional 30-second spot on ABC's "Wide World of Sports" vignettes. The MasterCard logo was superimposed over the game clock on the television screen for a total of 17½ minutes per game. In the case of injury/official time-outs and expanded post-games, each gold sponsor received additional exposure on a rotation basis. This format minimized the risk of ambush marketing.

Sharing the Sponsorship Expenses

MasterCard headquarters decided to cover 50% of the estimated $15 million cost of the sponsorship rights and allocate the rest across its regions. An event's commercial impact depended largely on the amount of regional or national media exposure it received. The participation of a country's national team in the final World Cup round increased the media coverage of the final matches in that particular country and increased the member banks' opportunities to exploit the sponsorship. The share of the cost allocated to each region was therefore based on the number of teams from a particular region that participated in the final round. The 30,000 tickets

Exhibit 6   *MasterCard World Cup Sponsorship Rights*

| Event | World Championship Soccer 1991–1994 Events[a] | | | |
	1991	1992	1993	1994
European Cup Winners' Cup Final	The Netherlands	Portugal	England	Denmark
European Champion Clubs' Cup Final	Italy	England	Germany	Greece
European Championship (Euro '92)		Sweden		
Under-17 World Championship for the FIFA/JVC Cup	Italy		Japan	
World Youth Championship for the FIFA/Coca-Cola Cup	Portugal		Australia	
FIFA Women's World Championship for the M&M's Cup	China			
FIFA World Indoor Championship		Hong Kong		
World Cup '94				United States
Projected Television Audience	1.9 billion	4.7 billion	1.2 billion	31.2 billion

[a]Representing 269 matches in total.

MasterCard was entitled to purchase were allocated to the regions in proportion to their shares of the funding.[23]

Although the funding of local promotions was the responsibility of the member banks, MasterCard provided seed money at the regional level to encourage member participation. For example, MasterCard's $1 million in seed money for World Cup-related projects in Europe stimulated a further $19 million in promotional expenditures by member banks in the region. The same ripple effect occurred in Latin America.

[23]The World Cup '94 finalists represented Argentina, Belgium, Bolivia, Brazil, Bulgaria, Cameroon, Colombia, Germany, Greece, Ireland, Italy, Mexico, Morocco, the Netherlands, Nigeria, Norway, Romania, Russia, Saudi Arabia, Spain, South Korea, Sweden, Switzerland, and the United States.

Cultivating the Global Sponsorship Property

Historically, many sponsors had viewed the World Cup as a good media buy primarily because of the brand exposure "embedded" in telecasts of the games, and they had therefore developed only limited World Cup-related promotions. In contrast, MasterCard viewed its sponsorship not just as an advertising opportunity, but rather as the basis for a total marketing program designed to:

- **Build brand awareness** through the events' television reach and a brand exposure of 7.5 minutes per 90-minute broadcast, an advertising cost estimated at $0.40 per thousand viewers reached. Pre- and post-consumer research showed that average recall of World Cup sponsoring brands increased 40%, even though some long-time sponsors already enjoyed very high awareness.

Exhibit 7   *MasterCard World Cup Sponsorship Rights**

Introduction

The introduction of the World Championship Soccer sponsorship rests on the rights granted to MasterCard International and our members through our worldwide sponsorship agreement. MasterCard encourages all members to capitalize on the sponsorship opportunities discussed herein to achieve their individual business objectives.

It is very important that all members understand the rights and obligations outlined in this section. All sponsorship-related promotion programs *must* be linked to MasterCard products and services, and approved in advance by MasterCard International. It is critical to note that your World Championship Soccer marketing programs may not be used with other services offered by your organization, whether or not they compete with MasterCard.

Sponsorship Rights

MasterCard and, as appropriate, its members are granted the rights outlined below on a worldwide basis:

A. Product category exclusivity
B. Official status designations
C. Use of official marks and emblems
D. Stadium advertising
E. Tickets
F. Display and franchise facilities
G. Program advertisements
H. Use of official music
I. Commercial broadcast time options
J. Use of marks on premium items
K. Use of marks on marketing, advertising, promotion, and public relations materials

These rights extend to all 16 international soccer events that are part of the sponsorship package. (see Appendix 1, World Championship Soccer Overview, for descriptions of the individual events)* World Championship Soccer events include:

World Cup '94 1994
European Championship (Euro '92) 1992
European Cup Winners' Cup Final (The European Cup Final) 1991, 1992, 1993, and 1994
Under-17 World Championship for the FIFA/JVC Cup 1991 and 1993
FIFA/Coca-Cola World Youth Championship 1991 and 1993
FIFA Women's World Championship for the M&M's Cup 1991
FIFA World Indoor Championship 1992

Please note that a number of additional soccer events are scheduled to take place in Africa, Latin America and Asia. The MasterCard sponsorship does not include right to these events (e.g. African Nations' Cup, Copa America, and Asian Cup) nor to the qualifying matches for World Cup '94.

continued

---

*Excerpt; rest of text and Appendix 1–4 omitted.

Exhibit 7   *(continued)*

Product Category Exclusivity

MasterCard is the exclusive worldwide sponsor in the product category of payment systems, which includes, without limitation:

- Credit cards
- Charge cards
- Check guarantee cards
- Travel and entertainment cards
- On-line and off-line point-of-sale debit cards
- ATMs and ATM access cards
- ATM networks
- Travelers checks
- Nonbank-branded wire transfers

The term of this exclusivity extends through the World Cup in 1994. However, the term for special cards issued by members which use the official marks extends through 1995.

Official Status Designations

MasterCard has obtained the exclusive right to use the designations "Official Sponsor" and "Official Card" in all marketing, advertising, promotion, and public relations materials in conjunction with the MasterCard logo.

When the MasterCard mark is used with World Championship Soccer marks—without member of affiliated local acceptance brand identification—examples of designations are:

- "Official Sponsor of World Cup '94"
- "Official Sponsor of Euro '92"

When affiliated local acceptance brands or member identification are used in conjunction with the World Championship Soccer and MasterCard marks, examples of designations are:

- "Official Card of World Cup '94"
- "Official Card of Euro '92"

The designations **"Official Sponsor"** and **"Official Card"** extend to all World Championship Soccer events. Per our agreement, only MasterCard can refer to itself as "Official Sponsor" of a World Championship Soccer Event. Members may call themselves the "Official Card" of such events, upon approval from MasterCard.

Use of Official Marks and Emblems

MasterCard has secured the rights to use the following marks on MasterCard payment systems products, services, promotional materials, advertising and company communications:

- Official Emblem and Mascot of World Cup '94
- Official Emblem and Mascot of the European Championship (Euro '92)
- Official UEFA Promotional Emblem
- Official Emblem and Mascot of the Under-17 World Championship for the FIFA/JVC Cup

continued

Exhibit 7 *(continued)*

- Official Emblem and Mascot of the World Youth Championship for the FIFA/Coca-Cola Cup
- Official Emblem and Mascot of the FIFA Women's World Championship for the M&M's Cup
- Official Emblem of the FIFA World Indoor Championship

Members may use official marks and emblems only in connection with the promotion of MasterCard brand products and services, and must follow the guidelines provided in Chapter III, Use of Marks and Approvals, and the graphics standards outlined in Appendix 4.*

World Championship Soccer marks may be used only by members and may not be used by affiliated merchants. Merchants may only display materials provided by MasterCard or its members.

Proposed use of emblems and marks must be submitted to MasterCard for prior approval. Please refer to the procedures outlined in Chapter II, in the section on Obtaining Approvals.*

Stadium Advertising

MasterCard will have perimeter advertising boards at all of the matches comprising the MasterCard World Championship Soccer program. A total of 169 events will display highly visible, strategically placed boards.

Tickets

MasterCard is provided with a limited number of complimentary tickets to each event, and may be able to assist you in purchasing additional tickets. As there will be a great demand for these tickets, we suggest that you plan your needs early and inform your MasterCard regional representative or MasterCard Global Promotions so that we may do our best to accommodate you.

Display Facilities

At all events, MasterCard has the right to use space for the display of MasterCard products and services on-site within the stadium area. As space may be limited, we request that members in event host countries who are interested in presenting displays forward their requests to MasterCard International as soon as possible

Program Advertisements

MasterCard will be featured in a full-page advertisement in official programs and various other official communications published by the governing bodies of soccer, FIFA (Federation of International Football Associations) and UEFA (Union of European Football Associations).

Use of Official Music

MasterCard has the exclusive use, within its product category, of the official music that will be composed for World Cup '94. This music may be used in conjunction with member advertising and promotion of MasterCard products and services.

continued

*Excerpt; rest of text and Appendix 1–4 omitted.

Exhibit 7   *(continued)*

Commercial Broadcast Time Option

In certain territories, MasterCard members may have the first option to buy advertising time on World Championship Soccer television broadcasts. However, because our rights to such options differ from event to event, we recommend that interested members contact their regional MasterCard representative or MasterCard Global Promotions as soon as possible in order to be informed about the availability of such rights.

In all cases, the right of first option is limited by the following three conditions: (1) if the network permits advertising, (2) if the network already has a conflicting advertising commitment, and (3) if MasterCard or its members are willing to make the minimum advertising purchase required by the broadcaster to obtain product category exclusivity.

For information concerning the availability of television advertising or telecase sponsorship in various markets, see Appendix 2*, World Championship Soccer Television Summaries. Members can contact the broadcaster directly to determine the availability of time and the minimum advertising buy required. For information on MasterCard plans for television advertising in your market, contact your regional MasterCard representative or MasterCard Global Promotions.

Use of Marks on Premium Items

Apremium item is a sponsor's promotional item that is either given away or sold at a subsidized price for advertising or promotional purposes. MasterCard and its members have the right to use the Official Emblem and Mascot of World Championship Soccer events in conjunction with the MasterCard mark on premium items to support marketing, advertising, promotional and public relations activities. Any item that is designed for use as a free giveaway or for sale may use the marks, with prior approval by MasterCard. If the premium item displays member identification, it must also indicate prominently that MasterCard is the Official Card of the particular World Championship Soccer event. Premiums bearing the Official Emblems or Mascots may not be sold for profit.

Specifics on the approval process are outlined in Chapter III, Use of Marks and Approvals.* MasterCard is preparing a worldwide premium program to make MasterCard branded World Cup premiums available to members. Information on this premium program will be sent to members in 1992. Preliminary information is provided in Chapter III, in the section on Sourcing of Premium Items, and in Appendix 3, World Championship Soccer Premium Program.*

Use of Marks on Advertising and Promotion Materials

Under the MasterCard World Championship Soccer sponsorship agreement, members have the right to produce advertising, marketing, promotion and public relations materials using the official marks. All uses of the marks must conform to the guidelines in Chapter III and Appendix 4,* MasterCard Graphics Standards, and must be approved in advance by MasterCard. All uses of the marks must be in connection with MasterCard brand products and services only.

*Excerpt; rest of text and Appendix 1–4 omitted.

- **Stimulate card usage and acquisition** by exploiting the global appeal of the World Cup. Members worldwide would have the opportunity to implement customized marketing programs targeted at specific usage, activation, and acquisition objectives. These programs would, it was hoped, increase cardholder interest in member products and services.
- **Provide business opportunities for members** through in-branch programs to build traffic, cross-sell other member products, such as Maestro and MasterCard Traveler's Cheques, increase ATM usage, and execute merchant-driven promotions to increase acceptance and preference for MasterCard products.
- **Enhance the perception of MasterCard as a global brand and payment system** by associating for the long-term MasterCard with the world's leading sport. It was hoped that this would enhance consumers' perceptions of the global utility of MasterCard products and services, position MasterCard as the industry leader, and bring together members, merchants, and consumers.

To achieve these objectives MasterCard headquarters had three tasks: obtain buy-in for the sponsorship concept; define, create and sell a multidimensional, equity-building marketing platform that could be used to achieve local, regional, and global marketing objectives; and, help regions and members with implementation. The first step was to communicate the sponsorship program and opportunities to regional organizations and member banks. Then, MasterCard Global Promotions prepared a worldwide marketing bulletin, a sponsorship manual, newsletters, a premium merchandise program, perimeter and outdoor advertising, and event-specific plans with each region. To minimize ambush marketing, which was expected to occur in the form of signage, premiums, customer service centers, or sponsorship of venue-specific events, MasterCard decided that "the best defense is a good offense." First, MasterCard secured sponsorship of the U.S. national team and secured advertising rights on Univision, the principal Spanish-language television network. Second, MasterCard's public relations agency secured the broadest possible press coverage of the sponsorship. Third, MasterCard planned to maintain high on-site visibility during matches. Fourth, MasterCard positioned itself as a conduit to other sponsors' goods and services. Finally, MasterCard strongly encouraged member banks to focus any World Cup-related promotions on reinforcing the benefits of MasterCard products and to exercise the option of sponsoring broadcasts of World Cup matches on commercial television networks in their markets.

MASTERCARD'S GLOBAL WORLD CUP '94 MARKETING PROGRAM

At the international level, MasterCard's objectives were also to build brand awareness, stimulate card acquisition and usage, provide business opportunities for members, and enhance the perception of MasterCard as a global brand and payment system. Regions and member banks had the opportunity to sponsor national teams, a first option on the purchase of television commercial time during the matches; access to card usage and acquisition programs, including statement inserts, hospitality events, and free tickets; and the ability to develop and use a variety of advertising media (print, outdoor, branch, and point-of-sale) around the World Cup theme.

Global Marketing developed a World Cup advertising campaign as well as a marketing kit for member banks. The television commercial for the campaign, featuring Pelé and the first commercial use of Leonard Bernstein's "America" score, was seen in more than 40 countries. Exhibit 8 presents a storyboard of the Pelé television commercial. Global Promotions also commissioned artwork to be included in all cardholder communications internationally and domestically. The Global Promotions Promotional Action Plan included Official Merchan-

Exhibit 8   *Storyboard for Television Commercial*

"WORLD CHAMPIONSHIP SOCCER"

MUSIC THROUGHOUT: "AMERICA"

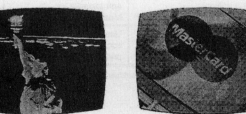

NO CARD MORE ACCEPTED...
NO ATHLETE MORE RENOWNED...

JOIN MASTERCARD

AND THE LEGENDARY PELE
IN CELEBRATING THE PASSION,
EXCITEMENT AND DRAMA

OF THE WORLD'S SPECTACULAR
SPORTING EVENT.
THE 1994 WORLD CUP.

(FINAL FRAME IF TAGGING COMMERCIAL
WITH YOUR LOGO OR MESSAGE.)

dise Offers, Decal Sweepstakes, MasterValues Program and Point-of-Sales materials. For most communications tools, customization was available, but legal approval from MasterCard headquarters and ISL was required.

Global Promotions provided resources as well as promotion ideas. For example, because Europay lacked personnel experienced in event marketing, MasterCard assigned one of its top Global Promotions executives to Europay to exploit Euro '92 and lay the groundwork for 1994. Subsequently, a Global World Cup Project Team was formed to exploit the sponsorship, promote knowledge transfer across regions and members, and provide guidance to MasterCard regions. The senior officer for every region nominated a team member. Quarterly meetings were held in New York and other United States and international locations. The type of effort required from MasterCard headquarters and the Global Team differed from region to region. Some regions understood the sponsorship concept but lacked the resources to fully exploit it. Others were well resourced and required relatively low levels of hands-on assistance.

Furthermore, members and regions could receive newsletters, promotion execution guides, sponsorship manuals, a promotional video, Pelé photos, Global Marketing bulletins, as well as corporate hospitality invitations and welcome kits. Pelé was very popular with international members. He made 76 appearances in 20 countries and was featured in 22 television commercials and print ads.

The marketing effort behind the sponsorship varied by country. It proved harder to persuade member banks to participate when the national team did not qualify or when regions had no local events to tie into,[24] when national interest in soccer was low, or when the image of soccer as a mass sport did not fit MasterCard's upscale positioning in certain underdeveloped credit card markets. For some members, limited funds, staff and experience, and a low priority assigned to the marketing of the World Cup sponsorship were further challenges. Some members, unaccustomed to proactive financial services marketing, felt uncomfortable about marketing logoed merchandise. MasterCard's World Cup sweepstakes programs could not be used in some markets because of regulatory restrictions. The need for language translation and local customization caused delays. Any item bearing a World Cup logo had to be approved by MasterCard's legal department and by ISL. Premiums shipped from the United States and some non-U.S. member banks had to pay customs fees.

Initial feedback also revealed that the sponsorship was exploited to different degrees in different regions. The Latin America region bought the rights to the Copa America and fully benefited from the region's passion for soccer. Member banks in the region spent $6 million on marketing the sponsorship.[25] Translated Master Values coupons were sent to cardholders for travel in the United States. In Canada, where interest in soccer was modest, the sponsorship was sold to members as a means of differentiation, but member bank investment was low. The Middle East/Africa region had bought the rights to the Seventh Pan Arab Games/Sixth Arab Cup and placed a World Cup commercial on airline flights within the region. Seven large member banks ran promotions with free trips to the World Cup finals. The biggest impact in the Asia/Pacific region, which had chosen to sponsor the Asia Cup, World Cup qualifying rounds as well as the Under-17 World Championship, was in Japan, where, as Alexander McKeveny, vice-president Global Promotions, pointed out:

We used Pelé to solve a specific problem in an important market. Japanese marketing is

---

[24]For example, regional championships such as Copa America in Latin America or Euro '92 in Europe at which World Cup qualifying matches were played.

[25]This figure does not include the region's share of the cost of the sponsorship.

heavily dependent on celebrity endorsements, so we developed television commercials featuring Pelé paying with his Master-Card in a Japanese restaurant and sporting goods store. Our brand awareness ratings tripled and we minimized the impact of the Japanese economic recession on MasterCard purchase volume.

Also, 14 out of 16 card-issuing Japanese member banks used statement inserts, cardholder magazines and brand posters to support World Cup promotions. In contrast, World Cup promotions were not so common in Singapore, where many cardholders, especially women, had little interest in soccer, and in Australia, where banks sponsored the more popular sport of rugby football.

In Europe, 26 member banks in 18 countries, including World Cup non-qualifying countries such as France, implemented programs. Total member expenditures on World Cup-related marketing programs[26] reached $19 million. The World Cup sponsorship proved to be an important marketing catalyst for Eurocard/MasterCard in Europe, since combined audiences of 7.8 billion Europeans watched the 52 final round matches.

The extent to which the sponsorship property was embraced varied from market to market. In France, the soccer sponsorship became a cornerstone of Europay France's marketing and advertising efforts, which included sponsorship of the French national team and World Cup television broadcasts. In Germany, where only 1% of adults held credit cards, MasterCard's licensee was GZS, owned by a consortium of German banks. GZS marketed the Eurocard MasterCard and had an agreed-upon joint-logo policy with MasterCard. However, the MasterCard brand rarely appeared in GZS advertising for Eurocard, which was budgeted at $20 million in 1994. The Eurocard brand enjoyed 84% aided

brand awareness versus 17% for MasterCard. GZS cherrypicked those programs from Master-Card's World Cup communications portfolio that did not depend on mass marketing. These are listed in Exhibit 9. GZS invested $800,000 in World Cup related promotions and insisted on Eurocard perimeter signage at all the European soccer matches (including the Euro '92 championship) that were part of the World Cup '94 sponsorship package.

Because the sponsorship's objectives had been to involve members, merchants and consumers, MasterCard's evaluation covered all these groups and included consumer interviews (in the United States, Brazil, Germany, Russia), spectator surveys (for the first and final U.S. match), brand awareness tracking studies in 12 countries, merchant participation and card acquisition/usage reports, as well as an estimate of "free" press/brand exposure. ISL provided a report on MasterCard's comparative aided share of mind (in the payment card categories). The sponsorship's positive internal impact on the MasterCard organization was already clear: improved relations with members, increased dialogue, greater cooperation and idea transfer across regions, cross-functional cooperation at headquarters, as well as improved employee morale at MasterCard and member banks. Exhibit 10 summarizes some of the success measures MasterCard used.

MasterCard also tracked the efforts of its fellow worldwide sponsors. M&M/Mars had launched a special edition Mars Bar featuring flags of the World Cup countries and soccer trivia on the packaging. McDonald's had hosted week-long McSoccer clinics across the United States and had signed spokesman Andres Cantor as the "Voice of the World Cup" for Univision, the Spanish-language TV network. General Motors had chosen to highlight a particular brand in each region rather than mount a global campaign (e.g., GMC trucks sponsored U.S. activities while GM's Opel Division sponsored European activities). GM had also produced a Soccer

---

[26]This figure does not include the region's share of the cost of the sponsorship.

Exhibit 9   *Summary of the GZS German World Cup Program, 1993–1994**

Event	Impact	Comments	Timeframe
Press conference with Pelé	Conference attended by 50 sports journalists in the GZS headquarters. Follow-up cocktail.	The conference received wide press coverage all over Germany.	October 1993
Promotion with member credit institutions (for their clients and employees)	Mailing to 4,000 credit institutions; 1,500 credit institutions ordered 11,000 packages.	Enabled clients to purchase merchandise with World Cup logo and thereby enter lottery.	November 1993
Mailing: Description of World Cup program in newsletter (circulation 10,000)	Reached 9,000 credit institutions.		January 1994
Point-of-sale display with possibility to win premiums or tickets	100 displays sold reached approximately 1 million clients of credit institutions.	400,000 entries returned for two programs.	January–March 1994
Statement inserts describing MasterCard/Eurocard World Cup involvement and possibility to win premiums or tickets	3 million statement inserts.	Prizes included a trip to the World Cup Final.	
Television commercial featuring Pelé with a Eurocard in hand ran during final rounds (did not choose to dub headquarters-made ad) Print ads featuring Pelé/Eurocard	Message: "You win with the one."	Ad developed in collaboration with Austria and Switzerland and used in three countries.	May 1994
Product placement: Pelé columns in weekly sports-magazine *Kicker* (circulation 2.3 million)	Four columns about soccer and his role as ambassador for MasterCard.		Spring 1994
Tickets: GZS purchased 650 tickets from MasterCard and sold to credit institutions	Used by credit institutions according to marketing priorities.		Spring 1994

*Source: Casewriter interview with Gesellschaft fuer Zahlungssysteme.

Exhibit 10   *MasterCard Measurement Criteria for World Cup '94 Sponsorship**

I. Leveraging of sponsorship by members/regions
   - Number of decals
   - Number of point-of-sale packages ordered
   - Number of global World Cup television commercials ordered/media value of ad schedule
   - Number/dollar value of premiums ordered
   - Number of Pelé appearances/impressions
   - Card usage increases—World Cup programs
   - Card acquisitions—World Cup programs
   - Number of members participating in programs
   - Member marketing dollar investment in leveraging the sponsorship property ("velocity spend")
   - Number of merchants participating in programs
   - Number of statement inserts/number of impressions/approximate media value

II. Brand exposure
   - Cumulative television viewership
   - Media value of brand identity exposure on television broadcasts of matches
   - Impressions/media value of ad schedule
   - Impressions on-site
   - Impressions from public relations programs

III. Qualitative indicators
   - Leveraging across the MasterCard organization: Maestro, CIRRUS, regions, departments, etc.
   - Integration of regions, departments, etc., working together on business-building programs
   - Members' reactions and perceptions of MasterCard and its sponsorship program
   - Consumer perceptions and brand imagery

*Source: Company records.

Instructional Video and distributed World Cup Sponsor Coupons for Value books in showrooms and via direct mail.

U.S. Marketing Program

Starting in mid-1992, the U.S. Promotions Department, with Advantage International, a marketing and special events agency retained throughout the entire project, prepared a full-scale marketing campaign and promotion plan tied to the World Cup. Mava Heffler, vice-president of U.S. Promotions, set out to "leverage the World Cup as a business-building opportunity incorporating usage and acquisition elements" through a consistent, visible, and comprehensive marketing program. It subsequently had to support MasterCard's new "smart money" positioning, introduced in early 1993, by providing value-added benefits; clearly establish Master-Card as World Cup host and preferred payment system; integrate within and through all Master-Card divisions and disciplines; maximize Mas-terCard's impact in the nine U.S. host cities; and finish "big."

The first challenge was to overcome the U.S. region's initial lukewarm response to the sponsorship. In the United States, soccer was considered an insignificant sport. Expected television audiences were one-ninth those achieved during

Exhibit 11 *MasterCard World Cup USA '94 Program and Timeline, 1993–1994*

National Programs

MasterCard's modular programming enabled members to accomplish individual objectives and profit priorities through the use of official World Cup marks and designations and officially logoed premium items, as well as the association with MasterCard's sponsorship/affiliation with Pelé and the U.S. national team. Point-of-sale materials were ordered through a 1–800 number and displayed in approximately 200,000 storefronts. To encourage display, the Decal Program included a sweepstakes entry for a free trip to one of the 24 qualifying nations. The nationwide **World Cup MasterValues** program was designed to increase awareness and usage. MasterCard also enlisted retailers such as Macy's and W.H. Smith bookstores in specific promotions, e.g., a free MasterCard/ World Cup poster for a purchase using a MasterCard card.

Through the **World Cup Soccer '94 Collection** MasterCard invited its members to participate in a revenue-generating statement insert program offering cardholders a variety of licensed World Cup merchandise and apparel, including commemorative coins and medallions, for purchase with their MasterCard Card. A Frequent Buyer Sweepstakes was available. The U.S. mint manufactured commemorative coins, and members marketed them through their own marketing plans. The **Mastering the Game of Soccer with Pelé Video** was the first Pelé instructional video produced in 15 years and could be used to create programs for acquisition, usage and retention. It brought the sponsorship into homes. Video orders by member banks exceeded 50,000.

SoccerBlast USA—Legends of Soccer Tour was a 36-city family soccer festival, including clinics and exhibits, in co-sponsorship with Procter & Gamble, Sprint, le Coq Sportif and members. It created additional awareness and visibility for MasterCard in supermarkets in Sunday free-standing inserts through mid '94, as well as advertising inclusion equal to over 200 gross rating points[1] in each market. At each event, 90% of all attendees (2,300 on average per event) passed through the MasterCard booth and 230 card applications were collected. Along the same lines, the uniformed MasterCard team's **Team Up with MasterCard** appearances received an estimated $500,000 in free local radio coverage. The **Ambassadors Cup** honored 24 winners of a nationwide search for individuals who brought the love of soccer to the U.S. The **Kick'in for Kids TV Special** involved the production of a 40-minute "show-within-a-show" in a tie-in sponsorship with the Children's Miracle Network, reaching 197 markets and 98% of U.S. households. A Watch-n-Win World Cup Ticket giveaway was held and 55% of all card pledges were made on MasterCard cards. Representatives of 40 member banks appeared on air in their local markets.

Host City Programs

Nine **MasterCard Welcoming the World Seminars,** organized in collaboration with local World Cup organizing committees and visitors bureaus, were attended by over 7,500 merchants, over 2,000 of whom requested follow-up materials; 61% of the requests were for additional information on current Merchant Acceptance programs. The seminars sought to help merchants leverage the World Cup as business opportunity. An estimated 36 million media impressions were created through local press coverage. A showcase **Main Street USA** area received over 3.6 million people over 52

continued

---

[1]**Gross rating points** represent the percentage of a target market reached by advertising in a specified period multiplied by the average number of advertising exposures.

Exhibit 11   *(continued)*

matches. **Host City Programs** Nine **MasterCard Welcoming the World Seminars,** organized in collaboration with local World Cup organizing committees and visitors bureaus, were attended by over 7,500 merchants, over 2,000 of whom requested follow-up materials; 61% of the requests were for additional information on current Merchant Acceptance programs. The seminars sought to help merchants leverage the World Cup as business opportunity. An estimated 36 million media impressions were created through local press coverage. A showcase **Main Street USA** area received over 3.6 million people over 52 matches.

Forty-two MasterCard/Coca-Cola **Welcome Centers** were strategically located in high traffic areas around match venues or at airports and provided a total of 10,000 hours of assistance to over 1 million people. Visitors sampled Coke products and received World Cup MasterValues booklets as well as a city information World Cup Value Guide which highlighted MasterValues merchants, Thomas Cook and key member locations. From May to July 1994, the **1–800-MC CUP 94** offered round the clock assistance to over 25,000 callers in five languages. **Thomas Cook** also expanded its services to MasterCard cardholders, including commission-free MasterCard Travelers Checks, currency exchange, lost and stolen reporting, emergency card replacements and cash advances.

Through **World Cup MasterValues** MasterCard launched its largest marketing initiative to date, in the form of nine city specific programs, involving more than 80 merchant partners and supported by 50 million statement inserts and free standing inserts (FSI). MasterCard provided the umbrella marketing program, the merchant and member point-of-sales materials, the inserts and training videos. **MasterCard at the Mall Programs** were conducted in 19 shopping malls. Consumer purchases with MasterCard cards were rewarded with World Cup premium items and a chance to have a picture taken with Pelé or members of the U.S. national team. Over 2,000 stores displayed MasterCard World Cup point-of-sale materials, over 4,000 applications for MasterCard cards were collected. Ten member banks co-sponsored local events.

Tailored **brand awareness programs** focused on creating a non-preemptable MasterCard presence in host cities during matches and positioning MasterCard as the global preferred payment system with visitors, residents, merchants, press and media. For example, in Chicago, New York, and Los Angeles the **MasterCard Hot Air Balloon** garnered an estimated 500,000 impressions. MasterCard and its members were also present at city-specific events such as The Embarcadero Festival in San Francisco, Amerifest in Dallas, and South Street Seaport in New York City. The world's largest soccer theme park, an interactive family festival called **SoccerFest,** was set up in the Los Angeles Convention Center.

Hospitality programs included free tickets, travel packages, and corporate events hosted by senior MasterCard management. The programs, organized and hosted by the Global Promotions division, were an opportunity to thank members for their support and demonstrate MasterCard's belief in global partnerships. Most of the free 30,000 tickets were used by MasterCard, regions and member banks for promotional and member relations purposes. The final week coincided with meetings of MasterCard's boards.

the Olympics. To sell the sponsorship internally, executives highlighted survey results showing that 80% of Americans had seen highlights of World Cup '90 and 50% had expressed an interest in watching World Cup '94 matches after learning that it would be held in the United States. The sponsorship would give MasterCard especially good access to suburban and ethnic markets. Over 16 million Americans played soccer, 79% of them lived in suburbs, and 29% lived in households with disposable incomes over $50,000. Finally, one-third of the U.S. pop-

ulation lived in, or close to, the nine World Cup host cities.

Then, outside partners and the three disciplines of promotions, public relations, and advertising had to be integrated into a comprehensive marketing program designed to reach three target audiences: potential and existing members, cardholders, and merchants. The buy-in of merchants and members required extensive education and communications. Participants within MasterCard included Member Relations, Global Marketing, U.S. Acceptance, Cirrus, and

Exhibit 12 *MasterCard World Cup USA '94 Promotional Summary* *

Promotion	Benefits	Communications Tools	Suggested Execution Dates
MasterCard/World Cup USA '94 *Official Merchandise Offers* (Issuer Promotion)	• Promotes usage • Offers high perceived value • Generates revenue • Builds brand preference • Offers flexibility for member customization	Statement Insert(s) 1. Cardholder collectibles insert 2. Members' choice insert	1st quarter 94–3rd quarter 94
MasterCard/World Cup USA '94 *Decal Sweepstakes* (Acquirer Promotion)	• Builds brand awareness • Enhances merchant relations • Promotes brand preference	• Decal • Decal folder with sweepstakes rules	1st quarter 94–2nd quarter 94
MasterCard/World Cup USA '94 *MasterValues Program* (Issuer Promotion)	• Associates MasterCard card with value • Encourages usage • Reinforces global acceptance • Differentiates MasterCard from competitive payment methods	Statement insert	Early 2nd quarter 94
MasterCard/World Cup USA '94 *Point-of-sale materials* (Acquirer/Issuer Program)	• Associates member with World Cup USA '94 • Builds brand awareness • Communicates excitement of World Cup • Offers flexibility for member customization	• Posters • Print ads • Counter card • Tent card • Postcard	1st quarter 94–early 3rd quarter 94

*Source: This fact sheet was enclosed in the MasterCard Promotional Action Plan folder sent to member banks.

Maestro. Outside "players" included advertising and design agencies, as well as the host cities, the U.S. national team, and Pelé. The rallying cry became: "Maximum integration for maximum leverage." Heffler recalled the process that led to the establishment of a multidepartment task force:

In event sponsorship, two things matter: what you have and what you do with it. What we had was the world's most important sporting event. It was hosted in MasterCard's most important market. However, it was not the highest impact event, given soccer's limited popularity in the United States. This meant that we could not treat soccer as an emotion, as the rest of the world could. It probably helped that I'm not a soccer fan and that my past experience was in packaged goods marketing. Soccer became a platform for solid, comprehensive, value-added business-building programs. MasterCard became the means by which our merchants could get a fair share of the $4 billion projected economic impact of the World Cup. For other sponsors we became the unifier, or host, of the event. Finally, we channeled the rights to our member banks. We did not just put together a few posters and premiums and call that a marketing plan. Our plan was a constellation of national and host city programs.

Exhibits 11 and 12 summarize the main U.S. programs and their timing during 1993 and 1994. The World Cup sponsorship was integrated in the $40 million MasterCard communications budget planned for 1994 with little additional investment. In 1994, 65% of these expenses were devoted to advertising, 25% to consumer promotions, 7% to merchant programs, and 3% to public relations.

PROGRAM RESULTS

When the results were in, television coverage of the 1994 World Cup amounted to 16,000 hours in 188 countries and achieved a cumulative worldwide television audience of 31.2 billion. The average number of matches watched per viewer varied widely from 7.3 in the United States, to 12.4 in Germany, and 15.7 in Brazil.

MasterCard brand perimeter signage exposure on television broadcasts averaged 8 minutes 16 seconds over the 52 matches (versus 7 minutes 30 seconds projected). MasterCard brand exposure during the final match was 12 minutes 8 seconds. Executives estimated that MasterCard would have had to have purchased media advertising valued at $493 million to achieve the same number of exposures delivered by perimeter signage. Even if a perimeter signage exposure achieved only 10% of the impact of a 30-second commercial, the media equivalent value of MasterCard's perimeter signage exposure was $49 million.

In the United States, MasterCard estimated that, in addition to the impressions generated by perimeter signage and media advertising, a further 8.5 billion impressions were created by out-of-home media, including street banners, billboards, painted buses, telephone kiosks, traincar and bus shelter ads. Media and public relations initiatives, which ranged from appearances and magazine articles by Pelé to personalized services for the media at the matches, also yielded substantial press and media coverage amounting to over one billion impressions.

More than 450 MasterCard members (including 75% of the top 100 card issuers) participated in one or more aspects of the global promotion. Together, they invested $38 million in sponsorship-related marketing. Some 87% of members stated that the sponsorship added value to their own marketing programs. The premium program was used by members in 59 countries. Some 42 million statement inserts for the MasterValues program were distributed by over half the MasterCard members in the United States and Latin America.

McKeveny and his colleagues tracked both consumer and member responses to MasterCard's World Cup '94 sponsorship. MasterCard objectives were achieved to varying degrees

Exhibit 13 *Evaluation of Sponsorship Impact Against Objectives**

CONSUMER OBJECTIVES

	Japan	France	Germany	U.K.	Argentina	Brazil	Mexico	U.S.
Build Brand Awareness								
Brand awareness increased	+	+	+	+	+	+	±0	±0
Closed gap against Visa	±0	+	+	++	±0	±0	±0	±0
Sponsorship awareness increased	+	+	++	+	++	+	+	+
Sponsorship higher than or equal to Visa Olympics	±0	+	++	+	++	±0	±0	NA
Enhance Worldwide Imagery								
Worldwide imagery improved	±0	+	±0	±0	–	±0	±0	NA
Closed gap against Visa	±0	±0	±0	++	–	±0	+	NA
Enhanced opinion of brand due to sponsorship	+	±0	+	±0	++	++	++	+

MEMBER OBJECTIVES

	Asia/Pacific	Canada	Europe	Latin America	Middle East/Africa	U.S.
Provide Membership with Business Building Opportunities						
Found sponsorship valuable	+	–	+	++	++	+
Sponsorship enhanced brand awareness	++	+	++	++	+	++
Sponsorship enhanced global imagery	+	+	+	++	++	++
Sponsorship offered new business opportunities	+	+	+	++	+	+
Stimulated Acquisition and Usage						
Sponsorship increased card usage	+	++	++	++	++	++
Sponsorship increased acquisition efforts	+	+	++	++	++	++
Other						
Enhanced image as a strong marketing organization	++	++	++	++	++	++

*Source: Company records. Note: ++: very positive; +: positive; ±0: same; –: negative.

from one region and country to another, as indicated in Exhibit 13.

THE 1998 WORLD CUP

The 1998 World Cup would be held in France. Japan seemed a likely candidate for the 2002 World Cup. Both Japan and France were important markets for MasterCard, where brand awareness had historically been below desired levels.

Exhibit 14 summarizes the events included in the World Cup 1998 sponsorship package. The 1996 European Championship would include 16 national teams (versus 8 in 1992). Cumulative television viewership of 6.9 billion was forecast, 8% above 1992, of which 45% would be outside Europe. The 1998 World Cup would include 32 national teams (versus 24 in 1994). A cumulative television audience of 37 billion was projected, 19% higher than in 1994.

Early indications were that the World Cup 1998 sponsorship might cost MasterCard $23 million. McKeveny estimated MasterCard and its members might need to spend around $60 million over four years to fully exploit the calendar of events.

A 1998 World Cup sponsorship raised a number of questions for McKeveny:

1. Should MasterCard renew its World Cup sponsorship?

2. What did it mean for MasterCard's strategy and organization that the final rounds would be held in France? How might the existence of two intermediaries between MasterCard and its member banks (i.e., Europay International and Europay France) influence MasterCard's approach?

3. How might the characteristics of the host country impact the theme and execution of the promotion in France and around the world? How could maximum exploitation of the sponsorship property be guaranteed?

4. How would MasterCard and Europay deal with the limited resources and experience of both Europay and its member banks? Should one or more executives be sent from the United States to transfer know-how? Should a permanent World Cup marketing team be created ?

5. Could the formula for sharing the cost of the sponsorship be improved? How should money be raised for local promotions? Could a Global Marketing Fund or World Cup Fund be set up?

6. Should the sponsorship focus only on the MasterCard brand or highlight other global (e.g., Cirrus, Maestro) or regional/national brands (e.g., Eurocard)? Should a single worldwide spokesperson or several regional spokespersons be retained?

7. How could MasterCard improve its evaluation of the sponsorship?

Exhibit 14 *World Championship Soccer 1995–1998 Events*

Event	1995	1996	1997	1998
European Championship		England		
Under-17 World Championship	Ecuador		Egypt	
World Youth Championship	Qatar		Malaysia	
Women's World Championship	Sweden			
World Indoor Championship		Spain		
World Cup '98				France
African Cup		South Africa		TBA

It was unclear whether MasterCard could—or should—replicate the scope and thrust of the 1994 U.S. region promotions in France in 1998. Since the U.S. national team was not guaranteed a spot among the final 32 in France, some MasterCard executives wondered what value sponsorship of the 1998 World Cup would bring to U.S. members and how it might help to consolidate MasterCard's recent market share gains in the United States. On a broader scale, if Master-Card committed to sponsor the 1998 World Cup and the "World Championship Soccer" package of international championships, a major challenge would be to continue the momentum built up in 1994. Finally, recognizing the significant financial and managerial resources required to plan and execute a worldwide integrated sponsorship marketing program, the viability and merits of alternative approaches to global brand-building needed to be addressed.

JURASSIC PARK

On June 11, 1993, *Jurassic Park,* Steven Spielberg's dinosaur movie based on Michael Crichton's best-seller of the same name, opened in U.S. theaters, to be swiftly followed by a worldwide rollout. For three years, and intensively over the previous 18 months, MCA; Amblin Entertainment, Spielberg's production company; Universal Pictures; MCA/Universal Merchandising; UIP (a company jointly owned by Paramount, Universal, and MGM), the film's foreign distributor; and licensing, promotional, and retail partners worldwide had all developed plans to promote and profit from the movie. In all, 690 licenses, more than ever before mobilized in support of a motion picture, were issued to market 5,000 different products. Management expected these products to generate $1 billion in worldwide retail sales.

Spielberg's *E.T: The Extra-Terrestrial,* which debuted in 1982, had generated more revenues than any other film by 1992; his 1975 *Jaws* ranked among the top five. While a Spielberg movie about dinosaurs seemed a sure-fire success, licensees and retailers viewed new motion picture properties as more risky than television shows, classic characters, celebrities and other time-tested properties.

THE LICENSING OF ENTERTAINMENT PROPERTIES

The licensing industry was estimated to generate worldwide retail sales of $98 billion in 1993. Two-thirds of these sales would be made in North America (see Exhibit 1). Licensing involved the granting of rights to use intellectual property on or in connection with specified goods and services. Entertainment licensing (24% of worldwide retail sales) encompassed properties associated with new movies and programs like The Simpsons, along with characters such as the Ninja Turtles, Bugs Bunny, and of course, the Disney pantheon. The licensing industry also covered a diverse set of property classes, including sports events such as the World Cup and advertising campaigns such as for the California Raisins. In the United States, licensors were estimated to obtain $1.9 billion in royalties from licensees in 1993, of which around 15% would be derived from sales of

---

This case was prepared by John A. Quelch. Barbara Feinberg and Jeremy Tachau also contributed to the development of this case. Copyright © 1995 by the President and Fellows of Harvard College. Harvard Business School case 596-014.

Exhibit 1   *1993 Worldwide Retail Sales of Licensed Merchandise by Geographic Area**

Territory	Total Retail Sales ($ millions)		Per Capita Spending on Licensed Products	
	1993E	1992	1993E	1992
U.S. and Canada	$66,500	$62,200	$232	$217
Western Europe	19,400	18,000	54	50
Eastern Europe/C.I.S.	35	10	<1	<1
Australia/New Zealand	1,300	1,200	65	60
Japan	9,500	9,000	76	72
S.E. Asia	385	250	<1	<1
South/Central America	285	200	<1	<1
Other	350	250	NA	NA
Total	$97,800	$91,100		

*Source: Adapted from *The Licensing Letter,* EPM Communications, Inc., 1994.
Note: Figures may not add up due to rounding. Per capita figures are based on population estimates from the Population Reference Bureau. E: 1993 figures are estimates.

licensed products and services linked to entertainment properties. Toys and videogames accounted for half of all licensed product sales, at 31% and 19% respectively (see Exhibit 2).

The highest per capita consumption of licensed products associated with entertainment properties was in North America, estimated at $232 in 1993, followed by Japan ($76), and Western Europe ($54).

A license was a contract between a licensor and a licensee. A license spelled out trademark rights, copyrights, and conditions for use of characters, likenesses, and logos. It also delineated geographic coverage and level of exclusivity, the duration of rights, procedures for renewal (if any), and performance and payment conditions. Income for the licensor could include not only royalties on merchandise sales (see Exhibit 3) and advance payments against future royalties, but also technical assistance fees, sales of materials or components to licensees, lump-sum payments for transfers of rights or technology, reciprocal license rights, and management fees.

In exchange for licensing rights, licensees agreed to the following broad responsibilities:

Product Manufacturing and Packaging

Criteria were set by the licensor to ensure (a) quality of product; (b) compliance with trademark obligations; (c) the honoring of names and likeness restrictions (protecting for example, live actors' images, voices, and recognizable lines). These restrictions were referred to as "publicity rights" and were not usually negotiable.

Marketing Commitments

A licensee's dollar commitments on marketing expenditures, the timing of these efforts, and the implications of failing to meet them were often negotiated and included in an agreement.

Exhibit 2   *1993 Retail Sales of Licensed Entertainment/Character Merchandise: Top Ten Categories**

Toys/games	31.2%
Videogames/software	19.1
Gifts/novelties	9.0
Accessories	8.5
Apparel	6.6
Publishing	4.3
Domestics[a]	3.5
Food/beverages	3.1
Music/video	2.9
Infant products	2.5

*Source: Adapted from *The Licensing Letter,* EPM Communications, Inc., 1994
[a]"Domestics" includes household merchandise such as a top-selling 1993 item, "Bibb's Barney."

Payment of Royalties and Advances

A percentage of gross or net sales was negotiated as the basis for most royalty agreements. The percentage varied according to the size of the market, the market share held by the licensee, the type of intellectual property being licensed, the relationship between licensor and licensee, and the product category involved. Risk-sharing in exchange rate fluctuations was also an important negotiating point in the typical two-year contract between a licensor and an overseas licensee.

Finally, a licensing contract usually included insurance and indemnification, as well as arbitration arrangements to settle disputes. For a global movie release, the licensor would typically establish intellectual property rights, including trademark registration in key coun-

Exhibit 3   *Average Royalty Rate and Range of Royalty Rates by Product Category, 1993**

Product Category	**Average Royalty**	**Royalty Range**
Accessories	7.7%	3%–15%
Apparel	7.8	4–12
Domestics	6.2	3–10
Electronics	7.7	5–10
Food/beverages	3.1	1–5
Footwear	6.1	3–11
Furniture/home furnishings	6.2	2–10
Gifts/novelties	8.6	3–12
Health/beauty	7.1	3–10
Housewares	6.2	3–10
Infant products	6.7	5–10
Music/video	8.7	5–20
Publishing	7.7	4–12
Sporting goods	6.2	3–10
Stationery/paper	8.7	4–12
Toys/games	8.2	4–12
Videogames/software	8.7	5–20
Total	**7.3%**	

*Source: Adapted from *The Licensing Letter,* EPM Communications, Inc., 1994.

tries early on—even before negotiating license agreements.

Given the complexities involved, the licensee had to think through in advance whether linking certain products to the licensor's property would enhance sales and profits. It was also important that the licensor research the potential licensee— and the respect for intellectual property in the prospective licensee's country. In some countries, the percentage of royalty payments or the duration of the royalty stream to foreign movie producers was limited by legislation.

Successful campaigns balanced the interests of the licensor, licensees, retailers, and promotional partners. Potential properties had to be identified, the terms of license contracts had to be negotiated, and the products had to be developed and merchandised. The budget and timing of marketing campaigns for licensed products based on a movie were a function of the launch date and expected run of the movie, and of how much publicity could and would be generated. Peak box office attendance and licensed product sales generally occurred in the six weeks following a movie's release.

Success Factors

The success of any movie merchandising effort depended primarily on the success of the film in appealing to its target audiences. For example, *Batman: The Movie,* which opened in 1989 and eventually joined the list of top ten grossing films, generated about $1 billion in licensed product retail sales. Batman enjoyed high consumer awareness thanks to regular comic book and TV appearances. As a result, the movie quickly generated strong demand for licensed products among both children and adults. In contrast, the sequel, *Batman Returns,* carried a PG-13 rating and put the pop character in a grim adult role that proved less popular. Yet for the sequel, McDonald's, a major promotional partner, had developed a Happy Meal tie-in targeted at young children; the disconnect between

the movie's tone and this merchandising effort sparked parental complaints.

When Spielberg's intent to film *Jurassic Park* became known, it spawned some concerns about audience fit. Crichton's book (and Crichton was co-author of the screenplay) was violent and cautionary: dinosaurs cloned from their amber-trapped DNA and populating a theme park run amok, threatening, among others, children. Meanwhile, in the U.S. marketplace, the most popular dinosaur for young children (under seven) was the fuzzy, purple, love-crooning Barney, a television character in a children's show, who had already generated around $100 million dollars in retail sales of licensed toys, videos, and clothing. For older children, replicas of "real" dinosaurs and other toys were being successfully sold in a variety of channels, from mass merchandisers such as K-Mart to museum shops.

Also of concern was the fact that Sony, Matsushita's archrival and owner since 1989 of Hollywood's Columbia/TriStar Studios, would be launching a major movie shortly after *Jurassic Park*'s opening. The movie was *The Last Action Hero,* starring Arnold Schwarzenegger, who had previously appeared in the successfully merchandised series of *Terminator* movies. Sony planned a full-scale merchandising effort for *The Last Action Hero* featuring action figures in everything from toys to videogames. The film's logo would even, it was rumored, be painted on a NASA Space Shuttle.

JURASSIC PARK LICENSING AND MARKETING STRATEGY

In June 1990, Universal, in stiff competition with three other studios, successfully bid for the movie rights to *Jurassic Park,* and preparations for the worldwide campaign surrounding the movie began. Industry sources estimated the successful bid at around $2 million. Spielberg typically kept details of his films secret before release; advance publicity rarely revealed

much. In the case of *Jurassic Park,* no full depictions of dinosaurs would be shown in advance. At the same time, there was tremendous
publicity surrounding the movie's (and the
book's) premise: was it in fact possible to clone
dinosaurs from their DNA trapped in amber?
This stirred significant scientific debate, facilitating publicity to maximize the film's value to
schools and to the media as well as its entertainment potential.

Exhibit 4 presents a projected income statement for *Jurassic Park.* The launch of the movie
(and the associated merchandising efforts of licensees) would be backed by a $60 million ad-
vertising and promotion budget (roughly equal
to the cost of movie production) paid for by its
producers, distributors, and promotional partners.[1] Of this, $25 million was set aside for
international advertising and promotion. Seventy-five percent of the budget in each country
would be spent prior to and during the first six
weeks following the title's release. The major
categories of licensed products to be associated
with the movie would be toys and videogames.
The principal tie-in promotions would involve
fast food.

By planning a compressed international release schedule for *Jurassic Park* and by scheduling media advertising for the movie over the
six months following the U.S. launch date,
MCA/Universal, Amblin, and UIP aimed to focus worldwide attention on the film, to make its
release a distinctive event and to maximize the
impact of free media exposure. A rapid worldwide release schedule would also generate revenues more quickly to cover production and
marketing costs and would limit losses in countries where audiovisual piracy was a problem.

---

[1] In 1993 the average Hollywood movie cost
$26 million to produce and was supported by
$14 million in marketing expenditures, of
which $12 million was media advertising.

Free publicity was especially important in those
countries where television advertising time was
expensive or in short supply; shots of people lining up to see the film, positive reviews by critics,
and recommendations by friends would be important supplements to any television advertising campaign.

Linda Berkeley, MCA's senior vice-president
for business development and chairman of the
merchandising group, and Brad Globe, Amblin's
vice-president of marketing, were responsible
for the worldwide JP merchandising strategy
and program. The development of a consistent
JP image and merchandising strategy outside the
United States was subsequently handled by
Gerry Lewis, Amblin's international representative, and Keith Isaac, senior vice-president international of MCA/Universal Merchandising.

Berkeley identified the five most important
challenges facing the JP team (which included
representatives from Amblin, MCA, UIP, and
Matsushita) in 1991 as:

1. Developing a coordinated event marketing
   strategy and distinctive logo;
2. Selecting licensees and bringing them together in events to build excitement into the
   campaign;
3. Coordinating marketing programs among
   MCA divisions (including Universal Pictures,
   theme parks, music, and publishing), Matsushita divisions (including those in charge of
   retail distribution of Panasonic products),
   and UIP's international offices, as well as
   among manufacturing licensees and retail
   channels;
4. Fashioning a "new breed" of branded dinosaurs (with the prominent JP logo) that
   consumers would identify as merchandise
   unique to the movie *Jurassic Park;*
5. Conducting joint presentations together with
   major licensees to retail buyers to build their
   marketing support for the movie and its licensed products.

Exhibit 4   *Pro Forma Model of Jurassic Park Filmed Entertainment and Licensing Revenues: June 1993* *

	Dollars (in millions)
Revenues:[a]	
Domestic gross	$346.3
Domestic theatrical rentals	207.8
International theatrical rentals	200 to 250
U.S. video sales and rentals	225 to 400
U.S. pay-per-view	4.0
International video sales and rentals	100 to 150
U.S. pay TV	12.5
U.S. free TV	9.2
International free TV	21.1
International pay TV	9.7
U.S. network TV	20.0
Net licensing revenue	100.0
Total revenues	$1,255.6 to $1,530.6
Costs:	
Production cost	$60.0
Interest	6.0
Overhead	3.0
Domestic prints[b]	4.5
Domestic advertising[c]	35.0
International prints[b]	3.5
International advertising[c]	25.0
U.S. video production, marketing, and distribution costs	75 to 130
International video production, marketing, and distribution	25 to 40
Domestic residuals	7.6
International residuals	6.1
Participations	150
Total costs	$400.7 to $470.7
Distribution fee (@ 20% of revenues)	$251.1 to $306.1
Gross profit	$603.8 to $753.8

*Source: Initial estimates calculated by Dave Davis, Motion Picture Analyst, Paul Kagan Associates, Culver City, California, June 22, 1993.
[a]These revenue projections were made during the first cycle of revenue generation. They do not include potential cash inflows from sequel movies, theme park rides based on the movie, and interactive game properties.
[b]A print is a copy of the movie that is shown in a cinema.
[c]Includes advertising for the *Jurassic Park* movie only, not for licensed products.

Selecting Licensees and Negotiating Agreements

In major entertainment licensing campaigns, the principal licensee category was usually toys and games. In the case of *Jurassic Park,* the principal toy licensee selected was Kenner, a division of Hasbro. Kenner designed a three-phase strategy for the rollout of merchandise to coordinate with the JP marketing program:

- June 1993: "action toys" timed to coincide with the movie's debut;
- September 1993: "counterpart vehicles" for collectibles;
- November 1993: movie "settings" for collectibles and counterparts.

Kenner also planned a relaunch of some of the above toy lines to capitalize on the anticipated October 1994 video release of the film. The timing and level of Kenner's marketing efforts were all spelled out in the licensing agreement. Excerpts from the catalog which subsequently merchandised Kenner's JP products to the trade are presented in Exhibit 5.

The key promotional partner was McDonald's, which decided to promote larger than normal "dino-sized" servings of beverages and french fries. Recalled Brad Globe:

The McDonald's ad campaign was fully integrated, linking as many restaurant offerings as possible in recreations of selected scenes from the movie. The McDonald's and Kenner advertising spots for JP merchandise were excellent examples of what a marketing partnership with a movie studio can accomplish.

Kenner Products, Ocean of America (which developed JP videogames for Nintendo), Sega of America, 3DO (computer games), and Topps (bubblegum) were the only five licensees to negotiate worldwide license agreements. In the case of McDonald's, although it was a global brand, it was necessary to negotiate the joint promotions country by country because McDonald's organization outside the United States was

highly decentralized. Once the MCA merchandising team secured the commitment of McDonald's in the United States, McDonald's headquarters staff and the JP team approached overseas franchisees.

Although the movie was based on the original best-selling novel by Michael Crichton, MCA Publishing Rights, a division of MCA Universal Merchandising, was able to create a complete publishing program for both children and adults that he fully endorsed. The U.S. program included an artwork tie-in edition of the novel, a behind-the-scenes book about the making of the movie (which was on the *New York Times* bestseller list for eight weeks, an unprecedented accomplishment for this type of book), five high-end children's books, including both fiction and non-fiction titles, several storybooks, coloring/activity books, comic books, and souvenir magazines.

According to Nancy Cushing-Jones, executive vice-president of MCA/Universal Merchandising and president of its publishing rights division:

The most challenging aspect of the publishing program internationally was to tailor book formats for each unique geographical territory to maximize the popularity of the publishing program and increase revenues. For example, in Japan, we licensed four publication book formats that were totally unique to that territory and not licensed elsewhere. In other territories, we may have only licensed foreign translations of our pre-existing books.

Royalties and other revenues from licensing agreements covering the United States and international territories were expected to exceed $50 million. Many of the international licenses were negotiated by MCA/Universal's independent agents in each country under the supervision of MCA/Universal's international office in London. In the spring of 1992, the MCA/Universal merchandising team organized several country-specific licensing groups to coordinate and

(continued on page 555)

Exhibit 5   *Excerpts from Kenner Catalog of JP Merchandise*

FIGURE ASSORTMENT

DENNIS NEDRY
Figure has removable arms to reveal Dino Damage™. Stands unaided and comes with a removable water squirting tranquiliser gun and backpack.

ROBERT MULDOON
Figure has articulated shoulders, neck & hips, stands unaided and comes with a detatchable backpack, pith helmet & spring loaded tranquiliser gun, which fires projectiles to a distance of 24".

TIM MURPHY
Figure has articulated shoulders, neck & hips, stands unaided and comes with a hatchling dinosaur, a cage which opens & closes and a rope snare accessory which fits over the small Dino Assortment figures.

DR. ALAN GRANT
Figure has articulated shoulders, neck & hips, stands unaided and comes with a spring loaded net launcher backpack which fits securely to his back. Comes with a hatchling dinosaur.

DR. ELLIE SATTLER
Figure has articulated shoulders, neck & hips, stands unaided and comes with a hatchling dinosaur and a backpack containing a spring loaded claw which snaps shut at the press of a trigger.

HELICOPTER
Features dinosaur net catcher and grappling hook suspended while in flight. Carries human figure and rotary blade spins around during flight.

BUSH DEVIL TRACKER
Jeep like vehicle fitted with dinosaur lead fitted to the left seat, which slides out away from vehicle. Missile launcher clips onto rear roll bar, and fires over 18".

JP EXPLORER
Brightly coloured Safari vehicle used to move visitors around Jurassic Park. Featuring Dino Damage™ to bonnet, detachable bumper, and blood sampling projectile, with a clear plastic cylinder which turns red when fired from the launcher.

COMMAND COMPOUND
Features a command tower housing the battery operated electronic computer console, and the biohazard hatchling set. Over 100 warnings can be heard. Surrounded by an electric fence and 2 strong wooden gates with a bar closure. Tower has Dino Damage™, the compound is guarded by a hypodermic injector tranquiliser gun, a diagnostic screen and a net launcher to catch escaping dinosaurs.

Exhibit 5   *(continued)*

DINO ASSORTMENT

PTERANODON
Inner and outer wings flap up & down by pressing on its back. The neck is articulated and the spring loaded jaw can firmly grasp a human figure's arm or leg when flying.

DIMETRODON
With articulated arms & legs, Dimetrodon's jaw opens when the left rear leg is squeezed. The "sail" on its back is made from a flexible, translucent material.

VELOCIRAPTOR (RAPTOR)
Articulated legs & arms, allow Raptor to stand on its hind feet or on its feet and tail. Neck and head dart forward & jaw snaps when leg is squeezed.

COELOPHYSIS (COMPIES)
The two poseable wire bodied Compies have articulated arms & legs and their jaws can be opened manually. The two are sold together and have 2 separate poses.

DILOPHOSAURUS (SPITTER)
With articulated legs & arms, Spitter stands on its hind feet or on its feet and tail. Squirts blinding venom (water) about 18" when stomach is squeezed.

BIG T-REX
Stands unaided with poseable neck, head, legs & knees. By pressing sides of the body, its massive jaw snaps open and activates a simultaneous electronic roaring sound. When the feet are banged on a hard surface, an electronic "stomping" sound is heard.

FOAM TRICERATOPS
Stands unaided with poseable neck, head, legs & knees. Has detachable Dino Damage™ section. When the sides of the body are pressed, the spring loaded head rams forward & can knock over a human figure. Once activated, the head can be pushed back to its original position.

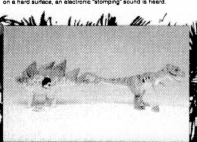

FOAM DINOSAUR ATTACHMENT
T-REX JR
Stands unaided, with poseable legs and knees. By pushing back on its head, the jaw snaps open & shuts when head is released. The arms can grasp a human figure. Has detachable Dino Damage™ section.
STEGOSAURUS
Stands unaided, with poseable neck & legs. Has detachable Dino Damage™ section. Manually activated tail whips from side to side & is strong enough to knock over a human figure.

DULUXE ELECTRONIC ASSORTMENT
DELUXE VELOCIRAPTOR
Stands unaided and has articulated hips. When tail is pushed down, or left leg pushed backwards, it activates a spring loaded arm-grabbing action and a simultaneous electronic roar is heard.
DELUXE DILOPHOSAURUS
Stands unaided, and has articulated shoulders & hips. By manually rotating one forearm, a jaw snapping action & simultaneous electronic 'hooting' sound is heard. Jaw snaps open by 1" and can firmly grasp a human figure.

Exhibit 6 *Selected List of Jurassic Park U.S. Licensed Products and Suggested Retail Prices*

Product	Features	Suggested Retail Price	Manufacturer
Toys[a]			
Jurassic Park Command Compound	Battery-operated electronic computer console with 100 audible warning messages, tower with Dino Damage™, electronic fence with alarm triggered by escaping dinosaurs, tranq gun and net launcher	$49.99	Kenner Products
Tyrannosaurus Rex	Dino Damage™, Realistic Feel™ flesh, Battery-powered dino roars and crashing footsteps	32.49	
Triceratops	Dino Damage™, Realistic Feel™ flesh	19.99	
Jurassic Park Capture-Copter	With tranq-missile and dinosaur net catcher	19.99	
Velociraptor	Battery-powered scream	10.99	
Dimetrodon	Clamping jaw	7.49	
Jurassic Park Action Figures	Accessories including tranquilizer gun and gear	5.99	
Electronic Games[b]			
Jurassic Park for Sega CD (CD-ROM)[c]	Players return to JP after the events of the movie to recover dinosaur eggs and leave before sundown. Includes dino education upon request, 360-degree field of view, digitized video of live action.	59.99	Sega of America (Publisher and Software Developer)
Jurassic Park for 3DO (CD-ROM)	Players take part in action from Jurassic Park with mission to save five characters. Includes video clips and music from movie.	57.99	3DO (Publisher) Universal Interactive Pictures (Software Developer)
Jurassic Park for Super Nintendo (16-bit)	Players participate in action from Jurassic Park (the book), including scenes not included in the movie. Includes overhead and 3-D viewpoints	63.99[d]	Super Nintendo (Publisher) Ocean (Software Developer)

[a]These products were targeted primarily at children ages 6–10. Toys priced under $6 are typically purchasable by children on impulse with allowance money.
[b]The videogame software market targeted children aged 6–16 and had achieved 80% penetration in U.S. households with adolescent boys.
[c]A 16-bit cartridge system retailed for $100 to $130. A Sega CD system carried a suggested retail price of $229.99.

Exhibit 6   *(continued)*

Product	Features	Suggested Retail Price	Manufacturer
Apparel and Plushes			
Boys knit sportswear	MeatEaters™ ("Bold colors, innovative designs"), Impact Dinos™ ("Blue and black clothes featuring arty images"), Urban Dinos™ ("Hip-hop culture-inspired designs")	$20–$45	Harleybrands
Jurassic Park T-shirts	30–40 T-shirt designs based on Jurassic Park scenes to be distributed at J.C. Penney, Kmart, Wal-mart, and Musicland	$12–$20	Winterland Productions
Jurassic Park stuffed dinosaurs	17"–30" stuffed brachiosaurus, spitter, raptor, or triceratops	$25–$50	Dakin Inc.
Confectionery Products			
Jurassic Jawbreaker dinosaur eggs, Spitters, and Raptor Bites	"Jawbreaker" candies, various flavors	$0.10 pc.	Creative Confection Concepts, Inc.
Jurassic Park gummy dinosaurs	Gummy fruit snacks, jellies, and ju ju's	$2.39	Ferrara Pan Candy Co.

maximize marketing efforts and to coordinate timetables for product distribution.[2] Ultimately, 690 licenses worldwide were negotiated (see Exhibit 6 for a partial list) to market 5,000 different products. Recalled Isaac, "The objective throughout with our international licenses was to establish a comprehensive licensing program in each country. All product categories had to be covered . . . but we never set a target for the number of licensees. We did, however, seek to work with prominent, creative companies."

In selecting licensees, depth of commitment and quality of product were key criteria. "We

wanted every last ounce of effort from our partners," explained Lewis, who indicated that *Jurassic Park* was such a major property that the licensor was in the driver's seat. Isaac commented:

> *We generally required royalties of 10% of wholesale prices plus advances of 50% of estimated royalties for the first year. Each licensee's marketing budget and other contingencies were also specified. In addition, product licensing activities associated not with the original movie but with a possible JP television series or sequel usually had unique royalty structures.*

"Ultimately," Isaac explained, "negotiation of the terms of a license contract is an art; it is a creative effort. The success of each deal hinges on the strength of the licensor-licensee relationship."

---

[2]Each group included UIP executives, MCA's country agent, and representatives of the principal worldwide licensees (i.e., Ocean of America, Sega of America, and Kenner-Parker).

A key challenge in the international JP campaign was coordinating the development and delivery of licensed merchandise. "Allowing sufficient time for signing up licensees in over 60 countries and enabling them to develop a range of quality products was critical. [We had] to coordinate artwork, packaging, trademark and copyright notices," said Isaac. All this had to be accomplished for product categories with widely varying development cycles (a video game, for example, required roughly one year to develop). Product launch dates and each licensee's advertising and promotion activities had to be carefully synchronized with the marketing program for the movie in each country. A further challenge was the variable quality and reliability of distribution channels across countries.

Internal and External Coordination

All MCA/Universal divisions were involved to an unprecedented degree in the marketing of JP and the merchandising of JP-licensed products. Under Linda Berkeley's supervision, the movie was in fact used as a vehicle to promote cross-divisional cooperation that could be exploited in subsequent movie releases. Exhibit 7 summarizes the collaborative involvement of other MCA divisions.

As one example of such collaboration, JP ad kits would be distributed to Matsushita's 25,000 Panasonic dealers in Japan (and to all of Panasonic's international sales offices). The kits suggested playing trailers for *Jurassic Park* on the Panasonic movie sets in retailer windows and floor displays. They also offered ways of tying sales of Matsushita's hardware (such as videocassette recorders and television sets) to MCA's software (such as JP videocassettes) through creative print advertising, elaborate dealer window and floor unit displays, and electronics trade show booth designs—all built around the *Jurassic Park* theme.

Internal coordination among MCA/Universal, Amblin, UIP, and Matsushita divisions went hand in hand with external coordination with and among all the licensing and promotional partners. The goal of a well-orchestrated advertising program that would appeal to JP's target audiences and easily transcend borders became common to all parties. The Universal Pictures marketing team and Amblin were responsible

---

Exhibit 7   *Participation in Jurassic Park Merchandising Across MCA Divisions and Companies** *

Universal Studios Hollywood and Florida	Jurassic Park Travel Destination Centers (promotional vehicle and merchandise outlet).
	Jurassic Park: The Ride (theme park attraction).
	Jurassic Park: Behind the Scenes (movie and video on the production of the film).
Spencer Gifts	Jurassic Park gift area (promoting awareness, providing sales outlet).
MCA Records	Recording rights (*Jurassic Park* soundtrack by John Williams).
MCA Music	Publishing rights (arrangements for marching band, concert band, orchestra, and "early learning series").
Winterland Productions	Official collection of Jurassic Park wear for mass-market distribution.
Putnam Berkley Group	Product-line of young adult and children's books.
MCA Home Video	Home video release of *Jurassic Park*.
Panasonic	Promotional program in 25,000 Panasonic shops in Japan.

*Source: MCA News, June 1993.

for producing theater and television advertising for the movie and approved ad campaigns developed by licensees and promotional partners. Amblin and MCA/Universal oversaw the design and presentation of JP merchandise and the licensees' advertising copy for JP merchandise. They coordinated the timing of point-of-sale merchandising and advertising to coincide with the movie's release in each country in order to reinforce movie attendance and maximize publicity for the JP event.

Finally, several marketing tools were considered to develop merchandising synergy between the licensor and multiple licensees including:

- Standardized in-store point-of-sale displays and materials.
- A catalog of *Jurassic Park* merchandise for a cooperative direct-mail campaign.
- A standard handbook of licensed merchandise specifications and store presentation and point-of-sale merchandising guidelines.
- A monthly *Jurassic News* periodical, inaugurated in February 1993, which treated the film as a real event—as if the Park itself existed—and included interviews with the principal protagonists.

Surrounding the JP media advertising campaign was a swirl of interest in and publicity about dinosaurs, much of which tied in to the movie. For example, in the United Kingdom, a competition was run for *Jurassic Park*-related coverage among the national newspapers, and the National History Museum in London announced special dinosaur-related seminars and established its own licensing program.

BUILDING A GLOBAL IDENTITY

While the coordination of such a vast worldwide campaign involved major headaches, no problem vexed the JP team at the outset more than the film's subject matter—dinosaurs. In and of themselves, these creatures were not protectable intellectual property. By embarking on an extensive merchandising effort, the team risked widespread counterfeiting—and a flood of legitimate dinosaur products to meet an expected surge of demand. "Dinosaurs were clearly in the public domain," said Brad Globe. "The challenge was to create a protectable program to ensure that retailers would support us rather than cheaper or more generic dinosaur products." The answer was a distinctive logo used to tie together all JP-related products, services, and communications.

The T-Rex Skeleton

The cover of Michael Crichton's book featured the skeleton of a Tyrannosaurus Rex, perhaps the most familiar of all dinosaurs. Recalled David Weitzner, head of worldwide marketing for MCA Recreational Services Group, "Steven Spielberg liked [the skeleton logo] so much that he incorporated it into the film itself. This reinforced the connection between the book, the logo, and the film. The skeleton logo stimulated the consumer imagination and was part of the larger strategy of not showing the actual dinosaurs too early in the advertising campaign for the movie."

The yellow, red, and black *Jurassic Park* T-Rex skeleton logo, shown in Exhibit 8, appeared on every licensed product and promotional item that was marketed, regardless of language. The logo was integral to the design of the ad campaign that promoted the film's release. The campaign began in late fall 1992, with the first of the following three movie trailers (i.e., an advertisement for a film preceding the showing of another film):

- In November 1992, the first trailer, unveiled in U.S. theaters, emphasized the scientific underpinnings of the film without including any actual footage; the logo, however, made its movie debut.
- In March 1993, at ShowEast (a trade event for theater operators on the U.S. East Coast), the second trailer underscored the film's "action/adventure" qualities, again not showing

Exhibit 8   Jurassic Park *Logo and Poster*

the dinosaurs but featuring the logo prominently. Introduced along with the trailer were various point-of-sale displays and other merchandising support materials.

- In May 1993, the third trailer, shown in theaters, hinted at what the creatures might look like, thereby demonstrating the sophisticated quality of the digital dinosaur images created for the movie.

Throughout the prelaunch campaign, the audio tag line, "An adventure 65 million years in the making," accompanied the trailers. Some 27 television ad spots were also created, targeting different demographic groups.

During 1993, the JP logo became one of the most widely recognized in the world, and all features of its design were rigorously protected. The slogan, "If it's not Jurassic Park, it's extinct," accompanied the skeleton logo on all licensed product packaging and movie posters. Specific instructions were issued to all licensees detailing the official JP symbols and precisely how they were to appear. A JP Trademark and Logo Manual included guidelines for final art, packaging, and merchandise design and guidelines, directed primarily at retailers on how to develop new applications for JP brand symbols. The latter were included to encourage retailer creativity in merchandising efforts for JP products and services. Excerpts from the Manual are presented in Exhibit 9.

Trademark Protection

Michelle Katz, vice-president and general counsel for MCA/Universal Merchandising Inc., recalled the principal methods used to protect the JP trademarks:

> First, we set out in our advertising to register in the minds of consumers and the trade our official logo, the ancillary (JP) logo and the phrase "If it's not Jurassic Park, it's extinct," which appeared on the packaging of every licensed product. A consistent "look" in the advertising and packaging of licensed prod-

ucts helped people remember the trademarks as a brand. Second, we used print advertising to warn of our intent to prosecute trademark infringements. In the United States, a widely publicized toll-free number (1-800-DINO-COP) was set up to facilitate reporting of unauthorized knockoffs. Third, we met with customs authorities and law enforcement officers throughout the world to familiarize them with our trademarks and enlisted their support. Fourth, we lined up a worldwide team of investigators and attorneys who responded promptly to any infringements spotted by our agents.

Added Lewis, "You always know when you have a successful logo—when political cartoonists use it in newspapers . . . and when other organizations use the logo in their ad campaigns without consent." *Jurassic Park* stimulated this level of response, harking back to the days of *Jaws,* when pounding theme music and sharks provided irresistible fodder for comedians, commentators, and trademark pirates around the globe.

Building Excitement Among Partners

In February 1993, MCA/Universal Merchandising orchestrated an unprecedented and highly publicized example of MCA synergy and collaboration at the Museum of Natural History in New York City. Steven Spielberg, the principal actors of *Jurassic Park,* and MCA corporate executives participated in a reception for International Toy Fair attendees that included the first clip ever to be seen from the movie and an overview of the merchandising support program for all JP-licensed products. At the Fair, toy manufacturers presented to thousands of retail buyers the new products they would develop for the fourth-quarter holiday season. All these events were the subject of a same-day front page story in *The Wall Street Journal.*

The timing of the museum presentation was in line with the annual calendar of interactions

Exhibit 9   *Excerpts from Jurassic Park Trademark and Logo Manual*

PANTONE 109
PANTONE Red 032

The official Jurassic Park Logo is as bold, distinctive and memorable as the movie itself.

There are two striking versions to choose from. The dazzling yellow logo and brilliant red logo are interchangeable. So pick the look that shows off your unique Jurassic Park product to best advantage.

In the movie, you'll see these logos just about everywhere you look. So make sure you reproduce them exactly as you see on this page. Consistency is the best way to make the most of your license. The more familiar people are with the official Jurassic Park Logo, the more they'll all want to get in on the excitement.

Remember, if it's not Jurassic Park, it's extinct!

PANTONE Red 032
PANTONE 109

INTERNATIONAL SYMBOLS

VELOCIRAPTOR

DILOPHOSAURUS

BRACHIOSAURUS

JP1

CAUTION! WARNING! DANGER!
Look out for the International Symbols used on all the signs throughout Jurassic Park because they're going to be everywhere.

CAUTION! BIOLOGICAL HAZARD! would be an appropriate placard in almost any dorm room.

CAUTION! HEARING PROTECTION REQUIRED IN THIS AREA! would look great over the stereo.

WARNING! WATCH YOUR STEP! would make a great refrigerator magnet to keep someone on their diet.

Jurassic Park International Symbols also make great backgrounds for packaging and ads.

CAUTION GOGGLES REQUIRED IN THIS AREA

CAUTION KEEP WINDOWS UP!

Finding new uses for International Symbols is just one more way to put your own personal stamp on one more corner of the Jurassic Park Licensing market.

Combine signs and symbols to make intriguing patterns for sheets and pillowcases.

CAUTION HEARING PROTECTION REQUIRED IN THIS AREA

involving toy manufacturers, motion picture studios, and toy retailers:

- February: At International Toy Fairs in London, Paris and Nurenberg, toy manufacturers presented to retail buyers brand line extensions, new licensed products, and other new product launches.
- June–July (United States) and September–October (international): Motion pictures that had the potential to become licensing blockbusters were released, often targeting the youth market and creating momentum for the fourth-quarter gift-giving season.
- Fourth quarter: In this promotional period, toy manufacturers and retailers launched major television and print ad campaigns.

The major toy retailers were increasingly involved as partners of licensors and licensees. For example, the international division of Toys 'R' Us operated 234 stores in international markets (there were 581 in the United States). Toys 'R' Us agreed to distribute a free JP box containing products and coupons to three million consumers in its U.S. outlets. Samples in the box included licensed products from General Mills, Keebler, Leaf, Lifesavers, and others.

Following the New York event in February 1993, a similar strategy was used to mobilize partners and energize licensees around the world. According to Gerry Lewis:

> One key to success in international licensing is to create the sense of a major event among the participating licensees. The various activities we planned affirmed that the licensees had a central role in the overall event and boosted their commitment. We coordinated premiere events at natural history museums around the world. In addition to adding credibility and generating excitement, these events attracted considerable media attention.

Outside North America, the JP effort resulted in 85 country-specific tie-in sales promotions worldwide—more than for any previous movie.

At the same time, explained Isaac, "The consistent 'look' of the advertising carried over to the packaging and design of licensed products. The logo was key. The uniqueness of *Jurassic Park* was the very strong logo we created early on that all licensees had to work with. . . . From there, our licensees developed products that incorporated their own interpretations."

The PG-13 Rating

Despite the tremendous effort behind the JP campaign, one issue lingered: the movie was about dinosaurs, which fascinated most youngsters, but the story was not appropriate for every child to witness on the large screen. Indeed, Spielberg himself admitted he would not let his children, aged eight and younger, see the film: "I took an R-rated book and turned it into a PG-13 movie . . . but I'm not going to let my youngest kids see it for a couple of years."[3]

Executives were concerned that *Jurassic Park* publicity could become a double-edged sword. On one hand, the free publicity, heightened by strategic leaks—and intended exposure—of the digital technology involved in creating the film's dinosaurs, was welcomed. On the other hand, it might generate interest among the very children least able to deal with some of the images the film promised to display. Dr. Jerome Singer, head of the Yale Family Television Research and Consultation Center, commented, "When kids play with toy dinosaurs in a fantasy kind of way, I don't see a problem. However, seeing dinosaurs on the screen is far different from having a toy dinosaur you can play with."

No one really knew how important an issue this would be. Hedging its bets, McDonald's

---

[3]In the United Kingdom, *Jurassic Park* received a PG rating, meaning children of any age could attend.

U.S. tied its principal JP promotion to "Dino-Sized" meals—bigger portions for adults and young adults. Another licensee, Western Publishing, created *Jurassic Park* coloring and story books that replicated only benign scenes of the movie's dinosaurs.

Toy manufacturers were especially concerned with the "play value" of licensed products. For five- to eight-year-olds, dolls and action characters relied upon a child's imagination. After eight years, children moved away from fantasies to a framework of reality. A motion picture could only create awareness of a toy, but play value depended on the quality of product execution.

CONCLUSION

As *Jurassic Park* made its U.S. debut, to be followed by a worldwide rollout, with years of work, publicity, and coordination behind it, the future growth of the entertainment-licensing industry hung in the balance. Already, MCA/Universal and Matsushita were attempting to build upon their JP licensing and merchandising efforts in preparing to launch *The Flintstones* movie in the following summer. Disney was gearing up for its animated potential blockbuster, *The Lion King*, also scheduled to premiere in the summer of 1994. And immediately waiting in the wings was Sony's bet, *The Last Action Hero*.

DISNEY CONSUMER PRODUCTS IN LEBANON

In March 1994, Jeremy Carter, Disney Consumer Products' vice-president and managing director for Disney Consumer Products Europe and Middle East (DCPEME), sat at his desk in his Paris office pondering expansion opportunities. DCPEME, a business unit of the Walt Disney Company, hoped to maintain its position as the fastest-growing division within the company. One growth possibility was in the Middle East. Penetrating Middle Eastern countries was attractive, given their favorable demographics and discretionary spending patterns. The company could also receive additional royalties from its licensees' sales of Disney-related merchandise. At the same time, DCP executives were concerned that successful entry into Middle Eastern markets could encourage unauthorized imitations or pirate versions of Disney products to be introduced; these, in turn, might be difficult to control.

In 1993, DCPEME signed a joint venture agreement with a Saudi partner, making Saudi Arabia the first country to be penetrated in the area. Did Lebanon, Carter wondered, represent a logical second step? Carter reviewed the market research DCPEME had undertaken in Lebanon and the sales potential of various Disney licensed products, and he was assessing the pros and cons of several distribution options. If he recommended that DCPEME enter the Lebanese market, he would have to explain how it could be accomplished to Dennis Hightower, DCPEME president for Europe and the Middle East.

THE WALT DISNEY COMPANY

In 1923, brothers Walt and Roy Disney founded The Walt Disney Company (WDC) as an animated-film business. By 1994, the company had become an entertainment giant comprising three major businesses (see Exhibit 1):

- Theme parks and resorts included major facilities in Anaheim (California), Orlando (Florida), Tokyo, and Marne La Vallée (near Paris).

This case was prepared by John A. Quelch. Jean-Marc Ingea and Barbara Feinberg also contributed to the development of this case. Copyright © 1995 by the President and Fellows of Harvard College. Harvard Business School case 596-060.

Exhibit 1   *The Walt Disney Company: Key Financial Data, 1991–1993 ($ millions)***

Year Ended September 30	1991	1992	1993
Revenues	$6,112	$7,504	$8,529
Theme parks and resorts	2,794	3,307	3,441
Filmed entertainment	2,594	3,115	3,673
Consumer products	724	1,082	1,415
Operating Income	1,095	1,435	1,734
Theme parks and resorts	547	644	747
Filmed entertainment	318	508	632
Consumer products	230	283	355
Net Income	637	817	300[a]

*Source: Company records.
[a]After loss from Euro Disney investment ($515 million) and accounting changes ($371 million).

- Filmed Entertainment comprised the Walt Disney Studios, which produced live-action films under the Touchstone, Hollywood Pictures, Miramax, and Caravan Pictures labels and animated films under the Walt Disney Pictures label. This subsidiary also provided programming for pay-per-view, network, and cable (including the Disney Channel) television and handled sales of videotapes.
- Disney Consumer Products (DCP) was responsible for all marketing and licensing activities and sales of Disney products through mail-order operations and retail outlets, including company-owned Disney Stores. Products consisted of publications, computer software, videogames, toys, personal care products, school supplies, party goods, watches, apparel, home furnishings, and food. DCP licensed the Disney characters, songs and music, and visual and literary properties.

WDC's objective was to remain the world's premier entertainment company. Adhering to Walt Disney's dream to "make people happy," the company's products were associated with such values as quality, integrity, and imagination. The company believed future growth lay in the worldwide character-licensing business; more Disney Stores, theme parks, and resorts;

accelerated output of feature-length animated films; and increased demand for motion picture software and TV programming. In addition, the video market was considered significant, as household VCR penetration worldwide began approaching that of the United States.

Disney Consumer Products

Of DCP's 1993 $1.4 billion in revenues, 1.3% came from Greece and the Middle East and 23% from Europe (excluding Greece). Table A summarizes DCPEME revenues by product category, while Table B provides more detail on DCPEME merchandise revenues:

Table A   DCPEME Revenues by Product Category, 1993

Publications*	61%
Merchandise	25
Music	6
Computer software	4
Other	4

*Note: Revenues for publications (80% magazines, 20% books) represent sales rather than royalties. Royalty revenues from publications approximated merchandise revenues.

Table B   Breakdown of DCPEME
Merchandise Revenues, 1993

Apparel	31%
Toys	24
Food	12
Home furnishings	12
Stationery	9
Gifts	8
Personal care	4

DCP tightly controlled its licensees to ensure a high level of design and creative integrity, and while royalties for product categories varied, they averaged about 9%. Among the characters DCP licensed were "classics" like Mickey and Minnie Mouse, Donald and Daisy Duck, Goofy, Peter Pan, and Pinocchio, along with characters from more recent Disney animated films such as *The Little Mermaid, Beauty and the Beast,* and *Aladdin.* Characters from *The Lion King,* opening in summer 1994, were also expected to be popular. Mattel, DCP's principal licensee, planned its largest-ever selection of toys for a Disney film. More than 100 *Lion King* publications—from coloring books to videogames—were also planned. And Donald Duck would turn 60 on June 6; special promotions, books, and other licensed merchandise would be launched to celebrate that event.

Licenses were usually granted for a specific territory, although worldwide or regional licenses were held by a few licensees—for example, Mattel (for infant and pre-school toys); Nestlé (for food products); and Seiko (for watches). In 1993, there were about 1,000 licensees for Disney products in Europe and the Middle East—a number that might decrease as more multiterritory deals were signed.

Disney Stores showcased the activities and products of the company's divisions via promotions and in-store videos. By early 1994, over 300 (26 in Europe) operated worldwide, 80% of which were in the United States; by late 1994, the company hoped to add 100 more. Given high startup costs, the European Stores had not yet turned a profit.

THE LEBANESE MARKET

In March 1993, DCPEME signed a 50/50 joint venture with a Saudi partner. The joint venture company became the legal entity that would manage Disney's Consumer Products' business interests in Middle Eastern countries, excluding Turkey and Israel. Saudi Arabia was the first country in which this joint venture would operate. The next step might be to extend distribution to Lebanon. Exhibit 2 compares DCPEME's operations in Saudi Arabia, France, and Lebanon.

Founded in 1943, the independent Republic of Lebanon, bordered by Israel to the south and Syria to the east and north, was roughly the size of Connecticut. During the ensuing three decades, the country prospered, with especially dramatic growth in the service sector, particularly tourism, financial services, and port-related activities; per capita gross domestic product was estimated at $1,070 in 1974. At that point, however, the country plunged into a civil war that lasted until 1990. According to United Nations' estimates, the resulting cost in damage to property and infrastructure was $25 billion. Nevertheless, the Lebanese economy subsequently displayed remarkable resilience. In 1991, GDP grew at 50% from the depressed 1990 level, and the World Bank forecast that real GDP would increase at 68% per year until 1999, as the infrastructure was restored. By early 1993, the economy was characterized by free market pricing for most goods and services, and by an unrestricted exchange and trade system. After years of devaluation, the Lebanese pound had stabilized (U.S. $1 = 1,700 Lebanese pounds). Most consumer products were priced

Exhibit 2   *DCPEME Operations in Saudi Arabia, France, and Lebanon, 1993*

	Saudi Arabia	**France**	**Lebanon**
Disney royalty revenues (Year 1):	$ 800,000[a]	$28,000,000[c]	$105,000
Disney royalty revenues (Year 5):	5,200,000[b]		(uncollected)
Merchandise	87%	69%	65%
Publishing	12%	19%	35%
Music	1%	12%	0%
Profit margin	30 to 75%	80%	NA
Distribution	Exclusive and nonexclusive nondistributors	Licensees' direct sales force and exclusive distributors	Not authorized except for worldwide licensees
Piracy	Exclusively on videotapes	Minimal	Exclusively on videotapes

[a]Objective for the first full year of operations.
[b]Objective for the fifth year of operation.
[c]Revenues include fully integrated businesses and have been restated on a royalty basis for comparison purposes.

in dollars. Exhibit 3 summarizes key demographic and economic data on Lebanon.

Although the Lebanese market was small, it offered several advantages. First, its population was much more literate than the populations of neighboring Arab states, and it was also more familiar with Western products, including those of Disney. Second, Lebanese distributors, many of whom occupied important positions in companies throughout the Middle East, might help DCPEME penetrate other Arab markets. Third, because Lebanese society was comparatively liberal, all Disney products could readily be sold.

In 1993, Disney products were distributed in Lebanon through one of three channels:

- Worldwide licensees, e.g., Mattel, that legitimately distributed Disney products through their Lebanese distributors.
- Non-worldwide licensees that distributed Disney products through Lebanese distributors even though they did not hold Disney licenses for Lebanon.

- Non-worldwide licensees unaware that several of their wholesalers were selling Disney merchandise to Lebanese distributors or retailers. For example, one publisher held a U.S. license for Disney picture books, but some of its U.S. distributors were selling them to Lebanese distributors.

Exhibits 4A and 4B list some of DCPEME's licensees and their products; Exhibit 5 compares the retail prices for such products in Lebanon and in the United States.

Market Research in Lebanon

In early 1994, DCPEME commissioned focus groups of Lebanese parents with children under the age of 18 to understand how parents entertained their children, which activities they encouraged, and which Disney products they liked and might purchase. The parents interviewed lived in Beirut and had household incomes among the top 25% in Lebanon. In ad-

Exhibit 3   *Key Demographic and Economic Data for Lebanon, 1992*

Population:	3.4 million (76% urban)
Children 0–12	650,000
Children 13–18	320,000
Households	670,000
Surface area	10,452 square kilometers
Literacy rate	80%
GDP	U.S. $6,460 million
GDP per capita	U.S. $1,900
GDP Distribution:	
Agriculture	7%
Manufacturing	14
Construction	7
Trade	29
Nonfinancial services	20
Financial services	9
Public administration	14
Imports	U.S. $3,565 million
Exports	U.S. $ 510 million
Balance of payments	U.S. $ 54 million

dition, 200 children aged 8 to 18 were interviewed to test awareness and appeal of Disney products. Research findings are summarized in Exhibits 6 and 7.

The studies revealed that parents viewed television as a way to stimulate their children's imagination—until the children were eight years old; beyond that age, television was considered more negatively, as a passive activity, although children were encouraged to watch cultural programs. Parents were much more positive about reading, starting to read stories to children as young as one year old. Read-along tapes were not widely used, given their limited availability in the market.

Plush toys (such as stuffed animals) were especially appealing to children aged 1–4, who formed very emotional relationships with these toys. Beyond the age of 4, most children switched to playing computer games, watching television, or engaging in outdoor sports. (Interestingly, Mattel's Barbie dolls retained their appeal for girls as old as 10 to 12 years.) But computer games were not appreciated by parents. Either the children purchased the games themselves or they insisted their parents buy them. In addition, parents felt that educational software for children was lacking in the market. Finally, teenagers were brand-conscious in their choices of clothing and accessories. Examples of "fashionable" brands included Lacoste apparel, Sebago shoes, and Swatch watches.

In cities of Western Europe, children began deciding what they wanted to do and play with as early as age four; in Lebanon, the transition tended to occur around ages 7 to 8. Parents purchased gifts for their children on major holidays and for birthdays of their own children and of friends of their children. Sixty percent of parents also purchased small gifts for their children on impulse, including videotapes, drawing kits, picture books, and Lego games. These impulse purchases were more frequent when parents had only one child, when children were too young to express themselves verbally, when mothers worked full time, or when parents had been away on trips and felt a need to compensate for their absence. Thirty percent of parents purchased small gifts as rewards for good grades at school or for helping out at home. Parents with several children felt that if they gave a gift to one child without a specific justification, they would be pressured to purchase gifts for their other children as well. Parents were also concerned about spoiling their children.

Regarding familiarity with Disney, 30% of the parents had heard of the company through television cartoons or video movies, and 30% had been to a Disney theme park. The Disney brand was regarded as a high-value label, and interviewees believed that using Disney apparel and other merchandise enhanced people's self-esteem

Exhibit 4A *Disney Licensees Distributing Products in Lebanon, 1993* *

Company	Country of Origin	Product Category	Retail Sales Value	Distribution Type
A	France	Picture books	$175,000	Direct sales
B	U.S.	Picture books	165,000	Three distributors
	France	Apparel	20,000	Appointed distributor
C	France	Picture books Puzzles	65,000	Direct sales
D	Figurines	U.S.	260,000	Several distributors
E	U.S.	"The Little Mermaid" figurine	50,000	Appointed distributor
F	Italy	Toys	40,000	Several distributors
G	U.S.	Plushes	20,000	Appointed distributor
H	Spain	Puzzles	10,000	Several distributors
I	Japan	Video games	100,000	Appointed distributors
J	Japan	Video games	80,000	Appointed distributor
K	Belgium	Towels	85,000	Exclusive retailer
L	U.S.	Toothbrush	80,000	Appointed distributor
M	France	Tapes, CDs	15,000	Several distributors
N	France	Rocking chair	5,000	Exclusive retailer

*Source: Distributors' estimates.

and perceived status. Many Lebanese had lived abroad during the country's civil war and were therefore aware of a wide range of Disney-licensed products beyond those legitimately distributed in Lebanon.

A Lebanese child's first contact with Disney characters usually occurred between ages 1–2, when parents began narrating Disney tales and children started watching cartoons on TV. Disney values and characters were then developed through videotapes, picture books, and plush toys.

Product Categories

In order to decide which products—if any—should be introduced into Lebanon, Jeremy Carter reviewed DCPEME's research findings on Lebanese parents' reactions to various Disney

Exhibit 4B *Retail Sales of Disney Products in Lebanon by Licensee Origin, 1993* *

Licensee Origin	Sales
Worldwide regional licensees	$ 455,000
Nonworldwide licensees, selling through selected Lebanese distributors	485,000
Nonworldwide licensees, selling through wholesalers in other countries	230,000
Pirate Disney Products (exclusively video)	650,000 to 1,200,000

*Source: Company estimates.

Exhibit 5   *Retail Prices of Disney products in Lebanon and the United States, 1993*

Product	Lebanon Retail Price	U.S. Retail Price
Video		
"Sing Along Song" tapes (pirate)	$5	$12
"Disney Classics" tapes (pirate)	7	19
Publications		
"Le Journal de Mickey" magazine	1.60	—
"Picsou" (Uncle Scrooge) magazine	2.50	—
"Disney Parade" magazine	1.80	—
Disney Hachette picture books (e.g., *Snow White*), 90 pages	11	7
Fernand Nathan picture books (e.g., *Bambi*), 45 pages	7	—
Toys/Plushes		
Mattel's Footlights	14	—
Hasbro's Disney Babies (e.g., Goofy)	28	—
Educa's Maxipuzzle, 150 pieces	18	3
Computer Games		
Nintendo's Mickey's Dangerous Chase (GameBoy)	40	—
Nintendo's Aladdin (SuperNintendo)	100	70
Nintendo's Who Framed Roger Rabbit (GameBoy)	35	—
Sega's Aladdin (MegaDrive)	80	60
Music		
Aladdin (compact disc)	22	22
Fantasia (set of two compact discs)	30	—
Pickwick's read-along tape	15	7
Pickwick's compact disc	27	15
Furniture		
Creapuzzle's rocking chairs	75	—
Mickey Office Chair made in Germany	250	—
Apparel/Accessories		
Ties	40	28
School Bags	20	13
Linen		
Sunday Junior's 1m80 wide sheets	52	—
Haplo's bath towel	20	—
Haplo's bath robe	75	—

Exhibit 6   *Awareness of Disney Products in Lebanon*

DCPEME commissioned two focus groups involving 15 mothers and fathers of children under age 18. Respondents were asked: "In which of the following product categories do Disney products exist?" In fact, Disney products were marketed in all categories listed.

Product Category	% Responding "Yes"
Magazines	60%
Picture books	100
Read-along tapes	100
Videotapes	100
Television cartoons	100
Watches	73
Apparel	93
Toys	100
Computer games	0
School supplies	93
Home furnishing	67
Food	87

---

products (see Exhibit 8). He also had collected preliminary data on Lebanese distributors' and retailers' margins by product category (Exhibit 9). With this information in hand, he set out to consider which product categories had the highest sales potential in Lebanon.

Apparel

This category included several product lines that varied in price/quality and age of the target audience. (Although Disney apparel was not sold legally in Lebanon, small quantities had been imported illegally.)

A high-end Disney line for teenagers would have to compete with such names as Benetton, Lacoste, Old River, and Compagnie de Californie. Lacoste, encountering piracy problems, had opened two stores in Beirut to enable cus-

tomers to buy its genuine products and to educate the market on how to spot them. Carter was concerned that if Disney built a high awareness for its merchandise in Lebanon, it too would face imported pirate products. This scenario had already developed in East Asia.

Research participants had looked favorably upon the price levels of a medium-quality line of apparel: Disney T-shirts at $20 and sweatshirts at $30 represented prices that Lebanese customers found reasonable. One source of concern, however, was that they perceived the value of such apparel by the added value *originality* would provide. On the other hand, T-shirts, sweatshirts, and accessories were often sold as gifts, and it was thought that gifts would represent a significant share of Disney apparel sales in Lebanon.

At the outset, Disney might work with international licensees to ensure product quality and creative standards. Although Disney apparel made by international licensees would find it hard to compete with low-priced, locally manufactured apparel or low-cost imports from Asia, the company would perhaps be able to penetrate the mass market with small accessories retailing at broadly affordable prices. The dollar sales of such products, if intensively distributed through many retail outlets, could be significant.

Publications

While such French-language Disney magazines as "Le Journal de Mickey" and "Disney Parade" were legitimately being distributed in Lebanon, representing as a magazine category annual sales of about $20,000, picture books were the principal Disney publications. Many Lebanese children were able to understand Disney publications in French and English (see Exhibit 10), but since French was more widely taught as a foreign language than English in elementary school, sales of Disney publications in French were higher.

Exhibit 7   *Selected Findings of DCPEME Market Study*

During January and February 1994, personal interviews were conducted with 200 children (50% boys and 50% girls) aged 8 to 18. Children were interviewed at school. Place of residence was as follows: 45% in East Beirut, 45% in West Beirut, and 10% outside of Beirut.

- Arabic was the predominant language spoken at home for 58% of respondents, French was predominant for 23%, English was predominant for 19%.
- Tom and Jerry were the characters preferred by 22% of the children, followed by Mickey Mouse with 8%. The overall distribution of first preferences was as follows (**Disney characters are in bold**):

Character Name	%
Tom and Jerry	22%
Mickey Mouse	8
Bugs Bunny	7
Pink Panther	7
Donald Duck	6
Tintin et Milou	4
Asterix et Obelix	3
Aladdin	2
The Little Mermaid	2
Ninja Turtles	2
Lucky Luke	2
Beauty and The Beast	1
Peter Pan	1
Pinocchio	1
Snow White	1
Uncle Scrooge	1

- 66% of respondents knew their preferred characters primarily from television, 12% from books, 9% from movie theaters, 9% from video, 3% from magazines, and 1% from computer software.
- 44% of respondents owned toys representing at least one of their favorite characters: 48% of these toys had been purchased outside Lebanon (mainly in Europe or the U.S.).
- 58% of respondents owned videotapes representing at least one of their favorite characters: 46% of these tapes had been purchased outside Lebanon and 64% were Disney tapes (either genuine or pirate).
- 31% of respondents owned apparel depicting at least one of their favorite characters: 66% of this apparel had been purchased outside Lebanon.
- 92% of respondents read at home, 17% of respondents had read the *Journal de Mickey* magazine: 38% of these children read it on a regular basis.
- 16% of respondents read *Piscou Magazine*: 50% of these children read it on a regular basis.
- 8% of respondents read *Mickey Parade* magazine: 43% of these children read it on a regular basis.
- 67% of respondents had at least one video game at home, 44% of whom had Nintendo games and 25% of whom had Sega games. 44% of these games had been purchased outside Lebanon.
- 99% of respondents lived in homes with a television, 87% lived in homes with a video recorder.

Exhibit 8   *Buying Intentions for Various Disney Products among Lebanese Consumers*

The following test was conducted in a focus group of parents of children aged 1–15. Focus-group respondents were shown a variety of Disney products and were asked which they would purchase at the prices indicated.

Disney Product	Suggested Retail Price[a]	% Who Would Buy Product
"Minnie" T-shirt	$23	40%
Baby suit in jeans	27	80
Baby suit in cotton	27	60
"Aladdin" towel	30	33
"Mickey" slippers	15	40
"Minnie" tennis shoes	15	87
"Mickey" toothbrush	6	20
"Aladdin" plastic watch	8	33
"Aladdin" beach plastic glass	11	40
"Donald Duck" school bag	21	40
"Donald Duck" plush	30	33
"Abu" plush	38	7
"Beauty" doll	24	40
Read-along tape	11	67
Musical television	50	20

[a]These retail prices represented a 50% premium over U.S. retail prices for the identical products.

One major French licensee was distributing a 30-volume series of picture books featuring classic Disney stories like *Snow White* and *Pinocchio;* the series was carried by almost every Lebanese bookstore, and a licensee representative was responsible for replenishing inventory. Annual retail sales of Disney publications represented about 10% of the licensee's total sales in Lebanon, roughly $140,000. Its licensing agreement with Disney did not include Lebanon, but Disney did not oppose the sales: they helped increase Disney product awareness and introduce the stories and characters to young children. Another French publisher was also selling Disney stories; its license for Disney books in France expired in 1992 so DCPEME assumed that the publisher was liquidating remaining inventories of Disney books. Any picture book in French,

however, faced competition from those starring such popular characters as Babar, Asterix, and Tintin, whose sales significantly outpaced Disney's.

One U.S. licensee sold Disney picture books in English through three local distributors; its annual retail sales in Lebanon were about

Exhibit 9   *Distributor and Retailer Margins by Category*

Category	Distributor Margin	Retailer Margin
Apparel	20%	30%
Publications	10	20
Toys/Plushes	15	20

Exhibit 10 *Percentage of Lebanese Population Able to Understand Foreign Languages by Age*

	Disney Target Audience		Overall Population	
	Under 12	12 and Over	Under 12	12 and Over
Arabic	100%	100%	100%	100%
French	70	80	50	60
English	20	60	10	30

$125,000. Price competition among the three was tough because there was no exclusive distributor for English-language Disney publications, and the licensee's publications were sometimes retailed at a loss.

Disney had signed licensing agreements with four publishers of books in Arabic. Several Lebanese book retailers had printing capabilities and wished to translate and publish Disney picture books and export them throughout the Arabic-speaking world. They argued that Lebanese printing quality was superior, citing an old proverb: "In the Arab world, Egyptians create stories, Lebanese publish them, and Iraqis read them!"

Plushes/Toys

Although retail sales of plushes and "figurine"-type toys in Lebanon were estimated at $16 million per year, Disney products were not widely available, for several reasons. First, Disney plushes/toys faced strong competition from both branded and unbranded products in Lebanon. Fisher-Price, for example, whose products targeted the age 3-and-under set, were 30% cheaper than equivalent Disney items. Further, Fisher-Price regularly inserted product catalogs in local newspapers and ran promotions on children's TV shows, offering free samples. Disney advertising was almost nonexistent in Lebanon.

Second, one important Disney licensee in the plush category did not market in Lebanon; the other was restructuring its Lebanese distribution as a result of disagreement over the kinds of merchandise the distributor received. Thus, in 1993, that Disney licensee selected another distributor for the Lebanese market, and the two were making ambitious plans for 1994.

Third, the category was limited to younger children, and Lebanese children rarely gave plushes as gifts to their friends.

Other Products

Most Lebanese were unaware that Disney watches existed, although focus groups indicated that plastic watches retailing below $15 were perceived as affordable and unique. More expensive watches would have to compete with such brands as Swatch and Timex, both widely available in Lebanon. Other categories in which Disney licensees' presence was very limited included home furnishings and food products.

At the same time, all major Disney computer games were available for use on Sega and Nintendo systems, though Disney faced stiff competition from non-Disney action games. Nevertheless, Disney's latest game, Aladdin, had been the 1993 best-seller in Lebanon, selling out after a few weeks on the market. Retailers were also interested in "read-along" tapes, but compact disc sales were limited to the 5% of Lebanese households with CD players.

Character

The Disney characters most widely known and appreciated by Lebanese consumers were Mickey and Minnie Mouse, Belle (of "Beauty and the Beast"), Snow White, and Ariel (of the

"Little Mermaid"). Concurrent with the release of "Beauty and the Beast" and "Aladdin" in 1992 and 1993, respectively, DCPEME had concentrated its merchandising on the principal characters in these films—with great success. With the highly anticipated release of "The Lion King" in summer 1994, DCPEME had high hopes for the Lebanese market: focus groups revealed that Lebanese youngsters liked animal-related plushes/toys, and boys especially appreciated the strength associated with lions.

Distribution

Fifteen Disney licensees had official distributors in Lebanon, but in many cases, their performance was not monitored closely because the country represented a small market. Given an improved political climate, licensees' interest in extracting more sales from Lebanon was expected to increase. Thus, one of DCPEME's distribution options was to rely on its licensees' current distributors while also encouraging its worldwide licensees not represented in Lebanon to sign agreements with one of these distributors. DCPEME would coordinate the distributors and encourage them to carry more Disney merchandise. Incentives might include establishing an advertising fund, sponsoring TV shows/special events, and offering Euro Disney entrance tickets and tour packages. A problem with this approach, however, was that current official distributors might not have the motivation or financial strength to distribute more Disney products, and might favor other products yielding higher margins. They also might not be the most appropriate to carry other Disney licensees' product lines; for example, Nintendo, a Disney licensee, had a Lebanese distributor that represented only Nintendo.

Another distribution option was to identify existing Lebanese distributors that might sell Disney products not yet present in the market. There were 10 top distributors in Lebanon in the product categories in which Disney competed; one carried a range of toy brands, including Fisher-Price, Milton Bradley, and Matchbox. A methodical study of the product line expertise, distribution ability, and financial strength of such distributors would take six months. If DCPEME increased the number of its Lebanese distributors, it faced the challenge of coordinating and supporting organizations unfamiliar with Disney products.

In the case of either option, DCPEME would have to determine how to handle requests for exclusivity. Most distributors required exclusive rights in Lebanon for the items they carried because the market was too small to support competing distributors. Traditionally, DCPEME encouraged its licensees to test new country markets and distributors for a limited time before granting exclusive rights. Yet granting exclusivity to local distributors might effectively combat diversion: Lebanese retailers could currently purchase Disney merchandise from U.S. or European Disney licensees' wholesalers and resell it in Lebanon.

Meanwhile, DCPEME had been contacted by several new distributors wishing to carry Disney products. One was an 18-store Saudi retail chain selling photographic and electronics equipment; it was interested in opening a Beirut store offering just Disney products and in acting as a distributor to other retailers. The chain had no previous experience in Lebanese retailing but recently purchased extensive space in Beirut for offices and a showroom, to be run by the current vice-president of marketing, a Lebanese citizen. Despite being advised that it could not have exclusive rights for any Disney products or use Disney store signage or any Disney character name or logo, the Saudi retail chain negotiated exclusive rights with 11 Disney licensees to sell a variety of their products in Lebanon. This merchandise comprised apparel, toys, school supplies, and gifts items. Other Lebanese distributors could continue to purchase products not included in the agreement from the same Disney licensees.

Exhibit 11   *Retailer Advertisement of Disney Products in Lebanon*

ALL PURPOSE BAGS!
Hand and Back Bags to French quality & design.

Always look out for
more of our products,
a newer collection
in our next catalogue!

STICKERS ON RELIEF!
All surface 3-dimensional plastified fun
stickers ranging from 10 to 90 cm.
Made in Spain.

T. F. BOWLES Ltd
Mar Mikhael
Fattal Bldg. 3rd floor
Close to Fichet-Bauche
Tel/Fax:01-581757

A second distributor had acquired from Disney licensees not yet present in Lebanon the rights to sell some of their Disney products, and had opened a retail store in Beirut in December 1993; it also began advertising its Disney products (see Exhibit 11 for a sample). Other Lebanese companies—frequently startups with little marketing expertise—were thought likely to try to acquire rights for certain Disney merchandise from international Disney licensees not yet distributing in Lebanon.

Finally, DCPEME could license one or more Disney Corners within existing retail stores. The licensee would lease the space for each Disney Corner from a storeowner. A Disney Corner would offer the full array of genuine Disney products properly merchandised and would ensure both continuity of supply and the aggressive promotion of new character-related products as they were launched. A Disney Corner could be a landmark for Beirut residents, increasing awareness and stimulating gift-giving of Disney products, while reaffirming company values and enabling DCPEME to market product not carried by current distributors. Startup costs for a 1,000-square-foot store-within-a-store were estimated at $125,000, including $30,000 of initial inventory. Inventory was expected to turn over four times a year and deliver a 30% gross margin. Beyond the costs, however, was the fact that opening a Disney Corner represented a serious commitment to a market whose potential had yet to be tested. Moreover, problems could arise with existing distributors of Disney licensees if DCPEME tried to direct all sales of Disney products through one or more Disney Corners where retail prices could be controlled.

DCP Organization in Lebanon

If DCPEME did decide to expand into Lebanon, should it set up an office in Beirut managed by full-time DCPEME employees, appoint a full- or part-time local marketing representative, or run Lebanon out of its Saudi office? An office would coordinate distributors' advertising and promotion efforts and mediate among them when necessary; ensure that DCPEME received all royalties to which it was entitled from sales of Disney merchandise; act to stop sales of pirated products or unauthorized imports; sponsor special promotional events; and in the long term, identify potential local manufacturers of licensed merchandise. Setting up an office in Beirut with full-time DCPEME employees would probably cost about $250,000 in the first year, whereas appointing and managing a half-time marketing representative would add perhaps $100,000 to DCPEME costs in 1994.

CONCLUSION

Jeremy Carter faced some tough choices. Should DCPEME enter the Lebanese market, and if so, how? Which products should be introduced, in what sequence, and through what distribution channels? How would copyrights, piracy concerns, and other protection issues be handled? Should Disney open an office in Beirut? The rewards in Lebanon seemed possible, but so did the risks.

PART VI

ORGANIZING AND MANAGING GLOBAL MARKETING OPERATIONS

Earlier in the book, we observed companies facing a diverse range of environmental forces and competitive pressures that were creating new strategic imperatives for them. While sensing, analyzing, and developing appropriate responses to these complex and often contradictory new demands is difficult, it is not where most global marketing programs fail. Far more frequently, companies develop a clear understanding of *what* they need to do, but struggle to understand *how* to do it. The greatest challenge usually comes in developing the organizational capabilities and managerial competencies to implement a clearly defined strategic intent.

GLOBAL VERSUS MULTINATIONAL ORGANIZATIONS

The tension between the powerful yet often competing forces shaping a company's global strategy—outlined in the introduction to Part I—has its analog in equally animated debates about whether a company should be organized around its products, its markets, or its customers. Like the arguments about the need for centralization versus decentralization, such polarization of the options misses the point. In order to build multiple sources of competitive advantage—global-scale efficiencies, locally responsive flexibility, and above all, an ability to develop and diffuse innovation—a company must build an organization that is multidimensional in its capabilities and flexible in its application of them.

Such an organization is difficult to build on the foundation of a decentralized federation of independent subsidiaries that often characterized the structure of older multinationals like Philips, Unilever, or ITT. But it is equally difficult to construct this organization on the centralized hub framework that has been favored by many comparatively newer global companies like Toyota, Boeing, or Matsushita. As they develop layers of competitive advantage, the subsidiaries in both these classic organization forms find that they can no longer relate only to the corporate center on the basis of either dependence or independence. To implement the multiple strategic capabilities in a flexible manner, they must be linked to the parent company and each other in an interdependent network of specialized operations.

In such an organization, resources are neither concentralized in the home country nor spread evenly around subsidiaries. Instead, they are allocated to the part of the organization where they offer greatest strategic advantage. Key strategic competencies are similarly built in the organization wherever the critical scarce knowledge and expertise exists. Thus, a subsidiary with a highly efficient plant might be designated the regional or global source for a certain line or business; another with an extremely creative development group might be named the company's center of excellence for a particular product or technology; and the unit with the most developed marketing capabilities may well become the lead company for the rollout of new product market strategies that are then leveraged worldwide.

This is an approach Unilever has taken as it adapts its decentralized federation structure into an integrated network. It developed its product market strategy for the fabric softener Snuggle in Germany; it led the worldwide rollout of the shampoo Timotei from Sweden; and its South African subsidiary developed a whole new category of product called body perfume, later transferring its new product Impulse to other subsidiaries worldwide.

MULTIPLE MANAGEMENT PERSPECTIVES

On top of this networked infrastructure, companies must create organizations in which the voices representing the multiple strategic imperatives can not only be heard but have influence on the key decisions. In the various worldwide markets, such organizations need strong geographic managers—whether at the country or regional level—who understand local consumer needs, national market structures, and host government requirements and are able to represent them in the company. They also need strong global product or business managers who can look across these local needs and interests and recognize the opportunities to capture economies of scale or develop coordinated competitive action. Finally, they need strong functional managers—technical directors, finance managers, HR professionals, and information officers—who can act as the repositories of the company's scarce financial, human, and knowledge resources and as the facilitators of their movement and application worldwide.

The reason ITT lost its dominant position in the world telecommunications industry was not through strategic blindness or technological incompetence, but simply because it was unable to develop the multidimensional management perspectives and capabilities it took to respond to the multilayered and fast-changing demands in that industry. Dominated by the all-powerful heads of the national companies around the world, ITT was never able to develop equally powerful global business and technology managers who could stop the parochial localization of their potentially powerful System 12 digital switch. After years of trying—and failing—to get all voices represented at the table, ITT sold its telecommunications business to allocate.

DIFFERENTIATED ROLES AND RESPONSIBILITIES

As a model, it is appealing to visualize a company as an integrated network of specialized, interdependent operations run by managers representing multiple diverse perspectives and capabilities. But how do companies translate that idealized model into practical reality? What are the specific roles and responsibilities and how are they allocated?

This is the most complicated and often the most sensitive part of developing a truly trans-

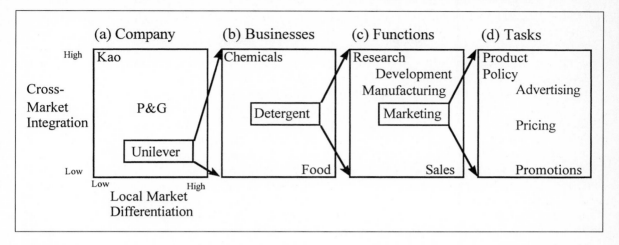

Figure 6.1

national organization, since it typically involves reallocating power long held by one group or another. To understand the shifts required, we can follow the way in which Unilever, the U.K.-Dutch packaged goods giant, adapted an organization that had operated for over half a century on a foundation of autonomous, self-sufficient subsidiaries.

Historically, this organization structure gave them an exceptional ability to be responsive to local market differences but not a strong capability in cross-market coordination (Figure 6.1[a]). During the 1980s, however, the company recognized that while the packaged food business (margarine, ice cream, frozen foods) was well served by the nationally responsive country-based structures, forces driving for cross-market integration required that they manage their commodity chemicals business in a much more centralized manner and that they coordinate many more of the activities in their detergent business (Figure 6.1[b]).

As Unilever's management analyzed what aspects of the detergent business could benefit from greater cross-market coordination, it was clear that research needed to be done on a global basis while sales continued to be a very local responsibility. In between these clear ex-

tremes, they decided that development capabilities in overseas countries could be specialized and integrated, as could production facilities. Marketing also needed to be more coordinated, but with some ability to respond simultaneously to local market needs (Figure 6.1[c]).

The particular detergent marketing responsibilities that had to be most nationally differentiated were local promotions decisions. On the other hand, the corporate product group wanted to keep clear control over basic product characteristics, market positioning, and other key aspects of product policy. Issues like advertising and pricing were recognized as requiring cross-market coordination and local flexibility; and these issues were coordinated by product manager-chaired teams with representatives from local subsidiaries (Figure 6.1[d]).

Such a portfolio of differentiated roles—often managed through cross-border teams and task forces—is a long way from the simple choices between centralized versus decentralized or product versus geography structures. But, as Percy Barnevik, CEO of ABB, said, "An organization that adapts to the new global reality will itself become a durable source of competitive advantage precisely because competitors will find it hard to match."

GLOBAL CLIENT MANAGEMENT

It was a Friday in mid-February, and Kadir Mahaleel, a wealthy businessman from the southeast Asian nation of Tailesia, was visiting London on a trip that combined business and pleasure. Mahaleel was the founder of Eximsa, a major export company in Tailesia. Business brought him to London every two to three months. These trips provided him with the opportunity to visit his daughter, Leona, the eldest of his four children, who lived in London. Several of his ten grandchildren were attending college in Britain, and he was especially proud of his grandson, Anson, who was a student at the Royal Academy of Music. In fact, he had scheduled this trip to coincide with a violin recital by Anson at 2:00 P.M. on this particular Friday.

The primary purpose of Mahaleel's visit was to resolve a delicate matter regarding his company. He had decided that the time had come to retire and wished to make arrangements for the company's future. His son, Victor, was involved in the business and ran Eximsa's trading office in Europe. However, Victor was in poor health and unable to take over the firm. Mahaleel believed that a group of loyal employees were interested in buying his company if the necessary credit could be arranged.

Before leaving Tailesia, Mahaleel had discussed the possibility of a buyout with his trusted financial adviser, who recommended that he talk to several banks in London because of the potential complexity of the business deal:

> The London banks are experienced in buyouts. Also, you need a bank that can handle the credit for the interested buyers in New York and London, as well as Asia. Once the buyout takes place, you'll have significant cash to invest. This would be a good time to review your estate plans as well.

Referring Mahaleel to two competitors, The Trust Company and Global Private Bank, he added:

> I've met an account officer from Global who called on me several times. Here's his business card; his name is Miguel Kim. I've never done any business with him, but he did seem quite competent. Unfortunately, I don't know anyone at the Trust Company, but here's their address in London.

After checking into his hotel in London the following Wednesday, Mahaleel telephoned Kim's office. Since Kim was out, Mahaleel spoke to the account officer's secretary, described himself briefly, and arranged to stop by Global's Lombard Street office around midmorning on Friday.

On Thursday, Mahaleel visited The Trust Company. The two people he met were extremely pleasant and had spent some time in Tailesia. They seemed very knowledgeable about managing estates and gave him some good recommendations about handling his complex family affairs. However, they were clearly less experienced in handling business credit, his most urgent need.

The next morning, Mahaleel had breakfast with Leona. As they parted, she said, "I'll meet you at 1:30 P.M. in the lobby of the Savoy Hotel, and we'll go to the recital together. We mustn't be late if we want to get front-row seats."

On his way to Global Private Bank, Mahaleel stopped at Mappin & Webb's jewelry store to buy his wife a present for their anniversary. His shopping was pleasant and leisurely; he purchased a beautiful emerald necklace that he knew his wife would like. When he emerged from the jewelry store, he was caught in an unexpected snow flurry. He had difficulty finding a taxi and his arthritis started acting up, making walking to the Global office out of the question. At last he caught a taxi and arrived at the Lombard Street location of Global Bancorp about noon. After going into the street-level branch of Global Retail Bank, he was redirected by a security guard to the Private Bank offices on the second floor.

He arrived at the nicely appointed reception area of the Private Bank at 12:15, where he was met by Miguel Kim's secretary, who told him:

Mr. Kim was disappointed that he couldn't be here to greet you, but he had a lunch appointment with one of his clients that was scheduled over a month ago. He expects to return about one o'clock. In the meantime, he has asked another senior account officer, Sophia Costa, to assist you.

Sophia Costa, 41, was a vice-president of the bank and had worked for Global Bancorp for 14 years, two years longer than Miguel Kim. She had visited Tailesia once, but had not met Mr. Mahaleel's financial advisor or any member of the Mahaleel family. An experienced relationship manager, Costa was knowledgeable about offshore investment management and fiduciary services.

Miguel Kim had looked into her office at 11:45 A.M. and asked her if she would cover for him in case a prospective client, a Mr. Mahaleel, whom he had expected to see earlier, should happen to arrive. He told Costa that Mahaleel was a successful Tailesian businessman planning for his retirement, but that he had never met the prospect personally. Then he rushed off to lunch.

GLOBAL CLIENT MANAGEMENT (B1)

The telephone rang in Peter Singer's London office. Singer was managing director of the European investment banking arm of Hart Grenfell. It was Friday, March 12, 1994, at 11:30 A.M.

> *Peter. This is Tony Gonzalez from the San Francisco office. There's a prospective client we're trying to contact to supply private wealth management services. Robert Stark. I hear you know him.*
>
> *Yes. What do you need?*
>
> *Would you be able to call him and give us an introduction. Stark's assets are concentrated with another company at the moment, but his key account manager just moved so we have an opportunity to go after this business.*

Singer wondered how to respond. He knew Stark well. They had been in the same class at business school 20 years earlier. Singer had successfully managed the placement of two IPOs for Stark's software companies in the early 1990s. During the past year, Stark had called Singer twice for informal advice on financial matters.

Singer had met Gonzalez but did not know him well. There were 150 partners in the firm. Gonzalez, aged 39, had become a partner in 1992, six years after Singer. Gonzalez had always worked in Hart Grenfell's asset management division. This was one of four lines of business at Hart Grenfell, the others being equities, fixed income, and investment banking. Hart Grenfell executives typically moved up the ranks to partner in one of the divisions; few executives moved from one line of business to another.

This case was prepared by John A. Quelch. Copyright © 1996 by the President and Fellows of Harvard College. Harvard Business School case 597-015.

BAUSCH & LOMB: REGIONAL ORGANIZATION

Daniel Gill, chairman and chief executive officer of Bausch & Lomb (B&L), a diversified multinational with sales of over $1.7 billion in 1992, believed that a change in organization structure was necessary to guide the further growth of B&L's international business. Despite a compound annual revenue growth rate of 17% since 1986 and an average return on sales of almost 10% over the same period, several internal problems had arisen that Gill attributed in large part to B&L's current organizational structure. The challenge was to manage B&L's rapid growth through an organizational structure that would respect the company's core values of autonomy and decentralization.

In 1992, Gill was considering creating an international organization structure based on three geographic regions: Europe, Asia/Pacific, and Western Hemisphere. However, he wanted to be sure that the organizational change would resolve the problems that had arisen, add value to customers, and enable the company to sustain a compound annual growth rate of at least 15%.

COMPANY BACKGROUND

In 1853, John Jacob Bausch, a German immigrant, opened a small optical goods store in Rochester, New York, and discovered a hard rubber called Vulcanite that could be used to make spectacle frames more durable and at lower cost than the metal and horn-rim frames then in use. By 1903, the company had added microscopes, binoculars, and telescopes to its eyeglass business and expanded its sales network and manufacturing capabilities. In the 1920s, B&L was asked by the U.S. government to develop an absorptive glass to help pilots overcome harsh glare conditions; the result, Ray-Ban sunglasses, quickly became a profitable business. Over the following three decades the company went public and developed several breakthrough optical products, such as the Os-

---

This case was prepared by Nathalie Laidler (under the direction of John A. Quelch). Certain proprietary data have been disguised. Copyright © 1993 by the President and Fellows of Harvard College. Harvard Business School case 594-056.

car-winning Cinemascope lens. Diversification via small company acquisitions expanded the product range to include scientific and industrial instruments, such as spectrometers and spectrophotometers,[1] which boosted sales to over $100 million by 1966.

In 1966, B&L purchased the rights to a contact lens made of hydrophilic material.[2] After five years of intensive product development, B&L received approval from the Food and Drug Administration (FDA) to launch the soft contact lens. Acquisitions and new investments reinforced B&L's dominant share of the contact lens and lens care products (including cleaning units and solutions). By 1981, when Gill was promoted to president and chief executive operating officer, the company's more traditional markets were experiencing increasing difficulty. Gill decided to exit the eyeglass business in 1981 and the industrial instrumentation business in 1984. In 1984, Gill also orchestrated a major organizational change, resulting in the creation of an International Division (ID).

THE INTERNATIONAL DIVISION

In 1983, B&L, with sales of $477 million,[3] had subsidiaries in 23 countries. Operations were organized into four worldwide product divisions: professional eye care products (contact lenses); personal products (contact lens solutions and accessories); consumer products (sunglasses and sports optics); and instruments. (Exhibit 1 depicts the organizational structure in 1983.) The four Rochester-based divisions had full functional capabilities and bottom-line accountability for their respective product lines.

---

[1]A spectrophotometer measures the relative intensities of the light in different parts of a spectrum.
[2]Hydrophilic material is a substance or material that has a strong affinity for water.
[3]Restated for 1984 writeoffs and discontinued lines.

The technology resided in the U.S. companies, which were each responsible for procurement, manufacturing, and R&D for the rest of the world.

In 1984, international sales accounted for 25% of the professional eye care division, 20% of the personal products division, 31% of the consumer products division, and 34% of the instruments division. International operations varied in size and sophistication, ranging from fully developed subsidiaries with product-specialized sales forces to distributor subsidiaries in which a handful of sales managers coordinated third-party distribution efforts. In the United States eye care and eyewear products were sold through seven different channels, whereas in most other countries opticians remained the dominant retail channel for both contact lenses and sunglasses.

The Drivers of Organizational Change

Headed by a country manager, each country subsidiary typically had a product manager and sales organization for each product line, resulting in duplication of selling effort and administrative inefficiencies. In 1984, for example, the French subsidiary was made up of three $10 million businesses, none of which had the critical mass of sales or earnings to retain quality management. Each product manager within a country reported to the worldwide product division manager at headquarters as well as to his or her country manager. Consequently, the country managers' decision-making power was low. B&L executives explained: "The problem was that no one had the authority to set priorities in a particular country and decide which business was more important."

By 1984, country managers started to complain that the U.S. divisions were not responding to their requests for specific products and/or were sending them products they did not want. On the other hand, Rochester-based product divisional managers, more focused on the de-

Exhibit 1   *Bausch & Lomb Organization: 1983**

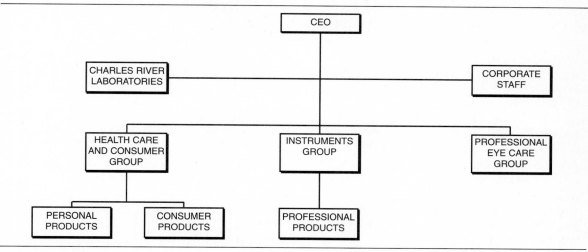

*Source: Company records.

mands of the U.S. market, protested that they could not customize their programs for each of 23 country managers. In addition, by 1984, some international subsidiaries had become larger than the smallest of B&L's seven U.S. businesses but had to go through two levels of decision making at headquarters to have their programs approved. In effect, the headquarters staff was slowing down the company's growth. Gill noted: "It was becoming increasingly apparent that B&L needed a better focus on its international business."

B&L asked the consulting group of Booz-Allen & Hamilton (BAH) to define organizational alternatives to best resolve these increasing conflicts. Following interviews with both Rochester-based and international staff, BAH proposed the creation of a new International Division with full functional capabilities. The ID was organized into regions encompassing a number of country subsidiaries, each run by a single country manager responsible for all B&L business in the country. (Exhibit 2 shows the new organizational structure.)

The shift to the ID was driven in part by a desire to achieve larger operating units in each country. The resulting benefits included a reduction in headcount and the emergence of a stronger country manager. The ID could now plan with each country manager how much emphasis should be placed on each product line and establish market-specific goals such as obtaining regulatory approval for lens care products. The achievement of these and other goals determined a country manager's bonuses.

Results of the ID Structure

By 1992, international sales accounted for almost 50% of B&L's revenues, having grown, on average, by 25% a year since 1987. B&L's international success was reflected by the market shares held by its major products outside the United States: B&L held over 25% of the contact lens market, over 40% of non-U.S. sales of high-quality sunglasses, and almost 25% of the lens solution market outside the United States.

Exhibit 2   *Bausch & Lomb Reorganization with International Division: August 1984**

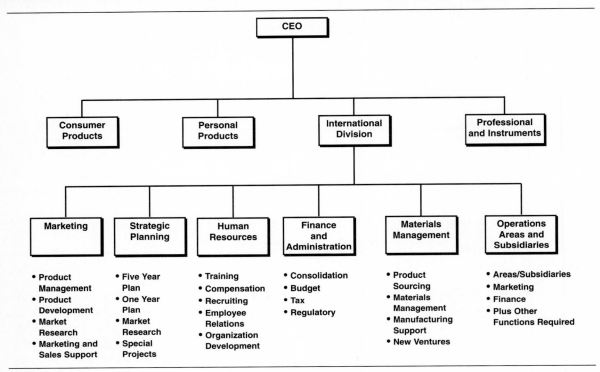

*Source: Company records.

B&L believed that this growth was driven largely by the entrepreneurship of local country managers. B&L executives explained:

> *Prior to 1985, we were a U.S. business with what we regarded as sales affiliates in international markets. After the creation of the ID, we recognized the importance of our international subsidiaries and chose a single country manager who could lead and develop each subsidiary.*

Selecting country managers proved difficult; it was hard to find managers equally excited about the challenge and competent enough to market fashion-intensive products such as Ray-Bans and technology-intensive lens care products. Most candidates had emerged from the lens care

business but, by 1992, fewer than 50% of the country managers who predated the ID were still in place. Gill was determined to find skilled, entrepreneurial country managers who could put into practice B&L's philosophy of "making every decision as close to the customer as possible."

The benefits of the ID included an expansion of international production facilities, faster response to local country and new capacity needs, and increased market shares and penetration in overseas markets. One B&L executive noted:

> *Prior to the ID, if a product division manager at headquarters had difficulty getting into a country market due to tariff restrictions, that particular country would have been ignored.*

Had the organization not changed, countries such as China, India, and Mexico would never have been developed by B&L.

THE SITUATION IN 1992

During the 1980s, B&L exited certain cyclical industrial product businesses and acquired growing, high-margin businesses with strong brand names (such as Interplak, a line of plaque-removing instruments). By 1992, B&L was focused on two business areas: Healthcare and Optics. Healthcare products, accounting for 60% of 1992 sales, included personal health products (lens care, oral care, eye care, and medications), medical products (contact lenses, prescription pharmaceuticals, and hearing care), and biomedical products. Optics, accounting for 40% of sales in 1992, included sunglasses, sports optics (binoculars and telescopes), and optical thin-film coatings that improved light

performance in medically related markets such as operating rooms. (Exhibit 3 lists the main products in each line and their sales volumes in 1992.)

B&L's major international product lines fell into two business segments: the Eyewear business, comprising mainly sunglasses; and the Vision Care business, comprising contact lenses and lens care products (contact lens solutions).

Eyewear

In 1992, sunglasses represented 75% of B&L's total Optical sales. B&L Ray-Ban sunglasses, making up over 98% of all B&L sunglasses sales, were considered to be global in appeal and availability; similar benefits were valued by consumers throughout the world regardless of the stage of economic development of the geographic market. In the early 1980s, B&L sunglasses were sold predominantly through opticians in the United States. However, by 1992,

Exhibit 3   *Bausch & Lomb Sales by Principal Product Lines: 1992**

	1992 Sales ($ millions)	Percentage Non-U.S.
Healthcare		
Personal:	$540	33%
Lens care products		
Oral care products		
Eye care products		
OTC medications		
Medical:	341	47
Contact lenses		
Prescription pharmaceuticals		
Hearing care		
Biomedical (Charles River Labs)	155	NA
Optics		
Sunglasses	500	53
Sports optics	100	35
Optical thin films	25	50

*Source: Company records.

sunglasses were no longer merely functional products but also fashion products, sold through a broad range of outlets including department stores and duty-free shops. B&L believed that this trend would also subsequently occur outside the United States, where sunglasses continued to be sold mainly through opticians.

In 1992, U.S. manufacturing supplied 70% of Ray-Ban's worldwide unit sales and 40% of international unit sales. Production facilities outside the United States included Waterford, Ireland, where plastic sunglasses were manufactured and all sunglasses could be assembled; Pforzheim, Germany, where metal parts were manufactured for European products; and Hong Kong, where there was an assembly plant. The B&L sunglasses product line comprised 350 stockkeeping units (SKUs)—a figure that had been constant for the past three to four years. Approximately 100 SKUs were replaced each year; it was estimated that, in 1993, 15% of sales would be derived from these new products. Headquarters R&D served all Ray-Ban markets.

Vision Care

Worldwide sales of contact lenses approached $300 million in 1992. Major brands included B&L traditional soft contact lenses; SeeQuence disposable soft lenses, designed to be discarded after being worn for one or two weeks; Medalist planned-replacement soft lenses, designed to be changed every one to six months; Quantum rigid gas-permeable lenses; and Boston Envision rigid gas-permeable lenses. B&L held 25% of the world market for contact lenses and planned to grow through new product development and geographical expansion. The SeeQuence line was strong in the United States, and B&L hoped to develop the Japanese and selected European markets. The Quantum line was strong in Europe and Asia, and the Boston Envision line had, in 1992, been heavily promoted in Latin America.

In 1992, lens care products worldwide sales were over $350 million, of which 67% came from North America, 16% from both Europe and Asia, and 1% from Latin America. B&L's ReNu multipurpose solution was the world's most advanced product for the care of soft contact lenses, and worldwide sales had risen from $57 million in 1988 to $152 million in 1992. The Boston line solutions were used with rigid gas-permeable lenses, and 1992 worldwide sales reached $66 million. B&L believed that the lens care market had become more technology driven and that more marketing and educational programs needed to be directed at eye care professionals. B&L supplied eye care professionals with care kits for new contact lens wearers and estimated that more than 80% of patients who started out using a B&L kit became loyal, long-term buyers of B&L lens care products. B&L intended to continue to streamline and simplify lens care regimens. Lens care sales depended highly on the volume of contact lens sales, and the marketing synergies between the two product lines were recognized and exploited.

Vision Care products were manufactured in Germany, Ireland, Italy, and the United States. B&L planned to open manufacturing facilities for soft contact lenses and lens care products in both India and China.

B&L Strengths

Gill described the company's strengths in 1992:

> *B&L has superior technology that results in quality products. Eighty-five percent of our sales are in product categories where B&L is the world leader. During the 1980s, investments were made to upgrade manufacturing facilities, so now B&L is the low-cost producer in the main categories we compete in.*

B&L executives described the company as highly goal-oriented and decentralized, unique in its managers' willingness to challenge the status quo and to do whatever it took to get a job done. Gill was seen as a catalyst for change; he communicated to employees that change was a way of life at B&L. Key managers were promoted through a variety of roles, broadening them beyond their areas of functional expertise and developing a top management team of seasoned generalists.

The main company driver was technology and the ability to narrow the time between conceptualization and commercialization of products. Future success depended on developing better products more quickly. R&D and productivity issues were expected to remain critical to B&L's success.

In marketing its products to consumers, B&L placed more emphasis on gaining the support of professional intermediaries such as opticians than on advertising. One B&L executive explained:

> We are not a typical consumer marketing company. We emphasize push rather than pull marketing. For example, we focus on educating dental professionals to recommend our Interplak product line, and we still rely heavily on opticians to recommend Ray-Bans even though they are now also sold through department stores.

Problems with the ID Structure

By 1990, a growing number of internal challenges had arisen. The U.S. domestic divisions and ID made separate marketing and manufacturing decisions. As a result, brands such as Ray-Ban sunglasses and B&L contact lenses could not be managed globally. Pricing disparities raised important diversion problems. For example, a typical pair of Ray-Ban sunglasses that sold to the trade for $25 in the United States were sold for $60 to the trade by B&L France. A pair of contact lenses that sold to the trade for $6.70 in the United States would be sold in Japan for over $30. Due to the high value-to-bulk ratio of these products, some distributors reshipped product bought in the United States to other countries for resale at below B&L's suggested prices, often through unauthorized channels. It was estimated that as much as 30% of U.S. Ray-Ban sunglass sales may have been diverted in this way.

Tensions between the ID and U.S. domestic divisions increased as the latter were criticized for shortchanging the ID of R&D and manufacturing resources. In addition, manufacturing plants tended to set production schedules without sufficient concern for the optimal allocation of global capacity. As the ID expanded, it gained increasing influence relative to the domestic U.S. divisions which, by 1990, were affected by a downturn in the U.S. economy.

Gill described the impact of these problems:

> Some competitors were fighting us globally, but we were only responding to them as local competitors. The lack of communication between the ID and U.S. divisions meant that we did not see that Johnson & Johnson was attacking us in the disposable lens business worldwide, not just in the domestic market. Incentive plans were geographically based so, for example, the Irish plant manager would not cut production on items that could be manufactured more cheaply in the United States, because this would have caused negative manufacturing variances and lowered his bonus. The culture at B&L has always been very profit-driven.

Country managers from France, Italy, and Spain complained that decisions were made too far away and too slowly. Optimization of manufacturing capacity worldwide and standardization of product quality levels were not being achieved. Some B&L executives believed that the successful growth of the ID had resulted in an increasing central bureaucracy in Rochester that was not responsive to local subsidiaries.

Gill's inclination was to push decision making down the organization and increase the autonomy of B&L's international subsidiaries. He believed that an organizational change was inevitable, given the rapid growth of international operations. However, it was clear that certain issues, such as global pricing, would require increased cross-border coordination in tandem with decentralization.

REGIONALIZATION

In January 1991, a task force was established to generate and review alternative organizational structures that would help resolve the conflicts and allow B&L to continue its international expansion. The B&L task force, working with McKinsey consultants, set three parameters for its work: speed of results, process to be driven by B&L executives, and input from as many B&L employees as possible. Some B&L executives were skeptical about the need for change, remarking that, in its international businesses, B&L had achieved a 25% compound annual growth rate (CAGR) and margins between 15% and 20% in the early 1990s. They argued: "If it ain't broke, why fix it?"

The Task Force

Six key B&L employees were assigned to the task force. They included the vice-president of marketing from the Polymer Technology Division, the vice-president of business development from the Eyewear Division, the vice-president of international marketing from the ID, the U.S. controller from the Personal Products Division, the staff vice-president of financial planning and analysis from corporate headquarters, and a senior executive who had just completed a Harvard Business School senior executive program and who became chair of the task force. The project comprised three phases: information gathering via over 20 workshops and 150 interviews with B&L employees worldwide, further in-depth interviews on issues raised in the first phase, the development of a list of organizational options, and a further refinement of the most attractive options. The team reported periodically to an Advisory Committee of corporate officers and eventually prepared final recommendations for the Management Executive Committee. The whole process was completed within seven months.

The project team concluded that the current organizational structure was no longer appropriate, given B&L's growing international revenues. The team considered several organizational options. These were, in order of the degree of change involved, fine-tuning of the current organization structure, a regional structure, a product-region matrix, and a global product structure. (These options are depicted in Exhibit 4.)

The Proposed Organizational Change

The Advisory Committee rejected the fine-tuning option: although it would be easy to implement (low risk and low cost), it did not improve the focus on specific businesses within the international division. The matrix organization offered a balance between a geographic and a business focus while resulting in little structural change at the subsidiary level. However, it was felt to be contrary to B&L's cultural emphasis on clear decision-making responsibility and, as a result, potentially confusing and difficult to implement. The regional and global product organizational structures were considered more favorably. (The pros and cons of each are summarized in Table A.)

The regional structure was eventually selected because it helped achieve B&L's strategic objectives and resolved key issues. In addition, it was thought to be flexible enough to accommodate subsequent revision if necessary.

In effect, the ID would be eliminated and replaced by three autonomous, self-contained regional headquarters: Europe, Middle East, and Africa; Asia/Pacific; and Western Hemisphere. The three regional presidents were expected to ensure that their countries' new product ideas and needs were developed quickly and that an integrated strategy was developed for each business line in the countries in their respective regions, approved by corporate headquarters.

Of the 160 people currently employed by the ID, it was expected that 50% would be reassigned to one of the three regional headquarters,

Exhibit 4   *Bausch & Lomb Organizational Options Considered by the Task Force: 1992**

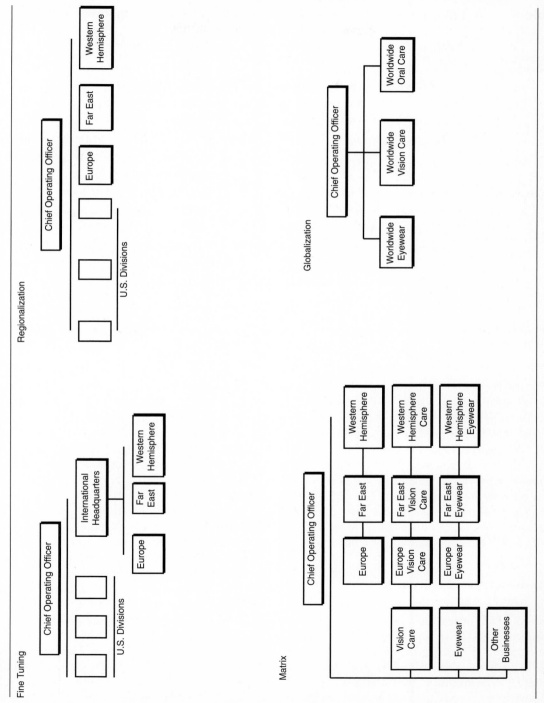

Fine Tuning

Regionalization

Globalization

Matrix

*Source: Company records.

Table A   Pros and Cons of the Regionalization and Globalization Options

	Pros	Cons
Globalization	• Improves coordination • Captures U.S. lens/lens care synergies • Provides individual business focus • Develops global managers • Fosters global-oriented decision making	• Reduces responsibilities of regions and countries • Decision making driven by the United States • Makes it difficult to capture synergies between international eyewear and vision care sales forces[a]
Regionalization	• Improves coordination • Moderate structural change • Elevates role of region presidents • Increases focus on non-U.S. operations • Provides global thinking • Moves decision making closer to markets	• Lack of product line focus • No cross-regional integration • Wide COO span of control • Dual role of regional presidents as corporate executives and champions of their respective regions

[a]In many international markets, eyewear and vision care product lines were marketed through the same distribution channels by different sales forces.

25% to corporate headquarters in MIS and finance positions, and 25% to the various U.S. divisions. Several B&L companies, including Charles River Laboratories ($155 million in annual sales), Sports Optics Division ($100 million), and Thin Film Technology ($25 million) would maintain separate responsibility for their operations outside the United States. The organization of U.S. operations would remain unchanged and structured around product lines. Almost all of B&L's R&D would remain in the United States.

Committees and Networks

To coordinate decision making between the regions and U.S. operations, business management committees (BMCs) and global business networks (GBNs) were conceived. Three BMCs would meet the need for high-level worldwide strategic coordination for B&L's three core product lines: Eyewear (sunglasses), Oral Care, and Vision Care (contact lenses and solutions). These BMCs would maintain communication of the individual division's strategic imperatives, identify elements of strategy of global importance, such as Ray-Ban sunglass and contact lens pricing, and coordinate initiatives and resolve conflicts with a common global perspective. The members of BMCs would include the U.S. division presidents, the regional presidents, and B&L's president and chief operating officer (COO) of the company. The latter's role would be to ensure that more decisions were made at the BMC level than in the Executive Committee.

Five GBNs were conceived, covering marketing and operations functions: Oral Care Marketing and Operations, Eyewear Operations, Eyewear Marketing, Vision Care Operations, and Vision Care Marketing. The purpose of the GBNs would be to facilitate communication across functions and to identify and coordinate decision making on issues of global importance.

As indicated in Exhibit 5, network participants would be senior middle managers with specific functional responsibilities drawn from both the U.S. divisions and the regional headquarters. For example, GBN participants might include the vice-president of operations from the Western Hemisphere Division, the vice-president of marketing from the Eyewear Division, and the vice-president of marketing from the European

Division. The responsibility for chairing each GBN would rotate every 18 months among the network members. GBNs would meet at least three times a year in addition to frequent tele-conferencing and video-conferencing. (Exhibit 6 outlines a sample agenda for an Eyewear Marketing Network meeting.)

The BMCs and GBNs were regarded as critical to the new organizational structure. B&L ex-

---

Exhibit 5   *Network Members*

Eyewear Operations Network
VP–Operations, Western Hemisphere (Chairman)
VP–Manufacturing, Eyewear Division
Director-Materials, Eyewear Division
VP–RD&E, Eyewear Division
VP–Quality, Eyewear Division
VP–Operations, Asia/Pacific Division
General Manager, B&L Ireland Sunglass

Eyewear Marketing Network
VP–Marketing, Eyewear Division
VP–Eyewear Marketing, Western Hemisphere Division
Director, Consumer Products, B&L Japan
VP–Eyewear Marketing, Europe Division
VP–Sales, Eyewear Division
VP–Worldwide New Product Marketing, Eyewear Division
Marketing Director, East Asia Region, Asia/Pacific Division
Market Research and Services Manager, Eyewear Division

Vision Care Operations Network
VP–Operations, Personal Products Division (Chairman)
VP–Operations, Contact Lens Division
Director-Manufacturing Operations, Polymer Technology Corporation
VP–Operations, Europe Division
VP–Operations, Asia/Pacific Division
VP–Operations, Western Hemisphere Division

Vision Care Marketing Network
VP and GM, Contact Lens Division (Chairman)
VP–Vision Care Marketing, Western Hemisphere Division
VP–Vision Care Marketing, Europe Division
VP–U.S. & Int'l Operations, Polymer Technology Corporation
Director–Marketing, Asia/Pacific Division
Marketing Product Manager–Contact Lenses, B&L Japan

Oral Care Network

VP–International Oral Care (Chairman)
VP–Operations, Oral Care Division
Division Director, Oral Care Division, B&L Canada
VP–Operations, Asia/Pacific
VP–Marketing, Oral Care Division

VP-Oral Care Marketing, Europe Division
Director Engineering/ Development-Oral Care Division
Director–Oral Care Business, B&L Japan
Manager–Oral Care, B&L Netherlands
Director–International Oral Care

ecutives sought to ensure that participation on these committees would be seen as an honor and that participation should be included in job descriptions and evaluation criteria. Some executives questioned how many GBNs should be set up and what issues they should address. On the one hand, B&L wanted to avoid too many networks, since this might result in confusion, second-guessing, and waste of management time. At the same time, executives in charge of functions such as quality control and regulatory compliance also wanted the status of having GBNs that would address their issues.

Gill believed that the effectiveness of the BMCs and GBNs would depend largely on each chairperson's leadership capabilities and coordination abilities. He felt that different product lines would benefit to varying degrees from the increased coordination. For example, lens solutions were subject to local regulations, and there appeared to be a limited opportunity for cross-regional or country transfer. On the other hand, contact lens solutions in the United States had moved from prescription status to widespread over-the-counter (OTC) distribution. This transition was thought likely to occur in other countries, and B&L executives believed that substantial information and expertise could be transferred from the United States to other countries to prepare for these market developments. In the case of sunglasses, the worldwide introductions of new product lines appropriately adapted to different markets would require considerable coordination.

The designated chairperson of the Vision Care Marketing Network did not anticipate any coordination problems within the network. He explained:

> There are no really contentious issues. The minor issues that may come up will be resolved pretty quickly. My guess is that the network will be highly cooperative. One reason is that, in the past, there have been no strong disagreements on marketing strategy in the vision care field.

The prospective chairperson of the Eyewear Marketing Network had a different view. He stated:

> One of the main issues at B&L is the relationship between the United States and ID concerning Ray-Ban sunglasses. It will take some time before network members start communicating, given the current level of distrust. Eventually the network will be able to add value because we will be able to create a common agenda and a clear set of goals. Achieving this however, will take time and effort.

Exhibit 6   *Sample Agenda for an Eyewear Marketing Network Meeting*

Role of Marketing Network
- Communication
- Coordination

Key Projects
- Coordination of market research
- Quality standards
- Bench-marking
- Pricing
- Warranty/returns
- Strategic plan volumes
- UV Issue[a]

Secondary Projects
- Opinion leaders of the 1990s

Core principles

New products

Review of financial results by region

Competition

---

[a]The U.V. (ultraviolet) issue concerns the holographic markings that could be used to identify the distributor source of product and reduce product diversion.

Benefits and Challenges

Regionalization was expected, first, to empower regional and country managers and encourage entrepreneurship in country subsidiaries. The transfer of marketing, product planning, and operational-support functions to the regions would enhance B&L's capabilities in the field. Support functions would be closer to the customer, enabling subsidiaries to respond quickly to local customer needs. Second, the increased emphasis placed by B&L on international experience would enable the company to create a pool of global managers to become future leaders in the company. Third, the BMCs and GBNs would stimulate communication within the company, facilitate worldwide strategic planning, and transfer the best ideas and practices to markets everywhere. Finally, it was expected that regionalization would encourage further sales growth in international markets, because regional managers would be more likely than the ID to focus on untapped country markets within their regions.

Gill believed that the key to growth and success lay with B&L's country general managers. The 27 subsidiary managers had been increasingly frustrated by the slow decision making of the Rochester-based ID. Regionalization would enable them to have decisions discussed and approved more quickly.

At the same time, there was concern that regionalization would not resolve the fundamental challenges facing B&L in 1992. First, it was not clear that the necessary coordination between U.S. product divisions and international operations would be achieved through the BMCs and GBNs. Under the current ID structure, a special staff liaised between the country organizations and the Rochester-based product managers. Under regionalization, each region would deal directly with U.S.-based product divisions, possibly adding to the complexity of coordination. In addition, the B&L culture, based on decentralization, entrepreneurship, and accountability, obviously did not mesh with the coordination culture required to make the BMCs and GBNs work effectively. Several B&L executives believed that the success of regionalization would depend on the success of the

BMCs and GBNs and that clarifying their terms of reference, membership obligations, and ability to implement decisions was critical.

Second, as the country subsidiaries continued to grow, the regional headquarters, particularly in Europe, could become obstacles to speedy decision making, just as the ID had become. As subsidiaries grew both in volume and product-line complexity, country general managers would have less time to oversee each particular product line. The same span-of-control problem might be true of regional presidents who would have to manage a growing number of ever-expanding country subsidiaries.

From the consumer perspective, potential benefits of the reorganization included products that would be locally adapted, higher service levels, more consistent positioning, and more new products brought to market faster. B&L intended to discontinue the traditional approach of rolling out a new product one market at a time in favor of simultaneous introductions in several countries across all regions.

REGIONAL ORGANIZATION AND MARKETING EFFECTIVENESS

The impact of the regional organization on the marketing function was expected to vary by region. In Europe, it was expected that there would be three marketing vice-presidents covering Oral Care, Vision Care, and Eyewear. Asia was thought to be behind Europe on the development curve, and, due to greater diversity of markets, a standard regional marketing approach seemed less likely. The regional marketing staff might specialize geographically, with some executives focusing on more-developed markets like Japan and others focusing on emerging markets like China, Malaysia, the Philippines, and Taiwan. In GBNs such as the Vision Care Marketing Network, it seemed likely that more than one marketing manager from Asia would have to be included. At the same time, there appeared to be more hitherto unexploited marketing coordination opportunities in the Asia/Pacific region than in Europe.

There was concern that the Western Hemisphere region would lack the critical mass to warrant a regional marketing organization. Canada, although included in the region, had frequent contact with U.S. operations because of geographical proximity and market similarity. For example, the contact lens solutions business in Canada was OTC driven (the only other country apart from the United States where this was true). While Canada's role in the new Western Hemisphere remained unclear, Latin America had been a "lost continent" under the ID structure and was expected to benefit from the visibility that regionalization would provide. Marketing in Latin American subsidiaries focused more on the basics of sales and distribution, whereas strategic marketing issues were equally important in the European subsidiaries.

In 1992, 27 subsidiaries, 6 joint ventures (China, Indonesia, Korea, Hong Kong, India, and Japan), and many national distributors sold B&L products around the world. Additional export operations existed in Geneva for Africa and the Middle East; in Miami for smaller Latin American countries; and in Hong Kong for East Asia. (Exhibit 7 lists the subsidiaries and joint ventures by region.)

Product Development

Prior to regionalization, all new product development decisions regarding which technologies and fashion trends to pursue were made in Rochester. ID Headquarters developed the products and marketing programs that were launched around the world. Under regionalization, each region would have its own product development team and be able to develop unique products for its own markets if it made economic sense. If a product manager in France had a new product idea that the French country manager endorsed, the idea's regional and worldwide potential would then be evaluated at

European headquarters. If the idea was deemed to have worldwide potential, the vice-president of marketing for Europe would present the idea to the relevant GBN. The U.S.-based development group, also represented on the GBN, would give priority to those ideas that promised to generate the most profits worldwide. Ideas specific to a single, small market would receive the lowest priority. The development group would then prepare production plans and decide where the product would be manufactured.

R&D groups in Rochester handled the various B&L product lines. If a subsidiary wished to develop, at its own expense, a local packaging variation that had no medical or regulatory implications, it would be able to do so under regionalization. If, however, the desired variation held implications for product stability (as, for example, in a switch from polyethylene to clear plastic containers for contact lens solutions), R&D groups in Rochester would have to be involved.

Market Research and Advertising

Under the ID structure, B&L's eyewear businesses outside the United States had sought out an advertising agency that not only could implement a global campaign but also be a global strategic partner. Young and Rubicam was selected as the Eyewear agency of record for all international subsidiaries and subsequently improved the coordination of advertising strategy around the world. A pool of print executions and television commercials with voiceovers was available to subsidiaries; they could also shoot commercials locally at their own expense, subject to ID approval. The process of formulating advertising strategy was not expected to change very much under regionalization, although it was expected that the European region, in concert with Young and Rubicam, would play a leadership role in copy development and that the other regions would follow suit. Some B&L executives believed that this would not result

Exhibit 7 *B&L Subsidiaries by Operational Activity: 1984–1992*

	Manufacturing			Marketing		
	1984	**1992**[a]		**1984**	**1992**[a]	
United States	21	25		0	5	
Bermuda	0	0		0	3	W.O.
Brazil	0	2	W.O.	0	2	W.O.
Canada	1	1	W.O.	2	2	W.O.
Colombia	0	0		0	1	W.O.
Mexico	0	1	MIN	0	1	MIN
Puerto Rico	0	0		1	1	W.O.
Venezula	0	0		0	1	W.O.
Austria	0	0		1	1	W.O.
Belgium	0	1	MAJ	0	0	
Czechoslovakia	0	1	W.O.	0	0	
Denmark	0	0		1	1	W.O.
Finland	0	0		1	1	W.O.
France	1	2	W.O./MAJ	1	1	W.O.
Germany	0	8	W.O.	0	1	W.O.
Great Britain	1	3	W.O.	1	3	W.O.
Greece	0	0		0	1	BRC (W.O.)
Hungary	0	1	W.O.	0	0	
Ireland[b]	1	1		0	0	BRC (W.O.)
Italy	2	2	W.O./MAJ	2	2	W.O., BRC (W.O.)
Netherlands	0	0	W.O.	0	1	W.O.
Norway	0	1		1	1	W.O.
Portugal	0	0		0	1	
Spain	0	2	MAJ/W.O.	1	1	W.O.
Sweden	0	0		1	1	W.O.
Switzerland	0	1	W.O.	2	2	W.O.
Australia	0	0		1	1	W.O.
Hong Kong	1	1	W.O.	1	0	
India	0	1	MIN	0	1[c]	
Indonesia	0	1	MAJ	0	1	MAJ
Japan	2	2	MIN/W.O.	1	1[c]	
Malaysia	0	1	W.O.	0	0	
New Zealand	0	0		0	1	W.O.
P.R. of China	0	1	MAJ	0	0	
Philippines	0	0		1	0	
Singapore	0	0		1	1	W.O.
South Korea	0	1	MAJ	0	0	
Taiwan	1	2	MAJ/W.O.	1	0	
Turkey	0	0		0	1	W.O.

[a]Type of subisidiary (1992): W.O. = wholly owned; MAJ = joint venture with majority ownership; MIN = joint venture with minority ownership; BRC (W.O.) = branch, wholly owned; DIS = distributor.
[b]Bausch & Lomb Ireland was a branch of Bausch & Lomb (Bermuda) Limited.
[c]Planned for startup in 1992.

in consistent global advertising. Subsidiaries would still be able to use local advertising developed at their expense, subject to regional headquarters approval.

There were no market research studies carried out in a consistent manner worldwide. It was hoped that the GBNs would be able to establish standardized market research tracking studies for each product line. Increasingly, product managers wanted to understand consumer trends in other geographical markets beyond their own and believed that market information gathered in a consistent way around the world would help. Recent market research, used to develop advertising copy strategies for sunglasses, had shown that very similar consumer drivers were at work in both France and the United States.

The B&L logo and most brand names were not expected to change. Some brand name variation across country markets might be rationalized. For example, the U.S. contact lens ReNu solution was marketed as ReNew in France and as Multipurpose in four other European countries.

Pricing

In 1992, the U.S. Eyewear Division's sales of sunglasses and manufacturing capacity utilization were being boosted by substantial product diversion. Distributors buying product in the United States could profitably resell a portion of their purchases in overseas markets where B&L factory prices were often higher than in the United States. U.S. Eyewear executives believed that to control diversion, they might have to discontinue about 15 U.S. distributors, resulting in a loss in revenues of approximately $30 million for the U.S. Division. It was hoped that the BMCs, with the help of the COO, would be able to coordinate pricing strategies and worldwide distribution to minimize product diversion. For example, to discourage diversion by permitting identification of the distributor source of product, each product could be marked with an invisible holographic marking that became clear under ultraviolet light.

IMPACT ON THE EYEWEAR AND VISION CARE BUSINESSES

Eyewear

B&L's Ray-Ban brand had benefited from the ID organization. Worldwide sales of Ray-Ban had skyrocketed from $60 million to over $500 million between 1985 and 1992, corresponding to a 30% compound annual growth rate. Under the ID's auspices, Ray-Ban sunglasses with fittings adapted to Asian faces had been developed for the Asian market. In addition, a new product development group had recently been established to determine where new products should be made and to help manufacturing plants reduce product start-up costs. Product development times had been reduced from 12 to 5 months, and ideas for changes in product design were solicited from B&L marketing executives worldwide. R&D and design were gradually becoming more customer driven. Consumer dissatisfaction with lenses that scratched had resulted in R&D developing a diamond-hard, nonscratchable lens. Development objectives for 1993 included a line for women aged over 30 years, based on a brief from marketing.

B&L Eyewear executives in Rochester believed Ray-Ban was a global brand that required global coordination of pricing and advertising strategies. Consequently, they felt that a worldwide product division headquartered in the United States was preferable to a regional organization that would encourage the regional presidents to build independent fiefdoms with their own manufacturing plants, design teams, and other functions. Despite being recognized throughout the world, there was no worldwide positioning or advertising strategy for the Ray-Ban brand. Under regionalization, this was likely to continue. There was also skepticism that regionalization would help resolve the pricing and diversion problems. Some executives feared that the GBNs such as the Eyewear Marketing Network might focus on old problems rather than new ways to share information and leverage good ideas. Under the ID structure, there were two decision-making entities, the United States and the ID, both located in Rochester. With regionalization, there would be four decision-making entities in different locations, adding to the complexity of communication and coordination.

Vision Care

Country markets varied in both preference and regulations governing the different kinds of lenses and chemical specifications of lens care solutions. Contact lenses in particular had to be adapted to meet specific country regulations. Lens care products also had specific packaging and labeling requirements depending upon the country. Neither product line could, in 1992, be described as global. Vision Care executives believed that regionalization would substantially benefit the business. However, some B&L executives argued that country-specific differences were still important, reflecting varying stages of market development, and that most markets would likely follow product trends set in the United States.

IMPACT ON THE EUROPEAN REGION

Regionalization would aid independent and faster decision making in Europe, the largest region. Money would be saved through the consolidation of certain back-room functions at the regional office and through regional sourcing of standard data processing and other equipment to be used in the country offices in the region. In addition, regionalization promised that new product initiatives could be pursued and launched in Europe even if the United States was not interested. The regional marketing manager would coordinate the development of pan-European strategies and marketing programs where consistency was considered appropriate and/or saved money. For example, common European product catalogs could be developed.

The European regional headquarters was expected to grow from 16 to 35 people. Most of the new positions would be in accounting and finance, since the European headquarters would consolidate results for the region before forwarding them to Rochester. Eight people would work in marketing, including three vice-presidents, each overseeing one of B&L's main product lines, and a vice-president of business development.

Following regionalization, the marketing manager of a country subsidiary such as France would participate in shaping regional marketing strategies and setting new product development priorities in conjunction with the European regional headquarters in London. The French marketing manager would report to a country general manager, as before, who in turn would report to the vice-president of field operations of B&L Europe. Product managers for all the country subsidiaries in a region would meet three or four times a year, in addition to a formal annual regional meeting. Sales and brand contribution in their own markets would remain the basis for their compensation while, at the country-manager level, 25% of the annual bonus would be based on pan-European performance to encourage coordination and communication.

Ray-Ban sunglasses had a similar brand image throughout Europe and a dominant market share of the premium sunglasses market in most European countries. In 1992, sales growth was derived from expansion into new distribution channels (such as airport duty-free shops) and new product development. The ability to influence new product development was considered by B&L executives in Europe to be critical to future growth. Contact lens solutions were also believed to represent an important growth opportunity in Europe. Idea transfers from the United States through the GBNs were expected to be useful, particularly for the ReNew product.

Conclusion

The principal issue for senior B&L executives was how to manage the company's international growth. Under the seven-year period of the ID, the subsidiaries' average annual revenues had grown from $20 million to $55 million, but some executives believed that the subsidiaries could have grown even faster had they been able to take more initiative in generating and developing their own marketing ideas. These executives hoped that the three regional headquarters would push more decision-making responsibility onto the subsidiaries.

HEWLETT-PACKARD CO.: EUROPEAN REMARKETING OPERATION

On November 8, 1991, Didier Philippe, European general manager of Hewlett-Packard's Finance and Remarketing Division (FRD) arrived early at his Geneva office for a meeting to discuss the future marketing strategy and organization of FRD's European Remarketing Operation (ERO). The mission of ERO was to refurbish and market used Hewlett-Packard (HP) equipment. Refurbishing for all of Europe was done in a plant at Boeblingen, Germany, while program managers located in individual European countries provided field-marketing support to HP's direct sales forces in the countries.

Recently, however, some program managers began marching to a different drumbeat. Instead of just remarketing used HP products sourced from the German plant, they began to act as local brokers, buying and reselling used HP equipment in their local markets. This trend provoked a blizzard of memos involving Geneva, Boeblingen, and the field.

Didier Philippe was considering several alternatives for ERO. One option was to close the central factory and hand over all operations and marketing responsibility to the country program managers. At the other end of the spectrum, he could replace the country program managers with an expanded pan-European marketing staff in Boeblingen. A middle-of-the-road option would seek further cooperation between Boeblingen and the field, redefine respective roles, and fine-tune marketing execution.

As Axel Wolff, ERO marketing manager from Boeblingen, was announced by the receptionist, Philippe reflected on a recent memo to Axel sent by Albert Solal, France program manager:

Axel,

I'm glad you identified "misunderstandings about the current focus and future direction of the local business." It was about time. I see two fundamental ambiguities regarding ERO's contribution to HP:

1. There are inherent conflicts of interest between ERO and country sales force objec-

---

tives. We are stuck in the middle. By assigning P&L responsibility to program managers, it's a cinch they'll try to maximize their profits locally even if it hurts ERO's bottom line. People on my team generate greater margins by reselling used equipment that they buy on the French open market than when they buy the same items from Boeblingen. Also, if you ask program managers to satisfy their customers, they'll put the interests of the domestic sales reps and their customers ahead of ERO's. It's difficult enough for me to convince French management that ERO works for them without being viewed as Mata Hari.[1] Where should my allegiance lie?

2. *There is a mismatch between the program managers' job description and the type of individuals hired to fill these positions. I took this job with the promise that I would run a P&L for HP. However, any moron can see that transfer prices and allocated costs rain monthly without human intervention. There are now five program managers in the European HP country offices[2] with a total of more than 30 years of experience. If you limit their role to that of an electronic mail box between ERO and the country sales forces, and if you ask them to sell antique products, you'll soon have to manage relationships with only four program managers . . . you don't really need me. French-speaking telemarketing reps located in Boeblingen could do the job just as well.*

Philippe was anxious to keep the meeting under control. Minutes later, Solal was announced.

---

[1]Mata Hari was a famous German spy during World War I. She was executed by the French.

[2]European country offices included France, Germany, Italy, the Netherlands, and the U.K.

INDUSTRY AND COMPANY BACKGROUND

Hewlett-Packard Co., with fiscal 1991 revenues of $14.5 billion,[3] was one of the world's leading manufacturers of electronic products and systems for measurement and computation (see Exhibit 1 for financial data). The company was founded in 1939 by two electrical engineers from Stanford, Bill Hewlett and Dave Packard, to design the world's first audio oscillator. Throughout its history, HP remained engineering driven, competing on the basis of technological features. In the past, HP had not been known for savvy marketing; it was sometimes said that "if HP made sushi, they'd market it as dead, cold fish."

The 1990s presented HP with an increasingly challenging environment. Overall growth in the electronics industry slowed as a result of a decline in U.S. capital spending, overcapacity in the computer industry, and reduced defense spending. As growth slowed, shorter product life cycles, a greater number of low-cost foreign competitors, and the movement toward "open" or nonproprietary information systems intensified competition.

Figure 1 illustrates the key role new products played in HP's growth. Each bar indicates the year's total product orders, with the top section of each bar showing orders for those products introduced in that year. More than half the 1991 orders were for products introduced in the preceding two years. Expenditures on new product development were 10% of sales.

Customers were also demanding greater returns on their computing and measurement investments. A general trend to downsize data centers and distribute corporate applications onto cheaper platforms affected mainframe vendors. HP's computers were increasingly challenged by networks of personal computers and workstations. In addition, more customers were

---

[3]HP's fiscal year ended on October 31.

Exhibit 1A *Hewlett-Packard Co. Financial Highlights: 1989–1991*

For the Years Ended October 31

In $ Millions Except Per Share Amount	1991	1990	1989
Total orders	$14,676	$13,495	$12,160
Net revenue	14,494	13,233	11,899
Research and development	1,463	1,367	1,269
Earnings from operations	1,210	1,162	1,212
Net earnings	755	739	829
Net earnings per share	3.02	3.06	3.52
Return on equity	11.1%	12.5%	NA
Capital expenditures	861	955	857
Total assets	11,973	11,935	NA
Shareholders'equity	7,269	6,363	NA
Long-term debt	188	139	NA
Number of employees	89,000	92,200	95,000

Exhibit 1B *Geographic Area Information*

In $ millions	1991	1990	1989
Net Revenue			
U.S.	$ 6,390	$ 6,025	$ 5,561
Europe	5,378	4,764	4,131
Other areas	2,726	2,444	2,207
Earnings from Operations			
U.S.	$ 1,191	$ 1,069	$ 881
Europe	292	363	359
Other areas	224	281	379
Eliminations and corporate	(497)	(551)	(407)

buying products from value-added resellers to whom HP granted higher discounts in return for the sales functions they performed. This lowered HP's average selling prices and increased cost of sales as a percentage of net revenue.

HP responded to these challenges by redefining its competitive strategy, revamping its product lines, and making frequent organizational adjustments. First, HP evolved from a manufacturer of "hot boxes" into a global supplier of information appliances. Management recognized the blending of computation and measurement technologies and the blurring of boundaries between consumer and professional electronic products. HP strived to satisfy the breadth of customer needs through partnerships and acquisitions when internal offerings did not exist and/or might take too long to develop. Second, the company succeeded at unifying its disparate lines of computers under a common RISC[4] ar-

[4]RISC (Reduced Instruction Set Computing) was a simplified yet very powerful computer architecture.

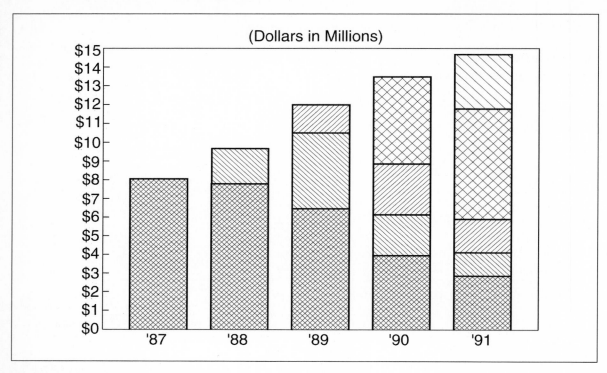

Figure 1   Mix of HP Product Orders by Year Products Were Introduced

chitecture code-named project Spectrum. This core technology positioned HP as the price/performance market leader, and, at the same time, the relative simplicity of the architecture enabled HP's marketing departments to introduce computers more rapidly.

Organization

At the heart of Hewlett-Packard's organization were divisional business units responsible for R&D, product marketing, and manufacturing. Most divisions had significant worldwide product line charters, and all were measured as profit centers. The divisions captured profits through transfer price mechanisms when they shipped products to HP's sales regions. Transfers between divisions and sales regions were mostly

made at market prices less allowances for subsequent manufacturing and/or marketing costs. HP's measurement system differed from those of IBM and Digital Equipment Corp., whose sales forces were organized as profit centers. Using a cautious pay-as-you-go budgeting process, HP allocated field personnel and capital expenditures among the divisions under the promise of additional profits. The sales regions were measured as cost centers and were responsible for revenues, field marketing, and customer service. One consequence of this organization was that two distinct cultures coexisted at Hewlett-Packard: one focused on long-term profit objectives, and another focused on achieving short-term quotas.

HP faced formidable competition not only from IBM and Digital in computers but also from emerging low-cost instrument companies. As a result, HP had to learn how to compete on cost while continuing to deliver quality. HP moved beyond boutique manufacturing to embrace high-volume, low-cost production. While remaining decentralized, HP grouped its divisions into three larger business sectors: Measurement Systems, Computer Products, and Computer Systems. This was even more necessary since the Spectrum project called for integrating design and manufacturing across 60 divisions that had previously operated with relative autonomy. Each sector had its own sales force and support organization.

As HP grew into a global company, the company's core values, known as the "HP Way," remained unchanged. HP Way principles included:

- Trust and respect for individuals
- Focus on a high level of achievement and contribution
- Uncompromising integrity when conducting business
- Teamwork
- Encouragement of flexibility and innovation

Said former CEO John Young:

The HP Way travels well and endures because it's the way people like to work. It's something people really value, and that's why I'm optimistic about it . . . We tend to see things pretty much the same way . . . we believe in the same value set, so those things are not even under discussion. But if somebody disagrees, that's a legitimate cause for concern and people make a real effort to understand the point of view.

Product Lines by Sectors

Hewlett-Packard was an international leader in computing and electronic measurement instruments. HP produced more than 18,000 products, including computers and peripheral products, test and measuring instruments and computerized test systems, networking products, electronic components, handheld calculators, medical electronic equipment, and instruments and systems for chemical analysis. Table A estimates the size of each sector by orders.

Measurement Systems Organization (MSO)

MSO manufactured general-purpose instruments as well as specialized test and measurement devices such as network analyzers and microwave components. MSO also had responsibility for analytical products such as chromatographs used in industrial process control and chemical laboratories. In addition, MSO included the Medical Products Group, which designed clinical information systems and ultrasound-imaging devices. MSO's most complex systems were sold through experienced sales engineers, while HP used catalog and telemarket-

Table A   Estimated FY 1991 Orders by Sector*

Sector	Orders %[a]	% Domestic (U.S.)	% International
MSO	25%	NA	NA
CPO	30%	50%	50%
CSO	40%	39%	61%

*Source: Casewriter estimates.
[a]Total less than 100% due to miscellaneous divisions (e.g., FRD) and products not included in sectors.

ing sales for entry-level instruments. Systems sales cycles were long and required extensive technical support. Customer discounts were low, ranging from 5% to 10%. Most MSO products and systems enjoyed long life cycles due to their complexity. HP pioneered the test and measurement industry and had established a leadership position over a 50-year period. However, MSO sales were declining due to a slowdown in spending by aerospace and defense industries, cutbacks in health care expenditures, and the emergence of low-cost foreign competitors. As a result, HP was forced to grant higher discounts and explore alternate channels of distribution.

Computer Products Organization (CPO)

CPO included personal computer and systems groups, as well as several mass-storage and printing divisions. CPO was a young organization within HP but quickly became the prime revenue contributor. Its success was based on affordable, high-quality, easy-to-use, and innovative products. For example, the LaserJet printer, launched in 1984, captured and maintained a 60% worldwide market share despite a flurry of competitive products. HP was a leader in peripherals such as inkjet printers, color plotters, and scanners for IBM-compatible personal computers as well as the Apple Macintosh. CPO's distribution policies departed from those of MSO and CSO: most products were sold through dealers and distributors. CPO products were characterized by low prices and very short product life cycles: a new version of the LaserJet printer was introduced every 18 months. To insure economical account coverage, CPO used a small number of direct reps whose role was to generate leads and then hand over logistics and order fulfillment to distributors. In return, HP granted discounts as high as 50% to large dealer chains. Although CPO operated in a very competitive marketplace, it enjoyed a healthy 15% growth rate.

Computer Systems Organization (CSO)

CSO included all the divisions designing and manufacturing computers, peripherals, system and application software, and networking products. HP computer lines included minicomputers used in business and industrial environments and technical workstations used by scientists and engineers for their high performance and sophisticated graphics capabilities. The minicomputers were marketed as two separate lines: the HP 3000 Series 900 family based on HP's proprietary operating system and the HP 9000 Series 800 family utilizing AT&T's popular UNIX™ system software. The HP 9000/800 had received good market acceptance because UNIX™ gave customers freedom to mix and match hardware from different vendors. HP positioned itself as the leader in open systems (systems with standard interfaces). Both lines used the same powerful RISC architecture. Despite technological innovations, HP's strategy had always been to maintain upward compatibility, thereby protecting customers' investments in software programs and peripherals.

Throughout the 1980s, HP's general-purpose minicomputers enjoyed robust sales and long life cycles. A well-trained direct sales force covered both major accounts and small businesses and pushed strong product features and excellent reliability to justify higher prices. Discounts ranged from 10% for small businesses to 25% for major accounts. HP introduced a hardware upgrade for its HP 3000 flagship family every two and a half years. However, as competitive pressure from microcomputers intensified in the early 1990s, HP strengthened existing models, broadened product lines, and reduced prices. This further shortened product life cycles. As of 1991, the HP 3000 life cycle had dwindled to 18 months, and some workstation models were on the marketplace for only about a year. The price/performance improvements were even more dramatic: each year saw prices fall by

20%, while new models boosted processor performance by 25%.

Shorter product life cycles and price reductions had two important consequences for HP. First, many customers postponed their computer expenditures and carefully monitored vendors' new product announcements. End users also tried to lessen their exposure to technological obsolescence by leasing equipment. Second, CSO reduced its number of sales reps and shifted its distribution strategy from direct to third-party channels like VARs (value-added resellers), OEMs (original equipment manufacturers), and distributors. The indirect channel was better suited to carry entry-level systems and workstations and could cover industry-specific niches and small accounts at a lower cost than HP could. As distribution shifted to indirect channels, HP's average channel discounts increased to 35%.

FINANCE AND REMARKETING DIVISION

The Finance and Remarketing Division (FRD) was an in-house leasing company and a vendor of used equipment that aimed to "help make HP the preferred solution by providing convenient and affordable services."

FRD Sales Finance provided leasing and rental offerings that encouraged the sale or use of HP products. FRD acted as the primary manager of financed HP equipment located at a customer site.

FRD Remarketing enhanced HP's competitive position by providing a lower-cost product alternative to price-sensitive customers. FRD was HP's major distributor of resalable used equipment. Customers were offered an array of refurbished products ranging from the technically complex (networked computers) to the standalone (instruments, workstations).

In 1991, FRD worldwide orders of $553 million included the value of products financed (72%) and remarketed (28%). FRD revenues of $227 million generated a 10.4% net profit. As of 1991, 80% of FRD's orders and revenues involved computer systems so FRD interacted mainly with HP's CSO divisions. Less than 4% of HP sales were on leases. The difference between orders and revenues stemmed mainly from the fact that Sales Finance revenues included only the value added to HP: interest income from leasing transactions, rental revenues, and purchase option revenues from customers who decided to buy equipment at the expiration of their lease contracts. Remarketing orders and revenues differed only as a result of time lags between order entries and actual shipments.

Compared with most HP divisions, FRD was a young organization. However, since its formation in 1985, FRD's orders, revenues, and net profits grew faster than HP as a whole, as indicated in Exhibit 2. The division employed 533 people worldwide, 240 being located at FRD's Sunnyvale headquarters in California. FRD Europe's headcount totaled 160, with Asia/Pacific and other international operations accounting for the rest.

FRD Mission and Organization

FRD provided (1) sales tools to increase customer appeal and to broaden HP's customer base and market position, (2) stronger account control, and (3) a means of recovering asset investments. With financing and remarketing to complement its technology, HP had a broader set of benefits to sell to additional customer segments. An internal leasing practice also reduced the ability of banks and independent leasing companies to move current customers to other vendors. In addition, Remarketing helped turn a profit on inventory positions assumed on equipment returned from leases, rentals, demonstration programs and upgrade credits. From a financial point of view, tax deferrals and benefits and superior return on assets more than compensated for high transaction costs. For these

Exhibit 2A *FRD and ERO Key Figures*

	FRD Worldwide Orders in 1991 (in millions)			
	U.S.	**Europe**	**Other**	**Total**
Sales finance	$276,698	$102,190	$19,239	$398,127
Remarketing	78,410	57,840	18,662	154,912
Total FRD	355,108	160,030	37,901	553,039

Exhibit 2B *ERO Orders Performance in 1991*

						Profit Contribution	
Region	**PL55 Orders ($ millions)**	**% Europe**	**% Quota**	**% Growth**	**Local Orders[a] ($ millions)**	**Net Profit PL55 %**	**Net Profit Local %**
EUROPE	57.8	100	103	40	20.3	100%[b]	0%
E.M.R	16.1	27.8	99	10	0	100	0
Germany	14.9	25.8	129	41	0	100	0
France	10.4	18.0	85	(24)	15.1	24	76
U.K.	10.3	17.8	78	(5)	3.5	68	32
Italy	6.1	10.6	206	101	1.7	74	26

[a]Non-PL55 orders sourced locally; they were not recorded in ERO's performance statements.
[b]ERO net 1991 profit was $8.5 million; local profit contribution was not officially recorded; net profits as a percentage of total orders ranged from 10.1% in E.M.R. to 23.4% in France.

Exhibit 2C *ERO Penetration Rates and Supply Analysis*

Region	**PL55[a] Penetration % Direct Sales**	**PL55[b] Penetration % Indirect Sales**	**Total PL5 Penetration %**	**Demo Shipments[c]**	**Sales[d] Finance Returns**
E.M.R	2.06	1.25	1.37	6.4	0
Germany	1.25	2.03	1.30	8.6	0.95
France	3.61	3.59	2.44	7.4	0
U.K.	2.92	2.75	2.25	7.6	1.42
Italy	1.96	1.58	1.90	1.0	0.34
Total EUROPE	2.17	1.99	1.67	31.0	2.71

[a]Penetration of PL55 used equipment in HP's direct channel (direct sales force).
[b]Penetration of PL55 used equipment in HP's indirect channel (VARs, OEMs, distributors).
[c]Demo shipments in millions of $ at book value.
[d]Sales Finance returns in millions of $.

reasons, almost all high-technology vendors, including IBM, AT&T, and Xerox, had set up captive leasing and remarketing programs. Both Sales Finance and Remarketing were measured as profit centers.

Despite the strategic advantages they provided, Sales Finance and Remarketing were inherently service-driven businesses conducted in a manufacturing environment. As one manager stated: "Managing a manufacturing company is difficult enough without the added burden of worrying about running a leasing company." Few managers outside of FRD understood the nature and complexity of leasing and remarketing. Most FRD managers had finance or tax backgrounds, in contrast to the traditional engineering and manufacturing training of typical HP managers.

In the U.S., U.K., and Australia, FRD was organized as a separate legal entity from the main HP country organization. For example, HP Finance Ltd. in the U.K. purchased equipment from HP divisions at list prices minus internal discounts. In the course of a tough negotiation, an HP finance rep had some leeway to increase the residual value of a computer two years hence to reduce customer monthly payments on a lease contract. Higher residual values translated into greater balance sheet exposure for HP Finance Ltd. given rapid technological obsolescence. In addition, regulations required that, as a financial institution, HP Finance Ltd. invest significant equity in the business and keep large cash balances.

In contrast, in other countries such as France, FRD was part of the main HP subsidiary. Since only banks were allowed to offer leasing contracts in France, FRD had to place all refinancing deals through them. Once a deal was signed, FRD would purchase the equipment from one or more HP divisions, sell it to a financial institution, lease it back from them, and then "lease" it again to the customer. FRD made a profit only on the interest rate spread, as opposed to receiving the lease payments in full, but no longer had

balance sheet exposure. From the customer's perspective, HP's FRD was the sole contract administrator.

Organizational diversity coupled with transaction complexity made the FRD business difficult to manage and increased administrative and back office costs. In addition, tax treatment of leases and rentals differed from country to country, making performance comparisons difficult. As part of a multinational corporation, HP subsidiaries maintained two sets of books: one to meet local reporting requirements and another for consolidation purposes.

Customers

As stated by Craig White, FRD's worldwide general manager:

Finance and Remarketing provide equipment acquisition and disposition services to customers who want to conserve cash, manage their balance sheets, hedge against technological obsolescence, or recover their equipment investments cost effectively.

Under this definition, FRD's target customers were all actual or prospective buyers of HP equipment. Sales Finance could be used to open new accounts as well as service existing HP customers. FRD only financed non-HP equipment when doing so could help displace another vendor from an account. There were two customer segments for financing. Fortune 500 and government entities represented 33% of lease orders, while small to medium-size companies accounted for the remaining 67%. However, as FRD planned to finance more instruments, workstations, and medical equipment, the number of large aerospace/defense and hospital customers was expected to increase the major account segment's share to 45%.

All Remarketing target customers were already HP accounts. Sales reps could not expect to penetrate new accounts with used equipment. Since 80% of products carried by Remarketing offices in the United States and Europe had been introduced within the last three years, HP had already spent time educating customers on product features. Remarketing targeted installed base customers who wanted peripheral add-ons, major accounts that needed bridging solutions before migrating to newer technology, government accounts that had standardized on older technology in previous public tenders, small businesses who did not have MIS departments, VARs whose software applications ran only on older technology, and rapidly growing cash-constrained companies. The customer mix varied dramatically by country and from year to year. For example, major accounts purchasing used equipment accounted for 55% of French remarketing orders but only 42% of U.S. orders. Since orders for used products accounted for a small fraction of total HP orders, one large deal in a given customer segment could alter statistics dramatically. For this reason, FRD tracked orders of used equipment via direct and indirect channels as indicated in Exhibit 2C.

FRD's internal customers were the HP divisions to which marketing, administration, manufacturing, and logistics services were offered. In the United States, FRD Remarketing had developed unique capabilities for managing used equipment. FRD executives sought to extend these capabilities to other HP entities in order to streamline operations and reduce costs. Remarketing positioned itself as a service contractor to HP, providing a cost-effective alternative to outside vendors. Remarketing charged a percentage fee for managing end-of-lifecycle products. Under this fee concept, used equipment remained the property of the new product divisions as opposed to being transferred to FRD. Management fees generated a smaller revenue stream, but FRD no longer had inventory exposure on its books. Examples of services provided by the U.S. FRD included:

- Used equipment market information and competitive positioning

- Marketing programs to move excess or end-of-life products
- Multiple channels of distribution focused specifically on reaching customers who purchased end-of-lifecycle products
- Open market purchases
- Refurbishment
- Returns management
- Warehousing

Although ERO executives toyed with the concept, management fees had not yet been implemented in Europe. In 1991, almost 97% of ERO's revenue was derived from external customers, whereas U.S. Remarketing already booked 14% of its sales in management fees.

Sales Finance

FRD offered a whole range of operating, capital lease, and rental products to better serve customer needs. Because HP sales reps had no expertise in financing techniques, FRD had its own sales force of finance reps located in HP's regional sales offices. Finance reps had sales objectives related to order volume and type of finance products sold. However, finance reps relied on HP's direct sales force for lead generation. When an HP account manager was about to close a deal, he or she would turn to a finance rep to design a lease or rental proposal. The account manager might invite the finance rep to the customer site to make a joint presentation of the HP solution or merely include the financing contract in his or her proposal. Cooperation between sales and finance reps was excellent because HP commissioned both parties for orders booked.

Despite being the premier lessor of HP equipment worldwide, FRD was facing trends which threatened to erode its profitability in both Sales Finance and Remarketing.

First, there was a trend away from "full-payout" leasing—no residual value assumed—to "residual-based" financing. Gone were the days when a lessor could transfer technological risk to customers. A tougher leasing market forced lessors to streamline lease payments and assume residual values. In addition, customers demanded more flexibility. More than 80% of all computer leases never went to full term without significant replacements, enhancements, or upgrades. Heavy discounting of new hardware products also hurt the value of residuals. Some aggressive independent lessors who had made overly optimistic residual estimates a few years back faced severe financial difficulty by the end of the 1980s. HP adopted conservative accounting whereby residuals on lease transactions were written off upfront. This, in turn, penalized FRD on short-term leases because early lease revenues could not offset depreciation.

Second, two product trends increasingly affected FRD: shorter product life cycles and more computer field upgrades.[5] As product life cycles contracted, customers used leasing to push the residual risk of equipment onto HP, resulting in an increase in the amount of equipment returned. Ultimately, this trend affected Remarketing's ability to recapture value. At the same time, the trend toward field upgrades as opposed to box swaps tended to reduce the flow of equipment returning to HP.

Third, with the development of open systems, customers were increasingly seeking multi-vendor financing, including financing for intangibles like software and services. FRD was reluctant to finance non-HP equipment because it had no expertise in other vendors' secondary markets. In addition, software could not be capitalized and had to be fully depreciated upfront, making the transaction less profitable in the early years of the lease.

---

[5]Upgrade programs enabled a customer to trade up his/her computer for a more powerful system for a fee. They included both *box swaps,* whereby whole systems were disinstalled and returned to HP, and *field upgrades,* whereby only processor boards were exchanged.

Fourth, the growing importance of third-party channels (VARs, OEMs, and dealers) and low-cost telemarketing and catalog selling posed a challenge to FRD. Compound annual growth between 1987 and 1990 had been 15% for the direct channel and 35% for the indirect channel. However, Sales Finance and Remarketing had always relied on HP's direct sales force to generate leads, so FRD executives were starting to design plans for HP third-party channel partners and direct marketing programs for small-ticket items.

EUROPEAN REMARKETING OPERATION

A sister organization of U.S. Remarketing, ERO was formed in 1987 when HP's early computer and instrument lease contracts began to expire. HP Europe also felt the need for a program to manage the flow of used equipment returning from customers as a result of upgrades. A small German team covering Europe was set up in Boeblingen. The program manager circulated a quarterly update on available products, with prices in U.S. dollars. European sales reps called Boeblingen for special product requests, additional discounts, or shorter delivery times.

In fiscal 1991, ERO's orders were close to $57.8 million, an increase of 40% over 1990. Net profit accounted for 14.7% of total revenues, posting a record growth of 138%. ERO employed 39 people, 28 of them being stationed in HP's factory in Boeblingen, near Stuttgart. The Boeblingen site served as HP GmbH Germany's headquarters and was by far HP's largest manufacturing operation in Europe. With a workforce of 6,000 people, Boeblingen also hosted the European operations of the computer systems divisions, the European Distribution Center, and the European Marketing Center whose mission was to coordinate and supervise all marketing programs across Europe. "Owning" Boeblingen gave HP Germany a pivotal role in shaping HP Europe's strategy.

Marketing Strategy

ERO positioned itself as "the lower cost alternative" that provided the same HP standards of quality and reliability. From its inception, FRD's management had decided that Remarketing managers should not try to act as brokers of HP's used products. Explained Axel Wolff, ERO's marketing manager:

> There are two distinct businesses out there. Brokers make money by bringing buyers and sellers together for a fee. HP's aftermarket is a private one, as opposed to IBM's or Bull's. Used HP equipment is not actively traded since it is not widely available, and there are no independent market makers or public price lists. Consequently, HP brokers tend to be niche players that focus on entry-level computers and instruments. They perform little refurbishment, if any.
>
> We are not in the used-equipment business. ERO's strategy is to offer fully refurbished systems and products, and remarket them as "equivalent to new." We remanufacture used equipment in Boeblingen and include services such as warranty, installation, and access to HP customer support. No broker can match our quality and benefits. Besides, ERO's cost structure is too high to compete against brokers: our markup on cost is 190% as opposed to brokers' 20% to 40%, so we focus on high-end computer systems and peripherals. The trick is to ensure that the level of refurbishment is exceeded by the margins generated. Our 1989 European survey indicated that customers were willing to accept a 15% premium compared to brokers' prices for quality and reliability.

Exhibit 3 summarizes the strengths and weaknesses of FRD's Remarketing competitors as of 1990. In addition to brokers, HP VARs occasionally competed in the used-equipment market by bundling their own software with used HP products, because margins on hardware tended to be higher than on software. However, some VARs also offered brokerage services by importing used equipment directly from the United States, where prices could be lower by as much as 25%, or by purchasing HP equipment on local open markets.

FRD estimated its global share of the HP used equipment market to be around 40%, although there were significant differences by country (see Table B).

Table B   Remarketing Market Share of HP Used Equipment by Country

Country	Share %
U.S.	40%
Germany	40%
France	50%
U.K.	25%
Italy	70%
E.M.R.[a]	30–70%

[a]The European Multicountry Region (E.M.R.) included Western and Eastern European countries in which HP had a limited presence. Share varied by country.

ERO market shares reflected varying competitive pressures in different countries. The U.K. was by far the toughest marketplace for used equipment, as British customers were very price sensitive. The U.K. also served as a European entry point for brokers importing used equipment from the United States. In France, HP sales reps would call on ERO to protect their accounts from regional brokers. Far more threatening was the entry into the used-equipment business of Paris-based ARES, HP Europe's largest VAR, which also signed an agreement to resell FRD's leases/rentals contracts for a fee. Within two years, ARES captured an estimated 30% of the French HP used-equipment market. In Germany, ERO competed against regional VARs in technical niches. ERO dominated the Italian market in part because Italy was too

Exhibit 3   *Strengths and Weaknesses of Principal Remarketing Competitors*

Strengths

BROKERS	VARS	HP REMARKETING
• Bundled-in services • Quick/immediate delivery • Products eligible to HP maintenance and support • Can buy back customer equipment on the open market • Can telemarket cheap products on HP's installed base • International sourcing • Low cost structure • Catalog/newspaper and direct marketing	• Country arbitrage (gray marketing) • Good customer relationships • Full service, technically competent • Benefit from HP support and offer HP warranty • Entrepreneurs/responsive • Discounts passed on • Bundle non-HP accessories and peripherals	• Product line breadth/depth • Refurbishment added-value • Access to HP information and resources • Coordination with new product divisions • Worldwide network • One-stop shopping: can bundle new and used equipment, software on same order • Customer preference for original vendor and factory program • Stability and financing

Weaknesses

BROKERS	VARS	HP REMARKETING
• Incomplete configurations • Lack technical expertise... but are catching up • Lack of capital, small inventory • Limited refurbishment if any • No long-term relationship with customers, opportunistic • Subject to timing of HP new product announcements (inventory exposure to obsolescence)	• Lack of capital (small VARs) • Limited financing options • Limited product configurations • HP control of VAR discounts and contracts (to limit gray market) • Sold "as is" as opposed to new	• High cost structure • Do not buy on open market • Little visibility on worldwide inventory • Lack of direct marketing tools (telemarketing, catalog) • Do not merchandise well/differentiate to external customers (rely on HP sales force to market products, no direct customer contacts) • FRD's small size within HP; not a core business; little management exposure • Long lead times • Restricted by mission and resources

small a market to justify the entry of foreign brokers.

ERO had to market itself within HP because it relied on HP's sales force to promote its product offering. Gaining access to senior management was also a challenge. As one former ERO general manager commented:

We still face difficulties such as lack of recognition, ignorance, or contempt because of our small size, and sometimes we face opposition instead of support. We are not really integrated and fully accepted as a service provider.

Product cannibalization was a source of tension between ERO and the new product divisions. All equipment sold by Boeblingen was labeled as PL55 product to track ERO's orders and revenues. However, new product managers did not record PL55 performance in their statements and feared that used equipment cannibalized sales of new products. ERO managers countered:

The customers who buy remanufactured products probably would not have bought from HP otherwise. In 1988, only two percent of the HP 3000 computer systems customers who bought new equipment also purchased remanufactured products from HP. And most of these were government accounts which still require older technology or value-added businesses which sell to price-sensitive customers.

ERO faced fewer problems with HP's sales force in part because PL55 product sales contributed to the achievement of sales quotas and were eligible for commissions. Unlike Sales Finance, Remarketing had no dedicated sales force and depended on HP reps deciding to involve ERO. This could arise when HP's latest technology was too expensive for a price-sensitive customer, when a broker attempted to penetrate an account with cheap used equipment, or when rapid availability of product was key to a sale. ERO personnel were therefore called in at the very end of the selling process and asked to "save the sale."

Reflected Solal, France's ERO program manager:

This is definitely not an ego business. ERO asks me to hit sales and profit numbers every month, but if I do too well, some marketing manager will come to me and play the cannibalization song and dance again. . . . We must run silent and deep, we can't blanket HP's installed base with direct-mail pieces, yet we must be on red alert for those times when sales reps come to us with unbelievable requests: give me a 50% discount, how come you guys can't ship yesterday, why don't you loan systems to customers, etc.

HP regional sales managers were ambivalent with regard to Remarketing's contribution. On the one hand, they understood that Remarketing brought additional profits to HP through management of the company's used-equipment assets. On the other hand, they were not accountable for profits and were far more concerned with order volume. They feared that used-equipment sales would yield lower quotas. Management was also reluctant to jeopardize HP's image by remarketing older technology too aggressively. (See Exhibit 4, a customer brochure for HP remanufactured products.)

Product Marketing

ERO's three product managers located in Boeblingen and reporting to Axel Wolff were responsible for separate product lines: minicomputers (HP 3000 and HP 9000), workstations, and peripherals (disk drives, tapes, and printers). Product managers performed a variety of tasks, including supply management, PL55 forecasting, product definition and positioning, and pricing. In addition, product managers worked closely with manufacturing to plan material requirements. Since ERO's product offering was by nature supply driven, product managers had to locate within HP inventories of critical parts

Exhibit 4   *Customer Brochure for HP Remanufactured Products*

Remanufactured products from Hewlett-Packard

When you buy Hewlett-Packard's remanufactured equipment you get a **worry free** solution. Why? Because the equipment has been **completely refurbished**—and a whole lot more.
You get:

- A **lower cost alternative** when your system has reached its capacity and your budget won't stretch any farther
- The **same warranty** HP provides new products
- **Engineering and software updates** developed by the engineers at the products original manufacturing division
- The **same sales terms and conditions** HP provides on new-product offerings (no added charges for de-installation of an old system, freight costs, insurance, manuals, documentation and installation of new system)
- A remanufacturing process that guarantees our products are **functionally and cosmetically equivalent to new**
- **Immediate eligibility** for a service contract. HP remanufactured equipment does not require a 30-day evaluation period
- A **varied selection of financing options** to choose from:
  —lease with option to buy
  —operating lease plan
  —rental plan
  —a 36-month, no-down payment finance plan
- HP's **top-rated reputation** for quality rehability and professionalism
- **Professional account management** to ensure that your long-term needs will be addressed and your problems resolved quickly
- HP's **one-vendor solution** which means continuity and stability for you
- **Coordination of all details**—from de-installation through delivery and beyond—saving your management team time and expense

All of this is backed by HP, a company with **50-plus years of customer commitment**.

The Worry-Free Solution

to remarket complete bundles. Product definition was more complex as new computer systems included dozens of options for customers to choose. ERO product managers restricted their offerings to selected configurations, depending on parts and options availability. For example, the original HP 3000 Series 932 computer included a 600-megabyte disk, a backup tape, and a system console. As used 600-megabyte drives were hard to find, the product manager would typically assemble two 300-

megabyte units in the same cabinet or simply offer the system with one drive. As long as a remarketed product was identical with the original, ERO simply added an "R" suffix to the original product number.

If defining bundles was a difficult task, managing a PL55 product portfolio was a real challenge. Exhibit 5 shows the price positioning of remarketed models in the HP 3000 Series 900 computer family in relation to their original prices. The Y-axis sorts systems by processor rel-

Exhibit 5   *HP 3000 Series 900 Product Lines*

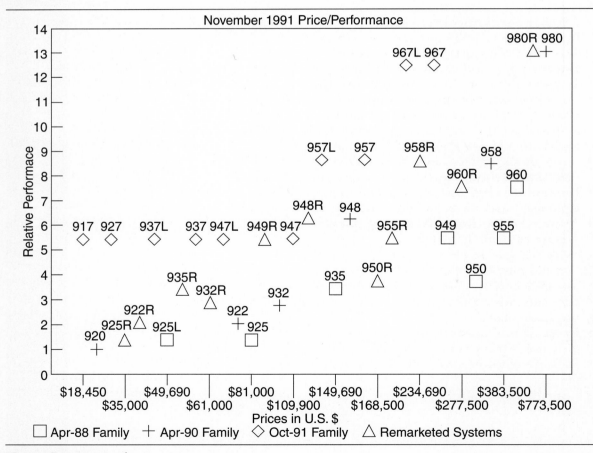

*Source: Company records.
Note: Some prices have been disquised.

ative performance, while the X-axis ranks system prices in ascending order. Pricing remarketed computers required marketing clout as well as negotiating skills. ERO's cost-plus strategy called for pricing used equipment at 15% below original product prices. However, given shorter product life cycles and price/performance improvements, ERO product managers were forced to lower their prices by as much as 55%: the remarketed HP 3000 Series 925 "R" was priced at $35,000 compared with the original Series 925 price of $79,690. ERO's price had to be lowered because, in October 1991, HP introduced the Series 927, which boasted performance six times better at a price of $33,000. Lamented Norbert Jensen, ERO computer product manager:

> Ich sitze zwischen zwei Stühlen![6] *Program managers always complain that we are too slow to introduce "R" products. To their credit, there is definitely a time-to-market issue. If I introduce a computer too late, ERO will incur the opportunity cost of lost orders, plus increasingly higher discounts to move the product at the end of its life cycle, and, finally, inventory write-offs when the product becomes obsolete. Having said that, I can only introduce products after building up enough supply for the whole of Europe. Moreover, new product divisions carefully monitor ERO prices and introductions for fear of new product cannibalization. I have very little latitude.*

Manufacturing

ERO followed a "focus and win" strategy, and a "10-step rebuilding process." Boeblingen received a steady supply of used equipment from across Europe. The equipment was refurbished, dismantled, sold "as is," or scrapped according to the value that could be captured. (ERO's value extraction process is presented in Exhibit

6.) In deciding what to do with used equipment, ERO product managers used criteria that included timing of returns in relation to new product life cycles, the quantity of used equipment on hand, acquisition costs, the source of the product, and the degree to which it had been used. The "focus-and-win" approach called for only 150 products to be added to HP's corporate price list under the PL55 label. These were almost all high-end computer systems and peripherals or products for which a sustained demand existed. Once a used product was deemed eligible for remanufacturing, a 10-step refurbishment process began. Products were disassembled, cleaned, tested, and repaired; software was updated; critical parts were replaced for preventive purposes; the complete configuration was tested; original documentation was added; and the product was packaged in standard HP boxes and finally shipped. The final result was a product "as good as new in function and appearance."

Products not eligible for full refurbishment could be sold to other HP divisions after some refurbishment, or be remarketed "as is" to VARs and brokers. However, a majority of the products returned from long-term leases or demo programs which had been obsoleted were written off HP's books and scrapped. In 1991, HP Germany incurred a $9.2 million charge as a result of ERO's write-offs.

Recent trends in leasing and remarketing motivated ERO to broaden its product offering and sell smaller-ticket products. As a result, manufacturing had to operate two production lines, one for high-volume, low-profit, short-cycle products (e.g., disk drives, accessories) and a second for low-volume, high-profit, longer-cycle-time products (e.g., HP 3000, HP 9000, printers). Dieter Muller, ERO manufacturing manager, operated a complex job shop:

> *We subcontract labor-intensive steps such as cleaning and painting and retain control of complicated processes such as testing. Testing*

---

[6] "I'm sitting on the fence!"

Exhibit 6 *ERO Value Extraction Chain*

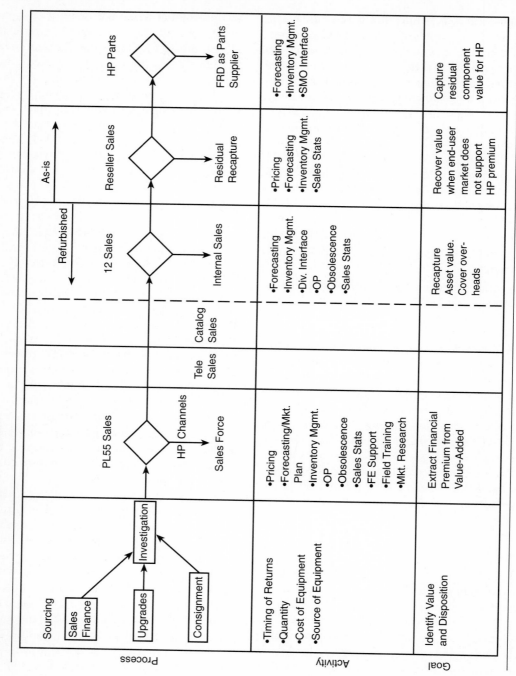

Sourcing	PL55 Sales	Tele Sales	Catalog Sales	12 Sales	Reseller Sales	HP Parts
Sales Finance → Investigation ← Upgrades, Consignment	HP Channels → Sales Force			Internal Sales	Residual Recapture	FRD as Parts Supplier
•Timing of Returns •Quantity •Cost of Equipment •Source of Equipment	•Pricing •Forecasting/Mkt. Plan •Inventory Mgmt. •OP •Obsolescence •Sales Stats •FE Support •Field Training •Mkt. Research			•Forecasting •Inventory Mgmt. •Div. Interface •OP •Obsolescence •Sales Stats	•Pricing •Forecasting •Inventory Mgmt. •Sales Stats	•Forecasting •Inventory Mgmt. •SMO Interface
Identify Value and Disposition	Extract Financial Premium from Value-Added			Recapture Asset value. Cover over-heads	Recover value when end-user market does not support HP premium	Capture residual component value for HP

Process | Activity | Goal

As-is, Refurbished

a complete computer configuration remains the bottleneck, no matter how fast we refurbish. We do use material requirement planning systems [MRP], but depend on an unpredictable product supply. We never really know what will be available tomorrow.

Supply and Procurement

U.S. and European Remarketing depended on HP divisions and sales regions for a steady supply of used equipment, since they did not purchase used HP products on the open market like brokers (see Exhibit 2C for sales regions' shipments of used equipment to Boeblingen). Remarketing would occasionally buy back equipment from an HP customer, if only to save an important new product sale. Four sources kept ERO supplied:

Demo/Consignment

In 1991, European sales regions held $74 million in demo and consignment inventories—at book value—provided by the divisions. Sales regions typically loaned equipment to HP customers and VARs/OEMs to test their applications and benchmark systems performance and also kept demonstration equipment in their showrooms. Divisions shipped products to the sales regions at list price minus demo discounts. Sales region demo coordinators could keep the equipment for only nine months, after which they had to resell it to ERO, sell it "as is" at "discretionary" discounts, or write it off. In 1991, $31 million—at book value—worth of equipment was shipped back to Boeblingen—a ratio of 42%. ERO product managers determined return credits, allowing the division to recapture some profit on a portfolio basis. They also committed ERO to buy back from the sales regions' equipment based on standard demo configurations. Over the years, demo/consignment became ERO's primary source of used equipment.

Sales Finance Returns

Leases/rentals returns to Boeblingen accounted for $2.7 million in 1991. There were too many transfer values in the European regions, so FRD was working toward unifying transfer prices worldwide. In the past, most equipment returning from long-term leases was written off and scrapped. However, leasing trends pointed toward an increasing supply and a greater variety of equipment returning to HP from this source.

HP Assets

ERO sometimes purchased end-of-life products or obsolete inventories from HP's divisions. ERO was considering adopting the U.S. Remarketing management fee approach to reduce its inventory exposure.

Upgrades

Although products obsoleted by upgrades were ERO's original source of supply, their importance dwindled as field upgrades of installed equipment replaced box swaps.

Decentralized Remarketing

As its business expanded, ERO established decentralized remarketing operations within the principal European countries, located at the host sales companies. The objectives of these operations were to (1) establish a local ERO presence, and (2) complement Boeblingen's PL55 product offerings with used products sourced locally to counter broker competition. In addition, ERO expected its local program managers to interact with sales region management and solve potential conflicts of interest. To facilitate this charter, each decentralized operation was measured as a management profit center, with quota, revenue, and profit objectives. ERO's first office in Paris was soon followed by operations in London, Milan, and Boeblingen. ERO later added offices in Amsterdam and

Stockholm. Remarketing operations in other European countries were coordinated from Boeblingen. In fiscal 1991, 11 people worked in decentralized remarketing operations. ERO France employed one program manager and four professionals. The ERO U.K. team consisted of one program manager and one professional. The other countries each had only a program manager.

Program managers reported directly to the FRD country managers and, on a dotted-line basis, to Axel Wolff. Their main responsibilities included managing the local profit centers, achieving sales quotas, tracking used-equipment inventories in a sales region and facilitating their return to Boeblingen, forecasting, administration, and field marketing. Field marketing entailed localizing Boeblingen's advertising campaigns and special promotions and converting U.S. dollar price lists into local currencies.

Dual reporting called for program managers to balance conflicting objectives. For instance, Remarketing's goal of managing *all* HP's used equipment meant giving priority to HP's huge demo/consignment inventories at the expense of lease/rental returns. Another issue was the management of transfer prices between two profit centers operating in the same division. Once the leases expired, Sales Finance was eager to transfer all capitalized assets to Remarketing at net book value, if only to stop depreciation expenses. For ERO, however, acquiring a one-year-old product at 35% of its original price was a risky proposition given rapid technological obsolescence and ERO's required markup. Regarding setting transfer prices, Craig White clearly stated in a memo:

The transfer prices are not to be used for setting residuals in leases or rentals. Transfer prices represent fair prices at which Remarketing can afford to buy the equipment, refurbish it, and resell at a profit. It is the responsibility of each region's FRD manager to balance what equipment will be returned from lease or rent at end of term, against lease/rental customer buyouts or renewals. In the United States, this ratio is 80% bought-out or renewed (at a high residual capture) and approximately 20% returned (at a low residual capture).

Program managers understood that transfer prices between Sales Finance and Remarketing merely shifted profits within FRD, yet they were less than sanguine to incur losses. In France, the non-PL55 local business was perceived as an additional source of profits and an effective way to cover residual exposures. Solal thus purchased an increasing number of products at the end of the demo/consignment period at "negotiated" prices, sometimes as low as one dollar. Being in a cost center, French sales-region controllers focused on U.S. reporting figures and did not record the difference between transfer prices to Remarketing and inventory values. Only at the end of the year did accountants reconcile the numbers to prepare HP France's tax return. In 1991, $4.8 million in write-offs was incurred by the French sales region as a result of transfers of equipment to local Remarketing. Solal countered that HP France's demo coordinators would have granted external customers excessive discounts just to move their inventories. He also highlighted the risks of letting VARs like ARES purchase truckloads of used equipment at up to an 80% discount and then remarket it to HP's installed base.

ERO RECENT DEVELOPMENTS

Since 1990, the Remarketing program managers in France and, to a lesser extent, in the U.K. saw a growing share of their orders, revenues, and profits come from local business. While this trend had been anticipated by FRD's management, it created serious tensions between Boeblingen and the field. First, local orders of products not officially carried by ERO could not be recorded under PL55. Program managers had no authority to add products to HP's corporate price list, so they booked local orders under original product lines. The booking mechanism was manual and cumbersome and created a revenue recognition problem for ERO, although each sales region posted the dollar amounts associated with sales of used equipment in its statements.

Second, program managers started developing their own local businesses at the expense of PL55 products. Solal for one became more and more engaged in buying and selling equipment on the French open market. As demand for new computer systems stagnated, HP sales reps put pressure on Remarketing to buy back customers' older technology in order to make their quotas. Much of this used equipment was not transferred to Boeblingen, because ERO's return credits were too low for country offices to make a profit. As a result, local inventories burgeoned. Wolff was also concerned about program managers retaining "hot" used PL55 computers and peripherals in the field for future sales. Program managers feared that if they delivered the used equipment they purchased to Boeblingen it would be shipped after refurbishing to other European countries, thus depriving them of potential revenue. Another motivation for retaining marketable products at the local level was Boeblingen's long lead times; the brokers with whom the program managers had to compete offered almost instant delivery. Such behavior was threatening ERO's profits since (1) Boeblingen could no longer supply critical used products when they were asked for, and (2) obsolete equipment returning from leases and consignment programs were still being shipped to the factory, forcing ERO to incur huge write-offs.

The following comments illustrate some of the frustrations felt by the program managers:

Boeblingen misunderstands what customers really want: is there really a distinction between used and refurbished equipment, since HP products will be fully supported? Is ERO's value chain relevant? Do we over-refurbish equipment? The emphasis on quality may be important in Germany, but in France and Britain, customers are very price sensitive. We are not in business to refurbish used products, but to sell them.

Product managers have a supply-driven mentality. Our computer configurations are based on what's available, as opposed to what the market wants. We should be ready to source missing parts from the open market if necessary. Customers, not ERO, must decide what products are obsolete or attractive. "If you can't sell what you have, it's because you have the wrong stuff at the wrong time at the wrong price."

Our discount approval and pricing delegation scheme is cumbersome; ERO is way too slow to react to a spot market.

Our cost structure is too high to counter brokers effectively. I understand FRD doesn't want to compete against brokers, but if those guys eat our lunch this year, we won't have jobs next year. I can't charge a 30% premium when the market will only tolerate 15%.

Remarketing should be used as a competitive weapon against brokers to protect HP's installed base. We forgo opportunities by not pursuing the secondary market more aggressively.

ERO's information flow between Boeblingen and the field is manual [quarterly price lists in dollars, promotional material in English] and not tailored to local requirements. We waste a lot of time creating localized price lists and ad campaigns every month. What we really need is online access to a record of all European inventories.

Right now, selling Boeblingen's output locally is a waste of our time and no fun; program managers just serve as mailboxes between field sales people and the factory. At the local business level, I can really manage my cost of goods sold. Given FRD's objective to finance more products from MSO and

CPO, Boeblingen will never be able to carry thousands of products and options, so the local business will inevitably take off. We must get ready now.

ERO executives at Boeblingen also expressed frustrations:

ERO exists to help HP remarket its own used equipment in the most profitable way; we are not brokers, nor should we attempt to compete against them. Buying and trading "hot" equipment on the open market only results in marginal gains for the company, while huge depreciation expenses and write-offs are incurred with our own used equipment. In addition, ERO's cost structure doesn't allow us to compete against brokers.

Storing small-ticket items or obsolete products for too long is not profitable, because it takes too much time and effort to manage this inventory and refurbish these types of products to meet customer needs. ERO's program managers should "focus and win" on a few products for which margins and barriers to entry [e.g., refurbishing standards] are higher. The real marketing challenge is to find niches for older technology; anyone can sell a computer that's nine months old.

We still need a central inventory to enable smaller sales regions [e.g., EMR countries] with no program managers in the field to sell used equipment. A central refurbishing operation also increases economies of scale in marketing and manufacturing. We should not duplicate Boeblingen's effort in all European countries. Decentralized offices will never be able to match Boeblingen's standards.

Program managers can't compromise HP's quality image by selling unrefurbished or untested products. According to our European survey, customers of refurbished HP equipment place more importance on image, security, product appearance, and service than on price. By selling unrefurbished or

as is products, ERO weakens its position against brokers while its cost structure remains too high to compete.

Program managers should not attempt to sell directly to accounts, nor should they rely mainly on HP's direct sales force. The handwriting is on the wall, so other channels for small-ticket items must be pursued [catalog, telemarketing, indirect distribution] that are more cost-effective.

Profits generated locally are an illusion at best. When local Remarketing operations purchase demo/consignment inventories at low price points, HP gets hurt anyway. ERO's marketing strategy should not be based on accounting rules.

Let's get rid of this them-and-us attitude. The program managers in the field and factory remarketing executives work for the same division. Challenging trends in Sales Finance will require much closer cooperation in the near future, so it's time we work together.

Future Prospects

Didier Philippe pondered several alternatives:

1. Gradually close the central factory and hand all manufacturing and marketing responsibility to the program managers. Proponents of this option argued that Boeblingen could never be responsive to a sales-and-trading spot market in which few economies of scale existed. However, a central warehouse enabled those country operations that were too small to have their own program managers to dispose of used equipment.

2. Clearly separate product responsibility. Apply the 80/20 rule and exhort program managers to return much-needed products to Boeblingen. In that case, the rules of the game would need to be changed, and the central factory should greatly improve its marketing responsiveness. In addition, it was not sure whether program managers would accept be-

coming merely Boeblingen's appendixes, after having managed independent profit centers.

3. Replace the program managers in the countries with an expanded pan-European marketing staff in Boeblingen. Coordination would be greatly simplified, but ERO would lose its presence in the countries and might become less responsive to local requirements.

On second thought, Philippe wondered whether the "focus and win" strategy made sense. Ultimately, he might have to broaden ERO's product portfolio, lower its cost structure, reduce remanufacturing efforts, and sell small-ticket items "as is." ERO would then need to adopt low-cost distribution channels. Maybe brokers could be used as a sales channel instead of being viewed as competitors. This approach would reduce headcount and SG&A expenses. On the other hand, HP could lose control of its installed base, as brokers would call on major accounts and cannibalize sales of new equipment.

BECTON DICKINSON: WORLDWIDE BLOOD COLLECTION TEAM

In the spring of 1993, Bill Kozy, president of Becton Dickinson VACUTAINER Systems (BDVS) division, discussed the challenges he foresaw for the Worldwide Blood Collection Team (WBCT) he led. Over his four and a half years chairing this team of managers drawn from BDVS operations around the globe, Kozy had seen great growth in the business. (See Exhibit 1.) He was particularly proud of the role the WBCT played in BDVS's two major new product introductions—the HEMOGARD safety closure and the plastic PLUS TUBE line—because they represented the first products developed and launched through the transnational management approach he was trying to develop.

Nonetheless, Kozy knew that he still faced difficult organizational issues as worldwide blood collection evolved from an international business treating overseas operations as appendages, to a genuinely transnational business managing its worldwide portfolio of resources and capabilities as strategic assets. Three major issues concerned him. First, there was the structure of the worldwide blood collection business. As Becton Dickinson's business grew outside the United States and the U.S. market matured, Kozy wondered if the configuration of roles and resources was appropriate. WBCT members were increasingly involved in discussions and negotiations over complex issues of where R&D resources and capabilities should be developed.

Kozy's second issue concerned the need to align human resource systems with the new worldwide strategies, the changing structures such as the WBCT, and the evolving processes for key decisions such as development of worldwide products. He had experienced the difficulties inherent in chairing a team of unevenly matched and skilled managers. And as larger numbers of managers became involved in decisions and

---

This case was prepared by Research Associate Kathleen Scharf (under the direction of Christopher A. Bartlett). Copyright © 1993 by the President and Fellows of Harvard College. Harvard Business School case 394-072.

Exhibit 1   *Becton Dickinson & Company—Income Statement**

Division and Strategy Center	1985 Actual $ (thousands)	1986 Actual $ (thousands)	1987 Actual $ (thousands)	1988 Actual $ (thousands)
Worldwide Blood Collection (including specimen collection)				
Net trade sales	$144,371	$172,770	$198,790	$236,736
Gross profit	62,815	77,902	90,443	109,201
Total expenses	37,188	40,156	46,897	55,114
OIBT[a]	23,046	34,950	41,441	48,680
RONA (pretax—average)	23.94%	30.60%	32.20%	31.00%
U.S. Blood Collection				
Net trade sales	$ 92,921	$102,823	$110,269	$123,018
Gross profit	44,400	48,327	50,723	56,711
Total expenses	22,780	22,218	22,975	25,013
OIBT[a]	19,421	23,978	25,955	29,730
RONA (pretax—average)	41.70%	41.10%	42.10%	41.70%
Europe Blood Collection				
Net trade sales	$ 30,204	$ 44,862	$ 56,669	$ 71,879
Gross profit	8,683	17,865	25,501	32,921
Total expenses	9,661	12,518	15,283	18,869
OIBT[a]	(1,055)	5,309	10,218	11,400
RONA (pretax—average)	(2.8%)	12.20%	20.00%	18.40%
Japan Blood Collection				
Net trade sales	$ 2,213	$ 3,421	$ 5,719	$ 7,438
Gross profit	1,237	2,382	3,380	4,626
Total expenses	1,084	1,532	3,883	5,130
OIBT[a]	154	850	(501)	(732)
RONA (pretax—average)	8.50%	45.00%	(16.7%)	(13.7%)

continued

*Note: Although data have been disguised, key relationships have been retained.
[a]OIBT: Operating Income Before Taxes for 1985–1987 includes little or no GCE for international units.

actions beyond their traditional areas of responsibility, he wondered how they should be measured and evaluated in terms of their contributions to BD's worldwide businesses.

Finally, Kozy was aware that some of his colleagues still wondered whether the WBCT was the right mechanism for managing BDVS's worldwide business in accordance with transnational concepts. While he believed this body had played a vital role particularly as it clarified its responsibilities in recent years, perhaps it was time to reevaluate its future role.

Exhibit 1   *(continued)*

Division and Strategy Center	1989 Actual $ (thousands)	1990 Actual $ (thousands)	1991 Actual $ (thousands)	1992 Actual $ (thousands)
Worldwide Blood Collection (including specimen collection)				
Net trade sales	$264,533	$293,940	$329,837	$363,376
Gross profit	118,353	133,234	147,000	163,714
Total expenses	59,518	65,436	75,970	82,614
OIBT[a]	52,562	60,110	60,344	72,732
RONA (pretax—average)	25.90%	23.00%	18.00%	23.00%
U.S. Blood Collection				
Net trade sales	$140,886	$149,910	$162,217	$170,670
Gross profit	62,595	66,860	71,375	74,753
Total expenses	27,269	38,693	32,759	34,712
OIBT[a]	32,990	35,539	33,559	36,529
RONA (pretax—average)	35.90%	29.60%	21.20%	25.30%
Europe Blood Collection				
Net trade sales	$ 75,275	$ 93,106	$111,751	$130,174
Gross profit	33,874	42,829	51,182	60,140
Total expenses	19,800	23,177	27,448	30,504
OIBT[a]	11,226	16,144	19,435	25,769
RONA (pretax—average)	13.00%	14.70%	14.30%	20.30%
Japan Blood Collection				
Net trade sales	$ 8,654	$ 9,074	$ 11,452	$ 14,735
Gross profit	5,338	4,339	4,972	7,100
Total expenses	4,978	4,877	6,149	6,692
OIBT[a]	95	(817)	(1,555)	(92.4)
RONA (pretax—average)	1.50%	(10.7%)	(17.3%)	(0.8%)

[a]OIBT: Operating Income Before Taxes for 1985–1987 includes little or no GCE for international units.

HISTORY AND CONTEXT OF BD'S INTERNATIONAL BUSINESS

Founded in 1897 as a manufacturer of clinical thermometers, Becton Dickinson and Company (BD) was a supplier of medical products and diagnostic systems to hospitals, physicians' offices, clinical and research laboratories, and pharmacies. BD had 10 core businesses organized into two product sectors: medical and diagnostic. Major medical sector products included hypodermic needles and syringes, medical gloves, diabetic products, and intravenous catheters. Diagnostic products included blood collection devices, prepared plated media, automated systems to detect and identify bacteria, rapid manual tests for doctors' offices, blood cell analysis systems, and immunocytometry products for cellular analysis.

Although about half of BD's 1992 sales of $2 billion were generated outside the United States, the company's international business had been developed relatively recently. In 1960, BD began to build a European organization whose central role was to expand the market for the very successful line of products the company had developed for the U.S. market. The European operation was built as a portfolio of country subsidiaries whose general managers reported to an area president who, in turn, was part of the corporate-level international group. Country managers were responsible for sales, marketing, distribution, administration, and compliance with local regulations, whereas U.S. division presidents managed R&D, manufacturing, and other operational issues. (See Exhibit 2.)

During the 1970s, BD transferred the locus of power from the functionally dominated regional office to the national subsidiaries, giving the country managers clear mandate to maximize sales in their countries. Evaluation and compensation still gave country managers little incen-

Exhibit 2   *Organization Chart, 1979*

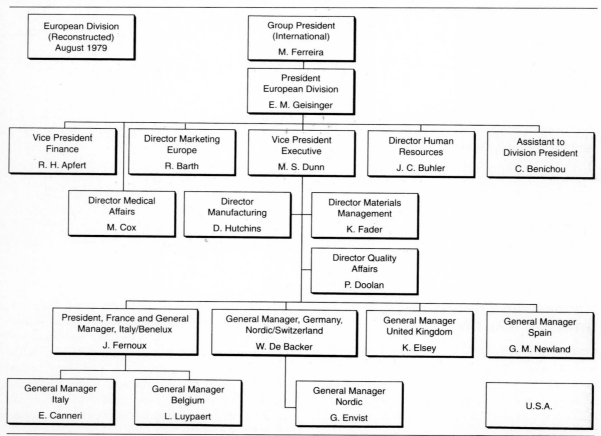

tive to risk short-term local results in the service of longer-term corporate goals for international market development. Their main complaint was that their performance was often limited because U.S. division managers often filled international orders only when the U.S. demands were covered, and routinely refused to consider new product requests from abroad.

European SBUs

In 1980, BD's senior executives saw the need to respond to several important developments. As the U.S. market matured, growing opportunities in Europe became increasingly attractive. At the same time, several international medical technology companies were focusing their attentions on Europe, posing a threat to BD's position not only in those markets but in the United States as well. As a result, pressure was increasing to reorganize sales and marketing activities in support of international growth, to rationalize international product flows, and to achieve more uniform cost and quality standards worldwide.

Expanding on the Strategic Business Unit (SBU) concept that had been overlaid on the U.S. product divisions to provide them with more strategic focus and discipline, top management decided to create corresponding European SBUs. The head of each European SBU was given the title of president, and treated similarly to a division president in the United States. This status level was higher than that accorded to country managers in Europe. Country-level sales and marketing personnel for these products now reported directly to the European SBU presidents rather than to their country manager. The country organizations retained responsibility for accounting, finance, human resource, and other administrative functions; BD's European headquarters coordinated these functions on a Europe-wide basis. The country presidents were still compensated based on their country P&L results, whereas SBU managers were rewarded for their SBU's results Europewide.

Although senior managers worked to prepare European managers for the new structure, a manager involved recalled making complex presentations to "a largely unresponsive audience." European managers had just adjusted to a shift from a regionally dominated functional organization to a stronger country system; now they were being asked to buy into a regionally driven structure once again. The changes were traumatic. Under the new hybrid structure, many country presidents felt their roles had greatly diminished. Although they were still BD's legal representatives and managed relationships with local regulatory agencies, unions, medical advisory panels, and the like, their role in broader strategy development, planning, and decision-making processes was unclear. In this environment, border disputes among SBU managers, country managers, and regional and corporate staff departments erupted frequently.

Differences over many issues such as marketing plans, sourcing, or managing manufacturing assets, arose periodically between U.S. and non-U.S. managers. But it was the conflict over new product development issues that often became the most emotional flashpoint for issues of autonomy, competence, and cultural bias. Because the U.S. divisions still controlled R&D, Europeans accused the U.S. divisions of a strong bias for products with U.S. markets. The U.S. division presidents, on the other hand, found most European product requests poorly documented and reflective of incomplete understandings of the real resource costs of the product development cycle.

Toward Transnational Management

Despite the continued spectacular growth of its European sales and market share, BD Europe posted operating losses for FY 1983–1984. The company was in an investment mode with respect to its European businesses, and the Plymouth plant, which had been built in 1981 as a regional plant for Europe, was not expected to turn a profit until the late 1980s. But senior managers feared that cost and quality goals would be difficult to achieve with the conflict that existed among pivotal players and organizational units, and it seemed unlikely that BD's European situation would permit it to contend successfully with a growing field of competitors.

By 1985, some senior managers were ready to reassess how the company managed its worldwide operations. As a result, BD engaged a consulting company to study the problem. The consultant produced two alternative models ("The Worldwide Product Division" and "Europe as Equal Partner"), each described in great detail as to the structural change required. Senior management decided it was not ready for another restructuring, with all the implied turf battles and inwardly focused energy. Instead, they sought a solution that would respond to the external forces for more cross-border coordination, but that would not compromise the country organizations' entrepreneurship and motivation, undermine their excellent relationships with their local markets, or interfere with their need to negotiate with national regulatory, medical and labor groups.

It was in this context that some senior managers met with Harvard Professor Christopher Bartlett, then undertaking a research project with his colleague Sumantra Ghoshal on worldwide organization.[1] In several sessions with the top team, Bartlett emphasized three core findings from the study:

- the strategic need for companies to build global efficiency, national responsiveness, and a worldwide innovation and learning capacity;
- the need of this multilayered strategic capability for a multidimensional organization, not one structured around traditional di-

chotomous choices between product and geography, centralization and decentralization; and

- the building of such organizations by changing management culture and values and developing organizational processes and relationships, and not just by changing formal structural design.

International Sector President Clateo Castellini, an Italian national, and Group President Ralph Biggadike, a British national, strongly advocated Bartlett's transnational approach because they saw it as providing a balance between the country structure and the SBU structure debated within BD. After many months of discussion, BD senior managers agreed to make the transnational approach the subject of the 1986 senior management conference. Then, in a series of three-day management conferences in 1986 and 1987, Bartlett exposed over 150 of BD's managers to transnational concepts. After analyzing the changes occurring in their businesses, the managers quickly realized the need to build multiple sources of competitive advantage and that doing so would require strong management capability in both the local and global dimensions.

Using frameworks similar to those illustrated in Exhibit 3, the managers spent most of the conference discussing and negotiating what needed to be managed in a more globally integrated manner, what needed to be handled in a more nationally responsive way, and what few issues needed to be handled jointly. As the exhibit suggests, they quickly discovered that there was no single formula and that they had to decide business by business, function by function, and even decision by decision.

Although most issues could be clearly allocated to country or business management, a few vital issues needed to be managed in a shared fashion. To provide a forum for these decisions, as well as a means to develop relationships between key managers, in late 1986 Worldwide

---

[1]Reported in Christopher A. Bartlett and Sumantra Ghoshal, *Managing Across Borders: The Transnational Solution* (Boston: HBS Press, 1989).

Exhibit 3   *Global Integration and National Responsibilities*

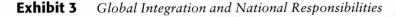

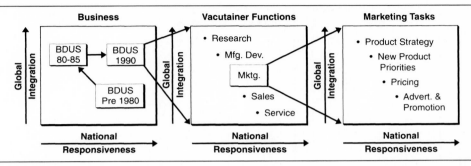

*This reflects the preliminary discussions and analysis done at the early transnational management seminars, where managers began to negotiate, business by business, function by function, and task by task, which responsibilities needed to be managed in a global manner (the northwest quadrant), which needed to be managed in a local manner (the southeast quadrant), and which *few key issues* needed to be handled in off-line forums where global and local managers could engage in the more intensive discussions and negotiations that transnational management required (the northeast quadrant).

Teams were established for each of the key worldwide businesses. Because each of the businesses had defined its organizational tasks differently, no attempt was made to impose a uniform set of responsibilities on the teams. Instead, senior management challenged each team to define its own role in helping manage the worldwide business. Some quickly became active in initiating worldwide projects and coordinating joint decision-making processes; others met less frequently and slipped into the role of communication forums.

THE CHANGES AT VACUTAINER SYSTEMS

One of the businesses affected by all the changes was the BD VACUTAINER Systems (BDVS) Division. BDVS included the U.S. business, which housed all R&D, and the European operations. Manufacturing plants in the United States and Europe reported to the BDVS president through the divisional director of Manufacturing. In Asia and Latin America, however, the VACUTAINER business still reported to the country presidents. (See Exhibit 4.)

BDVS as a Worldwide Business

The first formal "worldwide" meeting of BDVS managers occurred in Annecy, France, in 1982. The meeting was quite formal, with the U.S. group explaining to the Europeans procedures for new product development, product support, and other divisional functions. In response, the Europeans explained the nature of their market with its diverse pattern of medical practice.

Encouraged by their influence as a united group, the Europeans continued to meet on a somewhat informal and *ad hoc* basis throughout the early 1980s. Then European BDVS President Karlheinz Müller, described the spirit of the group:

> *After that [Annecy meeting] we had fairly regular meetings and product training for our sales force. It was a relationship we benefited mutually from, initiated really by the people, and tolerated by management.*

Through this process of opening communication channels, the non-U.S. managers became conscious that they might be able to have an input into BD's worldwide strategy. This encouraged managers in Europe and Japan to propose

Exhibit 4 *Organization Chart, 1986*

Organization Chart, 1986

President & CEO
J. Howe

- Sector Pres.: Medical
  W. Miller
  - Division Pres.: BDVS
    A. Battaglia*
    - Finance
    - Human Resources
    - Info Tech
    - Quality Assurance
    - Div VP Manuf
      W. Peters
      - Plant Mgr Puerto Rico
      - Plant Mgr Plymouth, UK
      - Plant Mgr Broken Bow, Neb.
      - Plant Mgr Sumpter, N.C.
    - Div VP Sls & Mktg
      H. Smith
      - Regional Sales Managers (US)
    - Div VP, R&D
      J. Welch*
- Sector Pres.: Diagnostic
  R. Gilmartin
- Sector Pres.: International
  C. Castellini
  - Pres., Blood Collection Eur.
    K. H. Muller*
    - Director, Mktg
      P. Dader*
    - Director Strat. Plan
    - Director Sales
      - Country Blood Collection Sales Managers
  - Japan Sub. GM
    - Mgr. Blood Coll.
      J. Abe*
  - Canadian Sub. GM
    - Mgr. Blood Coll.
      J. Robbins*

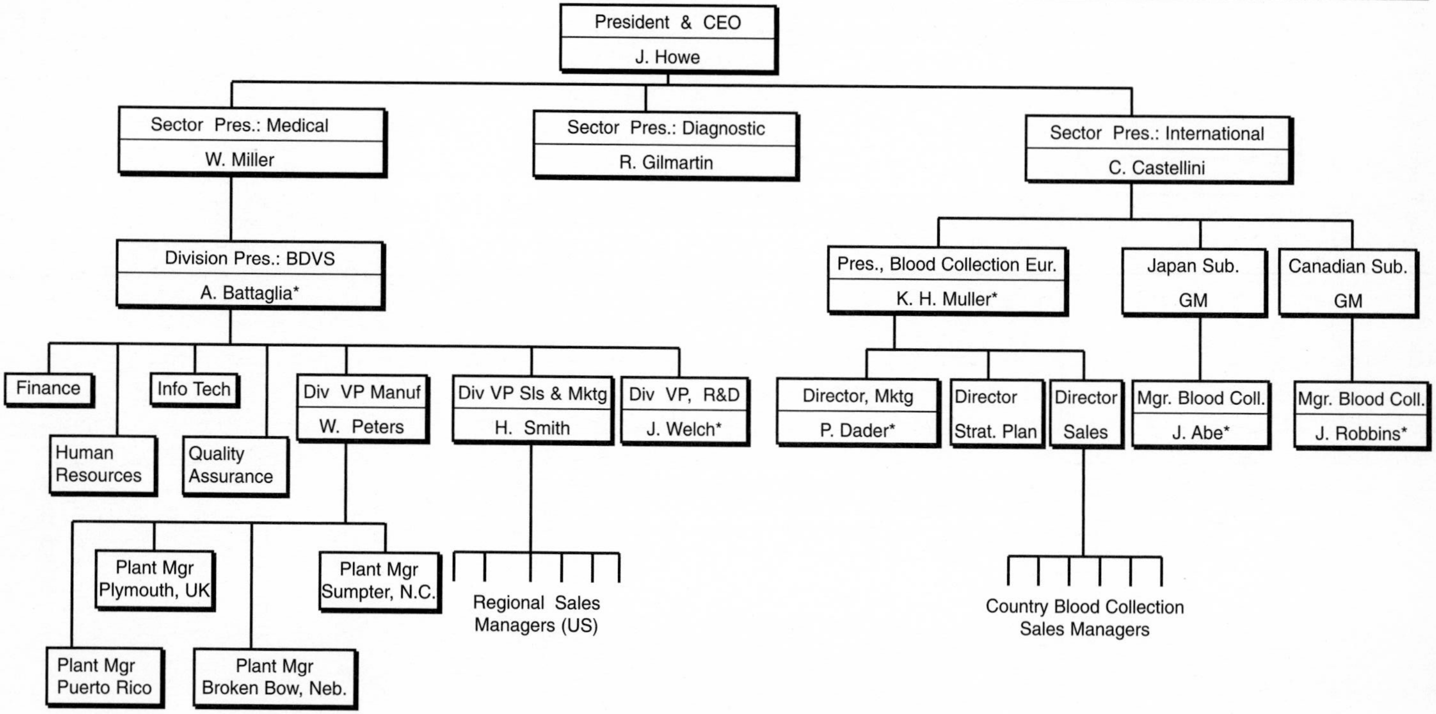

new product ideas to the worldwide SBU group in the mid-1980s. The initial response, however, was greatly disappointing for both non-U.S. groups, and by 1985 there was growing cynicism that the worldwide meetings were little more than a means of imposing U.S. strategy on overseas operations.

The stories of the development of two products—HEMOGARD and the PLUS TUBE—will illustrate the challenges BD faced in developing an integrated worldwide management approach.

HEMOGARD™: The European Proposal

In 1980, BD's European sales force began a push to convert European customers from conventional syringes to the VACUTAINER™ blood collection system that had been a major success in the U.S. market. In Europe, however, there was some resistance because of the perceived risk of blood exposure safety problems for laboratory personnel removing the VACUTAINER™ rubber stopper, which had to be popped off in order to remove blood for testing. Because this action broke the vacuum in the tube, there was some danger blood would "aerosolize"—spray out of the tube onto the worker's skin—or that the tube would actually break, posing a danger of cuts and infection with blood-transmitted diseases such as hepatitis.

The issue became a major topic of discussion in early 1983 at a VACUTAINER™ Europe sales meeting in St. Paul de Vence, France. Several sales and marketing managers reported that some of BD's competitors were developing closures that reduced the danger of worker contamination. Furthermore, they confirmed that BD's ability to convert was being slowed down most in the high-potential markets of the United Kingdom, Germany, and Italy, where safety concerns were the greatest. Following their diagnosis, the group developed drawings and preliminary specifications for the screw-on plastic closure device they envisioned and sent them

off to Joseph Welch, head of BDVS's R&D department.

The proposal met with little response due to a number of factors. There were no formal organizational means to translate regional interests into potential R&D priorities. Even new product and product extension ideas generated in the United States were not placed on a clearly prioritized list for R&D attention. Since the proposed screw-on cap represented an expensive product development commitment, U.S. marketing people saw little reason to develop it, believing it would be a niche product with limited demand, even in Europe. Furthermore, BDVS had several large-scale projects on the board, and the Americans saw little need to take a major risk without strong support within R&D and with thinly documented paybacks.

As Müller later acknowledged:

Since we had 100 million [annual unit sales of tubes] versus 500 million for the United States, it was hard to interest R&D. And our marketing group was not very effective then in submitting the Project Initiation Review properly. Without formal processes, it all had to be done through an informal relationship with Joe Welch.

Nonetheless, within Europe there was a growing sense of frustration as time passed and the screw-on closure was not forthcoming from U.S. R&D. The promise of truly worldwide management seemed hollow.

In June of 1984, after considerable pressure from Müller and his team, Welch agreed to a compromise. He directed his R&D department to develop a mold for an interim product, a press-on plastic cap called the Safety Cap that could be added to existing VACUTAINER products for use in hematology labs. The design was a good deal simpler than the European proposal, and the mold itself was produced in a weekend in BD's machine shop.

In October of 1984, four months after the first Safety Cap molds were produced, Alfred

Battaglia became BDVS president and committed himself to "lighting a fire" under the division's product development process. He saw his new division's R&D function as one with many projects but no clear sense of their relative importance and business potential. Instead of relying on personal contacts and the "squeaky wheel" approach that had been the division's *de facto* research priority system, Battaglia encouraged his staff to pursue a clearer and more informed approach to allocating BDVS's resources. To help in this regard, he developed and began to use an R&D priority matrix on which proposed projects were ranked based on a combination of development cost and potential return.

Early in 1985, BDVS began to ship small quantities of Safety Caps for field trials in Europe. The company's accounts were protected more against the incursions of competing safety products, and field data could be fed back to the U.S. R&D engineers still working on the project. Unfortunately, the trials were not very successful, as an engineer involved with the project recalled:

> The Safety Caps didn't exactly take off. They didn't fit in everybody's holders. They didn't fit with competitive needles. We didn't have a very good needle at the time, so a lot of places were using our tube with someone else's needle. . . . It was a son of a gun to push on; it took about 30 pounds of force to put it on . . . [and] it was very smooth and straight-sided, so it was hard to grip with a wet glove.

As BDVS engineers went back to work on the project, Battaglia urged the R&D group to look at the project as one with worldwide significance. Not only did it respond to a growing concern for health care workers' safety, but it also offered a differentiating benefit that could allow BDVS to standardize on a smaller global blood collection tube size, thereby reducing costs.

From the European perspective, however, all they saw was a further delay. Therefore, when key U.S. and European figures met in 1985 at BD's plant in Plymouth, England, Müller expressed his frustration to Battaglia. By this stage, the European team had buttressed its initial proposal with market studies and physicians' endorsements and lined up significant support for the product through direct contacts at the U.S. corporate level. (Müller later characterized his own approach as "table banging.") Battaglia was sympathetic and agreed to commit to the project.

Following this meeting, Welch assigned more R&D resources to the project and moved more aggressively to secure agreement to specifications. New European trials provided input into design decisions, and by March 1986, marketing groups in the United States, Canada, Europe, and Japan had signed off on the specifications for the Safety Cap. Now the challenge was to implement the launch of a product called HEMOGARD™.

PLUS TUBE: The Japanese Proposal

When members of the Blood Collection SBU met in Tokyo in 1985, Japanese managers talked with leading team members about what they saw as a key to VACUTAINER market share in Japan: unbreakable specimen collection tubes. Breakability was much more than an issue of safety to Japanese users. Because of a strong cultural aversion to blood loss, recollecting specimens because of tube breakage was a major problem, and resistance to breakability was seen as a core measure of overall product quality. Although European management viewed the plastic tube as a less urgent, longer-term need, the Japanese group saw it as an urgent priority to defend BD's fragile market share against competitive Japanese products that were already selling well.

Many BDVS observers realized that demand for relatively light, unbreakable collection tubes would grow as environmental and safety concerns increased worldwide. In both Austria and Japan, local firms had already introduced plastic tubes, and although their market share was small and localized, they looked to be potential threats to BD's penetration of these markets.

Again, the sense of local Japanese managers was that their requests had fallen on deaf ears. Japanese managers felt they had struggled against uncertain supplies and inattention to quality concerns for several years; between 1982 and 1984 BD actually lost part of its small market share in Japan. From their perspective, the HEMOGARD™ project had finally captured attention, and by 1985, was "winning" development resources while their project (dubbed the PLUS TUBE) "lost" because of the originating market's small size. U.S. R&D managers rejected this view and pointed out that the costs and technical challenges entailed in the two projects differed greatly. Whereas HEMOGARD could be developed with existing technologies, the projected plastic tube would require substantial retooling and the location or development of high-performing polymer materials that would not only meet medical standards but also guarantee shelf life, transparency, and other performance characteristics glass-tube users had come to expect.

THE WORLDWIDE BLOOD COLLECTION TEAM

The frustration and confusion managers were experiencing on the HEMOGARD and PLUS TUBE projects were symptomatic of the interpersonal tension that existed as BD struggled with how best to manage international expansion. The transnational organizational structure designated to help BD deal with these issues was the Worldwide Blood Collection Team (WBCT) in 1986. (See Exhibit 5.) It was hoped that the new organizational structure, and the changed management approach it required would help resolve some of the problems.

Exhibit 5   *Worldwide Blood Collection Team, 1986*

- Alfred Battaglia, President, BDVS US
- Hank Smith, Vice President, Sales/Marketing BDVS
- Joe Welch, Vice President/R&D BDVS
- Bill Peters, Vice President/Manufacturing BDVS
- Karlheinz Muller, President, Blood Collection Products Europe
- Pierre Dader, Director of Marketing, Blood Collection Products Europe
- Jun Abe, Manager, Blood Collection and Diabetic Products Japan
- Canadian representative (rotating)
- Periodic attender:
- Representative, Latin America

Early Years: Defining the WBCT's Role

Although the WBCT decided to focus on strategic issues, ability to fulfill that objective was limited by two factors. First, worldwide plans were part of the U.S. division's strategic/operational/financial planning process (SOF), developed by the U.S. staff with limited worldwide consultation. And second, few non-U.S. managers had been trained in BD's strategic planning system, which senior BD managers viewed as central to the firm's management system.

As a consequence, during the first two years of the WBCT's official existence, the team was seen largely as an information-sharing group. Basically, the organization continued to operate as it had under the old SBU model: the U.S. division determined strategy, directed R&D, and controlled manufacturing resources, while overseas operations focused on sales and marketing. Non-U.S. WBCT members, designated by their country or regional managers, tended to be junior to the U.S. team members and less able to commit their own organizations to the WBCT agenda. Some regions' delegates appeared irregularly at team meetings, changed frequently, and did not always command English well enough to participate fully in discussions. As a result, for both HEMOGARD and the PLUS TUBE, continued progress was determined by the originating region's ability to convince the BDVS president and R&D director of the projects' potential.

The creation of the WBCT, however, soon had an impact on the development of the HEMOGARD project. In 1986, it was becoming clear to U.S. epidemiologists and to the general public that the AIDS virus outbreaks were early warnings of a pandemic, and the worldwide humanitarian and business potentials of a safety tube closure became more obvious. A BDVS R&D engineer explained:

> The driver was Europe originally, and even in 1984 and 1985 . . . Europeans tended to have a longer view of some trends. They knew about AIDS, and that it was important, and would get worse. In the United States, we were a year or two behind on that curve; awareness peaked around 1986. . . . It was only after the scare hit the United States that we really started cranking [HEMOGARD] up.

With this more widespread support for HEMOGARD, the WBCT provided a useful forum in which to discuss and drive the project. At the team's urging, BDVS R&D director Joe Welch pursued the project aggressively. The WBCT also decided to use the Plymouth, England, plant as the major source for the product.

The PLUS TUBE found a more difficult time claiming the WBCT's attention. First, the team's role was unclear in its early days, and nobody seemed sure of what function to play. Second, the project overlapped with the HEMOGARD launch, and the BDVS R&D and manufacturing staffs were heavily involved with both.

Japanese managers were convinced that the HEMOGARD closure on a glass tube had no future in Japan. They were also greatly alarmed by

news that Terumo, BD's major competitor in Japan, was working steadily toward a plastic tube. While the persistent Japanese concerns convinced the U.S. managers to raise the priority of getting a viable product into Japan, even without the breakthrough in plastic technology they had been seeking, there was continuing debate within the WBCT about the worldwide application of plastic tube strategy. In contrast to HEMOGARD, which everyone believed eventually would be a crucial product worldwide, PLUS TUBE was seen by many as a uniquely Japanese product. Most of the Europeans, for instance, were unconvinced that rapid plastic tube development was necessary to their short-term regional strategy, although some, like Eckhard Lachenauer, believed it would be a key competitive product by 1995. A U.S. participant recalled the flavor of the discussion in 1987 and 1988:

> There seemed to be two camps about whether plastic was necessary. There was a lot of discussion of profits and ROA. We also had to decide how fast we would push the plastic tube, if we did decide to develop it. That was very important because in some instances the coexistence of glass and plastic was an important business strategy for us.

The division and the corporation agreed in 1987 to a staged development scheme, which aimed at supplying the Japanese market as quickly as possible, and moved on toward ultimate goals of shelf life, appearance, cost, and other factors with the help of BD's Research Center in North Carolina.

The debate of PLUS TUBE in the WBCT meetings did serve to increase overall awareness of the project and, as a result, led to some progress in locating suppliers. BD managers in Europe and in Japan ferreted out promising suppliers, licensers, and business partners who were able to supply technology and materials. For example, Müller introduced Welch to representatives of Greiner, the Austrian company manufacturing plastic blood collection tubes, and Jun

Abe of BD's Japanese company put him in touch with Sekisui, a Japanese company interested in a marketing partnership for its plastic technology. In 1987, BD agreed to purchase Greiner's molds and Sekisui's plastic technology.

The Maturing WBCT: Launching World Products

In October of 1988, when Battaglia was promoted to group president, Bill Kozy became BDVS president. By this time the WBCT composition and role had evolved considerably, and Kozy saw the team as a major means to achieve the ambitious growth in international business he and BD expected.

However, from his first meeting with the WBCT, Kozy was aware that it was still struggling with the notion of "transnational management." It was difficult for managers to grasp and embody a change process that was focused not on a structural prescription but on changing processes and relationships and on broadening management mentalities ("creating a matrix in managers' minds," as the transnational model proposed). Kozy described the division's early operating committee discussions:

> In terms of worldwide roles and responsibilities, no one had a clue. A bunch of basically command and control people suddenly became "team members" or "team leaders." Everyone wanted to know what his role was, what he was responsible for. People were still in the political mode of "If you're not going to develop my products, I'm going to tell."

To spark discussion on the team's role, Kozy asked his entire senior staff to read Bartlett and Ghoshal's book *Managing Across Borders*, so that the group could discuss it chapter by chapter during its regular meetings. The new division president saw the reading and discussions as a valuable exercise, although some of his staff greeted references to it with wry laughter.

Kozy himself recounted an epiphany of sorts that occurred on a plane during a conversation with his Japanese seatmate. The two men discussed the challenges of international business management, and the Japanese manager said Kozy was lucky to work for a company with the patience to adopt an approach like transnational management, which would clearly require at least 10 years to implement. The extent to which transnational management really was built on changing managers' mentalities and relationships rather than just restructuring reporting relationships suddenly struck Kozy with full force, and the amount of time required to achieve genuine transnational management became clear. He realized that it probably *was* a 10-year process, and that his own division had been struggling with it for only three or four years.

Kozy's commitment to clarify the WBCT's responsibilities and increase its role as a key forum for transnational management exchange was greatly facilitated by the ongoing operations relating to the two new products under development.

HEMOGARD launch

As the HEMOGARD launch neared, the WBCT was increasingly involved in marketing decisions, some of which did not meet with field sales approval. For technical reasons and to reduce manufacturing costs, BDVS wanted to minimize the number of individual HEMOGARD catalogue numbers. But every time they reduced the size of the product line, the European marketing group would have to lower its forecasts, triggering long debate within the group. Eckhard Lachenauer described the WBCT discussions of the number of VACUTAINER products to be offered with HEMOGARD closures and debates over sales projections as "a constant battle."

Finally, the HEMOGARD line was launched in July 1989. European Director of Operations John Hanson described the launch as the most successful in which he had ever participated, representing to him a truly cross-functional and trans-Atlantic team effort. He recalled the plan's execution:

> By the end of 1988 the real final stage was to involve the plants to bring the product to market. That was the part that was highly successful. It was the first real transnational effort that brought the product to a very aggressive launch date of June 1989. And we slipped by only one month, to July 1989. That I always quote as being truly successful in a worldwide team sense—the plants, R&D, the Supply Chain group, sales and marketing. We had very detailed plans, and they actually happened—that's the amazing part.

Hanson attributed the success of the HEMO-GARD launch effort to two central characteristics. First, team roles were made an integral part of members' regular jobs rather than side assignments:

> All of the team assignments and the additional responsibilities these jobs implied were formalized within the framework of their job description. People did the job as they were meant to, this meant that rather than being asked to take on a team assignment on the side.

Second, Hanson believed the launch process was effective because project participants agreed to bypass any existing management information systems that were slow and bureaucratic. For example, new materials management models were developed on local personal computers because existing systems seemed unlikely to support the manufacturing schedules BD contemplated. Furthermore, minutes of the meetings of far-flung teams and committees were faxed to Kozy and Welch within hours. In turn, these managers and their staff responded rapidly to queries, requests, and issues. Hanson recalled:

> The whole key was focus and communication and holding people responsible for what they're actually supposed to do. There's no project now with that weekly communication

and weekly meetings. The coordination is not as clear and crisp.

PLUS TUBE launch

The launch of the PLUS TUBE went less smoothly, but the WBCT's role was also critical in bringing this product to market. The main problem stemmed from BDVS R&D's agreement to a launch-date schedule before they completely understood how challenging a shift from glass to plastic would be. The molds purchased from Greiner produced tubes that did not fit the HEMOGARD closure and had to be modified. In making adjustments, the group quickly learned that plastic was a very different material from glass. But having the WBCT forum at least allowed the problems to be identified quickly and for corrective action to be agreed on and assigned.

Although BDVS originally planned to release the first PLUS TUBEs in late 1988 or 1989, by that date they had not even begun the first Japanese field trials. Eventually trials were conducted and the first products were shipped in 1991. The division and the WBCT were learning that agreement to a marketing strategy did not produce manufacturing capability, as one manager pointed out:

> It took us a year to figure out how to make it work; the schedules were very aggressive. We have learned from this. For the PLUS TUBE we put schedules on products before we figured out how to do it. We're now using a planning method that won't let you commit to a date until you've proved a technology.

Structural Change in the WBCT

At the same time the WBCT was handling the implementation of the two new product launches, it was also engaged in a variety of other issues that required the input and involvement of managers worldwide. Meanwhile, the size and diversity of team membership had grown substantially. By 1990, a few of the most active and influential team members felt that the WBCT was too large and too diversely skilled to make all of the decisions the team's projects required. As Lachenauer explained, "Bill (Kozy) and I realized one day that we could not make all the decisions in the big team. It was taking too much time on tactics and not enough on strategy." The decision was made to form three smaller subteams that could move more efficiently to deal with the strategic, operating, and marketing issues that were becoming increasingly important. (See Exhibits 7 and 8.)

In 1991 the three members of the Worldwide Strategy Team—Kozy, Lachenauer, and Abe—embarked on a worldwide profiling tour, using BD's long-established strategic profiling process to examine regional strategic potentials and advise regional managers on their role in the worldwide business unit's international strategy. The trio met in Tokyo with managers in BD's Japanese and Asia/Pacific blood collection businesses, in Mexico City with their Brazilian and Mexican counterparts, with Canadian managers, and with managers in Europe and the United States. They visited customers in Brazil and Japan. The visits exposed the Strategy Team to the realities of the business outside its major markets, and Kozy returned newly impressed by the potential of markets such as Latin America.

The trip also sensitized the team to the different needs of local markets (e.g. Japanese needs for smaller tubes and some labeling changes). In fact, the Strategy Team members were engaged enough in the problems presented by the Brazilian business that they arranged to visit Brazil. As these visits and exchanges continued, managers recognized that a new level of understanding and cooperation was emerging in subsequent WBCT meetings. Abe commented:

Before when we talked about "worldwide strategy" we really didn't know—we talked only about surface things. That really changed; there were much better suggestions, *and much better advice. Now we could see how to use U.S. and even European resources to help.*

The other major structural changes related to the management of R&D and technology support. As the HEMOGARD and PLUS TUBE experiences had shown, overseas managers had often experienced difficulty in getting support from the U.S.-based R&D group. The situation was even more difficult for those trying to get technology assistance for older products no longer marketed in the United States, because most R&D staff were tied up in current projects.

The situation gradually began to improve in the late 1980s, particularly after the arrival of Steven Sous, a BDVS quality assurance (QA) specialist. As a sideline to his domestic responsibilities, Sous took on the role of QA liaison to Japan and from that base gradually expanded his international role. Because of the personal contacts he made during those meetings and in trips to BD locations outside the United States, Sous was increasingly identified as the best person to contact for technical support—especially in the problematic area of support for products deemphasized or discontinued in the United States. As issues in which he was involved came up, he began to attend the WBCT meetings in an unofficial capacity, eventually attending regularly.

When Joseph Welch left BDVS in January of 1990 to become president of BD Labware, and Steven Savitz took his place as vice-president of R&D, Savitz defined his role as "doing worldwide R&D for the division." His non-U.S. colleagues viewed him as "genuinely transnational." Savitz strengthened the international role Steven Sous had taken, in 1991 giving him the new title of manager, Research and Development Worldwide Technical Support. Sous and his group were responsible for working with the non-U.S. businesses to support and extend products, including responsibility for relatively small projects such as label changes, producing VACUTAINER tubes for high-altitude applications, and packaging variations necessitated by government regulations or differences in device-dispensing practices. Most of these "do it now" projects did not require large financial investment and did not need to wend their way through the division's major project approval and resource allocation process. To deal with demand, Sous hoped to expand his staff by four permanent positions in FY 1992.

During the same period, Kozy and Savitz responded to Lachenauer's long-term lobbying for a Europe-based R&D manager by appointing Chris Dufresne, Manager R&D VACUTAINER Systems Europe in BD's European headquarters. He reported to Lachenauer with a dotted line to Savitz, and was responsible for helping to manage the interface between European manage-

ment and the U.S. R&D organization, particularly for expediting European new product and product extension ideas. Dufresne's position was a compromise between the European desire to be fully integrated vertically and the U.S. division's desire to maintain control over worldwide R&D efforts.

Dufresne lost no time in becoming a champion for European products. During the May 1992 meetings, he presented an ordered list of potential products for European applications. Many present agreed that his reputation and U.S. experience increased the likelihood that European ideas would be accorded serious consideration by the WBCT and by Kozy and Savitz.

During the May 1992 Toronto meeting, members of the WBCT discussed two important

---

Exhibit 6   *Worldwide Blood Collection Team Role, 1992**

- Develop the worldwide strategy and the strategic goals for the Blood Collection Strategy Center.
- Support development of the regional strategies congruent with the worldwide strategy.
- Recommend the worldwide resource allocation to achieve the maximized effectiveness and efficiency in implementation of the worldwide strategy.
- Review the worldwide business performance to monitor the progress to worldwide strategic goals and to recommend the corrective strategies, if necessary.
- Develop and update the worldwide competitive strategies by integrating the competitive information from the worldwide regions.
- Support developing the regional competitive strategies by releasing the collected competitive information to the worldwide regions.
- Evaluate and prioritize the new product concepts in the worldwide R&D agenda to maintain the optimum resource allocation in PACE.
- Support non-PACE regional product development requirements based upon specifically local customer needs by the worldwide technical support function in the BDVS organization.
- Coordinate worldwide product strategies and rollouts.
- Make recommendations on "global" vs. "local" business activities.
- Coordinate transfer of key skills/capabilities from "Centers of Excellence" to regions.
- Maintain good communications with regional senior managements to help them to develop and implement the well-integrated regional operations strategy with the Blood Collection Strategy Center strategy.
- Identify and locate medical/QA/RA support to the worldwide regions.
- Identify and allocate technical/selling skill training support to the worldwide regions.

*Source: *Worldwide Blood Collection Operating Manual.*

Exhibit 7   *Transnational Organizational Concept, September 1992**

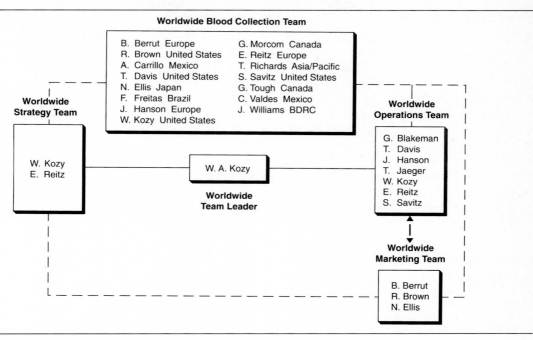

*Source: Worldwide Blood Collection Operating Manual.

new developments in their technology management. First, BDVS was working with a consultant to refine the project approval and project management processes. Second, they discussed the need for greater non-U.S. participation in the R&D function. Although budget constraints prevented him from further expansion of the R&D organizations in regions outside the United States and Europe, Kozy was sympathetic to the requests. After much discussion, he and WBCT members from Mexico and Japan developed the idea of creating a position within the U.S. R&D organization to be funded jointly by Mexico and Japan.

All WBCT members saw clear evolution toward genuine transnational management in the team's operation. Roles and structures were clarified in practice and in the "Worldwide Blood Collection Manual" (on which Exhibits

6, 7, and 8 are based). But historic difficulties in achieving a real balance between the power of the U.S. division staff and the rest of the company's interests persisted. During the 1992 Toronto meetings, Lachenauer and Kozy and his staff clearly dominated many discussions from which their non-U.S. colleagues sometimes seemed disengaged. A rapid assessment of the development costs and sales potential of a list of proposed new products and product extensions yielded a priority list intended to guide the U.S. R&D function in its work over the company year, but some team members wondered privately whether they had either the time or the expertise to assess every project fairly. They cited examples of products such as the European-sponsored SEDITAINER tube, whose further development still languished in the face of the American medical

---

Exhibit 8   *Worldwide Blood Collection Team, 1992**

- President, BDVS US
- President, Blood Collection Europe
- Vice-president/R&D BDVS
- Director of Marketing, BDVS
- Director, Worldwide Manufacturing and Logistics
- Vice-president, Worldwide Business Development
- Corporate Medical Director
- Marketing Director, Blood Collection Europe
- Vice-president/General Manager, Diagnostic Canada
- Marketing Manager, Blood Collection Canada
- Sales and Marketing Director, Blood Collection Japan
- Business Director, Blood Collection Asia/Pacific
- Sales and Marketing Director, Diagnostic Mexico
- Sales and Marketing Director, Blood Collection Brazil
- Director, Manufacturing Europe (Director Plymouth plant)

Worldwide Strategy Team
- President, BDVS
- President, Blood Collection Europe
- Vice-president, Worldwide Business Development

Leads Worldwide Strategy development in the Worldwide Blood Collection Team.

Worldwide Operations Team
- Director, Worldwide Manufacturing and Logistics (Chair)
- President, BDVS US
- President, Blood Collection Europe
- Plant Manager, Sumter, North Carolina
- Director, Manufacturing Europe
- Vice-president/R&D, BDVS

Acts as Worldwide Operations Management Team for Manufacturing, R&D, and Supply Chain Management.

Worldwide Marketing Team
- Director of Marketing, BDVS
- Director of Marketing, Blood Collection Europe
- Director of Marketing, BDVS Japan

Speaks for "Worldwide Marketing" on key product strategies or new product decisions.

---

*Source: *Worldwide Blood Collection Operating Manual.*

directors' disapproval and American marketers' indifference.

THE WBCT IN 1993: ACHIEVEMENTS AND CHALLENGES

After the WBCT met in Geneva in May of 1993, many participants sensed that the group was continuing to evolve toward a genuinely transnational position. Where they once struggled to achieve consensus around uniform global strategies and goals, they were now comfortable with regional variations consistent with overall worldwide strategies and business goals. For example, because European members preferred a marketing strategy that emphasized choice between glass and plastic, the group discussed selling the PLUS TUBE under another name in Europe to avoid implying invidious comparisons to the glass tubes they planned to sell alongside plastic for a few years. U.S. participant Tom Jaeger saw this and other local market-specific discussions as good indications of the WBCT's evolution toward a genuine transnational mentality:

> Even in the most recent meeting before this, we felt there had to be a worldwide consensus on business strategy; now a consensus has arisen that we can have different strategies . . . we need to have everyone understand, and decide on a regional basis exactly what to do. I believe in that—that everyone is the keeper of their own markets.

Furthermore, the WBCT's ability to respond rapidly to worldwide needs had developed considerably. When members representing Japan pushed for rapid expansion of catalogue numbers to include smaller tubes and a wider range of coatings and additives, many were elated by a six-month concept-to-release process for a new additive tube for Japan undertaken in 1992, remarking that without the R&D proposal review and priority-setting capacities of the evolving WBCT, such speed would have been inconceivable.

The group also broadened international participation in R&D decision-making. The European director of Operations and a senior European marketing manager joined the worldwide Project Approval Committee, thereby bringing the group to U.S./European parity. Furthermore, WBCT members had already agreed to place sponsored engineers from Europe, Japan, and Latin America on the U.S. R&D staff.

Members saw considerable change in WBCT team members' ability to communicate and negotiate shared and divergent strategies and operational parameters. A frequent WBCT participant with both R&D and manufacturing experience at BD observed that each member's understanding of the whole range of the business had deepened, and that members had learned how to argue for the projects they supported:

> Because of the Worldwide Team meetings, each of the different regions now looks at their marketplace a little bit differently because at meetings they have to explain to people from other parts of the world what's really going on. They have to get outside their tunnel vision, put a perspective on the whole thing. Someone can't just say, "This is the way it is," so he prepares his data to explain why his perspective might be different from theirs.

However, as he reviewed the WBCT's achievements, Kozy could not help wondering what additional changes would be required to keep the group operating effectively. Questions that particularly concerned him were:

- Does the business have the right configuration of assets and resources? In particular, what are the implications of our recent changes in the R&D function for the future of that key task? Should we try to keep our resources concentrated in the United States and expand the "sponsored liaison" positions, or should we yield to the European lobby for a more fully integrated European development capability? How can we balance

Exhibit 9   *Senior Management Bonus Plan Changes, 1993*

Corporate Officers	Sector Presidents	Division Heads
Old Formula		
50% Company (65% EPS vs. budget, 35% strategic)	25% Company (65% EPS vs. budget, 35% strategic)	25% Company (65% EPS vs. budget, 35% strategic)
25% Strategic (function/company)	50% Sector (65% OIBT vs. budget, 35% strategic)	50% Unit (65% OIBT vs. budget, 35% strategic)
25% Individual performance	25% Individual performance	25% Individual performance
New Formula		
75% Company EPS[a] budget	25% Company EPS[a] vs. budget	25% Sector (65% OIBT vs. budget, 35% strategic)
	50% Sector OIBT	50% Unit OIBT
25% Strategic (function/company)	25% Strategic (worldwide sector)	25% Strategic (worldwide teams)

[a]As reported for executive officers; FX neutral for other corporate officers.

the large-scale businesses in the United States and Europe, against the smaller businesses in the rest of the world?

- What changes do we need to make in our human resource policies and practices to move us further towards transnational management? What changes can we make to our human resource management system so we can send people on overseas assignment with some assurance that their careers won't be compromised? The new compensation system has been favorably received [see Exhibit 9], and should help us get over the conflict between the WBCT and the regions caused by

regional managers' being rewarded for maximizing the local budget, but what else can be done to increase WBCT effectiveness?

- Finally, how should the WBCT's role evolve as we move into the future? Is there need for more structure and more clearly defined roles as some advocated, or should it continue to be managed on a more flexible process-driven manner? What impact will changing membership have on its operation, and can such personal dependencies be managed? Do a few strong managers dominate team meetings, and do we need to find ways to foster broader participation?

ABB'S RELAYS BUSINESS: BUILDING AND MANAGING A GLOBAL MATRIX

It was a casual conversation between the chairmen of Asea and Brown Boveri in 1987 about the dismal state of the utilities equipment market that eventually led to merger talks between these two giant power equipment companies. Within weeks of the announcement in August 1987, Percy Barnevik, the CEO of Asea who was asked to lead the combined operations, had articulated a strategic vision for Asea Brown Boveri (ABB). Convinced that the decade-long decline in new power generation capacity would soon reverse itself, he believed that the new technologies and scale economies required to meet the new demand could only be developed by companies operating on a global scale. At the same time, however, he felt that because of the high level of government ownership or control of power companies, the vast majority of new orders would continue to go to companies with a strong national presence. His strategy was to build a company that could exploit these two major industry trends.

Having articulated his broad vision, Barnevik formed a ten-person top management work group to analyze how the operations of Asea and Brown Boveri could best be linked to achieve it. Because ABB would start operating as a merged company on January 1, 1988, Barnevik wanted quick action. Within two months the top management team had decided on a matrix structure that would balance the global business focus of an organization built on around 60 global business areas (BAs) with the national market focus provided by 1,300 local companies grouped under the umbrella of several country-based holding companies (see Exhibit 1).

Barnevik then set about selecting the management team that would staff the new organization. To select the 300 key managers who would lead the change process, Barnevik personally interviewed hundreds of Asea and Brown Boveri executives. He was seeking those with good technical and commercial backgrounds who

---

This case was prepared by Christopher A. Bartlett. Copyright © 1993 by the President and Fellows of Harvard College. Harvard Business School case 394-016.

Exhibit 1   *ABB Matrix Concept**

The ABB organization is built on a federation of 1,300 operating companies charged with managing the front-line operations. In each major country or region, these companies are administered through a national holding company, which is responsible for ensuring effective performance of ABB's total market presence. At the same time, each operating company reports to one of 58 Business Areas (BAs) responsible for developing global strategies.

   Conceptually, the matrix operates as follows:

Business Areas: / National Companies	Company A	Company B	Company C	Etc.
BA₁				Worldwide Strategy
BA₂				
BA₃				
Etc.		All BA Operations		

*Source: Company documents.

were "tough skinned, fast on their feet, and able to lead" yet also "open, generous, and capable of thinking in group terms."

   In January 1988, he assembled this hand-picked group of 300 for a three-day meeting in Cannes. In presentations supported with 198 overhead transparencies (an approach that was to become a signature of his communications-intensive management style), Barnevik detailed industry trends, analyzed market opportunities, and profiled ABB's economics and cost structures. But mostly he focused on how the new organization would allow ABB to manage three contradictions—to be global and local, big and small, and radically decentralized with central control. (Exhibit 2 presents excerpts from some of his overhead slides). At the end of the meeting, each manager received a 21-page "policy bible" outlining the major policies and values to be communicated to the next level of the organization.

   Barnevik's management model focused on the twin principles of decentralized responsibility and individual accountability. To emphasize the former, he ensured that most of ABB's key resources were controlled directly by the

Exhibit 2   *Cannes Top Management Meeting—Excerpts from Barnevik's Slides*

BA Management Responsibilities
- Worldwide result and profitability
- Establishing a management team—preferably consisting of members from different countries
- Developing a worldwide strategy
- Basic development (typically CAD)
- Coordinating delegated development
- Market allocation scheme and/or tender coordination

Country Management Responsibilities
- Size and complexity of local structure in line with ABB's business presence
- In smaller countries: single company with departments
- In larger countries: holding structure with many subsidiaries and operating units
- Local entities serve their respective markets in line with BA objectives, strategies, and guidelines—they have responsibility for operational results

General Principles of Management Behavior
1. To take action (and stick out one's neck) and do the right things is obviously the best.
2. To take action and do the wrong things is next best (within reason and a limited number of times).
3. Not to take action (and lost opportunities) is the only nonacceptable behavior.

Policies for Change
- Identify necessary changes implemented as fast as possible. Small risk that negative changes not considered enough.
    - Concentrate on the ones with biggest profit improvements (80-20 rule).
    - 10 times more common to delay than the opposite.
- Get over with "negative" changes in a lump sum and avoid prolonging the process and cut it up in pieces. Packages with "positive" and "negative" changes desirable. Important to quickly focus on new opportunities. Means earlier focus on positive changes.
- No "fair" reduction in terms of equality between locations—improvements of group profitability counts as main criteria in a broad sense.
- Most major changes must be started first year.
    - "Honeymoon" of small changes would be detrimental.
    - What is not started the first year will be a lot more difficult later.
- The merger creates unique possibilities ("excuses") to undertake long overdue actions which should have been undertaken anyway.
- Upcoming merger problems must be resolved fast and on lowest possible level.
- Example:
    - First cutting capacity, merging and streamlining costs;
    - Then with increased competitiveness—growth and new opportunities.
- Volume increase is solution to cost problems.

federation of 1,300 front-line companies, whenever possible set up as separate legal entities. To ensure that managers inherited their results from year to year, he gave them control over their balance sheets, including the right to borrow and the ability to retain up to 30% of earnings. Furthermore, he implemented his "30/30/30 rule," in which he decreed that all headquarters organizations—from corporate to business area to regional—should be dramatically downsized by relocating 30% of the headquarters personnel to the front-line companies, by having another 30% provide their value added as outsourced services, and by laying off an additional 30%. To set the example, the staffing level at ABB's combined corporate headquarters was reduced from over 2,000 to only 150.

To ensure accountability, Barnevik assigned a team to develop a new transparent reporting system which aimed at "democratizing information." Dubbed ABACUS, the system was designed to collect uniform dollar dominated performance data at the level of ABB's 4,500 profit centers. By allowing comparisons against budget and forecast to be aggregated and disaggregated, ABACUS facilitated analysis within and across businesses, countries, and companies or profit centers.

Given control over key resources and provided with current relevant information, managers on the front lines were expected to act. Barnevik's "7–3 formula" reinforced the notion that it was better to decide quickly and be right seven times out of the ten than to delay or to search for the perfect solution. "Better roughly and quickly than carefully and slowly" he said. "The only thing we cannot accept is people who do nothing."

He took these and other aspects of his strongly held beliefs and values out to the field, traveling some 200 days a year, always with his large bag of overhead transparencies. Through continued acquisition and rejuvenated internal growth, within four years ABB grew to become a $29 billion company with over 200,000 employees worldwide—the giant of its industry, dominating previous first-tier players like Siemens, Hitachi, and General Electric (see Exhibit 3). To understand how this rapid growth and geographic expansion was managed, this case focuses on the birth and development of one of ABB's business areas (BAs) out of almost 60 (Exhibit 4).

Exhibit 3   *ABB Key Performance Data: 1988–1991*

	1988	**1989**	**1990**	**1991**
Revenues	17,832	20,560	26,688	28,883
Operating earnings after depreciation	854	1,257	1,790	609
Net income	386	589	590	609
Acquisition expenditures	544	3,090	677	612
Property, plant, and equipment expenditure	736	783	961	1,035
R&D expenditure	1,255	1,361	1,931	2,342
Operating earnings/revenues	4.8%	6.1%	6.7%	6.6%
Return on equity	12.5	16.8	14.5	13.9
Return on capital employed	13.6	17.0	19.7	17.1
Number of employees	169,459	189,493	215,154	214,399

BUILDING THE RELAYS ORGANIZATION

In August 1987, Göran Lindahl, Asea's executive vice-president responsible for power transmission, found himself on Barnevik's ten-person top management transition team. After presenting a proposal for merging the two power transmission businesses, Lindahl was tapped to head this important segment for ABB as of January 1, 1988.

Creating the Management Team

In the relays business, as in each of the other eight BAs reporting to him, Lindahl's first task was to identify the managers who would drive the integration and capture the synergies that were fundamental to ABB's strategy. He described the process:

For me, the key qualifications were proven performance in their business, and broad experience in more than one discipline. But, as important as their career background was their personality—their flexibility, integrity, and statesmanship.

He named Anders Fraggstedt, general manager of Asea's relay business based in Västerås, Sweden, to assume the additional role of BA head for ABB's relays business worldwide. To support Fraggstedt in his new role (and also to help minimize the number of decisions escalated to the corporate level for resolution), Lindahl created a BA board with Fraggstedt as chairman and the relay business managers from Baden, Switzerland, and Vasa, Finland, as the two other members. (The Vasa business had come as part of the acquisition of Stromberg, the Finnish electrical giant.)

At the same time, Lindahl felt that he needed to keep a close personal involvement in the process. But this did not imply that he had an army of staff to monitor operations and control performance against targets. Like others at the group executive level, Lindahl maintained a small staff to help manage his $5 billion global business. Besides himself, it numbered four persons—two controllers, a business development manager, and a secretary.

He saw his key role as providing an environment in which those below him could be most effective. As a first step, he believed he had to create the uncertainty necessary to encourage "unlearning" of old assumptions and behaviors. Through what he referred to as "the framework," Lindahl set challenging goals and objectives for his newly appointed managers—tightly defined at first, but gradually expanding and loosening:

People are as good as you make them. We have about 8,000 engineers in our 35,000-person segment. They are bright, capable people who make excellent managers. My first task is to provide the frameworks to help them develop as managers; the next challenge is to loosen and expand the framework to let them become leaders.

In his definition, leaders were the individuals who had displayed the requisite personal characteristics (which he identified as flexibility, statesmanship and generosity), and who were ready to take responsibility for setting their own objectives and standards. "When I have developed all the managers into leaders," he said, "we will have a self-driven, self-renewing organization."

Communicating the New Philosophy and Values

As he met with his new team, one of the most important items on Lindahl's agenda was to communicate the company's guiding principle of decentralization. He explained:

The newspapers may describe ABB's power transmission power segment as a $5 billion operation with 35,000 employees, but I think of it as almost 200 operating companies further divided into 700 profit centers, each with about 50 employees and $7 million in revenues. Although the BAs play a vital role in

Exhibit 4   *ABB Organization Structure (1991)*

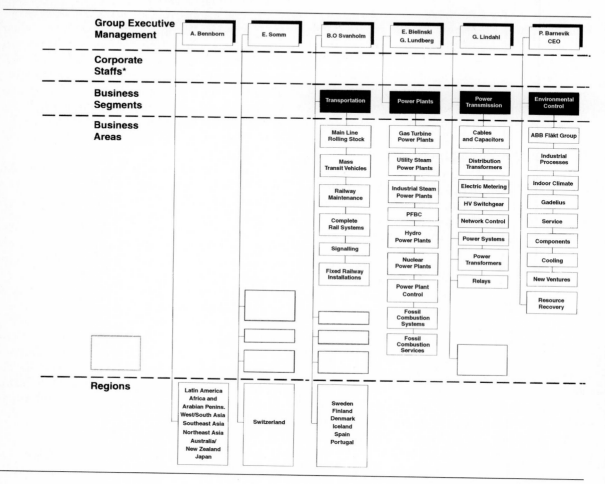

setting strategy, only the local companies can implement the plans and achieve the objectives.

The message was well received by most front-line managers. Don Jans, who had come with Westinghouse's power transmission and distribution business when ABB acquired it in early 1989, reflected the attitude among his colleagues at the time:

The prevailing view when ABB acquired our business was that we'd lost the war. We were resigned to the fact that the occupying troops would move in and we'd move out. But to our surprise, they not only asked us to stay on, they gave us the opportunity to run the whole relays business—even the Allentown operation that was ABB's own facility in the United States.

To do so, however, required Jans and his colleagues to make major changes in their business assumptions, organizational practices, and management styles. In Westinghouse, Jans had

Exhibit 4   *(continued)*

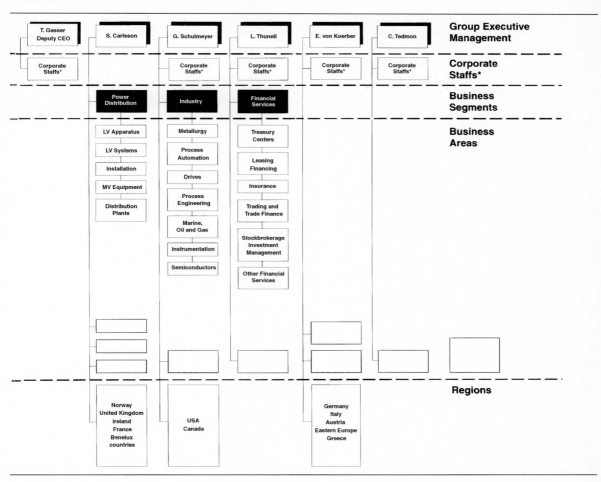

five layers of management between himself and the CEO; in ABB there were only two. In Westinghouse, he had been constantly frustrated by the bureaucracy imposed by a 3,000-person headquarters; in ABB he had to adjust to the need for self-sufficiency in an organization with only 150 people at corporate. In Westinghouse, decisions had been top-down and shaped by political negotiations; in ABB Jans found many more were delegated and were driven by data and results. He described the first few meetings

when he and his colleagues were exposed to the ABB philosophy and values as "an exhilarating experience":

It was amazing. We were constantly seeing the top guys in meetings and seminars— Barnevik, Lindahl, Schulmeyer (the North American regional VP). They came with stacks of transparencies and could talk for hours about how the industry was developing, where ABB wanted to be, how it was going to get there, and so on. It was spell-binding; a real education.

Just as important was their willingness to listen to our proposals and invest in the relays business. In Westinghouse, capital allocations had always been tightly managed, but after the mid-1970s, it seemed as if they were even less willing to invest in old core businesses like relays. Not so after 1989. ABB is really committed to this business, and if we can justify an investment we can usually get the resources.

One of Lindahl's main objectives in his non-stop communications was to instill a clear and strong value system to guide management action. "In the end," he said, "managers are loyal, not to a particular boss or even to a company, but to a set of values they believe in and find satisfying." He identified the core values as being an emphasis on quality, not only in products but also in organizational processes and relationships; a commitment to excellence in technology to ensure the business remained at the forefront of the industry; a dedication to productivity and performance, not just in the plants but at all levels of the organization; and a belief in people—both customers and employees—as the means to achieving the first three.

Lindahl also used his company visits to emphasize the importance of individual accountability. The company's broad philosophies were translated into specific task requirements for managers at all levels, and Lindahl devoted a substantial amount of time to communicating the appropriate roles, responsibilities, and relationships summarized in a chart that he had discussed with every profit-center manager in his segment (**see** Exhibit 5). While BA management was responsible for setting worldwide strategy and overall operating objectives, local company managers controlled operations and were responsible for profits. The integration of the different interests took place through a rigorous planning and budgeting process; the assurance of appropriate im-

plementation through a sophisticated set of formal and informal controls. Because he believed firmly in the need to control performance against "the framework," one of Lindahl's earliest and most important appointments was "a controller who was sensitive to operations rather than just a number cruncher."

Defining the Agenda

In the early days, Lindahl's "framework" was fairly tight. He wanted his businesses to focus on restructuring themselves rapidly:

If you want to bring about change, you need to force it, and that means giving the organization a clear vision of your expectations and pushing for results. Eventually, the change process becomes natural and develops its own momentum. . . . I told each BA board that our objective was to conquer the globe in power transmission. At the same time, I kept reminding them of the need to focus on the customers, watch competitors, and deliver current results. To do that, they would have to deal with the overcapacity we clearly had, and capitalize on the best technology in the combined operations. Which plants were the most efficient? Which technology should become standard? It was a huge undertaking to do all the analysis and negotiate sensitive agreements.

In the early stages of the restructuring process, Lindahl reported getting lots of issues coming up for his review and resolution, but typically he pushed them back down for further discussion. Many such issues involved the painful process of closing plants, reallocating historical market relationships, or cutting traditional product lines. He saw his major job as trying to convert the "winner/loser" mentality into a recognition that the new organization could become "winner/winner."

After a full year of difficult analysis, discussion and negotiation, Anders Fraggstedt and his

Exhibit 5 *ABB Management Philosophy**

The Matrix Organization

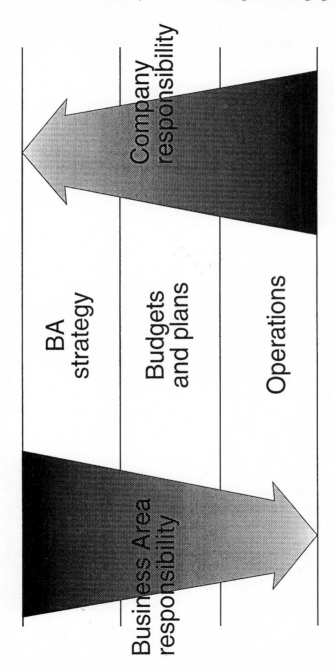

BA strategy

Budgets and plans

Operations

Company responsibility

Business Area responsibility

Power Transmission Segment

*Source: Company documents.

relays BA board decided on the BA's basic restructuring concept. Vasa, Finland, would assume the leadership role in developing and manufacturing relays for distribution protection, the lower-voltage products that had been Stromberg's specialty and for which it was clearly the technological leader. In high-voltage protection, where both Asea and BBC had strong capabilities, the major overlap in development, manufacturing, and marketing was resolved by giving Västerås, Sweden, primary responsibility for high-voltage products, and Baden, Switzerland, the lead role for project and systems deliveries that engineered multiple products into integrated forms or turnkey installations. Furthermore, to eliminate marketing overlap, Sweden would assume overall responsibility for sales into Europe, North America, and Australia, where bids were mostly for individual relay products, while Switzerland would focus its marketing efforts on Latin America, Africa, and Asia, where project business was more important.

A senior manager of the Swiss relays company reflected on the outcome for his unit:

Sure, there was concern in Baden. People talked about the Swedes dominating the management, they were concerned that most of our production was being transferred out, and they complained that we lost well-established markets like Germany and France while retaining only the "poor man's countries" in the developing world. But the company was committed to keeping the existing know-how, and Mr. Fraggstedt reassured us that our relays R&D group would be retained. After a long talk with Mr. Lindahl I was convinced, and I took on the job of persuading the organization to look at the changes more positively.

Restructuring the Business

In December 1988, Göran Lindahl approached Ulf Gundemark, the manager of ABB's Swedish low-voltage switch gear operations, and offered him the opportunity to replace Anders Fraggstedt as the business-area head for ABB's $250 million worldwide relays business. It was an attractive opportunity for a 37-year-old engineer who had spent ten years of his twelve-year career with Asea in its relay business.

Like other BA heads, Gundemark would continue to be responsible for his national company's operations, but would also wear a second hat as a worldwide BA manager. To assist him in this new role, he would have a staff of two—a controller and a coordination/business development manager. His first challenge was to integrate the disparate relay operations of Asea, Brown Boveri, Stromberg, and now Westinghouse.[1] It would be a difficult task to integrate companies that not only had vastly different management cultures, but also had been bitter competitors.

Gundemark saw his first priority being to communicate the broad rationalization principles that had been hammered out in a year-long negotiation process and to implement the major changes. Recognizing that ABB planned to take a one-time restructuring charge against its 1989 results, he initiated the Revaba Project (**Re**structure **Vä**sterås and **Ba**den) to implement the most difficult part of the rationalization plans as quickly as possible. Overall coordination of the project was assigned to a team headed by the R&D manager at Baden and the production manager at Västerås. After allowing the team to set its own goals within the framework defined by the board, Gundemark held all members ac-

---

[1] In January 1989, ABB acquired a 45% share of Westinghouse's transmission and distribution business with an option to buy the remaining 55%. The joint venture was fully integrated into the ABB. In relays, for example, Don Jans, the ex-Westinghouse relays head, joined the relays BA board now chaired by Gundemark.

countable for achieving their results, reviewing progress every two weeks.

Due to the complexity of Revaba and the acquisition of the Westinghouse operations, the restructuring project took longer than expected. By the end of 1990, however, the new structure of ABB's worldwide relays business was emerging. Production was specialized in four global production centers, development activities in each company were coordinated by a worldwide R&D head, and local manufacturing and engineering activities were defined and legitimized in the 12 noncore relays companies around the world (see Exhibits 6 and 7).

The process linking the worldwide structure was developed and defined by scores of day to day decisions that continually confronted Gundemark and his BA board. Soon after the production rationalization had been implemented, for example, Gundemark found himself confronting questions about the recently negotiated allocations of export markets. The issue was raised around the Swiss company's responsibility for coordinating sales into Mexico, which earned it a markup on products sourced from other ABB relays operations. Several senior managers felt the company had to shorten the company's lines to its customers and minimize the non–value-added work in the system. Gundemark delegated the issue to a team composed of the marketing managers from the four key supply companies and asked them to develop a proposal. After considerable negotiations, the team reported to the BA board that they could not find a solution. Gundemark pushed the task back to them for further discussion and analysis. Some days later, the team indicated they had reached a majority recommendation supported by three of the four members. Again Gundemark rejected the proposal, demanding a unanimous recommendation. Finally, after three full and exhausting days of negotiation, the marketing managers decided that local companies with strong engineering capabilities should be able to order directly on any production center.

Another piece of policy and structure was in place.[2]

New Organizational Structures and Processes

While he was overseeing the restructuring, Gundemark knew there would be significant coordination of operations built on a foundation of specialized yet interdependent operations. In 1989, the only effective integrating mechanism was the BA board Lindahl had established, and Gundemark was concerned that it had become a monthly forum swamped with current operating issues. He wanted to create an organization that would not only relieve this pressure, but also be truer to ABB's decentralization philosophy.

Building on an Asea practice in place for many years, Gundemark established a steering committee for each of the national relays companies. These were, in effect, small local boards with membership drawn from the local relay company, other closely related ABB units, the national holding company, and the corporate relays BA management. Two to four times a year, each steering committee met to discuss its local relay company's operating performance and long-term strategy. At the operating level, such meetings became vital forums for senior-level business and regional managers to review the operations of the local units, and to ensure that the objectives and priorities they were giving to those front-line operations were consistent. To the company general managers, they offered an important opportunity to communicate key issues and problems, elicit input and support, and reconcile conflicts.

Although he was relatively new to ABB, U.S. relays general manager Don Jans was quickly

---

[2]This management approach mirrored Barnevik's philosophy of decentralized responsibility and accountability. "You can escalate conflict once, you can escalate it twice," he said, "but if you escalate it three times I'll remove both of you."

Exhibit 6   *Relays BA Organization*

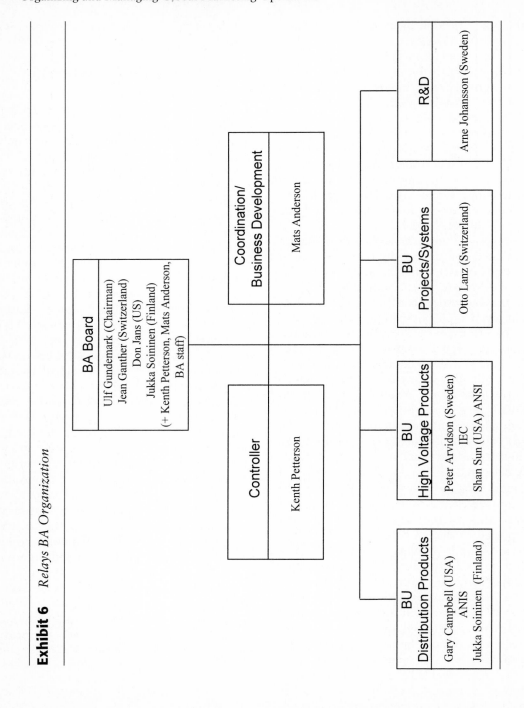

Exhibit 7 *Relays BA Worldwide Operations*

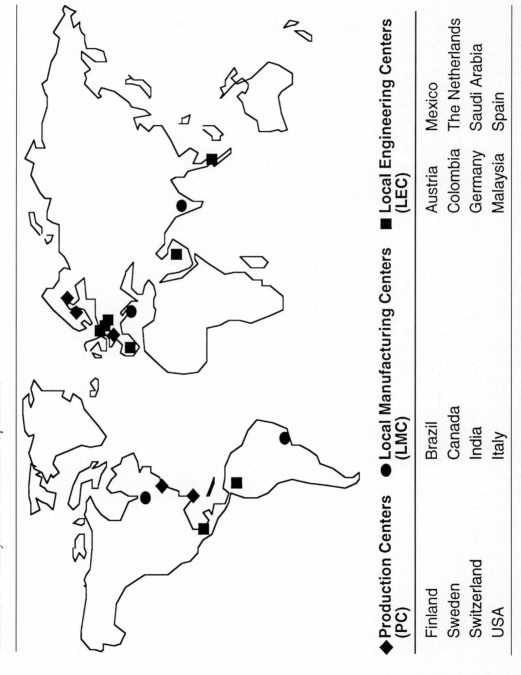

◆ Production Centers (PC)	● Local Manufacturing Centers (LMC)	■ Local Engineering Centers (LEC)	
Finland	Brazil	Austria	Mexico
Sweden	Canada	Colombia	The Netherlands
Switzerland	India	Germany	Saudi Arabia
USA	Italy	Malaysia	Spain

becoming accustomed to ABB's collaborative team management style.[3] He found the steering committee to be a "powerful concept." In addition to himself, his relays steering committee, which met quarterly, consisted of Ulf Gundemark as the BA representative, the strategic planning manager, marketing manager, and controller from the U.S. power transmission and distribution (T&D) regional headquarters, and the general manager of the closely related network control company. It was chaired by Joe Baker, the regional ABB Power T&D head, who reported both to Göran Lindahl, his business boss, and to Gerhard Schulmeyer, the president of the U.S. holding company, ABB Inc. (See Exhibit 8 for a representation of the matrix relationships.)

Relays steering committee chairman Baker, a 39-year veteran of Westinghouse, had entered ABB via the acquisition as a self-admitted skeptic of the matrix organization. In 1979, Westinghouse had imposed a matrix structure on its international division and the results had been "a complete failure," according to Baker. Eventually, however, he began to acknowledge that the ABB system seemed to be working, and he reflected on the differences:

In Westinghouse, we recruited first-class people, did an outstanding job of management development, then wasted all that investment by constraining them with a highly authoritarian structure. In ABB, we spent much of our first year thrashing out how we would work together. . . . In the end, it was this culture of delegated responsibility and intensive communication that made this organization work. . . . It was an amazing change; I felt

---

[3]As well as serving on Gundemark's relay BA Board, he was also a member of the steering committee for his own relay company, ABB's network control company in the United States, and for the relay subsidiaries in Canada and Puerto Rico.

like I'd rediscovered management after 39 years.[4]

In addition to providing local companies with more guidance, Gundemark also wanted to exploit synergies, particularly across the four core companies. To achieve this, he formed functional councils for R&D, total quality, and purchasing and charged each with the task of developing policy guidelines that captured "best practice." Each council was composed of specialists from several operating units, including the four major centers. They met quarterly, usually at a different site not only to expose managers to the various local practices, but also to send a clear signal to the organization. Chairpersons of the councils also rotated on an annual basis, allowing different national units to share the leadership.

All three councils were extremely successful in creating contacts among specialists in diverse geographic locations and providing them with a forum at which to share knowledge. For example, Bill Wallace, manager of total quality in the U.S. relays business, reported enthusiastically on the value created by the council on which he served:

It's had an enormous impact. There is a lot of cross-fertilization going on. For example, we had been working on time-based management for several years and had delivered impressive reductions in cycle time and inventory levels. In 1990, a team from Finland visited Coral Springs to see what we were doing. Nine months later on a plant tour during

---

[4]After seeing how quickly ABB turned around a business they had struggled for years, senior management at Westinghouse invited Baker to explain how they did it. After he described the change in organization culture and management philosophy that had revitalized the business, a Westinghouse EVP said, "We can't manage with so little direction and so much conflict." Replied Baker, "That's the problem."

Exhibit 8   *Partial Matrix Relationships in Relays BA*

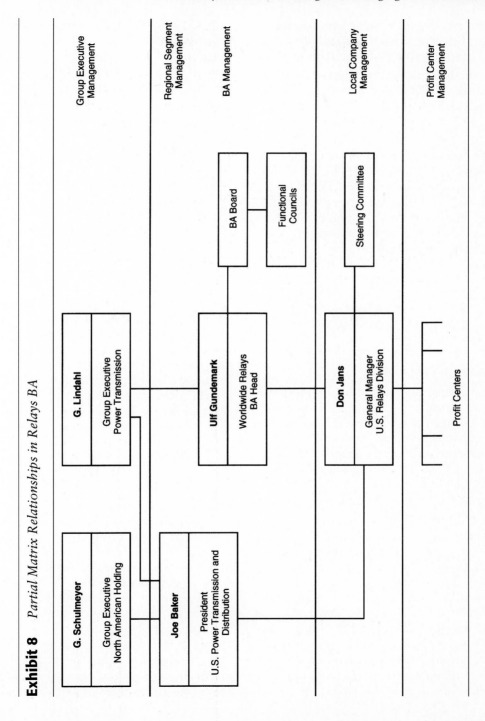

a council meeting in Vasa, I was amazed to see how they adapted and successfully implemented our JIT and Kan Ban system.

Larry Vanduzer, Coral Springs purchasing manager, was equally proud of progress on the council on which he served:

Because material costs can represent 35%–40% of sales value, there is huge potential for economies. Even in our first year when we were focusing mainly on developing the appropriate metrics to evaluate purchasing, we still squeezed out $1 million in cost savings. Now we work mainly on setting goals, certifying and consolidating suppliers, and sharing our learning. Each year we report back to the BA board on progress, and I'd have to say the measurement has created some healthy internal competition. Vasa reduced its lead time to an average ten-day delivery, and we want to challenge them!

New Strategic Process

Having delegated most operating responsibilities to the steering committees, Gundemark wanted to change the role of the BA board to a higher-level policy group that only met quarterly but focused more on strategy, policies, and overall objective setting. In introducing this longer-term focus, he was determined not to make strategic planning the hollow exercise he had both seen and experienced:

I wanted to sweep aside a lot of the old assumptions about strategy we inherited from the 1970s and 1980s—that it was defined primarily by top management, that it was communicated through confidential copies kept in locked files, and that it was updated annually, but usually without challenging the underlying assumptions or objectives. I wanted it to become a process that involved all levels of management, was widely communicated, and constantly open to challenge.

In March 1990, he formed a nine-person task force with members drawn from the high-potential middle managers of companies in Brazil, Germany, Finland, the United States, Sweden, and Switzerland, and charged them with the task of creating a clear vision for the relays BA. He set the tone by raising sensitive but important questions that he knew the team would have to confront if they were to develop a worthwhile proposal: How well are each of the companies implementing their new organizational responsibilities? Are we becoming too short-term focused? Is there too much of a Swedish bias in our management? He urged them to be bold, direct, and creative in taking a completely fresh look at the business, and to report back to the BA board in six months.

In September, propelled by a request from Göran Lindahl for a clear global relays strategy by year's end, the BA board heard the group's presentation, which proposed a broad vision focused on seven core elements of the relays business future development (total quality, customer focus, technology, human assets, organization, image, and growth). With further input and refinement by the BA management team, the task force's broad conclusions were developed into a 24-page document titled "Strategy 2000." Once approved, Strategy 2000 was formally unveiled at a worldwide relays management meeting and, within weeks, communicated to the entire organization via specially prepared materials and presentations (see Exhibit 9 for an overview).

Lindahl saw his role in the strategic process as much more than the approver of formal business plans such as the one developed by Gundemark's team. He saw strategy as an ongoing part of management and used his bimonthly transmission segment management meetings to shape the strategic thinking of his key executives. Here he not only reviewed current performance, but also challenged his nine BA heads (like Gundemark) and ten major regional managers (like Baker) to stretch their thinking. He would pre-

Exhibit 9   *Relays BA Strategy 2000: Excerpts and Overview**

Vision
Our vision is to contribute to a better living standard for the world by producing technically advanced products which are essential to ensure the safe and reliable supply of electric power.

Key Concepts (Excerpts)
- We must communicate our organization, vision, strategy, and results to all employees and tie their activities to the BA goals.
- Employees must feel they have jobs with personal development opportunities and team spirit.
- We will expand . . . through aggressive marketing, refined segmentation . . . and innovative sales concepts.
- Management will communicate a commitment to total quality . . . and we will improve total performance through systematic measurement and analysis of key elements of total quality.
- We will make customer focus plans and follow performance to bring the customer focus culture to all employees.
- We will create a team spirit and make teamwork the method for working together.
- We will push responsibility and authority to the operational level.
- We will have volume growth of 6% p.a. and a return on capital employed of 40%.
- We will reduce product development cycle times to one year by 1994.
- Will develop COMSYS as a evolutionary process for creating modular, locally acceptable products using common tools, methods, and design.

*Source: Company documents.

sent them with issues such as environmental legislation, trade barriers, or north-south political conflicts and ask them to develop scenarios for how such issues might affect their businesses and how they might deal with the changes. "I try to make such exercises fun," he said, "but you always have to be thinking a little bit ahead."

New Systems and Controls

Throughout this period of orienting and restructuring, Gundemark and other BA managers in the power transmission segment were constantly being reminded by Lindahl not to let the internal changes distract the organization from the marketplace. The historic performance of ABB's various relays units was mixed, with the portfolio of profits and losses about equalizing each other at the time of the merger. After 1989, his big challenge would be to get consistent profitability across all operations, while building an organization that could leverage the restructured business.

With ABACUS in place, budgeting had become a serious and demanding process. In May, Lindahl and his staff prepared a tentative broad gauge budget by BA and by region for the following year. The BA and regional managers in turn allocated their proposed breakdowns to the local company level. By August, a bottom-up response was returned to the corporate office, where it was consolidated and tested. Lindahl would identify gaps or concerns and contact the local manager and the BA head to challenge and negotiate, typically asking what additional support they needed to reach the proposed target. It was a communications-intensive process.

Exhibit 10A   *Relays BA Performance League: Letter to Local BA Managers*

February 22, 1991

Dear Friends:

BA Performance League: Actual, 1990

First of all, congratulations on a very successful year. As you know, we exceeded the budget for orders received, revenues, and earnings after financial items (EAFI). This year we reached an important milestone—having all Relay operations contributing with positive earnings.

Congratulations to Attila Magyar and his team in Austria. They have won the 1990 Performance League, outperforming the budget on three of the four measures. . . . The prize, a Minolta camera, will be presented at the next Steering Committee meeting.

- Digging into the year's results, we recognize:
- 67% of the units achieved over-budget gross margins. Good!
- 80% of the units beat their budgets in EAFI. Excellent!
- Only 40% of the units, however, have been able to keep S&A costs below budget.

And only two countries reached their budgeted inventory and receivable goals.

We are concerned about these developments on the cost and capital side. . . . We suggest that these items be brought up at your next Steering Committee meetings, and that targets and action plans be agreed on so we can together break these negative trends.

Finally, thank you once again for a very positive year. We look forward to a 1991 as successful as 1990.

Yours sincerely,

Ulf Gundemark

continued

Exhibit 10B   *Relays BA Performance League: Overall Rankings*

Position	Gross Margin % (Rank)	S&A/ Revenue % (Rank)	Inv. & Rec./ Revenue % (Rank)	EAFI/ Revenue % (Rank)	Total Points (Ranking)
1 Austria	35,3 (02)	15,2 (05)	38,5 (06)	20,0 (02)	15 (1)
2 Finland	32,0 (04)	18,9 (06)	41,8 (08)	17,3 (03)	21 (2)
3 Canada	30,9 (05)	19,4 (08)	28,6 (02)	14,4 (07)	22 (3)
4 Allentown	44,3 (01)	29,4 (15)	38,0 (05)	20,1 (01)	22 (4)
5 Spain	29,5 (06)	13,7 (04)	48,6 (09)	17,2 (04)	23 (5)
6 Coral Springs	35,1 (03)	23,3 (14)	31,7 (04)	15,2 (06)	27 (6)
7 Mexico	21,5 (14)	13,0 (03)	12,1 (01)	12,2 (11)	29 (7)
8 Brazil	28,4 (08)	19,4 (08)	56,3 (10)	15,8 (05)	31 (8)
9 Germany	25,1 (11)	19,3 (07)	28,6 (02)	6,9 (13)	33 (9)
10 Saudi Arabia	23,7 (13)	11,2 (02)	87,9 (14)	14,1 (08)	37 (10)
11 Sweden	25,4 (10)	19,9 (11)	41,1 (07)	13,3 (10)	28 (11)
12 Italy	28,7 (07)	20,0 (12)	78,9 (13)	13,6 (09)	41 (12)
13 India	12,1 (15)	8,0 (01)	124,9 (15)	6,9 (13)	44 (13)
14 Netherlands	26,6 (09)	21,1 (13)	68,2 (12)	8,1 (12)	46 (14)
15 Switzerland	25,0 (12)	19,7 (10)	62,2 (11)	5,7 (15)	48 (15)

Note: All figures from ABACUS.

Throughtout the year, Lindahl tracked the monthly results, and with the help of his controller, tried to identify trends or uncover problems. He had no problem in reaching across levels in the formal organization to check up on emerging problems. Typically, he asked managers "What went wrong? What are you doing about it? What can we do to help?" This ongoing awareness of current business developments and involvement in key decisions throughout the organization was what Lindahl described as "fingers in the pie" management:

Many companies, particularly in the United States, have evolved towards a kind of abstract management approach with senior executives controlling operations through sophisticated systems. I try to deal directly with the critical issues and the people managing them, and that means I need to put my hands on major changes. Even if I'm wrong, I need *to initiate the change, to shake things up, to create an environment of learning. Once that process is initiated, it gains its own momentum.*

At the BA level, Gundemark also exploited the new system by supplementing the broad budgeting process with more tailored reporting formats which he selected from the 30 measures tracked by ABACUS. For example, he created a Relays Performance League, which rank-ordered the companies on the basis of their quarterly gross margin, expenses, inventory, and net income percentages. The comparative data was circulated to all relays profit centers, and an award was given for the best overall performance of the year (see Exhibit 10). Those on the bottom of the league table desperately sought out ways to improve their standing, seeking input and support from their higher-ranked colleagues.

But Gundemark emphasized that Göran Lindahl was constantly asking him questions and proposing targets that were not measured by the formal systems. He commented:

ABACUS is fine, but it can only provide historical financial information. To manage the business properly—and to respond to questions from Göran—I need to be able to anticipate problems and understand alternative courses of corrective action. And that requires a strong personal management network. We work intensely at that!

MANAGEMENT CHALLENGES

At the end of 1991, Göran Lindahl seemed satisfied with the record that the relays BA had racked up in its first four years. The restructuring of assets and resources had largely been accomplished, and with help of the new operating systems and controls, current performance had been greatly improved. Compared with three years earlier when half the units were in a loss position, by 1991 all 16 major companies worldwide were contributing to the significantly improved profits. Furthermore, return on capital employed that had almost doubled since 1988.

As in most other businesses, ABB's relays management was still trying to fine tune both its strategy and its organization. In Coral Springs, for example, Don Jans was aware of two important issues that would have implications not only for his U.S. relays operation, but also for the worldwide relays BA. First, he would need to learn how to operate in ABB's complex matrix; and second, he would have to monitor the growing concern several of his managers were having about the BA's Comsys strategy.

Adjusting the New Organization

Although Jans was enthusiastic about the opportunities created by ABB's unique organization structure and management philosophy, he was also becoming increasingly aware of the difficulties of making it work effectively. While acknowledging that ABB's matrix organization brought his relays business much more attention and support than it had received in the old Westinghouse hierarchy, he was becoming aware that the process of obtaining such commitments could often be difficult and frustrating:

This kind of structure becomes frustrating when your two bosses' priorities don't coincide. For example, we recently got strong support from Gundemark to invest in people to push forward our long-term technical development priorities, but Joe Baker says he needs current operating profit and has crunched down on our proposed development funds. I'm not sure where we will end up, but right now it's confusing and frustrating.

Joe Baker agreed that the situation was frustrating, but felt that such negotiations were inevitable:

At Ulf Gundemark's urging, Don asked for approval for $1.5 million for new hires in product development, and at the time I indicated it looked OK. But I live in the matrix too, and when our regional transmission performance started slipping behind budget, I started hearing from Lindahl and Schulmeyer. Don understands that if one business is down, another one has to step up to the plate. I didn't tell him he had to cut R&D, but I did ask him to help with our shortfall.

Well, Don got really mad and wrote me a strong letter. In Westinghouse he probably would have been removed, but here we encourage people to kick back. I didn't like it, but I'm glad he did it. In the end, I talked to Ulf and suggested that if he really wanted the R&D done, maybe he could support it out of Sweden.

Although the issue was dormant for the moment, all the players recognized that conflict over resources was an ongoing issue. Balancing the need for short-term profit and long-term business development was expected to be a continuing challenge, particularly for Don Jans.

The Comsys Challenge

Although Jans was very supportive of ABB's philosophy of coordinating key strategy decisions across national boundaries, he had serious concerns about a major BA development project known as the common systems (or Comsys) project. Soon after announcing its formation in 1990, Gundemark challenged the relays R&D council to develop a common platform for future product development across units. As he described the problem:

Despite our coordination and specialization, we are still too compartmentalized. We are captives of our history, and each company tries to position and protect itself by creating products for its assigned markets. Rather than emphasizing differences in the needs across the European, American, and developing countries markets, we need to develop a common base of hardware and software that can be adapted to local needs and individual customers.

To implement the Comsys project, a cross-country team was formed consisting of two technical experts from each of the four major centers. By early 1992, the nine subproject teams were still hammering out the details of product design, operating standards, and overall project implementation, and the feeling was that they were years away from having tangible

---

Exhibit 11 *Evaluation of Relays BA Integration: Excerpts from Don Jans' Presentation to BA Board, February 1992*

Success Elements	Areas for Strengthening
• Clear vision and expectations from the top	• Tension between BA and country management (long-term vs. short-term)
• Responsibility pushed down—consensus teams, not "top down"	• Internal competition (marketing and technology)
• Good collaborative managers without strong egos—mutual respect	• Profit center concept creates unmet resource needs—psychological impact
• Strong ethic of "what/how/deadline"	• Tension between meeting operating objectives and participating in time-consuming integration processes
• Synergy through integrating devices (Boards, Councils, Centers of Excellence)	• Barriers to technology sharing
• Linking world capability (market access, technology, etc.) to become world class	• Still resistance to lead centers taking leadership in market/business planning
• Best practices—internal benchmarking—internal competition	• Reduce inventories through better support of engineering centers, reduced lead time, and on-time shipments
• Key programs share knowledge, provide focus (TQM, TBM, Supplier Partnering, Customer Focus, etc.)	• Need more people exchanges and benchmarking
• Constant communication	

results. Because most local development had been curtailed to focus resources on Comsys, the grumblings of many front-line profit center managers were becoming more audible. Said Gundemark:

> It was essential to get middle managers from the various countries involved rather than doing this centrally, even if it does slow things down. But these missionaries are confronting the old views back in their home organizations and are having a hard time selling the new ideas. It may mean we lose some time initially, but we will gain that back multiplied when we get everyone pulling in the same direction.

Don Jans felt that the Comsys problem was not only polluting his team's growing feeling of independent initiative, it was also compromising his unit's current performance. Yet he felt conflicted about his response. Should he wear his BA board member's hat and tell his managers to buckle down and make the project work? Or should he put on his company general manager's hat and defend the interests of his Coral Springs profit centers and ask Gundemark for relief from Comsys to focus more local resources back on projects to meet the immediate market needs?

The Future

As Jans prepared for the quarterly BA board meeting in early 1992, he drafted a "balance sheet" of achievements and challenges that would become the basis of a presentation he would make to his colleagues on the relays integration process to date (Exhibit 11). He was pleasantly surprised with the length of the asset side of his balance sheet but realized that most management attention needed to be focused on the "liabilities" side. Jans wondered what the company could do to deal with the kinds of problems he faced. It was a concern that was shared by Ulf Gundemark and Göran Lindahl.

PART VII

SPECIAL ISSUES IN GLOBAL MARKETING

Global marketers have to operate in an increasingly complex environment. Although tariffs are falling and regional trade pacts are inching the world economy towards freer trade, the selfish, protectionist trade policies of national governments, the varying adherence to intellectual-property rights, and the occasional specter of hyperinflation combine to impede global marketing. At the same time, the fax machine and the Internet are proving to be important liberating forces in international commerce.

International trade policies affect many marketing management decisions. First, tariff levels and proposed changes in tariffs affect the price of imported products and may influence decisions regarding whether or not to manufacture in-country. On the other side of the coin, government subsidies to domestic manufacturers affect their export competitiveness and may lead to allegations of dumping (i.e., selling below cost) in foreign markets.

Second, trade policies can affect international marketers' access to a country's distribution net-

works. Nontariff barriers (in the form of government standards and approval procedures that favor local suppliers) often remain (or are created) after tariff barriers are eliminated as a more subtle form of protectionism. European companies have frequently complained about the obstacles to distributing and selling their products in Japan. At the same time, European governments impede agricultural imports from the United States and emerging markets.

Third, trade policies that address but fail to enforce the intellectual property rights of pharmaceutical and software companies, for example, diminish the value of the marketers' brands and require them to invest in pursuing counterfeiters and educating their customers on how to spot the genuine article. In some emerging economies, the attitude towards the intellectual-property holder is: "You steal our labor by paying $2 a day to the workers who make your $150 Nikes, so we steal your ideas." Increasingly, multinational companies have to confront these ethical issues, which are often relevant to the younger target customers of the hollow corporations that leverage cheap third-world labor. At the same time, they must ensure that they register their brand trademarks quickly and correctly around the world whenever a new product is launched.

The challenge of intellectual property piracy is also found on the Internet. The Internet and the World Wide Web are rapidly becoming important forces in international commerce. The Internet empowers the consumer, enabling him or her to scan the globe to find the lowest-price supplier of whatever he or she wants. This empowerment is especially relevant in emerging markets, where choice is limited and national importers with exclusive distribution have historically charged high prices as a result of their quasi-monopoly questions. The Internet also empowers smaller suppliers who can become global marketers overnight. Several U.S. computer spare-parts companies already obtain over 40% of their Internet-based revenues from sales outside the United States.

Of course, there are implementation issues related to payment and data security, and many government agencies are scared of the loss of control and the reduced ability to collect cross-border tariffs (e.g., on financial and software transactions that are simply downloaded). But the Internet represents a powerful new distribution channel for many products and services and will command an increasing share of commercial transactions.

Compared to 10 years ago, there are fewer countries in the world affected by hyperinflation. However, the international marketer still needs to be aware of how marketing practices have to be adjusted in a hyperinflationary economy. Sophisticated marketers who sell their products before they have to pay their suppliers and who invest their cash in the "overnight" financial markets can often end up making more money out of financial engineering than out of merchandising. In such situations, marketing rules from the "developed world" are inapplicable. For example, a temporary sales promotion in a hyperinflationary environment might, for practical purposes, amount to imposing a price increase in the afternoon rather than first thing in the morning of the same day.

WEISSBERG GMBH

At 2:00 A.M. on Sunday, April 7, 1990, Frank Degmann was asleep in his São Paulo, Brazil, apartment when the doorbell rang. Degmann was the Dutch-born brand manager for Raysol, one of the leading brands of dishwashing liquid in Brazil. Degmann found two policemen at his door, who wanted to know why the retail price on Raysol at a local supermarket was higher than that permitted under recently introduced government price controls.

COMPANY AND BRAND BACKGROUND

Raysol was marketed by the Brazilian subsidiary of Weissberg, a German consumer-goods multinational. Weissberg had had operations in Brazil for 35 years. The wholly owned subsidiary was established in the 1960s following Weissberg's acquisition of a prominent Brazilian soap marketer. By 1990, Weissberg was one of the largest and most visible consumer goods multinationals in Brazil.

Weissberg was organized into three divisions, handling various brands of processed foods, detergents, and toiletries. Raysol accounted for around 30% of the detergent division's sales and 10% of total company sales.

Raysol was sold through Weissberg's sales force. Six regional sales managers each supervised around 40 salespeople who called regularly on the most important trade accounts. Because of the fragmentation of the grocery trade in Brazil, Weissberg supplemented its sales force with 240 merchandisers, who helped to ensure that the company's brands were in stock and prominently displayed in retail outlets. These merchandisers traveled by bus, called on about 15 shops a day, and often had to pull Weissberg products from a shop's stockroom and place them on the shelves. Both salespeople and merchandisers reported to Weissberg's regional sales managers.

In 1989, retail sales of dishwashing liquids in Brazil amounted to 220,000 tons. Retail sales volume had grown, on average, by 13% per year between 1986 and 1989. Around 78% of Brazilian households used dishwashing liquids in 1989, with annual per capita consumption of 1.5 liters. Since per capita consumption in Western Europe averaged 2.9 liters, analysts believed

---

that there was still substantial growth potential in the Brazilian market. Sales growth of dishwashing liquids depended significantly on economic conditions, since consumers could substitute less-expensive hand soaps.

Four brands accounted for almost all retail sales of branded dishwashing liquids: Weissberg's Raysol (21%); Lever's Minerva Plus (30%); the Limpol Brand of the Brazilian company Bombril (21%); and the ODD brand of the Brazilian company Orniex (28%). All four brands were similar in functional performance, range of package sizes, and cost and price structures. Raysol variable costs (including sales commissions and distribution costs), were 75% of net sales (after trade discounts). Raw materials accounted for half of variable costs. Nonvariable marketing expenditures were 10% of net sales. Trade margins were 16%. Due to heavier advertising than their competitors, Minerva Plus and Raysol achieved higher unaided brand recall and enjoyed a stronger image with consumers. Raysol, in particular, was believed to have a concentrated formula that provided the consumer with good value for the money.

Weissberg's objective for the dishwashing-liquid category was to increase the penetration and share of Raysol in the mainstream segment of the market, while trading some consumers up to new higher-margin formulas and packages.

BRAZILIAN PRICE CONTROLS

During the 1980s, the Brazilian economy was plagued by hyperinflation. In the 12 months prior to April 1990, the monthly inflation rate averaged 30%. As a result, changes to manufacturer list prices and retail prices were frequent. Manufacturers focused on pricing ahead of inflation and collecting receivables quickly, often offering incentives like early-payment allowances.

Each year, from 1987 to 1990, successive trade ministers in the Brazilian government tried unsuccessfully to control inflation by imposing price controls for three- to six-month periods. Whenever price controls ceased or collapsed, a wave of price increases followed, and inflation returned at an even higher monthly rate than before as marketers tried to compensate for their margin losses during the control periods.

In December 1989, Fernando Collor de Mello was democratically elected as president of Brazil. Five days before his inauguration, on March 10, 1990, Collor announced a surprise economic-reform program to bring inflation under control. The rate of consumer price increases had risen to 80% in February 1990, up from 10% a year earlier. The Collor reform package included the imposition of stringent price controls on a broad spectrum of widely used consumer products.

Under the Collor plan, many raw material prices as well as manufacturer list prices and retail prices were frozen. The items subject to price controls were not announced in advance but included the best-selling items in product categories with high household penetration. The allowable retail prices were published in an official list (called the "Tabela Sunab") that was reproduced in daily newspapers; responsibility for ensuring compliance rested with the manufacturer as well as the retailer. Consumers typically went shopping with the Tabela Sunab in hand and were encouraged to report any cases of overpricing to the police.

Degmann explained how consumer goods marketers responded to price controls:

Because we never know when price controls may be imposed under a new economic plan, we closely monitor our list prices and retail margins to ensure parity pricing with our face-off competitors at all times. Although grocery retailing is much more fragmented in Brazil than in Europe, our salespeople and merchandisers try to stay close to our retailers to ensure that prices on our brands are in compliance. The major chains—Pao de Açucar and Carrefour—usually present no problem;

their own public images are at risk. Compliance problems occur much more frequently in small stores.

Occasionally, the price of a controlled item could be increased during the control period if a manufacturer could demonstrate inflation in input costs. However, only one in four of Weissberg's applications for price increases was accepted between 1988 and 1990. A further challenge was how to obtain supplies of raw materials under price controls when suppliers were often seeking premium payments over the official prices. Weissberg typically held one to two weeks' worth of raw material supplies on hand and could not easily switch suppliers due to stringent quality standards. Multinational companies like Weissberg were wary of engaging in government lobbying or unofficial pricing for fear of negative media publicity. Executives in multinational companies believed that some of their local competitors received preferential treatment when applying for price increases and that they also received inside information that enabled them to raise prices just ahead of the announcement of price controls.

CONTROLLING WORKING CAPITAL

In an inflationary environment, one of Degmann's most important tasks was to control the working capital exposure of his brand. This meant keeping raw-material investments to a minimum, collecting accounts receivable quickly, and paying accounts slowly. Weissberg applied an "inflation charge" against each brand manager's profit-and-loss statement based on how much working capital was tied up in accounts receivable less accounts payable and in raw-material and finished-product inventories.

Weissberg's policy was to pay raw-material suppliers in 16 days and give its trade accounts 28-day payment terms. Astute retailers like Carrefour (which sold 18% of Raysol volume) paid Weissberg on this basis but turned over their inventory of the brand every seven days

and invested their sales revenues on the financial markets for the remaining 21 days. To gain further advantage, some larger chains tried to delay payments beyond 28 days. Degmann and his fellow brand managers were not permitted to extend trade terms without top-management approval. However, larger chains were gaining share from smaller, less sophisticated retailers who did not manage their inventories and working capital as well. Because of trade fragmentation and inefficiencies in the distribution system, as well as lack of sophistication, the trade stocks held by many retailers were equivalent to six weeks of retail sales.

MARKETING CHALLENGES UNDER PRICE CONTROLS

In the early hours of April 7, 1990, Degmann was required by the São Paulo police to accompany them to the local police station to provide an explanation. The police had been unable to locate the Brazilian regional sales manager, but his secretary had identified Degmann as the relevant brand manager. After an hour at the police station, Degmann was released on condition that he call back with further information from his office the following day. On Monday morning, Weissberg's head of legal and government affairs debriefed Degmann and took charge of follow-up negotiations with the police.

Ironically, a marketing-management meeting had been previously arranged for the afternoon of Monday, April 8, to discuss how Weissberg's marketing plans for its detergent brands should be changed (if at all) as a result of the Collor plan. The following questions were on the agenda:

1. Should advertising budgets be cut to preserve margins, or should they be increased since, as some executives argued, the existence of fixed prices meant that the consumer's focus could be shifted from price to brand attributes?
2. If cuts were made, should they be made evenly across all brands or should they be

disproportionately greater on smaller brands and/or lower-margin brands?

3. Should Weissberg go ahead with a consumer promotion planned for late April that offered tiny gold ingots as prizes in a contest open to consumers who submitted entries with Raysol proofs-of-purchase? The brand group had selected gold for prizes, because it symbolized the concentration of Raysol's product formula.

4. Should the launch of a premium-priced line extension to the Raysol range, previously scheduled for May, be postponed? Some executives argued that Weissberg should, instead, launch a lower-quality line extension or new brand to obtain an attractive price listing on the Tabela Sunab. It was unclear whether the launch of any line extensions to brands already listed on the Tabela Sunab would require government approval.

LEXUS AND THE USTR

On Tuesday, May 16, 1995, Mickey Kantor, the U.S. trade representative (USTR), announced the imposition of 100% tariffs on 13 luxury-class imported Japanese automobile models (including all four Lexus cars) arriving at U.S. ports after midnight on Saturday, May 20. The tariffs would, however, not be formally imposed until June 28. When asked at a news conference what message he would give Lexus owners, Kantor said: "Take a good look at some very attractive American cars."

THE DISPUTE

The USTR action was prompted by dissatisfaction with the level of U.S. auto parts exports to Japan. In July 1993, Japanese officials had committed to voluntary targets aimed at increasing Japanese imports of U.S. auto parts. These targets had not been met and USTR pressure on the Japanese for improved performance and further extensions had proven unsuccessful. U.S. auto parts exports to Japan were $1.5 billion in 1994 (1.4% of the Japanese market) and $1 billion in the first three months of 1995, while Japanese auto parts exports to the United States were $14.3 billion (12% of the U.S. market) and $10.4 billion for the corresponding periods. The resulting $12.8 billion gap in 1994 ($3 billion higher than in 1993) accounted for around 20% of the United States–Japan merchandise trade deficit of $66 billion. Japanese officials noted that, in 1994, Japanese car makers bought $17 billion in U.S. auto parts that were used in their U.S. plants—more than twice their purchases in 1990. The USTR also complained about the difficulties U.S. car manufacturers faced in setting up dealerships and selling their vehicles in Japan. In 1994, imported cars accounted for 8.1% of new Japanese auto sales versus 16% of new U.S. auto sales.[1] European imported cars accounted for 5% of sales, U.S. cars for 3%. Despite the intense competitiveness of the domestic Japanese market, sales of imported cars rose

---

[1]Some of the cars imported into Japan were Japanese-branded vehicles manufactured in foreign plants. In the United States, Japanese auto manufacturers had set up 10 manufacturing plants by 1995, so over one-half the new Japanese brand autos sold in the United States were no longer imported.

This case was prepared by John A. Quelch. Certain names have been disguised. Copyright © 1995 by the President and Fellows of Harvard College. Harvard Business School case 595-127.

40% in the first four months of 1995 over 1994. This increase was partly a result of the rise of the yen against foreign currencies which made imported cars more competitive in price.

The USTR also stated that the 13 luxury cars subject to the 100% tariff were priced lower in the United States than in Japan. For example, on May 15 when the dollar-yen exchange rate was 83.79, the Lexus LS400 retailed at $51,200 in the United States and the equivalent of $66,834 in Japan—30% more. The United States accounted for over half of Lexus unit sales worldwide in 1994.

The Japanese government responded swiftly to the USTR announcement, filing a complaint with the World Trade Organization (WTO) and asking it to urgently arbitrate the dispute. Trade experts believed the United States would lose, because WTO permission to impose the unilateral tariff had not been obtained. However, resolution of the dispute might take months and, during this period of uncertainty, U.S. sales of the affected vehicles were expected to decline, pressuring the Japanese manufacturers and government to give ground. President Clinton and Prime Minister Murayama were scheduled to meet at an economic summit in Canada on June 15, providing an opportunity for the dispute to be resolved. On the other hand, Mr. Ryutaro Hashimoto, Japan's minister of international trade, was known to have prime-ministerial ambitions and was likely to stand firm. There was concern that the dispute could result in Japanese retaliation against U.S. manufacturers in other industry sectors—like Boeing and Motorola—who were successfully exporting to Japan.

Initial reaction to the tariff announcement from the Japanese car makers was cautious. A Toyota representative stated: "We do not want to take any actions based on the assumption that sanctions will go into effect." Analysts estimated that if the Japanese car makers absorbed the 100% tariff and maintained current U.S. sales of the affected models, Honda would see a 21% decline in total profits, Toyota 14%, and

Mitsubishi 11%. On the other hand, if they did not absorb the tariff, and sales of the affected models in the United States collapsed, Toyota, Nissan, and Honda would lose around 2% of their worldwide sales, Mitsubishi 1.3%, and Mazda, 2.9%.

AFFECTED MODELS

The 13 targeted models accounted for 11.6% of the 1.8 million imported cars sold in the United States in 1994 and 2.3% of the total U.S. car market.[2] The 13 models, all retailing for at least $26,000, were sold through 2,035 of the 48,625 dealerships in the United States with 87,000 employees. Exhibit 1 summarizes the 1994 sales data, while Exhibit 2 provides dealership information.) The 1994 sales value of the affected models was $5.9 billion. The impact was likely to be greatest on dealers for Acura (a division of Honda), Infiniti (Nissan), and Lexus (Toyota). The Mazda and Mitsubishi models on the targeted list represented smaller proportions of the unit sales of those manufacturers and dealers.

The Japanese luxury car imports were advertised heavily. The unit prices permitted a high per-unit advertising investment, and recognition of the Acura, Infiniti, and Lexus brand names, launched as recently as the late 1980s, was still being developed. Combined media advertising in 1994 for these three brands was valued at $345 million. Increased advertising had been expected for 1995; Infinity was spending $35 million to launch its new I30 model, ironically on May 17.

REACTION AT LEXUS U.S. HEADQUARTERS

Senior managers at Lexus Division U.S. headquarters in California, who were responsible for importing all Lexus cars into the United States

---

[2]Japanese marques accounted for 23% of U.S. new-car registrations in 1994.

Exhibit 1   *U.S. Unit Sales of Japanese Luxury Car Brands* *

Year	Acura	Lexus	Infiniti
1986	52,869[a]	—	—
1987	109,470	—	—
1988	128,238	—	—
1989	142,061	16,302[a]	1,759[a]
1990	138,384	63,534	23,960
1991	143,708	71,206	34,890
1992	120,100	92,890	44,387
1993	108,291	94,677	50,547
1994	112,137[b]	87,419[c]	51,449

*Source: Adapted from *Automotive News* and *Advertising Age*.
[a]Partial year.
[b]Only 40% of Acura unit sales were subject to the tariff.
[c]In 1994, Toyota assembled 384,048 cars in North America and imported 293,677 cars under the Toyota brand in addition to the 87,419 imported Lexus cars.

from Japan, met early on Thursday, May 18, to discuss possible reactions to the USTR announcement.[3] The mood was somber. The finance manager commented:

> Toyota's overall sales in Japan have been sluggish due to the prolonged recession there. The rise of the yen against the dollar has squeezed our margins[4] in the United States and forced us to pass price increases along to our dealers, making our cars less of a value versus BMW and Mercedes than they used to be. Our sales in the last few months were 7% below last year. Now a 100% punitive tariff will put us out of business. Why did Washington pick on us and not target all Japanese vehicles?

The North American advertising manager replied:

> We can't worry about that now. The problem is that sales will dry up if we don't take action.

---

[3]Lexus U.S. took a markup of 10% on the landed cost of imported Lexus cars before invoicing the U.S. dealers.

[4]As the importer, Lexus U.S. took a markup of about 8% on the landed price of imported Lexus cars before selling them to Lexus dealers.

> The consumer will not buy a Lexus if he or she is not sure there'll be dealers to service their cars down the road. Our whole image depends on reliability. We have to reassure our current owners and prospective buyers that we're in this market to stay, whatever the tariffs. Overnight, I have prepared a mock-up of a full-page ad [see Exhibit 3] which I propose we run tomorrow in USA Today and the principal newspapers in our six biggest city markets.

The general manager called for a report on the new-car inventory position. There were 12,100 Lexus cars already at ports, in transit, or

Exhibit 2   *Number of U.S. Dealers and Dealer Employees for Targeted Japanese Car Imports* *

	Dealerships	Employees
Acura	281	11,000
Infiniti	153	3,340
Lexus	171	7,500
Mazda	906	50,000
Mitsubishi	504	15,000

*Source: Adapted from *Advertising Age*.

Exhibit 3   *Proposed Lexus National Print Advertisement**

An Important Message to Our Valued Lexus Customers

As you may know, the United States Trade Representative's Office recently announced proposed trade sanctions that will affect Japanese luxury cars, if the governments of the United States and Japan are unsuccessful in their attempts to settle a trade dispute. Nothing final has been decided; negotiations are underway. We hope that both sides of this issue recognize the importance and value of a strong economic relationship and that nobody wins in a trade fight.

In the meantime, please be assured that it's business as usually at your community's Lexus dealership. Lexus Division is part of a strong organization that is here to stay, with the resources to continue providing quality products and unsurpassed customer satisfaction, which have become benchmarks in the industry.

On behalf of our 171 Lexus dealers and the 7,500 Americans they employ.

(Signed)

General Manager—Lexus Division

Source: Excerpted from Bradley Johnson and Raymond Serafin, "$345M in Car Ads Hanging in Balance," *Advertising Age,* May 22, 1995, pp. 1–2. Reprinted with permission. Copyright, Crain Communications, Inc. 1995.

---

on dealer lots in the United States. This represented a 45-day supply. Another 3,000 Lexus cars were aboard ships headed for U.S. ports, but none would reach shore until after May 20. Reports suggested Infinity had 16,000 cars in the United States, including a 70-day supply of its new I30 model. The manager of dealer relations further reported:

> As rumors of the tariff on Japanese imported cars surfaced during the last month, some of our dealers ordered more cars than usual, but most did not change their order levels. If we start running low on pretariff cars, we may find dealers and consumers competing for the remaining available vehicles. That will make it harder to allocate vehicles fairly among our dealers and to balance supply and demand around the country.

The sentiment of the meeting was to hold prices to dealers at current levels, at least until June 28. The negotiated sale or lease prices of cars already ordered by consumers that had not arrived in the country by May 20 would certainly be honored. Lexus U.S. headquarters had not yet heard whether Toyota would "eat the 100% tariff" on cars arriving after May 20 to ensure that Lexus sticker prices could continue unchanged. Such a move would be expensive but would protect dealer investments in the Lexus brand and would demonstrate the parent company's long-term commitment to Lexus in the U.S. market. It was also unclear whether Lexus would slow down or halt production of the cars in Japan, pending clarification of the dispute.

After an hour-long discussion, the Lexus U.S. division president focused those attending on the following issues:

Do we need to communicate promptly with our dealers, our consumers, and the media? Assuming the answer is yes, what do we want to say? Is the proposed ad to consumers appropriate? Do we need to supplement it with direct mail to our owners? Beyond that, should we continue in a "business-as-usual" mode, running the same value-oriented advertising around our "relentless-pursuit-of-perfection" theme, maintaining the same prices to our dealers, and accepting cars arriving at the ports while praying all the time that the dispute is resolved before the tariff goes into effect? Or should we change course? If so, what should we do?

REACTION AT LEXUS DEALERS

On the morning of May 19, staff at individual Lexus dealerships throughout the United States met to discuss the proposed tariff and how to react. Banner Lexus, located in the northeast United States, was a typical Lexus dealership. It was one of the 20 dealerships owned by Banner Auto, a megadealer that operated free-standing dealerships that sold a variety of American, European, and Japanese cars. In 1994, Banner Lexus accounted for 3% of the megadealer's unit sales, 6% of dollar sales, and 7% of profits. Banner Lexus employed 30 sales, service, and management personnel in a dedicated sales-and-service facility, built to Lexus specifications in 1990 at an investment cost of $5 million. In 1994 Banner Lexus sold 550 units at an average gross margin of $3,500. Additional profits, about half the total, were derived from service, parts, and used-car sales. Banner Lexus carried 60 cars in inventory valued at around $24 million. As shown in Exhibit 4, Banner's model-by-model 1994 unit sales mix was similar to the national pattern.

Price increases had been substantial in recent years. The LS 400 sedan, for example, carried an average sticker price of $53,000 compared with $47,000 three years earlier. Banner leased 85% of the new Lexus cars it sold. In May 1994, the monthly payment on a 36-month LS 400 lease with option to buy was $950, including taxes and interest payments. Around 90% of leased cars were returned at the end of their leases; few owners took up the option to buy. Banner Lexus enjoyed a good business in sales of pre-owned models. A three-year-old LS 400 retailed for around $30,000 in May 1995.

Banner Lexus salespeople were aghast at the 100% tariff announcement and believed that their own livelihoods were being unfairly threatened. However, one or two of them thought the threat of the tariff might improve business in the short term. According to one salesperson, "If you talk to 10 people, four don't believe Clinton's got the guts to go through with it and the

Exhibit 4   *Banner Lexus Unit Sales Mix, Sticker Prices, and Unit Margins**

	% of 1994 Unit Sales	Average Sticker Price April 1995[a]	Banner's Average Unit Margin
LS 400 (sedan)	40	53,000	4,000
SC 400 (coupe)	5	52,000	4,500
GS 300	10	45,000	3,500
ES 300 (sedan)	45	36,000	3,000

*Source: Casewriter's estimates.
[a]Average sticker price included destination charge and some optional equipment above the price of the base model.

other six are buying cars." At the May 19 meeting convened by the general manager and sales manager, the following issues were on the agenda:

1. How will the tariff announcement impact (a) new car sales, (b) the mix of models sold, and (c) the mix of purchased versus leased vehicles in the short term (the next four weeks) and in the long term?

2. Should Banner Lexus run its planned advertising, featuring new monthly lease rates on the LS 400, in the local Sunday newspapers, or should "beat-the-price-increase" copy be substituted to build dealer traffic? One Lexus dealer in Texas was already advertising a "half-off sale" under the headline, "Our Lexuses are half-priced compared to what they're going to be if we have this Arkansas foreign policy."

ASTRA SPORTS, INC.(A)

In November 1986, a group of executives from Astra Sports, Inc. met in Seoul, South Korea, to discuss how to curtail the increasing number of counterfeit Astra shoes made in Korea that were appearing in retail outlets worldwide. The counterfeits were unauthorized replicas of Astra shoe designs that also carried near-perfect imitations of the Astra brand name and logo.

COMPANY BACKGROUND

Astra, a leading U.S. brand of athletic footwear and apparel and one of the three leading brands in the world, held an estimated 20% and 7% of the U.S. and international markets for branded athletic footwear. The company expected to sell 15 million pairs of shoes for basketball, tennis, and other sports in 1986. Thirty percent of these sales would be made outside the United States in 1986—up from 5% in 1982. International sales were made mainly through independent national distributors appointed by Astra rather than through wholly owned Astra subsidiaries. Astra was rapidly becoming a well-known global brand, especially among young people.

Astra's sales had doubled between 1982 and 1986, thanks to well-regarded product innovations and aggressive advertising. Supplies were short, especially of the most popular designs. There were 60 styles in the Astra line—a third of which were replaced each year by new designs.

All Astra athletic footwear was produced under contract in Asia by independent manufacturers. In 1986, around 60% of Astra's requirements was made by nine South Korean companies in 14 plants employing 3,000 workers. The percentage of the company's requirements made in South Korea was down from 75% in 1985, as Astra sought to develop sources of supply in other Asian countries with even lower labor costs. Full-time Astra employees were attached to the Korean subcontractors to advise on manufacturing processes and to ensure on-time production and quality control. Some of Astra's subcontractors also manufactured competing brands but in separate plants; Astra and its competitors worked hard to preserve the confidentiality of their designs until they appeared on retail shelves.

This case was prepared by John A. Quelch. Names and data have been disguised. Copyright © 1994 by the President and Fellows of Harvard College. Harvard Business School case 595-007.

Finished Astra products were shipped in containers from South Korea to ports all over the world. Because of their high quality and innovative design, Astra shoes were distributed selectively through service-oriented sports specialty stores and department stores. A typical pair of Astra shoes for which the company paid a Korean subcontractor $12 would sell in a U.S. retail store for $50. Astra's gross margin on its $27 selling price margin was around 50%; after-tax profits in 1985 were 8% of sales.

THE COUNTERFEIT PROBLEM

Counterfeiters manufactured low-cost and low-quality imitations of well-known branded products. These imitations were sold through unauthorized distribution channels to unsuspecting consumers who aspired to own the brand. These consumers either did not know enough to differentiate the genuine article from a fake or simply could not afford the real item and were happy to buy a good imitation at a bargain price. The market for counterfeits was strongest in countries where brand awareness was high but distribution of the genuine product was low or nonexistent.

Counterfeits were usually manufactured in countries such as South Korea with low labor costs. In the street markets of Seoul, buyers could purchase counterfeit watches, electronic products, whiskey, and apparel, sometimes openly advertised as "genuine fakes." The production and availability of counterfeits were marks of a strong brand name. Counterfeits of Astra shoes and those of the major competitor brands became increasingly evident in 1985 and 1986.

Astra executives believed that its South Korean subcontractors were not directly involved in manufacturing counterfeits, although one subcontractor whose order volume had been cut by half in early 1986 due to quality control problems was under suspicion. Most Astra counterfeits were believed to be made to order in small, family-run shops. They were commissioned by South Korean export companies who solicited and received orders for specific counterfeits from overseas distributors, contracted for production, consolidated orders, and arranged freight forwarding through Korean shipping companies.

Astra counterfeits first began to appear in the United States in 1985. By late 1986, Astra's international distributors were reporting their availability in street markets and lower-quality retail outlets in the major cities of Europe, Asia, and Latin America. The vast majority carried labels stating "Made in Korea."[1]

Estimates of the number of Astra counterfeits sold in 1986 ranged from 50,000 to 200,000 pairs. Most counterfeits were of simpler, classic models in the Astra line rather than the latest high-performance or high-fashion items that were harder to make. Astra executives were concerned not only by the increasing evidence of counterfeits but also by the quality of those they came across. One executive stated:

The counterfeits we saw last year just made us laugh. This year, we're seeing counterfeit products that, to the untrained eye, look very similar to the real thing. Of course, the construction quality is still poor so the shoes will come apart after a couple of months.

THE MEETING

On November 20, 1986, Astra's vice-president of international marketing and vice-president of corporate counsel met in Seoul to discuss Astra's options with Astra's senior managers in Korea and counsel from the Korean affiliate of a major U.S.-based international law firm.

The counsel from the Korean law firm was not encouraging about the possibility of a legal solution:

---

[1]Most countries required that the country of origin be clearly stated on all imported products.

Although counterfeiting of foreign brands is technically illegal in Korea, the practice is widespread. There is no point pursuing the counterfeiters through the courts. First, they are small fry just trying to make a living. Second, this type of legal action would be considered unusual in Korea and would take years. I think your best option is to lobby the Korean government, both directly and through the U.S. government, to put pressure on the exporters who are placing the orders for the counterfeits.

The vice-president of international marketing asked whether Astra's manufacturing subcontractors in Korea might help in this effort. Astra's general manager for Korea commented:

We are pressing our manufacturing partners to the limit to meet the surge in orders. I don't want to distract them. But I think one of them is related to the Korean minister of trade, and I know the brother of another is the chief of police in Seoul. Perhaps I should have a word with them to see if we can organize a few police raids.

Astra's manufacturing manager in Korea added:

Our partners are producers, not marketers. They don't understand how counterfeits may cannibalize their sales and profits. Or even if they do, they're making good money and don't want to rock the boat.

ASTRA SPORTS, INC. (B)

In January 1991, the vice-president of the Latin American division of Astra Sports, Inc. and the company's corporate counsel were discussing their options of a meeting with a Venezuelan manufacturer who had for seven years manufactured and marketed athletic shoes under the Astra name.

BACKGROUND

In 1982, Gaviria S.A., a Venezuelan footwear manufacturer, had filed an application to register the Astra brand. Two months later, the application—of which Astra only later became aware—was approved, having gone unchallenged. Astra's general counsel commented on how this same problem had arisen not only in Venezuela, but also in Peru, Guatemala, and Honduras:

In the early 1980s, Astra management had to focus on trying to meet the explosive growth in demand for our products in the United States. We simply didn't have the resources or experience to get our brands properly registered in all the overseas markets.

Today, there are trademark-consulting services that we subscribe to that report filings from all over the world that might infringe our trademarks. We get about 20 notices a week that require further action. But in 1982, these trademark watch services didn't exist.

Venezuela was not a signatory to the major international intellectual-property conventions that protected international brands. Trademark piracy was widespread in Venezuela; well-known brands such as Land Rover and Galeries Lafayette had suffered the same fate as Astra.

Under Venezuelan law, Astra had five years after the trademark registration was approved to sue for its cancellation. The case had to be made that Gaviria knew the Astra brand existed outside Venezuela before its application. However, Venezuelan law gave Astra almost no rights of discovery (i.e., requiring Gaviria to reveal internal documents), so no case could be pursued on this basis.

By 1990, the only legal recourse was for Astra to appeal to the Venezuelan government both directly and through the Office of the U.S. Trade Representative to rescind an earlier unjust

---

This case was prepared by John A. Quelch. Copyright © 1994 by the President and Fellows of Harvard College. Harvard Business School case 595-008.

decision by its own courts. This was considered a long shot, given the prevalence of trademark preemption in Venezuelan business, since a favorable decision might set a precedent for similar appeals by other international companies whose brands had been preempted. On the other hand, Venezuela had to compete with other countries for foreign direct investment by multinationals, and its reputation as a nonenforcer of intellectual-property conventions was an increasingly important impediment.

ASTRA SALES IN VENEZUELA

Between 1983 and 1985, Gaviria made and marketed few "Astra" shoes. By 1986, however, Astra's worldwide brand recognition meant that the brand was known in Venezuela and consumers were willing to pay a premium for it. Astra executives estimated that Gaviria produced 30,000 pairs of Astra athletic shoes in 1986, increasing to 500,000 pairs in 1990. These shoes were of mediocre (but gradually improving) quality, were sold by Gaviria at an average price of $6.50 per pair, and retailed for an average price of $13.00 in Venezuela—$3.00 per pair more than shoes of equivalent quality that did not carry the Astra name. By 1990, Astra executives believed that "Astra" shoes accounted for two-thirds of Gaviria's production and one-quarter of the Venezuelan market for branded athletic footwear and that 750 employees depended on "Astra" sales for their jobs. Astra was the only brand that Gaviria had preempted in this manner.

Genuine Astra shoes did find their way to some of Venezuela's 16 million consumers through the free-trade zone established by the Venezuelan government on the offshore island of Margarita. Since 1983, Astra's Central American distributor in Panama had transshipped Astra shoes to Margarita. Venezuelan citizens were not permitted to purchase goods in Margarita beyond their personal needs, but many did so, reselling the surplus on the mainland. In 1990,

100,000 pairs of genuine Astra shoes were sold to Venezuelans through this channel at an estimated average retail price of $65.00. Astra was unaware of any efforts by Gaviria to curtail its sales through Margarita.

ASTRA LATIN AMERICAN STRATEGY

In 1989, Astra began to place increased emphasis on penetrating international markets. All Astra shoes were manufactured in Asia, and fewer than 5% were then shipped to Latin American countries. Many of these countries imposed high tariffs (often between 100% and 300%) on imported footwear to protect their domestic producers. Brazil had a total ban on imported shoes. Astra had considered licensing one or two established shoe manufacturers in the larger Latin American countries to produce some of Astra's designs in return for royalties based on a percentage of sales, but had rejected the idea. Apart from quality control concerns, Astra feared that these manufacturers would simply apply Astra's designs to their existing domestic brands and would not put sufficient marketing effort behind the Astra brand. Given the import restrictions and the absence of local manufacturing, Astra found maintaining its trademark registrations to be a constant challenge, especially in countries like Brazil where prospective "free riders" repeatedly claimed Astra was not using its trademark and should, therefore, be denied continued protection.

Astra's Latin American vice-president believed that it was essential to protect the Astra brand equity against low-quality imitations. Counterfeits shipped from the Far East through Korean agents in Paraguay and Panama found their way into the major markets of Brazil and Argentina. Genuine Astra shoes were also transshipped in the same manner. In 1990, around 4 million pairs of genuine Astras were believed to have been sold in Latin America. Astra's gross margin per pair averaged $17.50, around 50% of its average selling price. The 4 million pairs represented 6% of branded athletic footwear sales to the 325 million people living in the region and 10% of the sales of international brands. Sales of international brands were growing at 10% per year.[1]

THE MEETING

A meeting with Gaviria's chief executive officer and owner was arranged by Astra's local legal advisers in Caracas. The Astra team realized that its bargaining power was weak but decided to develop a framework for computing the price Astra would be prepared to pay to buy back the rights to the Astra brand name from Gaviria.

The Astra team realized that there were other possible "solutions" to the situation, in addition to continuing to supply the Venezuelan market via Panama and Margarita. These included:

1. Appoint Gaviria as a manufacturing subcontractor and provide the necessary technical assistance and manufacturing investment to ensure that Gaviria could make the simpler models in the Astra line to Astra-quality standards. Astra might have to invest $1 million and concede an agreement on minimum-purchase quantities from Gaviria. A further problem with this option was that Venezuelan law did not allow Astra to enjoin Gaviria from exporting its production to other countries as part of any agreement.

2. Appoint Gaviria as Astra's Venezuelan distributor in exchange for a return of the brand rights and a cessation of unauthorized production. Gaviria had some distribution experience and contacts with the relevant retailers but would not have been Astra's first choice to be its Venezuelan distributor under normal circumstances. However, such an arrangement might enable Gaviria to earn a distribution margin after expenses of around $2.00 per pair, compared with an estimated $1.00 per pair profit on its current production of "Astras."

---

[1]One of Astra's international competitors, Adidas, dominated the Latin American market as a result of long-standing agreements with local manufacturers.

TRADE'EX: THE STOCK EXCHANGE OF THE COMPUTER INDUSTRY

SAABRE? NASDAQ? VISA? We see ourselves as a mixture of a credit card, an airline reservation system, and the stock market. We want TRADE'ex to become the de facto standard for electronic commerce over the Internet.
—*Daniel Aegerter, CEO, TRADE'ex*

TRADE'ex was an electronic transaction system that used the Internet as the communications conduit to link wholesale buyers and sellers worldwide. TRADE'ex was essentially a "virtual mall" where buyers and sellers from around the world could come together 24 hours a day to conduct business. Since going on-line in July of 1995 to serve as a whole marketplace for the sale of new computer equipment, TRADE'ex was attempting to define itself as the industry standard for conducting wholesale electronic commerce. Its powerful and proprietary software permitted on-line negotiation and bidding and the secure execution of buying and selling orders from computer dealers, distributors, manufacturers and resellers worldwide.

TRADE'EX HISTORY

Daniel Aegerter founded DYNABIT, a wholesale distributor of Macintosh computer peripherals, in Switzerland in 1986. In 1989, he established DYNABIT USA in Tampa, Florida as a domestic sourcing and purchasing office and moved to the U.S. to oversee its operations. DYNABIT specialized in servicing small and medium-sized resellers in Eastern Europe, the Middle East, and South Africa. The new division soon entered into agreements with other European distributors to represent them in the U.S. on a commission basis. As this business grew, Aegerter recognized the need for a software system to track the large volume of up-to-date product and pricing information DYNABIT needed to maintain.

In the spring of 1994, Aegerter and his colleague, Thomas Gustoff, began working on the development of a software system called TRADE'ex to answer that need. They wanted to create a system which would allow customers to

This case was prepared by Lisa R. Klein (under the direction of John A. Quelch). Confidential data have been disguised. Copyright © 1996 by the President and Fellows of Harvard College. Harvard Business School case 597-019.

Exhibit 1 *TRADE'ex Monthly Transactions and Sign-Ons, 1995–1996*

	July	Aug.	Sept.	Oct.	Nov.
Sign-ons	1,000	1,650	2,500	3,300	3,900
Transactions	200	300	400	450	600
Percent	20%	18%	16%	14%	15%
Per Transaction Analyses					
Volume/transaction	$44,434	$19,376	$21,014	$17,614	$14,401
Potential commission/ transaction	1,333	581	630	528	432
Total costs/transaction	2,961	2,025	1,517	1,447	1,103
General and administrative/ transaction	1,528	1,185	813	821	603
Operations/transaction	136	909	73	63	47

continued

source computer products anytime, day or night, with accurate information on price and availability. With test versions in hand by early 1995, Gustoff and Aegerter enrolled 40 vendors prior to the system's launch in July of 1995. Upon launch, one industry trade publication reported that TRADE'ex was "something akin to a supermarket where the shelves weren't all full," since it carried only 15,000 products.[1] Shortly thereafter, TRADE'ex signed on IngramMicro, Merisel, and Tech Data as vendors—each had product lines of over 30,000. In total, 120,000 different products were for sale on the TRADE'ex system as of April 1996. Thus, only 19 months after its launch, TRADE'ex was processing orders for 70 vendors and 650 wholesale buyers of computer products in 38 countries around the world; over 6,000 transactions were made using the system between its launch and April 1996 (see Exhibit 1).

In February 1996, DYNABIT USA, Inc. changed its name to TRADE'ex Electronic Commerce Systems, Inc. to reflect the company's new

business focus. The company's U.S. headquarters were in Tampa, with several offices in Europe and Asia. The DYNABIT companies (including TRADE'ex and the DYNABIT divisions worldwide) realized consolidated sales of over $30 million in 1995, 85% in North America, 7% in Asia and 8% in Europe.

THE TRADE'ex BUSINESS MODEL

The TRADE'ex System

TRADE'ex served as an electronic gatekeeper, earning a percentage of the dollar value of each system transaction. The TRADE'ex policy was to hold no inventory of its own. (However, the company had been taking advantage of good prices on some top-selling products by taking ownership and marketing them directly via the system.) Typically, vendors from around the world, including wholesale computer product resellers of branded components, distributors, and some small manufacturers offered items online and specified price, availability, warranty, delivery and credit information. Customers, mainly computer dealers, connected through the Internet using the TRADE'ex proprietary

[1]Ken Yamada, "Online Merchants Find Open Market in Internet," *Computer Reseller News,* October 16, 1995, p. 61.

Exhibit 1   *(continued)*

	Dec.	Jan.	Feb.	March	April	Total
Sign-ons	4,200	4,600	5,000	5,300	5,800	37,250
Transactions	700	750	800	900	1,000	6,100
Percent	17%	16%	16%	17%	17%	16%
Per Transaction Analyses						
Volume/transaction	$10,697	$8,272	$12,528	$11,903	$9,560	$13,715
Potential commission/ transaction	321	248	376	357	287	411
Total costs/transaction	923	996	901	850	824	1,118
General and administrative/ transaction	502	630	518	531	473	640
Operations/transaction	39	47	38	40	45	51

browser,[2] could see these offers upon signing on, and could compare the terms and conditions of different vendors and then place orders on-line. The system automatically verified payment terms and forwarded an order to the vendor, who then shipped directly to the customer, via a commercial carrier. The customer was invoiced by TRADE'ex, who in turn paid the vendor after deducting a transaction fee of 3%. The system was currently set up for cash purchases exclusively via wire transfer or credit card with plans to offer credit terms to qualified customers in the near future.

TRADE'ex vendors could change the prices or lists of products instantly from their own computers and could control which offers were seen by which buyers. Vendors could choose which TRADE'ex customers saw its offers by category, geographical territory or on a company-by-company basis. They could even decide not to sell to certain markets or customers or to sell at different prices in different markets. A vendor could see the offers of competitors in its region and could therefore price an offer to be attractive to target customers. Customers could also send out "price requests" via e-mail for specific items, which were automatically forwarded to all vendors carrying such items.

While each vendor paid an annual access fee based on its size and program choices, the service was free for customers. Without a distributor's overhead or markup and with direct competition among vendors, customers could usually obtain products for lower prices than through other channels. Online ordering also enabled customers to overcome the barriers created by time zones, language and culture differences, and distance. The minimum order price was $600.

TRADE'ex Marketing Programs
Seller Programs

TRADE'ex currently offered three programs[3] for vendors around the world. An overview of these is presented in Exhibit 2. They differed

[2]A demonstration of the software is available at the company's World Wide Web (WWW) site at http://www.tradeex.com.

[3]Information for all of the programs can also be found on the TRADE'ex WWW site.

Exhibit 2   *TRADE'ex Seller Programs, April 1996*

Major Program Components	Vendor	Reseller	Commerce Partner
Software	Standard TRADE'ex front-end system front-end system	Customized front-end to standard TRADE'ex system	Customized front-end to standard TRADE'ex system
Product Line Options	Select from own product line	All available on TRADE'ex	Select from all available on TRADE'ex plus own
Annual Fees	$800	$800	$800
Transaction Fees	3%	3%	3%
Other Fees:			
Software Maintenance in Year 1 Per 100 Users	0	4,500	14,500
Annual Support Per 100 Users	0	2,500	6,500
Customer Software Per User	0	50	0
Transaction Fee Per Order (First $1,000	0	0	$10
Transaction Fee Per Order (Each beyond $1,000)	0	0	$5
Number of Participants, April 1996	70	5	2

only in the amount of flexibility and customization offered to sellers. The Vendor program was the most limited, offering sellers the opportunity to sell only their own product line to an expanded customer base.[4] The Reseller program gave sellers the opportunity to serve as "middlemen" only by offering the complete TRADE'ex line to their customers. The most comprehensive program, Commerce Partner, allowed sellers to select among all of the TRADE'ex products of-

fered and to add their own product lines. Both the Reseller and Commerce Partner programs provided sellers with customized interfaces to the standard TRADE'ex software. The benefits to all sellers included:

- Pricing control by country and by customer type (e.g., reseller, direct marketer).
- Instantaneous pricing changes.
- Minimization of channel conflict when expanding internationally due to the ability to control price and availability on a market-by-market basis. In addition, TRADE'ex was "blind," so that sellers' identities were never

---

[4]Participants were often resellers but could also be original-equipment manufacturers.

known to buyers or other vendors prior to purchase.[5]

- Guaranteed payment by TRADE'ex. All sales were conducted similar to credit card sales in that vendors were paid by TRADE'ex who invoiced and collected from buyers, thereby assuming all of the credit risk.
- Sales without inventory risks and costs. Resellers did not have to own any product, but could offer a range of products to customers worldwide.

Although the three different vendor programs had been available since the launch, the Vendor program had attracted the most interest while the Reseller and Commerce Partner programs had been less popular than originally expected. TRADE'ex offered several options for vendors to update and maintain information about their product lines on TRADE'ex, including EDI and SQL-links for vendors with large amounts of data.[6] TRADE'ex's five salespeople encouraged vendors to use the system for cross-border transactions, commodity products, and overstocks.

Marc Young, the TRADE'ex marketing director, explained that the fees TRADE'ex charged to vendors were not based on any cost formula, nor was the prime motivation to generate revenues. The principal purpose was to provide an incentive for participants to use the system since they had paid for it.

Young described the sale of the system as a "concept sell." It had proven difficult to sell TRADE'ex to potential vendors without demonstrations. In the first few months, Young and his staff had attempted cold calling to sign up potential vendors. Young had many years of experience in the computer industry, including owning several computer superstores. He also had a strong entrepreneurial spirit and sales skills, having launched a successful local magazine several years before. However, given the newness of the technology and the low level of familiarity with the Internet, a short phone call was not sufficient to convince vendors of the system's value. Once potential vendors saw the software demonstrated, however, they became more enthusiastic. Nonetheless, the salespeople continued to use cold calling, aiming to persuade interested contacts to download demo copies from the TRADE'ex Web site before continuing discussions.

Another early challenge was to generate the critical mass of buyers and volume of transactions necessary to encourage vendors to devote time and energy to keeping the product lines they offered through TRADE'ex comprehensive and up-to-date. For example, some vendors became lazy about updating the pricing information when the volume of sales online did not meet expectations. Often, a vendor salesperson was assigned to the TRADE'ex account as one of his or her customers, with little incentive to invest time in the online information system unless it generated sufficient volume.

Marketing Partners

Aegerter understood that he would need assistance to expand globally, even within the computer products industry. Although the current staff could mange the U.S. business, given their familiarity with the computer industry and their personal contacts, they could not do the same worldwide. Hence, Aegerter gave Gustoff the responsibility of establishing a network of "Marketing Partners" who would build the business around the globe. In return for a commitment to

---

[5]This was implemented through a vendor numbering scheme. Vendor numbers were changed randomly and regularly so that tracking any one vendor was impossible.

[6]EDI, or Electronic Data Interchange, was a set of standards that defined electronic versions of common business documents and forms, e.g. purchase orders and invoices. SQL, or Structured Query Language, was a widely used programming language to extract information from computer databases.

Exhibit 3   *Marketing Partner Program*

TRADE'ex

M A R K E T I N G   P A R T N E R

BUILDING A BUSINESS AROUND TRADE'EX

TRADE'ex is quickly becoming the global standard for conducting wholesale commerce of computer products via the Internet. The number of worldwide on-line buying and selling transactions continues to grow at an incredible pace. Corporations around the world are investing millions of dollars in preparation for total electronic commerce. Within a few years there will be more on-line wholesale transactions for computer products than by traditional "off-line" means. Electronic commerce is here to stay and the business opportunities are immense.

TRADE'ex has developed several electronic commerce pro-

grams that are successfully operating worldwide. In order to accelerate the use of TRADE'ex and to create a global presence, we are recruiting qualified Marketing Partners who will use their established and new contacts to bring more participants to the system and resell the different programs in their area. Only companies who are prepared to make the necessary investment in time and resources to succeed will be considered. We believe the rewards will be great for those companies who have the foresight to become TRADE'ex Marketing Partners.

PRODUCT & TECHNOLOGY

TRADE'ex is an open on-line trading system operated and developed by TRADE'ex Electronic Commerce Systems, Inc. which establishes the marketplace for trading computer products among manufacturers, resellers and distributors worldwide over the Internet. TRADE'ex is comparable to a credit

card company that pre-qualifies buyers and sellers. We also own the "virtual" marketplace where buyers and sellers from around the world come together 24 hours a day to conduct business.

MARKET ENVIRONMENT

We are seeing explosive growth of the Internet. This growth will create immense opportunities in on-line commerce. We believe that the first area where the promise of on-line commerce will produce significant results is in the wholesale trad-

ing of computer products. TRADE'ex is being rapidly accepted because it provides both buyers and sellers with instantaneous access to comprehensive market data where such data has not previously existed.

CONCEPT OF THE TRADE'EX PARTNERSHIP

Due to the overwhelming response by customers, TRADE'ex Electronic Commerce Systems, Inc. the sole owner of TRADE'ex, seeks to accelerate the development of TRADE'ex by entering into marketing partnerships in select strategic markets around the world. In return for a commitment to market TRADE'ex, the Marketing Partner will receive certain rights to TRADE'ex in the target market area and can potentially receive an ownership interest in TRADE'ex.

This strategy enables a Marketing Partner to establish a valu-

able business by providing local marketing expertise for the rapid development of TRADE'ex. Therefore, the prospective Marketing Partner should have extensive contacts in the computer products industry and a proven ability to market a business to business service.

As of March 1996, TRADE'ex marketing partnerships have been established in Western Europe, Japan, Korea, Australia, and the Middle East. Partnerships are now under discussion in other major markets around the world.

Table A   Marketing Partners

Marketing Partner	Sign-On Date	Number of Local Customers	Partner's Average Monthly Transaction Volume
Germany	October 1995	14	$80,000
The Middle East	December 1995	4	0
Japan	February 1996	23	20,000
Korea	March 1996	6	10,000

market TRADE'ex within a designated geographic boundary, each partner received exclusive marketing rights and a minority equity interest (40%) in the TRADE'ex operation within his or her region. Currently, they were seeking partners with extensive contacts in the computer products industry and local business-to-business marketing expertise. The details of the Marketing Partner program are summarized in Exhibit 3. TRADE'ex currently had four Marketing Partners covering Germany, Korea, Japan, and the Middle East.[7] The volume of transactions and number of customers achieved by each Marketing Partner varied widely, as shown in Table A above. Most of the efforts of the Marketing Partners were devoted to selling licensing agreements for the TRADE'ex system to other industries, such as electronic components and original equipment manufacturing (OEM). Less attention was devoted to marketing the existing system to buyers and vendors in the computer products industry. Aegerter believed that this was the best way to leverage the skills and contacts of each Marketing Partner. In addition, local obstacles impeded rapid expansion of the service. In Korea, the language problem had prevented large-scale adoption of the system. In the Middle East, Internet access was not widespread.[8] Although access was expanding rapidly in Germany, it was expensive and unreliable.

The Japanese office (TRADE'ex Pacific) had opened at the beginning of April, 1996 under the leadership of Takashi Nakagami, vice-chairman of the Japanese Electronic Products Importers Association. Plans were already underway for Nakagami to license the TRADE'ex system in Asia for other industries. Gustoff and Aegerter had also recently begun to consider establishing regional marketing partnerships within the United States in order to grow the computer products business.

TRADE'ex Europe opened in October 1995 under the guidance of Dieter Kondek, who was credited with building C2000, the leading German distributor of computer equipment. Kondek was part of the top management team, ran the German company and, as a minority owner of TRADE'ex Europe, was responsible for selecting Marketing Partners in other European countries.

---

[7]The Middle East partner was based out of the United Arab Emirates and had responsibility for all Arab-speaking countries.

[8]For example, according to a January 1995 Internet domain survey by Mark Lottor, Egypt had only 600 host computers for a population of over 60 million. In contrast, the U.S. had nearly 214,000 for a population of 260 million. See http://www.isoc.com for further information on international domains.

Customers

TRADE'ex had to provide sellers with a critical mass of potential customers to justify their effort and investment. User fees for buyers were assessed based upon a buyer's total annual sales, according to Table B below. As with the annual vendor fees, these nominal amounts were only collected to discourage sign-up without usage. There was very little incremental cost associated with signing up new buyers, regardless of their size. Almost 30% of TRADE'ex's 650 buyers were companies with annual sales of less than $500,000, as shown in Table B.

Approximately 70% of revenues were accounted for by sales from U.S. vendors to European and Asian customers, as shown in Table C on the next page.

Five people sold TRADE'ex software to customers—Young, Gustoff, and three sales representatives. Each was responsible for approximately 130 customer accounts. Sales commissions were based on "sign-ons" (system accesses) rather than "sign-ups," so the salesperson needed to encourage customers via phone calls and e-mail to access the system frequently by promoting specials and the addition of new vendors. Sales commissions were $20 per account signed up and $10 per system sign-on afterward. Young anticipated needing five to six additional salespeople within the year to continue expanding just within the computer industry. TRADE'ex had one full-time technical-support person who handled any technical problems customers had when signing on to the Internet. New customers had unlimited use of an 800 phone number. In the first several months of operation, customer difficulties in Internet access had often dissuaded them from signing on, prompting TRADE'ex to provide such support. Young anticipated that these problems would abate as more companies acquired Internet access and became more comfortable with its use.

Three full-time programmers worked on the development and maintenance of the TRADE'ex software and databases. In early 1996, TRADE'ex had released version 2.0 of its software, which added:

- A Currency feature. This allowed buyers to see local currency-dollar comparisons in over 40 currencies, with exchange rates updated every 24 hours.
- A Price Request feature. This allowed buyers to send bids through TRADE'ex to all vendors of a specified product.
- A Product Inquiry feature. This allowed buyers to ask TRADE'ex directly about products not available on the system. TRADE'ex guaranteed a 24-hour response to these inquiries.

Table B   Profile of TRADE'ex Customers

Total Annual Sales Volume	Annual Fee[a]	Current Number of Customers	TRADE'ex Average Transaction Volume Per Customers July 1995–April 1996[b]
Less than $500,000	$250	187	$ 67,100
$500,000 to $5 Million	$100	303	124,200
Over $5 Million	None	160	209,100

[a]The annual fee was credited toward the customer's first purchase.
[b]Figures include multiple transactions.

Table C   Geographical Breakdown of TRADE'ex
Customers and Vendors Since Launch

Region	Buyers	Vendors
U.S.	410	47
Asia	176	11
Europe	24	9
Rest of World	40	3
Total	650	70

Competition

The only existing large-scale computer equipment "marketplaces" on the Internet were IBEX and Industry.net. (See the IBEX home page on the WWW at http://www.ibex-ga.com and Industry.net at http://www.industry.net for details on each of the system's features.) Both IBEX and Industry.net offered product lines quite similar to, although smaller than, TRADE'ex's. Both earned revenue from advertising, in addition to buyer and vendor fees of approximately $250 each per year. IBEX also charged fees of $10 or more per transaction to both buyers and sellers, depending on the number of rounds of negotiation and the number of buyers and sellers shown the offer. TRADE'ex management had resisted accepting advertising, believing that this would be seen as compromising the company's impartiality. In June of 1996, AT&T's New Media Services unit merged with Industry.net. AT&T revealed plans to the press and business community for aggressive growth of the business. Jim Manzi, former CEO of Lotus, had become Industry.net's CEO in early 1995 and was named CEO of the new company, Nets, Inc. The Nets, Inc. mission was to become the biggest business-to-business marketplace on the Web.

Several trading systems for used computer equipment, targeted at businesses and consumers, had recently launched on the Web. Given the growing supply of high-quality used equipment, and the inefficiencies of the current pre-owned market, these organizations anticipated fast growth. For example, the United Computer Exchange (UCE) had recently expanded its successful phone-based resale service to the Internet.[9] Neither buyers nor sellers were charged for listing equipment, but commissions of 10 to 15% of sales were collected from sellers. Buyers and sellers could use UCE not only to locate interested parties but also to mediate the transaction. This reduced the perceived risk that could deter such transactions between parties unknown to each other.

Stewart Bertron, the director of licensing, also explained, "Someday, I may be sorry I said this, but we actually wouldn't mind more competition. I think a greater awareness of the capabilities of such market-making systems would make for an easier concept sell." Many potential buyers and vendors seemed overwhelmed by the pace of change and were thus hesitant to commit to any new technologies.

Marketing

TRADE'ex had spent almost $700,000 on marketing since the system launch in July 1995. Of this, less than $100,000 was spent on traditional print media in trade publications. Because of the complexity of the sale and the importance of

---

[9]See http://www.uce.com.

real-time demonstrations, TRADE'ex had found industry trade shows to be its most valuable marketing tool. Buyers could easily be convinced to try the software, and TRADE'ex logins surged following each trade show. Equally valuable were the potential global-marketing partner contacts which could be made at shows. For example, initial contact with the Australian Chamber of Manufacturers had been made at MacWorld in Boston in the fall of 1995. Trade shows were, however, expensive: travel and equipment costs totaled about $30,000 per show. They also consumed valuable staff time. In 1996, Young planned to attend about 10 trade shows, concentrating on those which were oriented towards businesses rather than consumers.

A second valuable marketing tool for TRADE'ex was its Web site. Although Young had not been keeping close track yet of the inquiries the Web site generated, he knew site accesses were running at about 2,000 per day, without any on-line advertising of the site. Of every 100 visitors, about two downloaded the TRADE'ex demo software—a limited version of the TRADE'ex browser which allowed interested customers to sign on to the system, use the search and browse tools, but not conduct any transactions.

One of Young's major concerns for the following year was to develop a consistent TRADE'ex brand image and a reputation for excellent service. In order to sell the system, TRADE'ex had to convince potential partners of its reliability and efficiency. He was currently also considering expanding the company's new one-day "training seminar" for marketing partners into a week-long program to ensure that each new partner would understand the basics of the system and be able to sell it to its own buyers. The first training seminars had been run in early 1996 for the new Japanese partner and had made its people proficient with the computer software and familiar with TRADE'ex sales techniques.

Licensing

Given the initial success of the TRADE'ex system in the computer industry, TRADE'ex management foresaw possible applications of its software and capabilities to other industries in which such on-line trading could also create more efficient markets. The most promising industries were likely to be those with standardized products and fragmented buyers and sellers. Early target industries included: office supplies, electronic components, medical equipment, commodity retail clothing, and OEM products. TRADE'ex management understood that, in such cases, it would probably not be able to take on the full operational and management role it had assumed in the computer industry. Aegerter believed it was essential to move quickly to organize these markets through licensing.

Stewart Bertron, who joined the company in August of 1995 as director of licensing, was responsible for establishing relationships with key individuals and organizations (such as trade associations) within the target industries. Bertron had a background in finance and commercial real estate before joining TRADE'ex. TRADE'ex would license its software for an annual fee based on transaction volume. As Bertron explained, "We see ourselves as facilitators in these industries, not middlemen. Our critical competitive advantage is in organizing markets, not controlling them. This is an age-old business model. It's just that an affordable technology has not existed to implement it worldwide until now." The standard licensing arrangement is summarized in Exhibit 4.

The Australia Partnership

In January 1996, TRADE'ex linked its first regional licensing agreement with the Australian Chamber of Manufacturers (ACM) under the sponsorship of Senator Peter Cook, minister of industry, science, and technology of the Australian federal government. The agreement

Exhibit 4   *Licensing Program*

TRADE'ex

L I C E N S I N G   P A R T N E R

TRADE'ex Technology For Other Industries

TRADE'ex is quickly becoming the global standard for conducting wholesale commerce of computer products via the Internet. The number of worldwide on-line buying and selling transactions continues to grow at an incredible pace. Corporations around the world are investing millions of dollars in preparation for total electronic commerce. Within a few years there will be more on-line wholesale transactions for computer products than by traditional "off-line" means. Electronic commerce is here to stay and the business opportunities in other "hard goods" industries are immense.

Due to the overwhelming number of inquiries about the availability of the TRADE'ex system in other industries, TRADE'ex Electronic Commerce Systems, Inc. is now entering into partnerships with select entities to implement a TRADE'ex-based system in certain strategic markets around the world. The

Australian Chamber of Manufacturers together with the Commonwealth Government of Australia have already licensed TRADE'ex as their electronic commerce standard. In general, the contemplated ownership and compensation structure is a Joint Venture or partnership where each party focuses on its core competency. The capitalization and ownership structure of each partnership is addressed on a case-by-case basis.

We intend to enter into partnerships with companies who know their industries and are the dominant players within their markets. Under such arrangements, we will supply and maintain the technology on an outsourcing basis and they will provide the marketing and implementation of the system using their established industry contacts. The benefit of this arrangement is that it allows each party to focus on its own area of expertise while allowing both parties to share in the success of the venture.

Competitive Advantages of TRADE'ex

1. Our system is easy to use and offers extensive customized features to find and buy products with optimized efficiency. We estimate our lead-time against prospective competitors in this area to be twelve months.

2. The name TRADE'ex is rapidly becoming well known in our industry as the premier on-line sales channel. Our marketing reaches all critical buyers and sellers. Companies worldwide will understand that TRADE'ex is the best way to easily find and buy products fast and at low prices. Vendors will realize that TRADE'ex is the lowest cost channel to expand their markets. We will capture the valuable brand awareness that comes with having the first mover advantage.

3. The most critical aspect of our system, and the most difficult to duplicate, is its content. The data on TRADE'ex will always be current and of the highest integrity. A tremendous

number of products are made available through the system at competitive prices. Each buyer has a broad choice of offers within each product category, guaranteeing competitive prices through on-line competition among vendors. We realize that vendor support is the critical aspect to make TRADE'ex a success. We work in partnership with vendors to make it as easy as possible for them to update their information on our system. Potential competitors will find it very difficult to duplicate the extensive content on our system.

A TRADE'ex licensee receives the benefit of these established competitive advantages. Rather than risk a great amount of time and capital in an attempt to reinvent a system similar to TRADE'ex, a licensee can hit the ground running with a proven system that enjoys an excellent reputation and is ready today.

called for the licensing of the TRADE'ex commerce browser and server technology, which would be enhanced jointly by TRADE'ex and Australian software engineers. The initial phase of the project would include more than 1,500 companies in the information technology and telecommunications, medical and scientific products, paper and printing, and stationary and office equipment industries. According to Senator Cook, "The Government is a major purchaser in these industry sectors. The program will help to develop supplier communities so that they are well-placed to respond to electronic government purchasing. The ACM is delighted to participate in this project that will deliver great benefits to its members and other Australian companies. It will . . . accelerate the take-up of electronic commerce by Australian business, particularly small- to medium-sized enterprises."

Although TRADE'ex planned to focus on global vertical markets rather than regional licensing arrangements, Aegerter believed that the ACM deal would add to TRADE'ex's awareness and credibility. TRADE'ex was also confident in the ACM's ability to make the arrangement work. Moreover, the contract specified that under certain circumstances the Australian system could be linked to other TRADE'ex markets and offered to other industries under a sublicense arrangement. Thus, although this was officially a licensing arrangement, TRADE'ex viewed it more as a marketing partnership that would give it access to new markets.

GROWTH OPPORTUNITIES AND CHALLENGES

A number of critical decisions faced Aegerter and his management team in April. During the previous three months, they had begun to meet with interested venture capital firms to secure additional financing. Summary pro forma income statements for TRADE'ex, as presented to the venture capital firms, are shown in Exhibit

5. The company could pursue any or all of the following:

- *A Beta-test Java-equipped version of its browser software.*[10] Java was rapidly becoming the development tool of choice, enabling a broader range of functionality for interactive sites such as TRADE'ex.
- *Translation of the browser into Japanese.*[11] Given the expected growth of the Japanese market in both the computer and OEM categories, Aegerter was considering working with the Japanese partners to translate the browser menus and fields into Japanese.
- *Launching the software in the OEM and electronic components markets by mid-1996.* Licensing of TRADE'ex in additional markets would be pursued aggressively in the following 18 months.
- *Expanding the regional and global penetration of the new computer equipment market.* In 1996, the worldwide computer equipment market was $100 billion and growing at about 10% per year.
- *Establishing a logistics partnership with UPS.* This would allow TRADE'ex to provide quick, inexpensive, and efficient worldwide delivery as an additional service option for customers.
- *Finding global financial partners to provide credit to TRADE'ex buyers.* This would increase the advantages that the TRADE'ex system provided for small buyers in relation to traditional purchasing channels, especially with respect to cross-border transactions.

---

[10]Java was the programming language developed by Sun Microsystems that appeared to be rapidly becoming the de facto standard language for creating World Wide Web sites and Internet applications.

[11]While TRADE'ex and its global partners thought translation of the browser menu items and buttons would be useful, using English as the standard for the trading system itself was widely accepted.

Exhibit 5 *TRADE'ex Monthly Income Statement 1995–1996*

1995–1996	July	Aug.	Sept.	Oct.	Nov.	Dec.
Sales	8,886,831	5,812,827	8,405,744	7,926,422	8,640,497	7,488,178
Cost of goods sold	8,284,660	5,300,811	7,693,718	7,258,822	7,901,187	6,928,965
Commissions	602,171	512,016	712,027	667,600	739,310	559,213
Marketing	80,798	46,956	50,739	51,000	72,098	44,055
General and administrative	278,400	325,740	296,180	341,100	333,680	324,120
Computer/tech. operations	27,112	29,762	29,004	28,410	28,348	27,624
Other expenses	205,929	205,180	230,841	230,678	227,736	250,598
Net income	9,932	(95,622)	105,263	16,412	77,448	(87,184)

Expenses as % of Sales

Marketing	0.9%	0.8%	0.6%	0.6%	0.8%	0.6%
General and administrative	3.1	5.6	3.5	4.3	3.9	4.3
Computer/tech. operations	0.3	0.5	0.3	0.4	0.3	0.4
Other expenses	2.3	3.5	2.7	2.9	2.6	3.3
Commissions	6.8	8.8	8.5	8.4	8.6	7.5

continued

Exhibit 5 *(continued)*

1995–1996	Jan.	Feb.	March	April	Total
Sales	6,203,847	10,022,377	10,713,091	9,599,663	83,659,477
Cost of goods sold	5,594,626	9,209,618	9,883,897	8,726,993	76,783,297
Commissions	609,221	812,759	829,194	832,670	6,876,181
Marketing	56,102	74,951	81,539	96,128	654,366
General and administrative	437,260	383,860	441,920	427,720	3,589,980
Computer/tech. operations	35,008	30,646	36,288	44,790	316,992
Other expenses	218,337	231,159	205,485	255,231	2,261,174
Net income	(137,486)	92,143	63,962	8,801	53,669

Expenses as % of Sales

	Jan.	Feb.	March	April	Total
Marketing	0.9%	0.7%	0.8%	1.0%	0.8%
General and administrative	7.0	3.8	4.1	4.5	4.3
Computer/tech. operations	0.6	0.3	0.3	0.5	0.4
Other expenses	3.5	2.3	1.9	2.7	2.7
Commissions	9.8	8.1	7.7	8.7	8.2

Aegerter knew he lacked the resources to pursue all of these avenues, but his goals for TRADE'ex remained clear:

- To pioneer the creation of truly efficient markets by linking buyers and sellers via the Internet.
- To become the number-one creator of wholesale markets over the Internet worldwide.

Aegerter was concerned that in the race (against existing and potential competitors) to establish TRADE'ex as a global standard, he might have to sacrifice some longer-term equity ownership, control, and exclusive relationships. However, the dynamics of this industry seemed to demand a rapid rather than guarded international-expansion strategy.